MOTOR CONTROL AND LEARNING

MOTOR CONTROL AND LEARNING

A Behavioral Emphasis

Richard A. Schmidt, Ph.D.
Professor of Kinesiology
University of California
Los Angeles, California

Human Kinetics Publishers
Champaign, Illinois

Publications Director
Richard Howell

Editorial Staff
Margery Brandfon, Managing Editor
Jan Gantz-Clemens, Copy Editor
Karen Hendricks, Proofreader

Typesetters
Cathryn Kirkham and Sandra Meier

Text Design and Layout
Denise Peters

Cover Design and Layout
Jack Davis

Library of Congress Catalog Number: 81-82449

ISBN: 0-931250-21-8

Human Kinetics Publishers, Inc.
Box 5076
Champaign, Illinois 61820

This book is dedicated to

JACK A. ADAMS
and
FRANKLIN M. HENRY

two former mentors
who profoundly influenced my life.

CONTENTS

CREDITS

Figure 1-1 from *The Reticular Formation Revisited* by J.A. Hobson and M.A.B. Brazier (Eds.), New York: Raven Press, 1980. Copyright 1980 by Raven Press. Reprinted with permission.

Figure 1-2 from *"Models of the Structural-Functional Organization of Certain Biological Systems"* by I.M. Gelfand, V.S. Gurfinkel, S.V. Tomin, and M.L. Tsetlin, Cambridge, MA: MIT Press, 1971. Copyright 1971 by the MIT Press. Reprinted with permission.

Figure 2-2 from "Motor-output Variability: A Theory for the Accuracy of Rapid Motor Acts" by R.A. Schmidt, H.N. Zelaznik, B. Hawkins, J.S. Frank, and J.T. Quinn, *Psychological Review*, 1979, **86**, 415-451. Copyright 1979 by the American Psychological Association. Reprinted with permission.

Figure 3-3 from *Patterns of Human Motion: A Cinematographic Analysis* by S. Plagenhoef, Englewood Cliffs, NJ: Prentice-Hall, 1971. Copyright 1971 by Prentice-Hall. Reprinted with permission.

Figure 3-4 from "Control of Fast Goal-Directed Arm Movements" by W.J. Wadman, J.J. Denier van der Gon, R.H. Geuze, and C.R. Mol, *Journal of Human Movement Studies*, 1979, **5**, 3-17. Copyright 1979 by Lepus Books. Reprinted with permission.

Figure 3-5 from *Invariant Properties of Sequential Movements* by M.C. Carter and D.C. Shapiro. Paper presented at the annual meeting of the North American Society for the Psychology of Sport and Physical Activity, Asilomar, CA, June 1981. Reprinted with permission.

Figure 3-6 from "Control of Fast Goal-Directed Arm Movements" by W.J. Wadman, J.J. Denier van der Gon, R.H. Geuze, and C.R. Mol, *Journal of Human Movement Studies*, 1979, **5**, 3-17. Copyright 1979 by Lepus Books. Reprinted with permission.

Figure 3-8c from "Specificity vs. Generality in Learning and Performing Two Large Muscle Motor Tasks" by J.C. Bachman, *Research Quarterly*, 1961, **32**, 3-11. Copyright 1961 by the American Alliance for Health, Physical Education, Recreation and Dance. Reprinted with permission.

Figure 3-11 from "Specificity vs. Generality in Learning and Performing Two Large Muscle Motor Tasks" by J.C. Bachman, *Research Quarterly*, 1961, **32**, 3-11. Copyright 1961 by the American Alliance for Health, Physical Education, Recreation and Dance. Reprinted with permission.

Figure 3-13 from "Motor-Output Variability: A Theory for the Accuracy of Rapid Motor Acts" by R.A. Schmidt, H.N. Zelaznik, B. Hawkins, J.S. Frank, and J.T. Quinn, Jr., *Psychological Review*, 1979, **86**, 415-451. Copyright 1979 by the American Psychological Association. Reprinted with permission.

Figure 4-6 from "Stimulus Information as a Determinant of Reaction Time" by R. Hyman, *Journal of Experimental Psychology*, 1953, **45**, 188-196. Copyright 1953 by the American Psychological Association. Reprinted with permission.

Figure 4-9 from "Perceptual-Motor Skills Learning" by P.M. Fitts. In A.W. Melton (Ed.), *Categories of Human Learning*, New York: Academic Press, 1964. Copyright 1964 by Academic Press. Reprinted with permission.

Figure 4-10 from "Tactual Choice Reactions: I." by J.A. Leonard, *Quarterly Journal of Experimental Psychology*, 1959, **11**, 76-83. Copyright 1959 by the American Psychological Association. Reprinted with permission.

Figure 4-13 from "The Information Available in Brief Visual Presentations" by G. Sperling, *Psychological Monographs*, 1960, **74** (11, Whole No. 498). Copyright 1960 by the American Psychological Association. Reprinted with permission.

Figure 4-14 from "Short-term Retention of Individual Verbal Items" by L.R. Peterson and M.J. Peterson, *Journal of Experimental Psychology*, 1959, **58**, 193-198. Copyright 1959 by the American Psychological Association. Reprinted with permission.

Figure 4-15 from "Short-term Memory for Motor Responses" by J.A. Adams and S. Dijkstra, *Journal of Experimental Psychology*, 1966, **71**, 314-318. Copyright 1966 by the American Psychological Association. Reprinted with permission.

Figure 5-3 from "The Role of 'Attention' in the Psychological Refractory Period" by R. Davis, *Quarterly Journal of Experimental Psychology*, 1959, **11**, 211-220. Copyright 1959 by Academic Press. Reprinted with permission.

Figure 5-4 from "The Role of 'Attention' in the Psychological Refractory Period" by R. Davis, *Quarterly Journal of Experimental Psychology*, 1959, **11**, 211-220. Copyright 1959 by Academic Press. Reprinted with permission.

Figure 5-5 from "The Role of 'Attention' in the Psychological Refractory Period" from R. Davis, *Quarterly Journal of Experimental Psychology*, 1959, **11**, 211-220. Copyright 1959 by Academic Press. Reprinted with permission.

Figures 5-9 and 5-10 from "Attentional Demands of Movement" by M.I. Posner and S.W. Keele, *Proceedings of the 16th Congress of Applied Psychology*, Amsterdam: Swets and Zeittinger, 1969. Copyright 1969 by Swets and Zeittinger. Reprinted with permission.

Figure 5-11 from unpublished data by P.A. Bender, University of Southern California, 1979. Reprinted with permission.

Figure 5-13 from "Preparatory Set (Expectancy): Some Methods of Measurement" by O.H. Mowrer, *Psychological Monographs*, 1940, **52**, No. 233. Copyright 1940 by the American Psychological Association. Reprinted with permission.

Figure 5-14 from "Effects of Foreperiod, Foreperiod Variability, and Probability of Stimulus Occurrence on Simple Reaction Time" by D.H. Drazin, *Journal of Experimental Psychology*, 1961, **62**, 43-50. Copyright 1961 by the American Psychological Association. Reprinted with permission.

Figure 5-15 from "Attended and Unattended Processing Modes: The Role of Set for Spatial Location" by M.I. Posner, M.J. Nissen, and W.C. Ogden. In H.L. Pick and I.J. Saltzman (Eds.), *Modes of Perceiving and Processing Information*, Hillsdale, NJ: Erlbaum, 1978. Copyright 1978 by Lawrence Erlbaum Associates, Inc. Reprinted with permission.

Figure 5-16 from "Errors in Motor Responding, 'Rapid' Corrections, and False Anticipations" by R.A. Schmidt and G.B. Gordon, *Journal of Motor Behavior*, 1977, **9**, 101-111. Copyright 1977 by the Journal of Motor Behavior. Reprinted with permission.

Figure 5-18 from "Motor Performance Under Three Levels of Trait Anxiety and Stress" by R.S. Weinberg and J. Ragan, *Journal of Motor Behavior*, 1978, **10**, 169-176. Copyright 1978 by the Journal of Motor Behavior. Reprinted with permission.

Figure 5-20 from "Effect of Anxiety, Competition and Failure on Performance of a Complex Motor Task" by R. Martens and D.M. Landers, *Journal of Motor Behavior*, 1969, **1**, 1-9. Copyright 1969 by the Journal of Motor Behavior. Reprinted with permission.

Figure 6-11 from "Visual Proprioceptive Control of Standing in Human Infants" by D.N. Lee and E. Aronson, *Perception & Psychophysics*, 1974, **15**, 527-532. Copyright 1974 by Psychonomic Society, Inc. Reprinted with permission.

Figure 6-12 from "Neuromuscular Control System" by D.J. Dewhurst, *IEEE Transactions on Biomedical Engineering*, 1967, **14**, 167-171. Copyright 1967 by IEEE. Reprinted with permission.

Figure 6-13 from "Dynamic Kinesthetic Perception and Adjustment" by F.M. Henry, *Research Quarterly*, 1953, **24**, 176-187. Copyright 1953 by the American Alliance for Health, Physical Education, Recreation and Dance. Reprinted with permission.

Figure 9-18 from "An Inverted-U Relation Between Spatial Error and Force Requirements in Rapid Limb Movements: Further Evidence for the Impulse-Variability Model" by R.A. Schmidt and D.E. Sherwood, *Journal of Experimental Psychology: Human Perception and Performance*, in press. Copyright by the American Psychological Association. Reprinted with permission.

Table 9-2 from "Movement Time and Velocity as Determinants of Movement Timing Accuracy" by K.M. Newell, L.E.F. Hoshizaki, M.J. Carlton, and J.A. Halbert, *Journal of Motor Behavior*, 1979, **11**, 49-58. Copyright 1979 by the Journal of Motor Behavior. Reprinted with permission.

Figure 10-11 from "Influence of Age on the Speed of Reaction and Movement in Females" by J. Hodgkins, *Journal of Gerontology*, 1962, **17**, 385-389. Copyright 1962 by the Gerontological Society. Reprinted with permission.

Table 10-4 from "A Comparative Study of Aptitude Patterns in Unskilled and Skilled Psychomotor Performances" by E.A. Fleishman, *Journal of Applied Psychology*, 1957, **41**, 263-272. Copyright 1957 by the American Psychological Association. Reprinted with permission.

Figure 11-1 from "Role of Kinesthetic and Spatial-Visual Abilities in Perceptual Motor Learning" by E.A. Fleishman and S. Rich, *Journal of Experimental Psychology*, 1963, **66**, 6-11. Copyright 1963 by the American Psychological Association. Reprinted with permision.

Figure 11-2 from "A Test of the Adams-Creamer Decay Hypothesis for the Timing of Motor Responses" by D.C. Quesada and R.A. Schmidt, *Journal of Motor Behavior*, 1970, **2**, 273-283. Copyright 1970 by the Journal of Motor Behavior. Reprinted with permission.

Figure 11-5 from "Learning Curves—Facts or Artifacts" by H.P. Bahrick, P.M. Fitts, and G.E. Briggs, *Psychological Bulletin*, 1957, **54**, 256-268. Copyright 1957 by the American Psychological Association. Reprinted with permission.

Figure 11-7 from "Efficiency of Motor Learning as a Function of Intertrial Rest" by G.E. Stelmach, *Research Quarterly*, 1969, **40**, 198-202. Copyright 1969 by the American Alliance for Health, Physical Education, Recreation and Dance. Reprinted with permission.

Figure 11-8 from "Efficiency of Motor Learning as a Function of Intertrial Rest" by G.E. Stelmach, *Research Quarterly*, 1969, **40**, 198-202. Copyright 1969 by the American Alliance for Health, Physical Education, Recreation and Dance. Reprinted with permission.

Figure 12-1 from "Cognitive Aspects of Psychomotor Performance: The Effects of Performance Goals on Level of Performance" by E.A. Locke and J.F. Bryan, *Journal of Applied Psychology*, 1966, **50**, 286-291. Copyright 1966 by the American Psychological Association. Reprinted with permission.

Figure 12-2 from "Observational Learning of a Motor Skill: Temporal Spacing of Demonstrations and Audience Presence" by D.M. Landers, *Journal of Motor Behavior*, 1975, **7**, 281-287. Copyright 1975 by the Journal of Motor Behavior. Reprinted with permission.

PREFACE

Most of us have marveled at one time or another about how highly skilled performers in industry, sport, music, or dance seem to make their actions appear to be so simple and easy—almost commonplace—with incredible smoothness, style, and grace. *Motor Control and Learning* was written for those who would like to understand how it is that these performers can achieve such accomplishments, while we, as beginners in a similar task, are clumsy, inept, and highly unskilled. In particular, this book was written as a textbook for university or college undergraduate students taking courses in skilled human performance or motor learning, primarily in fields such as kinesiology, psychology, or physical education. Others from the neurosciences, physical therapy, biomedical or industrial engineering, or human factors (ergonomics) should find the concepts contained here to be of interest in their own fields, as movement behavior is a part of all of them. And, for those who are (or are becoming) practitioners in these fields, the principles of motor behavior outlined here should provide a solid basis for the intelligent design of man-machine systems, training programs in sport or industry, or teaching progressions in dance or music.

The emphasis of the text is behavioral. That is, the primary focus is on movement behaviors that can be observed directly and the many factors that affect the quality of these performances and the ease with which they can be learned. In this sense, the book has strong ties to the methods and thinking of experimental psychology and motor behavior. Yet, at the same time, we focus on the neurological and mechanical processes out of which these complex movement behaviors are crafted. Brain mechanisms that allow the detection of errors, spinal-cord processes that are capable of generating patterns of skilled activities in locomotion, and various biomechanical constraints that act to determine the nature of our movement behaviors are all important if we are to understand high-level skilled performance. This blending of behavioral, neurophysiological, and physical levels of analysis reflects the fact that the fields of motor behavior and motor learning, movement neurophysiology or motor control, and biomechanics are rapidly moving together toward the mutual understanding of complex movement behaviors.

The text is written in a simple, straightforward style, so that it will be readily understandable to the undergraduate with little or no background in experimental psychology or the neurosciences. Comprehension is enhanced by the organization of the text, with each chapter adding to a framework for understanding motor control so that by the end of the text a well-integrated, cohesive viewpoint about how movements are controlled will be achieved. The chapters reflect natural divisions of knowledge, but they are ordered in a way that presents a logical progression and steady build-up of understanding of human movements.

The book is divided into three sections. In section I, we begin in Chapter 1 with an introduction to the field and a brief history of it. Then, Chapter 2 presents a discussion of the methods of science, which provides basic scientific terminology and thought processes that are helpful in understanding the material in later chapters.

Section II deals with human skilled performance and motor control. Chapter 3 focuses on methods of studying motor behaviors, emphasizing various measurement techniques and the logic behind their use in experimental settings. Chapter 4 investigates how individuals process information in movements, focusing on how information from the environment and from the limbs is used prior to and during actions, and how such information is related to memory structures. Chapter 5 deals with attention, when and under what circumstances attentional capacities are involved in movement planning and control, and how these processes are influenced by emotional conditions. In Chapter 6, we turn to fundamental mechanisms of movement control, focusing on closed-loop mechanisms in which feedback from the responding limb or from the environment is used to modify on-going actions. We continue this direction in Chapter 7 to discuss open-loop mechanisms, in which the actions are planned in advance and are carried out without feedback by structures called motor programs. In Chapter 8 the motor-program concept is expanded, and the nature of these open-loop mechanisms is investigated in more detail. Chapter 9 presents a discussion of models of movement, where the fundamental variables in movement, analogous to the fundamental laws of mechanics in physics, are discussed. Section II ends with Chapter 10, which discusses individual differences, or how individuals are different from each other in their movement behaviors or underlying capabilities.

Section III is about motor learning, or the acquisition of skill through practice or experience. Chapter 11 addresses some fundamental problems of scientific method in studying motor learning and provides a basis for understanding the chapters that follow. Chapter 12 deals with the conditions of practice—those factors that affect the ways that motor skills are learned—providing an outline of the factors that must be considered in the design of teaching situations of various kinds. Chapter 13 continues in this direction, emphasizing one of the most important of the variables affecting motor learning—the information feedback received either during the response or after it, providing a basis for modifications in future attempts. Chapter 14 deals with the various ways that scientists have attempted to integrate the knowledge about human performance and learning presented in the earlier parts of the book, and it describes a number of theories of how movements are performed and learned. In Chapter 15, focus is shifted to the memory for movement skills, asking about the factors that determine how well skills can be retained over months or years of no practice.

This organization, in which discussion of motor control or human performance principles are followed by motor learning principles, is quite different from a traditional organization in textbooks discussing these materials. But I believe it makes the understanding of the field far more easy and coherent for the student. Most of the concepts about learning discussed in the later portions of the book use language and concepts discussed in conjunction with human performance presented in the first half of the text. Thus, by the time that the student has mastered the notions of human performance, the discussion of human motor learning is reasonably easy and natural. Such an organization contributes much to the integrated knowledge about skills that should result by the time the reader has finished the text.

I wish to thank a number of individuals who helped make this text possible. My wife, Gwen B. Gordon, tirelessly typed the original manuscript, aided in obtaining permissions, and prepared the index, helping at times when I know she had other things she would have preferred to do. Technical assistance was provided by Madalynne Lewis, Edie Hammond, Chuck Walter, and Ridge McGhee during revisions, and many useful suggestions were made by copy editor Jan Gantz-Clemens and by Margery Brandfon. Probably the most important help was produced by reviewers Beth Kerr, Rainer Martens, Karl Newell, and Tara Scanlan—fellow researchers in motor behavior—who generated many useful suggestions for improvement of the original manuscript. The resulting text is much better because of their efforts, and I am very thankful.

TO THE STUDENT-READER

The particular order of the chapters and concepts in this book were selected for the benefit of those student-readers completely unfamiliar with motor behavior and motor control. For those with some prior knowledge, however, certain deviations in the order may be used without a great loss in continuity. Chapter 2 could be skipped by those familiar with the methods of science, and Chapters 3 and 11 could be omitted by those with a working knowledge of research methods in motor behavior. Chapters 4 through 9 present a reasonably closely ordered set of ideas about motor control, however, and Chapters 12 through 15 do the same for motor learning and memory; therefore, these sections should probably be kept intact. Also, Chapters 12 to 15 should probably follow Chapters 4 to 9, but this is not absolutely critical. Finally, for those not interested in individual differences, Chapter 10 could be omitted without a loss in continuity.

Another aspect of the text should be mentioned for those new to the field of motor behavior. Reference citations are presented throughout all the chapters; these serve to document that the point being made in a certain sentence is in some way dependent on the materials in the cited reference. They invite the reader to examine the original sources for him or herself in order to gain additional information about a particular point or even to check my accuracy and integrity in reporting the facts to you. Complete bibliographical information for all reference citations are listed in the back of the book. Those entries in the Reference List are widely available, whereas those in the Reference Notes are more difficult to obtain. Readers who wish to gain simply a more general understanding of motor behavior, however, could probably ignore these citations and read the book as though they were not even there. If this is your goal, I apologize for the fact that these citations can be somewhat distracting, and I hope that you will understand the need for them to be included.

SECTION I

INTRODUCTION

This first section introduces the field of motor control and learning. In Chapter 1 the area is described, and the important distinctions separating motor control and learning from other, related, fields of study are made. Then, a brief history of the field is given, showing how knowledge about movements from psychology and physical education, as well as from the neurosciences, have recently been combined. The second chapter deals with scientific methods in general; it discusses how these methods are used in motor-behavior research and describes a number of principles of science used in later sections of the book.

CHAPTER 1

Description and Origins of a Field of Study

Movement is truly a critical aspect of life. Without movement, we could not feed ourselves, we could not reproduce, and we would not survive. Life as we know it would not be possible without the capability to move. Our capacity to move is more than just a convenience enabling us to walk, play, or manipulate objects; it is a critical aspect of our evolutionary development, no less important to understand than is the evolution of our intellectual and emotional capacities. In fact, ethologists (those who study animal behavior) assert that our highly developed cognitive capacities evolved so that we could make the movements essential to survival—the construction of shelter, the making of tools, and communication. Surely the study of movement needs no further justification than its significance in terms of the evolution of mankind.

Movement takes many forms. Some forms can be regarded as primarily genetically defined (inherited, or "self-differentiated" according to developmental biologists) such as the control of our limbs or the ability of the centipede to simultaneously keep track of all those legs. Other examples are the "scratch reflex" of dogs or the rapid blink of the eye in response to a sudden puff of air. Here, the patterns of action appear to be determined by genetic makeup and/or through growth and development, and these actions appear to be quite stereotyped across members of the same species. A second class of movements can be thought of as "learned," such as those involved in controlling an automobile, operating a typewriter, or performing a triple-twisting somersault. These learned movements are often termed *skills*. They do not seem to be inherited, and they require long periods of practice and experience in order to master them. Skills are especially critical in the study of human movement, as skills are involved in operating industrial machines, controlling vehicles, preparing meals, playing games,

3

and so on. Both skills and genetically defined movements can be very simple (e.g., snapping fingers or blinking eyes), or they can be very complex (e.g., pole vaulting or breathing).

This book is about all these kinds of movements, whether they be primarily genetically defined or learned through practice. In particular, the concern will be with how these various movements are *controlled*—how the central nervous system is organized so that the many individual muscles and joints become coordinated in movements. The concern will also be how sensory information from the environment and/or from the body is used in the control of movement and how such information allows a person to select a movement. The scientific field of study concerned with these issues is known as *motor control*—the study of the control of movements in humans and animals.

In this book, I will add one important aspect to motor control which is usually not included—the study of how movements are learned. Thus, in addition to the study of how movements are produced (or controlled) by the central nervous system and the muscles is the study of how movements are produced differently as a result of practice or experience. Indeed, we believe many of the movements mentioned already are made up of a complex combination of genetic determinants coupled with modifications made through practice or experience. Understanding how movements are learned is the major concern of a field of study called *motor learning*. I see no good justification, however, for separating the study of motor learning from the study of movement or of motor control in general, as this artificial separation inhibits the understanding of both issues. For these reasons, as the title reveals, the subject matter of the book is motor control *and* learning.

UNDERSTANDING MOVEMENT

Levels of Analysis

How can knowledge and information about movement be acquired? A logical way to proceed would be to study some relevant aspect of the movement-control process using scientific methods. But which processes should be examined? One possibility would be to focus on the nature of biochemical interactions that occur within cells as individuals move; this level of analysis would involve research techniques and scientific questions based on biochemistry. Or, we could focus on the cell itself, asking how cells interact with each other in the control of movement. In a similar way, we could consider groups of cells, such as a whole muscle, the spinal cord, or the nerves, asking how these relatively more complex structures are involved in movement control; this level of analysis would involve research techniques that focus on the electrical and mechanical actions of neurons, muscles, and the like. Another possibility would be to focus on the movements of the freely moving animal or human, concentrating on the factors that determine movement accuracy, the choice of movement, or the patterns of action. Here, the research techniques involve the measurement of overt movements rather than electrophysiological or biochemical recordings. Along the same lines, we could study movement in a more global context, asking about the role of movement in society, the choice of certain skilled occupations or sports, movement in groups or teams, and so on.

Clearly, there are various ways to consider the same phenomenon. They have been termed "levels of analysis," and analogous levels are present in any area of scientific concern. Illnesses, for example, can be considered at levels that range from the biochemical determinants of disease right up through the effects of disease on entire societies. Because these various ways of considering a single problem are so diverse, scientists usually focus on one, or at most two, of these levels of analysis.

A Behavioral Level of Analysis

The focus of this text will be primarily at the behavioral level of analysis. That is, the primary (but not exclusive) concern will be on movement in largely intact and normal animals and humans, disregarding special populations with various movement disorders. The major goals will be to understand the variables that determine motor performance proficiency and to understand the variables that are most important for the learning of movement behaviors. Also of interest is how such information can be used in the solution of certain practical problems such as in the design of equipment that humans must control, in the selection of individuals for occupations, and in the teaching of skills in sport and industry.

This behavioral level of analysis, however, is more interesting and complete when combined with two other fields of study, each representing a deeper level of analysis. *Biomechanics* is concerned with the mechanical and physical bases of biological systems. Certainly in order to understand movement we must understand something of the body itself, with all its joints, levers, and associated mechanical characteristics. Also related to the study of movement, *neurophysiology* is concerned with the functioning of the brain and central nervous system and how they control the contractions of muscles that move the limbs. And, there will be a concern for how the biomechanics of movement is related to the nature of the neural-control system, or with the nature of the task that is to be produced. Yet, the major focus of the book is behavioral, the main reason for the qualifying subtitle. The study of movement will be attacked at various levels of analysis—the behavioral level and the levels of biomechanics and neural control.

Emphasizing Movements

In considering movements, especially skills, it is often difficult to isolate a movement from its environment. In driving a car, for example, there are the coordinated actions involved in changing gears (clutch, accelerator, shift lever, etc.) as well as the movements of steering. These parts of the skill are the means through which the driver affects his or her environment. But, further analysis reveals that these skills, while they clearly affect the environment, are also *affected by* the environment. For example, whether or not the road turns or whether or not there is snow present determines the driver's movements of the vehicle controls. Such reciprocal relations between the environment and the individual make it very difficult to pinpoint the various determinants of motor behavior, since the interaction of the many motor control and environmental factors is extremely complex and difficult to study with experimental procedures. For these reasons, the area of study must be subdivided into smaller, more workable units. With research on driving, for example, this division is often made by holding constant the automobile's controls and systematically varying the environmental factors, so that changes in movement behavior can be attributed to the changes in the influence played by the environment. Alternatively, the environment could be held constant, so that changes in driver behavior could be associated with other factors within the motor control system.

The solution to this problem adopted in this text is to concentrate on *movement,* on the output of the motor control system, and to consider mainly those situations in which the influence of a constantly changing environment on the movement is minimized. We cannot accomplish this division completely, for to do so would clearly limit any useful discussion of many everyday skills; but the focus will be on the *movement* components of the skill with perceptual and environmental factors downplayed. This kind of solution is also appropriate for skills in which cognitive or intellectual processes play a very strong role. Consider, for example, the chess master who cleverly defeats an opponent or the cook preparing an exotic French meal. These skills involve very little movement; and when movement is involved, the actions seem almost trivial. The chess master could just as easily defeat the opponent over the telephone. Obviously, the success in tasks like these is dependent on the *choice* of which of many nearly trivial movements to make at the appropriate time rather than on the processes involved in any of the movements themselves.

The role of sensory information from the environment and from the performer's body are obviously important in making decisions involved in many high-level skills, such as swinging at a baseball or avoiding hitting a pedestrian who suddenly emerges from behind a parked car. No text dealing with human motor behavior would be complete without a treatment of such factors, and in Chapters 4 and 5 these questions are treated. Even so, the emphasis in the book is on the *movement* behaviors of the performers and on how the movements are controlled, focusing on those skills for which the primary determinants of success are in the movements themselves.

Varieties of Movements

Given an understanding of some of the processes underlying the control of movements, where can these principles be applied? High-level sports, games, and athletic events come to mind as areas for application, as these activities often involve the same kinds of processes studied in the area of motor control and learning. But potential generalizations should not be limited to this kind of activity. Many apparently genetically defined actions such as walking and maintaining posture are under consideration here.

Many industrial skills, such as using a lathe, typing, woodcarving, and handwriting, are of critical importance to this field of study. Many artistic performances, such as the playing of musical instruments, the creation of a painting, or the production of a dance, are certainly under the heading of motor behavior as treated here. The evocation of sounds, whether they be from the vocalist in an opera or from the student learning a new language,[1] is also a motor task, as the sounds are controlled by muscular activity of the vocal apparatus in ways analogous to the control of the hands and fingers of the skilled typist. (Indeed, the control of the musculature in speech is a problem for the field of motor control and learning.) The potential applications for the principles discovered in the field of motor control are present in nearly every aspect of our lives.

Factors Limiting Movement Proficiency

In defining the field of motor control and learning, it is helpful to consider the factors limiting the successful production of an action. One type of skill I will not consider is that in which the movement is nearly irrelevant for success in the task, since the limiting factor is primarily the intellectual capability related to decision making and strategy. In the 26-mile marathon, as another example, there is a strong cardiovascular or muscular component that seems to determine success, and we would not want to study these activities as representative of what I have defined as motor behavior. Similarly, I would not be comfortable including activities that involve only the application of strength, as such limiting factors seem to depend on other areas of investigation, such as exercise physiology. In all of these activities motor behavior principles must be of *some* relevance for a complete understanding of them, but other factors are probably more important, and thus overshadow any contribution that motor control factors might play.

ORGANIZATION OF THE BOOK

These distinctions provide a definition of the field of knowledge that is represented by the book. In attempting to understand this area, it has been useful to divide the book into essentially three sections. The first is an introductory section which defines the field and presents a short history of its development, followed by some basic concepts about the structure of science. The second major section of the book deals with issues about measurement and the methods of studying skills, and then shifts emphasis to the topic of movement control. I begin with a cognitive information-processing viewpoint, by which the human is considered as a processor of information from the environment, then move to some of the neurological

---

[1]Learning the rules (grammar) of language would probably not be of much relevance for the area of motor control, but learning to make the gutteral sounds involved in German or the nasal sounds inherent in French could logically be included in the area of motor control (MacNeilage, 1970).

mechanisms in movement control, and finish with a chapter on how people differ from each other in their capabilities for movement.

The third section of the book discusses motor learning, or the acquisition of skills via practice and experience. After an initial concern with questions of measurement, I examine the variables that define the most effective practice methods, as well as some theoretical ideas about the nature of learning and forgetting.

ORIGINS OF THE FIELD

In an examination of the early research on movement and learning, it will be evident that the field, as we know it today, emerged from two isolated bodies of knowledge. These two areas are (a) the branch of neurophysiology primarily concerned with the neural processes associated with (or that were causes of) movements, with only slight reference to the movements themselves, and (b) the branch of psychology and related fields primarily concerned with high-level skills with very little reference to the neurological mechanisms involved. For nearly a century these two fields developed knowledge at different levels of analysis but with little mutual influence. Only toward the end of the 1970s did these two fields come together.

Early Research

Some of the earliest motor skills investigations were done around 1820 by the astronomer Bessel (cited by Welford, 1968) in trying to understand the differences among his colleagues in recording the transit times of the movements of stars. This skill involved estimating the time required for a star's image to move across the cross hairs of a telescope. Bessel was interested in the processes underlying this complex skill, as well as in why some of his colleagues estimated accurately and others could not.

Considerably later, studies were made of the visual contributions to hand movements in localizing targets (Bowditch & Southard, 1882), and Leuba (1909) studied the accuracy of limb movements. Other workers in this early period were Bryan and Harter (1897, 1899), who studied the learning of telegraphy and Morse code; Galton (see Boring, 1950), who studied the relations among strength, steadiness, and body configuration in over 9,000 British males and females; and Book (1908), who investigated typing skills for very large samples of subjects ranging widely in ability and age. One of the earliest systematic approaches to the understanding of motor skills was conducted by Woodworth (1899), who sought to identify some of the fundamental principles of rapid arm and hand movements. This work, together with that of Hollingworth (1909), uncovered principles still being discussed by motor skills researchers.

A major influence of the time was provided by Thorndike (1914), who was concerned with processes underlying the learning of skills and other behaviors. His Law of Effect, which continues to have its influences in psychology, states that responses followed by a reward tend to be repeated, while those that are not (or that are punished) tend not to be repeated. This idea formed the cornerstone for much of the theorizing about learning that was to follow in this century.

Most of the work mentioned here originated from the field of psychology, and much of the field of motor behavior today has its legacy in this early thinking and research. But this research, which is similar in method to at least some of today's research, marked a severe break in tradition from the pre-1900 views of behavior. The pre-1900 research involved *introspection,* including subjective self-reports of feelings that were unobservable. Skills were studied only because they were thought to provide "access to the mind." As the century turned, there was a shift to more systematic and objective approaches to the study of skills. And, of equal importance, skills were beginning to be studied because investigators wanted to know about the skills themselves.

Toward the end of this period, there was a slight increase in the number of studies conducted on skills. Some of these concerned handwriting proficiency, ways in which practice sessions could be structured to maximize motor learning, and whether or not skills should be "broken down" into their components for practice. In the 1930s, skills research placed greater emphasis on industrial applications. So-called time and motion studies analyzed production line assembly movements; these methods became the target for criticism by workers because of the strict standards of performance it imposed on them. Interest rose in the most efficient ways to perform tasks such as carrying mortar and shoveling coal, and how work could be better conducted in extremely hot environments. Some early theories of learning were published (e.g., Snoddy, 1935), and some work by physical educators concerned with sports and athletic performances emerged (e.g., McCloy, 1934, 1937). An interest in factors associated with growth, maturation, and motor performance began to surface, and studies by Bayley (1935), Espenschade (1940), McGraw (1935, 1939), and Shirley (1931) led the way to the formation of the subarea that we now call *motor development.*

The development of the study of the neural control of movement paralleled the motor behavior area during this period, but there was little contact between them. Early investigations on the neural control of movement were conducted by Jackson in the 1870s, well prior to the advent of electrophysiological techniques which were to revolutionize the field. Jackson studied epileptic seizures, hypothesized about their causes, and provided considerable insight into the function of the cerebral cortex in normal movements.

After the discovery by Fritsch and Hitzig (1870) that the brain was electrically excitable, various early electrophysiological recording techniques were soon developed. These gave rise to studies by Ferrier (1888) on monkeys that investigated the responses in the cortex to artificial movements, as well as to the work by Beevor and Horsely (1887, 1890) that investigated sensory and motor areas of the brain.

One of the more important influences in the neural control area was the work on reflexes at about the turn of the century by Sherrington and his co-

Figure 1-1. Sir Charles Sherrington (1857-1952); from Hobson & Brazier, 1980.

workers. He studied and classified the major responses to stimuli presented to the extremities, and he believed that most of our voluntary movements resulted from these fundamental reflexes. Sherrington is credited with the creation of a number of classical concepts of motor control, most of which are still in our thinking today. For example, he first talked of *reciprocal innervation,* the idea that when the flexors of a joint are activated, the extensors are automatically deactivated and vice versa. Also, Sherrington coined the term *final common path,* which referred to the notion that influences from reflexes and sensory sources as well as from "command" sources from the brain eventually converge at the spinal levels to produce the final set of commands that are delivered to the muscles. Indeed, Sherrington's early writings (e.g., Sherrington, 1906) are still interesting reading today. (See also a tribute to his work by Gallistel, 1980.)

Somewhat later, Sherrington was one of those involved with research on various sensory receptors associated with the perception of movement. Various sensory receptors were identified, such as the Golgi tendon organ that was thought to signal changes in muscle *tension,* and the muscle spindle that was thought to be involved in the perception of muscle *length* and hence joint position. Sherrington coined the term *proprioception*, which refers to the sense of body position and orientation thought to be signaled by the various muscle and joint receptors together with receptors located in the inner ear.

Somewhat later, research on various brain structures was conducted. Herrick (1924) proposed numerous hypotheses about the functions of the cerebellum, many of which seem at least reasonable today. Also, patients with accidental cerebellar damage were studied (e.g., by Holmes, 1939) in an attempt to pinpoint some of the movement control deficits that were associated with this structure. Other brain structures were also studied using patients with various kinds of brain damage.

Early neural control research was done mainly on very simple movements. Indeed, sometimes isolated nerve-muscle preparations were

Figure 1-2. N.A. Bernstein (1897-1966); from Gelfand et al., 1971.

used or animals with various degrees of experimentally induced spinal cord damage were studied, with the concern about movement usually being secondary to the neurological processes. When movements *were* studied, it was often done without considering the movement in very much detail; and measures of the speed, the accuracy, or the patterns of movement were usually missing from these reports. The motor behavior work, on the other hand, typically involved very complex actions (e.g., typing, telegraphy) but with very little concern about the underlying neural or biomechanical mechanisms that controlled them.

An exception to this general separation of the neural control and motor behavior areas is found in the research of the Soviet scientist Bernstein and his colleagues in the 1930s and 1940s. His research integrated behaviorally based notions with neurophysiological, neuromuscular, and biomechanical data in the study of gait and locomotion primarily, and of other movements to a lesser extent. Unfortunately, other scientists involved in the study of movements, both from behavioral and neural control areas, were ignorant of Bernstein's contributions until a translation of his early papers appeared in the late 1960s (Bernstein, 1947, 1967). Thus, while the two areas were being blended in Russia, these trends were not seen in the U.S. or in England, where most of the work on movement was being conducted.

Post-War Research

World War II had profound effects on the world, and it is not surprising that it had major effects on movement research. One of the earliest and most direct effects was created by the need to select the most suitable people for pilot training, which resulted in the creation of the U.S. Army Air Force's Psycho-Motor Testing Program initiated by Arthur Melton in the early stages of the war (see Melton, 1947, for a description of some of this work). Important studies were conducted on underlying motor, perceptual, and intellectual abilities as they related to the selection of pilots and other military personnel (see Chapter 10). Similar studies were conducted in England. In addition, studies of gunnery, physical training in the heat and cold, vehicle control, and many other issues that related to combat performances were conducted.

When the war ended in 1945, the prevailing attitude in the U.S. was that the efforts related to selection and training of military personnel should not be abandoned. Consequently, this research continued for many years, with many of these programs still existing today. The military research effort was sustained by Arthur Melton's creation in 1949 of the U.S. Air Force Human Resources Research Center, which carried on many of the wartime programs but expanded to include studies of more general interest. A major contribution of this program was Fleishman's (e.g., 1965) work on individual differences and abilities. The wartime programs, devoted to personnel selection and motor abilities, did not result in the success in pilot selection that had been anticipated. Researchers began to realize that training—not selection—was perhaps more important to the development of proficient pilots. Hence, much attention was directed toward procedures for teaching motor skills, the transfer of motor skills from one activity to another (see Chapter 11), and the retention of skills (Chapter 15).

In addition to the formal laboratories that were supported by defense funds, federal funding was increased for individuals who were willing to conduct research relevant to the military. This funding, in the form of contracts, grants, and training programs, was responsible for a great shift of attention among psychologists toward motor behavior research. The directions imposed by federal funding agencies had, and continues to have, a profound influence on what behaviors were studied and what research questions were asked. At the time, the area of motor behavior was important, and a great deal of funding was directed toward its study, convincing a large number of psychologists to become interested in this area of research.

A second big influence that created the boom in motor behavior research in the post-war period was the emergence of various theories of learning, most notably that of Hull (1943). In scientific inquiry, theories generally provide an organization of the conceptual issues and findings as well as strong suggestions for future research. Theories stimulate and provide focus for the research of others, and Hull's theory was no exception. His was a general learning theory—applying to animals and humans, to verbal and motor behavior—and tests of it were often done with motor tasks. A major emphasis of the theory was the fatigue-like process associated with long practice periods. The theory attempted to explain how fatigue and recovery processes combined to determine the learning of motor skills. Thus, a large number of scientists worked with motor tasks to investigate Hull's predictions. Most of this work has relevance to the structuring of practice sessions (see Chapter 12) or to the effects of fatigue on performance and learning. Hull's theory later proved to be an inadequate account of the processes and variables that determine motor learning and performance. However, as emphasized in Chapter 2, theories like Hull's provide strong directions for research and contribute experimental data for use by future generations, even though the original theory may be shown to be inadequate (as all theories must, in the end).

As the complexity of machines increased in this period and industrial methods became more complicated, it became obvious that many machines were exceeding the capabilities of humans to operate them effectively. For example, a number of serious airplane accidents which were attributed to "pilot error" were eventually traced to how the instruments and controls in the cockpit were arranged (Chapanis, 1965). Thus, shortly after the war, there emerged a study of man-machine interactions, variously termed *human factors, ergonomics* (in England), or *engineering psychology* (a subarea of industrial psychology). The primary focus was that humans were an important link in most of the machinery involved in industry, and that such machinery must be designed with humans in mind. This thinking, while it began in the military, is now seen in automobile design (seating, suspension, steering), the organization of assembly lines and workspaces, the design of home appliances, and in many other areas.

This period also saw a great deal of experimental effort in England. One of the most important contributions was by Craik (1948), who proposed that we should consider the brain as a kind of computer in which information is received, processed, and then output to the environment in the form of overt actions of the limbs. An important part of this general idea is the notion of *central intermittency,* in which the human is seen as responding in discrete bursts rather than continuously, as it might appear. Craik's idea paved the way for other English psychologists such as Welford, who in 1952 proposed the still relevant *single-channel hypothesis* (see Chapter 5) associated with the *psychological refractory period*—the delay in response to the second of two closely spaced signals. Also, a great deal of work was done in ergonomics, on training and conditions of practice, and on hand movement control, particularly with respect to anticipation and timing (Poulton, 1950).

The ideas about central intermittency and the analogies of the brain to the computer were accompanied by similar new directions in psychology and related fields. One of these ideas was represented by Wiener's (1948) book *Cybernetics,* which outlined an information-processing basis for human behavior. Also, Shannon and Weaver's (1949) *Mathematical Theory of Communication* established important principles of information processing that later led to systematic attempts to study the motor system in terms of its capabilities and limitations in processing information.

In keeping with the information-processing basis for behavior suggested by Craik and others, Fitts (1954) presented some now-famous fundamental relations among characteristics of hand movements—their movement time, their movement extent, and their accuracy (see Chapter 9). This formulation, which has since come to be known as Fitts' Law, was an early attempt to apply mathematical and information-processing principles to the understanding of human movements, and it suggested that more complex limb control could be understood by future application of such methods and thinking. Even as a young man, Fitts was regarded as one of the future leaders in this area, but he died unexpectedly in the mid 1960s before his full potential could be realized.

In the middle of this post-war period, there was a great deal of motor

Figure 1-3. Paul M. Fitts (1912-1965)

behavior research being conducted, sufficiently so that Robert and Carol Ammons, themselves researchers in this area, created a journal in the late 1950s entitled *Perceptual and Motor Skills.* The journal now publishes both motor and nonmotor research, but it served as a major outlet for motor behavior work during its early years. In addition, the *Research Quarterly,* a physical education research journal, published a great deal of motor behavior research during this period.

Toward the end of the post-war period, the number of psychologists interested in motor behavior research gradually declined, while the number of physical educators interested in these problems strongly increased. The psychologists' disinterest may be attributed to decreased federal support for motor behavior research, disillusionment with Hull's theory, and increasing interest in other types of human behavior such as the learning of verbal skills. This trend reached its peak in the mid 1960s when an ''academic funeral'' sponsored by Ina and Edward Bilodeau was held at Tulane University. Renowned motor behavior psychologists gathered to read the last rites and to bid each other farewell, as each moved on to other related topics in psychology. Their eulogies were recorded in a volume entitled *Acquisition of Skill* (Bilodeau, 1966), which describes well the attitude of the times.

Motor behavior research was dead, or so the psychologists thought; but they did not consider a man named Franklin Henry, trained in psychology and working in the Physical Education Department at Berkeley, who was increasing his interest in motor behavior research. Fittingly acknowledged as the father of motor behavior research in physical education, he advocated an approach using psychological techniques, laboratory apparatus, and careful measurement. Unlike the psychologists, though, he used whole-body activities (as well as the psychologists' traditional fine-motor tasks) in his research, and many of these tasks used violent motor actions representative of activities in sports and games. Henry educated many doctoral students who used his general method and point of view as they took their places in physical education departments during the college growth boom of the 1960s. Many of these disciples created Ph.D. programs and trained more students in this basic tradition, resulting in Henry's influence being

Figure 1-4. Franklin M. Henry (1904-)

pervasive by the 1970s. With the leadership of A. T. Slater-Hammel, these new motor behavior scientists organized the North American Society for the Psychology of Sport and Physical Activity (NASPSPA); the Canadian Society for Psycho-Motor Learning and Sport Psychology soon followed. These groups flourished during the 1970s. During this period, the first text-book devoted strictly to motor behavior and motor learning was published by Cratty (1964), and many more (including this one) followed.

Not all psychologists of the period were bored with motor behavior research. Fitts and Peterson (1964) presented influential experiments on limb movement accuracy, Bilodeau and Bilodeau (1961) and Adams (1964) wrote needed reviews of motor behavior research, Adams (1968) wrote a theoretical treatment of the role of sensory feedback in movement learning, and Keele (1968) wrote an often-quoted review of motor control. But these were the exceptions. As the 1970s approached, the cluster of scientists in physical education and (to a limited extent) psychology began to grow in new directions. Posner and Konick (1966) and Adams and Dijkstra (1966) presented seminal articles dealing with short-term memory for motor responses. Henry and his students (e.g., Henry & Rogers, 1960) were con-cerned about motor programs, Posner (1969) studied attention and move-ment control, Pew (1966) examined levels of organization, and Adams (1971) initiated a return to theorizing about motor learning. These em-phases provided strong leadership for the motor behavior area in the 1970s.

As in the early period, the neural control and motor behavior scientists were oblivious to each other, but important contributions were being made in neural control that would later be important in joining the two areas. One of the more important contributions was the work on muscle-spindle mechanisms by Merton (1953; Marsden, Merton, & Morton, 1972), dis-cussed in Chapter 6. While the specific mechanisms by which Merton pro-posed that these adjustments occur now appear to be incorrect (Houk, 1979; Smith, 1977), Merton's original ideas about automatic regulation of movement are reasonable in very general terms. Merton's contribution was one of the first in which the measurement of movements *and* neurophysiological processes were accomplished in the same investigations, creating a beginning for a blend of behavior and neurological emphases that were seen later.

At about the same time, a great deal of research was devoted to the sensory receptors associated with movement perception and kinesthesis. Skoglund (1956) published a classic paper showing that the various receptors in a joint capsule appear to be activated only at certain specific joint angles, suggesting that these receptors have a large role in the perception of joint position. This point of view is currently being seriously questioned, as newer data suggest that the joint receptors operate only at the extreme range of movement. This debate is discussed in more detail in Chapter 6.

Numerous studies on the nature of muscle and its contractile and mechanical (i.e., spring-like) properties were also completed during these post-war years, and these studies have attracted the attention of contemporary researchers in motor behavior and motor control. These physical characteristics of muscle and of the motor apparatus were utilized by scientists in the Moscow laboratories who were following the earlier traditions of Bernstein. The extensive work on movement control by this group, originally published in Russian and thus generally unknown to American and British researchers, has recently attracted a great deal of attention through various translations (e.g., Gelfand, Gurfinkel, Tomin, & Tsetlin, 1971; Kots, 1977). This research has special relevance for the control of locomotion and provides important links between the neural control mechanisms and behavioral principles. But despite the efforts by the Soviet group, by 1970 almost no association existed between the behavioral scientists interested in more global and complex skills and the neurophysiological scientists interested in simple movements and neural control.

Motor Control Today

The 1970s brought massive changes in the field of movement control and learning. The strict stimulus-response (S-R) orientation that had such a strong foothold during most of the century was overshadowed by the cognitive information-processing approach, arising in large part from the impact that Neisser's (1967) *Cognitive Psychology* had on the field of experimental psychology in general and (later) on motor behavior in particular. The move toward cognitive psychology was a reaction to oversimplified S-R theories of behavior, and ideas about internal and mental and motor processes, together with many methods and paradigms for understanding them, took their place. Perhaps more than anything else, Neisser's book legitimized the study of processes such as response selection and movement programming, whose existence must be *inferred* from the behaving individual rather than directly observed.

Influenced by cognitive psychology, the motor behavior field seemed to undergo a transition from a *task orientation,* which focuses primarily on the effects of variables on the performance of certain motor tasks, to a *process orientation,* which focuses on the underlying mental or neural events that support or produce movements (Pew, 1970, 1974; Schmidt, 1975b). Humans were considered processors of information, and it was necessary to understand how movement information is coded and stored, how actions

Figure 1-5. Jack A. Adams (1922-)

are represented in memory, and how information is processed about errors so that learning can occur.

Led by such researchers as Adams and Dijkstra (1966) and Posner and Konick (1966), the process orientation helped to create the area of the *short-term motor memory*, the study of the processes underlying the memory loss in simple movements over short periods of time. Many studies were conducted in this area during the late 1960s and early 1970s (see Chapter 15). Studies were also completed on information-processing activities during the learning of simple motor tasks (see Chapter 13).

More importantly, theorizing returned to motor behavior and learning, a style of inquiry that had been relatively dormant since the failure of Hull's (1943) theory. Adams sparked the interest in theory when in 1970 he presented a feedback-based theory of verbal learning (Adams & Bray, 1970), followed the next year by a similar theory devoted to motor learning (Adams, 1971). In 1974, Pew presented important theoretical ideas about movement schemas (abstract hypothetical structures responsible for the conduct of movement) which are discussed in Chapter 14. And, one year later, I presented a schema theory for the learning of simple motor skills (Schmidt, 1975b). Together, these theoretical ideas have generated a great deal of interest in motor skills, as is made evident later in the text.

The motor behavior field not only changed its direction, but it grew rapidly during the 1960s and 1970s. Formal courses of study in universities flourished, and new journals appeared. In 1969, I founded the *Journal of Motor Behavior,* which was closely followed in 1972 by the *Journal of Human Movement Studies* created by the English motor behavior scientist John Whiting. A review journal entitled *Exercise and Sport Sciences Reviews* was created in this period, and it devotes a major portion of its space to motor behavior research. And the psychological journals (e.g., *Journal of Experimental Psychology, British Journal of Psychology,* and *Ergonomics,* to name a few) continued to publish some motor behavior research.

As the field grew, motor behavior textbooks proliferated. No fewer than twenty textbooks written subsequent to Cratty's (1964) initial book and a large number of chapters in edited volumes on more specific topics are currently available.

Also, the 1970s saw the beginning of a long-needed merger between the neural control and the motor behavior scientists. While this merger is far from complete, many people were trained formally in both motor behavior and neural control, and these people complete the bridge between these two levels of analysis. More and more behavior-oriented scientists are asking questions about movement control and making increased use of various electrophysiological and biomechanical techniques to understand the functions of the central nervous system in movement. The neural control scientists are shifting from studies that examine only the neural mechanisms to studies investigating these mechanisms during complex movements. Much of this latter work is done with animals, principally monkeys and cats. Records from electrodes implanted in the brain, spinal cord, or muscle are taken while the animal is engaged in motor activity. Representing this approach are Grillner and his colleagues (1972, 1975), who studied locomotion in cats; Evarts (1972, 1973), who studied a number of separate brain structures in monkeys; and Houk (1979) and Granit (1970), who studied the gamma motor system in monkeys and man. Much important work in this general area has also come from Matthews (e.g., Goodwin, McCloskey, & Matthews, 1972; Matthews, 1964).

The essential feature of all this work is the strong attempt to find an association between movement behaviors and neurological processes in order to provide a more complete understanding of how movements are controlled. This marks a refreshing change from the earlier research in which the movements per se were hardly considered. The surfacing association between motor behavior and motor control has resulted in several reviews written toward the end of the 1970s, such as those by Brooks (1975, 1979), Grillner (1975), Wetzel and Stuart (1976), and Gallistel (1980). Also, a number of scientific meetings have recently taken place in which both behaviorists and neurophysiologists have participated.

An additional change has occurred recently—one far more subtle than those just mentioned. The field of motor control is acquiring an independent identity rather than being a mere blending of two different fields. It is becoming a field of study in its own right, complete with its own journals and methods for asking research questions and collecting data. Such methods involve the use of sophisticated biomechanical techniques for recording and analyzing movements, such as electrophysiological recordings, cinematographic analysis, and measurement of the kinematics of movement, together with the more traditional techniques.

Also, Bernstein's ideas have resurfaced lately through the writings of Greene (1972) and Turvey (1977). Their views, a departure from the information-processing approaches, have a strong tie to physical biology and ethology. There is a strong ecological emphasis, stressing the notion that our motor system was created through evolution and interactions with the physical characteristics of the environment and that we should therefore attempt to understand the structure and function of the motor system by using more natural research settings. Also attached to this view are the ideas that perception and action are functionally inseparable, that understanding the motor system will be dependent on understanding the physical principles of our actions and how they interact with biological functions, as well as a reluctance to use cognitive-psychological styles of inquiry with hypothetically defined brain structures such as memory, motor programs, schemas, and the like. This approach, while yet in its infancy, may prove to be the next big shift in emphasis in attempting to understand motor behavior.

Motor behavior has strong roots in experimental psychology, for years using its methods, theories, and journals. But a number of us have felt that it is time to develop a field with its own methods, journals, and theories. We are now undergoing such a trend. The combination of biomechanical techniques and knowledge about movement, the neural control field as it is associated with movement, and experimental psychology and physical education as they are associated with movement are all blending together to form a unique area called *motor control and learning*.

SUMMARY

This text is fundamentally concerned with movements of human beings. Some of these movements are probably genetically defined while others are *skills,* for which practice or experience is required. Even though most of the field of human behavior is concerned in one way or another with movement, in this text I focus primarily (but not exclusively) on those movements that are relatively free of cognitive involvement, and for which the nature of the movement itself rather than the choice of the movement from already learned alternatives is the primary determinant of success. I will focus on movements that do not have heavy concentration on cardiovascular endurance or stength, as these responses seem to be more closely aligned with other fields of study. Finally, the focus is on many different movements meeting these restrictions, such as in musical performances, movements in industry, movements in sports and games, as well as movements in walking.

The field of movement control and learning, viewed from an historical perspective, emerged from separate but parallel fields of motor behavior and neurophysiology. Both fields showed steady growth through the beginning of World War II, then increased in growth and sophistication after the war and through the 1960s and 1970s. These two fields, however, were largely separated until the early 1970s, when these fields began to share common problems and methods. Today, we have the initial stages of a new field of motor control and learning with its own subject matter (movements), research methods, and journals.

GLOSSARY

Ecological viewpoint. A point of view emphasizing the study of movement in natural environments, and the evolution and physical and biological constraints of movement.

Ergonomics. The study of human beings in work environments; subsets of areas called human factors or industrial psychology.

Information-processing viewpoint. The study of movement in which the human is viewed as a processor of information, focusing on storage, coding, retrieval, and transformations of information.

Motor behavior. An area of study stressing primarily the principles of human skilled movement generated at a behavioral level of analysis.

Motor control. An area of study dealing with the understanding of the neural, physical, and behavioral aspects of movement.

Motor learning. An area of study focusing on the acquisition of skilled movements as a result of practice.

Movement. Changes in joint angles, the position of the entire body, or both; in the present context limited to those in humans and animals.

Process orientation. A point of view of the study of movement emphasizing the study of the mental and motor processes underlying movement.

Skills. Movements that are dependent on practice and experience for their execution, as opposed to being genetically defined.

S-R viewpoint. A tradition in psychology and motor behavior stressing the responses produced as a function of stimuli presented, without regard to the intervening mental events or processes.

Task orientation. A point of view of the study of movement focusing on the effect of certain variables as they affect the performance of various movement tasks, without relevance to the underlying processes; similar to the S-R viewpoint.

CHAPTER 2

Scientific Methods and Motor Control

Most undergraduate students, and some graduate students, find science to be a mysterious enterprise, and they hold numerous misconceptions about it. A good understanding of the scientific method is helpful in the study of any science, including motor control and learning. Actually, the workings of science are not all that difficult to understand, for many of the procedures used are essentially the same ones that people use "naturally" to make decisions about everyday problems, although the terminology used in research settings is often somewhat different.

Understanding the methods of science will not only help in understanding the remainder of this book, it will also contribute another dimension to the understanding of motor control and learning. This added aspect of knowledge is based on how "correct" the information we have at hand is, and how secure we are in using this knowledge as a basis for making decisions about various aspects of our lives. In order to truly understand the principles of motor control and learning, it is essential to know where the research results have come from, how they were achieved, what the limitations were on the techniques that were used to generate them, and how these results can be generalized to other situations. In order to understand these limits of knowledge, it is necessary to understand how science operates.

Such is the purpose of this chapter. I will examine some of the goals of science, its major methods, and its major strengths and weaknesses as they contribute to a field of knowledge. Only occasional reference will be made to the field of motor control and learning, as the fundamental methods in any science are essentially the same, with differences being only in how data are collected and experiments are run. An understanding of these ideas will aid in evaluating the major research findings presented in the later sections of this book.

GOALS OF SCIENCE

If I were to ask nonscientists about the purposes and goals of the scientific activities of their local universities, I would probably receive a variety of answers. One commonly held view—even among scientists—is that the purpose of science is to serve mankind, to provide solutions to problems that are important to society. A less commonly held view among nonscientists, but more often accepted by scientists, is that the purpose of science is to understand the various phenomena present in our universe. This understanding implies that we be able to account for the behavior of the objects under investigation, as well as to predict the behavior of these objects in future situations.

These two overall goals of science might at first glance appear to be contradictory. Scientists who believe that the overall goal is application operate somewhat differently than do scientists who believe that the goal is understanding, but these differences tend to be somewhat superficial. (See the section on basic and applied research later in this chapter.) The common feature of both approaches is that understanding is required for each of them, with this understanding being more or less a final goal for some scientists, and a step toward application for others. Seen this way, the basic goals of all branches of science are related to understanding and explanation of all of the behaviors of the objects under study. For most, this goal of understanding (or explanation) means the development of formalized explanatory structures called *theories* to encompass all phenomena in the area, as well as to predict new phenomena before they actually occur. In order to understand how these theories are developed, the fundamental elements or components of scientific thinking and how they relate to and result in the development of theories must be discussed.

CONCEPTUAL LEVELS OF SCIENCE

I will begin this discussion of science and its methods by mentioning some of the basic structures of scientific thinking and how they relate to each other. Most scientists agree that four distinct levels of conceptualization exist: (a) observations and facts, (b) laws, (c) theories, and (d) models. Very "young" sciences may lack one or more of these components, which are discussed in the next sections.

Level 1: Observations and Facts

Basic to any science are the observations of the objects under investigation. This level of science involves the collection of data about the objects under study, and it implies measurement procedures, with systematic recording of the observations (often called *results*). Scientists usually demand more than just observations, though, because what two people might observe in the "same" situation can be considerably different. Rather, there must be some kind of social consensus or agreement about the observations, which is usually based on more or less standardized procedures. When observations have this social consensus, they are frequently termed *facts*.

From the outside, this level of science may be viewed as the most important, perhaps because of the stereotype of scientists in white lab coats gathering information from objects of study. However, while the fact-gathering level of science is essential, it is not the level of primary importance. Some would even see this phase of science as routine and dull.

Facts take the form of statements about the results of reproducible procedures for measurement (e.g., "John threw the ball 22.6 meters"). In some situations, facts are easy to gather (e.g., counting the number of people in a room), while in other situations obtaining facts requires years of study to understand and develop the apparatus and techniques necessary for measurement. But whatever the difficulty, the basic aim of this level of science is the recording of data about the behavior of the objects under study.

Variables

When data are gathered or phenomena are observed, the object being observed is placed on a continuum—either imagined or real—that represents an underlying dimension. For example, imagine a dimension called "distance thrown," with numerical values along it. Other examples might be the weight of an object along a "heaviness" dimension, or the amount of error in performance on an "accuracy" dimension. These dimensions are often called *variables*, and they are usually represented by names or symbols.

Continuous variables. Conceptually, continuous variables can have any (real number) value. The differences between successive "points" on the dimension are limited only by the accuracy of the measuring techniques. For example, it would be difficult to read a millimeter ruler to the nearest 1/10 mm, but it is nevertheless possible conceptually.

Continuous variables can be further subdivided into three categories: *ordinal, interval,* and *ratio* variables. Ordinal variables are those for which the values are ordered, such as small, medium, large; but there is no implication that the amount of change between small and medium is the same as that between medium and large. Interval variables have this same ordering property, but the distance between successive points represents the same amount of change. An example is the Fahrenheit temperature scale, on which the amount of temperature change between 20°F and 30°F is the same as that between 50°F and 60°F. Finally, ratio variables have all the properties of interval and ordinal variables but also have an absolute zero. Thus, for a ratio variable, a value of "4" represents twice as much as a value of "2," whereas this is not the case with interval variables (e.g., 30°F is not twice as hot as 15°F).

The distinction between ordinal, interval, and ratio variables is important for the measurement of motor behavior. Just as it is not meaningful to say that 15°F is half as hot as 30°F, it will not be meaningful for some motor tasks to say that producing 30 units of error is half as skillful as producing

15 units of error, since skillfulness is measured as an ordinal or interval variable instead of ratio variable. One useful measurement of skill, though, is time to complete an action; it is often the case that the skill in these situations can be regarded as being measured on a ratio variable (Chapters 3 and 11).

Discrete variables. Some variables have only discrete values, such as "yes," "no," or "don't know" in response to a questionnaire; or "hit," "out," "walk," or "error" as an outcome of a play in baseball. Other variables can have only two values, such as "hit" or "miss," "male" or "female," or "right" or "wrong." These two-value variables are called *dichotomies.* Discrete variables are called *nominal* variables when the "value" of the variable simply names some characteristic of the object, such as male or female, hit or miss. These nominal variables do not have the order implied at all, as a hit and a miss do not stand in any fixed size relationship to each other; they are simply different things. Also, conceptually continuous variables can be used as discrete variables, such as in dividing a group of people into two classes on the basis of height (tall/short), or a group of performances in terms of skilled/unskilled. All of these types of variables are used in motor behavior research.

Relationships

Although the location of a particular object or behavior along some dimension (or variable) is fundamental to collecting data and experimentation, scientists are generally interested in more than this single piece of information.[1] Usually, the concern is with how the data on this variable are related to the data on another variable. That is, scientists are generally more interested in the relationships among variables than they are in the value of any one of the variables. Put another way, scientists are concerned with how one variable changes as another changes. An example is the observation that as the value on a variable called "practice time" increases, the value on another variable called "skillfulness" tends to increase as well.

Related to these relationships of variables is the desire to establish statements (either verbal or mathematical) that describe the value of one of the variables as a function of (i.e., depending on) the value of some other variable. For example, I might be able to estimate that, on the average, people who have typed on the job for 6 years or more can type at least 50 words per minute. Being able to make such a statement implies that there is some orderly way in which the behavior of one of the variables (practice time) relates to the behavior of the other (skill in typing).

Essentially, the establishment of relationships involves the measurement of an object or behavior on two variables simultaneously, noting the regularities between them. For example, we could take a large group of people, measure "simultaneously" their previous years' experience and typing speed, and create a graph such as is shown in Figure 2-1. Each dot is

---

[1]There are many exceptions, of course. A researcher might be interested in knowing that a certain presidential candidate is favored by more than 60% of the population or that 49% of the people in the U.S. are male, to name but two.

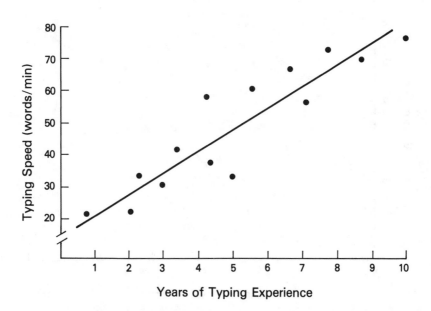

Figure 2-1. A hypothetical relation between years of typing experience on the job and typing speed. (Each dot represents a different individual.)

representative of a single person, with the location being determined by the joint values of each person on the "years of experience" and "typing speed" variables, respectively. From the arrangement of the points on the graph (called a *scattergram*), it appears that there is a relationship between these two variables, with a tendency for "speed" to increase as "years of experience" increases. Notice that this relationship is based on the separate evaluation of these two variables on different people.

A relationship could be established by using the *same* people for each of the data points. An example is the relationship between the error in hitting a target with a handheld stylus and the distance from the starting position to the target. In Figure 2-2, the results from such an experiment (Schmidt, Zelaznik, Hawkins, Frank, & Quinn, 1979) are presented. The subjects moved the stylus from various starting positions to a target, so that the movement distance was either 10, 20, or 30 cm. The error was measured as the variations about the target (called W_e, see Chapter 9). Errors tended to increase as the distance from the target increased. Thus, there is a relationship between errors and movement distance, based on this set of data.

It is useful to consider two fundamentally different kinds of relationships: causal and noncausal. These are considered in the next sections.

Causal relationships. In causal relationships, the change in one variable causes a change in a related variable. An example is that heating water (changing its value on the "temperature" dimension) will cause it to boil (changing its value on the "stillness" dimension). Notice that one change leads more or less directly to the other, and that the resulting change would not have occurred unless the value of the original variable ("temperature") had been changed. Also, the *direction* of the relation is critical; heating led to the boiling, not vice versa. In addition, there is usually a *temporal* order

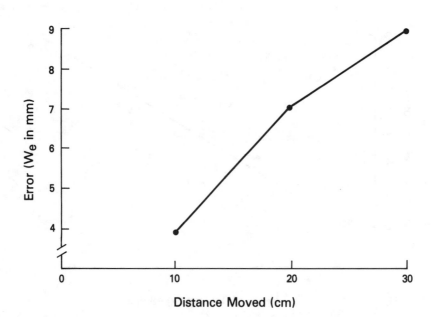

Figure 2-2. Relationship between the distance moved (140-msec movement time) in an aiming task and the error (W_e) produced in hitting a target. (Each data point is based on the same individuals; from Schmidt, Zelaznik, Hawkins, Frank, & Quinn, 1979, Figure 8.)

to causal relations: one event must happen before another can happen. Of course, most changes in variables have many causes—especially when considering the complexities of human behavior. For example, whether or not I make an error in a movement task may be related both to how rapidly I was responding and to whether or not I was paying attention.

Not all relationships are as direct as is implied above. In many situations, the relationship might be phrased as a *probability statement*. The probability of a certain behavior occurring (e.g., of making an error) will be related to the value of some other variable (e.g., the speed of a motion). For example, as is shown later, there is an increased probability of hitting a target as practice continues, but such a relationship does not imply that for every person on every attempt the accuracy will be greater as practice continues.

Noncausal relationships. Other variables are not related causally. A classic example of a noncausal relationship is that between the variables "mathematical ability" and "shoe size." For elementary school children, it was found that as the shoe size of the individual increased, mathematical ability increased as well. These variables are not related causally, however, because increasing the level of mathematical skills (through a lesson, perhaps) will not lead to larger feet and because stretching the feet (in a mechanical torture chamber) will not lead to an increase in mathematical ability. It is more reasonable to think of these two variables as related because of their mutual relationship to a third variable: age. As age increases (from first to sixth grade), mathematical ability increases (because of lessons in school), and shoe size increases through normal growth. It is an important task of scientists to determine which variables are related and whether these variables are related causally or noncausally. If they are related noncausally, the scientist usually is interested in knowing what the fundamental causes of the relationship are, such as discovering that age was mediating the relation between shoe size and mathematical ability.

Independent and dependent variables. Scientists often use the terms *independent variable* and *dependent variable* to distinguish the two fundamental ways in which variables can be employed. For causal relationships, the independent variable, when changed, leads to changes in the dependent variable. The independent variable "temperature" causes the dependent variable "stillness" to change in the example of boiling water. An easy way to remember this distinction is that the value of the dependent variable "depends on" the value of the independent variable.

For noncausal relationships, however, the distinction between dependent and independent variables is far less clear. In these cases, the "independent variable" is usually the one that is predicted from, while the "dependent variable" is the one that is predicted. For example, I may wish to predict the throwing accuracy (the dependent variable) knowing age (the independent variable), without these variables being related causally. Note that it is possible, in this example, to reverse the roles of the independent and dependent variables by predicting the age, given the level of throwing accuracy.

It should be emphasized that the label of "independent" or "dependent variable" is applied according to the way in which the variable is being *used,* not to the nature of the variable itself. For example, the variable "temperature" was used as an independent variable in the example of boiling water (increasing it caused the water to boil). It could just as easily be used as a dependent variable: increased "duration" of heating the water causes "temperature" to increase.

Causation. When I say that increasing the temperature causes the water to boil, I mean that changing the value of one variable produces changes in the other, not that changing the temperature was the "fundamental," or only, cause. I could just as easily say that the cause of boiling was the increased activity of the molecules as the temperature increased or that it was the change from liquid to gaseous state. I use the term "cause" to mean only that changes in one variable lead directly to changes in others.

Determining the Nature of Relationships

There are two fundamentally different ways to discover the relationship between variables, plus a third that is a combination of the first two. These may be termed (a) experiments, (b) natural experiments, and (c) pseudo-experiments.

Experiments. Students often refer to scientists "doing experiments," meaning the overall process of collecting and analyzing data, but scientists use the term experiment in a much more restrictive way. By their definition, an experiment is a set of operations designed to determine the extent and nature of the causal relation between two variables. In the simplest and most classic form, the experimenter creates (very much in the artistic sense) a situation in which the value of one variable is varied (scientists often use the term manipulated); this variable becomes the independent variable. Then, the effect of this manipulation on some other (dependent) variable is

measured. Actually, many experiments systematically vary a number of independent variables and/or study the effects on a number of dependent
variables, but these more complicated experiments are beyond the scope of
this discussion. The goal of the scientist is to systematically isolate some independent variable, so that the changes in some dependent variable can be
attributed only to the effect of the changes in the independent variable.

A simple example would be to study the effect of the amount of caffein
on motor performance. I could perform the experiment in a number of
ways. One would be to divide a group of 100 people into two groups randomly (or without bias) provide the members of one group with coffee, and
the members of the other group with no coffee, and then measure their performances on a dart-throwing task. If the performances of the two groups
of people are different, the changes in accuracy on the dart-throwing task
can (probably) be related to the effects of caffein.

A second way to do the experiment would be to use 50 individuals and
test them under both experimental conditions at different times. For example, for Individual 1, I would on one day administer coffee and then
measure the performance; on another day (when the effects of the coffee
could be argued to have disappeared) I would not administer coffee and
measure performance. I would balance the order of presentation of the coffee and no-coffee treatments "across subjects," so that half of the subjects
receive the coffee treatment first and half receive the no-coffee treatment
first. In both of these examples, the key feature to note is that the experimenter—and no one else—has determined the level of coffee in the subjects; put another way, an experiment always involves the active manipulation of the independent variable(s).

The experiments just described could be criticized on several grounds.
One important criticism is that, while I would like to attribute the changes
in performance to the consumption of caffein (because of the known effects
caffein has on steadiness, for example), we see that there are other independent variables that are varying along with "amount of caffein." One is that
people know that they are drinking coffee and perhaps they expect to
behave in a certain way as a result; and the observed changes in performance (if any) could be due to changes in this expectation. Therefore, it is
not known whether to attribute any changes in dart-throwing accuracy to
the independent variable "caffein" or to the independent variable "expected inaccuracy" which was varied along with it.

To correct this problem we must "control for" the effects of the second
independent variable, holding it constant while the amount of caffein is
varied by the experimenter. To do this we could use a *placebo* or a treatment
that has all of the characteristics of the "live" treatment except for the particular aspect under consideration (i.e., caffein). The subjects could drink
decaffeinated coffee in place of the no-coffee treatment or take tablets, one
with caffein and one without. In this case, both treatments would have the
same value on the variable "expected effects of coffee," and we would say
that the effect of the "expected effects of coffee" would be controlled, so
that any observed changes in accuracy would be due to some other variable
(e.g., "amount of caffein"). A group used to control for some independent
variable other than the one of major interest is called a *control group;* the

experimental condition is called a *control condition*. If there is more than one such independent variable to be controlled, there can be more than one control group (or control condition). There will be many examples of this principle later on in the text.

Apart from the control procedures used in the previous example, in which the experimenter wishes to control for the systematic effect of some independent variable, situations occur in which the experimenter wishes to control for the random effect of some independent variable. One such random effect might be that some individuals are more accustomed to drinking coffee, so that the effect of caffein would be less for them. This is one reason why experimenters often use many individuals in their treatment groups, so that the effects of such random factors as susceptibility of the experimental treatment can be more or less "spread" throughout the entire experiment. Another example is that individuals often show very different performances (behaviors) on different trials; a way to solve this problem is to provide many trials for each subject, so that the random variability will be "spread" across the various trials. This is a very common technique, especially in behavioral research.

Natural experiments. Natural experiments (sometimes called *field studies*) differ from "true" experiments described in the previous section in one important regard. The independent variable is not actively manipulated by the experimenter. Rather, the independent variable is allowed to vary "naturally," and the associated effects on some dependent variable are noted. This kind of experiment is used in research when it is impossible to vary the independent variable experimentally (e.g., in research on the prediction of tornados). Certain independent variables (temperature, humidity, wind velocity, and direction at various altitudes) could be measured and associated with the dependent variable, which is the instance or severity of a tornado. In motor behavior research, similar techniques can be used, as, for example, in studying a high-jumper's variations in technique as they are associated with success in clearing the bar.

A more common kind of natural experiment is that in which the variation in the independent variable is associated with different individuals; that is, individuals are chosen who have different values on some independent variable, noting the associated variation of some dependent variable. In such studies, I may take a large number of individuals (e.g., 50) and measure the independent and dependent variables on each subject; an example would be to measure age and throwing skill as independent and dependent variables to determine what "effect" age has on throwing. (See also Figure 2-1.) Through the use of correlational techniques (which I will describe more fully in "Individual Differences" in Chapter 10), the scientist can determine the direction and strength of the relationship between the two variables in question.

The interpretation of the results of natural experiments is quite different from that of "true" experiments. Since the experimenter in natural experiments did not actively manipulate the independent variable, there is no certainty that the changes in the independent variable were the cause of the changes in the dependent variable. A more proper interpretation is that it is possible that the changes in the independent variable caused the dependent variable to change, but other possibilities are not excluded. The example of mathematics ability and shoe size illustrates the point. There is a strong relationship between mathematics ability and shoe size, but it is not necessarily true that the changes in shoe size caused the changes in the math scores, or vice versa. Scientists often use terms like Variable A is *associated with* Variable B, or A is *related to* B, in describing the interpretation of natural experiments; they avoid using language that would suggest that changes in A were *caused by* B.

Pseudo-experiments. A third class of investigations may be called pseudo-experiments. They use the same techniques that "true" experiments use, but they are not actually experiments because of the way in which the independent variable is manipulated. A good example is the use of a dichotomy (such as sex) as the independent variable, dividing a large group of individuals into male and female categories. Then I might measure the "effect" of this independent variable on some dependent variable, such as throwing skill. The procedure appears to be an experiment, because I have two groups (males and females) and because I am concerned with the differences in group performance; but it is not an experiment, because the experimenter has not actively varied the independent variable. Notice that in order to actively vary the independent variable, the experimenter alone must decide which of the subjects are given which treatments, and this certainly cannot be done using sex as an independent variable. The result is that the sex of the subjects may not be the only factor to be varied in dividing the subjects in this way, and it would be reasonable to think that other independent variables such as "amount of experience" and "sex-role stereotypes" might vary together with sex, thus causing the differences. For this reason, pseudo-experiments are usually considered in the same way as natural experiments—that is, the effects are not taken to be causal effects—but they are often mistaken for "true" experiments because of the similarity in techniques.

Interpreting Relationships

The "raw" relationships that result from an experiment are not very meaningful or interesting until they are interpreted in some way. Usually it is not so much the relationship among the variables as what this relationship means to motor control and/or learning that is of interest. However, in making these interpretations, there are often a number of difficulties. Some of these are presented next.

Measurement disrupts behavior. First, in attempting to do an experiment, we always interfere (at least to some extent) with the very thing that we are trying to understand, even in the physical sciences (Zukav, 1979). In placing subjects in an experimental setting, researchers invariably alter the subjects' motor control so that the behavior in the laboratory setting is not quite the same as it is in a more "natural" setting.[2] This is especially true when the

---

[2]On the other hand, the outside world is, at best, an inexact and incomplete approximation to the real world of the laboratory. This statement, while used largely tongue-in-cheek, does raise the question about where "reality" really is. Is it to be found in the outside world or isolated in the laboratory?

subjects know that they are being observed. In many other situations, these biases are very strong, and in some cases, negligible. But there is almost always a bias of unknown strength present in experimental procedures.

Technological errors. Experiments and relationships are subject to various kinds of errors. First of all, there is nonsystematic error in determining the subject's score for a particular kind of behavior, such as in reading a clock or measuring the limb's acceleration. These errors can be handled in most situations by recording data from a large number of responses from each subject, so that these technological errors "average out" in the long run.

Intra-individual variability. A second kind of error is not really an error at all but is related to the fact that individuals tend to be inconsistent in their behaviors from trial to trial, even in the simplest of motor tasks. Some of this variation may be related to the subject's trying new strategies and movement methods, but certainly some of the variability is related to the inability of oscillating biological systems to produce identical behaviors on two different occasions. This kind of variation tends to produce variations in the relationships observed, and these relationships will perhaps be slightly different if a different set of trials were analyzed or if the same experiment were done on another occasion.

Individual differences. A third kind of error is also not really an error but is related to the fact that individuals tend to be consistently different from each other in a wide variety of ways. These individual differences (Chapter 10) lead to what is called *sampling error,* or the tendency for the mean score (or some other statistic) from a sample of individuals to be different from sample to sample simply because of the different scores of the various individuals who by chance will be included in the sample. One could have a situation where an experiment done on one sample of people showed that Treatment A produced larger scores than Treatment B; if the experiment were done again with different individuals, the opposite result (or no changes) could be produced, although it is unlikely.

Rosenthal effects. There are a number of potential biases related to the expectations of the experimenter. Together, these are named "Rosenthal effects," after the experimenter who expected to find these effects and uncovered them in various experimental situations (Rosenthal, 1966). Essentially, when an experimenter expects an experiment to turn out in a certain way, there is the possibility that knowingly or unknowingly the experimenter will influence the behavior of the subjects in such a way that the expected outcome is actually achieved in the data. Of course most experimenters are very concerned about the possibility of such effects, and they take precautions to ensure that these effects do not appear in their data; however, we can never be certain that such effects are totally absent.

Hawthorne effects. Related to experimenter expectancy are some findings on subject biases. In the Hawthorne Works of the Western Electric Company, a number of studies were done in the 1930s on worker productivity, investigating variables such as working hours, lighting, pay, and so on. Generally, each time there was a change in the working conditions, there was progressively higher productivity. In fact, even when the original working conditions were restored, productivity again increased! These findings suggested that the workers, conscious of being the object of a large experimental investigation, were motivated by this attention, causing them to work harder. The increased productivity probably had little to do with the changes in working conditions. These "Hawthorne effects," as they have come to be called, point out the difficulties in making inferences from studies of human beings (Roethlisberger & Dickson, 1939).

Questioning results. Recognizing these potential problems, scientists generally do not question the data from an experiment very much. Usually, the results of an experiment are taken at face value, and there is not much argument about whether the results are "correct" or not. Sometimes, however, a particular experimenter will not believe the results, and he or she is then free to conduct a *replication,* wherein the experiment is repeated with a different set of subjects to determine if the same result will occur again. But these replications are relatively rare, and it is safe to say that most experimenters accept the results of published experiments essentially without question.

Interpreting results. On the contrary, there is often a great deal of argument about what results mean, or about how a particular result is to be interpreted. For example, if I report that Mary is taller than Bob, there would be only minor concern about how I measured the heights, etc. But, if I were to say that girls are taller than boys as an interpretation, I would likely receive a strong argument. The interpretation that some girls are taller than some boys is less strong, and naturally less controversial. Facts alone are not very controversial or interesting without some sort of interpretation. And, the capability to interpret a future experiment in a certain way if certain results are achieved is a major source of motivation for the experimenter. In the next section, I will deal with the formation of *laws*, the process of formally interpreting related facts or observations.

Level 2: Laws

Laws are general statements that describe (or summarize) findings in terms that are more general than were the original findings. More specifically, a law is *a statement describing a stable dependency between an independent and dependent variable.* Laws are statements that result from the logical process of induction, which usually involves reasoning from specific facts to general principles—"generalizing." An example: when the weather is warm, my car starts normally; but when it is cold, my car does not start. I might generalize from these 10 or so separate observations that "When the weather is cold, my car doesn't start." Laws—especially "good" ones—are based on many separate observations, and they provide a summary of those separate observations in more general terms, as can be visualized in Figure 2-3.

Most scientific fields—especially the more mature ones— have a large number of well-established laws; the younger fields (such as motor behavior) have far fewer. In physics—generally recognized as the most mature science—a common example is Hooke's law of springs, which states that the amount of elongation of a spring is directly proportional to the ad-

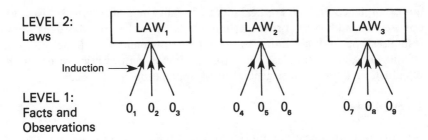

Figure 2-3. The relations between laws and observations in science.

ditional weight applied. In motor behavior, a law of information feedback states that failure to provide information about errors results in markedly less learning (as compared to providing such information). Both laws have been generalized from the original experimental results. In both examples, the exact objects of concern and the specific situation need not be specified, at least within broad limits. Hooke's law applies to all kinds of springs, in all parts of the world, and with all kinds of added weights; and the law of feedback does not specify the kind of task nor the nature of the learner.

Laws have earned a rightful place of importance in science. First, laws summarize a greal deal of experimental evidence (i.e., facts and observations). In this sense, a law is a very efficient way to "encapsulate" in a single statement a wide variety of separate facts. Second, laws allow scientists to generate new facts before they are found. For example, Hooke's law of springs allows the engineer to design a spring for a particular vehicle without having to experiment. For motor behavior, knowing that a particular law of information feedback holds for learning, allows us to design classroom settings to maximize learning, being certain to provide information about errors for each of the learners. Because of these two features, some scientists say that laws are the major goal of science, since they allow us to *predict* behavior. However, laws do not provide an explanation, or understanding, of various phenomena; they only provide a generalized description or summary. Most scientists feel that laws are important steps toward this understanding, which is the major goal of science, but not ends in themselves.

Law Formation

Since laws are the product of human creativity, different laws can be formulated by two different individuals who are examining the same observations. Laws do not automatically spring forth from the facts (unlike the image on a piece of exposed film that springs forth from the colors of the separate molecules of pigment on it), so how are we to know which of the laws is the "correct" one? Scientists have general rules by which these decisions are made. First, a law must account for all of the facts that presently exist for a given class of object. A good law of feedback must account for all of what we know about the behavior of feedback information, provided that certain limitations (termed boundary conditions) are not exceeded. These boundary conditions provide limits to the law's applicability, and in this example, could limit applicability to certain kinds of feedback (visual as opposed to auditory), or to certain kinds of tasks (rapid versus slow responses). Second, given that two different statements seem to account for all the facts, the "simplest" law (using simple mathematics rather than calculus), or the one most general in its application, is chosen.

Testing Laws

In the early stages of law formation when there are not many facts from which to generalize, the statements of laws are apt to be quite tentative; and frequent changes in the statements are made as new facts are collected. Often, studies are done with the express purpose of refining the statement of a law. Essentially, the existing statement of a law allows scientists to deduce (*deduction*, the opposite of induction through which the law was formed in the first place) the outcome of an experiment. Hooke's law allows us to predict the amount of elongation of a new spring, and then do an experiment to determine if the actual amount of elongation agrees with the amount predicted. If it does not, then something is incorrect in the statement of the law or there is an error in the experiment.

Testing the predictions of a statement of a law allows for the continual refinement of the statement (or its abandonment). Or testing may provide a stronger definition of the boundary conditions associated with the law. Recall one of the benefits of laws: they allow scientists to generate new facts. Through deduction, these new facts can (a) be used for testing the correctness of the law or (b) be put to practical use.

Level 3: Theories

The process of theorizing has to do with the explanation or understanding of the reasons behind facts or laws. Given that an area of study has some well-established laws, the natural curiosity of the scientist leads to questions about why these laws and facts exist and what the underlying explanation for them must be. The scientist wants to understand the fundamental nature of the objects of investigation that behave according to the laws.

Usually these questions about understanding and explanation are attacked at a level in science that deals with theories. Theories are abstract explanations for the various laws and facts that exist in an area of study. Basically, a theory relates a group of laws together by providing a set of processes or mechanisms that seems to account for the relations among the independent and dependent variables specified by the laws. And, since these mechanisms and processes are necessarily at a level of analysis "deeper" than that represented by the facts and laws, theories can be thought of as explaining the facts and laws by resorting to a shift in the level of analysis. As I discussed in Chapter 1, it is helpful to understand the laws of movement behavior by theories that are phrased in neurological terms—one level of analysis "deeper." It will be useful in understanding theories to define the basic elements contained in each theory: hypothetical constructs, postulates, and coordinating definitions.

Hypothetical Constructs

In creating a theory to explain a set of existing laws, the theorist begins with a set of hypothetical constructs that serve as "building blocks" for the theory. A familiar example is atomic theory, for which the constructs are the atom, molecule, electron, and proton. In the 1930s when atomic theory was developed, physicists had no way to "see" these elements directly, so they were created in the theorist's imagination. Examples from motor behavior and/or psychology are short-term memory (a hypothetical system for briefly holding information in store—see Chapter 15) and schema (a relation between the goal of a movement and the "instructions" given to oneself in order to produce it). Other examples are the concept of an ability (a stable underlying state of the motor system). These are rough definitions of hypothetical constructs; strictly speaking the construct is defined only by a set of postulates, to be discussed next.

Postulates

Postulates are statements that relate hypothetical constructs to one another and thereby provide a kind of definition for them. A simple example comes from geometry: the constructs *point* and *line* are not defined except by the postulate "two points determine a line" or "two straight lines can intersect in one and only one point." It is important to note that, although this example uses everyday words (point, line) for the constructs, there is no need to do so. The theorist could easily have used such terms as *dop* and *ked*. The postulate that defines dop and ked would be the statement "Between any two dops one and only one ked can exist." Current atomic theory uses constructs such as *quark* and *gluon* that have characteristics such as flavors and colors. Thus, postulates define the constructs and state how the theorist thinks the constructs relate to one another.

Given the constructs and postulates, deductive logic (the opposite of induction used in the formulation of laws) can be used to make specific statements. For example, in Euclidean geometry, beginning with a very few constructs and postulates, many more complex statements can be made using only the additional rules of deductive logic. These are often called *theorems*.

In order to understand how these derived statements can be used, it is necessary to understand how the abstract elements of the theory can be related to the concrete variables that are used in the statement of laws. This relationship is provided by the third element in the theory—coordinating definitions.

Coordinating Definitions

An important part of any theory is the set of "rules" for translating the "behavior" of the hypothetical constructs into events that can be observed by the scientist or used by the practitioner. Remember, constructs are imaginary entities that are not directly observable, and thus some method is needed to provide an experimental test of the logical deductions. As the name implies, the coordinating (or operational) definition provides a way for the construct to be defined in terms of actual measurement techniques. An example from the physical sciences is density (the construct), whose coordinating definition is stated in terms of the weight recorded on a scale relative to that of an equal volume of water. In terms of motor skills, the construct of memory for an event is defined in terms of how well the individual can produce an observable response related to the event in question. Learning is another important construct, and its operational definition, as discussed in Chapter 11, relates to a relatively permanent change in performance (behavior) as a result of practice.

All "good" theories must have clear operational definitions in order to be tested. It is easy to state theories that cannot be tested due to lack of coordinating definitions, but theories that cannot ever be tested are essentially useless.

Theory Building

Theories are created in a variety of ways but through a common process. First there must exist a set of laws, defined and generated in the ways discussed earlier and based on well-conducted experiments with repeatable findings or possibly on informal observations. The laws at this stage are not under very much dispute, and most of the scientific community feels that the methods for generating the laws (sometimes called *paradigms*) and the laws themselves are reasonably satisfactory. At this point, scientists begin to ask questions about the underlying causes of these lawful relations.

The theorist proposes hypothetical systems (to oneself or to a colleague at first) to explain the findings. These thought processes usually do not begin simply because the scientist decides that it is time to propose a theory. Rather they may begin at very odd times, for seemingly no good reason. Scientists have spoken of receiving a critical insight while taking a shower, driving to work, listening to a conference presentation, or discussing research over a beer with their colleagues.

The scientist then formulates the hypothetical constructs, postulates, and coordinating definitions and attempts to deduce the laws that exist in the area of study (Figure 2-4). This is a very important step in theory building, because the scientist must be able to use the rules of logic to deduce the specific statements that are the laws existing in a given field. If the scientist decides that one or more of the predictions does not agree with what has already been found (for example, the theory predicts that increasing Variable A should decrease Variable B, when the laws in the area show that increasing Variable A increases Variable B), then the theory is probably incorrect right from the start, and the scientist abandons that particular formulation. If the scientist is very creative, the original idea is modified to allow the laws in the area to be derived either by changing the statement of the theory or by generating an entirely new theory (the latter is far less likely). The basic principle is that the new theory must be able to predict all of the established laws in the area of study, and thus the theorist provides this initial series of "tests" before presenting the theory to other scientists.

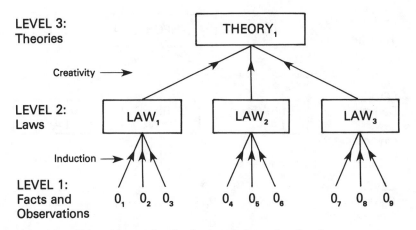

Figure 2-4. The relations between theories, laws, and observations in science.

A second, closely related method for theory construction is often used in which a scientist may react to a theory that is already in existence. For example, the scientist may interpret existing experiments differently so that their results are not predictable from that theory. A common situation is that the theory may be in opposition to the scientist's fundamental beliefs. Or there may be new experiments produced since the original theory was proposed that are in opposition to that theory. In such cases, there is a special motivation to formulate a theory that will account for the data and laws in a more effective way. The overall methods for creating a new theory (or a drastic modification of the earlier one) are basically the same as described above, but now the theorist is more or less driven to create the new structure by a serious failure in the earlier theory to account for the laws and facts in the field.

Theory Testing

The process of testing the new theory then begins in earnest. Often the scientist will deduce some new predictions from the structure of the theory (just as in high school geometry). These predictions are first generated as new "laws" that have not been found previously; then each of these new "laws" is translated into new "observations" that also have not been found previously (see Figure 2-5). In this instance, I have used the terms "law" and "observation" somewhat differently than earlier, as here the "law" is derived from the theory (not from the existing evidence) and the "observations" are derived from the "law" (not from experiments). These predicted experimental outcomes are frequently termed *hypotheses,* to distinguish them from actual laws; they can be seen as "potential laws," as the level of hypothesis and law in the organization of science is the same.

Next, the scientist might conduct some experiments to test these predictions. If the theory is a "good" one, he or she will be able to demonstrate this in the laboratory. At this stage, when the theorist has a system that can account for all of the laws in an area and the new predictions seem to hold in the laboratory, the theory is often presented to the scientific community

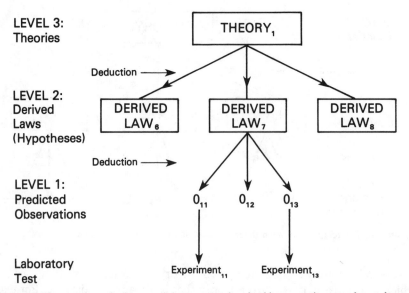

Figure 2-5. The structure of science and the processes involved in generating experimental tests of theories.

as a paper in a scientific journal or as a presentation at a scientific meeting.

Often, after hearing or reading about the new theory, other scientists become interested in it. A fundamental problem facing the new theory is whether or not other scientists believe that the constructs can be measured in the way the theory says they can be; that is, there may be debate over the nature of the operational definitions. Some scientists will go further to provide tests of the theory in their own laboratories. This involves using deductive logic to derive some new prediction, applying the operational definitions to "translate" the predictions into an experiment in which the behavior of the constructs is potentially observable, and then conducting an experiment to determine if the prediction holds in the laboratory. A great deal of the scientific activity in universities involves testing specific predictions from theories that others have created.

Support or rejection of theories. It is important to understand how the results of these experiments relate to the theory in question. There are two basic outcomes: (a) those in which the predictions from the theory hold in the laboratory and (b) those in which the predictions from the theory do not hold in the laboratory. If the scientist finds that some prediction from a theory holds in the laboratory situation, he or she says that the theory in question was "supported," not that the theory is "correct" or that it is "proved." The key issue is the logical meaning of the term *supported.* Here, it simply means that a prediction from the theory seems to hold experimentally.

Why is it that the theory has not been proven correct? Imagine that two scientists have independently produced two different theories to account for the presently existing laws, and which also derive the same new prediction (or hypothesis). Showing that this new prediction holds in the laboratory cannot prove both theories correct, because at most one theory can be correct at any one time; otherwise, all of the theories (even the incorrect ones) that can derive this prediction must be true. This, of course, is impossible. The following (incorrect) syllogism illustrates the flaws in this kind of logic:

1. If A is true, then B is true.	1. If the car's gas tank is empty, it will not run.
2. B is true.	2. The car will not run.
3. Therefore, A is true.	3. Therefore, the tank is empty.

In the first example to the left, consider A and B as "sentences" analogous to "The car's gas tank is empty" and "The car will not run" shown at the right. The methods of sentential logic enable us to analyze the appropriateness of the conclusion (Line 3) based on the earlier steps. The conclusion "Therefore, the car is out of gas" does not necessarily follow from the earlier sentences (although this may be one of the reasons the car will not run). But other reasons may exist to explain why the car will not run (e.g., the battery is dead, the spark plugs have been removed) even though the car may have a full gas tank.

In relation to the testing of theories, Line 1 of the syllogism is the derivation from the theory; if the theory is correct, then this result should hold experimentally. Line 2 of the syllogism is the experiment that tests the prediction in the laboratory; the predicted result holds. Then Line 3 is the conclusion based on the two previous lines. Now it is evident why it is illogical to conclude that the theory has been proved correct. What has been done, however, is to provide additional evidence that there is another law that can be predicted from the theory, perhaps giving some comfort to those who believe that the theory may be correct. But we have not proved the theory to be true; in fact, theories can never be proved correct with these procedures.

How then does science eliminate the "bad" theories and embrace the "good" ones? The answer is that science usually proceeds by disproof, by showing that some alternative theory is incorrect. This means that scientists must show that the prediction from the theory does not hold in the laboratory so that this theory can be excluded from consideration. Here is an example of this kind of logic in sentence (sentential) form (based on Adams, 1967, p. 120):

1. If A is true, B is true.	1. If the car's tank is empty, it will not run.
2. B is false.	2. The car runs.
3. Therefore, A is false.	3. Therefore, the tank is not empty.

Again, consider Line 1 as the prediction from the theory; if the theory (A) is correct, then B must hold in the laboratory. Line 2 is the experiment; B is found to be incorrect. In this case, Line 3 (conclusion) is that A of the first line must be incorrect; that is, the theory (A) from which the prediction (B) is derived is incorrect since the prediction (B) does not hold in the laboratory.

Seen in this way, the processes of theory testing are relatively simple. The scientist seeks to derive predictions from some theory (which, perhaps, is suspected to be incorrect or which is a "rival" to one believed to be more reasonable) which will not hold in the laboratory. If the predictions do not hold, this is reasonably strong evidence that the theory is incorrect and should be rejected. If the scientist finds that the prediction holds in the laboratory, this "supports" the theory in the sense discussed earlier. The theory is not proved to be true, but the probability that it is true is increased slightly as a result of this experiment.

Thus, the most powerful (and useful) experiments are those with results which are counter to the predictions from a theory.[3] These experiments force scientists to formulate other theories to account for the earlier set of laws plus the new law generated as a result of this last experiment. Each new theory has more laws to account for, and consequently it must be that much more accurate in its formulation.

Thus the process of theory formulation and theory testing begins again, the result being better theories at each step. Because of the importance of rejecting theories, I have used this technique frequently throughout this text to show why certain theories about human performance or learning are not acceptable.

Finally, I should not leave the impression that one experiment is sufficient to reject a theory. One initial difficulty is that experimenters may not believe that the interpretation of the experiment in relation to the theory is correct, and thus they may not see that the experimental outcome relates to the theory at all. This can happen due to the way in which the constructs are manipulated in the experiment; perhaps the experimenter has chosen to operationalize the constructs in a way that is not consistent with the operational definitions of the theory. A second problem is that the result of the experiment could be in error, for some of the reasons specified earlier in this chapter. This is a major reason for a scientist to replicate an experiment, as the results may be different, removing the shadow of doubt that the experiment casts on the theory. For these reasons, scientists usually demand a number of experiments that counter the predictions from a given theory before they are willing to say that the theory is incorrect.

Null results. There is one class of experimental outcome that deserves special mention. Say that some theory predicts that if Variable A is increased, then Variable B should increase also. I then operationalize this prediction and do an experiment, the results of which show that Variable B does not change at all as a result of increasing Variable A. Does this failure to show that the prediction holds provide evidence that the theory is incorrect? Usually not. One reason is that I cannot be sure that the experiment was sensitive enough to detect any changes in Variable B. Dipping my leg into the ocean displaces water and raises the level slightly in all parts of the world; but if I were to conduct this experiment, perhaps measuring the water level on the Santa Monica Pier with and without my leg in the water, I would have trouble showing a change in the level of the water.[4] Alternative-

---

[3]As Polya (1954, p. 10) has said, "Nature may answer Yes or No, but it whispers one answer and thunders the other; its Yes is provisional, its No is definitive."

[4]Thanks to Herbert A. de Vries for this example.

ly, one may ask, "Simply because I do not observe some phenomenon, does that guarantee that the phenomenon did not occur?" Of course not. This difficulty exists in motor control research, as many experiments fail to show any change, causing uncertainty about the theory under test.

A more powerful way to experiment is to generate predictions from some theory in such a way that, if the theory is correct, then no change in the dependent variable is predicted. But, if the theory is incorrect, then a change in the independent variable is predicted. In this case, we have the experiment that shows that "something happened," with this change being logically related to the theory being incorrect. Creating these experiments is very difficult. It is hard enough to create an experiment that is a clear-cut test of the predictions from a theory without having the added restriction that, if the theory is correct, no change in the dependent variable should occur. But this kind of experiment is a strong goal of most scientists.

Another kind of experiment is that in which the outcome should lead to an increase in the dependent variable if Theory A is correct and lead to a predictable decrease in the dependent variable if Theory B is correct, or vice versa. This is termed a *crucial experiment* and provides a possibility for rejection of one theory and support of another. Obviously, these kinds of experiments, while they are extremely difficult to create, represent a very efficient use of experimental resources and time in coming to an understanding of the phenomena under consideration.

Theory testing in the courtroom. The principles just described apply to many aspects of life (e.g., repairing cars, diagnosing illnesses), not the least of which is our justice system. When two lawyers are arguing about whether or not Individual A is guilty, they are really discussing evidence about two rival theories—one having A as the culprit, the other having A as an innocent citizen. There are many aspects of theory testing that are analogous to the courtroom. One important one is that, logically, the prosecutor has a particularly difficult time, since strictly speaking there can never be "proof" that a certain theory (e.g., that A is guilty) is correct. All that can be done is to present evidence to support that particular theory. To the contrary, the defense attorney has a much more powerful position logically. Evidence can be presented that makes the prosecutor's theory incorrect. For example, if it can be shown clearly that the defendent was somewhere other than the scene of the crime when it was committed, this is strong evidence against the theory that A is guilty. In a number of ways, the legal system is very similar to the scientific system, with its rules on the acceptability of evidence, public test, rejection of theories, and so on.

Level 4: Models

Many writers seem to disagree about the inclusion of models as the fourth major component of the scientific structure (Lachman, 1960), but I believe that models should be included. Many students mistakenly assume that the terms *model* and *theory* mean essentially the same thing, but most scientists see models as *analogies* to theory that enable the theory to be visualized more easily. A good example is atomic theory. As I said before, the con-

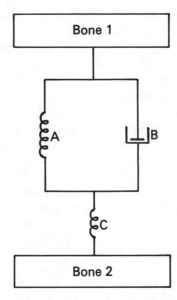

Figure 2-6. A simple mechanical model of muscle and tendon. (A represents the spring-like elastic properties of the contractile element, B is a dashpot, or a device for damping oscillations caused by a spring A, and C represents the spring-like qualities of the tendon.)

structs electron and proton (at the time atomic theory was developed in the 1930s) were imaginary, yet they were often "brought to life" as collections of little balls, with neutrons and protons clinging to each other in a nucleus and electrons spinning around them in orbits. In psychology, statistical sampling and mathematical models of decision making and learning are used, and computer models of the brain are often seen. In motor behavior there are mechanical models of muscles and joints (see Figure 2-6), feedback models of motor control (see Chapter 6), and computer models of movement programming (see Chapters 7 and 8).

Models have a number of important purposes. First, since they enable us to visualize theories more effectively, they suggest predictions that might be overlooked using only the logic of the deductive method. Thus, models suggest experiments, although the model's "predictions" must agree with the predictions from the theory. Also, models are good teaching devices. Throughout this book are examples of theories of motor performance and learning that are more easily understood by making reference to a model. We can even simplify the model somewhat to use it in lower academic levels, as in high school; plumbing/pump models of the circulatory system, and phonograph record models of movement control (see Chapter 8) seem easily understood by those who could not otherwise understand a complete theory behind them.

But models must be used carefully. A model is not a theory, but an analogy to it. Substituting the model for the theory in our thinking can lead to improper deductions and to wasteful experiments. Likewise, the brain is not a computer, although it may act like one in certain regards. This aspect of models has led some (mainly mathematicians) to suggest that models are a "refuge for weak minds"; but I believe that, properly used, models are useful.

HOW SCIENCE OPERATES: INTEGRATION OF THE LEVELS

Varieties of Scientific Activities

There is much more to the scientific endeavor than simply collecting data in the laboratory. The public often thinks that this is the primary role of the scientist, but there is a great deal of thought involved in the generation of experiments. For example, it is not always clear how to operationalize a certain variable or how to conduct the experiment so that the effects of one variable are not *confounded with* some other. Formulating laws requires a great deal of insight and creativity, as well as familiarity with the published literature where the separate facts and observations (the results of experiments) are recorded in journals and reports. The creation of theories requires a great deal of creativity also, perhaps more than the creation of laws; that very few of the scientists in a given field engage in theorizing attests to its difficulty and requirement for special abilities. Thus, actually doing experiments can be a rather routine part of the scientific procedure, with other aspects being more demanding and hence interesting.

Self-correction in Science

In examining the various levels of science and how they operate, one feature that stands out is that science is self-correcting. Science systematically eliminates incorrect explanations and creates more correct ones. Furthermore, it is the natural curiosity of the human that leads it to question a statement of a law. An experiment is created and perhaps the law is revised or abandoned as a result of it.

The same is true of theory testing, but at a somewhat more abstract level. Often definite "camps" of scientists exist who tend to believe in particular theories, and a great deal of competition among these groups exists. Much activity relative to the theories is generated, and many discussions result. Eventually one of the theoretical positions falls from favor because of the weight of evidence brought to bear against it.

A part of this self-correcting process of science is the constant demand to make one's experimental results subject to the scrutiny of public examination. Experimenters are not rewarded (in terms of pay raises or prestige) for experiments that they do not publish, and this is for good reason. Results and thinking that are open to public inspection are subject to criticism, and any experimenter has the right to replicate some other experimenter's findings. Also, most of the journals in which experimental results are published are *refereed,* with groups of established scientists reviewing the manuscript prior to publication to rule on the suitability of experimental procedures and methods of a proposed article. This aspect of science is often criticized because it creates a situation in which young scientists must adopt the techniques of the older scientific establishment, but it does prevent clearly inappropriate or misleading experimentation from becoming public.

Objectivity in Science

The original purpose of the various scientific methods was to provide a system of rules and procedures whereby scientists could come to an understanding of the nature of the world unaffected by prejudices and biases. Some of the major forces that have stood in the way of such an understanding are moral, religious, and political beliefs; think about the religious forces that have stood in the way of discussions of evolution, for example. The experiment is presumably one device that allows us to examine the state of the relationship among variables, hopefully unconfounded by prior beliefs about it. Great pains are taken to prevent the opinions of the experimenter from affecting the results of an experiment.

This sounds very "pure," but there are a number of ways in which the processes of science are biased. Obviously, which field I choose to enter is based on many subjective factors; and, once in the field, which problems I choose to study are subjectively determined. How I choose to conduct the experiment and the kinds of interpretations I place on the data are, to some extent, determined by personal preferences rather than by objective procedures. The choice of theories to believe in and to test is also very subjective. And, there are the findings by Rosenthal (1966) showing that even in the experiment itself, beliefs about how the experiment "should" come out may affect the data in a variety of ways.

In the discussion about theory in the previous section, I suggested that there was a larger pay-off for doing an experiment that tends to reject a theory. For these reasons, scientists often attack a theory by experiment with a strong suspicion—or hope, even—that the experiment will turn out a certain way, because that particular outcome (e.g., rejection of a theory) means a great deal more than another outcome (e.g., "support" for a theory) in terms of understanding the world. Of course, the scientist must constantly guard against allowing personal biases about the possible outcome to actually affect that outcome, and it is certainly not clear how successful scientists are in this regard. To be sure, the stereotype that most undergraduates have of the scientist as a highly objective and value-free individual who passively observes the nature of things in the world is an incorrect view of the typical scientist.

Empiricism

To this point, I have suggested that most scientists operate in the same way, their goals being theory development and testing. There are wide differences, however, in the degree to which scientists believe in this theory-based method, and an alternative orientation has been called *empiricism* (Adams, 1967). The term empirical means depending on experience (i.e., data or the results of experiments) without regard to theory. Imagine a continuum that defines the extent to which the scientist uses theory in his thinking. Label one end of the continuum "empirical" (the scientist operates totally without regard to theory), and the other end "theoretical" (the scientist has total regard for theory).

Empirical ——————————————————————— Theoretical

The true empiricist collects facts and observations from experiments for their own sake and without regard for the theories upon which these experimental outcomes might bear. The scientist operating at the other end of this continuum conducts experiments only because the study will tell him something about a theory that is under consideration. It is interesting to note that the experiments that these two scientists might conduct could be identical in method and result; the only difference is the reason that they were done. The empiricist wanted to find out about a particular set of experimental variables, while the theorist wanted to determine the relation between these two variables only because the relation is (or is not) predicted from a theory.

Many have argued (e.g., Adams, 1967) that there is a great deal of empiricism in both psychology and motor behavior today. In motor behavior, many feel that the field is too young for theorizing and that more facts are needed (which lead to laws) before advancing to the theory level. Others believe that there are sufficient facts and that it is time to advance to the theory stage in our science. The theorists argue that more facts simply "clutter up" the journals, since they do not directly relate to an understanding. Forscher (1963) likens this glut of facts to randomly placed bricks in a brickyard, with additional bricks just adding to the chaos; what is needed, he argues, is the unifying effect of a plan for a building (a theory, in the analogy) that can structure or order the bricks in some meaningful way. The brickyard does not need any more bricks (facts).

On the other hand, perhaps the most famous psychologist in the world today, B.F. Skinner, is a self-proclaimed empiricist. He argues (Skinner, 1956) that the theoretical method has a number of drawbacks. First, the method often places "blinders" on the experimenter, since the experimenter is looking only at those aspects of the data that have relevance for the theory under test. Skinner feels that important and meaningful relationships are often overlooked in these cases. He cites an example that the discovery of the important principle of *intermittent reinforcement* (rewarding an animal for an act only occasionally leads to increased probability of the response) was discovered by accident. Apparently, the machinery that automatically dispensed the pellets of food (the reward) through the night began to malfunction, dispensing the pellets only occasionally. The records showed that the animals were responding at a very high rate under these conditions. The empiricist would argue that the theorist would throw out the data because they did not provide a good test of the original theory and do the experiment over again when the machinery was repaired, apparently missing the principle. The theorist, on the other hand, would argue that accidental findings are rare or that even the most avid theorist would not miss such an obvious result (Adams, 1967; Platt, 1964).

A major difference between the theoretical and empirical methods relates to the efficiency with which each will lead to an understanding of the subject under study. If scientists accept the logic of the scientific method, for which the major goal is understanding and explanation and experiments are effective ways of ruling out incorrect theories, then the empirical method

seems to be relatively weak. The empiricist would counter this claim by saying that this understanding will come automatically as the number of
separate facts and laws are multiplied. It seems to me that this is as likely as
a monkey at a piano composing "Blowin' in the Wind" through an unsystematic combination of the notes. To be sure, operating theoretically is
not as easy as operating empirically, as the experiments must always be
designed with the rejection of a theory in mind; but the potential for
establishing explanations of motor behavior seems to be worth the extra effort.

Basic versus Applied Research

There is a second dimension to research that is independent of the empirical theoretical dimension. This dimension relates to the extent to which
the research was done to solve some practical problem.

Label one end of a continuum "Applied," where the motivation to do a
particular experiment was that it led to the solution of some immediately
pressing practical problem. For example, I might need to know if it were
more efficient for workers on an assembly line to perform Operation A
before Operation B, or vice versa. I could do the experiment, having half
the employees work in A-B order and the other half work in B-A order. If
the B-A order is more effective, then this order should be considered in setting up the assembly line. The motivation for the experiment was the solution of a practical problem.

Label the other end of this continuum "Basic." The motivation for an
experiment is interest in the problem, but there is absolutely no practical application for the result. I overheard a conversation between two mathematicians who were discussing the fact that a set of theorems discovered around
1910 were finally being put to use for the first time in the design of computers. The mathematician who did the work in 1910 probably had no practical application in mind. A combination of this dimension and the em-
pirical/theoretical dimension is shown as:

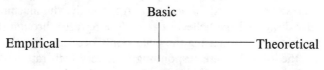

The major advantage to applied research is that it has immediate applicability to the specific problem that motivated it, but seldom do the findings contribute to the development of theory. Thus, applied research, from
the broader perspective of establishing an understanding of motor control,
seems somewhat inefficient.

Basic research, on the other hand, since it is not tied to specific variables
as is applied research, has more generality. More importantly, basic
research often leads to modifications in theory because the results are more
generally applicable to a greater number of situations, some of which might

be the concern of some particular theory. It has been said that "There is nothing more practical than a good theory" (Kerlinger, 1973, p. 10). A "good" theory enables scientists to predict new laws, some of which have immense practical applicability. Understanding the underlying mechanisms and processes makes possible intelligent application of the theory, perhaps even to the solution of practical problems.

This might, at first, seem backwards. Perhaps, in the long run, answers to practical problems are found through basic research. The disadvantage is that practical application must wait for sufficient knowledge to be accumulated. Hopefully, coming to an understanding of how the motor system operates through theories and principles will contribute more to application than will studying the areas of applicability directly.

SUMMARY

The goal of motor control research (indeed, the goal of all branches of science) is the generation of knowledge leading to an understanding of the phenomena under investigation. Science can be thought of as having three distinct levels, each contributing toward this overall goal.

At the most fundamental level are *facts, observations,* or *results,* usually derived from the outcome of *experiments* or other data collection methods, in which the effect of some *independent variable* on some other *dependent variable* is measured. These effects lead to the establishment of *relationships* between two or more variables. When a number of separate relationships have been found, these can be generalized into verbal or mathematical statements called *laws.* As the second level in the scientific structure, laws represent statements of stable dependency between independent and dependent variables and serve as summary statements for the experiments. When a number of laws have been established, attempts to *explain* these laws lead to the generation of *theory,* which constitutes the third level in the scientific structure. Theories are hypothetical structures that provide an underlying explanation of the phenomena of interest, and they contain (a) *hypothetical constructs,* (b) *postulates,* and (c) *coordinating definitions.* Theories can be tested by deriving *potential laws* (called *hypotheses*) from them and then by conducting experiments to determine if the predicted outcome holds in the laboratory. Finally, *models* provide analogies to the phenomena under consideration and are useful companions to theories.

Scientists engage in research in a number of different ways. One is termed *empirical,* in which the collection of facts is a major goal. Another is termed *theoretical,* in which facts are collected only because they have a bearing on some theory. Furthermore, many scientists have a primary interest in practical applications of their work (an *applied* orientation), while others are more concerned with the establishment of fundamental principles (a *basic* orientation). The principles discussed in this chapter should contribute to the student's understanding of the research on motor control which is presented later.

GLOSSARY

Causation. An experimental outcome in which a dependent variable necessarily changes as a result of a change in an independent variable.

Continuous variable. A variable whose values can take any real number.

Coordinating (operational) definition. A part of a theory which defines the behavior of the constructs in terms of measurable variables.

Deduction. The logical method of reasoning from generalizations to specific relations or facts.

Dependent variable. The variable which is measured in an experiment and which is studied in relation to the value of other variables.

Discrete variable. A variable which can take only specified real number values, such as high/low or small/medium/large.

Experiment. An operation in which the effects of artificial manipulations of some independent variable on some dependent variable are measured.

Hypothesis. A conjectured statement about the relationship between an independent variable and a dependent variable, which is often deduced from a theory.

Hypothetical construct. An abstract, imaginary entity which serves as a fundamental element in a theory.

Independent variable. The variable which is manipulated in an experiment, with resulting effects on a dependent variable which are studied.

Induction. The logical process of reasoning from specific facts to general principles.

Interval variable. A variable for which different values have order relations and for which the intervals between successive values represent the same changes in the behavior being measured.

Law. A statement of a stable dependency between an independent variable and a dependent variable.

Model. An analogy to a theory which helps in visualizing the theory; often used as mathematical or mechanical simulation of phenomena.

Natural experiment. A procedure for collecting data in which an independent variable is allowed to vary naturally, with the relation between this variation and that of a dependent variable being measured.

Nominal variable. A variable for which values represent the names of things, with no order implied.

Observations (facts). The measured values of dependent variables, usually produced from an experiment.

Ordinal variable. A variable for which values have order relations implied.

Postulate. A statement inherent in a theory that describes the relationship of the hypothetical constructs.

Pseudo-experiment. A procedure for collecting data in which objects are classified on some dimension, and the relation between this classification and a dependent variable is assessed.

Ratio variable. A variable for which different values have order and interval relations and which also possesses an absolute zero.

Relationship. The tendency for variations in one variable to be associated with variations in some other variable.

Theory. An abstract hypothetical explanation for a group of laws and facts.

SECTION II

MOTOR BEHAVIOR AND CONTROL

This second section is concerned with notions variously called motor behavior, motor control, or human performance. It deals with the principles of, and processes underlying, motor performances, ranging from simple movements, to rather stereotyped responses in animals and humans such as locomotion, to highly flexible and complex behaviors that receive a great deal of practice. First, methods are described for studying motor skills. Chapters 4 and 5 deal with cognitive-psychological approaches to skill, emphasizing information processing, memory, and attention. Then, Chapters 6 through 9 treat the neurophysiology of movement control and motor programming, and the control of various kinds of responses are described. The section ends with a discussion in Chapter 10 of factors that tend to make individuals differ in their skilled behaviors.

CHAPTER 3

Methodology in Studying Motor Behavior

I will now turn to the application of the scientific method to the study of motor behavior and motor control. A major goal of this book is to present not only relevant principles and theories about the nature of motor performance and control, but also to present the research evidence that supports (or, in some cases, refutes) these principles and theories. In evaluating this evidence, it will be necessary to understand something of the methods of this research and how the motor behaviors are measured, so that the relevance of this evidence to the particular principle or theory in question can be more effectively established.

CLASSIFICATION OF BEHAVIOR

In any field of study, the objects under investigation are usually classified according to some scheme or framework, in order to simplify the discussion. The field of motor behavior is no exception. Classification of movement responses and motor tasks is important for two fundamental reasons. First, in the research literature in motor behavior and control, various terms are used to describe the tasks and movements. These terms must be understood to communicate about the field. The second reason is that the laws of motor behavior seem to depend on the kinds of performances under consideration. That is, the relationship between certain independent and dependent variables is often different for one kind of task or behavior as compared to another. So classification is done for good reason; without it, the laws of motor control would be far more complicated than they are.

Motor versus Verbal-Cognitive Responses

I will begin the classification by considering all of human behavior. One distinction which has already been made is between (a) motor behavior and (b) verbal or cognitive behavior. There is really no objective way to make this division, so the division is more conceptual than practical. Even so, it is helpful to distinguish between those movements for which the determinant of success is primarily related to the verbal or cognitive elements and those movements for which the primary determinant of success is the motor behavior itself.

In Chapter 1, I emphasized that the major focus of the text is on motor responses, those for which decision making and cognition are minimal. To completely exclude these cognitive processes from a study of motor behavior would produce a very unnatural division, however, so reference is made to these processes when they are particularly relevant (e.g., in Chapters 4 and 5).

Classifications of Motor Responses

The Discrete/Continuous Dimension

Discrete movements. Discrete skills are those with a recognizable beginning and end. Kicking, throwing, striking a match, and shifting gears in a car are examples (Figure 3-1). A film of one of these skills would show the beginning, the middle, and the end. This finishing point is defined by the skill in question, not arbitrarily by when an observer ceased examining it, as would be the case for swimming, jogging, etc. Another characteristic of discrete skills is that they are usually rapid, seldom requiring more than a second to complete. While this may be a characteristic of discrete skills, it should not be taken as a definition of them.

The discrete skills are also often very cognitive in nature. For example, a common task is to press one of four buttons when one of four lights comes on (there are many variants on this basic theme), the problem being for the subject to decide which light goes with which button. Thus, the decision about which button to push is paramount, and the "how" of pushing the button is clearly secondary in importance. While many discrete skills have

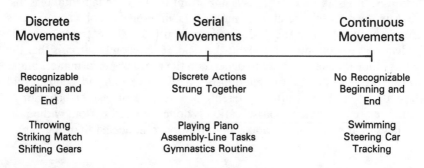

Figure 3-1. The discrete-serial-continuous classification for motor behavior.

large verbal-cognitive components, there are certainly examples that are highly "motor" in nature as well.

Continuous movements. At the opposite end of the continuum (in Figure 3-1) are *continuous movements*, defined as having no recognizable beginning and end, with behavior continuing until the response is arbitrarily stopped. Examples are swimming, running, and steering a car. Notice that if we were to film these responses, there would be no way to determine the beginning, middle, or end of the response, as the "end" would be determined purely arbitrarily. Continuous tasks tend to have longer movement times than do discrete tasks (they might continue all day), but, again, this should not be taken as the basic definition of them.

A common class of continuous skills, both in everyday experiences and in the laboratory, is the tracking task. It is characterized by a pathway (track) that the individual is to follow and some device that the individual attempts to make follow the track via certain limb movements. In steering a car, for example, the track is the road, and the follower is the car. A very common laboratory example involves two dots on a TV-like screen. One of the dots is moved by the experimenter (or by a computer), and it moves in either an uncertain or predictable way back and forth on the screen. The second dot is moved by the subject via a hand control, and the subject's task is to attempt to keep the two dots aligned. In a sense, this is like steering a car. If the car is fixed with the road moving under it, the road becomes a moving target to be tracked with the steering mechanisms of the car.

There are basically two kinds of tracking tasks: *pursuit* and *compensatory*. In pursuit tracking, experimenter-produced actions of the target and the subject's own movements are both displayed in relation to each other for the subject to monitor. A practical example is steering a car. In compensatory tracking, the experimenter-produced variations in the track are combined with the subject's movements to produce a single displayed value, and the subject's goal is to maintain this value at some constant location. Practical examples of compensatory tracking are often seen in aircraft instruments, such as the glideslope indicator; here the difference between the proper altitude and the actual altitude is displayed, and when the dial is in the middle of the screen, the pilot's altitude is correct. Compensatory tracking tasks are almost always more "difficult" than pursuit tracking tasks, especially if the behavior of the track is irregular and unpredictable. Probably this results because the movements of the track and of the hand tend to be easily confused. For some reason, aircraft designers often have pursuit displays adjacent to compensatory displays on the instrument panel (e.g., a glidepath indicator and an altimeter), which would seem to be quite confusing, at least for the novice pilot.

Tracking tasks also vary in terms of the aspect of the display that the subject controls. The most simple is the *zero-order,* or positional, display. If the subject moves the handle from one position to another and then stops, the indicator on the display moves a proportional amount and also stops; that is, the handle movements control the pointer's position. In a *first-order,* or velocity control, movement of the handle causes changes in velocity of the pointer. Moving the handle farther in one direction causes the velocity of the pointer to increase in the same direction, and stopping the handle movement off center results in a constant velocity of pointer movement. Finally, in a *second-order* task, the movements of the control produce changes in the pointer's acceleration. Keeping the handle centered produces zero acceleration, but moving the handle to a new position off center results in the pointer accelerating off the screen in the same direction. Each of these kinds of tracking tasks is used in research, and there are real-world examples of each in various control systems (see Poulton, 1974, for more details).

One final type of tracking task deserves mention—*step tracking*. In this task, the track "jumps" from one fixed location to another, often unpredictably, and the subject's task is to move the control as quickly as possible to correct for this sudden change in the track's location. Step-tracking tasks can be either pursuit or compensatory in nature.

Serial movements. There are a number of skills that seem neither discrete nor continuous, as they seem to be made up of a series of discrete actions strung together in time to make some "whole." Examples are starting a car, filling and lighting a pipe, and many tasks on production lines in industry. Such tasks may require many seconds to complete, and they may appear to be continuous, although they might have discrete beginnings and ends. Serial tasks can be thought of as a number of discrete tasks strung together, with the order of the actions being important. It is sometimes very difficult to classify responses, since the categories seem to overlap in important ways.

Open versus Closed Dimension

Open movements. Another way to classify skills is in terms of the extent to which the environment is predictable during the performance (Poulton, 1957). *Open skills* are those for which the environment is constantly (perhaps unpredictably) changing, so that the performer can not effectively plan the response (Figure 3-2). A good example is the football player about to return a punt. While there might be a general plan about the side of the field on which to run, the specific actions must be determined by on-the-spot decisions regarding potential tacklers. Other examples of open skills are those involving an opponent whose behavior is unpredictable, such as in fencing and wrestling. Success in open skills seems to be determined by the extent to which the performer is successful in adapting the behavior to the changing environment. Often this adaptation must be extremely rapid, and

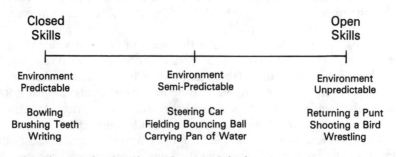

Figure 3-2. The open-closed continuum for motor behavior.

the effective responder must have many such different actions at his or her disposal.

Closed movements. At the other end of the continuum shown in Figure 3-2 are closed skills, for which the environment is predictable. An environment may be predictable because it is perfectly stable, such as for skills like archery, bowling, signing one's name to a check. Also a predictable environment can arise when the environment is variable, but the changes are either very predictable and/or have been learned as a result of practice; examples are juggling or industrial production line tasks. Here, the essential feature is that the environment for the next few seconds or so is essentially predictable, so that the movement can be planned in advance. The successful performer can anticipate the behavior of the environment in the near future. Of course, some skills have environments that are semi-predictable, and these can be classified somewhere between the ends of the open/closed continuum in Figure 3-2. Farrell (1975) has provided additional distinctions that help us to classify movements on this dimension.

The observation that open skills seem to require rapid adaptations to a changing environment, while closed skills require very consistent and stable performances in a predictable environment, raises interesting questions about how the two classes of responses might best be learned and/or taught. Should the methods for teaching open and closed skills be different? Do different individuals perform better in one skill or another? Are the laws of performance different for the two kinds of skills? Evidence suggests that the answer to these questions is "yes," and I will discuss these issues in more detail in later chapters.

BASIC CONSIDERATIONS IN MEASUREMENT

A fundamental issue in any science concerns how the behaviors of the objects of study are measured, and the field of motor behavior is no exception. We are often faced with operationalizing a construct we might term *skillfulness* so that we can assign numerical values to certain performances according to where we think they fall on this dimension. Scientists must be able to measure the degree of skill exhibited by a performer in scientifically acceptable ways. Some of the criteria for good measurement systems are (a) objectivity of the system, (b) reliability (or stability) of the measuring system, and (c) the validity of the system.

Objectivity

The term *objectivity* is important in measurement, because of the scientific demand that observations be subject to public verification. A measurement system is objective if two observers evaluating the same performance arrive at the same (or very similar) measurements. Measuring the distance that a javelin was thrown with a tape measure yields very similar results no matter who reads the tape. By comparison, evaluation of performances such as diving, gymnastics, and figure skating is more subjective, although elaborate scoring rules, complete with certification tests for judges, help make them more objective. From the point of view of research in motor behavior, it is important to use performances in the laboratory that have as much objectivity in scoring as possible, and this necessarily limits the usefulness of tasks such as figure skating for coming to an understanding of motor behavior in general.

A second aspect of objectivity is related to the sensitivity of the measuring device to changes in the skill of the performer. How high did the girl jump when she set the school record in the high jump? The record books say that she jumped 5 ft. 6½ in. But I say that she jumped *at least* 5 ft. 6½ in. The measurement system for the high jump (and for the pole vault) only indicates whether or not the bar was struck during the jump. It is possible that the successful jumper may have cleared the bar by 2 ft; and the system cannot discriminate between a slight "tick" of the bar and a missed jump. In such situations, the scoring system is *insensitive* to the variations in the performer's actual level of skill. Other examples of insensitivity are seen in tasks such as driving; we can measure certain aspects of driver behavior (steering movement, smoothness, etc.), but these do not seem to capture (or are insensitive to) other aspects of the skill of driving, such as the skill in avoiding an accident in a crisis situation, or one's ability to traverse a road course in a race car. Often measurements of performance on simple or highly practiced tasks do not tell much about the person's level of skill in that activity.

In the example with the high jumper, the scale of measurement itself was acceptable in sensitivity; in fact, we often see officials in track meets measuring the height of the bar very carefully, perhaps to the nearest ¼ in. What was lacking in that example was the successful interpretation of that accuracy in terms of the jumper's performance. However, sometimes the scale of measurement itself is lacking in precision. Often, continuous measures are artificially categorized, such as hit/miss with respect to basketball and golf putting, and hit/lean/miss in the case of horseshoes. Here, the details of the movement, together with information about the performer's skill level, are lost in this oversimplified measurement method. Such methods make it very difficult to determine if an individual has improved on the task with practice or which of two individuals is the more skilled performer, both of which may be critical questions in the study of movement.

Reliability

A second aspect of the measurement system important to motor behavior is reliability, the extent to which the measurement is repeatable under similar conditions. A lack of reliability can result from random technological error, such as the stretch in measuring tapes, errors in clocks, and errors in reading instruments. These errors, while they might seem to be important sources of unreliability, probably contribute very little, provided that a high quality recording apparatus is used. The most important source of unreliability is the performer's not being able (or willing) to perform the

same act twice in exactly the same way. Some of these intra-subject variations are caused by momentary changes in the internal state of the subject,
such as attention, fatigue, boredom, etc., while others are caused by
systematic changes, such as the level of learning of the task, changes in
strategy, and the like. Both of these factors contribute to unreliability in
measurement and interfere with the scientific goal of understanding the
laws and theories of motor performance because the constructs that scientists are attempting to measure are obscured by this variability in the
measurement system.

Experimenters seek to minimize these sources of variability through experimental control in the testing situation. Researchers typically use tape-
recorded instructions to subjects to eliminate variability in what is said; they
use testing rooms that are either silenced or sound-deadened; subjects are
tested one at a time to eliminate variability due to another subject in the
room; and the entire experimental session is often quite formal and imper-
sonal. These procedures tend to reduce these sources of variability so that
the experimental effects can be more easily observed. This is the primary
reason why motor behaviorists tend not to measure skills in everyday settings, such as in ball games or on the production line in industry. In these
situations, the environment is not well controlled, there being many sources
of variation from other players or workers, from the changes in the score in
the game, from the level of proficiency of the opponents, and so on. For
reasons of experimental control primarily, motor behavior tends to be most
profitably studied in the laboratory, away from these sources of variability.
To be sure, this makes the situation less life-like, and the measures we take
are not quite so directly related to practical settings, but the alternative of
studying skills during a football game seems particularly hopeless.

While the procedures mentioned above can reduce variability in experimental settings, there is one source of variability that apparently cannot
be reduced by such methods—variability due to biological causes. Even in
situations where the task is well learned and simple, where the experimental
situation is well controlled, and the subject is trying hard to do well, there is
still a great deal of variability due to the fact that biological systems are
oscillatory. Experimentally, the best method for countering this type of
variability is to provide many observations of the "same" behavior on the
same subject, taking the average of a large number of measurements under
essentially identical conditions. By so doing, the variations in the subject's
performance tend to "average out," raising the reliability of the measurement system, so that the mean of a large number of observations more
closely represents the construct we are attempting to measure.

Validity

Another aspect of the measurement process is validity, the extent to
which the test measures what the researcher intends it to measure. An important aspect of validity (called construct validity) is the extent to which
the measures taken actually reflect the underlying hypothetical construct of

interest. We would be reasonably comfortable with a 10-min. typing test to operationalize typing skill, but we would perhaps be less comfortable with a measure of finger tapping speed to assess the same construct. This issue relates back to the questions raised relative to coordinating definitions (see Chapter 2). Thus, the validity of a test can be seen as the extent to which the measures taken reflect the appropriate use of the coordinating definition. The problem becomes increasingly difficult when measuring abstract and/or complex constructs, such as intelligence or balancing ability; and interpretations of research frequently depend on what individual researchers believe the measures to mean.

There are, on the other hand, situations where validity does not seem to present much of a problem. One of these involves what is often called "face-valid" tests, which are so obviously measures of the concept in question that they usually are not questioned. For example, if I am interested in who of a group of individuals has most skill in javelin throwing (a construct), I might have them all throw the javelin as a standardized test.

Another class of measurement situations in which the importance of validity is minimal is in experiments on motor learning. In these situations, an arbitrary task is created that represents a motor performance that is novel to the subject, and the experimenter studies how the subject attempts to learn it and/or what variables influence that learning. The particular constructs being measured (e.g., balance, timing, movement speed) frequently are not important to the experimenter, because the primary focus is on the variables that affect performance and learning generally (see the discussion about the "task-oriented" approach later in this chapter for more on this issue).

MEASURING MOTOR BEHAVIOR

In the field of motor behavior and control, the problem of measurement can be approached in two different ways. First, there is concern for quantifying the nature of the actual movements that the person made. These can be expressed in a variety of different forms, each of which describes various aspects of the movement itself. Second, there is concern for how well the movement achieved some environmental goal that was inherent in the task (e.g., whether or not a target was struck). These two classes of measurement are discussed in the following sections.

Describing Characteristics of Movements

Countless methods could be used to describe movements, depending on the characteristics of the movement that were of interest to the observer. For example, movements have been described in dance notation created by Laban (1956), in terms of units of work behavior called "Therbligs" in time and motion studies, and in scientific settings in terms of descriptors that are used in the physical sciences (Plagenhoef, 1971). Because of their widespread use, this latter group of measurement methods—collectively called *kinematics*—will be treated here.

Movement Kinematics

Kinematics, a branch of mechanics in physics, involves the description of "pure" motion, without regard for the forces and masses that are involved. As applied to movement behavior, then, kinematic measures are those that describe the movement of the limbs and/or the entire body. A moment's reflection will reveal that there must be many separate ways to describe such movements. The locations of various parts of the body during the movement, the angles of the various joints, and the time relations between the movement in one joint and the movement in another, can all be recorded. The devices that can be used to collect this information are widely varied also. For simplicity, I will mention here only some of the most common kinematic methods.

Recording locations. Perhaps the most common of the kinematic methods involves recording the locations of the limbs during a movement. Early in the history of motor behavior and biomechanics, researchers used cinematography to record the movements, and then these films were studied frame-by-frame to measure the locations of certain landmarks (e.g., the location of the wrist, ankle, and so on). These positions on successive frames were separated by nearly fixed periods of time, so that a graph of position of the landmark against time could be generated from these data.

Figure 3-3 shows such an example, in which the locations of the ball of the foot, the ankle, knee, hip, wrist, elbow, and shoulder are plotted during a jumping motion from a squatting position (Plagenhoef, 1971). From such a record, one can plot any number of different location-time curves, such as the height of the shoulder or the angle of the elbow as a function of time. Which of these data one chooses to study will depend on the particular scientific questions that are being asked.

Similar data can be obtained through other methods that have tended to replace film analysis. For example, light-sensing devices can detect the locations of tiny light bulbs (called light-emitting diodes, or LEDs) attached to the limbs and record their location automatically by computer; another device can detect the locations of tiny sound-emitting devices attached to the limbs. Such devices have relieved the scientist of the time-consuming job of reading locations from each frame of film, as had been done previously. But, because they are expensive and require more technological expertise, film is still used for many applications.

Another way of determining the location of the performer as a function of time is to have the performer move a lever or other mechanical device and then to record the positions of the device. For example, in a technique used quite often, the subject makes a simple arm movement (say, an elbow flexion to a new position), that moves a lever attached to a potentiometer, a device that produces a voltage proportional to the angle to which it is moved. The potentiometer output is recorded on a recording device, either a stripchart recorder on which the changes in voltage are represented as changes in the locations of a line, or a computer in which the voltages are stored electronically.

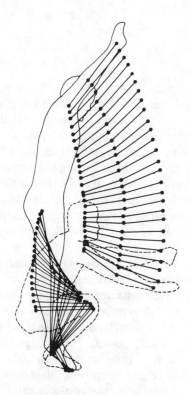

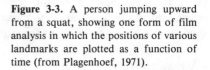

Figure 3-3. A person jumping upward from a squat, showing one form of film analysis in which the positions of various landmarks are plotted as a function of time (from Plagenhoef, 1971).

An example of one of these records is shown in Figure 3-4, taken from Wadman, Denier van der Gon, Geuze, and Mol (1979). For now, consider only the top trace, that labeled "position." This trace, read from left to right, represents an arm movement of about 17 cm. It began where the trace leaves the horizontal axis, the largest amplitude (about 20 cm) achieved about 125 msec after it started, and then the limb reversed direction to stabilize its position at the final location. The value of the peak velocity (shown by the steepest inclination of the curve) can also be estimated, as well as the location in the movement where the peak velocity occurred (about 75 msec after the movement started). However, such additional information can be obtained more precisely by measuring the velocity directly.

Recording velocities. In the second trace in Figure 3-4 is a record of the velocity of the response at each moment in time, placed on the same time scale as the positional trace for each easy comparison. Here, the velocity trace was determined by computer, which read in the position information from the potentiometer and then computed the slope or inclination of the line at each moment (which is, by definition, the movement velocity).[1] Then this information is output on the same record as the position information. Such a trace is quite useful in showing that the maximum velocity (Vm) was

---

[1]From calculus, the slopes (called derivatives) of the positions at each moment in time yield the velocities at corresponding moments, and the slopes of the velocities yield the accelerations. From physics, the velocity is the rate of change in position, and the acceleration is the rate of change in velocity.

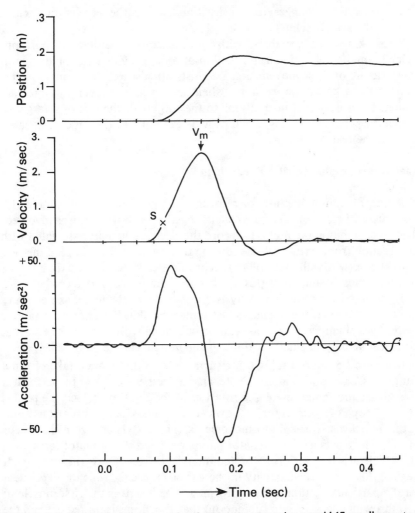

Figure 3-4. Position, velocity, and acceleration traces representing a rapid 17-cm elbow extension movement (from Wadman et al., 1979).

about 2.7 msec and that the maximum velocity occurred at about 75 msec through movement. Also shown is a gradual increase in velocity until the peak velocity (the midpoint of the movement) and then a decline toward the end. Also, there was a velocity in the negative direction (i.e., a backward movement) when the slight overshoot occurred near the end of the movement. Such a trace gives a more complete description of the movement than does positional information.

Recording acceleration. In the third trace in Figure 3-4 is a record of the acceleration at each moment of time. This record is also obtained by the computer, which calculated the slope or inclination of the velocity curve at each moment and then output it along with the other two traces on the same time scale. There is an acceleration that lasts about 100 msec until the acceleration trace returns to zero. Then there is a deceleration (indicated by a negative acceleration trace) that lasts for about the same length of time. Also, the peak velocity of the movement is achieved at the point at which the acceleration changes to deceleration (where the acceleration curve crosses the zero baseline).

These kinematic variables, with simultaneous recording of position, velocity, and acceleration as a function of time, provide a reasonably complete picture of these movements. Scientists often search for changes in certain of these kinematic variables when certain independent variables are changed, for example, instructions to the subject or the size of a target to which the person is moving. I will provide examples of this kind of research later in the text.

Electromyographic (EMG) Recordings

Another common method for recording a movement is to measure the involvement of a muscle in a movement, together with when it was involved. The most common method is to record the electrical activity associated with contraction from certain muscles during the response. The simplest method is to attach (with adhesive collars) recording electrodes to the skin over the involved muscle and have this weak signal amplified and recorded on a polygraph recorder for later analysis. Occasionally subcutaneous electrodes are used; the electrode is placed just under the skin but above the muscle belly. Or a small wire electrode can be imbedded within the muscle so that electrical activity in small portions of the muscle can be recorded.

In Figure 3-5 is a recording using surface electrodes in man, taken from a study by Carter and Shapiro (Note 1). Subjects were asked to perform a four-phase movement involving rotation of the right wrist, and the record at the top of the figure shows the clockwise (supination) and counterclockwise (pronation) movements. The EMGs are from the biceps muscle which acts as the supinator (clockwise) and the pronator teres muscle which acts as the pronator (counterclockwise). Once the movement begins, there is marked activity in the various muscles, which is dependent on the particular action being performed. The biceps is the first muscle to act, throwing the wrist into supination; then the biceps is turned off and the pronator acts to brake the action and reverse it; then the biceps brakes and reverses that action; and so on. These records indicate something about the temporal patterning of the movement segments. Also, it is possible to say something about the intensity of contraction from the amplitude of these records, with larger EMG amplitudes being generally indicative of larger forces. However, while there is a good relation between EMG amplitude and force under controlled conditions within a given muscle, many situations arise that can degrade this relation, so that the amount of force produced is usually not well reflected by the amount of EMG being produced. Generally, EMG records like this are useful for obtaining information about the temporal structure of movement patterns but are of limited utility in determining the forces involved in the action, although the EMGs can serve as rough indicators of the latter.

In Figure 3-6 is a record of the transformed EMG activity taken during a rapid elbow extension (from Wadman et al., 1979). Here, a number of changes have been made in the raw EMG signals before they were recorded. First, the EMGs have been *rectified;* that is, the negative voltage values have

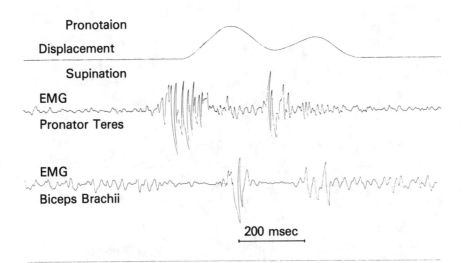

Figure 3-5. A typical EMG tracing taken during a movement (from Carter & Shapiro, Note 1).

been given positive signs, so that the resulting record is positive. (Notice that Figure 3-6 has two such records and that the record for the biceps muscle is inverted so that the two patterns can be compared more easily.) By rectifying the EMG, the pattern of electrical activity, a contraction can be seen more easily than is the case with the raw signals in Figure 3-5. Second, these records are averages for a number of similar responses, mainly so that the important patterns of contractions can be seen over and above the trial-to-trial variations. These patterns are more reliable than they would be for a single trial.

Such records are very useful, as they provide one kind of description of what the central nervous system "tells" the muscles to do. In the example shown, it appears that the central nervous system causes the triceps muscle to contract for about 100 msec; then it is turned off and the biceps muscle contracts for about 50 msec; then the triceps muscle comes on again for another burst of about 100 msec. These records are even more helpful if they are superimposed on other records of kinematic information, such as shown in Figure 3-5, so that the changes in the muscle actions can be associated with the actions of the limbs. This is frequently done in motor control research.

Describing the Outcome of Movements

The second aspect of measurement in motor behavior is the quantification of the extent to which a given movement achieved the goal that was intended or instructed. For example, did the movement result in striking the target, or was the movement made at the right time? Such measures are generally concerned with the movement in relation to some object or other performer in the environment, although some movements (e.g., modern dance, diving) may not be strongly tied to the environment. While it may seem that there are a wide variety of ways that the achievement of such en-

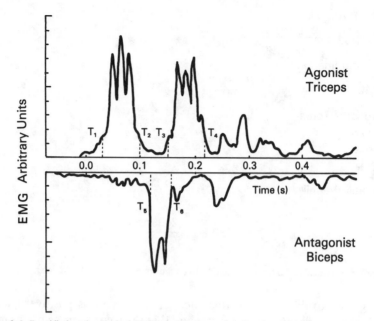

Figure 3-6. Rectified and averaged EMG signals from the triceps and biceps muscles during a rapid elbow extension (from Wadman et al., 1979).

vironmental goals can be assessed, they can be measured in three fundamental ways: (a) error, (b) speed, and (c) response magnitude.

Measures of Error

Many of the performances studied require that the subject do something with minimum error, thus the performance measures are some form of accuracy score. The goal of accuracy can be imposed in a wide variety of ways, such as moving with a certain amount of force, hitting a certain spatial target, or moving at a certain speed. An important class of tasks requiring accuracy is *timing tasks,* in which the individual must perform some act at a particular time (e.g., hitting a baseball).

In all of these cases, there can be defined a correct force, distance, speed, or time that is the subject's target; then deviations of the subject's performances with respect to this target are measured. At the most crude level, the performances can be scored as hit/miss, or right/wrong, such as in shooting a basketball or judging which of two lifted weights is heavier. The accuracy score can be refined by dividing the possible outcomes into hit/almost hit/miss, or by dividing a target for dart throwing into 10 or more zones, but motor performance is complex and more sophistication in the measurement of accuracy is required. Thus various methods have been developed for studying both the amount and nature of errors by using simple statistical error scores.

In the discussion that follows, assume that the performer is striving for accuracy in arriving at some target (e.g., a force, a speed, a location in space) and that the responses can be placed along some measurable dimen-

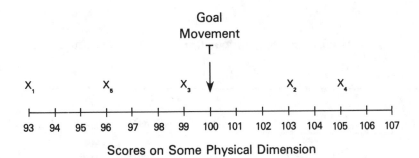

Figure 3-7. An arbitrary measurement scale, showing locations of a target (T) and of five hypothetical movement attempts ($x_1, \ldots, x_5$).

sion (e.g., kilograms, centimeters/second, centimeters) as in Figure 3-7. Let the correct value along this dimension—the tartet—have the value T. The values that the performer actually achieves are abbreviated by x_i, where i is a subscript notating a particular trial. That is, x_{23} is the score on the twenty-third trial. In the simple formulae that describe these fundamental statistical accuracy scores, the symbol Σ means "the sum of." For example, Σx_i means to add up all of the values x_i, where i ranges progressively from 1 through 5. That is, $\sum_{i=1}^{5} x_i = x_1 + x_2 + x_3 + x_4 + x_5$.

In the explanation of the various measures of error that follows, assume that there is some physical measuring dimension, that the target the person is attempting to achieve is 100 units on this dimension, and that the individual does not always achieve this target score. Here then, T (the abbreviation for the value of the target) is 100 units. In Figure 3-7, there are five scores: 93, 103, 99, 105, and 96 units for Trials 1 through 5 respectively.

It is obvious that no single trial will be very effective in describing the subject's behavior, as the scores possess a great deal of variability. One solution, therefore, is to combine these scores to achieve a more representative measure of the subject's capability. In the study of motor behavior, researchers have typically focused on four methods for combining scores. Each has a slightly different meaning in terms of the performer's capability. These four methods are described in the next sections as (a) constant error, (b) variable error, (c) total variability, and (d) absolute error.

Constant error (CE)—computation. The first statistic to be considered as a measure of the subject's accuracy is the *constant error* (CE), which measures the average error in responding. Its formula is

$$\text{Constant error} = \frac{\sum_{i=1}^{n} (x_i - T)}{n}, \tag{3-1}$$

where x_i is the score on Trial i, T is the target, and *n* is the number of trials the subject performed. It is very easy to compute this measure from Table 3-1, which provides a "worktable" for computing all of the statistics presented in this section on error measures. In Column A, the trial numbers are listed; the obtained scores (x_i) are given in Column B. All other values in the table are computed from these initial values.

Table 3-1

Worktable for Computing Various Components of Response Error

A	B	C	D	E	F	G
Trial #	x_i	$(x_i - T)$	$(x_i - CE)$	$(x_i - CE)^2$	$(x_i - T)^2$	$x_i - T$
1	93	−7	−6.2	38.44	49	7
2	103	+3	+3.8	14.44	9	3
3	99	−1	−0.2	0.04	1	1
4	105	+5	+5.8	33.64	25	5
5	96	−4	−3.2	10.24	16	4
Sum	496	−4	—	96.80	100	20
Mean	99.2	− .80	—	19.36	20	4
Square root	—	—	—	4.40	4.47	—

To compute the CE, the numerator calls for subtracting each of the scores on the test (x_i) from the target (100), and these are shown in Column C, headed ($x_i - T$). Notice that the sign of the difference is retained in this column. Next, the summation sign calls for adding values for each of the trials (in this case, 5), and this sum is presented at the bottom of Column C, or −4. (Note: The easiest way to do this by hand is to add up all of the negatives and positives separately and then subtract the two subtotals, assigning the sign of the larger.) Then the formula calls for dividing by n, the number of responses, and the final CE score is −4/5, or −.80.

Interpretation of CE. The score of −4/5 or −.80 indicates that on the average the subject fell slightly short of the target (by .80 units). Notice that the CE is given in units that represent the amount of *deviation,* sometimes called *bias.* One could also ask the subject's scores *on the average* by consulting the mean for Column B. Thus, the average score was 496/5 = 99.2 units, meaning that the subject fell short of the target by 99.2 to 100 units, or −.80 units. The CE represents the average magnitude of the response and measures the direction of the errors on the average.

While a measure of average error might, at first, seem satisfying to students as a measure of accuracy, notice that the value computed for the subject (−.80) was far smaller than the error for any of the single responses that contributed to the average. The responses were scattered a great deal, with the center of responses being roughly the target that was the goal. What the CE does not consider is this amount of scatter, variability, or inconsistency in performing the movements. (Notice that a second hypothetical subject with scores of 99, 99, 99, 99, and 100, representing a very small scatter, would have precisely the same CE score as the subject we have just been considering; compute the CE to verify this.) For this reason, the variable error (VE) is used to describe this aspect of the subject's inconsistency in responding.

Variable error (VE)—computation. The variable error (VE) measures the inconsistency in responding. It is the variability of the subject about the mean response and is calculated by the formula

$$\text{Variable error} = \sqrt{\frac{\sum\limits_{i=1}^{n} (x_i - CE)^2}{n}}, \tag{3-2}$$

where x_i and n are defined as in the previous example. CE is the subject's constant error, calculated as in the previous section and measured in the same units as the scores for the task, so that for this example the CE has the value of 99.2 units, not $-.80$ error units.

To compute the VE for this subject use Table 3-1 again. Notice that the formula indicates first to compute the difference between the performance score and the subject's own CE, so the first step is to compute the subject's CE. Computed in the previous section, the CE for these responses was 99.2 units. Now, the values in Column D of Table 3-1 represent the differences between the scores on the trials and 99.2. For example, $93.0 - 99.2$ equals -6.2, the first entry in Column D. The next instruction from the formula is to square each of these values, and these values are given in Column E. Next, obey the summation sign and add the squared values, the sum of which (96.80) is shown at the bottom of Column E. Then divide by the number of cases to get 19.36 and take the square root to arrive at the final answer of 4.40 units.

Interpretation of VE. The VE is sensitive to variability or inconsistency in responding, as can be seen from the "ingredients" in the formula. The numerator is the important feature in the difference between the subject's score on each trial and his or her own average score (or CE). Thus, if one subject always responds very consistently, then the VE will tend to be small. If the subject always receives the same score, even though it is not the correct one (such as 99), then the VE will be zero. This is so since the subject's CE will be 99, and the difference between each of the scores and the CE will always be zero as well.

One other feature of the VE needs emphasis. Its value does not depend on whether or not the subject was close to the target, since VE is the measure of spread about the subject's CE. To illustrate this point, the VE for the set of scores (43, 53, 49, 55, and 46) achieved while aiming at a target of 100 units will be precisely the same (4.40) as that calculated in the previous example. (These five new values were achieved by subtracting 50 from each of the raw scores in Table 3-1.) Note that the value of the target has nothing to do with the size of VE.

These two measures of performance—the CE and the VE—seem to represent two distinct aspects of responding. The CE represents the average location of the group of responses with respect to the target but without regard to their consistency, and the VE represents the amount of variability in these responses regardless of their locations. These two measures can be combined in various ways to determine measures of "overall error."

Total variability (E)—computation. The total variability around a target (or error) for a set of responses (labeled *E* by Henry, 1976, and often called *root mean square error*), can be thought of as the measure of "overall accuracy" in responding, it being a combination of the VE and CE. E can be defined as the square root of the sum of VE^2 and CE^2:

$$E^2 = VE^2 + CE^2. \tag{3-3}$$

Or, E can be computed directly from the formula

$$\text{Total variability} = \sqrt{\frac{\sum\limits_{i=1}^{n} (x_i - T)^2}{n}}, \tag{3-4}$$

where x_i, T, and n are defined as before. To use the formula, we can use Table 3-1 again. Notice that the major "ingredient" is the difference between the score x_i and the target, and this difference (with the sign included) is given in Table 3, Column C, the same values that were used to compute CE. The next instruction from the formula is to square each of these values, and these are given in Column F. The summation sign then says to add the squared values, and the sum (equal to 100) is given at the bottom of Column F. Next, divide by n (the number of responses included, or 5), which results in a value of 20; then find the square root, so that the final value for E is $\sqrt{20}$, or 4.47.

Interpretation of E. The total variability (E) is the total amount of "spread" of the responses about the target, and so it represents a kind of overall measure of how successful the subject was in achieving the target. The key to understanding this formula is the expression in the numerator $(x_i - T)^2$. E is based on the sum of a group of squared differences, where each difference is the amount by which the subject missed the target. This is in contrast to the VE, where the numerator $(x_i - CE)^2$ represented the deviations from the subject's own CE, not necessarily the target. In many cases, the CE tends to be very close to the aimed-for target, so that E and VE come to represent very similar aspects of the subject's responses. But because E represents accuracy with respect to the target, a number of writers recommend E (e.g. Henry, 1976) as the best overall measure of performance accuracy.

Absolute error (AE)—computation. A statistic that is closely related to the total variability (E) is absolute error (AE), which can also be thought of as a measure of overall accuracy in performance. It is the average *absolute deviation* (without regard to direction) between the subject's responses and the target, and its formula is

$$\text{Absolute error} = \frac{\sum\limits_{i=1}^{n} |x_i - T|}{n}, \tag{3-5}$$

where x_i, T, and n are defined exactly as in the previous examples. The vertical bars (| |) are the symbol for "absolute value of" and mean to take away the sign of the difference inside before summing.

AE is computed by referring again to Table 3-1. The first step is to compute the values for the numerator terms, and this is done in Column G headed $|x_i - T|$. Notice that each of the values in this column is the score received by the subject on that trial, subtracted from the score for the target (in this case, 100), with the sign removed (i.e., with the absolute value taken). The summation sign Σ is an instruction to add up these values from 1 to n (n is 5 in this example), and the sum is given at the bottom of Column G as 20. The next step is to divide by the number of trials included, and so the final answer is 4.0.

Interpretation of AE. In providing an interpretation of the absolute error (AE), it will be helpful to consider the ways in which it is similar to E. First, notice that the numerator is essentially the same for the two statistics, both having a difference between the obtained score (x_i) and the target as the major "ingredient." Second, the values for E and AE (4.47 and 4.0, respectively) are very similar; the two values will be equal only in special circumstances but very close in most situations. Third, both of the formulas involve methods for eliminating the sign of the difference between the score and the target; for the AE, the method is to take the absolute value, while for E, the method is to take the square of the difference to eliminate the sign and then take the square root of the sum.

Absolute error versus E. The absolute error is a very "logical" measure to use to describe the subject's overall accuracy in a task because it is sensitive to the extent to which the subject was "off" in his or her responses. It is far more common than E in the research literature, and it is used for many different applications. A controversy, however, has been raised about the use of absolute error by Schutz and Roy (1973). Chiefly because of their thinking, the use of absolute error has decreased in recent years. This is primarily because absolute error can be shown to be a complex combination of constant error (bias) and variable error (variability), and it is difficult to be certain of the relative contribution of each. Because of the relationship among E, CE, and VE (namely, $E^2 = VE^2 + CE^2$), E can be shown to be an exact combination of the variability and bias and thus is preferred to absolute error. The tendency today is to use E in place of AE, because (a) E measures essentially the same component of responding as AE and (b) E is more easily interpreted since it is calculated from a simple combination of CE and VE. However, I will use absolute error a great deal in this text, because much of the earlier research was done using only this measure.

Relationships Among the Error Measures

The previous sections have shown that $E^2 = VE^2 + CE^2$ and that AE measures essentially the same component of human responding as does E. But there are some other relationships that should be understood. Often in motor behavior research it is not clear whether the measure of overall error represents the bias of the subject away from the target, the variability of the subject about the target, or both. Consider a subject with no bias (CE = 0) and a total variability of 4.0, and a second subject with a bias of 4.0 and no variability (VE = 0). Clearly both subjects have the same E of 4.0 (since $E = \sqrt{VE^2 + CE^2}$), but they performed very differently to receive their respective Es. The first subject was inconsistent in spreading responses about the center of the target, while the second subject was consistent but the "aim"

Table 3-2

**Error Measures for Two Hypothetical Subjects
on an Accuracy Task**

	E	CE	VE	AE
Subject 1	15.61	− 15.2	3.54	15.2
Subject 2	3.55	− 0.2	3.54	3.0

was consistently off. In motor behavior research, it is often important to know why the subject received a large E (or absolute error); it may have implications for understanding the causes of behavior, or it may have implications for reducing the error with practice.

One way to evaluate the relative contributions of the various measures of error is to consider the following cases. At one extreme, when CE is very large (the extreme is when all of the person's responses lie on one side of the target), then the absolute error, the total variability, and the constant error all tend to measure the same component of responding—the bias or directional deviations of the errors. In the following case, the target is again 100, but Subject 1 produces five responses—80, 90, 85, 82, and 87, all considerably short of the target. Table 3-2 gives the four measures of error for this subject. Notice that the statistics E, CE, and AE are all around 15, but that the VE is very much lower at 3.54. This suggests that when the CE is large in either direction (I have not shown this for the positive direction, but the statement is still correct), the measures of overall error tend to measure the bias, and VE alone measures the variability.

Now consider Subject 2 in Table 3-2. This subject has the same spread of responses as Subject 1, but with much less bias. I did this by adding 15 to each of Subject 1's scores to get Subject 2's scores: 95, 105, 100, 97, 102. Table 3-2 gives the four error measures of this set of scores. Now notice that the measures of overall error tend to be very close to the VE, all around 3. The CE, however, is now nearly 0. Here the overall error measures now represent the variability of the responses (VE), exactly opposite from the situation with Subject 1.

From these observations a rule can be stated about the relationships among the error measures, as summarized in Table 3-3. When the CE is large in either direction, the measures of overall error (E and AE) tend to represent the amount of bias in the measures. When the CE is small, E and AE tend to represent the amount of variability (VE) in the scores. When the CE is intermediate in value (with some bias, but with scores falling on both sides of the target), the measures of overall error represent both the bias and the variability. This observation should make it clear that simply examining a subject's overall error statistics does not provide a very complete picture of the responses.

Table 3-3

Rules for Interpreting the Various Error Measures

If CE Is Large	If CE Is Small
AE and E tend to represent CE (bias);	AE and E tend to represent VE (variability);
VE represents variability	CE represents bias

Using the Error Scores

An additional aspect of error scores is important not only from the point of view of research in motor behavior but also from the point of view of practical application. What if I have two performers with the same overall error scores (e.g., both subjects have an E of 10.0), but Subject 1 has a large VE and small CE while Subject 2 has a small VE and large CE. If I had to use these data to select the subjects for a team which competed in this task, which subject would I choose?

My answer would be Subject 2, the person with a small VE who is highly consistent, because consistency is far more important in performance than bias. An example frequently cited concerns two archers. The one with the small VE is very skilled, but her sights are "off." I can improve her performance to reduce her CE easily by changing her sights, bringing her already consistent performance very close to the target. But the other subject, being inconsistent, is very difficult to improve, since she is either lacking in skill or in the basic abilities to perform this task (see Chapter 10 for a discussion of the distinction between ability and skill). The study of motor learning will show that the measure of error that is most sensitive to the effects of practice is consistency (VE); bias (CE) changes quickly in the first trial or two and remains near zero thereafter, even after years of practice.

To summarize, VE and E are the most important measures of skill, and should be used to select the best performer on tasks like those in the examples. I will have more to say about this issue in the discussion of learning in Section III. Situations exist, however, for which CE is preferred to VE, but these are specialized applications.

Other Measures of Accuracy

There are many tasks in the motor behavior literature and in the outside world that cannot be scored so simply as I have outlined. A task for which accuracy is important is the *tracking task,* for which performance is ongoing thus preventing the computation of a discrete performance error. A common tracking task is the *pursuit rotor,* shown in Figure 3-8(A). There are many varieties, but all have a target (usually a small circle) that is imbedded the surface of a turntable-like structure, and it rotates at a speed of 40 to 80 RPM. The subject holds a stylus in the preferred hand and attempts

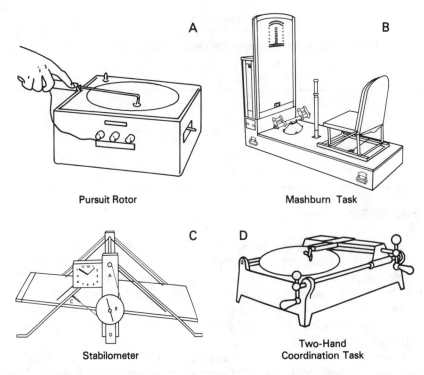

Figure 3-8. Four movement tasks frequently used in motor behavior research: (a) pursuit rotor, (b) Mashburn task, (c) stabilometer, and (d) two-hand coordination task.

to keep its tip in contact with the target as it rotates. A trial might last from 10 sec to 1 min, and performance is scored in terms of the amount of time in the trial that the subject maintained contact with the target. The performance measure is usually called *time on target* (TOT), and can range from zero, if the subject never touched the target, to the duration of a trial, if the subject was always in contact with the target. TOT is a complex combination of bias (if the subject is consistently behind the target, for example) and variability (if the subject is alternately ahead of and behind the target).

Other common variations of tracking tasks are shown in Figure 3-8. The *complex-coordination task* (or *Mashburn task*) is shown at the top right (B). It was designed to simulate certain features of airplane controls. The control panel contains three double rows of lights. One row of each pair is controlled by the movements of the subject (left-right and forward-backward movements of the stick, and right-left movements of the pedals), while the other row of each pair is controlled by the experimenter. The subject attempts to match the experimenter-determined lights with appropriate movements of the controls. The task is scored in terms of the number of correct matches that can be achieved in a trial of fixed duration.

The *stabilometer* is shown in Part C of Figure 3-8. The standing subject attempts to keep an unstable platform level; the scores are in terms of either time in balance or the number of times the platform edge touches the floor (indicating extreme loss of balance), during a trial of perhaps 30 sec. The number of times a stylus touches the sides of a maze is another example of this kind of measure (or the amount of time in contact with the walls, as a variant of this idea). Part D shows the *two-hand coordination task*, in which the subject attempts to follow a target by moving a pointer with two crank handles. One handle controls the right-left movement, and the other controls the forward-backward movement, much as in the "Etch-a-Sketch" game. The score is again TOT, or the amount of time in a trial that the subject was over the target. All of these measures, including TOT, are measures of overall accuracy, because they tend to confound the bias with variability in performance.

In each of the foregoing examples, the experimenter does not keep a record of the subject's actual behavior, although critical events are recorded. There are other tracking tasks for which a continuous record of the movements of the subject and the target are kept. One example is a tracking task in which a wavy line is drawn on a long strip of paper pulled past a slit; through the slit the subject can view only a small segment of the line at any given time. This small segment appears to move back and forth, and the subject's task is to keep a stylus (frequently a pencil or pen) aligned with the track. A continuous measure is recorded of both the target's and the subject's behavior from which is computed a measure of overall accuracy, the root-mean-square (RMS) error.

Essentially, the RMS error is based on taking small "slices" of time (perpendicular to the direction that the paper is traveling) and measuring the deviation of the subject's line from the target at each of these times, as shown in Figure 3-9. This can be done every second (or more frequently) over the entire course of a 20-sec trial, providing 20 measures of error. To compute the RMS error, square each of these deviations from the track, add up the squared deviations (20 of them), divide by the number of measures (20), then take the square root, giving a measure of the amount of deviation over the course of the trial. With modern computer techniques, this basic process can be done by recording both the movements of the subject and the

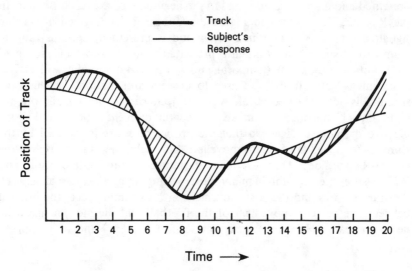

Figure 3-9. Hypothetical record from a tracking task, showing the basis for computation of RMS error.

track on magnetic tape for later analysis or by presenting them to the computer directly, sampling the difference as frequently as every millisecond. RMS error in each of these cases represents essentially (but not exactly) the area between the subject's responses and the target, as shown by the shaded areas in Figure 3-9. As with TOT, the RMS error is a measure of overall error and is sensitive to both the bias and the variability in performing.[2]

Measurement of Time and Speed

The second fundamental way that skills can be measured is by statistics that are sensitive to the speed with which the subject responded. Fundamental to this idea is the notion that, other things being equal, the performer who can accomplish more in a given amount of time or who can produce a given amount of behavior in less time is the more skillful. In such tasks, the dependent measures are usually expressed in terms of the number of units of behavior per time (as in the case of the number of units produced on a production line per day, or the number of taps of my finger that can be produced in 10 sec). Alternatively, these scores can be expressed as the amount of time required for a given behavior (e.g., the time for a 100-yd dash, or the time to move the hand from one place to another). These two measures are fundamentally the same, since a time measure (time/unit) can easily be converted to a speed measure by taking the reciprocal; that is, $1/(\text{time/units}) = \text{units/time}$, or a measure of speed. Both speed and time measures have been used a great deal in motor behavior research, and two very common cases of them are given next: reaction time and movement time.

Reaction Time (RT)

Reaction time (RT) is a measure of the time from the arrival of a suddenly presented and unanticipated signal to the beginning of the response to it. In the RT paradigm shown in Figure 3-10, the subject is given a warning signal, a randomly determined foreperiod is presented (perhaps ranging from 1 to 5 sec), and the stimulus is presented. Thus the subject is prevented from anticipating when (temporal anticipation) the stimulus will arrive. Sometimes "catch trials" are used to prevent anticipation, in which the stimulus is not presented at all. Also, subjects can be prevented from anticipating which response to make (i.e., spatial or event anticipation) by using two or more choices, so that the proper response is signaled by the stimulus (e.g., red light means move left, blue light means move right—the choice-RT method). There are many variations of this basic method, and RT measures are common in many sports settings (e.g., the interval between the starter's gun and the first movement in a swimming race, the interval between the center's movement of the football and the movement of the defensive team). However, as we shall see in Chapters 7 and 10, it is prob-

---

[2]Notice that RMS error is analogous to E described earlier. Both are root-mean-squared deviations of the behavior from some target, computed on successive "trials."

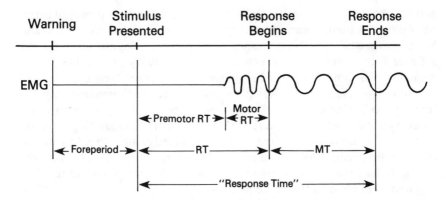

Figure 3-10. Critical events involved in the reaction time paradigm. (The trace is a hypothetical EMG record taken from the relevant muscle.)

ably not as important in understanding performance in other settings (e.g., boxing) as is commonly thought.

One variation of the RT method is to partition RT into its "central" and "peripheral" components (Weiss, 1965). In Figure 3-10, a hypothetical EMG trace is shown, taken from a muscle involved in the movement to be made. During a substantial part of the RT, the EMG is silent, indicating that the command to move the finger had not yet reached the finger musculature. Then late in the RT, the muscle is activated, but no movement occurs for 40 to 60 msec. The interval from the signal to the first change in EMG is termed *premotor RT* and is thought to represent central processes (e.g., perception, decisions, etc.); the interval from the first change in EMG to finger movement is termed *motor RT* and represents processes associated with the musculature itself. Such methods are useful in gaining additional information about the location of the effect of some independent variable on RT.

RT measures are very common in research on skills for two basic reasons. First, RT mesures are components of real-life tasks (e.g., sprint starts). A more important reason (amplified in Chapters 4 and 5) is that RT presumably measures the time taken for mental events, such as stimulus processing, decision making, and response programming. These two motivations for using RT measures differ considerably. In the first case, RT is a measure studied for its own sake; in the second case, RT allows the researcher to understand the kinds of mental processes that lead to movement (e.g., Posner, 1978). Regardless of the motivation, the measurement of RT is the same.

Movement Time (MT)

Movement time (Figure 3-10) is usually defined as the time from the initiation of the response (the end of RT) to the completion of the movement. Clearly, MT can be just about any value, ranging from a few milliseconds for a very quick movement to a few weeks if the movement is jogging from Los Angeles to Chicago. Some sports skills have minimal MT as a criterion (e.g., time to cover 100 m or time for a quarterback to "set up" for a pass), and MT is used a great deal in skills research as a result of its overall external validity in these practical settings. Sometimes researchers use RT and MT tasks together in the same response, such as requiring the subject to lift a finger from a key and move to a button as quickly as possible after a stimulus. The sum of RT and MT in these situations is frequently termed *response time* (Figure 3-10). Research has consistently shown that very different processes or abilities are required to react quickly than to move quickly once the reaction is over, and this has justified separating response time into RT and MT. (Note that what is frequently called "brake reaction time" in driver education tests is really response time, since it consists of the time to initiate the foot movement from the accelerator pedal and the time required to move it to the brake pedal.)

Often when using measures of speed, the degree of accuracy in the task is not taken into account. A well-known phenomena in motor behavior is *speed-accuracy tradeoff,* meaning simply that when performers attempt to do something more quickly, they typically do it less accurately or less well (exceptions are discussed in Chapter 9). In most measures of speed, therefore, accuracy requirements are kept to a minimum so that speeding up the response (which is the major goal for the subject) does not seriously affect accuracy. In some situations, though, measures of speed are badly confounded with measures of accuracy, and the speed with which the subject performs is dependent on the amount of error the subject is willing to make or the amount of error that the experimenter will tolerate. Such tradeoffs are particularly troublesome for experimenters, since it is not always clear to subjects how much error will be tolerated, and experimenters are unsure of how to interpret an independent variable that produces increases in speed but decreases in accuracy. Methods based on the theory of signal detection (e.g., Swets, 1964) have been developed to solve this problem, but they are not used very much in motor behavior research. Due to their complexity, they will not be described here. One solution to this problem is to hold accuracy constant by various experimental techniques, so that a single dependent variable of speed can be assessed. Or speed can be held constant via instructions, so that accuracy can be assessed (e.g., Quinn, Schmidt, Zelaznik, Hawkins, & McFarquhar, 1980; Schmidt et al., 1979).

Measures of Response Magnitude

A third way that skills can be measured is by the *magnitude* of behavior that the performer produces, such as the distance that a javelin was thrown or the amount of weight that was lifted. These measures have important applications to sports settings, as many sports use such measures as the primary determinants of success in the activity. Surprisingly, these measures are not used much in motor behavior research, as the scientists apparently believe that skills are more easily assessed by measures of accuracy or speed. This is but one instance in which research on motor behavior does not align itself very well with the applications of this knowledge.

One exception, though, is the Bachman (1961) ladder climb task, shown in Figure 3-11. The subject uses a free-standing, specially constructed lad-

Figure 3-11. The Bachman ladder climb task (adapted from Bachman, 1961).

der. At the beginning of a 30-sec trial, the subject begins to climb the ladder without skipping rungs until balance is lost and the subject topples over. The subject quickly returns to the starting position and begins climbing again, and so on until the trial has been completed. The score is the number of rungs accumulated in a given trial. A variant of the task is to climb as high as possible in a single trial, which ends when balance is lost.

While it might seem that the tasks requiring response magnitude measures are considerably different from those requiring speed and accuracy, the case will be made in subsequent chapters that the primary determinants of skill are not all that different. Readers new to motor behavior might have the idea that increased proficiency in tasks like javelin throwing, because they are measured by response magnitude methods, requires that the performer simply perform the muscular contractions "harder." A more reasonable view is that these skills require precise timing of the forceful contractions and that the amount of force contributed by the relevant musculature must be precisely adjusted.

Even in the most forceful of skilled tasks (such as weightlifting), all the muscles do not contract with maximum force; some of the muscle groups do, most do not, but all must be graded precisely in force and time to obtain maximum results. Seen in this way, tasks requiring maximum goals require accuracy in the minute muscular actions and timings that contribute to the skilled pattern; thus success in these tasks might be ultimately related to the same underlying processes as tasks requiring the most demanding accuracy.

Of course, consistency in these processes (in the sense of minimum variable error) is important for these tasks as well, since the javelin thrower must perform this precise muscular pattern over and over. Also, the performer must perform the precise pattern correctly on a *given* attempt, as in a meet, and movement pattern consistency is essential for this goal to be realized. More will be said about these patterns of movement and factors that lead to their success in Chapters 8 and 9 on motor programming.

Measurement of Secondary Tasks

There are instances both in research settings and in practical applications in which none of these basic methods of measurement will be sensitive to differences in skill among individuals or to differences in skill caused by some independent variable. Generally these situations involve tasks for which differences in performance are not evident because they are well learned (driving a car down an open road) or that do not "tax" the motor system very much because they are so simple (drinking a glass of water without spilling). Perhaps these are examples of the same principle: even complex tasks such as driving a car become simple after much practice. This is one of the most important generalizations about the acquisition of skills to be discussed in Section III. How are skills assessed in such situations?

One method is to use some measure of *critical incidents*. In the driving example, accident rate might be used as a measure of skill or with pilots "near misses" (midair near collisions) might be used as a measure. But these techniques are very difficult to utilize in the laboratory because (fortunately) they occur so infrequently. A more useful technique is to use some sort of secondary task, performed simultaneously with the primary task, as a measure of the skill in the primary task. For example, Brown (1962) has used a verbal task in which the individual is presented with a series of eight-digit numbers at 4-sec intervals. Each group had seven of the same digits as in the previous group, and the subject's task was to detect the eighth digit that was different and to provide a response. Errors were counted as omitted responses, incorrect responses, and late responses.

In Figure 3-12 are the scores on the verbal task alone and on the task when performed while driving under various conditions. The mean percentage of correct responses when the verbal task was performed alone was 90.6%. But when the task was performed while driving in quiet residential areas the mean percentage dropped to 83.8%. And when the task was per-

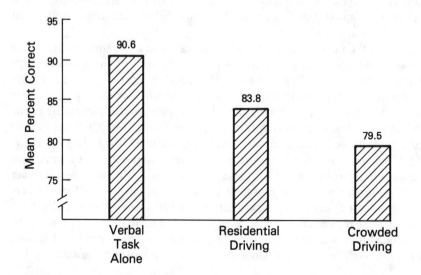

Figure 3-12. Mean number of correct digit detections alone and while driving in various experimental conditions (adapted from Brown, 1962).

formed in heavy traffic conditions, the percentage again dropped to 79.5%. Yet it was very difficult to see any differences in vehicle control in light and heavy traffic or for average or excellent drivers, largely because the task of driving is so well learned by most people. This secondary task has provided evidence about the difficulty of the driving conditions when the driving task itself would not provide such a measure.

The fundamental basis for this measure is the assumption (which is often questioned—see Chapters 4 and 5) that humans have a relatively fixed capacity for processing information. When the verbal task or the driving task is performed alone, the individual can perform either well since the required capacity is below the performer's limits. But when the verbal task is combined with the driving task, they are both competing for the performer's capacity and the performance on the verbal task is impaired in direct relation to the difficulty of the main driving task.

A wide variety of these secondary tasks can be and have been used in such situations. In addition to the digit-detection tasks used by Brown, researchers (e.g., Kerr, 1975) have used RT tasks as measures of *spare capacity*. The assumption is that the RT task, with the signal presented during the performance of a main task such as moving a lever or driving, requires some of the capacity, and thus a slower RT indicates increased capacity being devoted to the main task. Measures of tapping regularity have been used, whereby increasing difficulty of the main task leads to increasing irregularity of the tapping task (e.g., Michon, 1966).

Rather than a task, secondary physiological measures of spare capacity can be used during the performance of a main task. One of the most promising measures is pupil diameter, as measured by photographic techniques. Pupil dilation is associated with circumstances in which effort, arousal, or information processing is demanded (e.g., Kahneman, 1973). Also, when the task is more difficult there are greater changes in pupil size than when the task is easy (e.g., Beatty & Wagoner, 1978). Similarly, measures of heart rate, heart-rate variability, oxygen consumption (as a measure of overall effort), or even EMG from the muscles of the forehead (to indicate the level of concentration) can be used, depending on the particular situation. In all these cases, these secondary measures become the focus of the investigator, especially when the main task does not provide sensitive measures of the subject's performance.

A variation of this technique is the "probe task," in which a single stimulus is presented at various times during the production of a movement. By evaluating the reaction time to this probe, the investigator hopes to estimate the amount of attention (or capacity) being devoted to the main task at that moment. Such techniques have led to the conclusion that a great deal of attention is required at both the beginning and end of a discrete movement, with less attention required in the middle (e.g., Ells, 1973; Kerr, 1975; Posner & Keele, 1969). However, these methods have come under attack lately (e.g., McLeod, 1978, 1980). The findings are discussed in more detail in Chapter 5.

Another variation of this technique is to use a secondary task as a distractor in order to increase the overall "load" on the performer. Normally fatigue may not have any effect at all on driving, since the driver can compensate somewhat for the fatigue by shifting attention from other sources to driving. However, if the driver is required to perform a simultaneous mental arithmetic task, then large differences between fatigued and rested driving may be seen. Here, the major interest is on the performance of the main task, and the secondary task has increased the sensitivity of the measurement system of the main task. However, care must be taken with these techniques as Brown (1962) has shown. When truck drivers were fatigued, their performance on the secondary digit-detection task actually increased, suggesting that the drivers were devoting less capacity to the driving task and overcompensating by devoting more capacity to the secondary task. While these techniques can be somewhat "tricky" to use, they have served well in a number of situations, mainly for continuous, highly learned tasks.

EMPIRICAL EQUATIONS

An important process for evaluating the outcomes of various experimental procedures comes after the main performance measures are generated from the experiment, be they errors, speed, magnitude, or secondary task scores. This process involves the determination of the relationship between some independent variable and a dependent variable based on the empirical data. One important kind of relationship is linear. In a graph, the dependent variable plots essentially as a straight line with the independent variable.

In Figure 3-13 I have plotted data from an experiment by Schmidt et al. (1979), for which the error in hitting a target with a hand-held stylus is plotted as a function of the average velocity of the movement.[3] A quick examination of the plot in Figure 3-13 indicates that the relationship between these two variables is essentially linear. I have placed a line through the points that seems to represent their general direction, and this line is called the *line of best fit*. The actual placement can be done accurately by various statistical techniques (e.g., regression), or it can be done "by eye" for a rough approximation.

The goal of this section is to express this line of best fit in terms of what is known as an *empirical equation,*[4] a kind of shorthand that enables us, with but two numbers, to convey information about a linear relationship for an empirically determined set of data points. This simple procedure is important in order to understand scientists when they describe their data in this way. These two numbers also will have special meaning in terms of various theories; that is, these numbers will be measures of certain hypothetical constructs.

I will begin with the general equation for a line,

$$Y = a + bX. \tag{3-6}$$

---

[3]The independent variable of movement velocity is produced by nine different combinations of movement distance (10, 20, 30 cm) and movement time (140, 170, 200 msec).

[4]Many varieties of empirical equations are available, with linear equations being the most simple and useful.

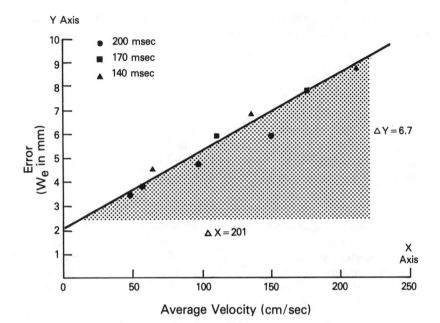

Figure 3-13. Graphical method for determining constants for linear empirical equations (data from Schmidt et al., 1979).

Y represents the values of the Y-axis (error), X represents the values on the X-axis (average velocity), and a and b are constants (Figure 3-13). The constant a is termed the Y *intercept,* and refers to the value of Y when the line crosses the Y axis; here the value is about 2 mm. The constant b is called the slope and refers to the amount of inclination of the line. The slope can be *positive* (upward and to the right, as in this example) or *negative* (downward to the right), associated with either positive or negative values of b. Once these values are specified from a given set of data, the empirical equation can be written that describes the linear relation of the data.

Computation of Constants

The computation of the constants needed for the empirical equation is simple. After the line of best fit has been applied to the data points, extend it leftward until it crosses the Y axis and read off the Y intercept, or a. In the data shown in Figure 3-13, a equals 2.08 mm.

Next, using the line of best fit, draw two lines, one perpendicular to the Y axis and one perpendicular to the X axis, as shown. It is best to place them somewhere near the extremes of the line of best fit for more accuracy, but the actual placement is irrelevant in theory. This creates a triangle, with two sides being the lines you have just drawn, and the third side being the line of best fit. The triangle is shown as a shaded area.

Then, the length of the line forming the base of the triangle will be called ΔX, and the length of the line forming the side of the triangle will be called ΔY. The symbol Δ means *change in;* measures of the changes in Y and the corresponding changes in X can be seen. Here, these values change from 17 to 218 cm/sec, or 201 cm/sec, for ΔX, and from 2.5 to 9.2 mm, or 6.7 mm, for ΔY. Then, the slope of the line is defined as

$$b = \frac{\Delta Y}{\Delta X} \tag{3-7}$$

That is, the slope is defined as the change in Y divided by the corresponding change in X. Here, the slope (b) is computed as $6.7/201 = +.033$. The interpretation of this slope is that each time the value of X increases by 1 cm/sec, there is a .033-mm increase in the Y value (error).

Uses of Empirical Equations

The slope and intercept are the only two values necessary to determine the linear relationship. Putting the slope and the intercept together into the general equation for the line, we have the empirical equation for these data:

$$Y = 2.08 + .033X. \tag{3-8}$$

By providing the calculated values of a and b found in California, someone in Georgia can reconstruct the line of best fit by using the linear equation. This is done by picking any two arbitrary values of X (say 50 and 250 cm/sec) and calculating the values of Y for these values of X:

$$\begin{aligned} Y &= 2.08 + .033 \ (50) = 3.73 \text{ mm, and} \\ Y &= 2.08 + .033 \ (250) = 10.33 \text{ mm.} \end{aligned} \tag{3-9}$$

Then, on a new graph these data points (X = 50, Y = 3.73; and X = 250, Y = 10.33) could be plotted, and the line in Figure 3-13 drawn between them. Thus, by saying that the intercept was 2.08 and the slope was + .033, a great deal of information can be conveyed about the experiment to someone who does not have access to the actual nine data points.

In addition, this relation can be used to predict new values of error before they are found. If I wanted to choose a velocity value so that the error was only 5.00 mm, I could take the empirical equation and substitute the value of the error as follows, then solve for the value of the velocity:

$$\begin{aligned} 5.00 &= 2.08 + .033X \\ -.033X &= 2.08 - 5.00 \\ X &= (2.08 - 5.00)/(-.033) \\ X &= (-2.92)/(-.033) \\ X &= 88.48 \text{ cm/sec} \end{aligned} \tag{3-10}$$

Thus, if I wanted the error to be about 5 mm, I would use a velocity of about 88.48 cm/sec. Having an empirical equation makes it possible to predict the result without actually having to go into the laboratory.

Interpreting Empirical Equations

In addition to the benefits provided by empirical equations in terms of description of the experimental results and prediction of new findings, the values of the constants a and b often have special theoretical meaning. This meaning will naturally vary depending on the nature of the data collected and the kind of independent variable studied. In the present example, the meaning of the constant a (the intercept) is related to the amount of error for the slowest movement possible, and thus the intercept seems to represent a kind of "background" or "baseline" error. On the other hand, the value of the slope (b) represents the amount of *increase* in error as the velocity increases, and it represents the "difficulty" of the task. For example, if another task had a slope larger than .033, I would say that this second task was more "difficult" than the first one. This interpretation will be clearer when this theoretical idea is discussed in more detail in Chapter 9. For now, just consider that the values of the intercept and the slope in these equations often have important meanings for a theory under investigation.

TWO APPROACHES TO STUDYING SKILLS

The previously described measurement techniques apply to the various ways that skills can be measured. The reasons for applying these techniques depend on which of two approaches is to be used in understanding skills. What makes these approaches different is the reason that the measures are taken, or the purposes that the measures are thought to serve. These two approaches have been named the *task-orientation* and *process-orientation* by Pew (1970, 1974).

Task-Oriented Approach

The older of the two approaches, this idea was to choose some performance task as a representative of skills in general and then to investigate the independent variables that affected skill as measured on this task. Many questions were asked about the effect of practice, fatigue, motivating instructions, information about errors, and so on, for the skill in question. The underlying assumption seemed to be that skill in all tasks was fundamentally the same, and so the choice of a task was one of convenience for the investigator. Performance measures tended to be quite "global" in nature, such as the TOT for 30 sec of rotary pursuit performance (with a single score representing 30 sec of behavior) or the VE for shooting 100 arrows at a target (with a single number representing 100 shots). There was not very much concern for the underlying processes that led to performance accuracy or for what the performer actually did (patterns of muscular action). These two criticisms have led to a general dissatisfaction with the task-oriented approach and have contributed to the adoption of the process-oriented approach.

Process-Oriented Approach

The process-oriented approach to the study of skills uses the same measures of performance (plus additional measures) as the task-oriented approach, but the reasons they are used are different. The researcher is interested in the underlying processes or mechanisms that contribute to performance, not simply in the outcome of the performance. There is a concern for the use of feedback, the use of error-detection mechanisms in performance, coding of information in memory, and programs of action. Each of these concerns involves some set of events, mechanisms, states, or processes that are internal to the subject and that are not directly observable. The idea is that these processes must exist for us to function in the world as we do. For example, assume that there are motor programs for the control of rapid acts (see Chapters 8 and 9); now the problem is to design tasks for measuring and studying these processes and how they change when independent variables change. The focus is no longer on skill in the general sense, but on measurements that will make it possible to study the underlying causes (or determinants) of skill.

As an example of the process-oriented approach, a blindfolded performer is asked to move a slide slowly down a trackway until a stop is contacted (presentation movement). The subject then returns to the starting position and, with the stop now removed, attempts to return the slide to the same position (reproduction movement). What kinds of processes are enabling a subject to perform accurately? Consider two possibilities. First, one hypothesis is that the subject remembers what it felt like to be at the stop and so moves down the trackway until achieving a position that feels the same way. The assumption is that the person "stores" the feedback information from the limb and compares the sensory information from the limb in the reproduction movement against it. A second hypothesis is that the subject remembers the distance moved during the movement to the stop, and then moves this same distance when asked to repeat the movement. This second hypothesis is different from the first because it does not require the subject to remember the sensory details of the correct endpoint, but only the distance from the starting point. Which of these underlying processes does the subject use? The processes-oriented approach to skills attempts to find out.

A very common solution to this question (used by Keele & Ells, 1972; Laabs, 1973) is to have the subject do the reproduction movement from a different starting position from that used in the presentation movement. If the presentation movement was 30 cm, the subject might be asked to travel to the same endpoint but from a starting position 5 cm to the right, so that the reproduction movement is now 35 cm in length. This arrangement is shown in Figure 3-14. Under these conditions, distance information is considered to be unusable (since the distance is different in the presentation and reproduction movements). But the location information is usable since it is the same for both movements.

Contrast this to a situation in which the subject has the starting position changed 5 cm, but now the goal is to move the same distance. The location information in the initial movement is not usable, but the distance informa-

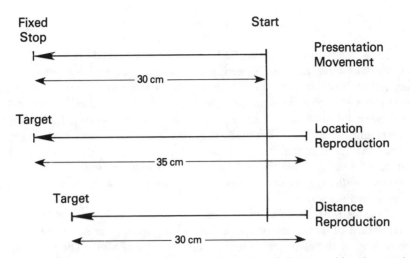

Figure 3-14. Diagram showing the method for the separation of distance and location cues in lever-positioning tasks.

tion presumably is, since the distance is the same for the two movements. This technique provides the researcher with information about the kinds of codes the subject uses in making the movements. Generally it has been found that distance information is far less accurate (and subject to greater forgetting over the time between the two movements) than the location information, suggesting that people move on the basis of position codes rather than distance codes.

There are many other examples of the process-oriented approach, such as the use of certain tasks to measure underlying abilities, information-processing capacity, or strategies that the subject might be employing in performance, the kind of feedback information the subject uses, and the like. In all of these cases, the focus is on what the performance means in terms of some underlying process that is of central focus, not simply on the performance of the task in question. Therefore, the choice of tasks and procedures, unlike the situation with the task-oriented approach, is far from arbitrary, as some tasks and procedures are far better for understanding the underlying processes than others.

A trend that is closely related to the issue of process-oriented versus task-oriented approaches is the increasing dissatisfaction with the tasks and methods that measure only "global" performance outcomes. Because researchers want to understand what the subject actually did in the performance, increasing use is being made of measures of movements themselves. A general increase can be seen in the use of biomechanical techniques, including movement kinematics and other sophisticated methods for recording the behavior of subjects. As mentioned earlier, the use of surface EMG is increasing, as are methods for recording subcutaneous electrical activities from the brain and spinal cord of moving animals. These various methods, coupled with the measures of movements just described, enable the fields of biomechanics, neural control, and motor behavior to be brought together as never before.

SUMMARY

Motor behavior can be classified according to several dimensions, such as *continuous-serial-discrete,* referring to the extent to which the movement has a definite beginning and end, and *open-closed,* referring to the extent to which the environment is predictable. Most of the tasks used in motor control work fall into one or another of these basic categories. In measuring movement, attention is devoted to a measure's *objectivity* (the extent to which two independent observers achieve the same score), its *sensitivity* to changes in skill, its *reliability* (the extent to which the score is repeatable), and its *validity* (the extent to which the test measures what the experimenter wants it to measure).

Movements can be measured in many ways, but common ones involve the calculation of kinematic variables (location, speed, acceleration) and the recording of the electrical activity from muscles (EMG). The outcome of movements in terms of the environmental goal can be measured in essentially three ways: in terms of errors, speed, or magnitude. There are many ways to measure errors in movement, and chief among them are *constant error* (a measure of average error), *variable error* (a measure of consistency), *total variability* (a measure of overall error), and *absolute error* (also a measure of overall error). Each of these error measures has a different meaning and is used in different aspects of the measurement process. Measures of speed are used when accuracy is less important and when rapid actions are critical. Measures of magnitude are used when the *amount* of behavior is critical. A fourth but related measure is based on the analysis of simultaneous secondary tasks, providing a measure of the spare capacity of the performer after devoting attention to a primary task.

Linear empirical equations provide a description of a linear relationship between a dependent and an independent variable. The parameters of the equation can be easily estimated, and they provide a means by which the relationship can be used to predict new facts before they are found. The field of motor behavior is changing from a task-oriented approach, which focuses on the effect of variables on the outcomes of a performance, to a process-oriented approach, which focuses on the movements themselves as well as on the processes underlying them.

GLOSSARY

Absolute error (AE). The average absolute deviation of a set of scores from a target value; a measure of overall error.

Closed skills. Skills that are performed in stable or predictable environmental settings.

Constant error (CE). The average, with respect to sign, error of a set of scores from a target value.

Continuous skills. Skills that appear to have no recognizable beginning or end.

Discrete skills. Skills that appear to have a definite beginning and end.

EMG. Electromyography, or the recording of the electrical activity from contracting muscles.

Empirical equation. An equation describing the outcome of an experiment in which the constants are estimated from the empirical observations.

Foreperiod. The interval from a warning signal to the presentation of a stimulus to respond.

Intercept. The value (a) on the Y axis when X is zero; one of the constants for linear empirical equations.

Motor reaction time. The interval from the first change in EMG to the movement's initiation.

Movement time. The interval from the initiation of a movement to its termination.

Objectivity. The aspect of measurement related to the extent to which two observers achieve the same score.

Premotor reaction time. The interval from the stimulus presentation to the initial change in EMG.

Reaction time (RT). The interval from the presentation of an unexpected stimulus to the initiation of the response.

Reliability. The aspect of measurement related to the repeatability of a score.

Response time. The interval from the presentation of a stimulus to the completion of a movement; the sum of reaction time and movement time.

RMS error. Root-mean-squared error, or the square root of the average squared deviations of a set of values from a target value; typically used as a measure of tracking proficiency.

Sensitivity. That aspect of measurement dealing with the possibility of detecting changes in a dependent measure in relation to varying experimental conditions.

Serial tasks. Movements in which a series of discrete elements form a complete response, with the order of elements being important.

Slope. The inclination (b) of a linear empirical equation; one of its constants.

Total variability (E). The standard deviation of a set of responses about a target value; a measure of overall accuracy.

Validity. That aspect of measurement related to the extent to which a test measures what the experimenter wanted it to measure.

Variable error (VE). The standard deviation of a set of responses about the subject's own constant error; a measure of response consistency.

CHAPTER 4

Information Processing and Memory Systems

Human functioning in the environment can be conceptualized and studied many ways. One of the most popular ways is based on the fundamental notion that humans are processors of information. It is assumed that information is available in the environment, that the individual accepts the information into various "storage systems" called *memory,* and that the information is *processed.* The term processed means that the information is coded, its code may be changed from one form to another, the information may be combined with other information, and so on. This chapter is about this viewpoint of information processing as it relates to human motor behavior. The kinds of information from the environment that are useful for movement, how the information is processed, how the information is used to control action, and how information is stored in memory for future use (see also Marteniuk, 1976) are discussed.

THE INFORMATION-PROCESSING MODEL

This model of functioning begins with the input of information from the environment through one or more of the sense organs, and considers what happens to this signal (or what the signal causes to happen) once inside the system. Conceptualize a "black-box" model as shown in Figure 4-1. The individual is considered to be the box, and information is put into it from the environment. This information is then processed in various ways inside the box, until eventually it is output as observable motor activity. In the S-R tradition (see Chapter 1), this model prevailed, which caused researchers to be primarily concerned with the relationship between what went into the box (the information, or stimuli) and the output (the response). With the

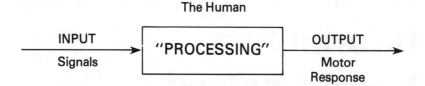

Figure 4-1. The simplified information-processing model.

emergence of *cognitive psychology,* however, interest has risen in the processes which occur *within* the box. Obviously, this is an abstract way to study the human, as it focuses on processes and events that are not directly observable. The knowledge about these processes is inferred from the overt behavior of the human under various experimental conditions.

Why not investigate these internal processes directly rather than make inferences about them? This is simply not possible, because the neural processes and their locations in the brain are not well understood. Adequate knowledge and techniques for studying complex human phenomena such as perception, decision making, and planning responses are not available at this time. However, by using the cognitive-psychological perspective, the events that occur in the black box can be studied in a variety of ways.

Some of these ways focus on the nature of the structure into which the information "flows," and some focus on the changes in the nature of the information as it proceeds through the system. Perhaps the most common approach is to consider the temporal aspects of information processing, concentrating on the duration of these various processes. This basic *chronometric approach,* as it is termed (see Posner, 1978, for a more complete statement), makes heavy use of the reaction-time (RT) method, whereby the chief measure of the subject's behavior is the interval between the presentation of a stimulus and the evocation of a response. This method is popular for a number of reasons, not the least of which is that RT is a very simple measure to collect on humans in experimental settings. In addition, RT seems to be a sensitive measure of the group of individual event-durations (added together) that occur between the presentation of a stimulus and the evocation of a response. Presumably, many different information-processing activities occur during this interval, but the measurement of changes in RT can, if the experiment is designed properly, describe the changes in the time required for a particular one of them. The different information-processing activities are usually termed *stages.*

STAGES OF INFORMATION PROCESSING

Although the notion that there are separate stages or processes between a stimulus and the response has been popularized by the cognitive-psychological viewpoint, the notion of stages of processing is quite old. Probably the first attempt to study the stages of processing was made by the Dutch physiologist Donders (1868) over a century ago. Although the exact formulation of his ideas about stages is probably not correct, the basic methods are still here today.

Table 4-1

Experimental Tasks and Logic Involved in Donders' Subtractive Method

Task	Stimuli and Action Required	Processes Involved
a-reaction (simple RT)	1 stimulus 1 response	
b-reaction (choice RT)	5 possible stimuli 1 response, different for each stimulus	Those in *a* plus Discrimination and Choice
c-reaction (discrimination RT)	5 possible stimuli 1 response, but only if a certain stimulus occurred; otherwise, no response	Those in *a* plus Discrimination

Duration of discrimination = $RT_c - RT_a$

Duration of choice = $RT_b - RT_c$

Donders' Approach: The Subtractive Method

Donders assumed the existence of a series of separate, nonoverlapping stages of processing between a stimulus and a response. The notion is that the processing that occurs in Stage 1 is different from the processing in Stage 2 and that Stage 2 cannot begin the processing until Stage 1 is completed. Donders studied this basic idea with RT methods and defined three different kinds of responses as shown in Table 4-1. In the first kind of response, which Donders termed an *a*-reaction, the subject was presented with a single, unanticipated stimulus which required a single response; this task is now called *simple RT*. In his *b*-reaction, the subject was presented with a choice. There were five possible stimuli that could be presented, and each of the stimuli required a different response; this task is now called *choice RT*. Finally, in his *c*-reaction, the same five stimuli could be presented but the subject was to respond only if a given stimulus was presented. This task is now called *discrimination RT* (also go/no-go).

Donders argued that the difference in RT between the *a* reaction and the *c* reaction would reflect something about the process of discrimination. Because both tasks have the same requirements for movement and choice and because they differ (presumably) only in terms of the need to discriminate among the possible stimuli, he reasoned that the difference between the RT for *c* and the RT for *a* was due to the processes involved in discrimination. More powerfully, he believed that the amount of time represented by this difference in RT was the actual duration of a stage of stimulus discrimination.

In a similar way, perhaps more relevant for motor behavior, Donders argued that the difference between the RTs for the *b*- and *c*-reactions was due to the processes involved in the selection of a response. Notice that the *c*-reaction and the *b*-reaction both involve the same element of stimulus discrimination, but the *b*-reaction has the added requirement that one of five responses must be selected. Thus, Donders argued that the difference between the RTs of the *b*- and the *c*-reactions was a measure of the time required by a stage devoted to the selection of a response.

As shown later, the answer is not quite so simple as Donders thought. Even so, his basic idea that the duration of stages could be understood by subtracting the RTs in various conditions was remarkable given the time of his work. This *subtractive method* and its basic assumptions serve as the foundation for more modern analyses of the stages of information processing (e.g., Sternberg, 1969).

Defining the Stages of Processing

Donders' work led to the suggestion that there could be other stages besides discrimination and choice. Besides there being more of these stages, they can act either *serially* (sequentially), as Donders had thought, or *in parallel* (simultaneously).

Serial and Parallel Processing

Imagine an automotive plant as a model of information processing, as in Figure 4-2. Some stages occur at the same time in different places, such as the fabrication of the frame, the assembly of the engine, and the assembly of the body, each representing separate stages in the manufacture of the car. But at some time in the overall process, these components combine to complete the final assembly stage. After final assembly, imagine another stage, the test-drive stage, wherein the drivers search for problems before the car is sent to the dealers, yet another stage. In this simple analogy is an example of parallel processing, with respect to the frame, engine, and body assembly stages. Yet these three stages must be performed before the final assembly stage, and the final assembly stage must precede the test-drive stage. So these three stages, the final assembly stage, and the test-drive stage are ordered serially. Thus, this system has both serial and parallel processing,

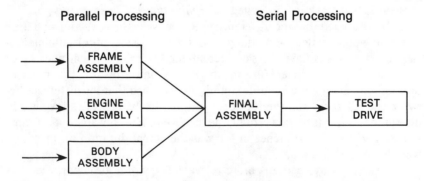

Figure 4-2. Examples of serial and parallel processing in an automobile assembly plant.

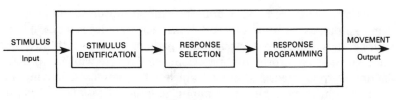

The Human

Figure 4-3. An expanded information-processing model.

but with respect to different times within the total sequence. Returning to the human, many have thought that the total RT has various stages, some of which can be performed in parallel, and some of which can be performed serially.

Three Possible Stages

In the work on information processing and motor behavior, some scientists have found it useful to consider a number of distinct stages of processing, tentatively assuming that they are serial and nonoverlapping in time. It could be argued that this kind of scheme is oversimplified, and I am sure that it is. At the same time, there is a great deal of merit in conceptualizing the human in this way, as this kind of scheme organizes a great deal of experimental data and provides a useful framework from which to gain a deeper understanding of human motor behavior.

At least three stages can be proposed that intervene between the presentation of a stimulus and the evocation of a response (see Figure 4.3). First, the individual must acknowledge *that* a stimulus has occurred and identify it. This stage is frequently called the *stimulus-identification stage*. Second, after a stimulus has been properly identified, the individual must decide what reponse to make. The decision can be to do one of a number of actions, or the stimulus can be ignored in favor of no action at all. This stage is usually called the *response-selection stage*. Finally, after the proper response has been selected, the system must ready itself for the appropriate action and must initiate that action. This stage is frequently called the response-initiation stage, but I will use the more inclusive term *response-programming stage* to mean the preparation of the motor apparatus and the initiation of the action. In the sections that follow, these stages are considered in detail, particularly with respect to the evidence that supports them, the kinds of processing that occur during them, and their limitations in the production of a response.

RT Analyses and Everyday Tasks

Before turning to the analysis of the stages, a word is in order about the usefulness of this kind of RT approach. What does the analysis of events that occur in an RT paradigm have to do with throwing a baseball, driving a car, or anything besides RT? The relevance to common skills is only present under a number of assumptions. For example, assume in driving a car that stimuli from the environment (vision of the road, horns honking) and from the driver's body (acceleration, vibrations) enter the information-processing system as input, as shown in Figure 4.3. As each stimulus is input, it is processed, perhaps leading to a response and perhaps not. Thus, the driver can be thought of as an information-processing channel, to which information is continually presented, and out of which come responses. Driving a car does not appear to have much in common with the RT task (except perhaps when a child runs from between two parked cars), but the assumption is that the processes within the individual are the same. This assumption could be wrong, and many (e.g., Turvey, 1977) think that it is. Consider the following analysis of RT in this light. I will discuss a different viewpoint later in this and other chapters.

THREE PROCESSING STAGES

This section is concerned with the events that occur during the RT interval, beginning when some stimulus is presented and ending when some response to it is begun.[1] The first of these stages is called the *stimulus-identification stage,* and it is concerned with the processes associated with entering the information from the environment into the system so that it can be processed further.

Stimulus-Identification Stage

Think of the stimulus-identification stage as beginning with an environmental stimulus on the body (e.g., the light entering the retina of the eye, or the sound entering the ear) being transformed (or transduced as the engineer would say) into a different code—the code of neurological impulses headed toward the brain. The stimulus is presumably processed further at each level of analysis until the stimulus *contacts memory*, meaning that some aspect of the stimulus is aroused, such as its name or some attribute of it to which it has been associated in the past (its red color, such as with apples or my Porsche). As we shall see, in order that the stimulus arouses the proper associate in memory rather than (a) improper associates, or (b) all possible associates (either of which would be confusing), much processing must occur. Processes within the stimulus-identification stage will be discussed later.[2]

What variables affect, or what determines, the speed of processing at this stage? In order to answer this question, it is necessary to know which

---

[1]The assumption that the stimulus starts the chain of events is arbitrary, of course. It could just as easily be said that the human is moving through the environment and that the change in what is seen (a stimulus of a different kind) is the *result* of movement, not the cause of it. The stimulus is assumed to be the beginning of the chain of events only for convenience.

[2]Some writers emphasize two stages in what I have called stimulus identification. One stage (stimulus encoding) is involved in transforming the stimulus from physical to biological codes, and another (stimulus identification) is involved in identifying it. This distinction is beyond the scope of this chapter, however, see Posner (1973) or Sternberg (1969) for details.

variables affect RT in the information-processing paradigm and to know which of these might affect the stimulus-identification stage. Scientists working in this area have assumed that the variables affecting the stimulus-identification stage are those having to do with the nature of the stimulus that is presented. For example, a variable called *stimulus clarity,* which refers to "sharpness" of the stimulus, has been used (it affects stimulus encoding; see footnote 2). The variable is manipulated in the RT experiment by presenting a visual stimulus in proper or improper focus. With increased focus the overall RT is shorter, and this change is attributed to the increased processing speed in the stimulus-identification stage. A variable called *stimulus intensity* (the brightness of a light stimulus or the loudness of a sound stimulus) also affects encoding in these RT tasks, and it has seemed logical to assume that the locus of the effect was in the stimulus-identification stage.

Although it makes sense that these variables affect only the stimulus-identification stage, workers in this area generally demand more than an assumption for this kind of conclusion. Variables such as stimulus intensity and stimulus clarity can be shown to have no effect on a subsequent stage (e.g., response selection) through *additive-factors logic* (Sternberg, 1969). For present purposes, though, assume that these variables affect only the first of the stages.

Pattern Recognition and Feature Extraction

In more realistic tasks, the stimuli that enter the system are seldom unitary, as they are in RT tasks, and we must usually extract a pattern or feature from the stimuli presented. Often these patterns have to do with the shape of a face, where a baseball is going and how fast, whether a picture is hanging straight, or whether two lines are parallel or perpendicular. Thus, some of the patterns are quite simple while others are complex. As well, some of these patterns can be thought of as genetically defined, such as verticality, whereas others may depend heavily on learning, such as movements of a defensive team in American football.

Important studies of chess players make the point about learned patterns very well (deGroot, 1965; Chase & Simon, 1973). With chess masters and good-to-average chess players as subjects, deGroot asked them to reconstruct the locations of the chess pieces in a half-finished game after viewing the board for 5 sec. As one might imagine, the chess masters were far superior to the good-to-average players. Even if they made small mistakes, the masters could easily correct them in a subsequent trial. It could be argued that the superiority of the chess masters in this task is not necessarily evidence that they have learned to remember chess patterns, but that they are superior in their inherent perceptual ability. This last hypothesis is doubtful, however; when the chess pieces were placed on the board in random fashion, the chess masters and average players were about equal in their ability to relocate the pieces. One interpretation is that the processes in the stimulus-identification stage were improved in the masters through years of experience in game situations.

Analysis of these static situations seems clearly important to many ac-

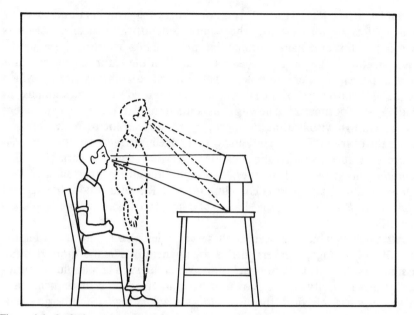

Figure 4-4. Optical arrays vary as the location of the observer changes in the environment (adapted from Gibson, 1966).

tivities; but even more important for an understanding of motor behavior is an ability to extract patterns of movement from the environment. In many situations, how the environment changes from moment to moment will determine the response. As well, patterns of movement of our own bodies, as detected from receptors in the limbs, muscles, eyes, and inner ear (balance), provide important information from which a pattern must be extracted.

A good example of genetically defined analysis of movement patterns comes from early work of Lorenz (see Lorenz, 1965, for a summary), later refined by a number of other workers (e.g., Schleidt, 1961; see Buss, 1973, for a good discussion). Schleidt found that passing a shape (a circle or a shape that resembled a hawk in flight) over young turkeys caused fear reactions but that these fear reactions were later *habituated* (weakened with repeated exposure). It is possible that there is a genetically defined mechanism for recognizing patterns related to dangerous events, but according to Schleidt, it is also possible that the fear reaction elicited in the wild by hawks overhead is related to the fact that responses to other more common patterns become habituated, leaving a strong fear reaction to the hawk (which is relatively rare and has not become habituated). Apparently, through a combination of genetically defined recognition of shapes, and experience with shapes other than hawks, the young turkey establishes a recognition of and reaction to the hawk shape that has obvious survival value.

A great deal of information is contained in the movement of the visual field, and it seems clear that individuals can use this information to provide unequivocal analysis of movements in an environment or of the environment's movements. Gibson (1966), for example, speaks of "optical flow patterns," which are the patterns made up of the rays of light that strike the eye from every visible part of the environment (see Figure 4-4).[3] As the individual and/or the environment moves, the angles of these rays change to allow the subject to extract a pattern of movement from the changing visual array. For example, I *know* that something is coming directly toward my eye if the rate of change of the angles of the rays of light from all edges of the object are the same. I have a rapid and seemingly involuntary response to avoid it. This is called *looming* and can elicit strong avoidance reactions even in children and young animals who have presumably not ever been hit in the eye, suggesting that these kinds of pattern recognitions may be genetically defined. Also, if the rays of light from the left side of an object are changing their angles more rapidly than are the rays from the right side, then this is evidence that the object will pass to the left. Presumably, these analyses of movement features are done in the stimulus-identification stage.

These interpretations are important for many fast-action sports and games. Patterns of opponent position, or patterns of action, arouse meaningful responses that lead to fast action in highly skilled players, while they may go nearly unnoticed by novices. For example, certain patterns of lineman movement coupled with backfield movement in American football mean that the play will be a run to the right side, and an effective response to this action by the defensive player often depends on recognizing it quickly and accurately. Pattern recognition in games has not been considered very much by coaches, and it seems that more could be done to train athletes to recognize patterns.

Abstraction

The processes of analyzing the complex array of stimuli for some environmental meaning can be termed *abstraction*. To abstract means to determine the general qualities of a situation based on the specific elements. For example, if a baseball is going to hit you in the eye, you are probably not aware that it has the same rate of change of visual angle from each side when you duck to avoid being hit. During the stimulus-identification stage this information is abstracted. The specific features of the ball's flight have not been retained; only the result of the analysis has. Specific elements have been coded and recombined into a pattern. It is even possible to imagine that two or more stimulus modalities, such as vision and touch, combine to form a very abstract and meaningful pattern that can be uniquely recognized.

Response-Selection Stage

At the end of the stimulus-identification stage, the individual presumably has analyzed the information in the stimulus input, providing a basis for "knowing" what happened in the environment. In the next stage, response

---

[3]Gibson and his followers would not wish to discuss optical flow patterns in relation to stages of information processing. Very generally, though, these patterns can be thought of as the inputs to early stages of processing.

selection, the subject decides on a response. This stage involves a number of events that serve to determine the choice of actions.

As mentioned in the previous section, one of the events that occurs in stimulus identification is memory contact, the activation of aspects of the stimulus associated with its name or associates of it. Many researchers think that aspects of the response associated with the stimulus are also activated at this time (e.g., Keele, 1973). For example, the sight of a ball looming toward my eye may arouse certain antecedents of the response to avoid the ball. In fact, Greenwald's (1970) *ideo-motor theory* assumes the stimulus arouses an image of the response which is instrumental in leading to the action.

Finally, and most important, a series of events allows the person to select an appropriate response out of a large number of responses that could be made. In performing in the outfield as a baseball player, when the ball is hit I must make rapid decisions about whether or not to attempt to field the ball at all, what direction to move to field the ball, and what to do with the ball if I am lucky enough to field it successfully. Such decisions can be quite important, and they apply to a wide variety of activities in sport, industry, driving, and so on. Presumably, the decisions about what to do are made in the response-selection stage. They can be studied in the laboratory by using the *choice-RT paradigm*.

The Choice-RT Paradigm

For over a century (since Donders' contribution) scientists have believed that the processing of information having to do with the selection of a response requires more time when there are a larger number of alternatives. Donders (1868) used such logic in defining his *b*-reaction (one of five possible stimuli comes on, and each requires a different response), and this has provided a justification for using the choice-RT paradigm to study processes involved in the response-selection stage. The idea is that if increasing the number of alternatives causes an increase in the choice RT, then the increased RT is associated with changes in the way the response-selection stage processed the information.

In the choice-RT paradigm, the subject might be presented with four stimulus lights and instructed that one of the four will be illuminated on a particular trial. Each of the four lights is associated (via instructions from the experimenter) with one of four different responses (e.g., pressing one of four buttons located under each of the fingers of the right hand). The task is to press the appropriate button as quickly as possible after the stimulus light has come on. Usually subjects are not able to predict exactly when the stimulus will occur, preventing them from initiating the response in advance. It seems reasonable that the time from stimulus to response will be sensitive to the variation in the speed of the processing responsible for the selection of the appropriate finger, as well as other factors. Also, by increasing the number of stimulus-response pairs (for example, eight lights and eight possible responses), the time for response selection would increase.

One of the earliest studies of this question was done by Merkel in 1885

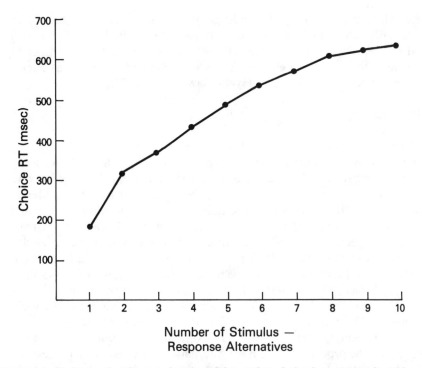

Figure 4-5. Choice reaction time as a function of the number of stimulus-response alternatives (data from Merkel, 1885, as cited by Woodworth, 1938).

(described by Woodworth, 1938). The digits 1 through 5 were assigned to the fingers of the right hand, and the Roman numerals I through V were assigned to the fingers of the left hand. On any given set of trials, the subject knew which of the set of 10 stimuli would be possible (e.g., if there were three possible stimuli, they might be 3, 5, and V). Merkel studied the relationship between the number of possible stimuli and responses and the choice RT. His basic findings are presented in Figure 4-5, where the choice RT is plotted against the number of stimulus alternatives. As the number of stimulus-response alternatives increased, so did the time taken to respond to any one of them. The relationship between choice RT and the number of alternatives was curvilinear; note that the increase in choice RT as the number of alternatives was increased from one to two was about 129 msec, whereas the increase in choice RT by adding another alternative when the number of pairs was nine was only about 3 msec. In addition, notice how long the RTs were with ten alternatives (over 600 msec). When one considers that, in high-level baseball, the ball can travel from the pitcher to the plate in as few as 460 msec (Hubbard & Seng, 1954), the lengthened RT might have important implications for the performance of certain rapid skills. The RT in Merkel's data was essentially the same as the entire pitch in baseball, making 600 msec seem like a very long time indeed!

This relationship between number of alternatives and choice RT has been studied a great deal since Merkel's original observations. The overall conclusion has not changed, although there have been some refinements in technique and some additional theorizing about the causes of the relationship. The most widely known findings and explanations of the effect was apparently determined by two people at about the same time—Hick (1952) and Hyman (1953). The relation they discovered between the number of stimulus alternatives and choice RT has since come to be known as Hick's law, or sometimes as the Hick-Hyman law (Keele, 1973).

Hick's Law

Hick (1952) studied the relationship between the choice RT and the number of stimulus alternatives in much the same way as Merkel had, using various numbers of lights that were associated with an equal number of keys that were to be pressed when the appropriate light came on. Just as Merkel found, choice RT increased as the number of possible stimulus-response alternatives increased. The RT values, as well as the overall shape of the function, agreed well with Merkel's findings in Figure 4-5. However, Hick's discovery was that choice RT appeared to increase by a nearly constant amount (about 150 msec) every time the number of stimulus-response alternatives *doubled*. This suggested that the relationship between the choice RT and the logarithm of the number of stimulus-response alternatives should be linear. The interpretation was that the logarithm of the number of stimulus-response alternatives was a measure of the amount of information that had to be processed, as if more alternatives required more processing. This relationship between the logarithm of the number of alternatives will become more clear in the next few sections.

At about the same time, Hyman (1953) studied similar relations in choice RT tasks. He was also interested in the relationship between amount of information processing and RT. In a series of investigations, he varied the amount of information that the subject had to process, doing so in various ways. First, just as Hick and Merkel had done, Hyman varied the number of stimulus-response alternatives, and he plotted these RTs against the Log_2 of the number of alternatives (which is a measure of the amount of information to be processed, as we shall shortly see).

The data from four subjects are presented in Figure 4-6; the data of interest at this point are the open circles, where the number of stimulus-response alternatives was varied. In each case, there was a strong linear trend between the amount of information [or Log_2 (N)] and choice RT. The empirical equations for each subject are shown on each subject's graph; for example, for Subject G.C. the slope (*b*) was 153 and the intercept was 212 msec. Notice that these "constants" from the empirical equations were considerably different for different subjects, casting considerable doubt on whether they are really invariant. Nevertheless, in each case the RT was linearly related to the amount of stimulus information.

The formal relation that has come to be known as Hick's law states that the choice RT is linearly related to the Log_2 of the number of stimulus alternatives. In equation form,

$$\text{Choice RT} = a + b[Log_2 (N)], \tag{4-1}$$

where N is the number of stimulus-response alternatives and *a* and *b* are the

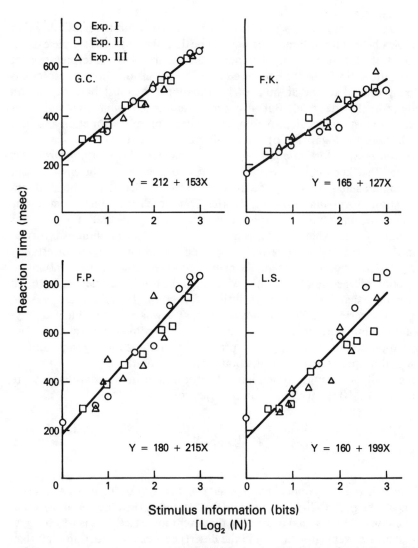

Figure 4-6. Choice reaction time as a function of stimulus information, or the Log₂ of the number of stimulus-response alternatives (from Hyman, 1953).

empirical constants. Notice that Equation 1 is somewhat different from the "typical" linear equation discussed in Chapter 3 (Y = a + bX); but if X equals [Log₂(N)], then Equation 1 means that choice RT is linearly related to Log₂(N), which what Hyman (1953) showed. The values of the constants a and b will be discussed later, to provide an explanation of their theoretical meaning for RT. I will now turn to a discussion of the meaning of Log₂ in terms of the information-processing model.

Interpreting Hick's Law

That the relationship between the choice RT and the logarithm to the base two of the number of stimulus alternatives should be so clearly linear is of considerable interest in its own right. A linear relationship is the most simple of relationships, and scientists become excited about the possibility that complex behaviors of human beings can be described by such simple expressions. But of even more importance is the nature of the interpretation of this relationship.[4] The time required to make a decision about a response is linearly related to the amount of information that must be processed in coming to that decision. But in order to understand what that statement means, I must digress slightly to discuss the notion of information and how it relates to the logarithm of the number of alternatives.

Measures of Information. To this point I have used the term *information* to mean that knowledge provided by various signals from the environment informing us about the state of the outside world. Scientists who study information processing, however, use the term more restrictively to mean the amount of uncertainty that is reduced by the fact that a signal was presented. Thus, when a signal is presented to you, the amount of information that is transmitted is affected by both (a) the amount of uncertainty that existed prior to the signal's being presented and (b) the amount of reduction of uncertainty. If while walking in the rain your friend says that it is raining, that signal conveys little information because there was no original uncertainty. You already knew that it was raining. But if he says that it is raining on the Sahara Desert, that signal conveys a great deal of information because there is (a) low probability that it is raining there and (b) you had no previous knowledge that it was raining there.

Generally speaking, the amount of information in a signal (usually abbreviated by *H*) is given by a simple equation:

$$H = \text{Log}_2 \frac{1}{P_i} \tag{4-2}$$

where P_i is the probability that a given event (i) will occur in a given situation. As the probability of an event (P_i) decreases, the amount of information conveyed by a signal describing that event increases; this is why a signal about a rare event (it is raining in the desert) carries more information than a signal about a common event (it is raining in Eugene, Oregon).

The amount of information contained in a signal is measured in *bits* (short for *bi*nary digi*ts*). One bit is defined as the amount of information necessary to reduce the original uncertainty by half. For example, your friend tells you that he is thinking of one of four people in your family, and he wants you to guess whom it is. If there are two males and two females in your family and your friend also tells you that it is a female he is thinking of, he has reduced the number of possibilities (and hence your uncertainty) from four to two (that is, by half). The amount of information in the message (the statement that the person is a female) has conveyed one bit of information. Next, I will connect the notion of reduction of uncertainty to the logarithm involved in the Hick's law.

First, the logarithm to the base two (Log₂) of a number (e.g., Log₂ (4),

---

[4]Actually, as seen in Chapter 2, there can be many different interpretations of such relationships, and we will simply consider only the most common of them here.

Table 4-2

Relation Between Number of Alternatives (N) and the Log$_2$(N)

Number (N)	Log$_2$(N)
1	0
2	1
4	2
8	3
16	4
32	5
64	6
128	7
256	8

read as "Log to the base two of four") is the power to which the base two must be raised in order to obtain that number. In this example, the base two must be raised to the power of 2 in order to obtain 4 (i.e., $2^2 = 4$). The Log$_2$ (8) is 3, since the base 2 must be raised to the power of 3 in order to get 8 (i.e., $2^3 = 8$, or $2 \times 2 \times 2 = 8$). Table 4-2 shows how the idea works. The Log$_2$ of the numbers (N) on the left of the table are given at the right; in each case, the Log$_2$(N) is the power to which the base two must be raised in order to reach N (e.g., Log$_2$(32) = 5, since $2^5 = 2 \times 2 \times 2 \times 2 \times 2 = 32$).

Now I will relate this notion to decision making. Consider the game shown in Figure 4-7. I have a number of boxes (N boxes) and only one of them contains a marble; your task is to ask me questions that can be answered by yes or no in order to determine which box contains the marble. How many questions must you ask in order to locate the marble?

The results of this game are tabulated in Table 4-3. If there is only one box, how many questions must you ask to determine where the marble is? The answer is none, of course, since there is no uncertainty about the marble's location. If the number of possible boxes is two, you ask, "Is it on the left?" to which I reply, "No," and your uncertainty is thereby reduced to zero by the answer because you now know that the marble is on the right. Alternatively, you could have asked, "Is it on the right?" to which I would have replied, "Yes," and your uncertainty would also have been reduced to zero. Since my answer to your single question (whichever one it may have been) reduced your uncertainty by half (from two alternatives to one) I have given you 1 bit of information. Notice that this 1 bit of information corresponds to the Log$_2$(2) where, according to Table 4-3, the Log$_2$(2) = 1 bit. Notice also that since each of the alternatives was equally likely (with a probability P_i of .5), the amount of information involved in the presentation of either of the alternatives is given by Log$_2$(1/P_i), or Log$_2$(1/.5) = Log$_2$(2) = 1 bit, according to Equation 2.

Now, consider the case to the lower left in Figure 4-7 where there are four possible boxes in which the marble could be. You ask, "Is it in either of the two rightmost boxes?" and I answer, "Yes." Then you ask, "Is it in the rightmost of these two?" and I answer, "No." By asking two questions you

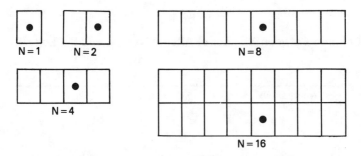

Figure 4-7. Marbles located in various numbers (N) of alternative boxes.

have reduced the uncertainty from four possibilities to one. You can reduce the alternatives by half once (from four to two) and then by half again (from two to one) with two answers, so that the amount of information required to find the marble when there are four alternatives is 2 bits. Notice that this is calculable from the equation $Log_2(4) = 2$ bits, as shown in Table 4-3. Notice also that since each of the four boxes was equally likely to contain the marble, the probability that it was in any one of the boxes (P_i) was .25, and the information required to reduce the uncertainty to zero is given by Equation 2: $Log_2 (1/P_i) = Log_2 (1/.25) = Log_2(4) = 2$ bits. Try the other examples in Figure 4-7.

These examples have shown that the amount of information necessary to locate the marble is related to the Log_2 of the number of possibilities that originally existed. More precisely, the amount of information required to decide where the marble is is linearly related to the $Log_2(N)$. Or, every time the number of stimulus alternatives is doubled (e.g., from 4 to 8), the $Log_2(N)$ and the amount of information to be processed is increased by exactly 1 bit (from 2 to 3). This is, of course, another way of saying that the $Log_2(N)$ is a measure of the amount of information to be processed.

Now, I will relate this observation to Hick's law. Consider the number of boxes in the marble example as analogous to the number of stimulus-response alternatives in the choice RT paradigm. In Figure 4-6 notice that

Table 4-3

Relation between number (N) of possible events (boxes) and the information required (Log_2N) in resolving the uncertainty about them

Original Number of Boxes	Number of Questions Asked	$Log_2(N)$ or Bits
1	0	0
2	1	1
4	2	2
8	3	3
16	4	4

the choice RT is linearly related to the $Log_2(N)$, and thus choice RT is linearly related to the amount of information needed to resolve the uncertainty about N things. Stated differently, every time the number of stimulus-response alternatives is doubled, the amount of information to be processed is increased by 1 bit, and the time required for choice RT is increased by a constant amount. Examine Figure 4-6 to check that this is correct. Therefore, the interpretation of Hick's law is: The choice RT is linearly related to the amount of information that must be processed to resolve the uncertainty about the various stimulus-response alternatives.

Additional evidence can be provided for this idea. Return to Figure 4-6, the plot of Hyman's (1953) data on choice RTs. To this point, I have only considered the open circles (Experiment 1), whereby the number of stimulus alternatives was varied in order to vary the amount of information to be processed. In his Experiment 2 (open squares), the amount of information was varied by changing the probability of the stimulus. Remember, as the event becomes less probable, having to process a signal about it conveys more information, as in Equation 2. When information was increased by decreasing the stimulus probabilities, RT again increased linearly. In Experiment 3, Hyman varied information by changing the sequential dependencies (the tendency for a given event to be followed predictably by another, such as a "q" to be followed by a "u" in English words). This had the effect of making a particular stimulus more or less probable, and the open triangles in Figure 4-6 also show a linear relationship between information and RT.

Resolving Uncertainty During Response Selection

If this interpretation is correct, it provides a very interesting view of what humans do during the response-selection stage of information processing. The response-selection stage can be thought of as being involved with reducing uncertainty about alternative responses when a given stimulus is presented. Furthermore, whenever the number of alternatives is doubled (that is we increase the Log_2 of the number of alternatives by 1), there is a constant increase in the time required to resolve the additional uncertainty. This kind of reasoning and evidence supports the view of humans as processors of information, especially in situations involving choice of response.

The practical implications of this observation are important and probably obvious. In games for which rapid reaction is important, if the player can double the number of likely alternatives for which the opponent must prepare (and the opponent cannot anticipate them), then the player increases by 1 bit the amount of information that must be processed in order to respond, and thereby increases by a constant the opponent's choice RT involved in initiating the appropriate response. (In Hick's data, this value—the slope—was about 150 msec, on the average, but there are wide variations among people as shown in Figure 4-6.) An additional 150 msec of time delay between one player's movement and the opponent's response to it can have serious consequences. For example, the time required by Muhammad Ali to complete a 16½-in. jab was only 40 msec (see *Sports Illustrated,* May 5, 1969; Keele, 1973), so an RT on the part of his opponent of 150 msec could have extremely serious effects if he were trying to avoid being hit by the punch. These kinds of effects are seen in most of the fast ball games popular today, as well as in reaction situations involved in driving a car, doing various industrial tasks, and so on. I will say more about this aspect of RT later in this chapter.

Finally, the strategy for processing the information in which the total number of alternatives is systematically cut in half on each round minimizes the number of "questions" that must be asked. If each of these "questions" requires time, such a strategy minimizes RT. However, the suggestion has been made that children may not use the most efficient strategy, perhaps using a more or less unsystematic search that requires more "questions" and more time. On the other hand, children's data do follow Hick's law, which suggests that the children might use the same processes as adults, but that they are simply slower. The literature is somewhat confusing on this point (e.g., Thomas, 1980).

Interpreting the Intercept and Slope. I will return now to the theoretical meaning of the intercept (a) and the slope (b) in Hick's law (Equation 1). From the earlier discussion of empirical equations (Chapter 3), recall that the intercept (a) was that value of Y (Y is choice RT) associated with $X = 0$ (when $Log_2(N) = 0$) or when the line crossed the Y axis. In the data from various subjects in Hyman's (1953) study (Figure 4-6), these intercepts were approximately 180 msec (212, 165, 180, and 160 msec). Also, recall that when $Log_2(N) = 0$, the value of N must be 1 (refer back to Table 4-3 to verify this), and this represents a situation with only one alternative. This is usually termed *simple RT* (Donders' a-reaction), and it is a situation for which theoretically there is no uncertainty about what to do, with the only uncertainty being about when to do it. Consequently, it has been reasonable to interpret the intercept of Hick's law as a measure of the overall "speed" of the perceptual and motor system exclusive of any time required for decision about which response to make. To this basic 180-msec time, then, is added the time to make additional decisions about choice when there is more than a single stimulus and response.

What about the slope? Also from Hyman's (1953) data, the slopes of the relation ranged from about 127 msec/bit to 215 msec/bit for the various subjects (Figure 4-6). Remember that the slope (b) is a measure of the amount of inclination of the line, and it is the amount of increase in the Y value (choice RT) as the X value [$Log_2(N)$] is increased by one unit (1 bit). So as the amount of information to be processed increased by one bit, there were from 127 to 215 msec of additional choice RT. Thus, the slope is the amount of time required to process one additional bit of information, or the "speed" of decision making by the response-selection stage of processing.

Seen in this way, the slope and intercept measure two different underlying processes involved in human performance. If this is correct, then the slope (b) and the intercept (a) should be affected by different experimental variables. Various of these have been reported in the literature (Fitts & Peterson, 1964). I will have additional information about the separability of the slope and intercept in Chapter 10, where I argue that a and b measure different abilities.

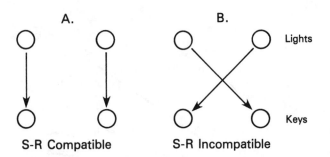

Figure 4-8. S-R compatibility as defined by the relationship between the stimuli and the response to which it is associated.

Qualifications to Hick's Law

Knowing that a relationship as strong as Hick's law holds over a wide variety of situations and kinds of people provides a great deal of encouragement for those who would like to be able to predict choice RT in "real life" situations. Information about choice RT as a function of the number of alternatives would be useful in designing highway and airport systems to minimize accidents as well as in designing successful football plays. Unfortunately, while the law holds in general, a number of variables have to be taken into account in order to predict choice RT, and a few situations exist where the law does not appear to hold at all. The key variables are (a) the nature of the relationship between the stimuli and the associated responses and (b) practice or experience with the task.

Stimulus-response (S-R) compatibility. S-R compatibility refers to the extent to which the stimulus and the associated response are connected in a "natural" way. Say a subject is to respond to one of two lights by pressing one of two keys with the fingers. The situation is said to be *S-R compatible* if the lights and keys are organized in spatially similar ways. In Figure 4-8, the configuration at the left is said to be compatible because the left light requires the subject to press the left key. On the other hand, the situation on the right of Figure 4-8 is said to be less compatible (or "incompatible") because the left light calls for the subject to press the right key, and vice versa.

In the experiment by Hick (1952) discussed earlier, the subjects pushed keys in response to lights. The S-R compatibility in this situation can be regarded as relatively low, since the match-up of the lights and keys was not particularly "natural." In these data, the slope was about 110 msec/bit. (Remember, the slope is interpreted as the amount of time required to process one additional bit of information.) This relationship is shown in Figure 4-9. Now consider the other two curves in the figure, which are from data presented by Fitts and Peterson (1964). For the bottom curve, the subject's task was to move the finger from a starting key to touch the stimulus light that was illuminated. Here the relationship seems compatible, in that the direction of the response in space is the same as the direction of the stimulus; the slope of the curve was only 17 msec/bit. The middle curve is from the same task as that just described, except that the hand and response targets were hidden from view by a screen, and the stimulus lights were

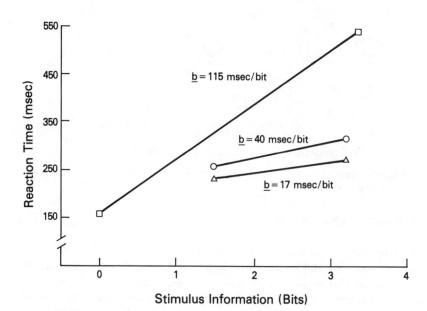

Figure 4-9. Choice RT as a function of stimulus information $Log_2(N)$ in bits (square data points are from Hick, 1952, and circles and triangles are from Fitts & Peterson, 1964; from Fitts, 1964).

presented on a vertical panel in front of the subject. Here, the relationship between the response and the stimulus is slightly less "natural," and the slope of the relation increased to 40 msec/bit. On the other hand, the response used by Hyman (1953) was signaled by various numerals. This task seems quite incompatible in comparison to the other examples, and the slope of line relating choice RT and $Log_2(N)$ averaged 174 msec/bit.

Thus the slope of the Hick equation can be changed easily (a 10-fold increase) by changing relationship between the stimuli and the responses. From these observations, it seems incorrect that the processing of a single bit of information requires a fixed amount of time; rather, the time required to process 1 bit of information (represented by the slope) clearly depends on the association between the stimuli and the responses, i.e., on S-R compatibility. It is also different for different people.

Can the situation ever be so compatible that the slope of the relationship between choice RT and $Log_2(N)$ will decrease to zero—that is, where there will be no increase in choice RT as the number of alternatives is increased? The answer seems to be a qualified "yes." Leonard (1959) studied choice RTs with one, two, four, and eight alternatives, but the situation was quite different from those seen earlier. The subject placed the fingers on the appropriate number of keys and was instructed to press as quickly as possible on the key that vibrated. It would seem that the relationship between the stimulus (vibrations) and the response (pressing that finger on the key) is very compatible, and that the slope of the relation between the number of possible choices and choice RT should be quite small.

Leonard's results are presented in Figure 4-10. There are two important aspects of the data to consider. First, related to the question of S-R compatibility, as the number of S-R alternatives increased from two to eight,

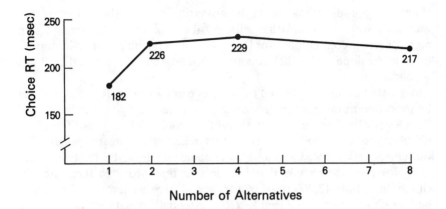

Figure 4-10. Choice RT as a function of the number of alternatives in a highly compatible task (from Leonard, 1959).

there was no further increase in choice RT. That is, the slope of the line was zero. The interpretation of this aspect of Leonard's data is that when the finger was vibrated, the connection between it and the response was so compatible that no additional time was required for decision making. Thus, there was a more or less "direct connection" between the stimulus and response. Perhaps very little decision making was required.

The second important aspect of Leonard's data is the observed increase from the simple-RT case (one alternative, RT = 182 msec) to the two-choice case (two alternatives, RT = 226 msec). Here, an increase in RT was found as the number of alternatives increased, contrary to the observation made when the number of alternatives increased from two to eight. One explanation is that in the one-alternative case the person could actually prepare for the response prior to the stimulus, perhaps doing some of the processing in advance that would normally follow the response-selection stage (e.g., Klapp, 1977a). But, in the two-choice case, the person presumably cannot do this, since the subject cannot prepare two contradictory responses at the same time. And, since humans cannot so prepare when the number of responses is two or greater, there is no further increase in choice RT with further increases in the number of alternatives. I will say more about this effect later in this chapter and in Chapter 8.

Another way in which the effect of compatibility can be seen is in relation to the direction from which the stimulus comes. Simon (1969a, 1969b) has shown that if a stimulus is presented on the subject's right and is paired with a right-hand response (not necessarily moving the hand to the right), the RT is more rapid (30-40 msec) than if the stimulus from the right is paired with a left-hand response. Such findings, together with the data from Leonard (1959), suggest that there may be natural patterns of S-R compatibility and that such patterns are not formed completely on the basis of experience. From an ecological point of view, we could imagine a survival advantage for motor systems that would react more quickly in the direction indicated by a stimulus, especially to block the attack of an animal leaping from behind a bush!

The effects of practice. It may be that difficulty with incompatible

stimulus-response arrangements is primarily due to the subject's un-
familiarity with them and that with sufficient practice, the arrangement
might "become compatible" for the subject. It is possible that an important
factor in the slope of the Hick equation is the amount of practice the subject
has had.

Many studies have examined the effects of practice on RT, but perhaps
the most important one for this discussion is the study by Mowbray and
Rhoades (1959). They used a two- and four-choice RT task and found, as
had been found previously by many researchers, that in early practice the
four-choice task showed a much slower choice RT than did the two-choice
task. However, their study is unique in that they provided their subjects
with an incredible 42,000 trials of practice! After this amount of practice,
the four-choice RT was reduced to a level essentially equal to the two-choice
RT. Thus, the slope of the choice-RT function between 1 and 2 bits (two
and four alternatives) was reduced by practice, eventually becoming essentially zero.

Another set of data that can be interpreted in similar ways comes from
Hellyer (1963). When the task involved digit-naming (the number of possible digits was varied, and the RT was measured by a voice microphone), increasing the number of possible digits to be named did not increase the
choice RT as predicted by the Hick's law. Since there is no reason to believe
that the relation between the numeral "4" and the vocal response "four"
should be genetically determined (such names and numerals are probably
arbitrary), the interpretation is that the names of digits are so highly practiced that the association between the digit and the name is nearly direct
(also, Fitts & Seeger, 1953).

Even though the association between stimuli and responses seems to
become more direct with practice, resist the idea that the movements have
become *automatic* or *reflexive* with practice. Automatic and reflexive imply
that the movements are being performed without awareness or attention,
and there is very strong evidence that this is not the case, as I will show in
Chapter 5. Also, simple RT, when there is very strong compatibility, is
never below about 120 msec at the least, which is found for kinesthetic
stimuli (e.g., Chernikoff & Taylor, 1952); the other stimulus modalities (vision, audition, etc.) produce RTs that are typically 160 to 200 msec. There
seems to be little basis in fact for notions such as "reflex volley" in tennis,
as even these highly compatible responses, when analyzed carefully, appear
to require a great deal of time and attention to produce.

Response-Programming Stage

Once the person has identified the stimulus and selected the response, the
organization and initiation of an overt response must be made. After
response selection, the task is to translate this abstract idea of a response into a set of muscular actions that will achieve it. These processes are thought
to occur during the *response-programming stage* (sometimes termed the
response-initiation stage). Like the processes in the earlier stages, the events
occurring in response programming are probably very complex, requiring

that some program of action be called from the performer's memory, that the program be readied for activation, that the relevant portions of the motor system be readied for the program (called *tuning,* see Chapter 8), and that the movement be initiated.

It is helpful to view the response-programming stage as the final set of processes that allows the individual to communicate with the environment, just as the stimulus-identification stage is viewed as the first stage that allows the environment to communicate with individuals. In keeping with this viewpoint, the variables that affect the stimulus-identification stage are *input variables,* affecting the nature of the stimulus given to the system. In a similar way, the variables affecting the response-programming stage are *output variables,* or variables that affect the nature of the movement that is produced. Between these two stages, of course, is thought to lie the response-selection stage, primarily responsible for associating the particular stimulus input with the appropriate response output. Thus, the response-selection stage is a translation between input and output. (In fact, these processes are called a translation stage by a number of authors, e.g., Welford, 1968).

In contrast to information about the first two stages of processing, knowledge about which was obtained very early in the history of motor behavior, information about the response-programming stage has been quite recent in its development. It seemed quite obvious to the early workers that variables like stimulus clarity and the number of stimulus alternatives would affect RT, but it was not until 1960 when Henry and Rogers performed an experiment on the nature of the movement to be produced in RT situations that thinking about the response-programming stage began.

The Henry-Rogers Experiment

Henry and Rogers (1960) studied the nature of the movement to be made in a simple-RT paradigm, in which the subjects knew on any given trial which response was to be made. In different series of trials, though, Henry and Rogers had the subjects make different movements, while keeping constant the stimulus that called for the movement, as well as the response alternatives. The first movement was the simplest; it involved merely lifting the finger from a key, so the movement was only a few millimeters in length and had essentially no accuracy requirement. For the second movement, the subject lifted the finger from the key and moved approximately 33 cm forward-upward to grasp a tennis ball suspended on a string, which stopped a timer measuring MT. The third movement involved a second suspended ball mounted 30 cm to the right of the first ball. The subject lifted the finger from the key, moved forward-upward to strike the first ball with the back of the hand, moved forward-downward to push a button, and then moved forward-upward again to strike the second suspended ball. Remember, the stimulus and response alernatives of these three movements were exactly the same (so that the processing speed in the stimulus-identification and response-selection mechanisms should be the same also); the only thing that varied was the nature of the movement. The primary measure, as before, was the RT, or the interval from stimulus onset until the movement began.

Table 4-4

Reaction Time and Movement Time as a Function of the Complexity of the Movement (adapted from Henry & Rogers, 1960)

Movement	RT	MT
Finger Lift	159	—
Single Ball Grasp	195	95
Double Ball Strike	208	465

Henry and Rogers used a number of different groups as subjects, but only the data from adult men and women are presented in Table 4-4. The medium-complexity movement (single-ball grasp) resulted in a 36-msec longer RT than the simpler finger-lift response. The most complex movement (double-ball strike) resulted in a further 13-msec increase in RT over the single-ball grasp. Since the stimuli were not changed for the different movements, these data suggest that the increased RT as the movements were increased in complexity was due to an increased amount of time required to program the movement in some response-programming stage. Henry's and Rogers' original idea was that more complex instructions, such as would be necessary to control the limb through several movement reversals and/or to produce grasping and striking actions, would require more brain centers to be coordinated and more extensive use of learned motor commands, in turn requiring more time for all of this neurological complexity to be organized during RT. In slightly modified form, the original idea still has a great deal of support today (see Henry, 1980; Klapp, 1980).

Response Complexity Effects

Since the publication of Henry's and Rogers' original data, a large number of separate experiments have shown essentially the same thing. Recent examples have been those produced by Klapp (see Klapp, 1977a, 1980, or Kerr, 1978, for reviews) using key-pressing movements of varying complexity, and those produced by Sternberg, Monsell, Knoll, and Wright (1978), who found that the RT was directly related to the number of elements in a sequence of action by studying spoken words and typed letters. The effect of movement complexity on RT is remarkably robust, and it appears both when the person knows the movement in advance (simple RT) and when the movement is indicated by the stimulus (choice RT). Regardless of the variations in method and movements, the effect of movement complexity on RT has been interpreted as relating to the time necessary to prepare the movement during the response-programming stage of RT.

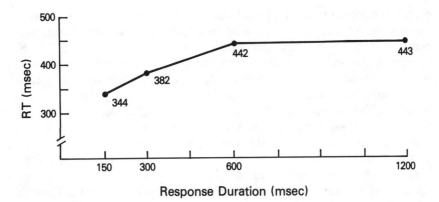

Figure 4-11. Reaction time as a function of the duration of the response (adapted from Klapp & Erwin, 1976).

Response Duration Effects

The movements studied by Henry and Rogers (1960) and by Sternberg et al. (1978) vary in at least one other important way besides their complexity: they vary in their *response duration*. From Henry's and Rogers' data (Table 4-4), notice that the more complex movement required much longer to produce (465 msec) than the simpler one (95 msec). In the Sternberg et al. experiments as well, time for the overall movements increased as the number of speech or typing elements to be produced increased. These and other findings have led various writers to suggest that a major variable in the response-programming stage might be the duration of the movement to be produced.

Klapp and Erwin (1976) asked subjects to make 10-cm movements of a slide along a trackway, with goal movement times of 150, 300, 600, or 1200 msec. The number of actions in the response was held constant, but the duration of the response was varied. As the response duration increased the RT to initiate the response increased as well (see Figure 4-11), especially when the response durations were below 600 msec. Similar effects have been found by Rosenbaum and Patashnik (1980), who varied response duration in terms of the time that a button had to be depressed, and by Quinn, Schmidt, Zelaznik, Hawkins, and McFarquhar (1981), who varied the MT for aiming responses of a stylus to a target. There is a great deal of evidence that the MT for the response is a determinant of the RT for that same movement. Perhaps many of the examples of response complexity effects on RT (e.g., Henry & Rogers, 1960; Sternberg et al., 1978) may be due to the fact that when complexity is increased, MT is also increased (Quinn et al., 1980). Whatever the cause of these effects, it seems clear that they "reside" in the RT for the movement, and the interpretation has been that these variables (complexity or MT) affect the duration of the response-programming stage.

MEMORY FRAMEWORKS

This chapter has been concerned with what happens to information as it enters the system and is processed, eventually leading to a response. The emphasis has been on a "dynamic" view of how man prepares a movement, without much focus on the nature of the information itself or on what happens to it as it is being processed. Also, information entering the information-processing system must be retained (some would use the word *stored*) for future use, just as a computer stores information. The systems that presumably hold the information for future processing and that are the location of the actual processing are collectively called *memory*. This section is about these systems as they contribute to movement planning and movement control. (See Baddeley (1976) for another review of this work.)

One common observation about how information is held is that some kinds of information appear to be held only for a few seconds (e.g., my realtor's telephone number that I just retrieved from the phone book), while other kinds of information appears to be retained for decades (e.g., what kind of car my father drove in 1946). These observations, coupled with a great deal of empirical evidence about the nature of the information that is stored, have led a number of researchers to speculate that there are three separate memory systems. These systems are different in terms of (a) the amount of information that can be stored in them, (b) the nature or form of the information that is stored in them, and (c) the rate of loss of this information (forgetting). This framework for memory systems can be thought of as a series of hypothetical "boxes" into which items are placed, with the information being transferred from box to box as a result of various kinds of information-processing operations that can be performed on them. These boxes are traditionally labeled *short-term sensory store* (STSS), *short-term memory* (STM), and *long-term memory* (LTM).

Another viewpoint on memory denies that there are discrete boxes into which the information is placed; rather, as the information is taken into the system, it is thought to be transformed into various codes and/or combined with other existing information, with these processes being continuous rather than discrete as the "box theory" would have it. In this view, the amount of time that an item can be retained is determined by the level (depth) of processing that it has received, as well as by the breadth (the amount) of processing that it has received. Therefore, the extent to which an item is retained is not determined by the particular "box" in which the information has been stored. This view has been termed the *levels-of-processing framework* by Craik and Lockhart (1972), and in many ways it represents an alternative to the "box theory" of memory just mentioned.

In the next few sections, evidence for these two frameworks for memory will be presented. In many ways, this evidence will appear to be complementary to the evidence just presented about stages of processing, and whenever possible, I will try to relate the stages to the discussion of memory. But the work on stages of processing was developed separately from the work on memory and was done by different scientists who used different methods, so the relationship between the ideas about stages and those about memory are not as close as they could be.

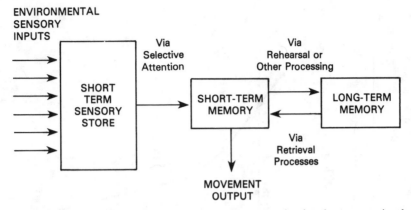

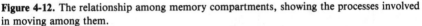

Figure 4-12. The relationship among memory compartments, showing the processes involved in moving among them.

"Box Theories" of Memory

There is no single "box theory" of memory. This label has been used instead to refer to those theories in which memory is thought to be comprised of various discrete compartments, each with somewhat different characteristics in terms of the length of time that items can be held, and the nature of the memory code (the "language" in which the information is stored). Without being too specific about particular theories, it is possible to discuss three such memory compartments that seem to be defined on the basis of the length of time that items can be held. These are (a) short-term sensory store, (b) short-term memory, and (c) long-term memory (see Figure 4-12).

Short-Term Sensory Store (STSS)

The most "peripheral" (i.e., close to the environment) level of processing is thought to be a memory system that serves to hold massive amounts of information presented to it for a brief period of time. When information is presented to the system, the short-term sensory store accepts it without much recoding and then loses it rather quickly as new information is added. Just as a red burner on an electric stove fades in color when it is turned off, the information in the short-term sensory store is thought to fade (or "decay," as psychologists put it) with the passage of time. Such a system can be proposed for each of the stimulus modalities—vision, touch, audition, kinesthesis, and so on. Perhaps there is even more than one short-term sensory store for each modality; hence, the many lines of input in Figure 4-12.

With respect to visual short-term sensory store, some of the earliest and strongest evidence comes from the work of Sperling (1960). He presented a matrix of three rows of four letters each on a tachistiscope, a device for presenting visual information very briefly and under controlled conditions. The matrix was presented for 50 msec so that the subjective impression was a bright flash of the letters. In addition, one of three tones was presented,

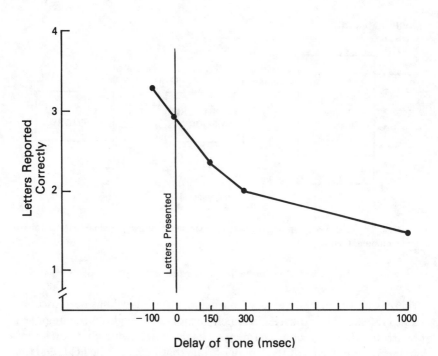

Figure 4-13. Number of items correctly recalled as a function of the delay of the tone indicating which row should be recalled (from Sperling, 1960).

and the tone indicated which of the rows of four letters the subject was to recall; a high tone meant the top row, the middle tone meant the middle row, and so on. The tone could be presented 100 msec before the letter matrix was flashed on, simultaneously with the letter matrix, or 150, 300, or 1000 msec after the matrix.

In Figure 4-13 the number of letters recalled is plotted as a function of the temporal location of the tone.[5] When the tone was presented before the letters, the recall was very good, about 3.3 letters (out of four). When the tone was presented 150 msec after the letters, the subject could recall only about 2.3 letters. When the tone was presented after a full second, the subject could recall only about 1.5 letters.

This evidence has been interpreted in terms of a short-term sensory store. The idea is that all of the letters are delivered by the flash to the short-term sensory store, where they are stored briefly. However, the subject does not know which of the rows to attend to until the tone is presented. If the tone is presented immediately after the letters are presented (150 msec), they are still available in short-term sensory store and the subject recalls them. But if the tone is delayed for a full second, the letters in short-term sensory store have begun to fade and the subject cannot report as many of them. This evidence suggests that (a) the short-term sensory store was capable of holding all the information presented to it (since the subject could report

---

[5]The number of letters recalled is what Sperling referred to as the "immediate-memory span" divided by three.

any of the letters in the row if the tone was presented immediately) and that (b) the short-term sensory store loses information very rapidly with the passage of time. Thus, according to this view, there is a continuously updated record of the visual events in the past few hundred milliseconds available in the short-term sensory store, and we actually "see" by "reading" the contents of visual short-term sensory store rather than by viewing the outside world directly.

Might such a system exist for modalities other than vision, such as audition, touch, and kinesthesis? For tactile stimuli, Bliss, Crane, Mansfield, and Townsend (1966) have shown relations similar to those of Sperling (1960), suggesting a short-term sensory store for this stimulus modality. Also, such a system would seem necessary for auditory stimuli in order to understand speech. Neisser (1967) has made the observation that any single piece of auditory information (lasting, for example, only 1 msec) would be uninterpretable to the listener. In order to understand a word, which might last for a few hundred msec, presumably the listener would have to retain the first sounds in a *buffer* until the later sounds arrived, so that they could be "put together" into a word. This buffer storage is really the same notion as that of auditory short-term sensory store, or "echoic memory," whereby the auditory information can be recycled in much the same way as an echo can be heard after sounds bounce off a canyon wall.

On the basis of later experiments, the information in visual short-term sensory store is thought to have a maximum duration of about 1 sec, with a more practical limit of about 250 msec. In the visual system, the information can be *masked* (blotted out) by the presentation of a bright light after the offset of the letter matrix (called *backward masking* effects), so that recall of the letters is not possible after the light is presented. Also, if in the same eye a target is presented for 15 msec followed by a second 15-msec masking stimulus, the subject's impression is that the *single* stimulus presentation was not clear (Turvey, 1973).

This and other evidence leads to the conclusion that short-term sensory store involves rather literal storage of information, in that the information is recorded in the same way that it came into the system, in terms of spatial location and form. A convenient analogy is how film records what comes into the lens of the camera, although we should not think that the information is stored *in* the eye. The information is continually entering the eye and ear and continually being replaced by later information, implying a loss of memory of the earlier information. These processes are thought to be happening in the stimulus-identification stage discussed earlier in this chapter.

A second important feature of short-term sensory store is the simple transformation of the literal information that is received. Many researchers believe that there are "analyzers" that interpret certain forms such as a right angle, verticality, roughness, or color, prior to their being stored. It appears that a number of such analyses can be performed simultaneously (earlier this was termed *parallel processing*) and that many such interpretations can be stored simultaneously in short-term sensory store. If these ideas are correct, the short-term sensory storage systems must have a very large capacity, since many different stimuli are being sent into the system and held at the same time. These features of the short-term sensory store are

Table 4-5

Characteristics of the Three Memory Systems

| | Memory System | | |
Attribute	STSS	STM	LTM
Storage duration	Less than 1 sec	1 sec to 60 sec	Seemingly limitless
Type of coding	Very literal	More abstract	Very abstract
Capacity	Seemingly limitless	6-8 items	Seemingly limitless

summarized in Table 4-5.

If this is the case, why doesn't the irrelevant information become confused with the relevant information? The answer most frequently given is that a mechanism called *selective attention* enables us to ignore the vast majority of irrelevant elements in the short-term sensory store. Presumably, information "screened" by selective attention is passed on to the next "box" in the memory structure, short-term memory (STM). The way in which selective attention, attention, and consciousness are thought to be related is discussed in Chapter 5.

Processing Information into Short-Term Memory

As mentioned above, the role of selective attention is to choose the relevant information in short-term sensory store for further processing, while allowing the remainder of the information to be ignored (refer to Figure 4-12). Presumably, the choices are determined by the nature of the task in which the person is engaged (such as attending to vision in fielding a baseball), or by the particular moment in time within a task (e.g., vision now, audition later). According to many such models, information that is processed further because of its *pertinence* to a particular situation is processed into short-term memory (see Norman, 1976).

A convenient analogy for this process might help. Imagine that you are in a dark room and that the walls consist of thousands of constantly changing letters, words, numbers, and images. You can gain access to this information by shining a flashlight onto the wall. But, the beam of the flashlight is narrow, and you can only see a very small part of what is on the wall at any time. If the light is pointed at one part of the wall you will miss something that came and went on some other part of the wall. In this analogy, you are short-term memory, taking in the information from the flashlight, which is selective attention; and the information on the wall is that contained in short-term sensory store. Furthermore, the beam of the flashlight can be very intense and concentrated, allowing us to be very precise in taking in information at which it is aimed but to miss adjacent information, or the beam can be very diffuse to take in a wider variety of signals but with less clarity. Presumably, then, all we ever see (or hear or feel) is information at which the flashlight was aimed.

Short-Term Memory (STM)

Short-term memory is thought to be a storage system for information delivered from either short-term sensory store or long-term memory. It is thought of as having a limited capacity and a relatively short duration and as being a kind of "workspace" for processing (Atkinson & Shiffrin, 1971). There are many common examples of the presence of short-term memory. When I look up a number in a phone book, I may say the number to myself (indicating that it has been processed from visual short-term sensory store through selective attention), but after I fumble in my pocket for a dime, I can no longer remember the number. This suggests that there is a conscious storage system of limited capacity and duration.

Verbal short-term memory. Peterson and Peterson (1959) and Brown (1958) provided evidence for this kind of system which was to have a strong influence on research in memory for the next two decades. Basically, Peterson and Peterson provided subjects with a single *trigram* (three unrelated letters), then removed the letters and had the subjects count backwards by three's from a three-digit number until recall of the trigram was requested from 0 to 18 sec later. The backwards counting was intended to prevent the subject from rehearsing the trigram during the retention interval. Thus, all the subject had to do was remember the trigram while counting backwards for up to 18 sec.

Peterson's and Peterson's results are shown in Figure 4-14, where the

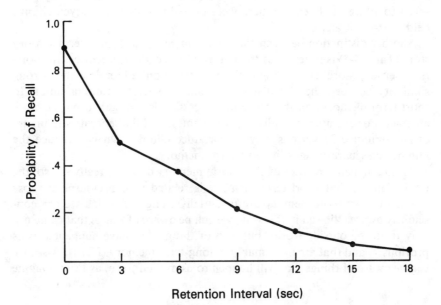

Figure 4-14. Probability of correct recall of a single trigram as a function of the retention interval (from Peterson & Peterson, 1959).

probability of successfully recalling[6] the trigram is graphed as a function of the length of the retention interval. When the recall was nearly immediate, the probability of recall was about .90; but when the retention interval was increased only by a few seconds, there was a marked decrease in the recall. This persisted until, at 18 sec, almost no trigrams could be recalled. This evidence suggests that a memory system exists that loses information rapidly (in about 30 to 60 sec) unless the information is rehearsed in some way.

A major difference between short-term memory and short-term sensory store (Table 4-5) is in terms of capacity. Earlier I mentioned that the capacity of short-term sensory store was very large, essentially limitless; however, evidence suggests that short-term memory has a capacity of only about seven (plus or minus two) items (Miller, 1956). Evidence for this conclusion comes from a variety of sources. One is the "memory span" experiment, in which the subject is presented with a long string of items and is asked to give the item that occurred some number of items earlier. The subject has to keep all of the items in short-term memory and can accurately remember only about seven previous ones.

This conclusion depends on the definition of an "item." Sometimes subjects group separate items into larger collections, so that each collection may contain five "items" of its own; this process has been termed *chunking* (Miller, 1956). The idea is that if there are 44 letters to remember, e.g., the letters in the first sentence in this paragraph, it would be impossible to remember them without rehearsing them. But by chunking the letters into larger, more meaningful groups (words or sentences) the 44 items can be recalled more easily. In this case, the capacity of short-term memory is thought to be seven chunks. Ericsson, Chase, and Faloon (1980) have shown that a subject, with 175 days of practice with a technique for chunking effectively, was able to increase the capacity of short-term memory from seven to 79 items! Even so, there were probably only about seven chunks held in store at any one time.

Another distinction between short-term memory and short-term sensory store (Table 4-5) is in terms of the nature of the coding processes. In short-term sensory store, the coding is thought to be quite literal, with a strong similarity between the coded materials and the actual stimulus input. In short-term memory, on the other hand, coding is thought to be far more abstract. For example, stimuli are given names, and the separate stimuli are often combined in various ways to produce chunks that can reduce the number of separate items in short-term memory.

Although many theories of short-term memory do not directly say so, the implication is that short-term memory is related to consciousness; those things in short-term memory are essentially things of which we are consciously aware. Viewed in this way, we can be aware of things that came not only from the outside world, but also of things that have happened to us previously, and that are presumably in long-term memory (LTM). Also, we can be aware of things that will happen to us in the future, as I can imagine

---

[6]Successful recall meant producing the proper trigram with a latency of no greater than 2.83 sec.

what it will be like walking to the university in the rain today. Many see short-term memory as a "workspace," in which information from short-term sensory store and information from long-term memory are brought together to be processed through the mechanisms that are thought to require attention (Atkinson & Shiffrin, 1971). For example, if I ask you, "What is the square-root of 9?" you enter the information from the question into short-term memory via selective attention being directed to short-term sensory store, and then retrieve the method (rules) for solving the problem (sometimes called an algorithm) from long-term memory. You then solve the problem "in your head" in short-term memory. This kind of thinking is the justification for the double arrow between short-term and long-term memory in Figure 4-12; information can be placed in long-term memory from short-term memory via rehearsal or other processes, and information can be brought out of long-term into short-term memory via retrieval processes.

Finally, it has been traditional to think of short-term memory as a storage location for sensory information, but from the previous paragraph it seems to be far more. In addition to storing information for brief intervals, short-term memory receives rules or methods from long-term memory and is a place where the processing can be done. An even more extreme view which appears to have merit has been forwarded by Klapp (1976), who believes that short-term memory is a storage location where action programs from long-term memory are "readied" and held briefly until they are run off. Thus, under this view, short-term memory might be the location of response programming. In keeping with this view, Figure 4-12 has an arrow leading from short-term memory to movement output, whereby the result of processing a motor program in short-term memory is a movement, such as saying the number three or throwing a ball.

Short-term motor memory. As with many aspects of the study of motor behavior, researchers followed the lead of experimental psychologists—in this case by Brown (1958) and Peterson and Peterson (1959)—and began to ask questions about the role of a short-term memory for motor information. Motor behaviorists attempted to reproduce the essential features of the verbal short-term memory experiments—namely, once-presented items, no rehearsal allowed, and short retention intervals. The lead was probably provided by Adams and Dijkstra (1966) (although others were doing similar work, e.g., Posner & Konick, 1966). These methods set the tone of short-term motor memory research for at least a decade.

Adams and Dijkstra asked blindfolded subjects to move a slide along a trackway until it struck a fixed stop which defined a criterion position. Then the subject moved back to the starting position to wait for the remainder of the retention interval (from 10 to 120 sec). Then the subject attempted to move the slide to the criterion position with the stop removed. The error in reproduction was measured as absolute error.

The major findings from their Experiment 2 are presented in Figure 4-15. The absolute error in recalling the position increased sharply as the retention interval increased from 10 to 60 sec and changed very little thereafter. These findings closely paralleled the early findings of Brown (1958) and Peterson and Peterson (1959) in that nearly all of the forgetting of the posi-

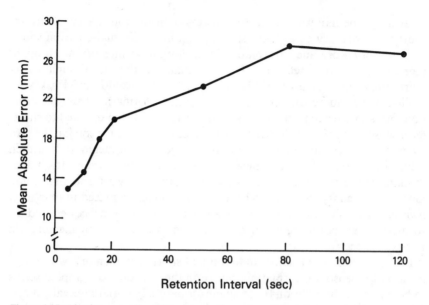

Figure 4-15. Absolute error in positioning recall as a function of the retention interval length (from Adams & Dijkstra, 1966).

tion occurred within the first 60 sec, which is taken to be the approximate upper limit for retention in short-term verbal memory.

I will say more about short-term motor memory studies in Chapter 15, but a comment about the interpretation of these studies is in order here. The idea has been (although it was never stated very emphatically until recently) that the subject moved to the criterion stop position, where some aspect of the criterion position was stored in short-term memory. Many, including myself (Schmidt, 1975b), believed that the subject stored the kinesthetic information about the position of the limb in the criterion position. Others believed that the subject stored information about movement length, about the pathway of the movement through space, or about some internal command that produced the movement. In any case, the subject held these items in short-term motor memory over the retention interval.

In the case of retaining information about the sensory qualities of the movement, we assumed that the subject's task at recall was to move to a position such that the feedback received matched the kinesthetic feedback that was stored in short-term motor memory. If the retention interval was long, the stored information would presumably fade from short-term memory, and the match would become more difficult, producing more error. A similar case can be made for the idea that subjects remember the command for movement; the command fades from memory, making the recall less accurate over time.

The short-term motor memory paradigm was very popular in motor behavior research for about 10 years, beginning in 1966, and a great deal of research was centered on the kinds of memory codes used, the retention characteristics for different kinds of movements, and so on, with most of the work using the linear-positioning task popularized by Adams and Dijkstra (1966). Today, however, there has been increased concern over the utility of extremely simple tasks such as linear positioning in coming to the understanding of motor behavior, and the questions about short-term motor memory are not asked very much any more. For good reviews of this area see Stelmach (1974), Kelso and Stelmach (1976), or Marteniuk (1976).

Long-Term Memory (LTM)

The major distinction between long- and short-term memory (Table 4-5) is with respect to the amount of time that information can be stored. According to most "box theories" of memory, when items are practiced (or rehearsed), which of course requires information processing activities, they are in some way transferred from short-term storage to long-term storage, where they can be held more permanently and "protected" from loss; refer again to Figure 4-12.

An example is learning a new phone number. The first time you hear it, you are likely to forget it quickly if you do not practice it. Repeated practice results in the number being transferred to more permanent storage. In some cases, this storage is indeed permanent; I can still remember the phone number I had when I was 8 years old—EMpire 3-1634. But, in some cases it is not so permanent, as I cannot remember my phone number from when I was 12 years old.

Long-term memory, of course, provides the capability for making movements that have been practiced before. In some ways the development of the long-term memory for movement is the major goal of the teaching/learning process in motor learning. Some of the variables that appear to determine retention of well-learned acts will be treated in Chapter 15. For now I can say that practice leads to the development of better and stronger long-term memory for movement and that these memories are often present after many years. Riding a bicycle is the most often cited example, as people appear to be able to ride acceptably well after 40 years or more with no intervening practice.

One way to think about memory loss is that the information in long-term memory weakens ("decays") automatically with the passage of time. A rival point of view is that the information does not spontaneously weaken but is actively interferred with by other activities that occurred either before or after the event was experienced (see Chapter 15). A variant of this interference theory for memory (see Adams, 1967, 1976) is that the information does not fade with time but somehow becomes inaccessible. This is analogous to the book which is stored permanently in the library; if the librarian forgets where it is located, it is as good as "lost." Some experiments with patients undergoing brain surgery while they are awake suggest that this view might be correct (Penfield, 1958); when the brain is stimulated with a very weak electrical current, the patients report experiencing past events in remarkable detail, sometimes in full color, even when these events had not been recalled for 40 years.

Another major distinction between long- and short-term memory relates to the *amount* of information that can be held (Table 4-5). Most argue that short-term memory has a functional capacity of about seven chunks, whereas long-term memory must have a very large capacity indeed. In fact, no one has ever determined a maximum value for the capacity of long-term memory, and it is probably safe to say that it is functionally limitless. In the motor realm, the analog of well-learned facts and principles is well-learned movements, and the functional capacity of long-term motor memory must also be very large if it is capable of retaining all of the movements that humans typically perform on demand. An interesting question—one which will be treated in Chapter 15—is whether verbal and motor long-term memory systems are the same system or functionally different systems.

When items are transferred to long-term memory, they are assumed to undergo changes in the coding with which they are stored (Table 4-5). For example, early work in verbal short-term memory has shown that the primary code of a once-presented item is acoustic; that is, information is stored in short-term memory primarily on the basis of what it "sounded like." Evidence comes from studies in which information in short-term memory is interfered with by other items that have similar sounds (e.g., rock versus sock). When the items are practiced further (into long-term memory), they appear to be coded according to their meaning (semantic coding) rather than according to their sound; thus, interference occurs between items in long-term memory if the items tend to have the same or similar meaning (e.g., rock versus stone) (see Adams, 1967, 1976).

One thing that appears to happen with practice or repetition is an increase in the number of associations with already-learned information (i.e., increased meaning), so that the recall of information is assisted by these associations. In this sense, the coding of the information in long-term memory is thought to be even more abstract than that in short-term memory (see Table 4-5), with elaborate rules and transformations of the stored information being necessary in order to, for example, remember my old phone number.

Levels of Processing Framework

In the "box theories" of memory, the information is thought to be "in" only one of the three discrete memory stores, with the nature of the codes for each being completely different. On the other hand, Craik and Lockhart (1972) argued that it is not necessary to postulate the existence of these discrete memory "boxes." Rather, they believe that the retention characteristics of information are determined by the levels of processing that the item received after being introduced, not by which "box" the information resides in. As an item is entered into the information-processing system, increasing the amount of processing for the item moves the information further into the system, and the extent to which an item will be retained is related to the "depth" (or level) to which the information was processed.

The idea of levels of processing is an attempt to account for the different kinds of coding processes that are used as items become increasingly well learned. When information is presented, it is processed at a very "shallow" level at first, since the amount of information processing devoted to the item is small; the information is still in a very literal form, and there are few associations formed with already learned information. This is analogous to what the "box" theorists consider information in short-term sensory store to be. As the item has more processing allocated to it, for example to detect features (right angles, verticality) out of an array, the information becomes more abstract as more of the subject's capacities and prior learning are combined with the original item.

This process is thought to continue if the item receives additional processing. Eventually, processing allows the item to be labeled and to become accessible to consciousness, which is analogous to the short-term memory store in the "box" theories. With further processing, such as rehearsal or elaboration, the information proceeds to deeper and deeper levels, with the information being coded more and more abstractly as the depth increases, and becomes associated with more and more similar information already in memory at each level. This increased depth of processing corresponds to the transfer of information from short- to long-term storage in the "box" theories. The increased meaning of information in more permanent storage is thought to be a result not only of greater depth of processing, but also of greater breadth of processing, whereby information at a given depth is associated with increasing amounts of similarly coded information already stored there. This notion of *breadth of processing* is closely related to the common view that it is far easier to retain information that is meaningful (that is, information that already has similar associates formed in memory) than it is to retain less meaningful information, as in learning by rote.

One of many tricks that people with exceptionally "good memories" use is to associate new information with already learned and easily reproduced structures in memory. For example, to learn a list of randomly presented words (e.g., car, cat, milk, coat, etc.), some people use a well-known saying like, "One is a bun, two is a shoe, three is a tree, . . ." to increase the associates of the to-be-learned information. Some memory artists form a mental picture of the first item with the bun, with the more bizarre the image the better. For example, I could picture an open hot-dog bun with a Porsche in the place that the hot-dog would be, with mustard dripping in the windows; then I could imagine a cat running with high-top tennis shoes, and so on. These techniques really work to increase memory strength, especially for nonsense materials (like the names of the cranial nerves).

Thus Craik's and Lockhart's (1972) idea appears to provide an explanation for the different retention characteristics of information in memory by postulating that information with increased depth and/or breadth of processing is coded progressively more abstractly and that increased depth implies increased retention. They feel that there is no good reason to assume that there are three discrete memory "boxes," and their view appears to be a rival for the earlier "box theories." It is perhaps too early to say which of these two theories is more correct, but current thinking generally favors the "box theories," largely because of the powerful body of evidence that supports them.

SUMMARY

A great deal about the way we move can be understood by considering the human as an information-processing system which takes in information from the environment, processes it, and then outputs information to the environment in the form of movements. Using the concepts of subtractive logic initiated by Donders (1868), *stages of processing* can be defined by using RT methods. The first stage, called *stimulus-identification,* is concerned with the reception of a stimulus, preliminary preconscious analyses of features, and extraction of patterns from the stimulus array. Variables like stimulus clarity and stimulus intensity affect the duration of processing in this stage. A second stage, called *response selection,* is concerned with the translation or decision mechanisms that lead to the choice of response. The duration of this stage is sensitive to variables such as the number of stimulus-response alternatives and S-R compatibility (the extent to which the stimulus and response are "naturally" linked). The final stage, called *response programming,* is associated with changing the abstract idea of a response into muscular action. The duration of this stage is related to variables affecting the response, such as response complexity and response duration.

Parallel to the ideas about stages of processing are concepts about information storage systems, or memory. In a common framework, memory can be thought of as consisting of three memory compartments; a *short-term sensory storage,* capable of storing a large amount of literally coded information for perhaps a second; a *short-term memory,* capable of storing only about seven (plus or minus two) abstractly coded items for perhaps 30 sec; and a *long-term memory* capable of storing very large amounts of abstractly coded information for long periods of time. Short-term memory has been visualized as a "workspace" where information from short-term sensory store and long-term memory can be brought together for processing. A rival to these "box theories" of memory is the *levels-of-processing framework,* which attempts to explain the nature of coding and rate of forgetting in terms of the amount and nature of processing an item has received, without postulating discrete memory compartments.

GLOSSARY

Bit. The amount of information required to reduce the original amount of uncertainty by half.

Choice reaction time. RT for a task in which each response to be made is associated with a different stimulus.

Chunking. The combination of individual elements in memory into larger units.

Cognitive psychology. A psychological tradition in which the nature of unobservable mental processes in human behavior is studied by indirect methods.

Depth of processing. A variable related to the nature of the coding processes in the levels-of-processing framework, with deeper levels being associated with more abstract coding.

Discrimination reaction time. RT for a task in which a number of stimuli can be presented, with a response being made only if a given stimulus occurs.

Hick's law. The mathematical statement that the choice RT is linearly related to the Log_2 of the number of stimulus-response alternatives, or to the amount of information that must be processed in order to respond.

Information. The content of a message that serves to reduce uncertainty.

Levels-of-processing framework. A framework for memory research that views memory as continuous rather than discrete.

Log_2 (N). The power to which the base 2 must be raised to achieve N.

Long-term memory. A functionally limitless memory store for abstractly coded information, facts, concepts, and relationships; presumably storage for movement programs.

Parallel processing. A type of information processing in which at least two processes can occur simultaneously.

Response-programming stage. A stage of information processing in which the previously chosen response is transformed into overt muscular action.

Response-selection stage. A stage of information processing in which the response associated with the presented stimulus is selected.

Selective attention. A mechanism for directing attention or capacity to a given stimulus input from short-term sensory store.

Serial processing. A style of information processing in which stages of processing are arranged sequentially in time.

Short-term memory. A memory store with a capacity of about seven elements, capable of holding moderately abstract information for up to 30 sec; analogous to consciousness; a "workspace" for processing.

Short-term sensory store. A functionally limitless memory store for holding literal information for only about 1 sec.

Simple reaction time. Reaction time from a task in which a single known response is produced when a single stimulus is presented.

Stimulus-identification stage. A stage of information processing in which the stimulus is identified, and features or patterns are abstracted; often divided into separate encoding and identification stages.

Stimulus-response compatibility. The degree to which the set of stimuli and associated responses are "naturally" related to each other.

CHAPTER 5

Attention and Performance

Attention! This chapter is about attention and how the concept can help in understanding the nature of information processing and its limitations in human performance. I will begin with a brief discussion of the concepts of attention and then turn to how attention relates to the stages of information processing presented in the previous chapter.

ATTENTION

Attention has always been of interest to motor behavior researchers. Even though the study of attention has enjoyed renewed interest lately, an acceptable definition of the phenomenon was written almost 100 years ago. William James, one of the earliest and most renowned experimental psychologists, wrote:

> Every one knows what attention is. It is the taking possession by the mind, in clear and vivid form, of one out of what seem several simultaneously possible objects or trains of thought. Focalization, concentration, of consciousness are of its essence. It implies withdrawal from some things in order to deal effectively with others (James, 1890, pp. 403-404).

But does everyone know what it is? As Norman (1976) and Moray (1970) have pointed out, many different definitions of attention (at least six) exist, and people use the term in a variety of ways. But inherent in James' statement are a number of features of the phenomenon considered important today, and these are discussed in the next few sections.

Attention and Consciousness

Roughly defined as "what we are aware of at any given time," consciousness has been one of the most important issues in psychology and philosophy since man began to ponder human behavior. As Posner (1973) has pointed out, beliefs about consciousness have ranged from the idea that (a) behavior is controlled by consciousness (humans behave in ways that are "willfully" determined by conscious activity) that (b) consciousness is the result of behavior (awareness results from our actions and is not the cause of them), to the idea that (c) consciousness is unrelated to behavior (awareness is a phenomenon that merely accompanies behavior). It is beyond the scope of this book to deal effectively with the notion of consciousness, but for interesting reviews of the early issues the reader could read Posner (1973, Chapters 1 and 6, and Posner, 1978, Chapter 6).

Scientists involved in human behavior have often avoided the notion of consciousness in spite of its inherent interest, because it cannot be studied easily. The usual definition of consciousness (if one is aware of something, it is "in consciousness") has troubled scientists because the only way to determine what is "in consciousness" is to ask subjects about those things of which they were presumably aware. The problem is one of experimental methods. Subjects are required to *introspect* (that is, "search their own minds"). It can be shown easily that people are not very good at introspecting accurately and consistently and that their perceptions of what is "in consciousness" can be biased by situational variables and expectations. Primarily for this reason, the study of consciousness has been avoided by most experimental psychologists, being thought of as nonscientific, despite recent arguments to the contrary (see Norman, 1976).

While for the purposes of this book I do not want to equate attention with consciousness, it is still useful for beginning students of the area to think of them as though they were equated. We all have a personal understanding of our own consciousness, and thinking of attention in this way will help in understanding what it is and how findings about it are related to human performance.

Attention Is Limited

From examinations of our own consciousness, and from James' (1890) definition of attention, it seems obvious that attention is limited. That is, there must be a limit to how many things can be attended to at any one time. Subjectively, consciousness seems to switch rapidly from one source of information to another, and we often have difficulties in dealing with two sources of information or two tasks at the same time. Attention and consciousness seem also to be limited in the amount of information that can be held "in consciousness" at a given time. As discussed in Chapter 4, people can remember only about seven (plus or minus two) items at any one time, suggesting a limitation in attention or consciousness (Miller, 1956). Thus, one major characteristic of attention is its limited capacity.

Another characteristic of consciousness, and perhaps of attention, is its temporal order or seriality. The things we attend to change from moment to moment, giving the impression that the experience of attention is sequential, in the same way that information on a film is. Again, this implies that attention switches among various activities over time, with some of these being the processing of information from the environment (sensory information) or from our own memory (my phone number, if I am asked to give it), or processes that transform or combine information provided from either the environment and/or memory (e.g., in doing mental arithmetic). The duration that attention remains fixed on some event or activity seems, on purely subjective grounds, to be very long in some situations (while working out a problem "in your head") but very short in others while walking in a crowd. The time required to switch attention from one source to another has been of interest lately (e.g., LaBerge, 1973; Posner, 1978). The mechanism that is "responsible" for the switching of attention among the various activities has been termed *selective attention* (see Chapter 4).

Modern Definitions of Attention

Largely because the definitions of attention in terms of consciousness (and the research methods) have proved to be so inadequate, other methods have been developed to investigate attention. A prevalent notion is that attention is a limited capacity (or resource) for handling information from either the environment or memory. If a certain activity requires attention, then some of the limited capacity must be allocated to that activity. Thus, some other activity also requiring attention will suffer in quality or be delayed as a result of its simultaneous performance with the first activity. For example, because driving in traffic requires a great deal of attention, another activity (e.g., remembering digits) cannot be performed easily at the same time (Brown, 1962). Similarly, since walking does not require very much attention, mental arithmetic can be performed relatively well while walking. These patterns of interference are the basis for the usual operational definition of attention: If two tasks can be performed as well simultaneously as individually, then at least one of them does not require attention, or a portion of the limited capacity. On the other hand, if one task is performed less well in combination with some other task, then both are thought to require attention.

Thus, attention is defined in terms of whether or not activities interfere with each other. If they do, then we are willing to say that they "take attention" to perform, or are "attention-demanding." This kind of definition has the advantage of lending itself to experimental operation (measuring the degree of interference between two tasks). This has enormous advantages over the definition of attention as consciousness, which was "measured" by the subject's introspection. (As is the case with many "modern" ideas, this one is not very new. In 1898 Welch used the decrement in maximum grip strength as a measure of the attention required for other simultaneous tasks, such as reading and calculation.)

There is more to this definition of attention than interference among tasks, however. A moment's reflection will reveal that there can be a great deal of interference among tasks at times when it would be hard to argue that it was due to some limit of central information processing. For example, if I ask you to steer a car through a twisting course and tune the radio at the same time, you would probably experience some decrement in both tasks simply because the hands are used for both, and the hands can perform only one activity at a time. A similar example involves two visual signals presented in separate locations; I can only look at one signal at a time, and the performance of the two tasks will suffer when the two signals are presented together.[1] The desire to define attention in terms of limitations of central capacities, rather than in terms of such peripheral mechanisms as exemplified above, has led to the notion of *capacity interference* versus *structural interference,* to distinguish between the two kinds of decrements when tasks are performed together.

Structural Interference

Structural interference means that if two tasks are performed together that have either a receptor system (as in the example of the eyes) or an effector system (as in the example of the hands) in common, then some of the interference will be due to competition between the two tasks for use of the same input and output system. In addition, it is useful to think of internal neurological systems (for example, a purely visual short-term sensory store) which could be occupied by two visual signal streams presented to the subject, one from each of two simultaneous tasks. These two streams could cause difficulty for the purely visual information-processing system. While this aspect of structural interference is far less easy to conceptualize than competition is for a given receptor or effector, the notion is useful because it separates the effects of peripheral interference from the more central information-processing capacity that is attention.

Capacity Interference

Capacity interference is thought to be the interference that results from the competition for the limited central information-processing capacity between two tasks that are being performed at the same time. Capacity interference is measured as the amount of decrement in one task because it is performed simultaneously with another also requiring capacity and is the operational definition of the amount of attention required by that task.

Notice that in order to provide an estimate of the amount of capacity inference (attention), there must be no structural interference between the two tasks. If the performer is asked in Task 1 to make hand movements to visual stimuli and in Task 2 to make vocal responses to auditory stimuli, it would be difficult to argue that these two tasks interfere structurally. The receptors are different (eyes versus ears), the storage systems are probably dif-

---

[1]Posner, Nissen, and Ogden (1978) have, however, shown that the person can direct the eyes at one signal source and be attending to another that is in peripheral vision. I will discuss this effect later on.

ferent (visual versus auditory short-term sensory store), and the response-programming and response-production systems may even be different (vocal versus manual). Thus, if interference occurred between these two tasks, it was probably due to some competition for capacity (see McLeod, 1980, for a further discussion of this issue).

Attention, Effort, and Arousal

Another way to operationalize the notion of attention is based on the idea that when people perform a task requiring attention, they are expending mental effort. Performing mental arithmetic, attempting to remember someone's name, and driving through heavy traffic all require effort and often result in fatigue. Even "paying attention" to someone at a noisy cocktail party seems to require effort. Based on this idea, it is possible to define attention in terms of various *physiological* measures that represent the amount of effort being expended.

Kahneman (1973) and Beatty (e.g., Beatty & Wagoner, 1978) have advocated effort measures of attention. One method measures pupil diameter by special techniques that do not interfere with eye movement. When subjects are asked to perform various memory tasks, the pupil diameter increases when the subject is under pressure to provide an answer, and the increase is larger for more difficult tasks. The diameter is smaller when the subject is relaxed or the attention demand is low.

In this sense, it is useful to consider attention as measured by pupil diameter as very similar to another physiological dimension termed *arousal*. Arousal is the extent to which a subject is activated or excited, with low arousal being associated with sleep or drowsiness and high arousal being associated with extreme excitement. Kahneman also shows the usefulness of other measures of arousal such as heart rate and skin resistance (resistance to a weak current passed over the surface of the skin associated with the number of active sweat glands). Thus, people are aroused when they are performing tasks requiring mental effort, but it is probably incorrect to equate attention and arousal, for other things increase arousal which are qualitatively different from attention (such as fear). It is useful to say that tasks involving attention are arousing and that the attention demand can often be measured in terms of arousal.

WHAT REQUIRES ATTENTION?

If attention is defined as the degree of interference between two tasks, it is useful to ask where or when attention is required in the course of a response. At a very superficial level, it seems clear that many tasks that interfere with each other do so because of limitations in capacity (e.g., driving a car in traffic and conversing with a friend). Does this interference arise because both tasks require some form of stimulus identification at the same time (watching traffic and listening to conversation), because both require the selection of responses at the same time, or because the two tasks require movements at the same time? Considering the stages of information processing presented in Chapter 4, which of these stages creates the problem for the subject in performing the two tasks together?

If it is correct that all of the processing from the presentation of a stimulus to the evocation of a response is contained within these three stages, then at least one of these stages requires attention. This stage can be thought of as a bottleneck for information processing. In the next section, some of the evidence is examined that reveals which of the stages are responsible for the attention demand and which of them are not. The evidence on this question is very complicated and often contradictory; thus we should not expect to answer this question definitively here.

Theories of Attention

Undifferentiated, Fixed-Capacity Theories

The early theories of attention (e.g., Broadbent, 1958; Deutsch & Deutsch, 1963; Keele, 1973; Norman, 1969; Treisman, 1969; Welford, 1952; see also Kerr, 1973), while different in detail, had some important features in common. First, they all assumed that attention was a capacity for processing information and that performance would deteriorate if this capacity was approached or exceeded by the task requirements. Second, early notions were that this capacity was fixed in size and that it did not vary from moment to moment, from task to task, or as a function of practice. Finally, these were theories of *undifferentiated capacity,* in that attention was thought of as a single resource that could be directed at any one of a number of processing operations.

The theories differed, though, in terms of the kinds of information processing that required attention. Welford's theory, which has been termed (by Allport, Antonis, & Reynolds, 1972) the *strong version* of the single-channel theory, assumed that all of the processes required attention; that is, the human can be regarded as a single information channel which can be occupied by one and only one stimulus at a time (see Figure 5-1, Line 1). *Weaker versions* of the single-channel theory denied that all of the stages of processing required attention yet placed a single channel later in the sequence of processing. Thus, these other theories (Broadbent, 1958; Norman, 1969; Treisman, 1969; Deutsch & Deutsch, 1963; Kerr, 1973; Keele, 1973) presumed that early stages of processing were done without attention, but that attention was required at the later stage(s) of processing. For example, processes that translate sound waves into neurological impulses in the ear and those that change mechanical stimuli into neurological activity in the movement receptors in the limbs can occur together presumably without interference. In other words, these theories assume that peripheral information processing occurred simultaneously and without interference, but they differed with respect to the stages in which the interference occurred.

Broadbent (1958) and Deutsch and Deutsch (1963) theorized that a kind of filter is located somewhere along the series of stages of information processing (see Figure 5-1, Lines 2 and 3). According to filter theories, prior to reaching the filter many stimuli can be processed in parallel and do not re-

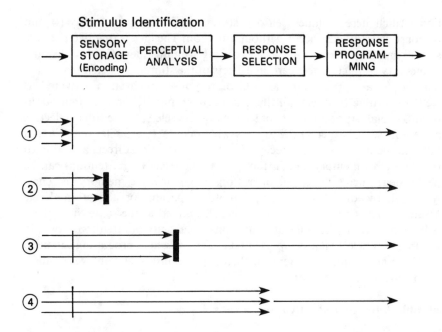

Figure 5-1. Utilization of attention in various stages of processing, according to various theories. [Line 1 represents the original single-channel theory (Welford, 1952), Line 2 represents Broadbent's (1958) filter theory, Line 3 represents the Deutsch and Deutsch (1963) and Norman (1969) theories, and Line 4 represents Keele's (1973) theory.]

quire attention. When the filter is reached, however, only one stimulus at a time is processed through the filter (the others being "filtered out"), so that the information processing from then on is sequential, requiring attention in the single channel. Which of the stimuli are filtered out and which one is processed further into the single channel presumably depends on which activity the subject is engaged in, which stimuli are expected, and which are relevant to the task in question.

Figure 5-1 shows the locations of the proposed filter for these two theories. The sensory storage stage can be thought of as the most "peripheral," involving the translation of the physical stimuli into neurological codes, while the perceptual analysis stage can be thought of as the process that abstracts some preliminary, simple meaning from the stimuli (e.g., perception of right angles, of verticality, and so on). (Notice that the stages labeled *sensory storage* and *perceptual analysis* can be readily combined to yield the stimulus-identification stage discussed in Chapter 4). Broadbent saw perceptual analysis and later stages as requiring attention, while Deutsch and Deutsch, Treisman, and Norman saw perceptual analysis as being automatic (i.e., not requiring attention), with later stages requiring attention. Thus, these theories are similar but they differ in terms of where the proposed filter is thought to be located in the chain of processes.

Keele's (1973) theory of attention places the bottleneck even later in the sequence of stages than the Deutsch-Deutsch theory. Keele's theory is not really a filter theory at all. Keele sees information processing as being in parallel and attention-free up to a certain point that may be likened to the location of the filter in the earlier two theories. All of stimulus identification (which here includes sensory storage and perceptual analysis) and response selection can occur without attention. The idea is that two possible stimuli can be processed in parallel during stimulus identification, leading to memory contact, where certain aspects of the stimuli are activated. There may be certain preliminary aspects of response preparation activated as well. According to Keele, all this can occur in parallel and without attention. Since all stimuli must contact memory, Keele supposed that selective attention (see Chapter 4) determines which contacts are relevant. When a relevant memory contact is received, selective attention directs attention to that aspect of memory and further processing (requiring attention) can be performed. Such subsequent operations might involve memory searches, rehearsal, recoding, or readying a motor program for activation. Keele assumed that if two such processes are demanded at the same time, there will be interference because of limitations in capacity or attention. Thus, in Figure 5-1, Keele's view is represented as Line 4, where processing can be in parallel and without interference through response selection, with subsequent operations requiring attention.

Flexible Allocation of Attention

In contrast to the theories of attention that saw capacity as fixed, are more recent theories that see attention as more flexible. For example, Kahneman (1973) argued that capacity should not be thought of as fixed, but that capacity changes as the task requirements change. For example, as the difficulty of two simultaneous tasks increases, more capacity becomes available and more of it is used in processing. Eventually, when task requirements for processing two streams of information begin to exceed maximum capacity, decrements are seen in one or more of the simultaneously presented tasks; that is, interference occurs.

Kahneman's theory also differed from the earlier views by suggesting that early stages of processing involve parallel processing but with some demand on attention. Kahneman believed that parallel processing could occur in all stages of processing, provided that maximum capacity was not exceeded. Kahneman's views that attention capacity is not fixed and that processing is always attention-demanding to some extent create a number of difficulties for certain secondary-task techniques for measuring spare capacity (see Chapter 3); with these methods, capacity is assumed to be relatively fixed.

More recent theories of attention have focused on issues of flexibility in information processing. For example, rather than assuming that processes requiring attention can process only one stimulus at a time, more recent theories suggest that these resources can be shared by parallel processing. How they are shared is presumably a function of the relative importance of the tasks, their relative difficulty, and other factors. Trade-offs between proficiency in two simultaneous tasks have been discussed by Norman and Bobrow (1975), Posner and Snyder (1975), and Navon and Gopher (1979). Such theories appear to have merit in coming to an understanding of the complex interactions that occur when people attempt to perform two reasonably complex activities at the same time.

Multiple Resource Theories

Recently some writers have argued that attention should not be conceptualized as a single pool of resources, but rather as a set of pools of
resources each with its own capacity and designed to handle certain kinds of
information processes. With such a view, resources for selecting the finger
to make a movement and resources for selecting the movements of the jaw
to say a word are separate. Hence, these two operations could coincide
without interference (e.g., McLeod, 1977; Navon & Gopher, 1979;
Wickens, 1976, 1980).

Similarly Shaffer (1971) and Allport et al. (1972) have provided evidence
that attention can be devoted to two separate stages of processing at the
same time. Such a view is inconsistent with fixed capacity theories, in which
the processing was thought to be confined to a single stage of processing,
although one or more separate operations might be able to be performed in
parallel. These views help to explain skill in complex tasks such as typing,
sight-reading of music, and so on, for which attention is thought to be
devoted to input (sight reading) and output (finger movements) stages at the
same time. Alternatively, Wickens (1980) thinks that separate pools of
capacity are responsible for information input and response output.

In the next sections, I will examine which stages seem to require attention.
An analysis of which of the stages requires attention will permit us to say
something about the correctness of the above theories of attention.

Attention during Stimulus Identification

From the discussion of the stimulus-identification stage in Chapter 4,
recall that a very large number of separate stimuli enter the system at the
same time. A major concern is the extent to which these simultaneous
streams of information are processed in parallel. As noted, most theories of
attention agree that processing must be parallel (and without attention) at
the most peripheral levels, but how far does this "pre-attentive" processing
extend into the stimulus-identification stage?

Processing Irrelevant Information

One set of findings that helps to answer this question relates to the *Stroop
phenomenon* (Stroop, 1935). In a modern study of the phenomenon, Keele
(1972) had subjects respond to the ink colors red, yellow, green, and blue by
pressing the appropriate one of four keys as quickly as possible after the
color was prsented (a four-alternative choice-RT task). In one condition of
the experiment, the colors were presented in various irrelevant forms such
as $\pm$ or $\sqrt{}$. These symbols were printed in the color to which the response
was to be made. In another condition, the colors were printed as letters that
spelled the name of a color that was different from the color of the ink in
which the word was printed. For example, the word RED was written in
green ink, and the subject had to respond with the "green" button, ignoring
the fact that the word "RED" was spelled. Even though in both conditions,

the color of the ink was the relevant stimulus, the latter condition produced slower RTs than did the first condition where the meaningless forms were used, suggesting that the spelled word and the ink color conflicted.

Why should an irrelevant dimension of the display (the words) interfere with the RT to the color of the ink? Why cannot the subject simply focus on the color of the ink and ignore the word that the letters spelled? The most plausible interpretation is that the color of the ink and the words are viewed as two simultaneously presented stimuli, or patterns. Both patterns are processed together during the stimulus-identification stage, and both arouse some meaning (i.e., they contact memory) about the nature of the stimulus and/or the response to be produced. These two meanings were different, and this conflict required additional processing time in order to resolve it, suggesting that the stimulus-identification stage processed stimuli in parallel and perhaps without attention. The fact that both stimuli achieved what Keele has termed *memory contact* approximately together implies that the processing of the two patterns in stages prior to response selection must have been stimultaneous. This line of evidence suggests that the processing in stimulus identification occurs in parallel and without attention.

Dichotic Listening Paradigm

Another important method for answering these kinds of questions is called the *dichotic listening paradigm*. The individual is presented (via headphones) with a different message in each ear. Usually the subject's problem is to ignore one of the messages and to concentrate on (and later report about) the other. Much has been learned about the kinds of information that can or cannot be ignored. A message that cannot be ignored (while another message is attended to) implies that the to-be-ignored message is being processed through the stimulus identification stage whether the individual tries to ignore it or not, perhaps without attention being required for that processing.

Cocktail Party Problem

The dichotic listening paradigm is a formal way to study the "cocktail party problem" described by Cherry (1953). At large, noisy parties, attending to one person's spoken message, while ignoring the many other conversations, is often quite difficult. But, with effort, the various conversations can be separated. Situations occur, however, when other messages cannot be ignored, such as when you hear your name spoken. The findings from the dichotic listening paradigm and common observations from cocktail parties lead to the suggestion that all of the auditory stimuli are processed through stimulus identification in parallel and without attention, and that some mechanism operates that prevents attention from being drawn to unwanted sources of sound. The mechanism, called *selective attention* by some, is such that when the sound is relevant or pertinent to us (e.g., our name or a loud noise), the stimulus is allowed to "pass through" for additional processing and attention. It is as if stimuli from the environment have entered the system simultaneously and have been processed to some superficial level of analysis, with only those relevant to the individual being processed further.

Taken together, these observations suggest that the filter theory of Broadbent (1958) and perhaps that of Deutsch and Deutsch (1963) are incorrect, with the theories of Keele (1973) and Kahneman (1973) providing a more reasonable explanation of the course of processing. See Kahneman (1973, especially Chapter 5) for a more complete discussion of this evidence and its interpretation.

Attention during Response Selection

Evidence from the Stroop Test

Can two responses be selected from two simultaneously presented stimuli in parallel and without interference? The Stroop phenomen can help to provide an answer. According to Keele's (1973) interpretation, the interference caused by the green ink and the word it spells (RED) is due to a conflict in the later response-programming stage, not a conflict in response selection. Keele's idea is that in the response-selection stage the color green activates the action for the "green" finger movement, while the word "RED" activates the response for the "red" finger movement, and that both of these processes occur in parallel and without attention. However, when the subject begins to prepare the finger action, attention is devoted to the selection of the movement, and the response conflict slows these processes, perhaps leading to increased errors.

Kahneman (1973) does not agree with Keele's interpretation. His argument is that the color green and the word "RED" written in green ink cause interference during response selection, so that the subject has difficulty in determining which movement to make. The additional RT then is presumably caused by the additional processing required to suppress the tendency to select the response to the word "RED" and to respond to the color green.

Some of the conflict between Keele's and Kahneman's theories is related to a decision about which processes should be contained in response selection. Keele believes that the ink color green arouses the selection of the response automatically (as does the word "RED" but for another response), and then subsequent operations (programming) are required to resolve the uncertainty. But these subsequent operations could also be legitimately contained in the response-selection stage, because they are involved with the choice among responses. This seems especially obvious if the S-R compatibility is low (requiring additional processing to "compute" the proper response) or if the stimulus is a statement like "What is the square root of 121?" Here, the choice of response must await a great deal of processing by the response-selection stage, all of which presumably requires attention and precedes the response-programming stage involved in the preparation of the vocal musculature for saying the word *eleven.*

Automatic Processing

More recent theorizing has been directed toward information processing in response-selection which does not seem to require any attention. Schneider and Shiffrin (1977; Shiffrin & Schneider, 1977) have proposed a theory of automatic and controlled processing that has interesting implications for complex movement behaviors involving two simultaneous activities, such as sight reading and playing piano music. They propose that many response-selection processes require attention, especially if they are relatively unpracticed and not very "natural" in their organization. These tasks undergo *controlled processing,* processing routines that are established for a particular situation and which require a large capacity. On the other hand, sometimes processing of complex stimuli does not seem to require any attention. This is called *automatic processing* and is characterized by relatively well-learned procedures such as sight reading in English. They propose that these automatic processes are learned after the use of controlled processing (when you were learning to sight read, the task required a great deal of attention).

Presumably these automatic processes can (a) be triggered by sensory events, (b) once initiated, control the flow of information in the system, (c) direct attention to some element in memory, and (d) govern overt responses. These automatic processes are analogous to motor programs (Chapter 6), whereby the routine is triggered and then runs its course without much modification from conscious sources. Perhaps these automatic processes were involved in the experiments such as Leonard's (1959) (Chapter 4), in which there was no increase in choice RT (beyond two choices) with an increased number of alternatives when the stimulus was a vibration of the finger to be moved; the "connection" between the stimulus and response was so "natural" that attentive processing was not necessary in response selection. Also, these kinds of processes are consistent with the ideas discussed earlier (Chapter 4) by Mowbray and Rhoades (1959), who showed that the slope of the equation describing Hick's law decreases to zero with extensive practice; in Schneider and Shiffrin's terms, this increased practice may have changed the processing in response selection from controlled to automatic.

Attention during Response Programming

In contrast to the debate about the attentional requirements of the response-selection stage, little disagreement exists about the response-programming stage. Probably the most important evidence on this issue concerns the *double-stimulation paradigm,* in which the subject must respond to two closely spaced stimuli, each of which requires a different movement.

Double-Stimulation Paradigm

This paradigm is diagrammed in Figure 5-2. Here, the subject is presented

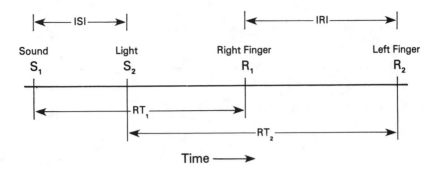

Figure 5-2. The double-stimulation paradigm (ISI = inter-stimulus interval, IRI = inter-response interval).

with a sound (Stimulus 1, or S_1) that calls for a response by the right hand (Response 1, or R_1). Also, somewhat later, a light is presented (S_2) that re-quires a response by the left hand (R_2). The two stimuli are presented in dif-ferent modalities and require responses by different hands so that structural interference is minimized.[2] The stimuli are usually separated by at least 50 msec, and they may be separated by as long as 500 msec; that is, the second stimulus could, in some experiments, come well after the response to the first stimulus, although this method is used infrequently. The separation between stimuli is usually called the *inter-stimulus interval (ISI)*. Further, the arrival of the signals is usually random, so that the subject cannot pre-dict the occurrence of a given stimulus (either S_1 or S_2) on a given trial. Thus, both stimuli must enter the information-processing system and be processed separately.

Psychological Refractory Period

For reasons that will become clear later, experimenters have been in-terested in the RT to the second of the two stimuli (RT_2). The critical com-parison has been between RT_2 when it is preceded by S_1 versus RT_2 when S_1 is not presented at all; that is, the "control RT_2" is a measure of RT_2 when the subject does not have S_1 presented at all. Using this method, ex-perimenters have shown repeatedly that the response to the second of two closely spaced stimuli is considerably longer than RT_2 in the control condi-tion. Apparently S_1 and R_1 cause a great deal of interference with the pro-cessing of S_2 and R_2. This important phenomenon was discovered by Telford (1931), who named it the *psychological refractory period* (PRP).[3]

---

[2]Even so, data from McLeod (1980) have suggested that because both *hands* are involved in the two tasks the response-programming stage for the right and left hands interfere with each other. What is needed, presumably, is a different response for the second stimulus.

[3]In a way, this label is unfortunate. The original idea was that the delay in the subject's response to the second of two closely spaced stimuli was analogous to the delay found when a single nerve fiber is electrically stimulated twice in rapid succession in physiological ex-periments. If the second stimulus is very close to the first (within .5 msec), no response at all will be recorded from the second stimulus. This effect has been termed the *refractory period*, meaning that the nerve was refractory to additional stimulation while it "recovered" from the effects of the first stimulus. These nerve processes probably have little to do with the psychological refractory period, as the time courses are very much longer in the behavioral work (e.g., 200 msec).

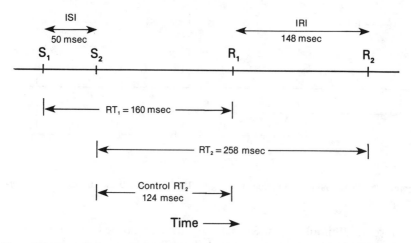

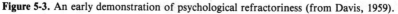

Figure 5-3. An early demonstration of psychological refractoriness (from Davis, 1959).

The findings from Davis (1959), presented in Figure 5-3, are typical. In this example, S_2 followed S_1 by 50 msec. The control RT_2 (RT for S_2 in separate trials in which S_1 was not presented) was 124 msec.[4] However, when it was associated with S_1 and its response, RT_2 was 258 msec, about twice as long. Thus, the presence of S_1 and R_1 caused a marked increase in RT_2. In other studies, the amount of increase in S_2 caused by S_1 and its processing can be 300 msec or more (Creamer, 1963), making the RT for the second stimulus around 500 msec!

Another important result in studies of refractoriness is the effect of the inter-stimulus interval (ISI) on the delay of R_2. In Figure 5-4, also containing data from the Davis (1959) study, are plotted the values of RT_2 for various values of the ISI, which ranged from 50 msec to 500 msec. Notice that since the RT_1 was about 160 msec in this data set, all of the ISIs greater than or equal to 200 msec occurred when the second stimulus was presented after the subject had responded to the first (see also Figure 5-3). In Figure 5-4, we see that as the ISI was increased from 50 msec to 300 msec, RT_2 progressively shortened, until there was no delay at all (relative to the control RT_2 shown in the figure) with longer ISIs. The most important points from Figure 5-4 are that (a) the delay in RT_2 decreased as the ISI increased and (b) there was considerable delay even though R_1 had already been produced (i.e., at inter-stimulus intervals of 200 msec or more).

One major exception to this generalization about the effect of the ISI should be mentioned. If the second signal follows the first one very quickly, with an ISI as short as, say, 10 msec, then the two signals are apparently dealt with as a single, more complex event. This effect is called *grouping*. The two signals elicit the two responses at the same time but with a slightly greater RT than if only one of the responses were made to a single stimulus

---

[4]This 124-msec control RT is considerably shorter than is typically seen in RT experiments. It is probably explained by the fact that the S_2 was auditory—which usually results in a somewhat faster RT than visual signals—and that there was a high degree of expectancy for its arrival time.

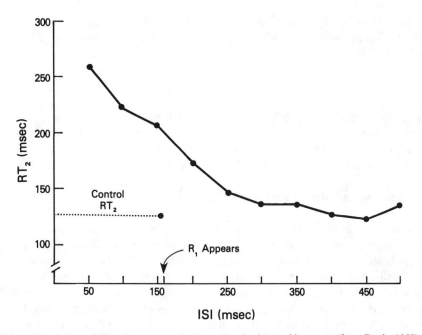

Figure 5-4. Refractoriness decreases as the inter-stimulus interval increases (from Davis, 1959).

(see Welford, 1968). This fact has important implications for understanding the nature of the delay in the processing of S_2, which will be discussed later.

The Single-Channel Hypothesis

A major contribution to the understanding of human information processing in motor tasks was made in 1952 when Welford proposed the *single-channel hypothesis* to account for the well-known findings about psychological refractoriness. In the original version of the theory, Welford hypothesized that the entire information processing system was structured as a single channel, or bottleneck, so that only one stimulus could be processed at a time. If S_1 entered the single channel and was being processed, then processing of S_2 must be delayed until the single channel is cleared. This was a strict serial-processing model, because S_1 and S_2 would not be processed together, with the processing of S_1 requiring attention. Of course, if S_1 is being processed and S_2 cannot be, then there is interference with RT_2; and this is, by the earlier definition, attention demanding.

How does this theory "work" to explain psychological refractoriness such as is present in Figures 5-3 and 5-4? Referring back to Figure 5-3, S_2 was presented 50 msec after S_1, and RT_1 was 160 msec. Thus, there was $160 - 50 = 110$ msec of RT_1 remaining when S_2 was presented. According to the single-channel hypothesis, S_2 must be delayed until the channel is cleared, and thus the actual RT_2 will be the control RT_2 plus the 110-msec delay. Note from the data that the control RT_2 was 124 msec, which makes the estimate of RT_2 in the double stimulation situation $124 + 110 = 234$ msec. If you look up the obtained value of RT_2 (258 msec) given in Figure 5-4, the estimate (234 msec) is fairly close.

According to the single channel hypothesis, the duration of RT_2 was thought to be the control RT_2 plus the amount that RT_2 overlapped with RT_1, or

$$RT_2 = \text{control } RT_2 + (RT_1 - ISI). \qquad (5-1)$$

It can be seen in Figure 5-3 and Equation 1 that as the size of the ISI increases, there is less overlap between the two RTs, and the predicted value of RT_2 decreases. This accounts for the finding that the RT_2 decreases as the ISI increases, as shown in Figure 5-4 and in other research (Welford, 1968).

Evidence against the Single-Channel Hypothesis

While the original single-channel hypothesis accounts for some of the data, a considerable amount of evidence—mainly produced since the hypothesis was proposed in 1952—suggests that the theory is not correct in its details. The most important part of this evidence pertains to the changes in RT_2 as the ISI is altered. Remember, according to the single-channel hypothesis, RT_2 lengthened as a direct function of the amount of overlap between RT_1 and RT_2, as can be seen in Equation 1. The first concern was that even when there was no overlap between RT_1 and RT_2—that is, when S_2 occurred after the subject had produced a response to S_1—there was still some delay in RT_2. Look at Figure 5-4. When the ISI was 200 msec, so that S_2 occurred 40 msec after R_1, there was still some delay in RT_2 (about 50 msec) which did not disappear completely until the ISI had been lengthened to 300 msec. How can there be refractoriness, according to the single-channel view, when the RT_1 and RT_2 do not overlap at all?

Welford (1968) suggested that after R_1 is produced, the subject directs attention to the movement, perhaps concentrating on the feedback from R_1 to confirm that the movement was, in fact, produced before processing S_2. Thus, according to his view, attention was required after the response, which delayed RT_2, as did the attention produced during the response.

But this explanation could not solve other problems, one of which was that the amount of increase in RT_2 as the ISI decreased did not correspond well with the predictions from the theory. Consider this example. What happens to RT_2 if the ISI is decreased from 150 msec to 50 msec? From Equation 1 and from previous discussions, the effect would be to increase RT_2 by exactly the same amount as the overlap in RT_1 and RT_2 was decreased. Because decreasing the ISI from 150 msec to 50 msec has the effect of increasing the overlap between RT_1 and RT_2 by exactly 100 msec, the RT_2 at an ISI of 150 msec should be exactly 100 msec shorter than the RT_2 at an ISI of 50 msec.

What do the data say? Considering the data from Davis (1959) again, I have plotted the relevant values from the two situations above in Figure 5-5. The ISIs of 150 and 50 msec and their RTs, as well as the values of RT_1, are shown. When the ISI was 150 msec, RT_2 was 209 msec; but when the ISI was decreased to 50 msec, increasing the overlap of RT_1 and RT_2 by 100 msec, the RT_2 was 258 msec, *not* 309 msec (209 + 100 msec), which the theory predicted. In this instance, the theory could not account for the fact

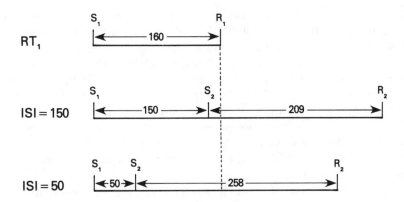

Figure 5-5. Empirically determined values of RT_2 contrasted with the values predicted from the single-channel hypothesis (from Davis, 1959).

that when the ISI was 50 msec the RT_2 was 51 msec too short. Davis' data are consistent with a number of the studies in this area in showing this deficiency (see also Kahneman, 1973).

How can these findings be accounted for more effectively? One possibility is that while the response-programming stage is preparing the response to S_1, the stimulus-identification stage is processing S_2, because the stimulus-identification stage had presumably been cleared of S_1 long ago (see the top panel of Figure 5-3). Therefore, as the ISI increases, more of the early stages of processing for S_2 are being done at the same time as the later stages of processing for S_1, providing systematic underestimates of the time required for RT_2. This hypothesis does not violate the assumption that the stages are serially ordered; all that must be assumed is that processing in the stimulus-identification stage is not attention demanding. If it is not—and it does not appear to be from earlier sections—then processing of S_2 in the stimulus-identification stage can occur at the same time as processing of S_1 in the response-selection stage—and without interference.

Another possibility is that S_1 and S_2 can be processed in parallel in the same stage. This possibility is most likely if the ISI is very short, so that the stimulus-identification stage can handle S_1 and S_2 simultaneously.

For these reasons, the single-channel hypothesis appears to be incorrect. It does not allow for the possibility of processing in two stages simultaneously or for parallel processing of two signals in a given stage.

Implications of Refractoriness

Aside from the theoretical questions that surround the refractoriness effect, with questions about whether processing is in parallel or sequential and in what stages, the phenomenon of psychological refractoriness is not under debate. For whatever reasons, the second of two closely spaced stimuli suffers a great deal in processing speed, and this fact can have important practical implications. For example, in many games players "fake out" an opponent by displaying the initial parts of one response (e.g., a slight movement to the right) followed immediately by another response (e.g., a movement to the left) which is actually carried to completion. If I am an opponent attempting to follow this player and I respond to the first "move," it will require a full RT (about 150 to 200 msec) plus the added time caused by refractoriness to begin to respond to the second move. Thus, my RT to the second move could be as long as 500 msec (see Creamer, 1963). Standing around "doing nothing" for 500 msec can be disastrous in many games. But this is not the only problem that my opponent has created for me. If I have "taken the fake," then I suffer not only a delay in RT to the "real" movement, but I must also overcome the inertia that my incorrect movement has produced and make up any distance that I may have traveled in the wrong direction. "Taking the fake" can provide disastrous effects in any rapid game.

An apparent principle of faking is that the actual move should follow the fake by sufficient time that the second move is treated separately rather than being grouped with the first one. Thus, the ISI should probably be around 50 msec or longer. Also, the second move must not follow the fake by so long an interval that the refractory effects of the first response have dissipated, probably not more than 250 msec (see Figure 5-4), although it is difficult to pinpoint the exact time without studying the task directly. It would be interesting to study the most effective fakes in football or basketball to discover if the most effective ISIs correspond with estimates from experimentation. Such information would be of great use to coaches.

Just as effective "fakers" have probably learned to produce the most effective ISIs, it may be possible that such intervals are a part of natural actions in other species. Watch a rabbit being chased by a dog. The rabbit runs with unpredictable directional changes, probably using intervals between directional changes that are highly effective in confusing the dog. Refractoriness might be an important survival mechanism in animals other than humans.

Separation among Responses

Evidence about the refractorines effect strongly suggests that it is not possible to respond simultaneously to two separate stimuli separated in time by a minimum of 50 msec. Rather, the first response is being produced in more or less the same time that it would be if S_2 had not arrived, and the second of the two responses occurs well after the first. Thus, it appears that even if we try to "drive" the motor system with two stimuli presented closely in time, the output is two responses greatly separated in time.

How close in time can two responses be produced, provided they are not grouped and produced simultaneously? In answering this question, Kahneman (1973) has suggested an examination of the *inter-response interval (IRI)*—the time separation between responses (see Figure 5-2)—as it is affected by bringing the stimuli closer and closer together in time. In Figure 5-6, I have plotted some of the data from M.C. Smith's (1969) study, as Kahneman (1973) did. ISIs were 50, 150, 300, and 500 msec, and the separation between responses that resulted from these intervals is plotted in Figure 5-6. As the time between stimuli decreased (moving leftward on the graph), the interval between the two responses decreased but only to a certain point. It appears that no matter how small the interval between stimuli—provided they are not grouped and emitted simultaneously—at

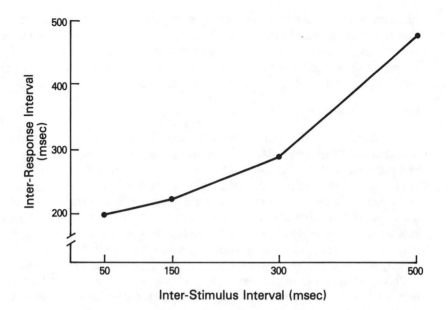

Figure 5-6. The relation between the inter-response interval and the inter-stimulus interval (data from M.C. Smith, 1969; adapted from Kahneman, 1973).

least 194 msec occurs between responses. This is a most important result.

This finding suggests that if a signal "gets into" the information-processing stages up to a certain point, a response to it is generated. If another stimulus is presented soon afterward, indicating that the system should do some *other* action, the second action must wait for at least 194 msec before it can be initiated. To explain this phenomenon some writers (see Welford, 1968) have suggested the idea of a "gate" that "slams" to prevent a second signal from entering the information-processing mechanisms and interfering with the response to the first signal. Welford suggests that the gate "slams" approximately 50 msec after the first signal is presented. If a second signal comes after this point, it must wait; if it comes before this point, the first *and* second signals are processed together as a unit, and the two responses are grouped.

Skilled piano players can produce many responses of the fingers in which the separation between responses is far less than 194 msec. How do they do this? I will discuss this issue in detail in Chapters 7 and 8 but for now will provide a very brief answer. Apparently the system can prepare a "response" to a given stimulus which, in itself, is complex and involves many movements in rapid succession. The "response" that is planned by the response-programming stage is still one response, but it has many parts that are not commanded separately. This can be thought of as "output chunking," whereby many subelements are collected into a single unit. This unit is called a motor program (Keele, 1973; Schmidt, 1976a).

It is indeed fortunate that S_2 cannot "get into" the system to disrupt the preparation of the response to S_1. If I am preparing a response to a dangerous stimulus (a lion jumping at me), I will be successful in emitting an avoidance response only if I can process the information and produce a response without interference from other conflicting signals. Thus, the function of the response-programming stage can be that of protection, in that the stage operates as a single channel, preventing the interference of other stimuli that will negatively affect the quality of the responses. Of course, such protective benefits in one situation (evading the lion) serve as hindrances in other situations such as fast ball games.

Responses in Bursts

One of the major conclusions from the data in Figure 5-6, as well as from data that will be presented later, is that the human motor system appears to be structured so that it responds in bursts, with each burst separated by approximately 200 msec (the estimate from Figure 5-6 was 194 msec). It appears that no two movements can follow each other by less than about 200 msec. (Remember, the definition of a "movement" was that it be initiated as a unit, a "movement" could have a very large number of separate actions, as in a piano trill.) It is, of course, possible that bursts last a second or longer, and in Chapters 7 and 8 I will have more evidence on this point.

This generalization might seem surprising, as it may seem that humans respond continuously and smoothly, with a constant flow of movement as a result of the flow of stimulus input. But the analysis of psychological refractoriness indicates that humans probably do not function in this way. This intermittent mode of responding was recognized long ago by Craik (1948), who provided a major lead in making this aspect of movement known. I will discuss this issue in Chapters 7 and 8, but for now the message is that though the stimulus inputs may come into the system continuously, the movement output is decidedly discontinuous, or discrete. This observation is fundamental to understanding human movement.

Attention Demands in the Stages

With all of the detail presented in the chapter so far, it is helpful to come to some general understanding of all these various results in terms of the stages of processing. Which stages of information processing require attention? Where is the bottleneck, if any, in the information processing system?

Figure 5-7 summarizes the findings. The hypothetical attention demand is plotted as a function of the stage of processing after a signal has been received. In the initial stages of processing, there appears to be nearly no attention demand, making a great deal of parallel processing possible. As the stimulus moves "deeper" into the system, however, there appears to be more and more attention demand and less and less parallel processing. In the final stages of processing there appears to be no parallel processing, and massive amounts of attention are required. All the theories of attention will make this general statement (see Figure 5-1), but the shape of the curve that I have drawn in Figure 5-7 will be slightly different for each, with some having attention required in nearly all stages, and some having attention required only in the later stages. This disagreement among theories is not large when considering information processing in this somewhat more general way.

Finally, a single channel *does* seem to exist, contrary to the conclusion drawn in the section about the single-channel hypothesis. But the single

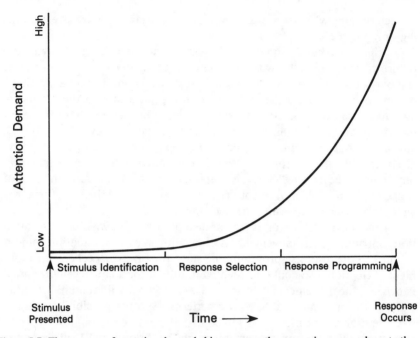

Figure 5-7. The amount of attention demanded increases as the processing comes closer to the response; a summary of existing data.

channel does not appear to apply to all stages of processing as the 1952 version of the theory stated. Rather, it appears that the single channel is properly placed very late in the information-processing stages. I have suggested that the single channel is in the response-programming stage, so that only one response can be prepared at a time. This version of the single-channel hypothesis has considerable support.

ATTENTION DEMANDS FOR MOVEMENTS

To this point, I have examined only the processes present during the RT, which, of course, is prior to movement. But this book is really about movements, and a study of their attentional requirements should follow at this point. Conceptualize a "stage" of processing that follows response programming in which the individual carries out the movement and keeps it under control. Strictly speaking, it is not a stage in the sense of the other three stages, as it does not occur during RT, but the attentional requirements of the processes that create movements can be studied by conceptualizing a "movement execution stage."

In thinking about our own skilled movements, we are perhaps left with the impression that skills require attention for their performance. A complex dive, for example, would seem to require that attention be riveted on the performance. We must be careful with these introspective analyses, though, because we cannot be sure whether it is the movement itself that requires attention or the programming and initiation of future movements (in the dive, when to "open up" to enter the water). We are in a weak position for determining whether or not movements themselves require attention, using only the methods of introspection.

On the other hand, sometimes it seems that a particular movement is peformed automatically, without attention, especially when the movement is a part of a well-learned sequence. Often when I am driving a car that is not my own, I depress the clutch at a stop sign, although the car has an automatic transmission with no clutch pedal. Only after I have made this movement do I realize that I have produced it. Have you ever found that, in buttoning your shirt and daydreaming sleepily about the upcoming day's activities, that the buttoning activities continue even though a particular button might be missing? These examples, plus others that you can think of, suggest that not all movements require attention for their performance, while others seem to require massive amounts of attention.

When a movement requires a great deal of attention, what does the attention contribute to the movement? As I mentioned earlier, attention could be devoted to the response-programming stage for future aspects of the movement. Attention also could be devoted to other aspects of the environment; in driving, the movements themselves are carried out with minimal attention while attention is directed to traffic patterns. Another possibility is that we pay attention to our movements to control them, to carry out any necessary corrections. Finally, our movements might be "monitored" with attention to see if they are being produced satisfactorily. Welford (1968) suggested this possibility in attempting to explain why attention was required even *after* R_1 in the double-stimulation paradigm (see Figure 5-4). So, having considered the role of attention in movement planning and initiation, I will now turn to the role of attention in movement *execution*.

Attention in Simple Movements

Experimenters began to study attention demands of movements with simple responses in the hope that the information gathered would later generalize to more complicated movements. A common tool for evaluating the role of attention in these movements is the "probe technique" discussed in Chapter 3. In this method, the subject performs a "main task" for which attention demands are of interest; but the person is also presented with an occasional stimulus (usually auditory) to which a response must be made with a limb not involved with the main task. The signal, or probe, can be presented at various places or times in the movement. A basic assumption is that some fixed amount of capacity or attention exists, that the "main task" occupies some proportion of it at any given moment, and that some capacity remains for the processing that will be required for the probe, as diagrammed in Figure 5-8. If the probe RT is rapid, then spare capacity was large and the amount of attention required by the main task was relatively small. If the probe RT slows when the main task is changed or when the probe is inserted at some other place in the main task, then it is argued that the main task was taking up a larger share of the fixed capacity. One disadvantage of this method is that it assumes a fixed capacity, an assumption which may be incorrect, as discussed earlier in this chapter.

Posner and Keele (1969) asked subjects to make 700-msec wrist-twist

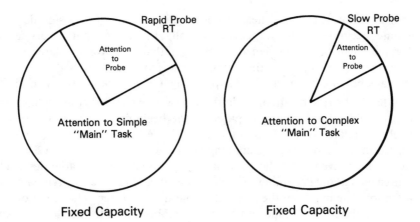

Figure 5-8. Assumptions of the probe-RT task: With fixed total capacity, attention to the probe decreases as the complexity of the "main" task increases.

movements of a handle through 150°, attempting to move a pointer to either a large or a small target area. The experimenters presented probe signals at various points throughout the movement—at the start or at 15°, 45°, 75°, 105°, or 135° of handle movement. The probe RTs are plotted as a function of the location within the movement in Figure 5-9, where the horizontal line represents the no-movement control probe RT. First, the finding that the probe RTs were always larger than the corresponding values of the no-movement probe RT is taken as evidence that the movements required some attention. Next, a marked slowing of the probe RT at the beginning of the movement was observed, with somewhat less slowing at the end. This finding suggests that attention to the movement is strongest at the beginning, that a relatively attention-free portion is near the middle, and

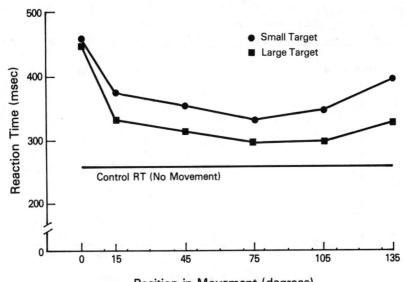

Figure 5-9. Probe RT elicited at various points in movements to large and small targets (from Posner & Keele, 1969).

that attention is required near the end again, perhaps for positioning the pointer accurately in the target zone. Finally, the finding that the probe RT for the small target movement was larger than that for the large target movement suggests that the small target required increased attention, perhaps because of the additional planning and control necessary to hit it.

What is the role of attention in these movements? First, the finding that considerable attention was required at the beginning of the movement is probably related to the findings seen in Figure 5-4: that attention was required in the response-programming stage, or perhaps a "response execution" stage, even after the movement was initiated. Such attentional requirements at the beginning of the movement could reflect the remnants of attention demand from the response-programming stage. The attention required at the end of the movement is presumably due to the need to position the pointer accurately at the target. But these interpretations do not answer the initial question about the role of attention in movement. All of the attention demands in this study could be due to the initiation and programming of parts of the movement, not to the conduct of the movement.

One way to approach the problem was to search for examples of movements that do not require any attention. If examples could be found, it would suggest movement per se may be carried out without attention and that it is the response-selection and response-programming stages that require attention.

Posner and Keele (1969) used the probe technique with various kinds of movements, one of which involved a 120° wrist-twist movement to a mechanical stop performed blindfolded. The task was analogous to pushing a door closed, the major requirement being that sufficient force be produced with no penalty for too much force. They used a measure of attention demand that was the difference between the probe RT when the movement was being performed simultaneously and the probe RT in the no-movement control condition. Presumably, this difference represents the extra RT that is caused by having to make the wrist movement.

The values are plotted in Figure 5-10. There was, as in the earlier experi-

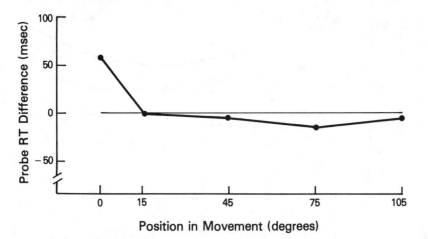

Figure 5-10. Differences between control and movement probe RT in a nearly automatic movement (from Posner & Keele, 1969).

ment (Figure 5-9), a fairly high attention demand at the start of the movement; but by the 15° point, the probe RT was as low as the control RT (i.e., the difference was zero), and the values thereafter were *negative* (the probe RT was slightly less than the control RT). Thus, except for the portion of the movement just following initiation, the blindfolded movement to a stop did not appear to require attention for its production. This is an important finding, suggesting that at least some movements can be performed without attention. Apparently, in such movements, the individual plans the movement with processes (response selection and response programming) that do require attention, but then the control of the response is shifted to a part of the system that carries out the movement automatically.

Other experiments have shown that even in rapid movements, with movement times of about 320 msec (Salmoni, Sullivan, & Starkes, 1976, Experiment 3), an elevation of the probe RT of about 50 msec near the end of the movement was found.[5] Thus, apparently only the most simple movements (those in Figure 5-10), those without much need for accurate control, can be executed without attention. But the experiments showing attention demands for simple movements typically have not used highly learned actions, and it is possible that the need for attention would diminish as the skills became more highly practiced.

Attention Demands for Expected Events

Evidence from Kerr (1975) shows that the expectation of the change in a movement requires attention. She had subjects move along a semicircular pathway which had choices between alternate paths later in the movement. Either before the movement began or during the initial stages she gave information about which of the paths was to be followed later in the movement. She presented a probe at the point in the movement at which the advance information was (or was not) provided. The probe RT was greater for the subjects who expected to receive information than it was for the subjects who had already received information, suggesting that some attention was required in expecting to receive information during a movement. As an analogy in sport, players sometimes look for certain signals (e.g., some action on the part of defensive team) which might slow responses to some other event, such as the presence of an unexpected would-be tackler in rugby.

Problems with Structural Interference

All of these studies suffer from a potential difficulty, as pointed out recently by McLeod (1980). In every case, the subjects are making a hand movement as the main task and another hand movement with the opposite hand to respond to the probe. McLeod has raised a number of objections to

---

[5]Earlier, Ells (1973) has apparently shown that these rapid movements could be performed without attention, but the experimental design he used appears to prevent such a conclusion; see Salmoni et al. (1976) for details.

this procedure. First, he has shown that when the probe task requires a hand response, there is more interference from a manual response than from a vocal response; this finding is serious for those who argue that the probe task measures (undifferentiated) central capacity, since presumably central capacity is devoted to either the hand or vocal response. Second, the procedure does not provide a good estimate of when the attention is involved in the movement; because of the lags in both the movement processing and the probe processing, there is interference, but it is not clear when this interference occurs.

Interference among Hand Movements

In our own laboratory, Bender (Note 2) has studied the simultaneous production of two different hand movements. In a preliminary session, she had her subjects learn to make, using a special pen, a "V" with one hand and a Greek letter gamma, "γ", with the other, one at a time. She restricted the movement times to less than 150 msec. The letters drawn by one of the subjects are shown in Figure 5-11. In the upper left corner are the letters drawn separately on the last of 225 trials, and there was little difficulty in drawing them properly in less than 150 msec. After the 225th trial, she asked the subjects to make these same figures using the same hands as before but simultaneously, and the first such "dual trial" is shown in the lower left. Here, the subject drew two gammas, and the movement times were very slow. Performance improved somewhat by Dual Trial 16 (upper right), but the figure on the right which should have been a gamma resembled the "V". Dual Trial 18 (lower right) was the subject's best performance. Generally, the subjects found the task to be very difficult. They produced distorted letters, duplicate letters, and letters in one hand that had features

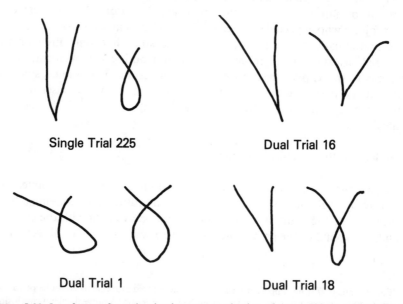

Single Trial 225   Dual Trial 16

Dual Trial 1   Dual Trial 18

Figure 5-11. Interference from the simultaneous production of two rapid movements (from Bender, Note 3).

of the letter done in the opposite hand (e.g., a "V" with a rounded bottom). Bender's data say that there was a great deal of interference between the two hands when the hands had to do different responses simultaneously (but see Chapter 7 for examples of two hands doing the same actions). Thus, the data lend support to the idea of hand-hand interference present in the probe-RT studies, as suggested by McLeod's data.

Response-Execution Stage—Single-Channel Control

I think that these data say even more than this. Remember the definition of attention: If two tasks are performed together and they interfere, then both require attention. That situation existed for Bender's data—two tasks were performed together with massive interference. I think that these data indicate that if there is a movement-execution stage of processing (following response programming), then it is strictly single-channel and no parallel processing is possible in it. That Bender's subjects were able to perform the dual movements at all was probably due to the generation through practice of a new movement program which contained both the gamma and the "V" and which executed them simultaneously. In support of this, notice that the dual "V"s and gammas did not resemble the same letters when they were drawn individually. The issue of single-channel operation in a response-execution stage is very interesting, and much more detail is provided when I discuss movement programs in Chapters 7 and 8. But, as I think you can see, this issue is somewhat different from the idea that these movements require consciousness. Here, then, is one way that the notions of attention and consciousness appear to diverge.

Attention Switching

Earlier in this section, I suggested that capacity or attention can be shifted from one aspect of the movement, or movement situation, to another. For movements, attention can presumably be shifted from the response-programming stage to a response-execution stage, or to a set of processes enabling fine adjustments of the movement near a small target. In driving a car, I can shift attention from the traffic flow, to the control movements, to the movements involved in tuning the radio, and back to the traffic flow. As I mentioned briefly in Chapter 4, the processes necessary for switching attention to the relevant aspects of a response have been called *selective attention*.

The ability to shift attention seems to be of great importance in many rapid activities. Shifting attention from the rear view mirror back to the highway quickly is important in freeway driving. Also, shifting attention from catching a basketball to other places on the court where I might pass, shoot, or dribble, is another example. Keele (Note 3) has been interested in developing tests to measure subjects' speed and flexibility in attention switching (see also LaBerge, 1973, for attention switching in detection tasks).

Adams (1966) and, more recently, Klein (1976) and Wickens (1980) have argued that attention switching may be a part of the skill itself—a part that has to be learned with practice just as the contractions of the musculature must be learned. For many skilled actions, knowing what to attend to and when could be a critical element. This idea is very close to the ideas of automatic processing discussed earlier (Schneider & Shiffrin, 1977), in that nonconscious mechanisms appear to have the capability to direct attention to the proper sources, with these automatic mechanisms requiring a great deal of practice to perfect. Instructing beginners to direct attention from vision to touch at a particular moment could be a large help in speeding the learning processes for a skill.

Finally, those aspects of the environment to which we are attending are not necessarily the same as those at which we are looking. For attention to auditory stimuli this is obvious, as we can attend to nonvisual stimuli with our eyes closed. But, Posner et al. (1978) have shown that, even for vision, I can be looking at one thing and be attending to some other visual event in peripheral vision. This observation agrees well with the subjective observations that highly skilled game players can look at one source of information while actually directing attention to another source of information in peripheral vision. Also, there is evidence that attention switching is more or less analogous to the flashlight model used for selective attention in Chapter 4. Posner et al. (1978) have shown that when attention has to be switched from one visual source to another, there is a "sweep" of attention across the visual field, analogous to the sweep of the flashlight on the dark wall as it is directed at a new signal source.

ANTICIPATION

In this chapter I have stressed the difficulties that performers have in handling environmental information indicating that a new movement should be made. The major conclusion was that if information was presented in unpredictable ways so that the individual cannot anticipate what is to be done when the signal comes on, or cannot anticipate when a given signal will come on, or both, a great deal of time is required to start some new response when the signal finally does arrive. The actual RT varies with a wide variety of factors, some of which have been discussed. Even so, RT is rarely found to be less than about 120 msec for kinesthetic stimuli (with artificially moved limbs as the stimulus) and essentially 160 to 180 msec for auditory and visual stimuli.

The problem with the previous discussion is that RT has been studied in highly unrealistic situations, in which stimuli are suddenly presented and cannot be anticipated. In fact, experimenters intend to make the situation unrealistic, in that there is careful randomization of foreperiods, the use of "catch" trials in which no stimulus would come on at all, and the use of choice-RT situations in which the actual response could not be predicted in advance. While much important information has been achieved from this paradigm, it is reasonable to ask what these RT methods have to do with the performance of everyday tasks that do not have such suddenly presented information (e.g., Turvey, 1977).

In just about every skill imaginable, there are almost never suddenly presented stimuli. The stimuli are a constantly moving environment (in walking or in driving a car) or the stimuli can be predicted in some way, either through advance information or through past experience that a signal will be expected at a certain time in an action. And often when the signal does arrive, it is not a discrete event but rather an ongoing pattern of activity (e.g., a ball rebounding from a bat). These objections are very important, and they form the basis of what has come to be known as the *ecological approach* for studying skilled movement (Turvey, 1977). It has been argued that by failing to recognize that stimuli are almost never suddenly presented, experimenters have uncovered a number of principles about human performance that are unrelated to performance in natural environments. To attempt to remedy this situation, in the next sections I will turn to one of the critical neglects of the RT method presented to this point—the failure to consider that one of the most potent variables for responding in natural environments is the anticipation of upcoming events.

Spatial or Event Anticipation

Being able to anticipate which action is going to be required provides strong advantages to performers. For example, both Leonard (1953, 1954) and Jeeves (1961) used an apparatus that had trackways arranged as spokes of a wheel. Subjects were asked to move repeatedly from the center position to the ends of the various tracks and back again as quickly as possible. When the appropriate spoke was indicated only when the subject had arrived at the center position, subjects could not anticipate which move to make next. Performance was slow, labored, and jerky. However, when subjects were informed of the next trackway to be selected when they were at the outside end of a trackway, subjects could presumably plan the next movement while they were moving toward the middle and avoid a delay at the center position. Overall performance appeared to be smoother, less labored, and, of course, more rapid.

A similar study was done by Leonard (1953). The subject had a six-choice RT task that could be conceptualized as a two-choice and a three-choice response. Leonard presented advance information as to which one of the two-choice stimuli would appear on a given trial, and this advance information preceded the actual stimulus by either 1 or 5 sec. He found that when the advance information was presented 5 sec before the stimulus, subjects responded with an RT that was essentially equivalent to that for a single three-choice response; apparently the subjects had used the advance information to reduce the six-choice RT task to a three-choice task, thus saving processing time when the stimulus arrived. Interestingly, this effect did not occur when the advance information arrived only 1 sec before the stimulus; apparently in this situation the advance information required greater than 1 sec in order to be used in reducing the number of stimulus alternatives.

Some of these effects can be demonstrated in a simple experiment. Arrange two columns of randomly ordered letters down the side of a piece of paper. Place the paper to the left of a typewriter and type the letters one at a time as quickly as possible with the right index finger only. First, type the letters by placing a file card over all but the letter you are typing at the moment, exposing only one letter at a time. This situation involves no advance information about the up-coming letters. Alternatively, without the card, run your finger down the side of the column of numbers, using it to keep your place. You can "look ahead" to gain advance information about the next letter(s) to be typed, and you will find that the typing is much smoother and far more rapid. Apparently, you are processing the next letter and preparing the response to it while you are responding to the present one (see also Allport et al., 1972; Shaffer, 1971).

Another example involves reading. Read the following sentence aloud: The words that you are currently speaking were viewed about 500 msec earlier. These "experiments" demonstrate some of the most common effects of anticipation in everyday tasks. Presumably, they occur while steering a car in traffic, running with the ball in rugby, or working on a production line. The advance information determines in part what stimuli are going to be received and what responses need to be made in the next few seconds.

Recently there have been efforts to determine what kinds of information can be used in advance and how much time can be "saved" in using it. Klapp (1977b) and Rosenbaum (1980) have used tasks in which various aspects of the response could be specified in advance, leaving other aspects unspecified until the stimulus arrived; the stimulus then provided the remaining information. For example, Rosenbaum used a task in which the movement was to be made (a) with the right or left hand, (b) toward or away from the body, and (c) to a target that was near to or far from the starting position. This is an eight-choice RT task ($2 \times 2 \times 2 = 8$ alterantives), but if subjects are given advance information about, for example, which hand is going to be required, it is possible to consider the task as a four-choice situation, perhaps saving processing time.

Rosenbaum found that providing advance information about any one of the features to be involved in the movement (the arm, direction, or extent of the movement) reduced the RT by about 100 to 150 msec. Apparently, when the subjects had advance information about one of the features of the up-coming movement, they could engage in processing before the stimulus arrived, thus saving processing time. Also, there seemed to be more advantage to information about which arm was to be used (150-msec savings in RT) as opposed to which extent of the movement was to be used (100-msec savings in RT), suggesting that the situation is somewhat more complex than merely having the number of choices reduced from eight to four.

Klapp's (1977b) work shows the same kinds of effects in a task in which the subject must make a Morse code "dit" or "dah"; a "dit" is a rapid press-release, and a "dah" is a press-hold-release. Klapp found that advance information about whether a "dit" or a "dah" was to be made saved processing time even though the subject did not know which finger to use until the stimulus light came on. This finding suggests that certain of the processing operations, normally done during the response-selection and/or the response-programming stage, can be done before the stimulus light comes on. These effects are important for understanding how people make use of advance information in many different tasks (e.g., driving, rapid ball games, etc.). Performers can take advantage of these capabilities by performing certain operations before the stimulus comes on. The advantage

No Advance Information

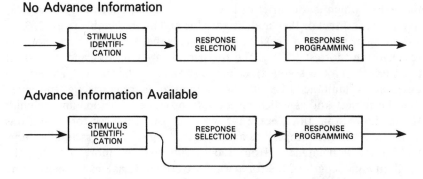

Advance Information Available

Figure 5-12. Bypassing the response-selection stage by processing information in advance.

is that such operations, then, do not have to be performed after the stimulus arrives, shortening the RT.

This evidence can be viewed in relation to the stages of information processing. In Klapp's situation (1977b), information about whether to make a "dit" or a "dah" allows the choice of program for "dit" or "dah" to be done in advance, thereby reducing the processing time required of the response-selection and response-programming stages, leaving only the selection of the finger to be involved after the stimulus arrives. Presumably, providing all of the aspects of the response in advance could enable the response-selection stage to complete all of its processing in advance. In that sense, the response-selection stage can be "bypassed" through the early processing of the advance information (Figure 5-12). It is also interesting to note in Leonard's (1953, 1954) and Jeeves' (1961) studies that the advance information allowing the partial selection of the next movement direction was presented (and therefore processed) while the subject was already moving to the center position. Although this result should not be particularly surprising, it does indicate that one response can be planned while another is being executed.

Temporal Anticipation

The previous evidence on spatial anticipation suggests that the performer can, by knowing the response to be produced, eliminate (bypass) or at least drastically shorten some of the stages. The shortening of RT here is rather modest, though, and the responder still has difficulty responding to environmental stimuli quickly. The evidence presented in the present section suggests that if the person can anticipate when the stimulus is going to come on, large reductions in RT can be made. Under the proper circumstances, the performer can eliminate RT altogether. First, I will consider some of the simple laws of temporal anticipation.

Foreperiod Regularity

Consider that the subject is in a simple RT situation (one stimulus and one response) and that there is a warning signal followed by a foreperiod,

the end of which is the onset of the stimulus. Foreperiods may be regular
(e.g., always 3 sec) or they may be variable and unpredictable (e.g., 2, 3, or
4 sec in some random order). It seems obvious that a regular foreperiod will
result in the shortest RTs. If the foreperiods are constant and very short
(e.g., less than a few seconds), evidence shows that the subject can respond
essentially stimultaneously with the stimulus after some practice (provided
that the subject knows which response to produce). Quesada and Schmidt
(1970) showed that the average RT with a constant 2.0-sec foreperiod was
22 msec. When the foreperiods are random, they result in essentially "normal" RTs, with latencies from 150 to 200 msec or more. Clearly, the
regularity and length of the foreperiod are critical variables in determining
RT.

It is probably not reasonable to think that the RT under a constant
foreperiod is actually shortened relative to the situation with a variable
foreperiod. Rather, it seems more likely that the person anticipated the arrival time of the stimulus and began the response processes before the
stimulus came on so that the overt movement was made at about the same
time as the stimulus. Anyway, the situation with constant foreperiods seems
not to fall under the usual definition of RT, which is the delay in responding
to a suddenly presented and unanticipated signal.

When the foreperiods are longer (e.g., 12 sec) but regular, subjects apparently cannot shorten RTs to zero as they can with the shorter
foreperiods. Mowrer (1940) showed that under these conditions RTs were
about 230 msec. Also, the RT in these long but regular foreperiods seems to
be similar to an RT when the foreperiod is short but irregular (Mowrer,
1940). With long foreperiods, the subject cannot anticipate the exact arrival
time of the stimulus because the person's time-keeping mechanisms are not
sufficiently accurate to time 12 sec. Attempts to respond in advance result in
many early responses (by 1 sec or so), which are usually not tolerated by the
experimenter. All the subject can do is prepare for the stimulus arrival and
respond very quickly when it does arrive.

Preparation versus Early Responding

The above evidence suggests that performers can anticipate temporally in
two fundamentally different ways (see also Posner, 1978). First, if the
foreperiods are both regular and short, and the response to be produced is
known, evidence indicates that the subject can initiate in advance the processes leading to the response so that the overt response appears at about the
same time as, or even slightly before the stimulus. This early responding implies that the individual engages the stages of information processing (as
discussed in Chapter 4) and at the appropriate time during the foreperiod
issues an internal "go" signal. If the "go" signal is timed appropriately, the
response will occur exactly when the stimulus does.

On the other hand, when the foreperiod is very long (e.g., 10 sec) and the
response known, the subject can perform certain processes in advance but
cannot know exactly when to issue the internal "go" signal to initiate the
response. In some situations, it is possible that the subject performs all of
the stages of processing except the triggering of the response, and then waits

for the signal to come on. When it does, the response is triggered but with a rather fast RT. Perhaps this is what is meant by the statement that the person is "fully prepared" to receive a stimulus and to respond to it.

Foreperiod Duration

In simple-RT situations, there is a great deal of evidence that irregular foreperiods averaging about 1 sec produce shorter RTs than do longer ones of 2, 3, or 4 sec (e.g., Klemmer, 1956; Welford, 1968). This effect seems to be quite small, however, and it is overshadowed by a larger effect that is apparently related to when the subject expects the signal. In these latter situations, the fastest RT is not associated with the shortest foreperiod as would be expected from Klemmer's results, but rather with the most probable foreperiod or, if the foreperiods are all equally probable, with the center of the range of foreperiods (Aiken, 1964; Mowrer, 1940; Poulton, 1974).

This *expectancy effect* can be seen more directly in an experiment by Mowrer (1940). He had subjects respond to tones presented every 12 sec during a training session, and RTs dropped to about 231 msec with practice. Then, without any break in the testing, he occasionally presented tones at times greater or less than 12-sec intervals. The data in Figure 5-13 show the RTs associated with these other intervals. Notice that the most rapid RT was at the interval that was most expected (12 sec) and that longer and especially shorter intervals resulted in slower RTs. These data say that subjects are most rapid in responding at intervals for which they are expectant.

It appears that as the set of expected foreperiods draws near, the subject begins to prepare for the stimulus and for the response. Since maintaining a prepared state is effortful for the subject, this readiness begins to increase

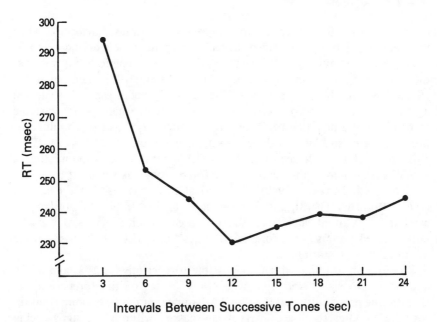

Figure 5-13. Minimum RT occurs at the most probable inter-stimulus interval (from Mowrer, 1940).

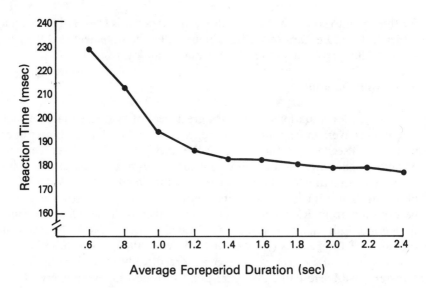

Figure 5-14. The aging foreperiod effect (from Drazin, 1961).

only when the first of the group of foreperiods is expected, reaches a maximum at about the center, and declines toward the end of the group of foreperiods. Presumably, the subject is most expectant for the signal when it is presented near the center of the foreperiods, and the RT is somewhat faster there as a result. This readiness is probably not due to early responding, as the RTs are far too long in these situations (over 230 msec in Mowrer's data).

Aging Foreperiods

There is a notable exception to the previous findings that occurs when there are no catch trials provided. In such cases, the subject does not appear to respond most quickly at the center of the set of foreperiods but rather at the last of the foreperiods (Drazin, 1961; Rothstein, 1973; Salmoni et al., 1976). Drazin's data are shown in Figure 5-14, where the RT is plotted against the average foreperiod duration. Here, there were variable foreperiods and no catch trials, and the RT decreased as the stimulus was presented later and later in the group of foreperiods.

At first, this result seems to be contradictory to the finding that a stimulus presented at the center of the foreperiods has the most rapid RT (Aiken, 1964; Mowrer, 1940). The critical difference is that the Drazin (1961), Rothstein (1973), and Salmoni et al. (1976) studies did not employ catch trials. Without catch trials, the subject can become increasingly expectant for the stimulus as the foreperiod "ages" toward the last possible time of stimulus presentation.

Consider an example with four possible foreperiods (1, 2, 3, and 4 sec) and no catch trials. Note that when only ½ sec of the foreperiod has elapsed, the probability that the signal will appear at the 1-sec point is one in four (.25). After the 1-sec interval has passed without the signal being presented, the probability that the signal will arrive at 2 sec increases to one in three (.33). After 2 sec has passed, the probability that the signal will arrive at 3 sec is .50, and the probability of the signal arriving at 4 sec increases to 1.0 beyond the passage of 3 sec. Thus, the subject has a basis for becoming increasingly expectant as the foreperiod "ages."

Temporal and Spatial Anticipation Combined

One of the important themes in the literature on temporal predictability (see Schmidt, 1968, for a review) is that subjects cannot make very good use of temporal anticipation unless they also know which response to make when the signal comes on. Consider two situations in which the subjects receive short and regular foreperiods. In one case (Quesada & Schmidt, 1970), the subject knew in advance which response to produce, and the RTs were 22 msec on the average, sometimes even negative. In another case (Schmidt & Gordon, 1977), the subjects did not know which of two responses to produce, and the RTs were long (150 to 200 msec) and never negative. It would seem that being able to respond early, so that the response is simultaneous with the stimulus, is critically dependent on knowing about which response to make when the signal comes on. That is, early responding cannot occur (successfully at least) without both spatial and temporal predictability.

Noble and Trumbo (1967) described some studies with temporal predictability in which certain aspects of the response were presented ahead of time. When short and regular foreperiods were used and subjects knew the movement distance (but not the movement direction, right or left) in advance, no early responding occurred, and the RTs were quite long. Apparently, knowing the extent of the movement (but not its direction) did not enable the subject to perform all of the processing in advance so that the movement could be triggered before the actual stimulus.

The effects of the structure of the foreperiods on RT have many applications to everyday tasks. The starter in a sprint race prevents anticipation by using an unpredictable foreperiod, requiring the athletes to wait for the signal before initiating the response. On the other hand, the dance instructor or the drill leader in the military uses predictable foreperiods so that all of the performers can respond simultaneously with the first count and with each other. Dance instructors use a count that has the first 1-2-3-4 presented without action, and the pupils know that the first action must begin with the "1" of the second 1-2-3-4. Drill leaders issue a command (e.g., "Column left . . .") to provide the soldiers with event predictability and then at a very predictable time will give another command "March!" which is the stimulus to perform the action; a good unit will respond as a single person. A similar case can be made of the conductor in an orchestra or the starting sequence (called *staging*) in a drag race.

These concepts are also important in American football, in which the quarterback provides a set of signals for his teammates just before the ball is snapped. The basic idea is for the quarterback to enable his team to anticipate without allowing the opposition to anticipate. From the principles discussed in the previous sections, it would seem most effective for the quarterback to provide a signal count that was regular (providing temporal anticipation), with his own teammates knowing to which of the signals they are to respond. This would provide a situation in which the team could respond simultaneously with the specified signal, causing the opposition to wait at least one RT before responding. The quarterback should be careful to avoid the aging foreperiod effect, as an alert defense could predict the onset of the snap with increasing certainty as the count "ages." Some teams use a warning signal, and then at some unpredictable time another single sound is provided and the team responds to that signal. This would seem to be a particularly ineffective way to handle this problem, since the opposing team could respond at the same time as the offensive team. Here, the offensive team has been denied temporal predictability, and this lowers their reaction speed.

Types of Anticipation

Anticipation is a powerful tool that enables us to avoid using the rather sluggish information-processing systems after a signal to respond has been presented, which is often too late. It is tempting to say that skilled individuals who can anticipate effectively behave as though they had "all the time in the world." In this section, I consider the various types (based on Poulton's, 1957, notions) of anticipation that enable people to behave so skillfully.

Perceptual Anticipation

Poulton's (1957) term *perceptual anticipation* refers to temporal predictions that are made where the subject cannot measure the true passage of time. Rather, the person has some "internal clock" which keeps track of time. A drummer producing a rhythm without a time-keeping device such as a metronome or band leader is an example. How people do this is open to question, but there is suggestion in the literature that when the intervals are greater than 2 sec, the person might use internal processes, such as monitoring feedback from his or her limbs (Schmidt, 1971b) or counting. When the intervals are less than 1 sec, the drumbeats could be part of a program of action, with the program defining the intervals between beats. These ideas are discussed more completely by Schmidt (1971b).

Receptor Anticipation

Poulton's term *receptor anticipation* refers to the situation in which the individual anticipates the arrival of some critical event by watching or listening to the relevant parts of the environment. We know when to close our hands to catch a ball because we have anticipated the time of its arrival by watching it come toward us. We know when it is safe to change traffic lanes, because we can detect the rate of approach of other vehicles. Obviously, this kind of anticipation is very common and provides the basis for responding to these signals at the appropriate times, avoiding accidents and performing smoothly without panic or rush. Naturally we must learn the regularities of environmental events in order to anticipate them effectively.

Perhaps one of the reasons that children do not perform as well as adults in ball games is their lack of experience in the critical skills of anticipation (see also Thomas, 1980).

Effector Anticipation

There is an additional type of anticipation called *effector anticipation.* Consider the situation in which the batter watches a ball approach from the pitcher. Presumably the person readies a batswing program, "holds it," then issues the signal to "Go," after which the movement begins. How does the person know when to give the "Go" signal? Clearly he or she must anticipate (with receptor anticipation) the time of arrival of the ball over the plate, but the batter must also know how long the swing will take and where the limb will go.

From film analyses, Hubbard and Seng (1954) found that the swing of the bat required about 100 msec for good batters. This was not the time of the entire swing action, which began with a stride well before the pitcher released the ball, but rather the interval from the first movement of the bat forward until the bat arrived over the plate. Prior to the initiation of the batswing, the individual must have decided critical details of the action, such as whether or not to swing and where to aim the swing. The individual must also have decided how long the batswing action itself will take. This is so because the "Go" signal only starts a chain of events that eventually results in the beginning of the swing, and then the swing itself must occur. So there are a number of processes between the "Go" signal and the arrival of the bat over the plate, all of which must be taken into account in deciding when to produce the "Go" signal. Estimating these intervals of time is what Poulton (1957) termed *effector anticipation,* or the anticipation of the duration of the effector system's action.

Benefits versus "Costs" of Anticipating

The previous sections have shown benefits to the performer of anticipating temporally and/or spatially. However, in both the outside world and in motor behavior the addage that "you don't get something for nothing" holds equally well, and there are necessarily "costs" of various kinds that result from anticipating. In this section, I will identify some of these costs and relate them to the benefits that can be achieved.

Attention Demands of Anticipating

One of the important concepts of this entire section is that when we are given advance information we "save" time during RT by processing ahead of time. Of course this processing requires attention. Rosenbaum (Note 4) has used a *precue paradigm* in which the individual is given in advance some of the aspects of the movement to be made (e.g., with which arm or in which direction). One of the important aspects of his study is the delay in responding to a given signal when it is contrary to the precue. As an example, suppose that the precue indicated use of the right hand and then the reaction signal indicated use of the left hand. In these cases, the response to the left hand signal is 50 msec longer than if the subject had not received a precue at all! By our usual definition of attention, we can see that the anticipation of the right-hand movement caused the left-hand movement to be slower, and thus we can say that the spatial anticipation of the right-hand movement was attention demanding. Larish (Note 5) has used a similar technique.

The same point was made by Slater-Hammel (1960). He had subjects watch a hand on a sweep timer (1 revolution/sec) and lift their right index fingers when the clock hand stopped at 750 msec. It seems clear that subjects must use receptor anticipation to monitor the movement of the clock hand and effector anticipation to know how long the fingerlift will take in order to stop the hand at exactly 750 msec. However, the subjects were told that when the clock hand stopped unexpectedly at various points before reaching the 750-msec point, they were to inhibit the response and leave the finger on the key. As the 750-msec point approached, the subjects became unable to inhibit the fingerlift response when the hand stopped (see Figure 7-4 and associated discussion in Chapter 7). This suggests that the anticipation of the fingerlift required attention, without which the subject could not respond to the second signal indicating that the response should be inhibited. This evidence suggests that anticipating temporally and spatially requires attention, since a second task (the inhibitory response) was interfered with by the primary task near the 750-msec point.

Finally, although there are not very strong data on this point, there has been the suggestion (Gottsdanker, 1970; Klapp, 1977a) that anticipating in some situations requires a great deal of mental effort and that subjects will tend to avoid anticipating unless they are highly motivated. This is another way of saying that anticipating is attention-demanding, especially when some (e.g., Kahneman, 1973) equate attention and effort. Situations may exist in which the benefits to be received by anticipating are too small and inconsequential for performers to invest the effort.

Cost-Benefit Analyses

What happens if we anticipate incorrectly? There are many common examples of this, such as the batter who anticipates a curve ball and receives a fastball or the boxer who expects a blow from his opponent's left hand but receives one from his right hand. LaBerge (1973) and Posner and his associates (1978) used a method of estimating some of the costs of anticipating incorrectly, called the *cost-benefit analysis*.

In Posner et al.'s method, the subject fixated on the center of a screen and received one of three precues. One sec after the precue, a signal would come on at one of two locations on the screen (which could be seen without an eye movement), and the subject's task was to lift the finger from the key as rapidly as possible when it did. Only one response was ever required (lifting a single finger from a key) regardless of which stimulus came on, and the foreperiod from the precue to the stimulus was constant. One of the precues was a plus sign, presented one-third of the time, indicating that either of the two signals could come on with equal probability. On the re-

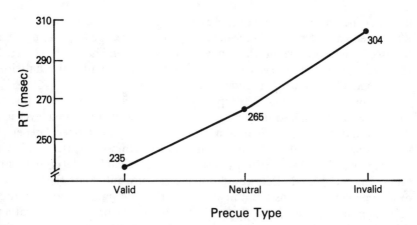

Figure 5-15. The cost-benefit analysis: RT as a function of type of precue (from Posner et al., 1978).

maining two-thirds of the trials, however, the precue was an arrow pointing to the left or to the right, and it meant that the signal would be presented on that side of the screen 80% of the time. On the remaining 20% of the trials, the subject was "tricked," with the signal arriving on the side of the screen opposite to that indicated by the arrow. Those trials for which the signals arrived on the same side as the arrow were called *valid trials,* while those for which the arrow pointed away from the eventual signal were called *invalid trials.*

The RTs to the valid and invalid conditions, as well as to the neutral (plus sign) precue, are shown in Figure 5-15. When the precue was valid, with the signal arriving where the subject expected it, there was a reduction in RT, relative to the condition in which the subject could not predict where the signal would arrive. In the figure, the benefit was about 30 msec (compared to neutral). However, when the signal was presented in the location opposite to that indicated by the arrow (invalid), the RT was increased over and above neutral. This can be seen as the "cost" of anticipating the direction incorrectly, and it produced about the same amount of RT increase (about 40 msec) as was gained when the anticipation was correct. Notice that this cost of incorrectly anticipating involves only the cost associated with the detection of the signal, since the response was always the same regardless of the signal that was presented.

These findings can also be viewed with respect to attention. During a trial, the subjects were gazing straight ahead. (The authors discarded trials in which the subjects actually moved their eyes toward the signal source.) This means that when the arrow came on the subject's attention was shifted to the indicated side of the screen without the subject moving the eyes there, and a "benefit" of 30 msec resulted on valid trials. This provides strong support for the concept presented earlier in this chapter that attention is distinguishable from "what the person is looking at."

The previous lines of evidence have indicated that (a) the RT for detecting a signal can be lengthened if the subject is expecting some other signal (LaBerge, 1973; Posner et al., 1978) and that (b) if the response to the expected signal is different from the response to the unexpected signal, presentation of the unexpected signal causes added costs in terms of the delays in RT (Rosenbaum, Note 4). These delays in RT can be quite large, as much as 50 msec in the Rosenbaum study in which only the hand had to be changed. However, there can be even greater costs associated with false anticipations—actually producing the incorrect response.

Schmidt and Gordon (1977, Experiment 2) used a two-choice RT task in which the subject had to produce a correct amount of force on a lever in a direction indicated by a signal light. There was a constant 1-sec foreperiod from a warning signal until the stimulus, so that temporal anticipation was possible. In one series of trials, the right and left signals were presented in random order, and subjects could not successfully anticipate the direction of the upcoming response. But in another series, the signals were presented in an alternating order, and the subjects would develop strong spatial anticipation about the next response. In this alternating series, however, a few signals were embedded that were opposite to the direction expected: e.g., we would present R, L, R, L, *L,* where the last *L* was expected to be an R by the subject. These false anticipation trials were studied to determine the frequency of error as well as the latency of the corrections.

On those trials for which the subject was anticipating one direction but was prsented with the unexpected signal, there were errors about 64% of the time, where subjects moved in the incorrect direction before they reversed their movement toward the correct target. This effect is shown in Figure 5-16, where it can be seen that the subject had a rather rapid RT (144 msec on the average), moved in the incorrect direction for another 144 msec on the average, and only then reversed the movement to begin to move in the direction of the correct target.[6] The RTs on trials for which the presented signal was opposite the expected one, but in which no errors were made, were slow (276 msec on the average).

These results have a great deal to say about the costs of anticipating when the anticipation is incorrect. First, if the subject is anticipating left but the right signal comes on, and the subject does avoid making an error, then the RT is somewhat longer (276 msec) than if the person were not anticipating at all (235 msec). Thus "unprogramming" the wrong response can require about $276 - 235 = 41$ msec. This value can be thought of as the cost of anticipating incorrectly (in terms of the cost-benefit analysis discussed in the previous section), and it is roughly similar to the 50 msec cost found by Rosenbaum (Note 4). Interestingly, though, in the Schmidt-Gordon study, there was an 83-msec benefit (i.e., $235 - 152$) of anticipating correctly, which is somewhat larger than benefits found by others (see Figure 5-15).

But a 41-msec cost is not a very long interval. But more important than the interval length is the finding that people actually moved in the incorrect direction on a majority of the trials (64%) for which they were falsely anticipating. They did not *begin* to move in the correct direction for 288 msec (see Figure 5-16). But this is compounded by the fact that the person now

---

[6]Attach no particular significance to the finding that (a) the RT to the beginning of the error and (b) the interval from the initiation of the error until the initiation of the correct move both happened to be 144 msec on the average.

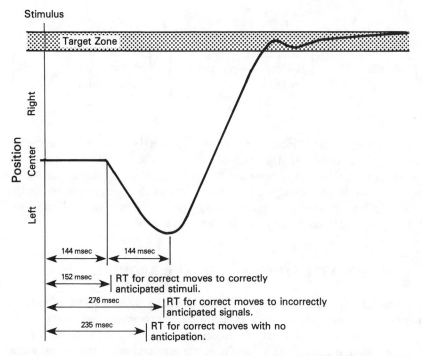

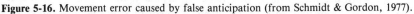

Figure 5-16. Movement error caused by false anticipation (from Schmidt & Gordon, 1977).

had farther to go to reach the correct target so that the arrival at the correct target was delayed even more over the situation where the subject anticipates correctly. And, as if this were not a sufficient price to pay, in having to move farther to the target after the reversal in direction, the errant performer is less accurate in hitting the target, because the accuracy in hitting a target is roughly proportional to the movement distance. When we put together all of these negative aspects of making an error, the cost of anticipation, if the performer guesses incorrectly, can be quite high.

Many theoretical questions arise from these data on error production, but the major importance of these findings is their application to various common activities. A tennis player anticipating that a shot will be hit to her left moves to the left, only to experience that sinking feeling when the ball is hit to her right; she is moving quickly in the wrong direction, and has no hope of making that point. The defensive lineman in American football expects to be blocked to his left so leans or moves to his right, only to find that he is now being blocked to his right, making the task a very easy one for his opponent who was going to block him in that direction anyway.

Effective coaching techniques should employ the notion that anticipating has certain benefits and costs, and that whether or not to anticipate in a certain situation should be determined by weighing the probable gains against potential losses. Such techniques are used in other fields, (e.g., in business forecasting, etc.), and a general way of expressing the gain to be expected in a certain situation is:

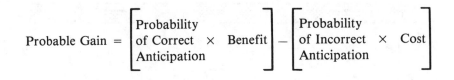

$$\text{Probable Gain} = \left[\begin{array}{c}\text{Probability}\\ \text{of Correct} \times \text{Benefit}\\ \text{Anticipation}\end{array}\right] - \left[\begin{array}{c}\text{Probability}\\ \text{of Incorrect} \times \text{Cost}\\ \text{Anticipation}\end{array}\right]$$

In many sport situations, the benefit of correctly anticipating might be very small compared to the cost of a false anticipation. In others, the reverse is true. Obviously, these factors will depend on the particular activity, as well as on particular situation (the score of the game, position on the field). To my knowledge, these methods have not been used at all in sport, but they certainly could be used to great advantage.

ATTENTION, STRESS, AND AROUSAL

I will shift emphasis slightly at this point to discuss some important aspects of human performance that are related to stress and arousal, and their relationship to ideas about attention. Stress is common, such as in high-motivation conditions as might be experienced in an important game or match, or when we are threatened with harm in some way, as in one's first parachute jump. How do stressful conditions affect the processing of information necessary for the successful performance in activities?

Consider this true story. An airline pilot, with over 20,000 hours of flying experience, returns to San Francisco after an all-night flight from Hong Kong. He drives home to Oakland (20 miles away), sleeps for a few hours, and drives to the local airport to check out his private plane for a flight. With his family of three aboard, he leaves for a destination a few hours away, watches an automobile race there, and late at night begins the return flight. At about 2:00 a.m. he radios that his heater is not working and that he is above a layer of clouds over the Oakland airport. A pilot with his experience would, in this situation, be expected to perform a relatively lengthy (20 to 30 min) instrument approach through the clouds to the airfield, but instead he radios that he is looking for a "hole" in the clouds, presumably to avoid the instrument approach. The plane crashed a few minutes later after a wing broke off, killing all aboard.

What happened? We might guess that the pilot was very fatigued from the overseas flight, from the two other flights that day, and from the car race. He was also cold from being without a heater in the plane. The fatigue and cold stress led to a bad decision to find a "hole." Also because of the fatigue, the pilot may have been handling the plane badly, perhaps becoming disoriented and diving too steeply through the "hole," and the wing failed. The combination of the stress of the situation and the fatigue and cold probably led to panic, to bad judgments, to ineffective control of the aircraft, and eventually to the crash.

Similar examples of panic come from underwater diving, as pointed out by Norman (1976) and Bachrach (1970, p. 122):

> A woman enrolled in a diving course but lacking experience, was reported to have . . . drowned while diving for golf balls in a twelve-foot (pool). When her body was recovered, she was wearing her weight belt, and, in addition, was still clutching a heavy bag of golf balls.

Again, something went wrong. Perhaps fatigue and cold led to panic. What effect do stress and panic have on information processing in these situations that causes people to abandon highly practiced techniques and resort to the skill level of an inexperienced beginner? I consider some possible answers to these questions in the next few sections.

Arousal, Stress, and Motivation Defined

First, although it is possible to make many fine discriminations among stress, motivation, arousal, activiation, and anxiety in terms of the way these words are used in everyday language, it is not so easy to demonstrate differences among these concepts in experimental settings. For example, high arousal (or any one of the other terms) implies a highly energized state, in which there is alertness, an elevated heart rate, increased sweating, decreased resistance to the passage of weak electric current over the surface of the skin, and slightly dilated pupils, to name but a few of the physical and physiological manifestations. A problem for the understanding of arousal, motivation, and stress is that they result in similar shifts in these physiological measures.

A related problem, as pointed out by Kahneman (1973), is that for any one method of generating a high arousal state the pattern of change in these various physiological measures is not uniform. Some of these measures may change in a way indicating more arousal, while others may change in a way indicating less arousal. Such observations make it difficult to measure with any confidence the individual's arousal state, since it is not clear which measures of arousal are the "proper" indicants of it. This evidence suggests that arousal is not a simple internal state at all, but that it has components that vary when individuals become aroused or activated by certain stimuli in their environment.

Even though there is a great deal of difficulty in measuring the arousal state physiologically, differences can be seen among arousal, stress, and motivation in terms of human behavior. For example, at a behavioral level, an individual who is highly motivated has different movement behaviors, facial expressions, and skill levels than does one who is afraid of an injury if the performance is not effective. How can individuals with roughly the same states, as indicated by physiological measures, behave so differently? An important distinction among arousal, stress, and motivation will help to answer some of these questions.

Arousal Is Neutral

As implied earlier, arousal can be thought of as a dimension that describes the extent to which the individual is energized. It ranges from deep sleep to the highly energized state characteristic of an individual fighting for survival in combat or competing in an important sporting event. In this definition, arousal is neutral, in that it represents the amount of energy or effort that the individual will apply to whatever action is being accomplished.

Stress and Motivation Are Directional

Stress and motivation, on the other hand, can be thought of as having a directional component. Stress is usually considered to be a negative emotional state, leading to avoidance or escape from unpleasant situations. Likewise, motivation implies movement toward some goal, as with motivation to win a game. But sometimes the motivation to win a game can lead to stress, as when anticipating failure to meet the demands. To summarize, motivation and stress define the direction of the action, while the arousal level determines the intensity with which that action will be approached or avoided.

The Inverted-U Hypothesis

One of the oldest and certainly one of the most interesting aspects of arousal and performance was discovered by Yerkes and Dodson (1908) in studying the learning of brightness discrimination in mice. They found that increased intensity of electric shocks delivered to the mice increased the rate of learning, but only up to a point. Beyond this point, further increases in the intensity of the shock seemed to impair the learning. If the shock is arousing, then there appeared to be an optimum level of arousal for learning; that is, the relationship between shock intensity and performance followed an inverted-U (see Figure 5-17). The basic notion is that increased arousal improves performance up to a point, but further increases cause performance to deteriorate. The principle has been called the Yerkes-Dodson law, after its originators, or, more commonly, the *inverted-U hypothesis* (Duffy, 1962).

The idea of an inverted-U relationship between arousal and performance seemed to be of great interest to motor behavior, especially since many coaches see arousal (or motivation) as an important part of a game situation. But until recently there had been very little evidence that the inverted-U principle applied to motor responses. Weinberg and Ragan (1978) have provided evidence for the phenomenon in motor behavior (see also Martens & Landers, 1970).

They asked college males to perform a task in which tennis balls had to be thrown at a 5-cm target 6.1 m away. After 10 trials of initial practice, the subject was asked to fill out a questionnaire, and he then received one of three feedback statements. In the High Stress condition, the subject was told that he was only in the 10th percentile and that 90% of the population of college males would have performed better than he did. The Moderate Stress condition placed the subject in the 40th percentile, with 60% of the population having better performances than his. In the Low Stress condition, the subject was told that his throws were in the 70th percentile, so that only 30% of the population were better at throwing. Because the subjects

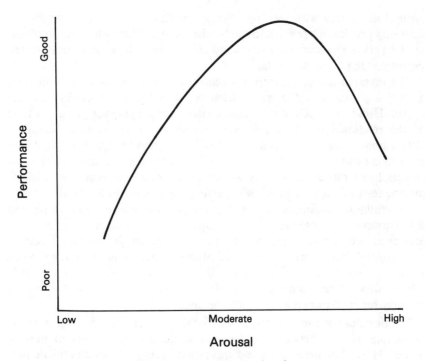

Figure 5-17. The inverted-U relation between arousal and performance.

were told that this task was an important predictor of success in most sport tasks involving throwing (which is not actually correct, as we shall see in Chapter 10), such (false) statements about their level of performance were expected to be arousing to differing degrees. Indeed, arousal data collected by Weinberg and Ragan indicated that this was the case.

In Figure 5-18 are the throwing scores for the subjects in these three stress conditions. Increased arousal from the Low Stress to the Moderate Stress condition produced strong gains in performance, but further increases in

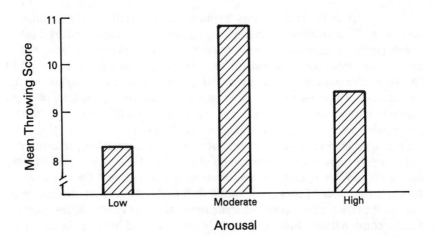

Figure 5-18. Throwing proficiency as a function of three arousal conditions (from Weinberg & Ragan, 1978).

arousal associated with the High Stress condition produced a decrease in throwing proficiency relative to the Moderate Stress condition. As predicted by the Yerkes-Dodson law, there was a clear optimal level of arousal for the performance of this motor task.

The inverted-U relationship has received a great deal of study in both animal and human subjects, as discussed in a recent review by Landers (1980). However, much of this research does not provide very clear-cut tests of the relationship between arousal per se and performance. Näätänen (1973) points out that, in much of this work, the idea has been that high arousal is measured by, for example, high heart rates, so anything that increases heart rate is incorrectly assumed to increase arousal. Or subjects may be tested on an RT task while performing at various levels of intensity on a treadmill, finding an inverted-U relationship between heart rate and RT. However, because the attention demand for running increases as speed increases, such findings can be interpreted as either due to the effects of high arousal (heart rate) or of varied attention demands of running. Even so, there are sufficient studies in the literature that support an inverted-U relationship between arousal and performance to warrant including such a relationship as a principle of motor behavior.

The principle of the inverted-U relationship clearly suggests that there is no simple relation between the level of stress and the quality of performance. How often do coaches and sportscasters suggest that an athletic performance was very good because the athlete or team was "up" for the game (see Nideffer, 1976)? The implication is that the "higher" we are, the better we perform. Actually, there is rather strong evidence that there is an optimal level of arousal and that too much or too little arousal or motivation causes marked deterioration in performance.

Attentional Mechanisms and Arousal

Easterbrook's Cue-Utilization Hypothesis

What attentional mechanisms explain the inverted-U relationship of arousal and performance? One interesting possibility suggested by Easterbrook (1959) is the *cue-utilization hypothesis*. The individual is assumed to take in cues from the environment or from his own movements that aid in future performances. In a game situation, such cues might be the movements of opponents, the movements of teammates, patterns of play, the time remaining in the game, etc. Then, as arousal increases there is a progressive narrowing in the range of cues that are utilized. When the arousal level is low, there are presumably many cues used for performance, but some of these are irrelevant. The *selectivity* of the cues is poor during low arousal. With an increase in arousal to moderate levels, there is a reduction in the number of cues used, with a shift to those cues that are more relevant to the task performance. At some optimal level of arousal, the most effective combination of attention to relevant cues and minimal inclusion of irrelevant cues seems to exist. However, when the arousal level is further increased, there is a further restriction in the range of cues used, many relevant cues are not included, and performance deteriorates. This may have occurred with both the pilot and skin diver discussed earlier.

Perceptual Narrowing

The Easterbrook view of cue utilization is very similar to the idea of *perceptual narrowing* that is described by Kahneman (1973) and others. With this notion, increased arousal causes increased narrowing of the attentional focus, with a progressive elimination of input from the more peripheral aspects of the environment. The term *peripheral* need not refer to events that are actually "in" the periphery (e.g., in peripheral vision), but the term refers to events that are relatively improbable. It just so happens that, with vision, events that are expected are usually in our central vision (because we direct our gaze toward them), and events that are improbable are in peripheral vision. With audition, however, probable and improbable events are neither central nor peripheral.

As arousal level increases, selective attention directs capacity toward those sources of information that are likely to provide the most meaningful information, and we tend to ignore those events that are judged as irrelevant. Attention becomes more narrowly focused on the relevant events, and attention is directed away from irrelevant ones. Such shifts in the attentional allocation make our performances rapid and effective when a likely event occurs, but very slow and erratic when an unlikely event occurs. This phenomenon is similar to the effects shown in the cost-benefit analysis discussed in the previous sections (Figure 5-15).

Considerable evidence is available supporting the notion of perceptual narrowing in a variety of tasks (see Kahneman, 1973). In an interesting and practical setting, Weltman and Egstrom (1966) studied novice SCUBA divers in air, in a controlled water tank, and in the ocean. The divers performed two main tasks (arithmetic and a dial-detection task), and the authors measured the response times to a light stimulus presented in peripheral vision in the diving mask. They found that, as the subjects were moved from air to tank to ocean, large increases (as large as 300 or 400%) occurred in the time taken to detect these peripheral signals. Their interpretation was that the stress of being in the tank or the ocean narrowed the focus of attention, rendering ineffective the processes necessary to detect the light in peripheral vision.

In addition to the reduced range of cues that can be attended to as arousal increases, there is an increase in the number of shifts in attention to different input sources. Some researchers (e.g., Kahneman, 1973) have referred to this effect as increased *distractibility*. Thus, high levels of arousal are likely to cause the individual to direct attention to many different sources from moment to moment, with some of these sources providing irrelevant information and causing the relevant signals to be missed. Apparently, the individual must discriminate between relevant and irrelevant cues during performance, and one effect of high arousal is deterioration in the quality of such discrimination.

Increased narrowing of attentional focus and increased distractibility to irrelevant cues seem to be common with many different sources of arousal.

For example, the arousal from working in loud, continuous noise or vibration, increased motivation to succeed or fear of failing, certain activating drugs, and very hot or cold environments seem to cause similar shifts in attention. In addition, certain depressive drugs such as alcohol, appear to cause such narrowing effects even though the effects are not caused by increased arousal. Mildly intoxicated drivers appear to perform effectively with respect to cues and responses that are common and relevant, but they do not respond effectively to an unexpected signal such as a child running from between two parked cars. Perhaps such effects can be explained by the idea that alcohol decreases overall capacity, causing the individual to increase the amount of attention devoted to the immediate aspects of the environment and enabling proper functioning under the majority of the circumstances. This, however, leaves little capacity for responding to unexpected signals.

A convenient model of this kind of effect is the flashlight analogy that I described in relation to selective attention (earlier in this chapter) and in relation to short-term sensory store and short-term memory in Chapter 4. As the level of arousal increases, the beam of the searchlight becomes more intense, more focused and narrow, which aids in the processing of those things that are actually "illuminated." But, at the same time, the narrowed beam eliminates some of the immediately adjacent cues that could be relevant to performance, and the increased distractability (increases in the number of shifts in the location of the beam) often causes relevant sources of information to have attention taken away from them. Such models should not, of course, be taken too literally, but they are useful in thinking about these kinds of concepts.

Direction of Attention

In addition to the ways in which attention is focused as arousal changes, Nideffer (1976) has considered how arousal affects the direction of attention. Figure 5-19 gives a diagram of the basic idea. The dimension of at-

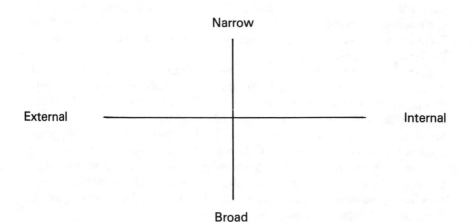

Figure 5-19. Nideffer's notion of two dimensions of arousal: Narrow/Broad and Internal/External (adapted from Nideffer, 1976).

tention labeled "Broad/Narrow" refers to the notion of perceptual narrowing discussed in the previous section. But a second, independent dimension, according to Nideffer, is labeled "External/Internal." It refers to the extent to which attention is directed at internal events, such as feelings, thoughts, or concerns about adequacy and failure, versus external events, such as an opponent's movements, the changing environmental setting, and so on. While Nideffer provides no evidence that this notion is correct, he argues that the effect of arousal on performance depends not only on the Broad/Narrow distinction, but also on the focus of attention. Further, he argues that people differ in terms of how arousal affects the Internal/External dimension, with some people becoming very externally focused and others becoming very internally focused at a high arousal level.

These shifts in direction of attention could result in large changes in the nature of the performance, depending on the task. Consider a task that involves directing attention toward opponents or at the instruments in an aircraft during landing. A high arousal level that could force attention to be shifted to internal factors could have serious negative consequences; if my attention were directed at thoughts of failure, for example, important signals in the environment could be missed. These are important ideas that provide a potential link between the changes in attention during arousal and related changes in performance, but more research needs to be done before Nideffer's proposals become principles of attentional mechanisms in movement control.

Arousal and the Nature of the Task

What kinds of performances should be improved by high arousal and what kinds of performances should be impaired by it? One very common observation in the earlier literature on attention and arousal is that complex tasks, in which there are many signal sources and many different things that might have to be done, with a great deal of decision making about possible choices of action, should be impaired most by high levels of arousal; common examples are the recent near accidents in the control rooms of nuclear power plants. On the other hand, very simple tasks with but a single or a few signal sources and relatively stereotyped responses might be enhanced by the same level of arousal. This observation suggests that one of the dimensions defining the kinds of tasks that would be benefited by high arousal is the open-closed continuum (Chapter 3). Open skills, in which the number of possible relevant signals is high and from which the subject must select the most relevant, might be more severely impaired by high levels of arousal than would closed skills. This fits with Nideffer's (1976) ideas, because open skills are those in which attention must be externally directed for success, while closed skills might demand a much more internal focus.

However, high levels of arousal do increase performance on tasks that require a high degree of rapid, powerful activity, especially if the amount of control required is not very great. A good example is the production of maximum force, when the high levels of arousal created by an unexpected gunshot behind the subject's head (aimed away from the subject, fortunately for him) produced marked gains in force (Ikai & Steinhaus, 1961). Along the same lines are reports of a mother actually lifting a car to free her trapped child. Such reports are difficult to confirm, but witnesses to such actions appear to be in agreement that the woman lifted the car.

It does appear that when the tasks seem to involve more control or precision, there is not so much of an advantage to high arousal levels. To the contrary, there can be a strong disadvantage if the patterns of skilled activity are disrupted by the arousal. Weinberg and Hunt (1976) provided a demonstration of this phenomenon, in which the electromyographic (EMG) patterns among the muscles involved in a throwing pattern were studied in children. When the subjects were told, erroneously, that they were not doing very well and that they should "try harder," there were numerous changes in the EMG patterns. For example, there was increased co-contraction during the throw, in that the agonist and antagonist muscles were contracting together to a greater extent, probably making the whole movement "stiffer." Also, greater background EMG activity was seen before and after the action, indicative of more tension. These changes in EMG are in a direction that would indicate less skill and less efficiency. The arousal levels produced by the instructions to "try harder" produced not only less "coordinated" EMG activities but also decreases in throwing accuracy. These negative effects were largest for subjects classed as "high anxious," people who say they worry a great deal. These data indicate that telling people to "try harder" does not necessarily lead to gains in skill, and may actually do the reverse.

From the above, it might be expected that those kinds of tasks that are going to suffer most from high arousal levels are (a) those that require very fine control, (b) those that require precise grading of forces and times of muscle contractions, (c) those that require steadiness, and (d) often skills that require proper decisions about a number of alternatives. On the other hand, the tasks that probably benefit from high arousal levels are (a) those that have high force requirements, (b) those that emphasize quickenss (as in simple RT), and (c) closed skills that have relatively stereotyped movements. See Landers (1978, 1980) or Martens (1974, 1975) for more complete discussions of these issues.

If these speculations are correct, they should have a great deal of potential applicability for both industry and sport. Knowing, for example, that a particular task is disrupted by high levels of arousal, the well-informed coach or supervisor will attempt to have the individuals perform calmly, rather than under highly motivating conditions or the stress of deadlines. Future application of these notions would seem to require that the tasks in question, as well as the role of motivation, be understood more completely than they are at present.

Individual Differences in Arousal

A discussion of the relation between arousal and performance would not be complete without mention of the differences among individuals in terms of "arousability." Some people seem never to become excited regardless of what happens to them, while others seem highly nervous and under stress most of the time. Such effects have been measured by paper and pencil tests that assess the variable anxiety. Two kinds of anxiety have been identified: *state anxiety* and *trait anxiety* (Spielberger, 1966).

State Anxiety

State anxiety is another label for the kinds of arousal so far discussed. It is often assessed by questions such as "Are you worried about your performance now?" "Yes" answers are indicative of the level of worry about this particular task. Of course, state anxiety can vary from minute to minute and from task to task.

Trait Anxiety

A second kind of anxiety is trait anxiety, which is a measure of the individual's general tendency toward worry or anxiety. It is assessed by questions such as "Are you usually worried about your performance?" "Yes" answers indicate a general tendency to be worried or anxious in life. This general tendency should not fluctuate very much from moment to moment or from task to task; it is a stable characteristic of the person. However, those individuals who are classed as high trait-anxious are those people who tend, under the specific conditions of a task or test situation, to become highly aroused. That is, high trait anxious people tend to be the most state-anxious on any given motor task. Seen in this way, trait anxiety is a variable that describes the ease with which an individual can become stressed by his or her environment. Scanlan and Passer (1978) have discussed *competitive trait anxiety*—a general tendency to be aroused by competitive situations in particular.

Anxiety and Motor Performance

If trait anxiety is a variable that determines one's "arousability" in motor tasks, it would therefore seem to be of importance in predicting the effects of motivating conditions in different individuals. That is, the effect of motivating conditions on human performance will depend somewhat on the nature of the people who are being motivated.

If a given level of arousal is optimal for a given motor task, an individual who is high trait-anxious will reach that level with less external motivation than will an individual who is classified as low trait-anxious. Put another way, there is a risk of over-motivating the high trait-anxious individual so that he or she begins to suffer from too much arousal for the particular task. And, Nideffer's view is that such increased arousal can result in either too much focusing or focusing too internally or externally for the task in question.

Arousal and Level of Learning

Another important factor in the relationship between arousal and motor

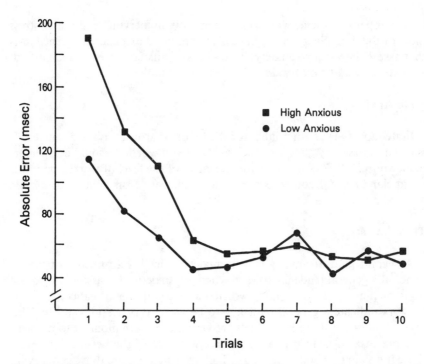

Figure 5-20. Performance of subjects classed as high- and low-anxious for early trials of a movement-timing task (from Martens & Landers, 1969).

performance seems to be the level of practice on the task being studied. Martens and Landers (1969) used a coincident-timing task in which a hand-held slide had to be moved so that a pointer coincided with the arrival of a target at an endpoint, more or less like a laboratory example of hitting a baseball. Figure 5-20 shows the absolute errors in this task for two groups of subjects, one classified as high-anxious and one classified as low-anxious. There was marked inferiority of the high-anxious subjects early in the practice sequence, but this difference dissipated with continued practice.

The reasons for this kind of effect are not clear. One possibility is that the high-anxious subjects, when presented with the next task in the laboratory situation, were over-motivated; the low-anxious subjects, being less excitable, remained more calm in the same experimental conditions. The excess motivation in the high-anxious subjects led to poor initial performance, until they established a lower level of arousal in later trials. This early-practice arousal can be seen clearly in dangerous tasks such as sport parachuting, in which beginners have very high arousal levels as the time of the jump approaches (Fenz & Jones, 1972).

These data, and this interpretation of them, suggest that very new tasks can be highly stressful, especially to high-anxious subjects. The results have obvious implications for teaching motor skills. Knowing that an individual is very highly anxious would lead to somewhat different methods of presenting information in the early stages of learning a motor task (see also Martens, 1971).

These overall principles about practice and stress are summarized in

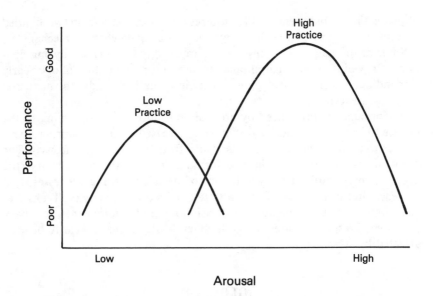

Figure 5-21. The arousal-performance relationship for two levels of practice on a motor task.

Figure 5-21. In this hypothetical situation, the performance of some task under different levels of arousal is estimated for two different levels of practice on the task. It can be expected that as the level of skill increases with practice there is a corresponding increase in the level of arousal that produces the maximum skill level. Also, attention may shift from internal thoughts of failure to the critical elements of the task. When skills are more highly practiced, so that the attention demands are less, presumably individuals can tolerate high arousal and motivation more easily. These particular effects have never been documented in experimental settings, but such effects do seem predictable from the other principles of stress that have been documented experimentally.

SUMMARY

Attention has been defined as a capacity for processing information that is related to consciousness, that is limited, and that is measured by the extent to which different tasks interfere with each other. *Structural interference* occurs when the same receptors, effectors, or storage mechanisms are used for the two tasks. *Capacity interference* results from limitations in attention. Most theorists agree that early stages of information processing may not require any attention and that attention requirements are increased markedly in late stages of processing.

Psychological refractoriness (the delay in responding to the second of two closely spaced stimuli) is taken as evidence that some single channel, or "bottleneck," in processing is present in the response-selection and/or the response-programming stage, requiring that movements be produced in discrete "bursts" even though the stimuli calling for them are presented continuously. In the production of movements, attention is usually required in all but the most simple actions, suggesting that a response-execution stage of processing, subsequent to RT, requires attention. Data from two-handed movements suggest that such a stage may be a single-channel mechanism.

Some of the stages of processing can apparently be bypassed by anticipation. Providing both spatial and temporal predictability allows early responding, whereas providing other information leads to increased readiness to respond.

Performance is influenced by arousal and motivation, according to the inverted-U principle which says that with increased arousal performance increases to a point and then decreases with further increases in arousal. The mechanisms that appear to limit performance under stress are related to the decrease in cue utilization, the failure of decision-making processes, and decreases in the accuracy of the patterning of muscular activity. Tasks that have high force requirements, low decision-making requirements, relatively stereotyped response patterns, and high levels of practice appear to be least affected by stress.

GLOSSARY

Arousal. An internal state of alertness or excitement; similar to activation.

Activation. An internal state characterized by potential action; similar to arousal.

Attention. A limited capacity to process information.

Capacity interference. Interference between tasks caused by limitations in attention.

Cocktail-party problem. The phenomenon, described by Cherry, whereby humans can attend to a single conversation at a noisy gathering, neglecting other inputs.

Consciousness. The mechanism or process by which humans are aware of sensations, elements in memory, or internal events.

Cost-benefit analysis. A method by which the benefits from anticipating correctly can be weighed against the "costs" of anticipating incorrectly.

Early responding. Processing all of the aspects of a movement in advance so that the movement can occur at or before the stimulus.

Effector anticipation. Predicting the duration of internal processes and of the planned movement so that the response can be made coincident with some anticipated external event.

Motivation. An internal state that tends to direct the system toward a goal.

Narrowing. The focusing of attention so that specific sources of information are more likely to be received but rare events are more likely to be missed; also called perceptual narrowing.

Perceptual anticipation. Anticipation of the arrival of a signal only through internal mechanisms or processes.

Preparation. Reorganization of attention and processing information so that a signal can be received and responded to quickly.

Psychological refractoriness. The delay in the response to the second of two closely spaced stimuli.

Receptor anticipation. Anticipation of the arrival of a stimulus due to sensory information about its time of arrival.

Single-channel hypothesis. A theory of attention which says the system can process only a single stimulus leading to a response at any given time.

Spatial anticipation. The anticipation of which stimulus (or the response to it) will occur; also called event anticipation.

State anxiety. A temporary state of worry or concern about a particular situation or activity; similar to arousal.

Stress. A negative motivational state that tends to direct the individual away from some particular situation.

Structural interference. Interference among tasks caused by the simultaneous use of the same receptors, effectors, or processing systems.

Temporal anticipation. The anticipation of when a given stimulus will arrive or when a movement is to be made.

Trait anxiety. A general tendency to be anxious or stresssed that is characteristic of a particular individual.

CHAPTER 6

Modes of Motor Control I: Control Systems and Closed-Loop Processes

Human motor response is based on the simultaneous integration and cooperation of many anatomical parts (the muscles, the brain, the receptors that send information about the environment, and so on). In this sense, it is useful to consider all of these parts as making up a system whose behavior can be studied as a whole, much as a car is a system dependent on the interaction of its various parts. With other kinds of systems that have to be controlled, it has been useful for engineers to define various *modes of control*—fundamentally distinct ways that the system's parts can work together. At a very superficial level, some systems "control themselves," with little or no involvement from humans (e.g., the control of temperature in a refrigerator). Other systems require a human to control them (e.g., a car). For those systems that control themselves, there are a number of different modes of control that can be described.

Just as there are different modes of control for the many machines that fill our lives, there are similar modes of control for the machine that is our body. For over a century scientists interested in movement have thought about how the human motor system might be controlled in ways similar to the control of mechanical systems. Figure 6-1 is a photograph of an early attempt to model movements of biological systems with inanimate mechanisms. Pictured is Jacques Vaucanson's seventeenth century "duck," which was designed to swim, flap its wings, preen itself, eat food, and even excrete the feces-like products of its "digestion" (Eco & Zorzoli, 1963; Gallistel, 1980). It was never implied that the biological system really was purely mechanical, but the ideas that were created for the control of mechanical systems seemed to provide a convenient frame of reference for coming to the understanding of human motor control.

Chapters 6 and 7 are closely related. In Chapter 6, the various ways that

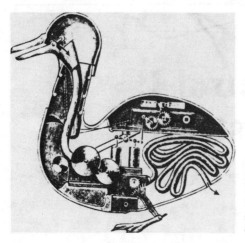

Figure 6-1. Jacques Vaucanson's mechanical duck, representing an early mechanical model of behavior (adapted from Eco & Zorzoli, 1963).

engineers and motor control scientists have conceptualized control systems are considered, with a primary goal being general understanding of how these various systems operate. Then, one general class of these various control systems that involves the use of feedback—called closed-loop systems—will be discussed. In Chapter 7, a major alternative view of movement control—open-loop control—is discussed. Evidence about this mode of control in human performance is provided. Chapter 7 concludes with an overview of the various control systems to provide some integration of the ideas into a unified picture of human motor responding.

CONTROL SYSTEMS

Closed-Loop Systems

For engineers and scientists who attempt to understand human motor control, a fundamentally important control system is the closed-loop system. These systems are important in a large variety of situations, most of which require a system to "control itself" for long periods of time. Examples are home heating systems and the gyroscopic steering systems in large ships.

A diagram of a simple closed-loop system is shown in Figure 6-2. It consists of three parts. First, input about the system's goal is provided to a *reference mechanism*. In the example of the home heating system, the system goal might be a thermostat setting of 68°, with the overall goal being the achievement of this temperature in the house. Next, the reference mechanism samples the environment that it is attempting to control to determine what the temperature actually is. This information from the environment is usually termed *feedback*. The reference mechanism then compares the value of the goal to the value from the environment, and an *error* is computed, representing the difference between the actual and desired states. The error is then given to an *executive level,* and decisions are made

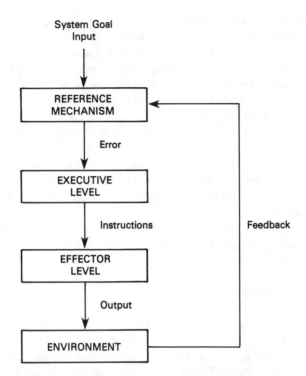

Figure 6-2. The elements of the typical closed-loop control system.

about how to reduce the error toward zero. In the case of the home heating system, the executive level decides whether the error is large enough to turn on the heater. If the error is large enough, instructions are sent to the *effector level,* and a mechanism that has some effect on the environment is activated—in this case, the heater. The heater raises the temperature of the room, and this raised temperature is fed back to the reference mechanism. This process continues until the diference between the actual and desired temperatures is zero, whereupon the executive level produces a decision to shut off the heater. In such a way, the heater cycles between being on and off as a function of the actual value of the room temperature and thus maintains the temperature somewhere near the value set as the system goal.

From the previous example, it can be seen that a closed-loop system has a number of features. First, there is a *system goal,* or a setting of some value that the system is attempting to achieve. Next, there is *feedback* about the actual state of the system. In a *reference mechanism,* an *error* is computed, representing the difference between the actual and desired states. And finally, there is an *instruction* given to an effector level based on the size and direction of the error. All closed-loop systems have all of these parts, but the parts themselves can take on many different forms. These self-regulating systems are often called *servomechanisms,* or more simply *servos,* and they are the heart of a number of larger systems that demand that some state be regulated. Such systems are termed *closed-loop* because the loop of control from the environment to decisions to action and back to the environment again is completed, or closed.

How does this model of the servo system correspond to the human motor system? Think of the reference of correctness and the executive level as being contained in the stages of information processing, so that the system can receive feedback information through short-term sensory store and the stimulus-identification stage. The system can calculate an error and decide what to do about it in short-term memory and the response-selection stage and then program instructions to the musculature to reduce the error in the response-programming stage. Instructions are then given to the effector level, usually thought of as the muscles or a program of action that actually controls the muscles. Then, the information from the various muscle, joint, and tendon receptors, as well as from the eyes, ears, and so on, is sent back to the reference mechanisms for analysis, and decisions about future action are again made.

It is useful to make a distinction between two different kinds of servo systems: continuous versus discontinuous. The distinction is based on the extent to which the system output "mirrors" the state of the environment.

Discontinuous Servos

A servo system in which the control actions of the effector are not continuously related to the state of the system being controlled is called a discontinuous, discrete, or sometimes sample-and-hold system. The home heater is a good example. Figure 6-3 shows that over the course of 15 min the room temperature fluctuates continuously, slowly rising and falling as the heater is turned on and off. Yet the heater does not behave in the same manner; it is either on or it is off. The system is designed to operate so that the heater remains on until the temperature in the room is elevated to a certain point, and then the heater is shut down to allow the temperature to fall.

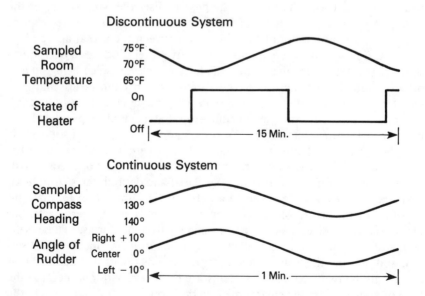

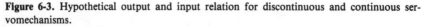

Figure 6-3. Hypothetical output and input relation for discontinuous and continuous servomechanisms.

The critical feature is that there is no one-to-one relationship between the minute-to-minute changes in the temperature and the minute-to-minute changes in the state of the heater. Some discontinuous systems sample data for a long while, obtaining an estimate of the average state of the system for that time period and then act based on all of this information. These systems are sometimes termed sample-and-hold systems, as they hold steady in their output while sampling data.

Continuous Servos

In contrast to the discontinuous servo that operates in distinct bursts, the continuous servo has a one-to-one relationship between the behavior of the effector and the feature of the environment that is to be controlled. In the bottom of Figure 6-3 is a hypothetical example from a steering mechanism of a ship. The "automatic pilot" senses the ship's direction from a compass and issues commands to a motor that controls the rudder angle. Notice that every fluctuation in the ship's direction is associated with a corresponding fluctuation in the rudder angle to compensate for it. Sometimes the actions of the effector are delayed in time with respect to the states of the environment, but there will always be a one-to-one relationship between them in the continuous mechanisms.

Negative and Positive Feedback

The examples that I have just shown are examples of *negative feedback systems,* in which the actions of the effector operate in a way opposite to the indicated errors, so that its effect is a reduction in error. A higher indicated temperature results in the heater being turned off, and a movement of 10° to the right in the ship results in leftward movements of the rudder to compensate.

A *positive feedback system,* on the other hand, operates in such a way that the behavior of the effector is in the same direction as the error, actually causing further increases in the error. A common example is the task of carrying a full bowl of water without spilling it. A slight adjustment in the bowl's position disturbs the water, your attempts to compensate disturb the water even more, and so on. Another way to think of positive feedback systems is to imagine how a ship would behave if the controls were reversed; if the ship deviated to the right, the compensation would be to move the rudder to the right, which would make the ship deviate even more to the right, and so on. Positive feedback systems are usually very unstable and result in the system's "blowing up" if they are not checked in some way. There are a few instances of positive feedback control in motor behavior, but the majority of systems employ negative feedback.

Embedded Feedback Loops

In many systems that we see in everyday life one servo system is embedded within another. A common example is the home heater just discussed; embedded within the temperature regulation system for the house is

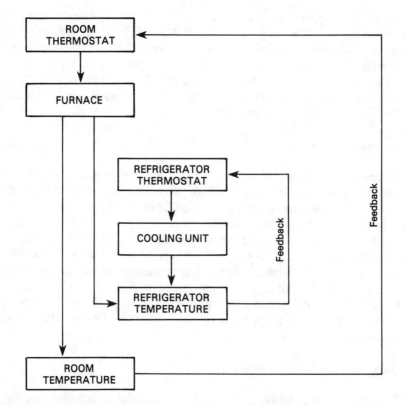

Figure 6-4. Embedded servomechanisms: the servo controlling refrigerator temperature is contained within the servo controlling room temperature.

another servo that controls the temperature of the inside of the refrigerator. In Figure 6-4 notice that the room heater's being on has two effects. First, it raises the temperature of the room. Second, it raises the temperature of the refrigerator which is in the room, and its internal temperature slightly as a result. The thermostatic control of the refrigerator compensates to maintain the refrigerator temperature regardless of the changes in the room temperature. (In doing so, the refrigerator gives off heat, which raises the room temperature a small amount.) It could well be that at the same moment the refrigerator is cooling itself from the inside the heater is warming it from the outside, and the two systems are working at cross purposes!

Open-Loop Systems

A second kind of control system often seen in everyday activities is the open-loop system, in which the instructions are structured in advance and are executed without regard to the effects that they may have on the environment. That is, the behavior of the open-loop system is not sensitive to feedback.

A diagram of a typical open-loop system is shown in Figure 6-5. The executive and effector mechanisms can be thought of in the same way as in the closed-loop system (Figure 6-2), but the feedback loop and the reference of

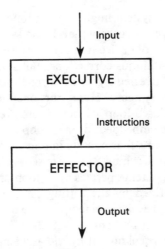

Figure 6-5. The elements of the typical open-loop control system.

correctness are missing. The executive is "programmed" to send certain instructions at particular times to the effector, and the effector carries them out without the possibility of modification if something goes wrong. A good example is the traffic signals at a major intersection. The pattern of red and green lights is controlled from a "program" that is usually located in a large box on the corner. The program controls this sequence without regard to moment-to-moment variations in traffic patterns. If there is an accident or if traffic is particularly heavy, there can be no immediate modification in the pattern because there is no feedback from the traffic conditions back to the executive.

Even though the program for the traffic lights is inflexible, we should not get the idea that it must be simple. We can imagine that the program can be structured so that the north-south street has a 20% longer green-light duration than the east-west street during rush hours, with this relation being altered in mid-day when the traffic flow decreases. But notice that the only way that such changes can occur is to have the programmer structure them into the program in advance. There are many other common examples of open-loop systems, such as the clothes washer that cycles automatically from wash to rinse to spin and the microwave oven that will turn itself on at a certain time, then defrost and cook the meal.

Hybrid Systems

Often with a large system, some aspects of it may be open-loop while other aspects of it are closed-loop. The term *hybrid,* which usually refers to a mixture of two distinct elements into a single one, is used by control engineers for such systems. For example, in a car the temperature of the engine is controlled in a closed-loop mode by a thermostat that senses the engine's temperature and controls the coolant flow, while the order and timing of the firing of the spark plugs is "programmed" in advance by a distributor.

Sometimes an overall system might seem at one level to be closed-loop, but at a different, more microscopic level, the system might be operating open loop. A speed-control device in a car ("cruise control") senses errors in speed and makes continuous corrections. But some of the internal parts of the engine that are affected by these corrections (e.g., the distributor) function as open-loop systems. Here, the open-loop control system is embedded within the closed-loop system. There are other examples where closed-loop systems are embedded in open-loop ones.

Finally, there are systems that operate in one mode at one time and in an opposite mode at some other time. If the house is cold and you turn on your home heater, the entire system operates open-loop until the house warms up to the temperature defined by the setting on the thermostat. Then the system acts closed-loop, because the temperature of the room feeds back on the operation of the heater and controls it.

A major point of the discussion of hybrid and embedded control systems is that frequently it will be difficult, if not impossible, to answer such questions as "Does some system behave as an open-loop system?" Answers are usually oversimplified, as the system will often be open-loop at some time or level and closed-loop at some other time or level. As we shall see in the ensuing sections, such simple classifications of human motor behavior will become very difficult to justify, as it will often make more sense to regard ourselves as complex combinations of open- and closed-loop systems.

Feedforward Control

The last fundamental mechanism for general system control is termed *feedforward control*. The term feedforward is an obvious attempt to represent the opposite of feed*back*. While feedback refers to information that is sent back to the executive level about the results of the action, feedforward is information sent forward by the executive level to ready the effector system in some way. The feedforward information can (a) ready the effector level for the arrival of future commands for action or (b) ready (or preset) sensory systems to "expect" a certain signal. All of these actions can be seen as anticipatory or preparatory, as they occur prior to the commands for the action and well prior to the feedback from the action itself.

There are examples of feedforward processes in everyday systems. An executive of a paint factory might send word to the factory workers that tomorrow they will be making a particular kind of paint. This feedforward information would then have the effect of readying the employees for the new task, perhaps by obtaining the relevant materials from storage and arranging them for action tomorrow. Here, the feedforward readies a system for future commands. Another example: When I come back from a weekend trip and the house is cold, I must reset the thermostat to 68° so that the heating process can warm the house. Here, feedforward involves the setting of a reference of correctness before the action occurs, with the action itself being the closed-loop achievement of this reference of correctness. This is an example of the second kind of feedforward process mentioned above, whereby the system is readied to receive a different kind, or particular value of, feedback from the system being controlled. As we shall see later in this chapter, feedforward mechanisms are important in the central nervous system's control of movement.

Control Systems in Human Performance

I will turn now to the analysis of the human motor system using these various concepts about control systems. The literature on human motor control contains a number of theoretical treatments of skills, and such points of view typically have at their base one or more of the fundamental mechanisms mentioned above. There are, however, too many theoretical ideas to treat in this volume. By considering the fundamental processes proposed by each theory and by grouping them according to the breakdown provided earlier in the chapter, a good understanding of the nature of a motor theorizing can be achieved. I will begin by considering a very important class of theory for movement control—the closed-loop theory. The focus will be on the role of feedback in movement control.

SENSORY INFORMATION AND FEEDBACK

As can be seen from the previous section, closed-loop systems depend heavily on the involvement of sensory information produced by the system as it responds. Such sensory information, in the context of closed-loop control systems, is often termed *response-produced feedback,* or simply feedback, implying that the sensory information to be considered is the result of the motions of the animal. Of course there are many other forms of sensory information that are not associated with the motions of the animal, and these are usually considered under the more general heading of sensation or perception. In this section, the various kinds of sensory information that can be used in the control of movement are discussed.

Varieties of Feedback

When speaking of the various kinds of sensory information that are available to the responder, these feedback sources are usually arbitrarily classified into three groups, which stem from a classification system suggested by Sherrington (1906). Perhaps the least important is the class of receptors called *interoceptors*. They tell us about the states of our internal organs, such as "hunger pains," and have questionable relevance for motor behavior. The remaining two classes of receptors are divided according to whether they provide information about our own movements or information about the movements of objects in the environment. These receptors have been called, respectively, the *proprioceptors* and *exteroceptors*. The roots *proprio* and *extero* refer to events in one's own body and events outside one's body, respectively. This distinction is somewhat misleading in terms of coming to an understanding of information contributing to movement control.

Receptors for Movement Information

Vision

Certainly the most important receptor for supplying information about the movement of objects in the outside world is the eye, and is often referred to as the "queen of the senses." Subjectively, we all know that in darkness we are critically impaired in many tasks, although we also know that vision is not critical for all motor performances. As well, blind people learn to respond to the environment with remarkable facility, although it is clear that blind people are at a large disadvantage in many situations. In terms of human performance, vision provides information about the movements of objects in the environment that is important for subsequent motor behavior (the movement of balls, the sizes of objects, their locations, and so on), and it appears that a large part of motor responding is involved in tailoring our behavior to meet the environmental demands.

The eye (and the visual system) has, traditionally, been classified as an exteroceptor, primarily because it was thought of as a receptor that provides information only about the movements of other objects in the environment. While it does have this capability, it has been learned recently that the eye can serve as a proprioceptor. That is, the eye can be viewed as a receptor that gives us information about our own movements.

Visual Proprioception

Recent discussions about vision (e.g., Turvey, 1977; D. Lee, 1980), stemming essentially from the ideas put forth by Gibson (1966), treat vision as a far richer source of information than is implied by passive observation of movements in the environment. Think of the retina (the light-sensitive receptor-segment of the eye) as being "bombarded" with rays of light from the objects in the visual field. The locations that these rays find on the retina are unique for each position that an eye can achieve in space. Moving the head changes the angles of entry of these rays into the eye and hence the relative locations on the retina (see Figure 4-4). For example, as I sit here thinking, essentially motionless, at the typewriter, I see that the edge of the carriage is in a line with the sill of a door beyond and that the lamp in front of me lines up with a doorknob. If I move slightly to the left, the angles that these objects make on my retina change. I see the typewriter carriage "slip by" the door sill, while the light and the doorknob remain lined up in the vertical dimension. If I move my head downward, I obtain predictable changes in the visual scene again.

Figure 4-4, in Chapter 4, is a diagram showing how changes in head position contribute to the changes in the angles of light rays entering the eye. The pattern of rays experienced is called the *optical array,* and it provides a unique specification of the location of the eye in space. The changes in the optical array when the eye is moved from one place to another are called the *optical flow,* implying that the visual environment "flows past us" as we move around. Of course, particular patterns of flow imply something about

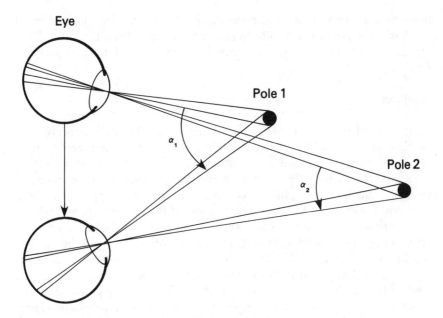

Figure 6-6. The detection of distance: the angles of the light rays from the distant pole change less than those from the near pole as the head and eyes are moved.

the particular kind of movement occurring in the environment. The essential point is that vision provides not only an indication of movement in the outside world but is also a rich source of information about our movements in that world.

The moving optical flow not only tells me about my movements in the environment, but is also tells me about the environment in ways that I could not achieve if I were not moving at all. For example, as I look outside the window, I see two poles, as in Figure 6-6. Which of them is closest to me? The question is difficult to answer if I remain still, but if I move my head sideways I can tell immediately. I notice that one of the poles seems to "move more quickly" as I change head position. This, of course, is the same as saying that the angles of the rays received from one object have changed more quickly (α_1 in the figure) than did those from the other (α_2), implying that Pole 1 is closer to me than Pole 2. Thus, the visual system through movement of the entire head or body can provide rich information about the nature of the environment.

This view says that vision is not merely an extroceptive sense, passively telling about the environment. It is also a proprioceptive sense telling us about our own movements.[1] As well, vision is dependent on movement in some situations for telling us about the environment. In this way, vision and

---

[1]D. Lee (1980) has argued that we should add the term exproprioception to Sherrington's (1906) original list. Thus, we can talk of three classes of receptors: exteroceptors for information about movements of the environment, proprioceptors (and perhaps interoceptors) for movements of our body per se, and exproprioceptors for movements of our body *in relation to* the environment.

movement are very closely and reciprocally linked. Excellent discussions of this basic idea are found in Gibson (1966) or D. Lee (1980), the latter showing relevance to many situations, including sport-related motions and bird flight.

Audition

Another of the senses that is traditionally classified as exteroceptive is hearing, or audition. Certainly, audition has a strongly exteroceptive role, informing us about the nature of movements in our environment, such as the approach of a bicyclist in the dark, the firing of the starter's gun, and so on. But at the same time, like vision, audition can tell us a great deal about our own movements. As we all know, most of the movements we make in the environment produce sounds, such as the sound of footsteps when we are jogging, the sound of our own speech, or that of the bat as the baseball is hit squarely. The nature of these sounds, then, can provide us with a great deal of information about our own movements, such as the kind of terrain on which I am jogging or the impact I have delivered to a baseball. Thus, to a limited extent, audition and vision are very similar, providing both exteroceptive and proprioceptive information.[2]

Vestibular Apparatus

Located in the inner ear is a set of sensors that provides information about movements of the head. One aspect of head movement that is critical for perception is its orientation with respect to gravity—i.e., whether the head is upside down, tilted, etc. Such information is provided by two small structures, the *saccule* and *utricle,* located in the inner ear that signal information about the relation of gravity to the head. If the head is spinning, they provide information about the rate and perhaps direction of spin (e.g., in a somersault). Located near the utricle and saccule are the *semi-circular canals,* three fluid filled canals, each of which is a half-circle. Because the canals are oriented in each of the major planes of the body (frontal, saggital, horizontal), these structures are in a position to sense particular directions of movement, as well as rotation. As one might imagine, these structures are probably important in balance, as well as in responses for which the individual requires information about forces and accelerations applied to the head (e.g., flying a plane, doing a somersault, etc.).

Joint Receptors

The joints of the various limbs are surrounded by a sheath called a *joint capsule,* which is primarily responsible for holding the lubricating fluid for the joint. Embedded within the joint capsules are different kinds of receptor cells (Ruffini endings, Pacininan corpuscles) known as the joint receptors.

---

[2]We can think of the bat, flying in a dark cave, as using audition from its radar-like sounds as exproprioceptive feedback for orienting itself in the cave.

They are located primarily on the parts of the joint capsule that are stretched most when the joint is moved, which originally led investigators to believe that these receptors were involved in the perception of position of the joint. By studying the cat hindlimb, Skoglund (1956) found individual receptors that fired at very specific locations in the range of limb movement. For example, a given receptor cell would fire only when the joint was in a particular range; (e.g., from 150° to 180° of joint angle); another cell would fire at a different set of joint angles; and so on. Such findings appeared to say that the role of the joint receptor is very great in signaling the positions of the limbs, as the central nervous system could "know" where the limbs are by detecting which of the joint receptors were active.

The conclusions have been seriously challenged, however (see Kelso & Stelmach, 1976, for a review). A number of investigators (e.g., Burgess & Clark, 1969) have found that only a small proportion of the joint receptors fire at specific angles; rather, most of the joint receptors tend to fire near the extremes of the movement in a joint. Further, others have found that the nature of the firing pattern is dependent on whether the movement is active or passive (Boyd & Roberts, 1953) and is dependent on the direction of motion of the joint (see Smith, 1977). The fact that the firing pattern of the joint receptors is dependent on factors other than the simple position of the limb has dimmed the enthusiasm for the hypothesis that the joint receptors are the means by which the system determines joint positions. It does seem clear that the joint receptors can provide some information about joint position, but their role in the perception of joint position is not as strong as was once believed.

Golgi Tendon Organs

Yet another receptor for the generation of movement information is the Golgi tendon organ. These structures are tiny stretch receptors located in the muscles near the musculo-tendinous junction, where the muscle "blends into" the tendon (see Figure 6-7). They seem to be ideally located to provide information about tension in the muscles, because they lie in series with (i.e., between) the force-producing contractile elements in the muscle and the tendon that attaches the muscle to the bone.

Early thinking about the role of the Golgi tendon organ was based on its neurological connections. The tendon organ is connected to the central nervous system via the Ib afferent (sensory) fibers.[3] The Golgi tendon organ has been shown to produce inhibition of the muscle in which it is located, so that a stretch to the active muscle would cause the same muscle to decrease its tension somewhat. Also, the finding that it appeared to require a very large stretch of the muscle (near physiological limits) to induce the Golgi tendon to fire led to speculation that the sensor was primarily a protective device that would prevent the muscle from contracting so forcefully that it would rupture a tendon.

---

[3]The label "Ib" provides two pieces of information; the "I" refers to the size of the sensory (afferent) fiber (Type I fibers are large), and the "b" refers to the fact that the fibers originate at the Golgi tendon organ.

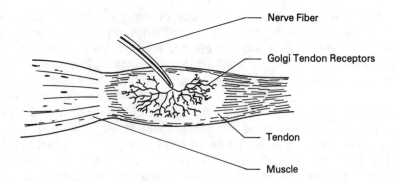

Nerve Fiber

Golgi Tendon Receptors

Tendon

Muscle

Figure 6-7. Anatomy of the Golgi tendon organ (adapted from Sage, 1977).

Recent data, largely from the work of Houk and Henneman (1967) and Stuart (e.g., Stuart, Mosher, Gerlach, & Reinking, 1972) have provided a very different picture of functioning of the Golgi tendon organ. First, new anatomical evidence revealed that each organ was connected to only a small group of from 3 to 25 muscle fibers, not to the entire muscle as had been suspected. Thus, the various receptors were sensing forces produced in different parts of the muscle. Moreover, there were only a few (up to 15) different motor units[4] represented in the muscle fibers attached to a single tendon organ, so that the tendon organ now appeared to be in a very good position to sense the tensions produced in a limited number of individual motor units, not in the whole muscle. Also, contrary to the earlier beliefs, this recent work has shown that the tendon organs are sensitive to forces produced in the motor units connected to them, responding with forces of less than .1 g (Houk & Henneman, 1967). Such evidence has nearly reversed the beliefs about functioning of the tendon organ, the current notion being that they are very sensitive detectors for tension in localized portions of a particular muscle.

It would seem that the Golgi tendon organ can serve a number of separate functions in movement perception. First, it has the well-known protective function discussed earlier. But more importantly, it probably has a role in the perception of tension in the contracting muscle, as it is uniquely located to provide such information when muscles are producing force. Furthermore, there must be some functional significance to the fact that the receptors are located with such strong association with particular motor units. Some writers have suggested that the individual tendon organs are responsible for providing very detailed information about the individual contributions to the overall muscle force provided by the different motor units activated. So, the view about the function of Golgi tendon organs has shifted

---

[4]A motor unit is defined as an alpha motoneuron and all of the muscle fibers that it innervates. In man, the number of fibers supplied by one alpha motoneuron might vary from a few (in muscles requiring fine control—in the hand, larynx, eyes) up to several thousand (in muscles requiring only gross control—in the trunk muscles). There could be from a few to several hundred motor units in any one muscle.

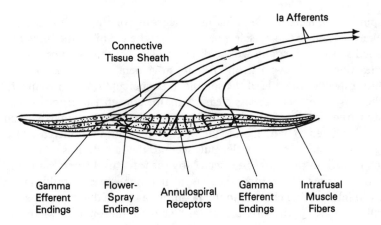

Figure 6-8. Anatomy of the muscle spindle (adapted from Sage, 1977).

from the view that they are relatively insensitive protective devices to the view that they are very sensitive detectors of what is going on in the various motor units that make up an overall muscle contraction (Stuart et al., 1972).

Muscle Spindles

Between the fibers of the main muscles of the body are small spindle-shaped (cigar-shaped) structures that are connected in parallel with the muscles. This orientation places them in a position such that they are stretched when the main muscle is stretched. The spindle is made up of two major parts. At the polar ends (see Figure 6-8) are very small muscle fibers called *intrafusal fibers* that are innervated by *gamma motoneurons.* These intrafusal fibers cannot contribute significantly to the tension in the overall muscle. Rather, they provide a tension on the central region of the spindle, called the *equatorial region.* A number of different kinds of sensory receptors are located here, all of which are sensitive to deformation of the equatorial region when the spindle is stretched. One of the major neurological connections to this sensory region is the *Ia afferent fiber,* whose output is related to the amount of deformation of the equatorial region, as well as to the rate of change in deformation of this region. Therefore, the Ia afferent seems to convey information about the length and the rate of change in length (velocity) of the muscle in which it is embedded.[5]

There has been a great deal of controversy about what the spindle actually signals to the central nervous system. Not under dispute is the fact that

_____

[5]Some help with the terminology: The greek letter gamma refers to the spindle system, thus the term gamma system. The term "Ia" refers to the fact that the sensory (afferent) fiber emerging from the spindle is a large Type I afferent, and the "a" refers to the fact that this fiber comes from the spindle (remember that Ib fibers come from the Golgi tendon organs). The root -fusal means fusiform or spindle-shaped; so intrafusal fibers are muscle fibers within the spindle, and the extrafusal fibers are those outside the spindle—i.e., the fibers of the muscle in which the spindle is embedded.

the spindle connects to the alpha motoneurons for the same muscle, providing excitation to the muscle when it is stretched. This is the basis for the so-called stretch reflex and will be discussed later in this chapter. Thus, the spindle appears to have a strong role in movement regulation.

With respect to the role of the spindle in the perception of movement, the conclusions have been far less clear. A major conceptual problem was the fact that the output of the Ia afferent that presumably signals stretch or velocity is related to two separate factors. First, Ia output is increased by the elongation of the overall muscle. But, second, the Ia output is related to the stretch placed on the equatorial region by the intrafusal fibers via the gamma motoneurons. Therefore, the central nervous system would have difficulty in interpreting changes in the Ia output as being due to changes in the overall muscle length with a constant gamma motoneuron activity, to changes in gamma motoneuron activity with a constant muscle length, or perhaps to both. Another problem was that there was no strong evidence that the Ia afferent fibers actually sent information to the sensory cortex of the brain, where other sensory events were thought to be registered. This was reinforced by Gelfan's and Carter's (1967) research on humans undergoing operations involving wrist-tendon repair under local anesthetic only. When the muscles were passively stretched and the subjects were asked what they felt when the tendon was pulled, subjects usually reported no sensations or sensations that were inconsistent with the direction of tendon pull. Primarily, for these reasons, researchers believed that the muscle spindles were not important for the conscious perception of movement or position.

Recent data from Goodwin, McCloskey, and Matthews (1972) and others have helped to change this point of view. In these studies, subjects had a rapid vibration applied to the biceps tendon at the elbow. The blindfolded subject was asked to "track" the passive movements of the vibrated arm with corresponding movements of the other arm; thus, the subject had to perceive where the right arm was and match that (felt) position with movements in the left arm. The vibration of the tendon is known to produce small, rapid alternating stretch and release of the tendon, which affects the muscle spindle and distorts the output of the Ia afferents from the spindles located in the vibrated muscle.

Goodwin et al. found as much as 40° misalignment of the vibrated arm with the unvibrated arm. The interpretation was that the vibration distorted the Ia information coming from the same muscle and that this distortion led to a misperception of that limb's position, and hence to improper decisions about the positioning of the opposite limb. The argument, then, is that this information from the Ia actually did reach consciousness and that the Ia was the basis for knowing the limb's position. (To control for the possibility that the vibration merely influenced the structures in the joint capsule, the authors placed the vibrator over the triceps tendon; the misalignment occurred in the opposite direction, much as would be expected if the perception of the Ia output from the triceps muscle were being disrupted.) Such evidence points strongly to the idea that the muscle spindle is related to the perception of limb position and velocity—quite a different view than that held earlier. There is still some question as to whether or not the spindle is sufficiently sensitive to detect small positional changes, and thus it may be only one of a number of sources for detecting position (see Kelso & Stelmach, 1976).

Cutaneous Receptors

A final group of receptors related to movement perception is located in various places in the skin. Although such receptors can signal a wide variety of separate states of the body, such as pain, pressure, heat, cold, or chemical stimuli, I will be primarily concerned with those receptors that seem to signal information about touch, and, to some extent, deep pressure. As well, pain sensations are certainly important for certain kinds of movement behaviors.

Essentially two main kinds of cutaneous receptors can be found. One of these, called the Pacinian corpuscle, is located deep in the skin and is stimulated by deep deformation as would be produced by a blow or heavy pressure. When it is deformed, the Pacinian corpuscle tends to fire more rapidly, sending sensory information to the central nervous system.

Other kinds of receptors in the skin can be identified as well, such as the Meissner corpuscles, Merkel's discs, and "free nerve endings." The latter provide especially strong signals when hairs on the body are deformed by light touch, as they are located close to the hair follicles. On less hairy portions of the body, such as lips and palms of the hands, there is a particularly strong concentration of Meissner corpuscles and Merkel's discs, which are sensitive to slight deformations of the skin in these areas.

Input to the Central Nervous System

The major pathways for transmitting signals from the periphery to the brain are the spinal tracts, located alongside the vertebra that make up the spinal column. There are 8 cervical, 12 thoracic, 5 lumbar, and 5 sacral vertebrae, defining a number of segments of the spinal cord. Except for the input from the structures in the head and neck (for our purposes here, mainly from the eyes, ears, and vestibular apparatus, entering through one or more of the 12 cranial nerves), the input to the central nervous system is through bundles, called "roots," that collect and guide the input to the spinal cord at each segment. Each segment serves a particular region of the body.

A diagram of a typical segment of the spinal cord is shown in Figure 6-9, where a "slice" of the cord is viewed from the back (dorsal side). Input from the various receptors comes together in the periphery into *spinal nerves,* collections of individual neurons (both sensory, or afferent, and motor, or efferent) which carry information toward and away from the spinal cord. Near the cord, these nerves branch into two roots, called the *dorsal* (posterior, or back) and *ventral* (anterior or front) roots, where they contact the spinal cord separately. There is almost complete division at this point of the neurons into afferent or sensory, which enter via the dorsal roots, and efferent or motor, which leave the cord via the ventral roots. Once inside the cord, the afferent neurons can either *synapse* (connect) with other neurons whose cell bodies are in the central gray matter (in the shape

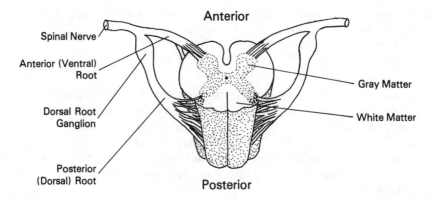

Figure 6-9. A spinal cord segment (adapted from Sage, 1977).

of an H), or they can travel to higher or lower levels in the cord or to the brain in one of the many tracts that form the white matter adjacent to the gray matter.

Kinesthesis and Proprioception

All of the above receptors and others that have not been mentioned contribute to a person's awareness of his or her body and its movements, which has been termed *kinesthesis*. Historically, kinesthesis, stemming from the roots kin- (motion) and -esthesia (sensation), was a term limited to a person's perception of his or her own motion, both of the limbs with respect to one another, and also of the body as a whole. Sherrington's (1906) term *proprioception* was originally used to mean the perception of movement of the body plus its orientation in space (even though it may not be moving). Over the years these two terms have become practically synonymous, and it is probably not important to continue this distinction. Also, as already mentioned, many of the classically defined exteroceptors (e.g., the eyes) can serve the function of proprioceptors and can lead to kinesthesis (Gibson, 1966; D. Lee, 1980; see Footnote 1).

Ensemble Characteristics

Kinesthesis enables us to tell with remarkable accuracy where our limbs are and how they are acting, but how do the various receptors mentioned in the previous sections contribute to our kinesthetic capabilities? An important concept is that any one of the receptors in isolation from the others is generally ineffective in signaling information about the movements of the body. This is because the various receptors are often sensitive to a variety of aspects of body motion at the same time. For example, the Golgi tendon organs probably cannot signal information about movement, because they cannot differentiate between the forces produced in a static contraction and the same forces produced when the limb is moving, with the muscle either lengthening ("yielding") or shortening during the movement. The spindle is sensitive to muscle length, but it is also sensitive to the rate of change in length (velocity) and to the activity in the intrafusal fibers that are known to be active during contractions; so the spindle confounds information about position of the limb and the level of contraction of the muscles (force). And the joint receptors are sensitive to joint position, but their output can be affected by the tensions applied and by the direction of movement, or whether the movement is active or passive (Paillard & Bruchon, 1968).

As a solution to this problem, many have suggested that the central nervous system combines and integrates information from the tendon organ, muscle spindle, joint receptors, and cutaneous receptors in some way to resolve the kind of ambiguity in the signals produced by any one of these receptors (e.g., Wetzel & Stuart, 1976). Producing an *ensemble* of information (*ensemble* in French means together, or the whole effect) by combining the various separate sources could enable the generation of less ambiguous information about movement.

As an oversimplified example of how this might work, consider the inputs signaled by the spindle and the tendon organ. I argued earlier that the spindle produces a signal that can be thought of as length + tension, whereas the tendon organ contributes a quantity that can be thought of simply as tension. If the central nervous system were to use both of these sources of information as an ensemble and, with a kind of "subtraction," compute the difference between the spindle's signal and the tendon organ's signal, the resulting difference could be thought of as:

Spindle − Tendon Organ = (length + tension) − (tension) = length.

Thus, muscle length, and hence limb position, could be determined by considering the ensemble from two other sources, neither of which indicates muscle length directly.

This hypothesis about the perception of muscle length is probably far too simple, and there is little direct evidence that the central nervous system integrates information in this way. Nevertheless, some kind of integration is assumed, and this simple example is meant to illustrate one of the ways that such a combination of inputs could occur. Furthermore, complex combinations of many different signal sources, such as those from the spindles, tendon organs, joint receptors, and cutaneous receptors, as well as from the eyes, ears, and vestibular apparatus, are conceivable. Complex combinations of the inputs could result in very sensitive and unambiguous sensations about our movements and positions in space. How the central nervous system does this and which sources of information are most strongly represented in which situations are important questions for the future.

Many aspects of kinesthesis may be discussed, including (a) tests of kinesthetic sensitivity, (b) issues about whether the kinesthetic sense is unitary or is comprised of an ensemble of smaller senses as discussed above, (c) issues about the role of kinesthesis in movement production and control, and (d) questions about the role of kinesthesis in the learning of skills. All of these questions and issues will be discussed either later in this chapter or in subsequent chapters.

In the next section, I will apply these ideas about feedback and kinesthesis to a simple and fundamental closed-loop model for movement control. In the subsequent sections, the term feedback will be used loosely to mean sensory information from any or all of the various receptors mentioned earlier. The concern will be whether or not, or in what ways, the various feedback sources operating as an ensemble contribute to movement control.

CLOSED-LOOP CONTROL OF MOTOR BEHAVIOR

The closed-loop ideas presented earlier have been considered in human performance in various ways, but one of the more common is to consider the closed-loop system as containing conscious decision making. (Of course, as discussed earlier, this does not rule out the possibility that other embedded closed-loop systems do not involve consciousness.) It is useful to consider the executive level of this system as consisting of the information-processing stages discussed in the previous two chapters. This idea is diagrammed in Figure 6-10. An original command for action, such as an external stimulus or an internal self-generated "go" signal, starts the action by progressing through the stimulus-identification, response-selection, and response-programming stages, eventually leading to the evocation of the movement commands to the muscles. This portion of the closed-loop model is similar to that involved in an open-loop system. The difference becomes apparent, however, when considering the actions subsequent to this first aspect of the response. First, a reference of correctness is generated that will

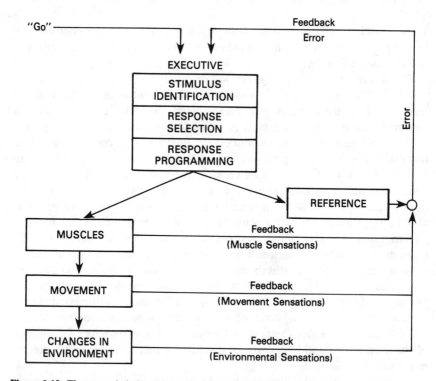

Figure 6-10. The expanded closed-loop model for movement control.

serve as the standard against which the performance (that is, the feedback from it) is judged. This reference of correctness can be thought of as an image (or some other abstract mental representation) of the feedback qualities associated with moving correctly, and it is analogous to the value to which you set your thermostat in the home heating system or the compass heading for the automatic pilot of a ship. Just as the reference represents the state of the feedback if the correct goal is being achieved, so too does the reference for the human closed-loop system represent the state of the feedback associated with the correct movements of the limbs during the intended action. The reference is something to be achieved.

According to this model, during muscle contraction and slightly afterwards, these actions cause movements of the limbs and body, as well as changes in the environment. Each of these kinds of movements generates response-produced feedback. The contracting muscles provide feedback about the lengths and tensions produced; the movement of the body produces sensations from the joints, the inner ear, and vestibular apparatus; and the visual and auditory systems provide additional information about movements. Another source of feedback is from the environment itself, for example, the sounds of balls that are struck or the vision of a ball as it moves away after it has been hit. The idea is that the system can "compute" the expected nature of these sensations in the form of a reference and can compare the feedback it receives on a particular trial with the feedback it expects to receive. If the two sources of feedback are the same, the implication is that the system is correct and that no corrections are necessary. But if a difference exists between the feedback received and the reference—that is, an error signal is present—some correction is required.

Closed-loop models such as the one in Figure 6-10 are thought of in essentially two ways. First, they provide a basis for knowing if a movement produced is correct or not. Imagine a golf swing. After the ball flies away, the sensations the swing produced can be analyzed. A professional golfer probably will be able to tell a great deal about the direction and distance of the golf shot just from the feel and sound of it. I will have more to say about this post-response feedback analysis later when I discuss motor learning; it is a basic idea in a number of learning theories (e.g., Adams, 1971; Schmidt, 1975b).

A second way in which the closed-loop ideas in Figure 6-10 are used concerns the control of ongoing movements. These kinds of models have obvious relevance to responses with very long duration, such as steering a car down a highway. Think of the reference as the set of sensations associated with being in the center of the lane, moving at a particular speed, and maintaining a certain distance behind a car. Each aspect of that response has certain visual and auditory sensations associated with it. If any one of these goals of the response is not met, the feedback received and the reference do not match and an error is fed back to the executive level in order to compute a correction. Thus, these theories view the control of a car on a highway as a series of corrections that keep the vehicle on the road safely, and the basis for these corrections is the reference of correctness.

Control of Long-Duration Movements

The closed-loop model presented in Figure 6-10 has been very effective and useful for certain kinds of responses. From the way the model is described, it seems to have the most relevance for tasks that require a great deal of time, because the processes involved in the analysis of the error information take considerable amounts of time and mental energy. Also, the model seems to have considerable appeal for movements in which something is regulated at some constant value, such as keeping the car at a particular speed by monitoring the speedometer or keeping the airplane on the proper glide path when guiding it onto the airport runway. These movements are called *tracking* responses (Chapter 3), as the performer's major goal is to regulate behavior or to follow some externally imposed track by movements of the limbs that, in turn, control some system such as a car or airplane. These kinds of movements constitute an extremely important class of motor behavior, and they occur in a wide variety of situations. Perhaps for this reason, tracking tasks have been the single class of motor behavior that has received the most study, and much of this work has been directed to problems in vehicle control, gunnery, and the like. A good review of the research on tracking has been provided by Poulton (1974), showing the major issues and the experimental evidence.

There are a wide variety of mathematical and physical models of tracking behavior, and they differ mainly in how the system uses feedback information and how the system initiates a correction when errors are detected. It is beyond the scope of this book to go into these different closed-loop models (again, see Poulton, 1974, for more on this topic). The most important generalization from this research is that if the models are used in computer and/or mechanical *simulations* of the human in which the computer or mechanical device is controlled in ways analogous to those in Figure 6-10, these nonliving devices "come alive" to behave in ways nearly indistinguishable from their human counterparts. By proper adjustment of certain mathematical or electronic elements in the devices (called parameters), the system can be made to show many human characteristics, and they track with essentially the same levels of error. For example, if the human is steering a car down a straight road, approximately 200 msec elapse between the appearance of an error and the initiation of a correction back toward the center of the road. Such lags and the character of the correction can be mimicked very well by computer stimulations using these closed-loop tracking mechanisms. The statistical agreement between the actual and simulated moves is good for this kind of task.

This large body of experimental literature suggests that because the human can be mimicked so well by computers that use closed-loop mechanisms such as shown in Figure 6-10, the human in these situations can be regarded as a closed-loop control system, responding essentially by analyzing the feedback produced against the reference of correctness and issuing corrections. This evidence does not prove that humans actually track this way, but the agreement between theoretical predictions and data is very strong, and alternative theories cannot boast of similar success.

I suggested earlier that such models of movement control should be most effective if the closed-loop system were operating to maintain some constant state of the system, such as the thermostat does. In considering the kinds of motor behavior that correspond most closely to this kind of goal, the first candidate must be the maintenance of posture. A related example might be the control of learned postures, such as a handstand or balancing on the circus high wire. Therefore, the first issues about closed-loop responses in motor behavior are directed toward this general class of responses.

The Control of Posture and Balance

Early thinking about postural control tended to focus on mechanisms that are seemingly obvious contributors to the skills. The first aspects of balance to be considered were the structures in the inner ear, the so-called vestibular apparatus discussed in the previous sections. The receptors are sensitive to deviations from the vertical, to the orientation of the body in space, and to the accelerations applied to the head when the body is moved. All of these aspects of balance possibly could be signaled by these receptors.

A second class of processes for the control of balance were the various receptors associated with the joints and muscles. These processes will be discussed in more detail later in this chapter, but for now consider that the system is organized to maintain given angles (or muscle lengths) for the joints associated with a particular position. When the body begins to lose equilibrium, the movement away from the balanced position can presumably be sensed by the joint receptors, or perhaps by the stretch of the spindles in the muscles that control the movement of the joint. (Remember, moving a joint must stretch one or more of the muscles that span it, providing the spindles with stretch.) Also, there could be tactile sensation from the feet or toes indicating loss of balance. Each of these receptors, alone or in some combination, could conceivably provide the input necessary to sense a loss of balance and could provide a basis for initiating a correction. Nashner and Woollacott (1979) have conducted experiments in which the balance of the subject is unexpectedly disrupted while standing or while walking, and have observed the compensations that are produced as a result of these perturbations. While it is not clear whether these compensations are based on the information-processing stages as seen in Figure 6-10, or whether they are reflexive in nature, it is clear that major receptor mechanisms are the structures in the muscles and joints. I will have more to say about the possible role of reflexive corrections later in this chapter.

A third source of feedback about balance has recently been emphasized by Lee (e.g., D. Lee, 1980, for a review). Gibson (1966) termed this source of feedback *visual proprioception*, an apparent contradiction in terms. I argued in Chapter 4 (see Figure 4-4) that vision has the potential for telling us where our eyes (therefore, our head and body) are in space and how they are moving (if they are) by the analysis of the patterns of optical flow received from the surrounding surfaces and elements in the environment. Could vision be involved in the control of posture? One common finding, as

Figure 6-11. Experimental apparatus and paradigm for the "moving room" (from **Lee &** **Aronson**, 1974); Lee is second from the left.

pointed out by D. Lee (1980) is that blind people are generally less stable in posture than are sighted people, with the former showing more swaying to and fro as they stand. An associated finding is that sighted people sway more when they have their eyes closed, and sighted people with their eyes closed resemble blind people in relation to the amount of sway. All this suggests that vision may have a role in balance.

But more convincing evidence for this assertion comes from some of Lee's experiments (Lee & Aronson, 1974). He has used a "moving room" apparatus, whereby a person stands on a stationary floor in a three-sided "room" with walls that can be moved backward and forward as a unit without moving the floor. The effect of this wall movement on the posture and sway of the subject is studied. The general arrangement is shown in Figure 6-11. Using small children as subjects, moving the wall a few centimeters toward the subject causes loss of balance, resulting in a rather ungraceful sitting response and great surprise on the part of the child. Moving the walls away from the subject causes a drastic forward lean, which results in a fall or a stumble. When adult subjects are used, the effect is less drastic, but increases in sway, in phase with the direction of the wall movement, can be seen.

How can these effects be explained? Remember, the floor of the room was fixed, so that the movements of the walls could not have exerted mechanical influences on the position of the subjects. The mechanisms associated with the joint angles and muscle lengths, as well as the vestibular apparatus, were not directly affected. The most reasonable explanation is that moving the wall toward the child changed the optical array. If the child was using the form of the optical array as a source of feedback that signaled posture and balance, the child could have interpreted the changed visual array as a loss of balance and produced a compensation in the opposite direction as a result. The walls appearing closer to the eye would, if the room were "normal," mean that the person was falling forward, and a compensation to move backward would be expected. This is just what Lee found: moving the wall toward the subjects caused them to fall backward. This kind of explanation holds that vision is operating like a proprioceptor, providing information about the body's position, hence the term *visual proprioception*.

It is not clear which of these various mechanisms for balance are most important, although it would appear that the visual sense tended to dominate the vestibular and muscle-joint senses in Lee's experiments. But in other circumstances, the reverse could be true. The main point is that all of these mechanisms operate in a closed-loop fashion to control posture. The system senses the feedback, detects errors, and issues corrections in order to maintain the body's position in space.

Changing the Reference of Correctness

The ideas about the maintenance of a given state of the system can be extended somewhat to include tracking tasks in which the desired state changes from time to time. As with steering a car, for example, if there is a turn in the road, such a turn will cause an error in the closed-loop system because traveling in a straight line will cause the car to go off the road. These errors are detected, and corrections are sent to the hand and arm musculature to move the car back into the center of the road. In this way, the closed-loop system explains how the driver is capable of staying on the road during mountain driving or on a race course.

I can extend this idea somewhat (as Adams, 1971, 1976, 1977, has done) to account for how the individual makes a limb movement such as would be involved in sawing a board or in reaching for a mug of beer. Here, the reference of correctness is not a single state as in the earlier examples, but rather a set of states that is changing at each moment in time. For example, the reference of correctness could be set for this position at time t_0, at another position at time t_1, at yet another position at time t_2, and so on. Thus, at each moment in time the reference of correctness would have a different specification for position of the limb. Because the reference is constantly changing, it can then be matched against the feedback from the moving limb which is also changing as the movement progresses, so that errors in the movement's *trajectory* can be detected and corrected. One possible example could be in the production of a reaching movement, in which the pathway of the hand and arm is monitored continuously and consciously (as in Figure 6-10), and corrections for deviations from the correct location are made through the information-processing stages while the movement is in progress. This kind of mechanism is the basis for Adams' (1971) theory of learning, whereby the subject learns the set of references of correctness (he calls this the "perceptual trace") that the closed-loop system is to "track" during the response. I will have more to say about Adams' ideas later in the book when I discuss learning theory (Chapter 14).

But these kinds of models have serious limitations. Engineers can design robots and other machines to behave in this way, using what they call *point-to-point computation* methods. The position of the limb at each point in space and at each time in the movement is represented by a reference of correctness, and the system can be made to track this set of positions across time to produce an action with a particular form. But the system must be very "smart," and it must process information very rapidly, even for the simplest of movements. All of these references of correctness must be stored somewhere, and each of the points will be different if the movement begins from a slightly different place or if it is to take a slightly different pathway through space.

Engineers have generally found that these methods are very inefficient for machine (robot) control, which has led many motor behavior researchers (see Kelso, Holt, Kugler, & Turvey, 1980; Kugler, Kelso, & Turvey, 1980) away from these kinds of control processes to explain human skills. But there is still the possibility that the system might operate in this way at certain times or for certain skills which demand very high precision (e.g., threading a needle). Also, such a mechanism might serve as the basis for recognizing errors at various places in the movement as it is carried out, without actually being the basis for making a correction. The performer could say, after a tennis stroke, that the elbow was bent too much on the backswing, and thus have a basis for making a correction in the movement on the next trial. Considerable debate about these issues can be found at the present time (e.g., Adams, 1971, 1976, 1977; Kelso et al., 1980; Schmidt, 1976a, 1980). Finally, the possibility exists that the system might make use of reflexive mechanisms (without using the information-processing stages) to hold itself on the proper track; these possibilities are discussed in the next section of this chapter.

A compromise position is that only certain positions in the movement are represented by references of correctness. One viewpoint is that feedback from the movement when it is at its endpoint is checked against a reference of correctness and that subsequent corrections are initiated to move the limb to the proper position. These views of motor control hold that the limb is more or less "thrown" in the direction of the endpoint by some kind of open-loop control and that then the limb "homes in on" the target by closed-loop control. Here, the actual trajectory of the limb is determined by how the limb is "thrown," in combination with mechanical factors such as gravity and friction. In this view, the trajectory is not determined by point-to-point computation as a purely closed-loop system might explain it.

Purely closed-loop models of movement control, such as that shown in Figure 6-10, appear to have a great deal of experimental support and logical appeal. But this kind of support is limited to movements such as tracking behavior, or movements in which the limb is moving very slowly through space, perhaps to a very carefully defined target. As shown in the next section, these models have difficulty in explaining how very rapid movements are controlled.

Control of Rapid Actions

One of the most important points to have emerged from the evidence presented in Chapters 4 and 5 was that the information-processing mechanisms, which lie at the very heart of the closed-loop system shown in Figure 6-10, require a great deal of *time and attention* for stimuli to be processed to yield a response. So far I have assumed that each error signal that the system receives must be processed in these stages and that the response (a correction) can follow only after all of the stages of processing have been completed. Thus, a correction is seen in the same way as any other response to a stimulus. It requires a great deal of time and attention.

But there is a problem. In the closed-loop models such as in Figure 6-10, with rapid actions sufficient time is not available for the system to (a) generate an error, (b) detect the error, (c) determine the correction, (d) initiate the correction, and (e) correct the movement before a rapid movement is completed. Muhammad Ali's left jab is a good example. The movement itself is about 40 msec; yet, according to our estimates, detecting an aiming error and correcting it during the same response should require about 150 to 200 msec—the time necessary to complete the activities of the stages of information processing. The movement is finished before the correction can begin. Other movements, such as the batswing in hitting a baseball, require about 100 msec (Hubbard & Seng, 1954), again leaving insufficient time for any corrections before the movement is completed. For this reason, the closed-loop models of movement behavior do not seem to be well suited for explaining rapid responses.

Another problem is that the time between two responses that are not grouped (see Figure 5-6) was found to be essentially 190 msec. Therefore, the time between any two successive corrections (because corrections are responses) should be similarly separated. This information has serious consequences for models of human limb control that demand a large number of attention-based corrections in a very short period of time. Point-to-point computation models have this basic problem when human performance is considered.

These and other limitations to the closed-loop models will be raised again in Chapter 7. For now, suffice it to say that the closed-loop mechanisms involving the stages of processing (Figure 6-10) appear to have a very difficult time explaining rapid movements. Because these models have a great deal of credibility with respect to very slow movements and/or posture and have little with respect to rapid movements, it is possible that there are essentially two fundamentally different kinds of movements: fast and slow. I will return to this distinction later in Chapter 7.

So far, I have intentionally ignored the possibility of closed-loop processes in movement that do not involve the stages of information processing. That is, I have ignored the possibility that feedback could be operating reflexively—i.e., without attention (and without the information processing stages). In the next sections, this vital aspect of movement control is considered.

REFLEXIVE CLOSED-LOOP CONTROL

In the previous section on the closed-loop control of movement, I dealt only with the kind of closed-loop model in which the determination of the correction was produced by the conscious information-processing mechanisms (see Figure 6-10). What about the possibility that the central nervous system contains closed-loop mechanisms that do not require any attention? Many examples are possible, such as the control of body temperature and the regulation of breathing during sleep. In this section I will present evidence that these nonconscious mechanisms are involved in the control of limb movements as well.

Latencies of Corrections

An experiment by Dewhurst (1967) is representative of a number of studies on this problem. The subject was asked to hold the elbow at a right angle to support a light weight attached to the hand. The subject could monitor the performance in this simple task through vision of a dot on an oscilloscope screen that provided information about the angle of the elbow. The experimenter recorded the position of the arm together with the rectified electromyographical (EMG) activity in the biceps muscle as the subject performed. Unexpectedly, the weight attached to the hand was increased, and, naturally, the hand began to move downward. After a brief period, the subject increased the EMG activity to the biceps muscle, which increased its force output and brought the limb back to the right-angle position.

Given that the lowered arm represents an error in performance that can be corrected, how much time must elapse before the increase in the EMG in the elbow flexors? If the subject must process the visual and/or kinesthetic feedback from the arm through the information-processing stages, there should be no increase in biceps EMG for approximately 150 to 200 msec.

Figure 6-12 shows the essential results. The weight was added at the point in time indicated by the arrow, and the limb began to move down immediately. The records show a small burst of EMG about 30 msec after the weight was added, and a larger irregular burst beginning about 50 msec afterward. Just after this second burst of EMG, the limb began to move back to the target position. This change in EMG represents a clear correction for the added weight, yet this correction was initiated far more quickly than can be explained by an attentionally based closed-loop process such as is shown in Figure 6-10. Because these corrections appeared to be initiated so rapidly, motor control researchers believe they cannot be based on the information-processing mechanisms shown in Figure 6-10. Rather, they are thought to be due to the operation of reflexes in lower, probably spinal, levels in the central nervous system.

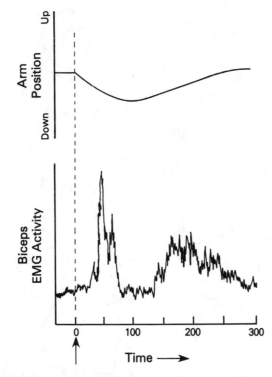

Time ⟶

Figure 6-12. Movement and rectified EMG record showing the latencies of two reflex-based corrections (from Dewhurst, 1967).

Attention Demands of Reflexive Corrections

Another aspect of reflexive corrections for errors, aside from their apparent rapidity, is that they might not require attention, as other corrections seem to. Evidence for this notion was provided in a little-known study by Henry (1953), in which subjects had to regulate the force they applied to a handle. The basic arrangement is shown in Figure 6-13. The standing subject (blindfolded in the actual experiment) is pushing against a handle attached to a mechanical device that could continuously alter the position of the handle. The arrangement was such that if the subject was not pressing against the handle, the handle would move forward and backward unpredictably. But there was a spring placed between the machine and the handle so that, by modulating the force produced at each moment, the subject could manage to hold the handle in a constant position.

Henry used three conditions. In a Constant Pressure Test, the subject's task was to keep the pressure against the handle fixed by varying the position of the handle. When the handle pushed against the subject, the correct response was to "ease up," so that the tension was held constant. In the second condition, the Constant Position Test, the subject was to compensate for the changing pressures exerted by the handle so that a constant position of the handle was maintained, but with constantly changing pressure exerted. A third condition assessed the conscious perception of pressure change; the subject attempted to hold the arm immobile, reporting through

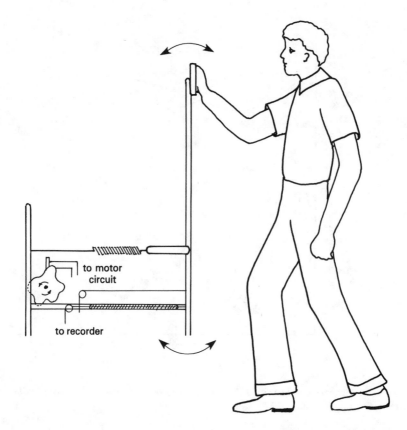

Figure 6-13. Apparatus and general arrangement in Henry's experiment (from Henry, 1953).

a left-finger movement when a change in the pressure exerted by the apparatus was sensed. The pressure changes were different for different segments in the testing period, and Henry could obtain an estimate of the amount of change required for conscious perception of change.

Henry's major findings are shown in Table 6-1, showing the average

Table 6-1

**The size of a change in the system response required
for subject response in the various conditions
in the Henry (1953) experiment**

Condition	Amount of Force Change Required for Response (dynes)
Conscious perception	.559
Constant pressure	.296
Constant position	.029

Note: One dyne is the force required to accelerate one gram at one centimeter/sec/sec.

values for the pressure change that was required for a response in the three different conditions. When the subject was to report when a change was felt, a change of .559 dynes was required for a response. But when the subject was to hold pressure constant, the size of a change required for a response was only .296 dynes. Even more striking was the finding that in the Constant Position Test the subject could respond to changes that were only .029 dynes. That is, the subjects were capable of responding to changes in force that were only 1/20 (i.e., .029/.559) of the change required for conscious awareness. Henry's data say that subjects in the Constant Position Test were responding to changes in the apparatus of which they were not aware! The adjustments were made unconsciously and seemingly without attention being required.[6]

Reflex-Based Corrections

These studies show two important things about movement control. First, experiments like Dewhurst's (1967) show that corrections for suddenly presented changes in position can be initiated far more rapidly than the earlier 200-msec estimates, with correction latencies being from 30 to 80 msec in the various investigations that have been done. This kind of result suggests that the information-processing stages are not involved in these corrections, as the stages require too much time for processing. Second, the data from Henry (1953) suggest that subjects can make adjustments for changes in position, and perhaps for changes in tension, that are so small that the subject cannot perceive them. Again, these data cannot be explained by theories that use the stages of information processing as a basis for determining a correction, because the response-selection and response-programming stages are throught to require attention and consciousness. Both of these results suggest that these kinds of corrections are being produced by reflexive mechanisms that do not require the stages of information processing or attention.

Muscle Spindles and the Gamma Loop

The mechanisms responsible for the effects just described probably involve the muscle spindle, the small fusiform (cigar-shaped) structure located between and in parallel to the main fibers of the skeletal muscles; review Figure 6-8 and the associated text. The (oversimplified) neurological connections of the spindle to the spinal cord are diagrammed in Figure 6-14. Recall from Figure 6-8 that the small intrafusal muscle fibers are innervated

---

[6]Caution is warranted in interpreting the result in this way. The estimate of the size of a pressure change required for awareness is based on the subjects' willingness to report that something was felt. Such techniques can be tricky, as results depend on the kind of instructions given, the nature of the experimental setting, and many other factors. Certainly the subjects' responses would be different if the experimenter had said "You felt that, didn't you?" rather than "You didn't feel anything, did you?"

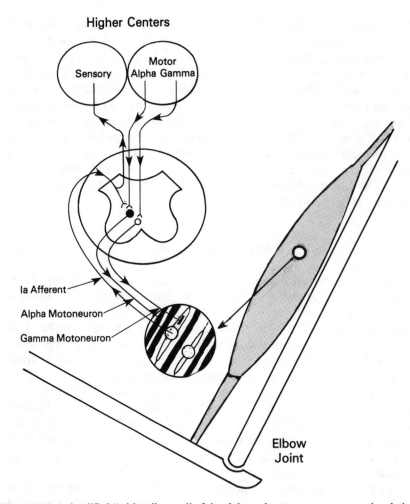

Figure 6-14. A simplified "wiring diagram" of the alpha and gamma motor systems in relation to the spinal cord and higher centers.

by efferent neurons (gamma motoneurons) which emerge from the ventral (front) side of the cord. When activated by the central nervous system, they cause the intrafusal fibers to contract somewhat, which distends the central sensory region of the spindle. When so distended, the Ia afferent fibers emerging from this area fire more rapidly, and this information is delivered to the dorsal side of the spinal cord through the dorsal roots (see Figure 6-9). Notice that the information from the Ia afferent is sent to essentially two places: the alpha motoneurons in the same (homonymous) muscle and upward to various sensory regions in the brain. Finally, notice that the alpha motoneurons are innervated by two separate sources of information. There is innervation from higher motor centers in the brain (the motor cortex, primarily), as well as innervation by the Ia afferent from the spindle. Although I have shown only one such circuit here, many of them operate together in the cord.

As mentioned earlier, when the overall muscle is stretched, the spindle stretches along with it, and the sensory region of the spindle causes the Ia afferent to fire more rapidly, delivering information about stretch to the central nervous system. However, the Ia afferent feeds back on the alpha motoneuron, in that when the Ia afferent is firing more because of a stretch it tends to increase the firing rate of the alpha motoneurons, which causes the same muscle that was stretched to increase its force output and oppose the effect of the stretch.

This process is the basis of what has been called the *monosynaptic stretch reflex,* experienced when the patellar tendon is struck lightly just below the kneecap when the knee is flexed. The "knee-jerk reflex" is caused by the rapid stretch of the muscle, which stretches the spindle, which increases the firing of the Ia afferent transmitted to the cord where it increases the alpha motoneuron firing rate, which causes the muscle to contract. This is called an *autogenetic reflex,* because it causes an action in the same muscle that was stimulated. The loop time, or the time from the initial stretch until the extrafusal fibers are increased in their innervation, is about 30 msec in man. Because this 30-msec value corresponds with the latency for the first burst of EMG shown in the Dewhurst (1967) experiment (Figure 6-12), this monosynaptic mechanism is probably responsible for this first compensation for the added weight.

Notice that the activity in the Ia afferent is determined by two things: the length of and rate of stretch of the extrafusal muscle fibers and the amount of tension in the intrafusal fibers, which is determined by the firing of the gamma efferent fibers (see Figure 6-14). Both alpha and gamma motoneurons can be controlled by higher motor centers, and they are thought to be "coordinated" in their action by a process termed *alpha-gamma coactivation.* Notice that the output to the main body of the muscle (through the alpha motoneuron) is determined by the level of innervation provided directly from the higher center and the amount of added innervation provided indirectly from the Ia afferent.

This information may explain how Dewhurst's (1967) subjects responded so quickly to the added weight. When the subject was holding the weight steadily, a coordinated pattern of innervation to the alpha motoneuron and to the gamma motoneuron produced (via the direct and the indirect routes) just enough tension in the muscle to hold the elbow at a right angle. Now, when the weight was added, the muscle was stretched; the spindles' sensory receptors were distended; and the additional Ia afferents firing caused a stretch reflex that tended to increase the activity in the main muscle, all within 30 msec. All of this activity occurs at the same level of the spinal cord as did the innervation of the muscles in the first place, and no higher centers were involved in this 30-msec loop. This helps explain why Henry's (1953) subjects were able to make corrections for position that they could not even perceive; some of the corrections for changes in position occur in the spinal cord, without the involvement of the information-processing stages.

Control of Posture

These monosynaptic reflexes have been known for many years, but their function in human motion is still under dispute. An early view was that the spindles were responsible for the control of muscle length in posture. They are particularly well suited to this role, because when the animal sways the muscles supporting the skeleton are stretched and reflex compensations occur quickly without requiring the animal's attention. Such mechanisms are probably responsible for horses' ability to sleep standing up and for the well-known headjerk reflex when we fall asleep and our head is jerked upright by the responsible musculature. This effect, which tends to wake us up because of the violent jerk on the head, has saved my life a number of times when I have fallen asleep while driving on a long automobile trip.

Control of Muscle Stiffness

The spindle is not the only mechanism involved in posture; I have already discussed the roles of vision and the vestibular apparatus. But the spindle seems to be related to the control of muscle stiffness, which is probably very important in the control of posture and other movements. Stiffness, which is one of the measures used to describe the characteristics of elastic materials, is defined in terms of the amount of tension increase required to increase the length of the object by a certain amount. Engineers define stiffness more precisely as the change in tension divided by the resulting change in length. A very stiff spring requires a great deal of tension to increase its length, while a less stiff spring requires much less tension. This is important because the muscle seems to provide a compliant (springy) interface between the performer and the environment.

While maintaining posture, it may be that the muscles supporting the skeleton are contracting under the influence of the gamma loop just described. This is conceptualized in Figure 6-15, where a bone is being sup-

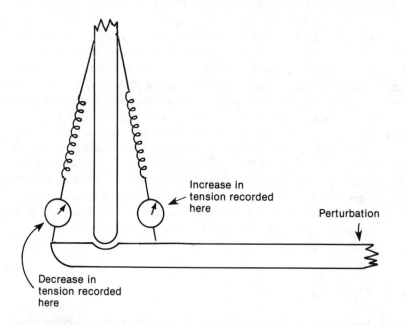

Increase in
tension recorded
here

Perturbation

Decrease in
tension recorded
here

Figure 6-15. Muscle-spring model with gauges for measuring tension in the "tendons" as a perturbation is applied.

ported by two opposing muscles that are producing force. As the system is perturbed, causing the bone to fall, the muscle on the right side of the diagram is lengthened slightly, causing two reactions. First, it causes the stretch reflex mentioned in this section. Second, and perhaps even more important, because the contracting muscle is a "springy" substance, as its length increases, more tension is produced in it by purely mechanical means. Furthermore, this change in tension is nearly instantaneous, just as the change in tension in a spring would be if it were stretched. Such increases in tension have the effect of opposing the perturbation, bringing the system back to the original position. Nichols and Houk (1976) have provided evidence that the muscle spindle is responsible for the maintenance of muscle stiffness when the muscle is stretched, so that it can continue to act as a spring in the control of posture and similar responses (see also Houk, 1979).

Reflexive Control during Movement

This kind of reflexive adjustment is applicable to situations other than those in which the limbs are being held in a static position. Numerous investigations have shown that these processes seem to keep an ongoing movement on course. For example, Marsden, Merton, and Morton (1972) had subjects move the last joint of the thumb back and forth in time to a metronome. At an unpredictable time, the movement of the thumb was resisted. The result was an additional burst of EMG within 30 msec of the perturbation. It is impressive that this occurred at any location or time in the thumb's cycle that the perturbation was applied. Similar findings have been shown in the breathing cycle by Sears and Newsome-Davis (1968), when the resistance to air flow was suddenly changed at various places in the cycle. Here, there was an increased EMG in the intercostal muscles (which control the rib cage volume), with a latency of 30 msec, regardless of where or when the resistance to air flow was changed. Also, Nashner and Wollacott (1979) have shown similar findings when the ankle joint is unexpectedly altered during normal walking.

To me (Schmidt, 1976a) and others, these findings mean that there is a reference of correctness that "moves with" the overall movement, so that at any time in the movement the limb's desired location is specified. Thus the muscle spindles can presumably detect if the limb is in a position different from that specified, and they can induce reflex-based corrections if it is not. Neurologically, these processes are probably handled by the phenomenon called *alpha-gamma coactivation,* whereby the gamma efferent activity to the intrafusal fibers of the spindle are "coordinated with" the alpha efferent activity that drives the main muscle. Since the gamma motoneurons constantly maintain the "tone" on the sensory region of the spindle as the overall muscle shortens, the spindle continuously "seeks" a new muscle length at each moment in the movement, with deviations from this length being corrected by the gamma loop. I will return to this topic in Chapter 8.

Long-Loop Reflexes

From Dewhurst's (1967) example, the monosynaptic reflex loop with a latency of about 30 msec can be seen, as well as another kind of activity that is responsible for the more sustained burst of activity occurring about 50 msec after the weight was added (review Figure 6-12). This activity occurs too rapidly to be explained by stages of information processing, yet it is apparently too slow to be accounted for by the monosynaptic stretch reflex. And it appears to be more important than the monosynaptic reflex; the early burst at 30 msec was very brief and did not result in much actual increase in force, whereas the burst at 50 to 80 msec was larger, more sustained, and probably resulted in the force changes necessary to actually move the limb back to the horizontal position. The response to muscle stretch with a 50 to 80 msec latency has been termed the *long-loop reflex*, or sometimes the *trans-cortical stretch reflex* (also *functional stretch reflex*).

Figure 6-14 shows how the long loop reflex fits into the overall picture of segmental limb control. When the spindle is stretched and the Ia afferent is increased in its activation, the information is fed back to the spinal cord where it activates the alpha motoneuron and is sent to higher segmental levels and/or to the brain. The Ia is integrated with other information in sensory-motor centers in the brain which can initiate a more complete response to the imposed stretch. It is not clear where this reflex "resides," but it may involve structures in the cerebellum and/or motor cortex. Because the information travels to a higher center to be organized, the reflex requires more time. The 50 to 80 msec loop time for this activity corresponds with the additional distance that the impulses have to travel, plus the fact that more than one synapse is involved.

But something appears to be regained with the loss in time. First, the EMG activity from the long-loop reflex is far stronger than that involved with the monosynaptic stretch reflex, and it is probably the primary determinant of the increased EMG activity in this example. Second, because the reflex is organized in a higher center, it is more flexible than the monosynaptic reflex. For example, Evarts (1973) has shown that if the subject in a task similar to Dewhurst's (1967) task is told to resist the stretch, a burst pattern like that in Figure 6-12 occurs. But if the subject is told to "let go" so that when the weight is added the subject simply lets his arm be moved by it, the second burst (presumably due to the long-loop reflex) nearly disappears but the first burst is unaffected. It appears that prior instructions can change the response to a given stimulus (the added weight), so that the reaction to the stretch is "tailored" to the particular situation. The monosynaptic reflex, residing at a very low level in the spinal cord, is probably not capable of being modulated by prior instructions to any great degree. It is fortunate that we are constructed in this fashion, as situations exist in which we must resist very strongly when perturbations occur (e.g., in tackling in football). Other situations arise in which a very strong resistance would mean a serious accident, such as in skiing over bumps; failing to "let go" would result in a very stiff leg musculature, when a very compliant (springy) one would be most desirable.

Other Functions of the Gamma System

Other roles that the gamma system seems to play in movement control have been identified recently. One of importance is the supposed capability to generate extra force in very rapid actions. In most violent actions, there is usually a backswing or "windup" of some kind. Such procedures generate extra movement distance for the limb's action, generate higher velocity, and "set up" the system biomechanically. But an additional effect of these procedures is related to the stretch imparted to the future agonist muscle. During a backswing, the future agonist muscle is put on a stretch and the Ia afferents should fire more rapidly, which tends to activate the alpha motoneurons in the cord to a greater extent. Many scientists think that this kind of activation of the cord results in a more forceful and rapid response when the agonist is finally turned on during the backswing. These procedures, then, might serve to "tune" the spinal motoneurons for the future action (see the section on Feedforward and Corollary Discharge later in this chapter).

Another function of the spindles is related to fine control. Recall that the spindles were most heavily represented in those muscles that require the most careful and precise action, such as those which control the fingers, the face, and the tongue, suggesting that the spindles in these muscles are in some way related to the capability to produce precise actions. Support for this kind of viewpoint was provided by Frank, Williams, and Hayes (1977) by having a subject point the index finger carefully at a visible target. They used a method called the "cuff technique" to block the action of the spindles, so that they could study these movements without the spindles being involved.

In this technique, the subjects have a blood pressure cuff placed around the upper arm and inflated to above systolic blood pressure, so that the blood supply to the arm is temporarily cut off. Leaving the cuff on for 20 to 22 min results in the arm's progressively going numb, because the afferent fibers become anoxic from lack of oxygen and stop delivering impulses to the spinal cord when their receptors are stimulated in the periphery. Interestingly, because the afferent fibers are generally smaller than the efferent fibers (primarily the alpha motoneurons), there is a period of around 20 to 25 min after cuff application during which there is hardly any sensation in the limb, yet the capability for muscle contraction is relatively unimpaired. Such a technique provides a situation in which control of the limb without the involvement of sensory feedback can be studied. The anoxia is easily reversed when the cuff is taken off—although not without "pins and needles." Laszlo (1967) and her colleagues have played a role in popularizing the technique, and it has been used extensively. It has not been without its critics, however, who claim that there is a serious motor deficit in addition to the sensory loss (Chambers & Schumsky, 1978; Kelso, Stelmach, & Wannamaker, 1976). In any case, it seems fairly clear that the cuff technique provides a safe method for temporary deafferentation (removing afferent feedback). I will have more to say about deafferentation in Chapters 7 and 8.

Frank et al. (1977) showed that, even when the subjects had vision of the target and of their finger, they were grossly inaccurate in positioning the finger when they were under the cuff condition; there was about five times the variable error in positioning as compared to the no-cuff condition. The subjects would move from one position to approximate the next, but would arrive with very large errors, produce a corrective movement often resulting in as much error as the original movement, and so on, until finally the subject would simply stop moving when he or she was relatively close to the target position. Of course, subjects with normal feedback channels can make these movements smoothly and accurately. The interpretation was that the spindle feedback is normally responsible for making these accurate movements of the fingers, and without it the subjects were seriously impaired. These data support the hypothesis that the spindles are involved in fine control of the finger musculature.

This hypothesis is nicely supported by data from Kelso (1977), using the cuff technique at the wrist to block the sensory feedback from the finger joints. The muscles controlling the fingers are in the forearm (above the cuff), so their spindles are functioning normally because the cuff is placed below them. Even though the subjects could not feel their fingers, Kelso showed that they could position the fingers normally. This suggests that the spindles, which were operating normally in Kelso's study but not in the Frank et al. study, were the critical determinant of the accuracy in positioning.

Smith, Roberts, and Atkins (1972) have provided another line of evidence for the role of spindles in movement. Again, temporary deafferentation procedures were used, but in this case the Ia afferents (and other afferent input) were blocked by an anesthetic injected into the brachial plexus, a collection of nerves from the arm. By properly adjusting the concentration of the anesthetic, the smaller afferent fibers could be rendered inactive, leaving the larger efferent fibers relatively unaffected. Smith et al. performed a number of tests when the subjects had the gamma loop from the triceps muscle blocked in this manner. One was a simple finger-to-nose-touching task. The subjects crashed violently into their faces with their fingers on the first trial, as if the "braking" aspects of the movement were impaired. Remember, the triceps muscle is the antagonist for this movement, and proper timing and force of contraction in this muscle is presumably involved in bringing the arm to a stop so that the fingers lightly touch the nose. These data say that the spindles, rendered inactive, did not provide the necessary braking function that they would have normally. The interpretation is that in the normal movements the gamma and alpha motoneurons are coactivated during the contraction, so that the gamma motoneurons can provide a reference of correctness about the location of the endpoint. Thus, the spindles seem to be involved in the achievement of locations in space, operating to provide precise braking activities for moving limbs. Of course, other afferent input was blocked here as well, such as the input from the joint receptors, tendon organs, and cutaneous receptors; and it is possible that the lack of feedback from these sources led to the lack of control.

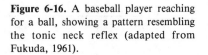

Figure 6-16. A baseball player reaching for a ball, showing a pattern resembling the tonic neck reflex (adapted from Fukuda, 1961).

Other Reflexes

Many reflexes can be elicited in humans, and some scientists have suggested that these reflexes play important roles in movement control. For example, Fukuda (1961) has collected a number of photographs of athletes, dancers, and other performers in critical situations, such as the baseball player shown in Figure 6-16 who is jumping and stretching his gloved hand high in the air to catch a ball. In this example the position of the head is such that it can elicit the *tonic-neck reflex* so often seen in infants. When the head is turned to the left, the left arm becomes extended and the right arm curls up alongside the neck. Fukuda's observations in the baseball task suggest that these built-in reflex patterns can perhaps be basic components of various skilled actions in adult motor behavior. In support of Fukuda's argument, there is evidence that in a force-production task if one turns the head toward the hand doing the gripping, there is an increase (see Figure 6-17) in force as compared to when the head is turned away (Hellebrandt, Houtz, Partridge, & Walters, 1956). Turning the head supposedly activates

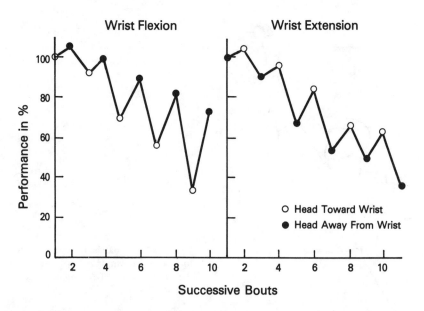

Figure 6-17. Turning the head toward the hand decreases the force of flexion actions and increases the force of extension actions (from Hellebrandt, Houtz, Partridge, & Walters, 1956).

the tonic neck reflex that provides a reflex-based facilitation of the alpha motoneurons on the same side of the body.

Turvey (1977) cited another example indicating that built-in reflexes can possibly be of use in movement control. He discussed the coyote chasing a rabbit, while the rabbit uses various abrupt changes in direction and speed to avoid being caught (see Chapter 5, PRP effects). As the coyote pursues, a leftward movement of the rabbit produces changes in the pattern of stimulation on the retina in the back of the eye, and these changes cause the animal to move the head slightly to the left. This change in neck position, originated by the changed visual signals from the rabbit, lead, according to Turvey, to a slight change in the gait, causing the coyote to begin to turn left. It is possible that the reflex changes that are caused by the neck movement to the left send signals to the spinal cord that bias the forces produced on the two sides of the body, with the forces in the right legs being larger than those in the left; the resulting behavior is a left turn, in the direction of the rabbit.

It is interesting to ponder the possible roles of the various reflexes in the control of behavior such as baseball-catching and rabbit-chasing, but the evidence on these roles is very slim indeed. Probably many mechanisms can change the coyote's running direction (see Chapter 5), and no strong evidence exists that the reflexes from the neck are responsible. In the baseball example, it is possible that the player is in this position (Figure 6-16) because he is merely looking at the ball, not because the reflexes are producing the classic tonic-neck pattern. It is certainly a suggestive set of findings, but it is far too early to tell if these reflexes as observed in isolation and in childhood are important determiners of the movement patterns seen in adults. A more advanced review of the possible role of reflexes in movement is provided by Easton (1972, 1978).

Triggered Reactions

From the examination of records like those shown by Dewhurst (1967) in Figure 6-12, it appears that three distinct processes lead to increased EMG activity that tends to compensate for the added weight. As discussed, the first is the monosynaptic stretch reflex, with a latency of about 30 msec and a very brief EMG response (see Figure 6-12). This response is segmental and is probably not modifiable to any great degree by instructions to the subject. The second is the long-loop reflex (or the trans-cortical stretch reflex) with a latency of about 50 to 80 msec. Unlike the monosynaptic reflex, the EMG response is quite large and can be magnified or eliminated by instructions to the subject such as "hold on" or "let go" when the weight is added. And, of course, a RT response can occur at about 180 msec which, presumably, involves the stages of information processing and attention (Chapter 5).

Crago, Houk, and Hasan (1976) have provided evidence that there is yet a fourth kind of response to the added weight that falls between the 50 to 80 msec transcortical loop and the 180 msec RT loop. They term these responses *triggered reactions*—prestructured responses to the added weight that are "triggered" into action by the sensations produced by the stretch receptors. According to these authors, the triggered reaction will have a latency of about 80 to 200 msec, with these latencies being far more variable than the latencies of the prior two stretch reflexes. Presumably the triggered reaction is like a "fast" RT, perhaps with some of the stages of information processing being bypassed. The system is presumably able to bypass certain stages of processing because the reaction to the stretch is so stereotyped, predictable, and practiced that the subject does not have to spend much time in processes like response selection and response programming. It is simply "triggered off."

What is the evidence for such processes in movement control? Crago et al. (1976) have shown that, compared to the situation where the subject always knows whether the weight will be added or subtracted, when the subject cannot predict the direction of weight change, there is a 10- to 80-msec increase in the portion of the reflex response that is subject to modification by voluntary instruction. Think back to the Chapter 5 discussion of Hick's (1952) law. The RT was dependent on the number of stimulus-response alternatives. Crago et al. have shown that a portion of the reflex response to added stretch, which is faster than a RT, is affected by the number of stimulus alternatives; or, the RT and the 80-msec EMG response are perhaps using some of the same processes. Thus, one interpretation is that the 80-msec response used the stages of information processing to initiate a triggered reaction, but that it bypassed certain of the stages so that the response can be more rapid; the stages that are used are sensitive to the number of stimulus alternatives.

However, it could be argued that when the subject knows the direction of the weight change, the spinal apparatus for the action can be prepared in advance (this is called *tuning*). For example, if the subject knows that an increase in the biceps EMG will be required, the activity of the neurons in the appropriate level of the cord can be adjusted, so that the action is more forceful when the stretch does come (e.g., Frank, 1980). But if the person does not know whether he or she will have to increase the EMG (if the weight is added) or decrease it and turn on the triceps muscle (if the weight is subtracted), two incompatible responses cannot be prepared at the same time. If the "triggered reaction" is more rapid when the subject can anticipate the direction of the movement simply because of increased ability to tune the spinal apparatus, then the Crago et al. results might not mean that the responses are triggered programs at all. Rather, these effects could simply be the increased speed of the RT response caused by the increased tuning at the spinal level.

A second criticism is that these reactions have always been shown in situations in which the muscle that is changed in its EMG response is the same one that it stretched (so-called autogenetic responses). It would certainly add power to the idea if it could be shown that the stretch in one part of the body would lead to a triggered reaction in some other part, and that this reaction could be accomplished more rapidly than would be expected on the basis of simple-RT effects. No one has done this experiment.

So the evidence about triggered reactions is mixed, and I am not sure that it is meaningful to add them to the list of reactions to muscle stretch shown in Table 6-2. But there is a potential role for such reactions if they can be shown to exist. In certain skills, when a particular event (e.g., a stretch or a sound) occurs it may be important to produce a very rapid and complex response in order to compensate. Further, this response might not necessarily be in the same muscles that were stimulated. One example is the stereotyped braking response when something comes in the path of your

Table 6-2

Four kinds of responses to environmental stimuli during movement, and some of their differing characteristics

Response Type	Category of Analysis			
	Loop Time	Structures Involved	Modified by Instructions?	Affected by # Choices
Myotatic reflex	30-50	spindles, gamma loop	No	No
Long-loop reflex	50-80	spindles, cortex or cerebellum	Yes	No
Triggered reaction	80-120	various receptors, higher centers	Yes	Yes
Reaction time	120-180	various receptors, higher centers	Yes	Yes

Note: Loop times are in milliseconds.

car. Its initiation could be faster than one RT, and would be found in only the most experienced of drivers. Such responses would presumably have been learned from experience, and they might not be genetically defined compensations for increased stretch like the monosynaptic stretch reflex. Such triggered reactions would have the advantage that an entire pattern of compensation could be brought into action without the delays required by the information-processing system, with the stimulus simply triggering the pattern of action. The problem is that no one has studied such reactions, and judgment must be withheld until more evidence is in.

FEEDFORWARD AND COROLLARY DISCHARGE

In this section I will consider evidence that the motor system operates with a feedforward control mode. In an earlier section in this chapter, I defined feedforward control as the sending of some signal "ahead of" the response that (a) readied the system for the upcoming motor command or (b) readied the system for the receipt of some particular kind of feedback information. Such processes appear to occur frequently in the central nervous system, and I will consider a few of these examples here.

Preparatory Postural Reactions

Consider a situation in which a standing subject awaits a signal to raise the arm quickly from a relaxed position at the side to a position in front of the body, as if to point straight ahead. According to earlier discussions about such actions, the commands for the shoulder muscles are generated after a RT of about 200 msec or so, and the EMG in the shoulder muscles is the first sign of the action after the stimulus. But if the subject is standing in balance, a sudden movement of the arm forward-upward will cause a shift in the person's center of gravity, and balance will be lost unless some compensation is provided along with the action itself. When is such compensation produced?

The Russian workers Belen'kii, Gurfinkel, and Pal'tsev (1967) recorded the EMG activity from the muscles of the legs as well as the shoulder in this action performed during RT conditions. After the stimulus came on, the first signs of the response were seen as EMG in the large muscles in the back of the leg (biceps femoris) on the opposite side of the body as the intended action, and these changes occurred about 60 msec before any action could be seen in the shoulder muscles. The actions of the EMGs in the legs could not have been caused by an imbalance resulting from the movement of the arm, because these changes occurred before the first EMG changes in the shoulder and even longer before any movement in the shoulder occurred. It is possible to consider these changes as an example of feedforward control, in which the motor system sends commands to the spinal levels associated with the leg musculature prior to the arm action, the purpose being to "ready" the legs so that the body does not lose balance when the arm finally moves.

A variant of the feedforward view of this action is that the changes in the pattern of EMGs in the legs prior to action were merely a part of the commands in the motor program for arm action. Usually the commands for a particular action begin with the muscles directly responsible for the action (in this case, the shoulder muscles), but here the action begins with some changes in the legs. W. Lee (1980), using this same action, has shown that the temporal aspects of the EMGs are quite closely linked, with the various muscles acting in the same order and with a nearly constant pattern of action for various trials supporting a motor-programming interpretation.[7]

Spinal Tuning

Investigators have been concerned with the neurological events that occur prior to overt actions. One class of events takes place in the spinal cord in the *alpha motoneuron pools,* which are clusters of alpha motoneuron cell bodies located in the gray matter of the spinal cord (see Figures 6-9 and 6-14). The pools are arranged to span up to three segmental levels, and they can be visualized as "cylinders" running up and down limited sections of the cord. A given pool contains cell bodies from alpha motoneurons that will exit the cord at the same or an adjacent level at which the pool is centered. Therefore, the cells in a pool tend to innervate the same muscle, or perhaps a group of muscles that are closely related anatomically. It is in these pools that the Ia afferent fibers from a given muscle terminate, so that they can activate the homonymous (same) muscle when it is stretched.

Figure 6-18 contains a schematic drawing of a "slice" of alpha motoneuron pools with some of the inputs to it and outputs from it. In earlier discussions of the spinal cord and the muscle spindle (Figures 6-9, 6-14), I did not complicate the story by saying that the pools contain many cell bodies and that the pools receive input from many different sources, such as cutaneous receptors, tendon organs, higher centers, and many *interneurons*—neurons which originate and terminate wholly within the spinal cord. In Figure 6-18, the pool is seen as providing an "environment" for the alpha motoneuron cell bodies that can be modified in terms of its activation level, or *gain*. If facilitative input from other sources is extensive, then the pool can be brought to a state at which little *additional* activation will cause some alpha motoneurons to fire, resulting in muscle action. If the gain in the pool is quite low, then a great deal of additional activation is required to make the alpha motoneurons fire. As mentioned before, one of the inputs to the pool is the Ia afferent, which originates in the muscle spindle for the same muscle as the alpha motoneurons in the pool in question. The situation allows the indirect measurement of the gain in the motoneuron pools by a method named the *Hoffman-reflex* (H-reflex)

---

[7]W. Lee found that the correlations among the EMG onset times were quite high, suggesting that the *phasing* of the events (i.e., the temporal organization of the events) was relatively constant, perhaps being a part of a unitary *pattern* of activity. I will discuss phasing and the measurement of movement patterns in Chapter 7.

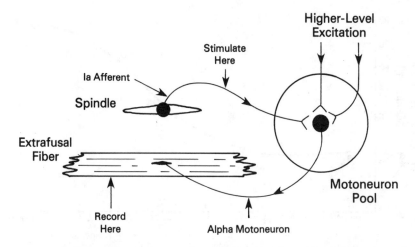

Figure 6-18. Simplified diagram of the gamma system, with input to the motoneuron pools from higher centers; the H-reflex is elicited when the Ia afferents are stimulated, and the resulting EMG is measured in the extrafusal fibers.

technique, after its originator (Hoffman, 1922).

In the H-reflex technique, the Ia afferent fiber is stimulated electrically with a weak shock (see Figure 6-18). The impulse travels up the Ia afferent, where it tends to increase the excitability in the alpha motoneuron pool for the same muscle. If the gain of the pool at this moment is high, then the Ia activity will cause many alpha motoneurons to fire, resulting in a relatively large EMG (twitch) in the muscle. A small gain, by contrast, will result in a relatively small, or no, EMG in the muscle. Simply, the H-reflex technique involves the stimulation of the Ia afferent directly and measurement of the amplitude of the EMG evoked in the muscles. Higher H-reflex amplitudes imply greater gain in the motoneuron pool from higher centers or other sources.

The Russian investigators Gurfinkel et al. (1971), Kots (1969), and Kots and Zhukov (1971) studied H-reflexes in the muscles involved in ankle movement. (It is relatively easy to obtain H-reflexes from ankle movement, because the nerve with the associated Ia afferents runs near the surface of the skin just behind the knee.) They used a standard RT technique with a visual stimulus, and the movement of the ankle was the response. They delivered the shock to the Ia afferent at various times during the RT interval to determine the state of the alpha motoneuron pool as the person prepared to produce the action.

The percentage of maximum H-reflex amplitude in a study by Kots (1977) is plotted in Figure 6-19 as a function of when in the RT interval the shock to the Ia afferent was delivered. The level of spinal tuning (as indicated by the changes in the percentages of maximum amplitude) began with a baseline level associated with the subject's being in an attentive state, and then it began to rise as the response approached. The beginnings of these changes appeared about 60 msec before the actual movement and continued to increase until the movement occurred. The interpretation of these findings is that the higher motor centers activated the pool associated with the muscles for the intended response prior to action, and thus probably

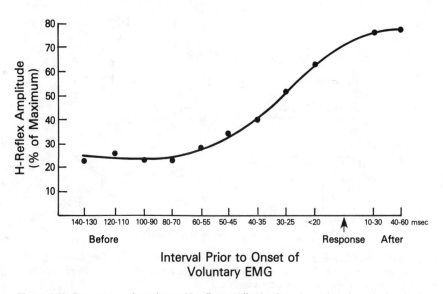

Figure 6-19. Percentage of maximum H-reflex amplitude plotted as a function of when in the RT interval the stimulation was applied (from Kots, 1977).

facilitated the signals for the action that arrived 60 msec later. In addition, this activation cannot be considered as a change in the general level of excitement as the response approached, because the H-reflex in the pools serving muscles that opposed the action (the antagonists) was not increased in amplitude during the same interval. This kind of process fits our definition of feedforward control, as the activity from the higher centers has readied the spinal cord for the upcoming action.

To what extent are these changes in the spinal motoneuron pools simply a part of the motor program for action? Is it necessary to consider the notion of tuning separately from the pattern of activity resulting from the RT stimulus? Some recent evidence by Frank (1980) indicates that tuning is not simply a part of the program. Frank used the H-reflex techniques with a task in which the subject had to make an ankle movement when a visible moving clock hand reached a certain point. The subject could anticipate the time of the response, unlike traditional RT tasks. Under these conditions, the subject might be able to "tune up" the motoneuron pools well ahead of the response and hold the level of activation for some time until the movement is to be made. Frank found that the H-reflex began to increase about 120 msec before the ankle action, 60 msec earlier than had been found previously. The fact that the beginning of the tuning could be decoupled in time from the movements of the ankle itself provides evidence that the tuning and the movement were not simply a part of the same action. If that were so, the time of tuning and the time of the action would be temporally locked, much as W. Lee (1980) found with respect to the time of the activation of leg musculature in relation to the time of the activation of the arm musculature. Thus, the pools can be increased in sensitivity prior to the action, presumably to ready the system for the movement.

Visual Perception

Numerous other situations exist in which the idea of feedforward control appears to be involved in the production and evaluation of human behavior. One of the earliest notions of feedforward control concerned the mechanisms of visual perception when the eye was rotating to fixate on some new target. When the eye "jumps" to a new location (during a *saccade*), the image on the back of the retina changes in response to the changed light patterns. How does the person who has made such an eye movement know whether the eye is moving in a stable environment or the environment is moving with a stable eye? The pattern of stimulation (optical flow pattern) on the retina could be exactly the same in both cases.

The answer that has been given by von Holst (1954), Sperry (1950), and others (e.g., Gallistel, 1980) was that the visual perception system was informed about the upcoming movement of the eye ahead of time, so that the pattern of changed visual input could be evaluated properly. This advance information, called feedforward in this section, has been termed *corollary discharge,* or *efference copy,* by these authors (see also Evarts, 1973, for a very readable discussion and review of this issue).

The idea is that a "copy" of the motor (efferent) command to the eye muscles is also sent to some other location in the brain, where it is used to evaluate the incoming visual signals and to "correct for" the fact that the image on the retina will have moved. Thus, the individual perceives the environment as being stable and "knows" that the eye has moved. How such a system works is the subject of much debate, but many scientists have argued that some such mechanism must exist in order for the individual to interpret incoming visual signals correctly.

Efference Copy in Limb Control

The previous example has shown how the efference copy of the motor command to the eye can apparently prepare the sensory system for the incoming information. Does such a system have a parallel in the control or perception of limb movements as well? The answer appears to be "yes" in a number of situations. First of all, as pointed out by Evarts (1973), there is strong neurological evidence that information destined for the muscles is also sent to places in the brain that are primarily sensory in nature. It is reasonable to suspect that the purpose of such activities would be to "tell" the sensory system what was ordered by the motor system and/or to ready it for receipt of the feedback and to evaluate it in terms of its correctness. Thus, the idea of efference copy is much like the establishment of the reference of correctness against which the feedback signals will be compared. If there is a deviation from the reference, then the system "knows" that an error has been made and that some correction should be initiated. One component of this feedforward must simply be the knowledge *that* the person moved voluntarily, so that the person can distinguish feedback from movement as due to active motion versus passive motion. Of course we all make such distinctions, and the idea of efference copy and feedforward seems to provide an explanation of the capability to perceive movement.

Related to the above example is the well-known heightened sensitivity to touch when the subject is moving actively versus passively. Do this experiment. Take a few different surfaces varying in roughness (various grades of sandpaper will do) and rank them in terms of roughness by rubbing them with the index finger (eyes closed). First, *actively* move your finger over the surfaces, being as consistent as possible in terms of speed and pressure. Then have someone hold your finger and move over the surface in the same way, without your muscular involvement. You will find that your perception of roughness is much impaired when you are moved passively. Why? One answer is that when the motor system sends the commands to move actively, it also sends an efference copy of the commands to some sensory area in the brain to enable the feedback from the fingers (resulting from the movement) to be evaluated properly. But when the finger is moved passively, no motor commands are issued to the muscles, hence no efference copy, and thus the "same" feedback signals from the finger are not perceived so accurately.

Detection and Correction of Errors

I have suggested that an efference copy of the motor command can aid in the interpretation of feedback from the responding musculature and limbs. Others have taken this argument further to suggest that movement errors may be detected and corrected using the efference copy. Efference copy presumably results when a command for action is initiated by the central nervous system. If the efference copy can be "analyzed" for errors in the same sense that feedback from the movement can be, then the central nervous system could use the efference copy to detect error. In this way, efference copy can be thought of as "feedback," only it does not come directly from the action produced, but rather from the command that will eventually result in that action. If I ask a friend to call my home from my office and she does so while I look on, then I have knowledge that the telephone is ringing at home even though I cannot hear it directly. I know that it is ringing because I "ordered it" to ring. Here, the knowing that I gave the order is almost as reliable as hearing the telephone ring.

If this notion is correct, then it would be reasonable to expect that this feed*forward* information could be evaluated in much the same way as feed*back* information discussed in earlier sections. That is, there could be some reference of correctness, and the efference copy could be delivered to it when the motor command was issued. If the subsequent analysis of the efference copy indicated that the command was going to result in an error, a correction could be initiated and a new movement command could be sent. Further, the time from the original command to the new command could be very short, perhaps even so short that the first "movement" could be corrected before it occurred, or very shortly after its initiation. That is, the error could be detected by this "central feedback loop" before the impulses reached the muscles, resulting in very rapid detection and correction of errors in movement before they could "do much damage" in the environment.

Various experiments appear to provide evidence that such processes may

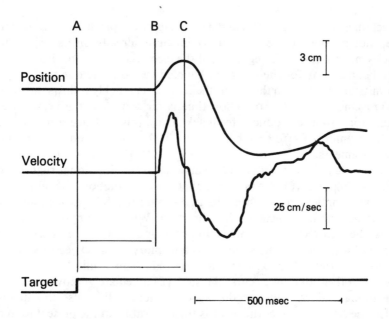

Figure 6-20. Position (top) and velocity (center) traces showing an error with "rapid" correction toward the target (from Angel & Higgins, 1969).

occur. For example, Angel and Higgins (1969) used a step-tracking task, in which the target would move suddenly in discrete steps to the left or right; the subject's task was to follow the target movement with appropriate limb movements. In such situations, particularly when the subject is highly motivated to minimize RT, the person will occasionally move in the wrong direction, reverse the move, and then move rapidly to the correct target. Figure 6-20 is a diagram of a typical trial, showing the initial incorrect move and the subsequent correction. Interestingly, the correction times, measured as the interval from the beginnings of the incorrect movement until the beginning of the correction (from B to C in the figure), can be as short as 90 msec. Because the usual estimates of RT are about 120 to 200 msec, it remained unclear how the subject could produce a response to an error so rapidly.[8] Angel and Higgins felt these findings meant that the subjects could not have been processing feedback from kinesthesis or vision in order to detect the error, because the correction for the false move was made more rapidly than could be accounted for by the usual feedback processing mechanisms.

A number of researchers feel that the processes involved in these rapid error corrections are based on efference copy (see Higgins & Angel, 1970; Megaw, 1972). They argue that the person sends a copy of the incorrect muscle command to a center in the brain where it is evaluated against a reference of correctness. If the command is determined to be incorrect, a

---

[8]Actually, Angel and Higgins showed that the error correction RT was even shorter than kinesthetic reaction time (about 110 msec), measured by passively displacing the limb and measuring the latency of a corrective response in the opposite direction.

correction is immediately sent, and a new response is produced. At the same time, though, the incorrect motor command is already on its way to the muscles and produces the beginning of the incorrect movement. Because the central corrections for the error are handled very quickly due to the short transmission distances in the brain, the correction quickly follows the incorrect movement, and the correction time is far shorter if the person were waiting for response-produced feedback. Thus, this evidence seems to provide an example of efference copy aiding in the control and correction of limb movements.

But our (Schmidt & Gordon, 1977) analysis of the situation is slightly different (see Figure 5-16). We proposed that in these situations the subject can occasionally anticipate which of the two stimuli will be presented and can prestructure the movement in that direction. When the opposite stimulus occurs, the incorrect movement is initiated anyway, but the response will be in error. In our model, the subject has a memory of the expected stimulus (he guessed "right," so expected that the right light would be presented). When the other stimulus occurs, the subject immediately knows that he is going to make an error and produces a correction. In this false-anticipation model, the time to correct the error is the interval from the presentation of the stimulus to the beginnings of the correction, or the interval from A to C in Figure 6-20. If this idea is correct, the interval from the stimulus presentation to the initiation of the correction should approximate one RT. In our data (Schmidt & Gordon, 1977), this interval was 288 msec, about what would be expected on the basis of this model.

At this stage, I am not certain whether these rapid error corrections are based on efference-copy mechanisms or determined by false anticipations, with the subject detecting the error visually. These quite different hypotheses do share the similarity of feedforward. In the efference-copy hypothesis, the motor command is fed forward and compared to a reference of correctness. In the false-anticipation hypothesis, the expected visual consequences (the image of the right-hand light) are fed forward, allowing a comparison of the actual visual consequences to those that were expected. How the motor system detects and corrects errors is a topic of great importance, and future research in evaluating these and other models should provide much insight into how the entire system works in everyday activities.

SUMMARY

Various modes of control for mechanical systems can be identified. Closed-loop systems involve the processing of feedback against a reference of correctness, the determination of an error, and a subsequent correction. Open-loop systems involve no such feedback analysis and error corrections, and the output is preprogrammed. Open- and closed-loop systems can be used in groups to form larger "hybrid" systems, and it is probably most reasonable to consider the human motor system as such a hybrid.

The receptors for the feedback supplied to closed-loop systems are the eyes, ears, and vestibular apparatus, as well as the Golgi tendon organs, the muscle spindles, the joint receptors, and touch receptors in various places in the skin. All of these sources provide input to the central nervous system, and then presumably combine into an ensemble for purposes of analysis of perception of movement—kinesthesis and proprioception. It has only recently been recognized that vision can serve as a strong motion detector, particularly in balancing tasks.

Closed-loop control theories seem to have their greatest strength in explaining movements that are very slow in time or that have very high response accuracy requirements. Tracking tasks are most obviously related to closed-loop processes. These theories have difficulty explaining the kinds of corrections seen in very rapid responses, however, and this fact leads to the suggestion that two fundamentally different kinds of movements exist: slow and fast. However, strong evidence exists for closed-loop reflexive control in limb movements. Most of this work suggests the involvement of the muscle spindle and the gamma loop, but other receptors are probably involved as well. Such reflexive corrections can be classified as (a) the monosynaptic stretch reflex (latency = 30 msec), (b) the long-loop or transcortical stretch reflex (latency = 50 − 80 msec), (c) the triggered reaction (latency = 80 − 180 msec), and (d) RT (latency = 150 msec or longer).

Feedforward control models involve the delivery of information to some other part of the system to "prepare it" for incoming sensory information or for an upcoming motor command; thus they involve anticipation. Feedforward processes appear to be common in the motor system and may involve segmental tuning processes and error detection, as well as serving as a basis for visual perception.

GLOSSARY

Alpha motoneuron. Large efferent (motor) neurons responsible for innervation of the extrafusal fibers of the skeletal musculature.

Closed-loop system. A control system employing feedback, a reference of correctness, computation of error, and subsequent correction in order to maintain a desired state of the environment; sometimes called a servomechanism or servo.

Continuous servo. A servo in which there is a one-to-one relationship between the instruction from the executive level and the state of the environment being controlled.

Discontinuous servo. A servo in which there is no one-to-one relationship between the instruction from the executive level and the state of the environment being controlled; sometimes called a discrete or a sample-and-hold servo.

Dorsal root. The collection of nerve fibers from the periphery into a bundle near the posterior side of the spinal cord at each spinal level; the major sensory input to the cord.

Ensemble. The combination of the various sources of sensory information that enable accurate perception of movement and position.

Extrafusal fibers. The muscle fibers of the major skeletal muscles, exclusive of the fibers in the muscle spindles.

Feedforward control. The sending of information ahead in time to ready a part of the system for incoming sensory feedback or for a future motor command.

Gamma motoneurons. Small efferent neurons that innervate the intrafusal muscle fibers of the muscle spindle.

Golgi tendon organs. Small stretch receptors located at the musculo-tendonous junction, providing very precise information about muscle tension.

Hybrid system. A large control system that consists of smaller systems of various types.

Intrafusal fibers. The small muscle fibers lying at the polar ends of the muscle spindle.

Joint receptors. Common term for a number of different receptors that are located in the joint capsules, presumably providing information about joint position.

Long-loop reflex. A stretch reflex with a latency of from 50 to 80 msec, modified by instruction, and mediated in higher brain centers.

Monosynaptic stretch reflex. A segmental reflex produced by stretch of a muscle and its spindles connecting monosynaptically with the alphamotoneurons in the same muscle and having a latency of about 30 msec in man.

Motoneuron pools. Collections of alpha motoneuron cell bodies in the gray matter of the cord which serve motor units in the same, or related, muscles.

Muscle spindle. Small spindle-shaped structures located in parallel with the extrafusal fibers that provide information about muscle length.

Open-loop system. A control system with preprogrammed instructions to an effector that does not use feedback information and error-detection processes.

Stiffness. A characteristic of muscles and springs defined as the change in tension divided by the change in length.

Triggered reaction. A response to an environmental stimulus that is faster than the RT yet slower than the long-loop reflex.

Vestibular apparatus. The receptors in the inner ear that are sensitive to the orientation of the head with respect to gravity, to rotation of the head, and to balance.

Visual proprioception. Gibson's concept that vision can serve as a strong basis for perception of the movements and positions of the body in space.

CHAPTER 7

Modes of Motor Control II: Open-Loop Processes and an Integration

In this chapter I will continue to explore the identification of the various modes of movement control. In Chapter 6, the focus was primarily on feedback mechanisms and closed-loop processes. In this chapter, I will emphasize open-loop processes, those fundamental modes of movement control that do not use feedback.

OPEN-LOOP PROCESSES

Response-Chaining Hypothesis

Certainly one of the earliest explanations of movement control was the *response-chaining hypothesis* (sometimes called the reflex-chaining hypothesis) proposed by the Nineteenth century psychologist William James (1890). The basic idea is diagrammed in Figure 7-1. James assumed that a movement began by an external or internal signal causing a contraction in a muscle or muscle group. This contraction generated sensory information (which he termed *response-produced feedback*) from the muscles and/or from the movements that the contracting muscles produced. This feedback, which James regarded as stimulus information just like that from any other stimulus such as light or sound, served as the trigger for the next contraction. This second contraction then produced its own response-produced feedback which triggered the third contraction, and so on until all of the contractions in the sequence were completed. With such a mechanism, James could explain how certain actions appear in the proper order in skill, as the response-chaining hypotheses ensured that the second

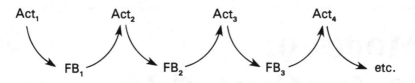

Figure 7-1. The response-chaining hypothesis. (The response-produced feedback from earlier portions of the action serve as triggers for later portions.)

contraction did not occur before the first one. Also, James thought that this mechanism could account for the timing among the various contractions so important for skilled actions; such timing (or *phasing,* as it is now called) would be determined by the temporal delays in the various sensory processes and could be relatively consistent from response to response to produce stereotyped and consistent actions. Although such a model seems most appropriate for series of actions (starting the car, buttoning a shirt), there is no conceptual reason why the model could not explain more rapid actions such as speech and throwing by assuming that the responses that are triggered are the contractions of individual motor units at the proper time within a sequence. Viewed in this way, the response chain shown in Figure 7-1 which consists of four units of behavior might last only 100 msec, or it could be seen as lasting a few seconds.

Coming at a time in history before the advent of electrophysiological recording techniques and the greater knowledge about neural systems, James could not be very specific about which feedback sources triggered which responses. The thought was that any feedback source that was contingent on the movement could be potentially involved. Thus, the system could use afferent information from the contracting muscle (e.g., from the spindle and the tendon organs), from the responses to movement (e.g., from the cutaneous receptors, joint afferents, vestibular apparatus), or from the movements created in the environment (e.g., from vision or audition) as triggers for the next action in the sequence. Also, the feedback from one action in the sequence could conceivably affect a movement in a completely different limb or it could be involved with an action in the same limb. Thus, the theory is quite general in its application, and it seems to account for a number of actions.

James (1890) had recognized that when skilled movements were produced they did not seem to require much attention for their control (see the section on attention demands of movement, Chapter 5). Under the response-chaining hypothesis, movements could be viewed as requiring attention only for the initiation of the first action, with the remainder of the actions requiring no attention. Also, James' view of *learning* motor skills saw the acquisition of the associations between a given feedback event and the next action as the fundamental basis for improving in skill. In the highly skilled, the proper aspects of the feedback are associated with the next act so that the movement can be carried out smoothly and effortlessly.

The response-chaining hypothesis is really a variant of an open-loop control mode, in spite of the presence of feedback. Remember that in a closed-loop system, the executive level is acting on the error that is produced, and such errors are computed as the difference between the actual state and the desired state defined by the reference of correctness. In the response-chaining hypothesis, though, there is no reference of correctness against which feedback is compared, and feedback simply serves as the trigger for the next act in the sequence. It is open-loop because the original stimulus sets the chain in motion, and the remainder of the events are determined by the learned associations between feedback and the next act in the sequence. Also, they cannot be modified if something goes wrong or if the environment changes, as is the case for a closed-loop model.[1]

One way that the reflex-chaining hypothesis can be tested is to examine the role of feedback in the production of movement. Of course if the feedback were disrupted by eliminating it, degrading its quality, or delaying it, the triggering of the next contraction in the sequence will be disrupted, and a loss of skill, or even paralysis, should result. In the next sections, I will review some evidence about feedback degradation in relation to this hypothesis.

Deafferentation

In Chapter 6, two temporary methods for interrupting the flow of sensory information into the cord were discussed. One involved the *cuff technique,* in which a blood-pressure cuff was applied to the arm or wrist with a pressure higher than systolic blood pressure, so that the afferent neurons returning to the spinal cord from the periphery were blocked from firing when they became anoxic (deprived of oxygen). A second, related method involved the injection of local anesthetic into the area surrounding a group of nerves, so that the action of the afferent fibers can be blocked selectively. In both cases, a near total blockage of afferent information occurs to the cord from the limb, but with only minor interruptions in the person's capability to contract the muscles in the same limb. (Review the sections on muscle spindles and the gamma loop in Chapter 6 for more information about these temporary deafferentation procedures.)

Permanent deafferentation procedures are also possible, but are limited in use to animal subjects. From Figure 6-9 in the previous chapter, recall that nearly 100% of the afferent input to the cord entered through the dorsal roots[2] on the posterior side of the cord. In an operation that is called a *dorsal rhizotomy,* the back of the animal is entered surgically, and the muscles are carefully moved to expose the dorsal roots. Then, at the particular spinal level of interest, the dorsal roots are cut, essentially preventing

---

[1]On the other hand, one could argue that the nature of the feedback is dependent on the outcome of the particular movement segment, so that the next action would be triggered in a way that is dependent on the correctness of that segment. The response-chaining hypothesis has not been considered in this form, however.

[2]A few small fibers have been isolated that appear to be sensory in nature, yet they enter the ventral (motor) side of the cord. The role of these ventral-root afferent fibers is not well understood, but it is doubtful that they could serve an important regulatory function since they are so slow in their conduction velocities and so few in number (Coggeshall, Coulter, & Willis, 1974; see Kelso & Stelmach, 1976, or Smith, 1977, 1978, for a discussion).

any sensory information from reaching the cord in the future (review Figure 6-9). This procedure can be done at a single spinal level or at many levels down the cord, with each successive level progressively eliminating more and more of the animal's sensations from the periphery. The operation can be done bilaterally, eliminating the feedback from both sides of the body at the same time. These procedures have been performed routinely on cats, monkeys, and other species in order to study the movement control that results in the deafferented state.

While normally these procedures are limited to animal experiments, a few examples of deafferentation in humans have occurred. Lashley (1917), in a study described in detail later, discovered a patient with a gunshot wound to the lower spine. The lesion had the same effects as surgical deafferentation, and it left the motor innervation of the subject intact, as this is transmitted through the ventral roots that are "deeper" and more difficult to injure accidentally (review Figure 6-9). Also, terminal cancer patients are sometimes surgically deafferented to relieve their pain. Herman (Note 6) has conducted some research on limb control with these deafferented patients who, he remarks, are remarkably cheerful and enthusiastic about being able to contribute to scientific investigations of limb control. Finally, Kelso (Kelso, Holt, & Flatt, 1980) has studied arthritic patients who have had the joints of the fingers replaced with artificial ones. This operation removes the joint and the joint capsule in which the joint receptors are located. Thus, while this is not really a deafferentation procedure in the strictest sense, it does provide a situation in which there is disrupted feedback from the responding limb. The results of some of these studies are discussed later in this chapter.

Early Deafferentation Studies

One of the earliest investigations using surgical deafferentation was conducted by Sherrington (1906). He severed the dorsal roots in a monkey, so that only the sensations from a single forelimb were lost, with the remainder of the body having normal sensory feedback. A major finding was that after recovery from surgery the monkey never used the limb, keeping it tucked against the chest and using the other limbs to eat and ambulate. At the time, this finding was regarded as strong support for the response-chaining hypothesis, because eliminating the feedback seemed to eliminate movement altogether, as it should if the hypothesis is correct. For decades, Sherrington's work was seen as support for the response-chaining hypothesis, as well as evidence that feedback from the responding limb was essential for movement production.

The conclusions that came from Sherrington's work were seriously challenged by a number of separate lines of evidence. On the one hand, at about the same time as Sherrington's studies, considerable research was completed on the control of locomotion in lower organisms such as fish, snakes, frogs, insects, birds, and the like (see Grillner, 1975, for a review of this early work). Some of this research involved severing the afferent (sensory) pathways for various segments of the animal's system, and the conclusions generally were that movements are not seriously disrupted by deafferentation. Considerably later, Wilson (1961) deafferented locusts, stimulating the insect electrically with a pulse near the head region, and wing movement patterns resembling flying resulted. The patterns were decreased in amplitude and frequency relative to normal flight patterns, but clear rhythmic activity nevertheless continued. Nottebohm (1970) found that birds sing even when one side of the vocal apparatus is denervated (severed nervous supply), with the portions of the song from the opposite side appearing at the same time as they would have if the bird were singing normally. Fentress (1973) amputated the forelimbs of mice, observing the grooming patterns that occur in this species. Normal mice go through a long sequence of face-washing behavior, in which the paws are brought to the mouth and licked, then the saliva is spread over the face in ever-widening patterns, finally washing behind the ears. The mice with amputated forelimbs licked their "paws," and "washed" their face and ears, even though no part of the foreleg touched the tongue, face, or ears. As well, when the mouse would pass the "paw" over the eye, the eye would blink, just as it would have if the paw were there, in order to "protect" the eye. The totality of such evidence suggests that the feedback from the responding limb is not essential for the production of at least some movement patterns. Another explanation for these fixed action patterns is that they are genetically defined movement programs which, when triggered by the appropriate stimulus, allow the complete behavior to occur without the involvement of feedback. See also Keele (in press) for more on this question.

Why is the locust's movement so well accomplished, when Sherrington's monkey did not move the deafferented limb at all? Could it be that the lower species and the humanlike monkeys are fundamentally different in terms of their motor systems. This is probably not the answer, as studies subsequent to Sherrington's on humans and monkeys have tended to show that movement is not strongly interrupted by deafferentation. For example, Lashley (1917), in his study of a patient who had received a gunshot wound to the spine rendering the legs deafferented, asked the patient to perform various positioning movements with the knee joint without vision. While sitting on the edge of an examination table, the patient was asked to extend the knee to 45°, and the error in producing the movement was compared to that of a "normal" control subject. Lashley found that the deafferented subject could position his leg as well as the "normal" subject and concluded that feedback from the responding limb, because it was not present in the wounded patient, was not necessary for movement production—a conclusion opposite to that of Sherrington's (1906). At the time, Lashley believed that the patient produced the movements through a central set of commands to the musculature that did not require sensory feedback. The implication is that the reflex-chaining hypothesis must be incorrect, because controlled movements were produced in the absence of sensory feedback from the limb, which, theoretically, leaves the system with no feedback with which to trigger future contractions.

How can the apparently contradictory findings of Sherrington and Lashley be reconciled? One possibility is that the deafferented monkey chose not to use the affected limb, which is quite different from saying that he could not use it. You know how it feels when you sleep on your arm the "wrong way," so that you cannot feel it after you awaken; the sensation is strange and unpleasant, and we probably would not use the limb unless it were important to do so. Would the monkey use a deafferented forelimb if both forelimbs were deprived of feedback, so that the monkey could not simply tuck one limb away and rely on the other?

Later Deafferentation Studies

In a long series of studies spanning a decade, Taub and his colleagues (see Taub & Berman, 1968, or Taub, 1976, for reviews) have answered this question by using surgical deafferentation affecting various portions of monkeys' bodies. When the monkeys had both forelimbs deafferented and had recovered from the operation, they were able to move the limbs nearly normally. I have seen films of these animals, and in activities such as climbing, swinging, eating, and grooming, they are different in only minor ways from the normal animals. The deafferented monkeys do, however, show some deficiencies in very fine manipulations, such as would be required to pick up a small piece of food. Perhaps this is related to the role of the spindle and the gamma loop in these responses (see Chapter 6; Frank, Williams, & Hayes, 1977). The conclusion to be drawn from these studies is that feedback from the responding limb is not essential for movement, but that it probably aids movement in some situations. Of course, these findings call into question the reflex-chaining hypothesis that claims the necessary involvement of feedback in the normal conduct of movement.

Deafferentation in Humans

Provins (1958) studied the role of joint receptors from the fingers by injecting anesthetic directly into the joint capsule. Although the movements of the finger could not be felt by the subject, there was nevertheless a strong capability to move, although the accuracy suffered somewhat compared to the condition without the anesthetic. Very similar findings were obtained by Kelso (1977; Kelso et al., 1980a) in studies of the joint afferents from the hand. When the feedback from the joint afferents was blocked either by the cuff technique (Kelso, 1977) or in patients who had artificial finger joints (Kelso et al., 1980a), little or no loss in movement positioning accuracy occurred without vision. Of course, all of these studies involved normal afferent feedback from the muscle spindles located in the finger muscles in the forearm, and it could be that this was the source of feedback that allowed the accurate control. Certainly, Frank et al.'s (1977) data, for which the whole lower arm was deafferented, suggest that this may be correct (see Chapter 6). All of these studies imply that the joint afferents are not essential for movement, as is often believed (e.g., Adams, 1977).

Using an anesthetic block of the gamma loop and other pathways from the right arm in humans, Smith (1969; Smith, Roberts, & Atkins, 1972) found that dart-throwing and grip strength tasks were only minimally disrupted by this kind of deafferentation. Although some impairments in performance occurred, the most important point is that the movement could be produced, even though no feedback was available from the responding limb.

Many studies have been done using the cuff technique popularized by Laszlo (1967). In a long series of studies using such tasks as rapid finger tapping, handwriting, aiming, and positioning, impairments in performance under the cuff conditions have been found; but the movements, although impaired, still remained, contrary to the expectations from a response-chaining hypothesis. See papers by Chambers and Schumsky (1978), Kelso, Stelmach, and Wannamaker (1976), and Laszlo and Bairstow (1979) for reviews and criticisms of this kind of work.

Deafferentation and the Response-Chaining Hypothesis

Even though the early work with various kinds of deafferentation reviewed in this section has shown clearly that feedback from the responding limb is not necessary for actions to occur, a number of qualifications must be added to such a statement. First, the earlier evidence is often taken incorrectly to mean that feedback in general is never used in movement control, because movement can occur nearly normally under deafferentation. The deafferented animals, however, are not normal in their movement, especially when the fine control of finger action is required. Also, it is possible, as Adams (1971, 1976b) has said, that other kinds of feedback could be substituted for the lost sensations in the deafferented animal; thus, the organism could simply be using a different channel of feedback (e.g., vision) as a substitute. And, finally, there are many cases in which feedback is almost certainly used in movement, such as those that I pointed out in Chapter 6. In these situations, we appear to respond much as though we were a closed-loop servo.

On strict experimental grounds, the evidence does not really show that the response-chaining hypothesis is incorrect, although it strongly suggests it. A more reasonable hypothesis would be that feedback is not essential for the production of at least some movements, although it is likely that feedback provides increased flexibility and improved fine movement control. The possibility remains that under some conditions or for certain kinds of skills the response-chaining hypothesis might be correct, but it seems fair to say that it is not correct in general.

CONTROL IN RAPID MOVEMENTS

I turn now to a theme discussed briefly in Chapter 6, where it was tentatively decided that feedback control with the kinds of mechanisms suggested in Figure 6-10 was limited in effectiveness. In this section, I will discuss these ideas in more detail.

Consider a very rapid movement, in which the pattern of action in the limb and musculature is initiated and completed in 100 to 200 msec. There are many examples of movements like this, such as the batswing in baseball (100 msec) and Muhammad Ali's left jab (40 msec). Because these discrete tasks are so highly represented in our everyday activities, they have been studied in laboratory settings in an attempt to understand how they are con-

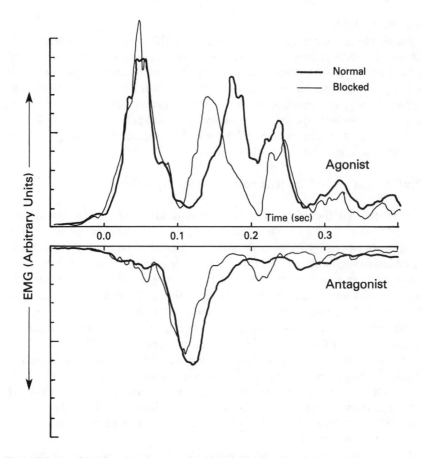

Figure 7-2. Agonist (triceps) and antagonist (biceps) EMG activity in a rapid elbow-extension action (from Wadman, Denier van der Gon, Geuze, & Mol, 1979).

trolled. A laboratory study might involve beginning with the elbow in one position, then rapidly extending it so that the hand comes to rest at or near a target 30 cm away. Although this movement at first appears to be very simple, the kind of neurological activities associated with it are very elegant and complex.

Although many examples could be presented, a recent one by Wadman, Denier van der Gon, Geuze, and Mol, (1979) makes the point particularly well. Figure 7-2 is a record from such a set of movements. The EMGs from the triceps (the agonist) and the biceps (the antagonist) are shown. The "raw" EMGs from the muscles have been *rectified,* meaning the negative swings of the EMG signals have been changed to positive values; and the area "under" this set of positive values is shown. The occurrence of peaks or "bulges" in the rectified EMGs represent periods of heightened activity in the muscle in question. Also, the record for the biceps (the antagonist) has been turned "upside down," so it can be compared to the triceps record. These records were determined from a number of trials, with the integrated EMGs from these separate attempts being averaged to produce the signals shown. (Ignore the lines in the figure that refer to the "blocked" movement and concentrate on the "normal" ones; I will return to the "blocked" movements later on.)

Figure 7-2 shows a pattern of EMG activity that has been common to many investigations using fast movements (there have been exceptions). Here, a distinct three-burst EMG pattern is evident. A burst of the agonist (triceps) muscle occurs first, then the agonist is turned off and the antagonist (the biceps here) is turned on, presumably to bring the limb to a stop. Then, near the end of the response, the antagonist muscle is turned off, and the agonist comes on again, probably to cause the limb to be clamped at the target, damping the oscillations that could be produced. This pattern seems to be degraded somewhat, or even absent, if the movements are slower (Desmedt & Godaux, 1979).

A question of interest for these kinds of actions is how the motor system "knows" when to turn off the biceps activity and turn on the triceps activity. This question can be extended to include skills for which many muscles come on and off at particular times, such as in pole-vaulting and running. The closed-loop account of movement behavior (Figure 6-10) involving the stages of information processing could account for these features of the response by saying (as Adams, 1977, has) that the system monitors the position of the limb (perhaps by sensing the joint angle by the joint receptors) and waits until the limb is at some particular position before turning off the triceps and turning on the biceps. That is, the system could use the feedback from the responding limb to trigger the end of activity in one muscle and initiate activity in the other.[3] However, a number of fundamental difficulties arise with this idea about the control of actions. These are (a) the notion just discussed that feedback is not necessary for actions, (b) the degrees of freedom problem, and (c) the sluggishness of feedback processing. These last two problems are discussed next.

The Degrees-of-Freedom Problem

One difficulty for the closed-loop model, and for any other model that holds that the contractions of the various muscles are handled by direct commands from higher centers, was raised by the Russian physiologist Bernstein who was writing in the 1940s (translated in 1967). The idea is that if the information-processing system were involved in the production of all the decisions about each of the muscles participating in a motor act, then imagine all of the mental work involved in producing a simple act like that shown in Figure 7-2. The fundamental concern is that the system has too many independent states that must be controlled at the same time. These independent states are usually called *degrees of freedom*. Each joint is capable of moving independently, and each joint represents at least one degree of freedom that must be controlled in an action. Actually, some joints have

---

[3]This view could also be related to the reflex-chaining hypothesis. The difference is that the closed-loop model would have the feedback evaluated against a reference of correctness, whereas the reflex-chaining view would have the feedback from the movement trigger the next action directly.

two degrees of freedom, such as the shoulder that can (a) allow the hand to move in a half-sphere with the elbow "locked" and (b) rotate the shaft of the arm, independently. This problem is compounded because each joint has a number of muscles acting on it, and each of these muscles is made up of hundreds of motor units (an alpha motoneuron and the fibers it innervates) that must be controlled. This would lead to an almost impossible situation for the central nervous system if it had to control all of these degrees of freedom separately by conscious decisions (see also, Greene, 1972).

This argument is related to ideas about the evolution of the motor system. It would seem that motor systems would have evolved in such a way that decision-making mechanisms would do as little as possible in the production of action, so they could be free to perform other functions, such as visual search for prey. Turvey's (1977) point is that this aspect of motor behavior should be considered when attempting to understand action. In searching for answers to how we coordinate movement, the question is, "How can the very many degrees of freedom of the body be regulated in the course of activity by a minimally intelligent executive intervening minimally" (Kugler, Kelso, & Turvey, 1980, p.4). First, the idea is that the executive should not be given much responsibility for determining the precise details of an action such as walking. Even if you are intelligent enough to make these decisions, do you believe that a hamster is? Or an ant? Second, the executive should be thought of as intervening minimally in the movement, so that the details must be handled by some structure other than the executive.

Finally, for years it has been thought that *movements* are controlled, not muscles. When we make an action we seem aware of the goal or the action pattern that we will make, but we seem hardly aware of the particular muscles we will use. Certainly, we are not aware of the particular motor units that are involved. Somehow, the system makes these determinations at an nonconscious level.

A solution provided by Bernstein (1967), Easton (1972, 1978), and Turvey (1977) for this degrees-of-freedom problem is the *coordinative structure*, related to the idea of a motor program discussed in the previous chapter and later in the present chapter. It is thought that the various degrees of freedom in the system are *constrained* by a particular organization imposed (either temporarily or permanently) on the motor system. The various muscles that operate at a joint, and the various joints that operate in a particular limb, can be constrained to act as a single unit, thus reducing the number of degrees of freedom from a very large number to one. Then, the information-processing system must produce only one action, the establishment of the particular coordinative structure or initiation of a motor program that will achieve the performer's movement goal. The performer controls the selection of the coordinative structure, which, in turn, is responsible for the enactment of the details of the action so that the various limbs are "coordinated" as if belonging to a single unit.

Tuller, Fitch, and Turvey (1981) discuss the example of the skilled marksperson. Numerous joints and muscles are involved in holding posture and keeping the barrel of the rifle still while the trigger is pulled. Each of these joints has a certain amount of variability, or movement, associated with it.

If I built a mechanical system with a number of joints, and each of the joints had independent variability, then the variability in the position of the rifle (which is determined by all of the participating joints acting together) would be a kind of summation of the separate variabilities of the partici- pating joints. But what one observes is that the variability in the aim of the rifle is far less than one would expect on the basis of such a mechanical model. One interpretation is that the various joints are coordinated by a coordinative structure, so that variation in one joint is counteracted by an "opposite" variation in one or more others, so that the resulting action of the rifle is very quiet and controlled. Also, the coordinative structure can operate at one level without the information-processing system being aware of the individual actions leading to the control.

The problem raised with respect to the EMG pattern in Figure 7-2 can also be explained by the motor programming idea. Here, the patterning of action in the various participating muscles is determined in advance and is called up as a unit. It is as if the individual said, "Do the arm movement," and a motor program was called up that handled all of the details, produc- ing the EMG pattern found. In this way, the number of degrees of freedom involved in the limb action, from the point of view of the stages of informa- tion processing, is reduced to one.

Limitations in Speed of Processing

Another argument against the idea that separate instructions are needed to terminate the triceps burst of EMG and to initiate the biceps burst (see Figure 7-2) are handled by the information-processing system is related to the available time for generating these events. A major conclusion from Chapters 4 and 5 is that the information-processing stages, such as those shown in Figure 6-10, seem to require about 150 to 200 msec for an en- vironmental stimulus to begin to produce some new response. This kind of model would explain the results in Figure 7-2 as resulting from some stimulus causing the initial triceps burst, and then some other stimulus, perhaps the feedback from the joint afferents (or other sensory receptor), turning off the triceps and turning on the biceps burst, with each of these "responses" determined by a "pass" through the stages of information processing. While this model might be acceptable with respect to very slow movements, it seems totally inadequate for the rapid actions under con- sideration. If the feedback from the joints, for example, is responsible for the pattern, then Muhammad Ali's jab and the movement in Figure 7-2 will have been completed before the feedback from the periphery can be pro- cessed and the modification in the pattern made. Some other process must be involved in switching the innervation from the triceps to the biceps mus- cle groups.

These arguments suggest that the stages of information processing, and attention, cannot be involved in the determination of the patterning of EMG activity seen in Figure 7-2. But what about the possibility that these patterns are determined by reflexive adjustments? As discussed in Chapter 6, reflexes probably do not require attention, and they are far faster than are those corrections produced by the stages of information processing. While debate continues about this question, some data do suggest an answer.

In the Wadman et al. (1979) experiment, there was an additional condition that I have not yet described. After the subject became accustomed to the apparatus and had made a large number of movement trials, the lever was unexpectedly locked in place, so that no movement could occur when the subject imparted force against it. The EMG patterns from these "blocked" trials are superimposed on the "normal" trials in Figure 7-2 (lighter lines). For about 110 msec after the initial agonist EMG burst, the two EMG patterns were nearly identical, with only minor modifications in the pattern after this point. These data suggest that the switching off of the triceps and switching on of the biceps was not due to reflexive involvement. If it were, then the pattern (i.e., the time of biceps EMG onset) would surely be influenced by blocking the movement. Rather, because the usual pattern of EMG activity was emitted, the movement pattern appeared to be structured in advance and run off as a unit.

Some other data (e.g., Angel, 1977), however, show a complete elimination or serious modification of the second burst when the limb is blocked. I believe that this occurred because the movements in these later studies were slower, allowing time (perhaps with the stages of information processing) to voluntarily turn off or reduce the intensity of the pattern. After all, producing a violent response such as this with an unexpectedly locked lever should be rather uncomfortable, and it would be understandable if the subject stopped responding as quickly as possible.

A second line of evidence against the hypothesis that the pattern of EMG bursts is determined by reflexes comes from the work on deafferentation in animals discussed earlier. Generally, when the animals are deafferented, they produce movements that are relatively normal. Examples cited by Grillner (1975) are walking and running in cats; ambulation, climbing, feeding, and grooming in monkeys; swimming in fish, and "slithering" in snakes. Remember, the deafferentation procedures completely eliminate the afferent feedback from the responding segment, and thus no reflexes based on this feedback can be operating to produce the movement patterns. The fact that these movements are slightly impaired probably means that feedback aids those actions to make them more smooth or precise but that they are not the primary cause of them.

Producing Modifications in Rapid Responses

In the next sections, some of the evidence about the performer's capability to change a movement once it has been initiated will be examined. This information is strongly related to the findings presented in Chapter 5 (e.g., psychological refractoriness), and the two kinds of findings seem to blend well to provide a picture of what happens during the course of a rapid action.

Anecdotal Evidence

Evidence from personal experiences is quite difficult to interpret, for the strong possibility exists that what we think we do is not accurate and leads to a false picture of movement control processes. Even so, some of our common observations guide us to experiments where the ideas can be studied more carefully.

Long after his work with the wounded patient, Lashley (1951) provided an example of a skilled pianist playing a piano with a broken key that could not be depressed. As the pianist played a string of notes, the attempts to press the broken key did not interrupt the series of actions at all. In fact, only after the entire sequence was completed did the individual notice and remark that the key was broken. This suggests that the movement sequencing was not dependent on feedback from the fingers. The actions do not appear to be structured with feedback to "verify" that a certain finger move has been made before the next one is commanded. The feedback appears to be present, though, or the person would not have known that the key was broken. But the feedback probably did not serve as a signal to initiate the next finger movement, and probably it was only minimally involved in the production of the movement sequence.

My favorite example is shirt-buttoning, which continues in its fine detail even if the button is missing. Again, feedback from the fingers is probably not critically involved in the buttoning movements. These ideas are interesting, but they lack good, solid data that document the time-course of the events that are happening in the fingers. In the next sections, some experiments that examine these questions are presented.

Initiation of Movement Modifications

Henry and Harrison (1961) asked subjects to begin with a finger on a key located by their hip and at a "go" signal to move forward-upward to trip a string located in front of their right shoulder. They were to do this as quickly as possible. The simple RT in this situation was 214 msec on the average, and the movement time was almost the same, at 199 msec. Sometimes a second light would come on indicating that the subject should avoid tripping the string or at least begin to slow the limb as quickly as possible. The "stop" signal could come on at one of four points: 110, 190, 270, and 350 msec after the "go" signal. Figure 7-3 shows the timing of the essential

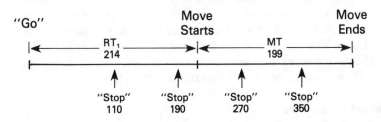

Figure 7-3. A time-line showing the critical events in the Henry-Harrison experiment. ("Stop" signals were presented at various times after an initial "go" signal; adapted from Henry & Harrison, 1961.)

details of the experiment, indicating where the "stop" signals could come on within the RT and MT intervals. Henry and Harrison measured the time to begin to decelerate the limb after a "stop" signal.

Their results are simple. Only when the "stop" signal was given at the 110-msec location was there a tendency for the subjects to start to slow the movement before it had been completed. But the more interesting feature of these data is the subject's response in the 190-msec condition. Notice here that the "stop" signal came on 24 msec *before* the movement even started, and yet the movement was carried out without interruption. That is, a signal presented before the movement was ineffective in modifying that particular movement, even when the movement lasted for 199 msec.

If the information-processing stages are too slow to be involved in details of a particular action [I have argued that these patterns are not produced by reflexive involvements because of the results when the lever was blocked in the Wadman et al. (1979) experiment], then the question is: What does produce these patterns of action? The best theory to have been proposed at this point is that these patterns are *preprogrammed*, structured in advance, and run off as a unit without much possibility of modification from events in the environment. To me, this is one of the strongest lines of evidence available that movements are controlled by motor programs. Before I describe the motor program notion, I will examine a number of additional aspects of the Henry-Harrison experiment that are of interest.

Internal "Go" Signals

The overall movement (the response to the "go" signal) must have been initiated internally considerably before the moment that the overt response (the arm swing) actually started. In Chapter 5, I discussed the idea that some internal "go" signal ultimately leads to action and that once this "go" signal is issued, the action occurs and it cannot be stopped, like pulling the trigger on a gun. In the Henry and Harrison experiment, when the (external) "stop" signal was presented 90 msec *before* the overall response was to begin, the response began anyway, and an additional 110 msec or so were required to even begin to stop it. This is an interesting phenomenon. When I perform in this experiment, I receive the impression that I see the "stop" signal, then a great deal of time passes, and then my arm begins to move as if the "stop" stimulus had never been presented. Subjectively, I feel that I have no control over my arm for a long time between the presentation of the "stop" signal and the initiation of the movement. Perhaps "I" really do not have control over it; perhaps the motor program does.

When is this internal "go" signal issued? At what point in the RT to a signal are we committed to action? The next experiment by Slater-Hammel (1960) helps to answer this question, as well as supporting some of the other points I have just made about programming of action.

Inhibiting a Response

Slater-Hammel (1960) asked subjects to watch a sweep timer (one revolution per second) and to respond by lifting a finger from a key to stop the

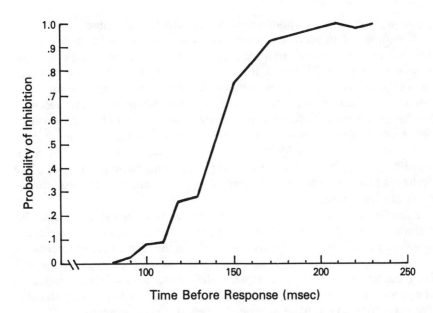

Figure 7-4. The probability of successfully inhibiting an anticipated finger lift as a function of the interval before the critical event (from Slater-Hammel, 1960).

clock at the moment when the timer reached "8," 800 msec after it started. The subject could not, of course, wait until the clock hand had actually arrived at "8" before initiating the movement, because the finger lift would occur well after that point, and the timer would stop well past "8." (Our previous understanding would lead us to expect that if the subject did wait for the hand to actually be at "8" before responding, the finger response would probably occur at around "10," 200 msec after it was initiated.) So the subject's task was to anticipate the movements of the clock hand and to anticipate the lags in the information-processing and neuromuscular systems, so that the finger was lifted at precisely the correct time.

Slater-Hammel added an interesting condition, however. Occasionally and unpredictably, the clock hand would stop before it reached "8." If this happened, the subject was instructed not to lift the finger from the key and to do "nothing." The hand could stop at anywhere from 200 msec to 750 msec after it started. Slater-Hammel studied the capabilities of successfully inhibiting the movement as the amount of time before "8" was varied experimentally.

A plot of probability of successfully inhibiting the finger lift against the time before "8" is presented in Figure 7-4. If the clock hand stopped 230 msec before "8," the subject should have no trouble inhibiting the movement; and, conversely, if the clock hand stopped only 50 msec before the clock reached "8," the subject should not be able to inhibit the movement. That is essentially what Slater-Hammel found. But notice that as the time before "8" decreased from 230 msec, the probability of successfully inhibiting the movement began to decrease, with the probability being about .5 when the interval before "8" was about 146 msec. Another way to state this finding is that, if the clock hand stopped 146 msec before "8," the subject could inhibit the response successfully only half the time.[4]

A number of important interpretations may be made from this single finding. First, the finding that the subject could not inhibit a response once it was planned and initiated internally supports the observations made about the Henry and Harrison (1961) study. Apparently, once the subject is committed to action, the action occurs even though some signal is presented in the environment indicating that the action should not be performed. Students do this experiment in the laboratory sections for my motor behavior course; their subjective impression is that they see that the clock hand has stopped, but that much later their hand responds anyway. The feeling is that "we" do not have control over the hand, where "we" means "our consciousness."

Another important outcome of the Slater-Hammel study is that an estimate is provided for the time before the response that the movement is absolutely committed—168 msec. This value is difficult to accept uncritically, however, because many kinds of processes have probably made this 168 sec estimate too large. For example, if the subject is providing attention to the processing of the internal "go" signal when the second "stop" signal is presented (the clock hand stopping), then the processing of the "stop" signal could be slowed markedly. For this reason, the evidence from Slater-Hammel probably means that the signal entered a stage where it cannot be revoked after the point in time at which 168 msec remained before responding. Even though it is difficult to pinpoint the time of this event exactly, the evidence suggests that the "go" signal is issued well before the actual movement occurs and that it cannot be revoked once it has been issued.

Finally, these data agree with those of Henry and Harrison (1961) that it is very difficult to change one's actions once they have been initiated. Notice that in the earlier experiment, the change was in terms of reversing or stopping movement that was already being produced. In the Slater-Hammel experiment, the movement had not yet been produced when the clock hand stopped, and thus the subject had to change the movement from one of doing something to one of "doing nothing." This implies that "doing nothing" is a response in itself that requires time and attention to "initiate" if the system is already doing something else.

Processing Vision in Movement: A Possible Contradiction

Certainly one of the most important kinds of feedback information in many, if not most, skills is vision. Unless one is specifically trained to perform without vision, one is severely impaired when vision is taken away. Because of the dominance of the visual modality, it has been important to ask how rapidly visual information can be used in movement control.

A famous and often-cited study of visual feedback processing time was

---

[4]Actually, Slater-Hammel found that the 50 percent point was at 146 msec before "8," but that the subjects on the average responded a little late (22 msec). If I add the 22 msec to the 146 msec as an estimate of how long before the response the inhibition could not occur, I obtain the 168 msec value reported in Figure 7-4.

Table 7-1

Proportion of target misses and mean movement times (milliseconds) as a function of the instructed movement time and lighting conditions (from Keele & Posner, 1968)

Lights	Instructed Movement Time							
	150		250		350		450	
	On	Off	On	Off	On	Off	On	Off
Prob of missing	.68	.69	.47	.58	.28	.52	.15	.47
Actual movement time	190	185	267	254	357	338	441	424

done by Keele and Posner (1968). They trained their subjects to move a hand held stylus (like a pencil) to a small target a few centimeters away. Knowledge of results about MT was provided, and subjects were trained to move in either 150, 250, 350, or 450 msec, in separate sessions. Then, when the subjects had perfected the MTs, on certain trials (unpredictable to the subjects) the experimenters would turn off the room lights when the subjects left the starting position, so that the remainder of the movement would have to be made in the dark. The logic was this. If, in the 250-msec conditions, for example, the lights-on condition produced less movement error than the lights-off condition, then the lights being on must have contributed to accuracy, and the implication would be that vision was being used in the movement control. Conversely, if no differences in accuracy were obtained between the lights-on and lights-off conditions, then the implication would be that vision was not being used in the response and that visual feedback processing time was greater than the corresponding MT in these responses.

Keele and Posner (1968) measured the probability of missing the target for the four MT categories for the lights-on and the lights-off conditions; their data are seen in Table 7-1. The most important finding is that, in the 150 msec MT condition (the actual MT was 190 msec), about as many target misses were recorded when the lights were on (68 per cent) as when the lights were off (69 per cent). The authors argued that when the MT was 190 msec or less, the vision of the hand or target did not contribute to movement control; thus, they argued that using visual feedback required at least 190 msec (one RT) to process. Also, as the MTs increased, an advantage began to develop for having the room lights on. When the MT was 260 msec, there were 47 per cent misses for the lights-on condition and 58 per cent misses for the lights-off condition. The lights-on advantage increased steadily as the MT increased, so that with a 450 msec MT, the lights-off condition had 47 per cent misses and the lights-on condition had only 15 per cent. This last finding is certainly consistent with the view that feedback processing requires substantial time, so that vision could be used only when time was available in the movement for the visually detected errors to be corrected. From these data, Keele and Posner suggested that the time required to process visual feedback information was between 190 and 260 msec.

Hawkins, Zelaznik, and Kisselburgh (Note 7) questioned the procedure used by Keele and Posner whereby the subjects were never able to anticipate whether the lights would be on or off on a particular trial. Their argument was that if the subject never could count on having the lights on, he or she would likely avoid a strategy employing vision. If the subject is expecting to use vision, and it is taken away unexpectedly, the person would have a poor basis for making the movement. Such a situation should cause a shift in strategy away from the use of vision, perhaps toward open-loop control. Their hypothesis was that the unpredictability of vision in Keele's and Posner's study forced the subjects to ignore vision, and thus the estimates of visual processing time in their study may have been too large.

Hawkins et al. performed a series of experiments much like that of Keele and Posner, except that their subjects practiced for a block of trials with vision always presented, and then a block of trials with vision always withheld, thus eliminating the problem of having the vision unexpectedly removed. They plotted the total variability around the target (see Chapter 2 for a review of E and its computation) as a function of the MT, and the plot is seen in Figure 7-5. The lights-on condition was beneficial at all MTs, even for those as short as 100 msec! These data suggest that vision, when its presence can be expected, can be used in far less time than the 190 msec that Keele and Posner (1968) suggested, perhaps with visual processing times as short as 100 msec. In subsequent experiments, Hawkins et al. showed that the advantage for the lights-on condition remained even if the procedures were reversed, so that now the lights would be off but come on suddenly. Another experiment showed that the advantage of the lights-on condition vanished when the MTs were 80 msec, suggesting that it required somewhere between 80 and 100 msec to process visual information in this situation.

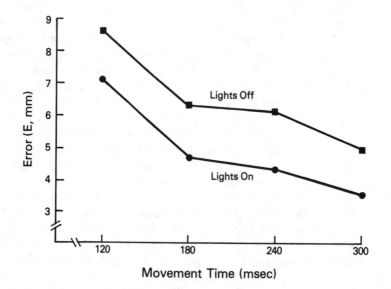

Figure 7-5. Target accuracy (E) in a stylus-aiming task as a function of MT and lighting conditions (from Hawkins, Zelaznik, & Kisselburgh, Note 7).

Other findings suggest the same thing. Carlton (1979) found that when the first half of a 270-msec movement was obscured from the subject's view, there was no decrement in the movement accuracy; the implication is that vision was used in about 135 msec, although this interval was not measured. Smith and Bowen (1980) showed that distorted and/or delayed visual information caused disruptions in movement accuracy when the movement times were 150 msec.

Taken together, these findings seem to provide a contradiction to the general notion that vision presented in the environment cannot influence a movement until all of the stages of information processing have been completed—that is, until about 190 msec have elapsed. How can the advantage of vision occur when the MT is far shorter than this 190 msec? One answer is that vision in these situations is not processed like a suddenly presented stimulus to which a response must be made, because more or less continuous vision of the hand and target occurs during the movement. Thus, it could be that what we are seeing is a distortion, caused by presenting the stimulus suddenly, such as in the Henry and Harrison (1961) and Slater-Hammel (1960) experiments. This viewpoint is favored by a number of writers who feel that suddenly presented stimuli do not provide a particularly realistic (ecologically valid) experimental setting (e.g., Turvey, 1977).

Another possibility is that vision "tunes" the motor system for accuracy (see Chapter 6 on feedforward). It is possible that corrections in the movement do not occur at all, but that vision prepares the spinal apparatus for the ongoing movement, with these tuning processes interacting with the program of action that is sent down, producing a slightly more accurate response. In this way, vision may operate in these situations without the usual information-processing stages. These ideas are speculative, but with the undeniable importance of vision in motor control, scientists must experiment further.

Limitations in Processing Speed: Summing Up

The evidence presented in the previous sections has strong implications for thinking about the control of fast movements. First, it says that a model in which the information-processing stages are involved in the moment-to-moment control of action must be incorrect, because the stages are simply too slow and limited to accomplish this kind of activity. Second, evidence suggests that the details of a rapid action are not determined by feedback processes.

Another major point is that the stages of information processing seem to be involved in selection and planning of fast movements, which was a major conclusion of Chapters 4 and 5, but are not involved in the conduct of these movements unless the movements are very slow, as seen in Chapter 6. Therefore, at least two levels of control appear to operate in the motor system: (a) a level for planning and initiating a complex pattern of muscular adjustments such as is seen in Figure 7-2, and (b) a level for controlling or producing that pattern of adjustment as the movement unfolds. The evidence suggests that once the movement is planned and initiated, the second level produces it whether the first level "likes it or not." The movement, in a sense, is not under the control of the planning level any longer, and will not be changed until enough time has elapsed for a new movement (perhaps a modification, or a cessation of the movement) to be produced. In this sense, the information-processing stages can be viewed as the executive level, and the motor program can be viewed as the effector level (see Figure 6-5).

If the system does work this way then it must plan rapid movements in advance, because time is not sufficient to prepare them once they have been triggered. The next sections evaluate evidence that the movement is, in fact, prepared in advance.

Planning the Movement in Advance: Preprogramming

I have already discussed some evidence for advance planning, or pre-programming as it is called, in Chapter 4 when I dealt with the stages of information processing. After the response-selection stage has decided about the nature of the movement, the response-programming stage readies the system for the action and initiates it. To this fundamental idea, add the idea that during the response-programming stage the person prepares a program of action which, when initiated, will result in a series of muscular activities that result in a movement. According to this model, the program must be structured completely, or almost completely, before the movement can be initiated.

In discussing the response-programming stage in Chapter 4, I provided evidence that certain variables concerned with the complexity of the movement or variables which influence the duration of the movement tend to affect the RT (e.g., Henry & Rogers, 1960). That is, the time required to initiate a movement is dependent on the nature of the movement that follows. (Remember, the RT is the interval from the stimulus until the movement is *initiated*.) We concluded that the more complex the movement, the longer the time required to ready the system for action and, hence, the longer the RT. The "location" of these effects was thought to be in the response-programming stage.

This same evidence can be viewed as showing that the movement is structured in advance. The variables—movement complexity and movement duration—which are concerned with the nature of the movement to be made, can be shown to affect a process that occurs before the movement is even begun. It has not been possible to explain how these effects could occur except by the hypothesis that the movement is structured in advance, with these variables affecting the time that will be required for this structuring.

Some other lines of evidence strengthen this position. First, if the movement is to be made in a simple RT situation, in which the subject knows in advance which movement is to be made, a number of authors have shown that the effect of variables like movement complexity or movement duration does not lengthen RT, especially if the subjects are highly motivated (e.g., Klapp, 1977a; but see Henry & Rogers, 1960, and Sternberg, Monsell, Knoll, & Wright, 1978, for counterexamples). Thus, when the RT situation is simple and the response is known in advance to the subject, presumably the person can program the movement before the reaction signal and merely wait for the signal to trigger it. If this happens, the extra time required for advance planning of a more complex movement will not be seen in RT, because these processes will have occurred prior to the reaction signal. This evidence, of course, is completely consistent with the idea that people structure movements in advance. It says, in addition, that people are flexible as to when they structure the movement—either before or after the reaction signal, depending on the circumstances (see Chapter 5).

Second, what happens if the movement is long, taking 1 sec or more? The closed-loop idea says that humans have difficulty processing information during short-duration movements, and this was the major reason why scientists think that such movements are structured in advance. But with long-duration movements, the details of the end of the movement do not have to be structured in advance, because the performer can preprogram the first part before the movement and wait until midmovement to program the ending. This idea is supported by some other studies done by Klapp and his colleagues (Klapp & Wyatt, 1976). They showed that if a movement was increased in its complexity at the beginning, then RT was increased. This is logical, because the more complex beginning would have to be preprogrammed before the movement started. But if the added complexity was at the end of the response, it did not affect RT. This makes sense, too, because the programming of the added complexity could then presumably be done during the movement.

CONTROL OF LOCOMOTION

To this point, evidence has shown that the central information-processing systems are probably not involved in the control of ongoing rapid movements, that feedback from the periphery is useful but not essential for movement control, and that rapid movements appear to be structured in advance. All of this evidence suggests that much of movement control is accomplished through motor programs, but the evidence has been indirect. In this section, I turn to the evidence about the control of locomotion, for which the details of the movement programs have been studied in more detail and with more direct methods.

Grillner (1975) reviewed considerable evidence about the control of locomotion and gait in a variety of species. One important set of studies concerns "spinal" preparations in cats or other animals. Here, the spinal cord is cut at a level below the brain so that the higher centers cannot influence lower ones, and often the cord is deafferented below the level of the cut as well. If the cord so prepared is then stimulated, it can be shown to display a definite periodicity in terms of the activity in the efferent fibers emerging from the ventral side of the cord (see Figure 6-9). Thus, the spinal cord itself is seemingly capable of producing a rhythm or oscillation, and this rhythm cannot be present without feedback from the limbs. In gait patterns, these rhythms in the cord were thought to first activate motoneurons that were to go to the flexors of the leg, then to activate motoneurons to the

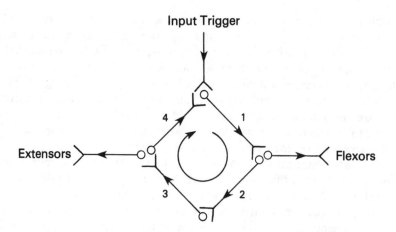

Figure 7-6. A simple possibility for the connections of interneurons forming a spinal generator.

extensors, then the flexors again, in a pattern more or less like that which would be displayed in locomotion. Apparently, the spinal cord has complex neural circuitry which is capable of producing these oscillations. These circuits have come to be called the *spinal generators* (or pattern generators).

The Spinal Generator

A schematic diagram of how such a spinal generator might be structured is shown in Figure 7-6. Many alternatives for this mechanism exist, and the present one is only one simple possibility. There could be a neural network in the cord made up of, say, four neurons (the cord probably uses many more). With a stimulus from some higher center (a chemical or electrical signal in the spinal animal), Neuron 1 is activated, which activates Neuron 2, etc., until Neuron 4 activates Neuron 1 again. This continuous cycling process would go in indefinitely or until some other process turned it off. Now, imagine that Neuron 1 also synapses with a neuron that drives the flexor muscles, and Neuron 3 also synapses with one that drives the extensor muscles. Every time Neuron 2 is activated by Neuron 1, the neuron to the flexors is activated too; the same is true for Neuron 3 and the extensors. Every time around this continuous circle, a burst of the flexors and a burst of the extensors occur, and they occur at opposite points in the cycle.

Such a model is obviously too simple to explain locomotion, but this basic concept of simple oscillating circuits helps to see how a neural network could be expected to produce rhythmic patterns of activity such as gait in animals.

Spinal Generators in Gait Control

To show that the spinal cord has some slow rhythmic capability is interesting, but to what extent is this activity involved in gait control? A very important surgical preparation in cats has allowed considerable insight into

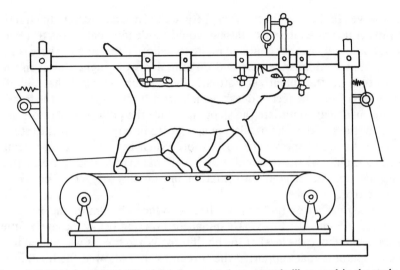

Figure 7-7. Mesencephalic (midbrain) cat supported on a treadmill as used in the study of spinal mechanisms in gait (from Shik, Orlovsky, & Severin, 1968).

this process. This preparation is called the mesencephalic (midbrain) preparation, or the *Shik preparation* after its originator (Shik, Orlovsky, & Severin, 1968). In this situation, the cat receives a cut of the spinal cord in the midbrain, totally severing the lower levels of the cord from the higher centers where perception and consciousness are thought to reside. The cerebellum, the small structure behind the midbrain, is left intact, connected to the spinal cord side of the cut. In this state, the cat is unable to sense any stimulation from the body (because the afferent pathways to the cortex are severed), and the cat is unable to perform voluntary movements of the legs. Shik et al. supported the cat above a treadmill, as shown in Figure 7-7.

A number of important observations have come from this preparation. First, when the animal was stimulated with a brief electrical current or a chemical called L-DOPA at the level of the cut, the animal began to produce stepping movements that resembled normal locomotion in cats. This stepping continued, although not indefinitely, when the stimulus was turned off. As the treadmill sped up, the cat walked faster, even trotting or galloping. It appears that some spinal generator(s) for walking must be turned on by some higher source (thought to be located in the midbrain in the intact cat) and that, once initiated, the pattern of flexion and extension continues without further involvement from the higher centers. Because the mesencephalic animal cannot sense the activity occurring in its limbs, such stepping activity must be independent of the animal's perception of the activity.

As it turns out, a stimulus from the higher center in the midbrain is not the only way to initiate the spinal generators for stepping. Using the same set-up, Shik and Orlovsky (1976) studied the cat's behavior when the treadmill was turned on. At first, the legs would trail off behind the animal; but then suddenly the animal would initiate stepping, with the total pattern of activity generated as a unit. As the treadmill increased in speed, the animal would walk faster, with little or no difference in the pattern of activity from that observed in the normal cat, except for some unsteadiness. As the tread-mill further increased in speed, the cat would suddenly break into a trot pattern. Occasionally the cat could be made to gallop. (Remember, there is no control from the higher centers and no stimulus from higher levels in the cord to turn on the spinal generators.) These results indicate that the afferent inputs from the feet and legs, which are at first dragged by the treadmill, are sufficient to initiate the stepping. Once the pattern generators are turned on, the speed of the oscillation appears to be controlled by the rate at which the treadmill moves the cat's foot. When the cat's feet are being moved so rapidly by the treadmill that a walk pattern is no longer effective in keeping up, the afferent information presumably triggers a new pattern—the trot.

An analogous set of findings has been produced by Smith and her colleagues (e.g., Smith, 1978). A cat's spinal cord was cut below the level of the forelimbs but above the level of the hindlimbs. When the cat was placed in a special apparatus that supported the forelimbs, but allowed the hindlimbs to be placed on a treadmill, the stepping of the hindlimbs could be initiated by the movement of the treadmill as in the Shik et al. (1968) experiment. The activities of the hindlimbs are not under voluntary control, and the cat has no awareness of the actions being produced. In fact, the cat may go to sleep while the stepping cycle is being maintained in the hindlimbs.

A General Model of Gait Control

As a result of evidence such as I have presented here, as well as the evidence reviewed by Grillner (1975), a general model of gait control has emerged. In this view, shown in Figure 7-8, the box in the center of the

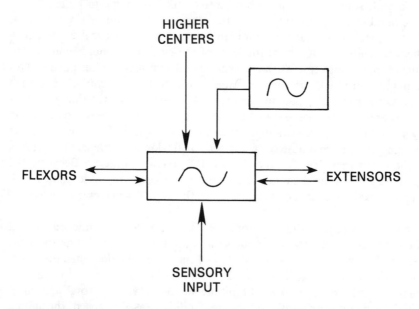

Figure 7-8. Spinal-generator model for gait, showing input to oscillators from sensory sources, from higher centers, from other oscillators, and from moving limbs.

diagram represents a central pattern generator, and it can be turned on or off by higher centers in the midbrain (heavy arrow). In some cases, this higher-level input appears to be but a single pulse that will turn on the generator, with no further higher-level activity necessary for the oscillator to continue to operate. In other cases, a continuous input (not necessarily a rhythmic one) appears to be necessary, with the action in the generator continuing only so long as the tonic input is on. These neurons that are capable of turning on spinal generators to produce a total pattern of activity are called *command neurons* [see the review by Kupferman and Weiss (1979) and the associated discussion of this topic].

The activity in the generator can also be turned on by sensory input. While the generator is operating, the activities in the flexor and extensor muscles are produced in a coordinated fashion, and feedback from the responding limbs also can serve to modify the output; this is shown by the two-way arrows from the various muscles to the spinal generator. And, finally, a number of spinal generators are thought to exist, perhaps one for each of the four limbs in the stepping cycle of the cat, so that the operation of the separate oscillators must be coordinated (coupled) by interneurons, neurons residing wholly within the cord. Thus, in the diagram, a connection is shown from another oscillator to indicate this kind of control.

Many details of these processes are not considered here, but a number of important concepts emerge from this work on pattern generators. First, for the control of gait and other stereotyped actions in a variety of species (e.g., tail-flipping/escape reactions in lobsters, eating in molusks, etc.), strong evidence exists that these patterns are controlled by "prewired" pattern generators that can handle most of the details of the actions. They can be turned on by a variety of sources of stimulation, and they can continue until they "run down" or until stopped by some other source of input. While the basic pattern is quite stereotyped, in "higher" animals (cats) extensive modification of the basic pattern is possible, either from higher centers to make the whole pattern more rapid or more forceful or from lower feedback sources (e.g., from the leg or foot) that serve to alter the particular pattern of force applied to conform to variations in terrain. And, finally, these pattern generators do not require the conscious awareness of the animal in order to operate. Once initiated, they can apparently continue without involvement of the higher centers. This is tantamount to saying that the pattern generator can operate without attention (see Chapter 5). However, in the operation of these generators while we are running, for example, attention seems to be required, perhaps to evaluate the upcoming terrain or to keep the oscillator running (e.g., try to do a complex addition problem in your head while jogging). Even so, the evidence from cats suggests that attention is not essential for the control of locomotion, with the coordination being handled automatically at lower spinal levels.

Reflex Involvement in Locomotion

The concept of the spinal generator tends to argue against an older notion of control in locomotion in which the patterns of limb action were thought to consist of fundamental reflex activities (e.g., Easton, 1972). This latter idea is somewhat different from the reflex-chaining hypothesis, in that the component reflexes were thought to be the identifiable, genetically defined patterns that we see so often in infants, whereas the reflex-chaining hypothesis involves any chained activity—even those that are learned. A good example of these genetically defined reflexes is *reciprocal inhibition*, whereby the flexors of a joint tend to be automatically inhibited when the extensors are activated. Another example is the *crossed-extensor reflex*, in which the extensors of one knee are activated when the flexors of the opposite knee are called into action. When we step on a tack, the flexors in the affected leg take the weight off the tack, while the extensors in the opposite leg help to prevent the individual from falling down. Another example is the *tonic-neck reflex*, whereby turning the head to the right causes facilitation in the arm flexors on the left, and in the arm extensors on the right (Figures 6-16 and 6-17).

That these reflexes exist is not questioned. They are especially easy to identify in infants, and they have been used in the diagnosis of various neurological disorders. But their involvement in gait is questionable because, as you recall, the spinal-generator evidence shows that the animal can produce a locomotion pattern even when deafferented. If so, how can reflexes be the critical element in the determination of the pattern since there will be no afferent input to the cord to initiate the reflex activity? Thus, I see the hypothesis that the reflexes are involved in locomotion in much the same way as I see the reflex-chaining hypothesis; deafferentation evidence tends to say that both are incorrect.

If the reflexes are not responsible for determining the basic patterns of action that we see in gait, what is their role? One role, to which I have referred earlier, is to ensure that the pattern specified by the program for locomotion is carried out properly in the face of changes in the environment. The muscle spindle and gamma system seem to fill this role. One function of the gamma system is to maintain muscle stiffness (spring-like properties) in the face of changes in muscle length (Nichols & Houk, 1976). If the animal steps on a patch of ground that is higher than expected, the spring-like properties of the contracting extensors can allow the extensors to yield without collapsing, maintaining a smooth gait. This view is expanded somewhat in Chapter 8.

A variation of this idea is that reflexes can be set up to actually provide an automatic and rapid deviation from the preprogrammed pattern. A good example of this kind of control was provided by experiments conducted by Forssberg, Grillner, and Rossignol (1975). In the locomoting cat, when a light touch or a weak electrical shock is applied to the top of the foot during the flexion portion of the swing phase of the gait cycle (i.e., the time that the animal is lifting the foot in preparation for the swing forward), an abrupt increase occurs in the flexion response (with an extension response in the opposite foot), as if the cat were trying to avoid an obstacle (such as a rock, curb, etc.) that would cause it to trip. (This crossed-extensor pattern is not voluntary, as it can be shown to exist in the mesencephalic cats described earlier in this section; thus, the response is spinal in origin.) However, when the same stimulus is applied to the foot during the phase of the gait cycle when the foot is on the ground (stance phase), essentially no reaction or perhaps a slight extra extension, takes place in the stimulated foot—a response opposite that shown in the opposite phase of the step cycle.

Given the mechanisms involved in the step cycle, such a pattern of compensation should be beneficial to the animal. If the tap is applied during the swing phase, the flexion response will cause the foot to be lifted over the obstruction, and the increased extension on the other side of the body will tend to keep the animal on balance. When the tap is received during the stance phase, however, the same response (increased flexion) would cause the animal to fall, and so this response pattern is inhibited. Thus, in such a view the reflex pathway is activated selectively during the step cycle so that it maximizes the animal's chances of avoiding a fall.

Because the same stimulus causes two different patterns of action depending on the phase of the stepping cycle, these effects have been termed the *reflex-reversal phenomenon*. Usually a reflex is thought of as a stereotyped response caused by a particular stimulus. Yet the evidence above indicates that the response to the stimulus depends on the location of the limb in the stepping cycle and is not simple and stereotyped. Thus, a simple view of reflex control cannot explain these effects.

This kind of evidence has been explained (e.g., Grillner, 1975) by assuming that the spinal generators for locomation, in addition to providing efferent commands to the relevant musculature, also provide signals to other locations in the cord that serve to modify the actions of various reflexes. The sense of this control is that if the pathways to the extensors of the right leg are being activated (during the stance phase), then the reflex that would serve to lift the leg in response to a tap is inhibited by the central generator, and is activated when the flexors are activated (in the flexion phase). In this way, the pattern generators involve the already structured reflex pathways and "play on them" so that they contribute maximally to the animal's overall movement goals. These kinds of interactions of spinal generators with the reflex pathways are just beginning to be understood, and there will certainly be more research on these questions.

The "Smart" Spinal Cord

Early in the thinking about motor control, the spinal cord tended to be viewed as a "freeway" that simply carried impulses from the brain to the peripheral receptors to the brain. Gradually, as many spinal reflexes were isolated and studied (e.g., Sherrington, 1906), the spinal cord came to be regarded as considerably more complex. The evidence that the spinal cord contains complex spinal generators for gait and other responses continues in the direction of seeing the cord as a complex organ where much of motor control is structured. Further, recent evidence suggests that the spinal cord is responsible for considerable integration of sensory and motor information, as shown by the following example.

Figure 7-9 shows a frog making a wiping response to a noxious stimulus placed on the "elbow." Fukson, Berkinblit, and Feldman (1980), like others before them, have shown that the frog is capable of performing these

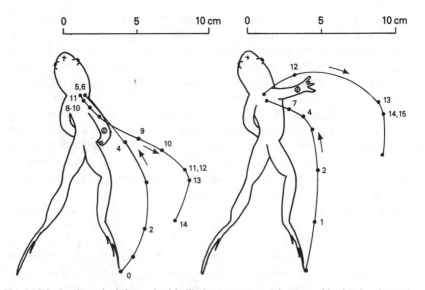

Figure 7-9. In the spinal frog, the hindlimb response to wipe an acid stimulus from the "elbow" is aimed to various elbow positions without the involvement of voluntary control from the cortex (from Fukson, Berkinblit, & Feldman, 1980).

hindlimb responses when spinalized, that is, with a transection that separates the cortex and "higher" brain centers from the intact spinal cord. The response always begins with a movement of the toe to the region of the shoulder area, followed by a rapid wiping action that is aimed at the elbow. It is interesting that the animal can use sensory information from one part of the body (the elbow) to trigger an action pattern in some other part (the hindlimb), even when spinalized. What is of more interest, however, is that the animal produces different wiping movements depending on the location of the elbow at which the response is aimed. That is, the spinal generator for this response appears to be modified in its action depending on the sensory information from the forelimb about the position of the stimulus. Or, as Fukson et al. say, the spinal cord takes into account the "body scheme" in making this response, indicating that the cord "knows" where all of the limbs are before making the action. Remember, the frog has no cortical involvement in this response, and thus no awareness of the limbs' actions, so this integration of sensory information was done at very low levels, perhaps completely within the spinal cord. Such observations indicate that the spinal cord is a very "smart" organ indeed, capable of handling much information processing that would otherwise be done by higher brain centers.

Spinal Generators and Human Skills

The evidence and ideas just presented provide support for a motor programming concept. However, these results on locomotion must not be generalized too far. First, they are produced in animals, and it is not clear whether humans have similar kinds of control in their locomotion, although we would certainly expect that they would. More importantly, remember that the movements studied in the cat are probably genetically defined and "prewired." To what extent are motor programs for movements like throwing a football structured in the same way? Are there programs in the spinal cord that can handle the production of a football pass if they are activated by a pulse from the midbrain, or do programs that are not genetically defined have some different origin? These questions are difficult to answer, as almost no research with animals has used tasks or skills that we could consider as learned, or which are not genetically defined. The hypothesis that workers in motor behavior have adopted is that the control of learned and genetically defined actions is fundamentally the same, but no good evidence supports this view.

An Impulse-Timing Model

These kinds of ideas about the control of locomotion and other skilled actions are really based on an *impulse-timing model* of limb control. The term *impulse*, from physics, refers to the aggregate of forces applied to an object over time. If I were to plot a force-time curve, which represents the amount of force applied to a bone at each moment of an action, the area under the curve would represent the impulse (see Figure 8-6 in Chapter 8). The impulse-timing label implies that the motor program or spinal generators time the application of the electrical activity delivered to the muscles and thereby determine impulses from muscles. The time of onset of the impulse, as well as the duration and amount of force of the impulse, are presumably controlled by the motor program. From principles of physics, the pattern of movement of an object (like a limb) can be specified by determining the forces applied to it and the onsets and durations of these forces, and hence the impulse-timing model is viewed as one way in which the motor system can control the trajectory of the limbs. I will have more to say about this impulse-timing model for limb control later on in this chapter, as well as in Chapter 8.

MASS-SPRING MECHANISMS

Muscles, and tendons which connect muscles to bones, have a certain amount of springiness, or *compliance*. In an older view of muscle (e.g., Huxley, 1965), the notion was that the contractile component of muscle was responsible for the production of forces, and a *series elastic component* (in the muscular connective tissue and in the tendons) provided elasticity. Recently, it was realized that the contractile portion of muscle has a certain elasticity as well, such that the entire muscle-tendon unit can be likened to a complicated spring. This concept has influenced thinking about what muscles do when they move bones in skilled actions.

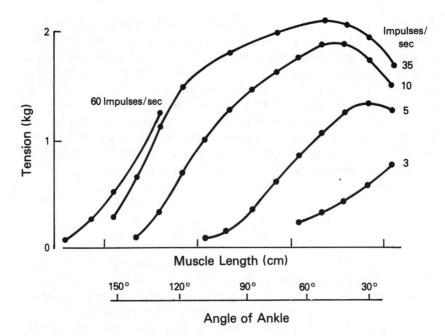

Figure 7-10. Tension produced by muscle as a function of the level of innervation (impulses/sec) and its length (from Rack & Westbury, 1969).

The Length-Tension Diagram

One way to study the properties of a muscle is to describe it in terms of a length-tension curve, or the relation between a muscle's length and the tension that it is capable of producing at that length and under a given level of innervation. These are usually produced in animal preparations. The length of the muscle can be predetermined, and the anesthetized animal is stimulated artificially in the nerve to the muscle so that level of innervation to the muscle can be controlled. Then the resulting tension is measured. Such a procedure can produce a family of *length-tension diagrams*, with one curve for each of the levels of innervation that the experimenter uses. Some of these curves from Rack and Westbury (1969) are shown in Figure 7-10, where four levels of innervation are used.[5] Notice that at all levels of innervation a generally increasing relationship was found between the length of the muscle and the tension it developed. This relationship is roughly what we would expect if the muscle were a spring attached to a lever (the bone). A fundamental mechanical principle about springs—Hooke's law of springs—is that for a given spring, the tension that the spring will produce is directly proportional to the amount that is elongated. Figure 7-11 is a simple hypothetical length-tension diagram that would be produced if a spring were used. The four curves indicate that four different springs were used, with the top curve being from a spring with high stiffness and the bot-

---

[5]The level of innervation is defined in terms of the number of impulses of electrical stimulus per second.

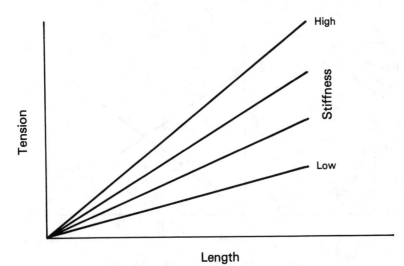

Figure 7-11. Idealized length-tension curves as would be produced from four springs, each with a different stiffness.

tom curve being from a spring with lower stiffness.[6]

A Mass-Spring Model

The realization by Asatryan and Fel'dman (1965) that muscles could, in certain gross ways, behave something like complex springs has revealed a possible mechanism for movement control known as the *mass-spring model*. Consider a lever, pivoted near one end, with two springs attached on either side. This set-up is shown in the left side of Figure 7-12. Think of the lever as the bone in the forearm; the pivot is the elbow joint; and the two springs are the groups of muscles that span the joint—the flexors and the extensors. The flexors are really three different muscles in our arms but consider them collectively as one spring for simplicity.

On the right side of Figure 7-12 are the hypothetical length-tension curves for these two springs, assuming a constant level of motor activation. First consider the curve labeled "flexors." Here, as the elbow angle is increased from 30° to 180° (that is, the elbow is extended), there is a progressively increased tension produced in the flexors because they are being lengthened or stretched. (Ignore the fact that as the elbow angle changes, the angle of attachment of the tendon to the bone changes as well; a more complex analysis could take this into account, but it is really not critical here.) Also, the curve labeled "extensors" represents the tension in the extensor muscles when the elbow angle is changed, and as the tension in the flexors increases the tension in the extensors decreases. This is because as the length of the

---

[6]Stiffness is a physical quality describing how much force is required to lengthen the spring. It is the change in tension divided by the resulting change in length, and is the slope of the length-tension curve. See also Chapter 6 and the section on the control of posture.

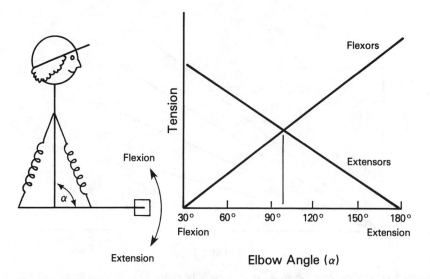

Figure 7-12. The mass-spring, or equilibrium-point, model. (Left, muscles seen as springs; right, the length-tension diagrams for the flexors and extensors plotted for different elbow angles, with the intersection being the equilibrium point where the tensions in the two muscle groups are equal and opposite.)

flexors increases the length of the extensors decreases, and the tensions they produce are related to their length.

If the springs are of the proper stiffness, the lever would move to an *equilibrium position* (or *equilibrium point*) in its range, where it would be stabilized by the opposing actions of the two springs. The equilibrium point is represented by the elbow angle where the tension (or, more properly, torque) in the flexor group is just equal to the tension in the extensor group. In the diagram, the two tensions are equal at only one elbow angle—that being the elbow angle at which the two length-tension diagrams cross each other, at about 95°.

What will happen if I deflect the limb from its equilibrium point to 120° and then I release it? At 120° the tension in the flexors will be higher than the tension in the extensors, which will result in more force being produced in the direction of flexion than in the direction of extension. This imbalance in forces causes the limb to move toward flexion, until the two forces are equal again at the equilibrium point. Notice that the mass-spring system will tend to move back to the equilibrium point after being deflected, regardless of the amount or direction of the original deflection. This view helps to explain how limbs can be stabilized in one position, such as in the maintenance of posture. See also Figure 6-15.

Such a view perhaps explains some simple things about how I can hold a limb in one place, but how can it explain movement? In the model, increasing the innervation to a given muscle is analogous to changing the spring from one of low stiffness to one of high stiffness. Consider what would happen if I substituted the flexor spring with one of greater stiffness while leaving the extensor spring in place. In Figure 7-13 are the length-tension diagrams for the original flexors and extensors, as well as the new length-

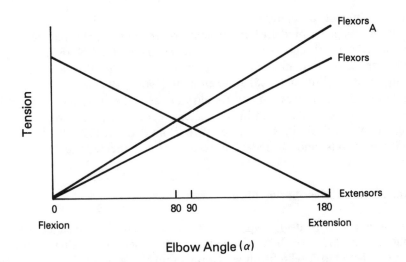

Figure 7-13. Length-tension diagrams for the extensors and flexors for various elbow angles. (The equilibrium point is shifted from 90° to 80° by increased activation in the flexors to produce a new length-tension relation A.)

tension curve for the higher-stiffness flexor spring. Notice that increasing the stiffness of the spring (or the slope of the length-tension curve) has the effect of shifting the equilibrium point to the left—that is, in the direction of increased flexion. If the limb is at the "old" equilibrium point and the new spring is added, then the limb will move in the flexion direction, eventually to come to rest at the "new" equilibrium point (about 80°). In this view, then, by appropriately selecting the innervation levels (i.e., the stiffness) of the two muscle groups spanning a joint, the joint can be moved to any position within its range. It will move to a position such that the torques from the two opposing muscle groups are equal and opposite—i.e., to the equilibrium point.

This model is quite unlike the other models discussed in earlier sections. First, it does not require any feedback, with the muscle moving the bone to the new equilibrium point by purely mechanical means; thus, it is considerably different from the closed-loop ideas discussed in Chapter 6. And, it is unlike the impulse-timing model of movement control discussed earlier in this chapter with respect to the control of gait and rapid limb actions. In that model, the critical determiner of the limb's action and trajectory was the amount of force programmed and the timing and duration of this force. With the mass-spring model, the muscle innervation is simply changed to a new level, and the timing of the onsets and offsets of the muscular impulses is presumably not involved. Finally, an important distinction is that the motor system does not have to "know" where the limb is starting from in order to move it to a new location. This can be seen in Figures 7-12 and 7-13, where the equilibrium point can be achieved regardless of the starting position. Thus, the mass-spring model is somewhat simpler than the impulse-timing view because all that is specified to the muscles is two levels of innervation. With the impulse-timing view, the system must know where the limb is at the beginning of the movement and then must specify the appropriate durations and intensities of the muscular impulses. I will return to these two models in a later section.

The mass-spring model of movement control is not new, having been mentioned in an obscure paper by Crossman and Goodeve (Note 8) in 1963, and then later and apparently independently by the Russian workers Asatryan and Fel'dman (1965) and Fel'dman (1966a, 1966b). However, this kind of model for movement control has not been taken very seriously until the recent work of Bizzi and his colleagues (e.g., Bizzi, Dev, Morasso, & Polit, 1978; Bizzi, Polit, & Morasso, 1976; Polit & Bizzi, 1978, 1979). Their evidence for this kind of model has been quite convincing, and I turn to it next.

Evidence for a Mass-Spring Model

Experiments with deafferented monkeys. Bizzi and his colleagues (e.g., Polit & Bizzi, 1978, 1979) have done numerous experiments using monkeys with deafferented forelimbs, in which the monkey was rewarded for pointing the hand and an attached lever, or turning the head, to a target light. The monkeys could not, of course, feel their limb move, and they could not see their limb either. The movements were made in the dark, with the target light being turned off as soon as the monkey began to move toward it. Thus, it seems reasonably safe to say that the animals were not capable of processing feedback from the responding limbs.

The major dependent variable of interest in these experiments was the terminal location of the movement on particular movement trials. Bizzi et al. studied these moves when the limb was perturbed in certain ways prior to or during the movement. For example, when the stimulus light was turned on and the animal looked at it, preparing to move, the experimenters would unexpectedly shift the initial position of the limb. (Of course, the animal could not feel this shift in position.) Or a mass would be unexpectedly applied to the lever that the animal was to move, or a brief pulse of force was applied that temporarily restrained or aided the movement.

Typical records of these arm movements are shown in Figure 7-14. The top three records are from the monkeys prior to deafferentation. An unresisted move is shown on the left (A) and a perturbation is applied (as indicated by the horizontal bar) to aid the movement in B and to resist the

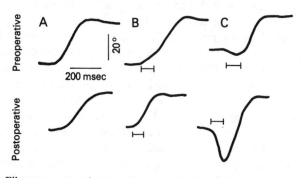

Figure 7-14. Elbow movements in normal (top) and deafferented (bottom) monkeys. (The endpoint is achieved even if a perturbation (indicated by horizontal bar) is applied during the movement; from Polit & Bizzi, 1978.)

movement in C. The same monkeys then performed the movements after recovery from surgical deafferentation. The unresisted move in A appears to be quite like the move before the deafferentation, except that it is slower. When the perturbation was applied to aid the movement in B or to resist the movement in C, the movement endpoint was achieved regardless of the direction of the perturbation.

In other experiments using head movements in deafferented monkeys, Bizzi et al. (1976) have shown that adding a mass to the head caused a slower rate of approach to the target, but the movement reached the same terminal location as when the head was unresisted. In other situations, when a pulse of force was added during the movement the limb showed a slowing—perhaps even a complete stop or a slight reversal in direction—but the limb always reached the target location when the pulse of force was withdrawn. Sometimes when the target location was close to the starting position, the shift in limb position would take the hand past the target. In these cases the limb moved "backward" toward the target and achieved nearly the same position as when it was unresisted.

These findings raise some interesting questions. First, the monkeys tended to move directly to the target reagardless of the mass that was applied to the limb and regardless of shifts in initial location. All of this was accomplished without feedback from limb position, so the hypothesis that the moneky "felt" the change in position or load and altered the motor command to compensate seems to be incapable of explaining these data. (Of course, such a mechanism probably exists for intact animals, but it could not be working in these experiments because of deafferentation.) It appeared that the motor program determined the endpoint in advance, and that position was achieved regardless of the changes in load or the initial position. The mass-spring model argues that when the command is issued to the muscles, the two opposing muscle groups are innervated such that the muscles achieve the equilibrium point by purely mechanical means. The limb "springs to" the target.

The results from Bizzi's experiments also tend to argue against an impulse-timing hypothesis which would assert that the monkey first determines where the limb is. Then the movement is initiated by a contraction of the agonist, the program turns it off, and then a contraction of the antagonist is initiated which brings the limb to a stop at the target. Of course, the durations as well as the intensities of these contractions are critical in determining the movement's endpoint.

Two pieces of evidence argue against the impulse-timing hypothesis. First, if the limb was shifted in its initial position before the movement began, the impulse-timing hypothesis would say that the animal would have to take this into account, because the program (if unaltered) would cause under- or over-shooting of the target. Of course, the animal cannot detect that the target position was shifted, yet the limb achieved the correct position anyway. It is difficult to imagine how the impulse-timing hypothesis can explain this finding. Next, recall that even when the monkey's limb was shifted past the target position before the movement, the limb moved "backward" toward the target. The impulse-timing hypothesis holds that the limb is moved by a contraction of the agonist first, then the antagonist, with this order of contraction being specified by the motor program. If so, then the initial movement should have been away from the target, not "backward" toward it. Thus, all of these lines of evidence tend to argue against the feedback-based idea that the limb moved to a position that the motor system sensed as correct, and they tend to argue against the impulse-timing view of motor programming. Apparently, a mass-spring model of motor programming can explain these findings satisfactorily.

Experiments with humans. These studies warrant skepticism for a number of reasons. First, the experiments were conducted with animals, and it is not certain that these processes also operate in humans. Second, it is never perfectly clear that the deafferentation procedures actually prevented sensory information about the movement from reaching the brain. Bone-conducted vibrations from the movement can be sensed by parts of the body that are not deafferented, for example. Also, the monkey may have "known" where the limb was at the end of the previous move, because a juice reward was given for being there. Finally, and perhaps most importantly, the monkeys may have adopted a mass-spring mode of control purely in response to the fact that Bizzi et al. had deprived the animals of all their usual movement mechanisms. Is it possible that the mass-spring mechanisms do not have any relevance for normal movement control, but have relevance only when other mechanisms cannot be used? A number of experiments with intact humans fail to support this view.

Kelso (1977) used the cuff technique, whereby a cuff was placed around the wrist to temporarily deafferent the receptors in the hand. Under these conditions, subjects could not feel passive finger movements. When given a blindfolded positioning test, though, the subjects were able to move the fingers to remembered positions as accurately as were subjects with all afferent channels intact. Kelso and Holt (1980) have provided similar findings with oscillatory movements of the finger joints. And Kelso et al. (1980a) used arthritis patients whose metacarpal-phalangeal joints (the large knuckles in the hand) had been replaced surgically. Again, these subjects had no sensations of passive movements in the hand, yet they were able to move to remembered positions about as well as normal subjects.

These studies show clearly that the joint receptors in the fingers are not responsible for accuracy in positioning the finger, evidence which helps to resolve some of the controversy about the role of various receptors in kinesthesis and movement control discussed in Chapter 6. Also, they tend to support the predictions from a mass-spring model, but they do not rule out the possibility that the moves were made using feedback from the muscle spindles, because the muscles (and spindles) lie above the cuff, in the forearm, and were not functionally deafferented. Credence is given to this possibility by Frank et al. (1977), who used a cuff on the upper arm which functionally deafferented both the hand (as Kelso and his colleagues had done) and the muscle (and spindles) that moved the hand. As discussed in Chapter 6, subjects had a very difficult time positioning the finger, even with vision. One possible explanation of all these findings is based on Nichols' and Houk's (1976) evidence that deafferented muscles do not maintain their spring-like character under stretch as do normally afferented muscles. If so, then the role of the spindles in the Kelso et al. studies could

Table 7-2

Constant errors (CE) and movement times (MT) under "normal" and "switch" conditions for movements in the horizontal and vertical planes (from Schmidt & McGown, 1980)

Horizontal: Mass Varied		Normal Trials	Switch Trials
Mass Added	CE MT	+6.36° 187	+6.81° 278
Mass Subt'd	CE MT	+5.78° 214	+6.28° 180
Vertical: Mass Varied		Normal Trials	Switch Trials
Mass Added	CE MT	+15.82° 202	+10.40° 243
Mass Subt'd	CE MT	+7.83° 196	+15.79° 155

have been to maintain the spring-like character of the muscles so that the mass-spring mechanism could operate, whereas it could not operate in the Frank et al. study.

We (Schmidt & McGown, 1980) have conducted experiments with normal, intact humans to study mass-spring control. Subjects produced rapid elbow-flexion movements of a lever to a target in 150 msec. Occasionally, without the subject's being able to predict it, the load on the lever was changed before the movement, and the subject made the limb movement with the changed load conditions. In the first of the experiments, the lever movement was horizontal, and the lever mechanism itself would support the weight. We were concerned with the constant errors in achieving the target on the normal trials (with expected weight) and on the switch trials, for which the weight was either added or subtracted unexpectedly.

Table 7-2 (top) shows the results from this experiment. When the mass was suddenly increased unexpectedly, the limb movement endpoint (the CE, or constant error) was nearly the same regardless of the load characteristics of the lever. And the same was true in the mass-subtracted portion of the experiment. However, the MTs shifted considerably, being far longer when the mass was suddenly added and far shorter when the mass was suddenly subtracted. These results are consistent with the mass-spring view, as the movements arrive at the target even when the inertial characteristics of the lever were unexpectedly changed, with the rate of approach to the target position being affected by the mass conditions.

However, like the Kelso et al. evidence discussed above, these findings do not rule out the possibility that the limb moved to the target position by some kind of feedback process. After all, all feedback channels were intact, and ample time was available to have made a spindle-based, or even RT-based, correction (see the earlier section entitled "Closed-Loop Reflexive Control" in Chapter 6). But the next experiment casts considerable doubt that the subjects use feedback in this way. Here, we did the experiment as was just described, but the lever movements were done in the vertical plane rather than in the horizontal plane. The spring-mass model, in this case, predicts that the limb movement endpoint should be affected by the changed weight. Because the target position is achieved by programming an equilibrium point, according to this hypothesis, the suddenly added weight will, because of gravity, tend to bias the equilibrium point downward, and a suddenly subtracted weight will tend to shift the equilibrium point upward. Thus, the prediction is that the limb will undershoot the target when the weight is added and overshoot it when the weight is subtracted. This is quite different from the predictions for the horizontal movement case, in which the mass-spring model predicts that no shift should occur in the movement endpoints (because gravity is not involved there).

The results of this second experiment are shown at the bottom of Table 7-2. When the weight was added unexpectedly, the switch trials were about 5° shorter in extent of movement than were the normal trials. And, when the weight was subtracted unexpectedly, the limb movement was approximately 8° longer than in the normal trials. (Contrast these shifts in endpoint to those shown in the horizontal experiment in the top portion of the table.) Larger shifts in MT also occurred, with the added weight slowing the movement and the subtracted weight speeding it. Interestingly, a reflexive closed-loop model would predict that the movement should achieve its desired endpoint, because the limb system would simply move to the position that it "recognizes" as correct. Added weight should have no effect on the terminal location of the limb. Seeing such large shifts in limb endpoint in this experiment casts considerable doubt on the hypothesis that the limb in these rapid movements is positioned by some feedback mechanism. Like the horizontal movement portion of this experiment, these findings support the mass-spring view very well.

Finally, like the work of Bizzi et al., these results fail to support an impulse-timing hypothesis, which predicts that the movement duration should be unaffected by the added or subtracted weight. This is so because the durations of the agonist burst, the time of offset of this burst, and then the onset of the antagonist burst are determined in advance by the program. The prediction would be that the limb would come to a stop in the correct time but would fall short if the weight were added and overshoot if the weight were subtracted. Both experiments show a shift in MT which is contrary to the impulse-timing hypothesis.[7]

Limitations of a Mass-Spring Model

The evidence just presented, both from animals and intact humans, cer-

---

[7]It is interesting that Mays and Sparks (1980) have produced data on human eye movements that are consistent with a mass-spring view of oculomotor control.

Table 7-3

Constant errors (CE) and movement times (MT) for "normal" and "switch" trials for the reversal movements in the horizontal plane (from Schmidt & McGown, Note 9)

Reversal Mass Varied		Normal Trials	Switch Trials
Mass	CE	28.3°	25.8°
Added	MT	139	163
Mass	CE	24.9°	28.6°
Subt'd	MT	144	123

Note: CEs are in total distance to reversal because no target was used in this experiment.

tainly presents a favorable picture of the mass-spring model as one of the fundamental mechanisms in movement control. However, the support for this hypothesis comes from only one kind of movement—simple, unidirectional positioning responses. To what extent is this kind of movement mechanism involved in movements that use more than one direction of a limb or in movements that involve more than one limb and that must be coordinated?

Schmidt and McGown (Note 9) have investigated this problem with various kinds of movements. One of these used the same kind of apparatus and experimental design as that just described for the single-direction moves, but the task involved a reversal in direction. The subject was to move in flexion, reverse the move, and extend the elbow past the starting position so that the time from the beginning of the initial flexion until the starting point was reached again was about 300 msec. The mass was added or subtracted from the lever exactly as described previously. Of particular interest was where and when the movement reversal occurred under the normal and switch conditions.

The major results are shown in Table 7-3. The reversal point became shorter when the mass was added and longer when the mass was unexpectedly subtracted. A mass-spring model would predict that this endpoint would be unaffected by the altered mass, just as it was in the unidirectional moves in Table 7-2. That this result does not occur is seen as evidence against the mass-spring model for movements requiring a reversal in direction that must be timed. The impulse-timing model can explain these results by saying that the motor program told the agonist when to turn off and that the movement with added weight could not go as far in this fixed amount of time, so the reversal point would be short of that in the normal trials. These findings indicate that the mass-spring model may be limited in its generality to movements that are unidirectional.

What about movements involving more than one limb? Schmidt and McGown (Note 9) did another experiment in which the weight of a stylus to be moved in 150 msec to a target was unexpectedly altered in a manner analogous to the techniques already described for the lever movements, but the task was somewhat more complicated. The subject initiated a right-hand movement of the stylus toward the target and also attempted to lift the left index finger from a key exactly on the arrival of the stylus. Presumably, both the stylus movement and the finger lift must be preprogrammed as a unit before the stylus move. What will happen to the time of the finger lift when the stylus is unexpectedly replaced by a heavier one? (As before, the subject does not know of the stylus change until after the movement begins.) The heavier stylus slowed the stylus movement considerably (from 150 to 159 msec), but hardly any shift occurred in the time of the left-hand finger lift which occurred at 150 msec (on the average) in both conditions. This would be expected from the impulse-timing hypothesis, in which the time of the left-hand onset is determined by the program, regardless of what may happen to the right hand after the movement begins.

As a side issue, these data fail to support the earlier reflex-chaining hypothesis and more modern versions of it (e.g., Adams, 1977), all of which would expect that the trigger for the left-hand movement is the joint position of the right arm. That is, the left-hand movement would be triggered when the left arm had reached a certain *position* in space (perhaps indicated by the joint receptors). But in this experiment, the arrival of the right arm at a particular position was delayed by the addition of the heavier stylus, while the time of onset of the left-hand response was unaffected. It certainly does not seem to be the case that the left hand was triggered by the position of the right hand during the movement.

INTEGRATING THE FUNDAMENTAL MECHANISMS

In Chapters 6 and 7, I have outlined the fundamental processes that seem to occur in the control of movement, to provide examples for or situations in which mechanisms may operate, and to provide evidence that these mechanisms of control work as they do. But the picture of the human that emerges from such an analysis is fragmented: it appears that the motor system is comprised of a group of unrelated mechanisms seemingly in conflict. Such a viewpoint is probably a natural outgrowth of the fact that various scientists have been occupied with small parts of the motor system in their research, developing seemingly contrasting theories. Obviously, these various mechanisms *do* fit together to produce a smoothly operating, skilled human motor system. How these mechanisms are combined and coordinated is the subject of the following section.

Centralists versus Peripheralists

Certainly one of the hottest debates has been that between the *centralists*, who argue that movements are controlled by centrally stored motor programs, and the *peripheralists*, who argue that movements are controlled by feedback-based mechanisms. The centralists cite evidence indicating (a) that movements can be produced in the absence of feedback (i.e., under deafferentation) and that (b) central pattern generators have been found for gait control in certain lower animals. The peripheralists, on the other hand, argue that when feedback is taken away, performance deteriorates, and that the evidence for central pattern generators is not sufficiently strong in humans to believe in them. The argument has been fueled by additional research from these "camps." The peripheralists would use experimental techniques and tasks that produce results most supportive of "their" point of view (e.g., tracking tasks and very slow movements), and the centralists would do the analogous thing (e.g., using rapid actions). For a more thorough treatment of this issue, see Schmidt (1980), or see some original statements of the issues by Adams (1971, 1976b, 1977), Kelso and Stelmach (1976), or Schmidt (1975b, 1976a).

It now appears that the polarization of views is decreasing. As discussed in Chapter 2, scientists cannot allow contradictory theoretical positions for very long. Some kind of reconciliation of the viewpoints will usually occur so that the contradictory evidence can be incorporated into a single, more encompassing position. In the next sections I will discuss how these opposing viewpoints about the control of limb movements are becoming less polarized.

Effect of Movement Time

One of the major ways in which the experiments claiming support for the peripheral notion have differed from those claiming support for the central notion has been the nature of the movements studied. A major factor in the difference between the tasks has been the MT. As I have argued before, a strong determinant of the system's capabiltity to use feedback information and the stages of information processing (i.e., as in Figure 6-10) is the duration of the movement. If the movement is too rapid in time, the limbs will have completed the response before the stages of information processing can complete the processing of any corections. In addition to the idea that not enough time exists to process feedback information, there is evidence that in very rapid movements the feedback information is actually prevented from entering the system (i.e., it is "gated out"), perhaps so that the feedback will not interfere with the execution of the preplanned movement program (see Evarts & Tanji, 1974). Further, as learned in the section on feedback control processes, as the movement becomes longer in duration, more time is available for feedback processes to have an effect. In tasks like steering a car, the analysis of feedback and the production of corrections is probably a major determinant of performance.

The important point is that it seems to make no sense to conclude that "Man is a closed-loop system" or that "Movements are controlled by motor programs," because conclusions about the nature of the control system seem clearly to depend on the kind of task studied. It makes far more sense to recognize that movement programs are critical for rapid actions and that feedback processes are important for slow actions when regulation is important.

Intermittent Control

A second way that scientists have attempted to resolve the conflict between the central and peripheral issue is to entertain theories encompassing both control modes. One example is the idea of *intermittent control*, sometimes called "sample and hold" (Chapter 6). The movement programs provide some action (e.g., moving the steering wheel to bring the car to the center of the road), then the incoming sensory information is sampled to determine an error. When enough information is received so that the system is "certain" that an error is being produced, a new correction is issued in the form of a program that eliminates the error, and so on. In the same theory feedback processes evaluate the sensory information and compute errors, and motor-program processes produce actions in the limbs to eliminate the errors.

The evidence for intermittent models of movement control is substantial. Evidence from studies of tracking behavior shows that a person can produce only about three corrections per second (when the track to be followed is unpredictable; Poulton, 1974), agreeing well with the previous analyses of how much time is required for the stages of processing to operate (Chapter 5). In addition, the delay from the presentation of a change in the trackway to the initiation of a correction is about 200 to 300 msec, which suggests that the person processes the feedback information through the information-processing stages for about one RT before the movement is seen. And, removing, degrading, or delaying feedback information in these tasks has a powerful negative effect on performance. This evidence seems to point to a model very much like that in Figure 6-10, where it is understood that the feedback processes and the motor programming processes alternate as the movement is completed.

Another recent example in which sensory processes are being integrated with motor-output processes comes from experiments relating the role of tactile sensations in movement. MacKay (Note 10) has recorded the activity in the sensory cortex in the brain resulting from the firing of a cutaneous receptor in the hand of a monkey. The monkey reached for an object. Then when he finally touched it, the cortical area where the touch receptor was connected was very active, showing that the touch receptor is very sensitive to the skin deformation produced by touching the object that is being achieved. But when the object is grasped, the area in the sensory cortex becomes relatively quiet, with almost no activity at all. Notice that the touch receptor in the hand is still being stimulated by the object as before but now that the object has been grasped, the information from the receptor no longer reaches the sensory cortex where it can be perceived. I interpret these findings to mean that the motor program for reaching allows feedback from the touch receptor to be transmitted to higher centers until the object is touched, where it could be that a response to grasp the object is triggered. Thus, feedback processes are apparently responsible for triggering a motor program process, such as grasping. The information from the touch receptor is then "gated out," presumably so that the monkey does not have unneeded information in consciousness. On the basis of this evidence, it would seem foolish to claim that reaching and grasping are a closed- (or open-)

loop process. It is almost certainly both alternating with each other.

Consider a rapid hand movement to a target. A leading model for these actions, initially proposed by Woodworth (in 1899!) and discussed more fully in Chapters 8 and 9, is that the initial phase of the movement is fired open loop, and then closed-loop corrective processes operate to reduce any errors that may have been produced in the initial open-loop portion of the response (Welford, 1968). Here, then, is a theory in which both open- and closed-loop processes are involved in a movement, but at different times with different purposes.

Feedback and Program Execution

Another way feedback processes and program processes can be considered together is to postulate that a feedback process is embedded within an open-loop process (or vice versa). (See the section on embedded feedback loops in Chapter 6 for a review.) Evidence for this was seen earlier, in the section on muscle-spindle-based corrections. A program for action was carried out open loop, but at the same time feedback-based corrections (see "Reflex-Based Corrections" in Chapter 6) seem to be able to correct for minor disturbances applied to the limb (e.g., a slight resistance added to an object that is to be moved). It is as if the open-loop process were responsible for determining the pattern of action and the feedback mechanisms embedded within this system were responsible for insuring that this pattern of action is carried out correctly. Again, it makes no sense to postulate that a movement is *either* a feedback-based or a motor-program-based process, for both mechanisms have clear, but different, roles in movement production.

A variant of this idea was mentioned earlier in this chapter on the control of gait. Recall that the reflex-reversal phenomenon in the running cat involved two different responses to the same stimulus applied to the top of the foot, with these responses being determined by where the foot was in the stepping cycle when the stimulus was applied. If the foot was about to be placed down, the tap to the top of the foot caused increased downward pressure. But if the tap were applied just when the foot had been lifted into the swing phase, the response was a sharp increase in the amplitude of the foot, as if the cat were trying to avoid tripping over an object. Here is an example of a programmed gait pattern in which is structured a feedback-based process for modification of this action under certain circumstances. Thus, it is reasonable to think of the motor programs involved in gait, for example, as being composed of commands for action combined with feedback processes that can modify the commands for action in various ways. Also, it is not certain whether such processes should be considered as purely closed-loop processes or as triggers for action. In either case, it is likely that sensory information is interacting with motor program output. It makes no sense to believe that the limbs are controlled by either one or the other process (see also Smith, 1978).

Flexibility of Control Processes

An important idea in biology is that organisms are structured with a great deal of redundancy, or duplication, so that various parts of the central nervous system can be destroyed with little or no loss in behavioral capabilities. Such redundancy has obvious evolutionary importance, as a damaged animal can survive on a "backup" system. Redundancy appears to have application to the motor behavior area as well, as there appear to be a number of ways that the system can perform a certain task or action, with performance being unimpaired (or only slightly impaired) when the primary system is fatigued or damaged.

An example of this idea involves the control processes in a long-duration movement, perhaps with a movement time of 2 sec. According to our previous reasoning, the person could control such an action by feedback-based processes, as ample time is available for such processes to have an effect. But it is also possible the performer could produce a program of action that would last for 2 sec or longer. Evidence from Shapiro (1977, 1978) indicates that a movement with a duration of 1.3 sec can be programmed as a unit (see Chapter 8). If so, then the performer would have a choice between performing the movement with a feedback process or a programming process. What are some of the determinants of this choice?

Level of Learning

One obvious factor in leading to a choice of feedback-processing versus programming mode of control is the level of learning of the task. In order to use a motor program for 2 sec, I would first need to have a program in my long-term memory that was "good" enough to control my limbs in acceptable ways. One of our fundamental beliefs about nongenetically defined motor programs is that they are "constructed" through practice. If there has been no practice at all on the task, then there will be no program, and the choice of feedback versus program will be obvious. If the program were highly developed, then the individual would be more likely to use it than if the program were not based on much practice or experience.

Attentional Requirements of the Situation

The processing of feedback in the information-processing stages during the course of performing a task in the closed-loop mode seems clearly to require attention and effort (e.g., Ells, 1973; Kerr, 1975). As discussed earlier (Chapter 5), this attention seemed to be attributed to the response-programming stage, and perhaps the response-selection stage. The implication of such an observation is that using the closed-loop control mode (i.e., such as in Figure 6-10, with the stages of processing being involved) is costly to the subject in terms of attention and effort. Obviously, any process that requires effort or attention (e.g., consciously controlling the limbs) will detract from some other process that also might require attention. Thus, if I attend to the details of a tennis swing, I will perhaps suffer in some other aspect of the game, such as higher-order decisions about strategy.

However, the production of a movement (or execution, once it has been initiated) with a program appears not to require very much attention; at least, there are examples of programmed movements that do not require attention for their execution (e.g., Posner & Keele, 1969). If the movement is very simple and does not require any decisions about where or when to stop, the movement can be produced without any attentional requirements at all (review the section "Attention Demands of Movement," Chapter 5). Thus, there is the potential for a trade-off of the "cost," in terms of attention, in producing a movement with a closed-loop process. The benefit is that, with closed-loop processes, the movement will perhaps be performed with less error. This leads to the notion that if the overall task has little likelihood of error, or if the "cost" associated with making an error is quite small, the human can presumably shift control to a program mode so that not much effort has to be exerted or so that the person can devote the limited attentional capacities to some other, more important aspect of the movement situation.

The same argument can be made about fatigue and performance, involving tasks that are mentally fatiguing or boring (as many assembly-line jobs appear to be). One way in which the individual could cope with fatigue might be to reduce the amount of effort expended on the task to be performed by shifting the control mode away from the relatively costly feedback-control processes in favor of programming. Such shifts could make the job more interesting, because when the person is programming the movements, more attentional capacity remains for use in conversing with fellow workers, thinking about something else, etc.

Inherent in the discussion about the flexibility of control systems thus far has been the implication that the movements are more accurate if a feedback-control system is used. This is obviously correct in most situations, as driving a car in an open-loop mode (blindfolded?) would be dangerous and fielding a ground ball in baseball would be nearly impossible without sensory information. But in other cases, shifting to a feedback-based control mode interferes with performance. A well-known example is that when a person playing a piano is asked to describe what the right hand is doing, it detracts from the performance. Attending to the hand to process errors in movement would presumably detract from performance for the same reason. It appears that when a person has a well-established movement program developed over years of experience, shifting to a feedback mode places the person in a control mode that is far less smooth and precise, and degraded performance may result. These ideas have existed for a long while, having been originally discussed by Bliss (1892-3) and Boder (1935) and resulting in what is now sometimes called the *Bliss-Boder hypothesis*: Attending to a well-learned action can interfere with performance (see also Keele, 1973). This hypothesis suggests that, if your golf partner is beating you regularly, buy her a golf book so that she can analyze her swing; that should degrade her to your level very quickly. Little experimental work has been done to test the Bliss-Boder hypothesis, so it is not known to what extent it is correct.

Complex Component Interactions

I hope to have provided an understanding of these various component mechanisms of motor performance, each of which can be isolated for study in the various paradigms, but none of which seem to operate independently during most everyday performances. It is important for students to understand these component mechanisms, but the real problem in coming to an understanding of motor behavior is to understand how these processes work together toward the smooth, elegant, and energy-efficient performances. In this regard, research has barely scratched the surface. I will close Chapters 6 and 7 with the idea that a complex interaction must be kept in mind when the component mechanisms are discussed. I hope that scientists will not lose sight of the total while examining the parts.

In the next chapter, however, I return to reductionism by considering one of these component mechanisms—the motor program—in more detail. My personal bias is that the field of motor behavior will come a long way if motor programs and how they are structured and learned can be understood. This belief, together with the increased research that the motor program concept has received lately, justifies the discussion of the subject in Chapter 8.

SUMMARY

The response-chaining hypothesis proposed by James (1890) was the first open-loop theory for motor control. It held that each action in a sequence is triggered by the response-produced feedback from the immediately previous action. Research on the role of feedback in movement performance, with animals under deafferentation conditions and with humans with temporary deafferentation, has tended to show that feedback from the responding limb is not essential for motor performance, although feedback is important in the smooth control of many actions. Thus, the response-chaining hypothesis cannot be universally correct, as it requires feedback from the responding limb in order to govern a movement sequence.

Scientists believe that motor programs exist for three major reasons. First, information-processing stages are too slow to exert ongoing control over all the details of a rapid movement, such as the EMG burst patterns seen in the quick limb-positioning movements. Also, movements cannot be inhibited once they are triggered; the pattern of action runs for one RT or longer without the possibility of modification. Second, the evidence from deafferentation studies shows some decrements in performance without feedback, but the performance still remains, suggesting that feedback information is not critical for motor behavior but may aid it. Third, findings that the RT increases as the movement complexity increases support the notion that rapid movements are structured in advance. Thus, for rapid actions and for primarily genetically defined actions research shows that both are governed by some set of central commands, called a *motor program* or *central pattern generator*. This structure handles the details of the individual muscle contractions, which frees the stages of processing for other tasks.

A theory regarding limb positioning, called the *mass-spring model*, has recently been isolated. It holds that the limb moves to a position defined by an *equilibrium point* between the opposing muscles spanning a joint and that the movement to this position is dependent on the spring-like characteristics of the muscles. Such a model is distinct from closed-loop theories of limb positioning, as described in Chapter 6, and it is different from an impulse-timing mechanism whereby the amounts of force and the times over which they are applied are controlled by the motor program. All three mechanisms might operate, but perhaps for different skills or under different conditions.

The various closed-loop mechanisms described in Chapter 6 and the various open-loop mechanisms described in Chapter 7 must be understood as operating as a part of a larger motor system, and it is probably wrong to believe that any one mode of control adequately represents the human motor system. Only by considering the human as a complex system composed of many separate mechanisms will a complete understanding of complex skilled movement behaviors be achieved.

GLOSSARY

Bliss-Boder hypothesis. An early, largely unsubstantiated hypothesis that attention devoted to well-practiced movements will result in their disruption.

Coordinative structure. The functional "coordination" of various muscles or muscle groups enabling them to behave as a single unit.

Cuff technique. A method of temporary deafferentation in which blood flow to the arm is eliminated by a blood-pressure cuff, rendering the afferent neurons anoxic so that they cannot deliver sensory information.

Deafferentation. Eliminating, usually by surgery (dorsal rhizotomy), the sensory input to the cord, while leaving efferent output intact.

Degrees of freedom. The number of separate independent dimensions of movement in a system that must be controlled.

Dorsal rhizotomy. The cutting of the dorsal roots at various segmental levels of the spinal cord, resulting in deafferentation from the associated areas of the body.

Equilibrium point. For a given level of muscle innervation, the hypothetical joint angle at which the torques from the two opposing muscle groups are equal and opposite; a construct in the mass-spring model.

Fixed action patterns. Patterns of action that appear to be stereotyped, genetically defined, and triggered as a single programmed action.

Impulse-timing model. A model of motor programming in which movement trajectory is determined by impulses—the amount and timing of applied forces.

Interneuron. Neurons originating and terminating wholly within the spinal cord that connect various segments of it; some are thought to be involved in the spinal generators.

Length-tension diagram. A graph of the tension produced by a contracting muscle as a function of its length.

Mass-spring model. A model of limb control in which a movement is produced through the specification of an equilibrium point between the agonist and the antagonist muscle groups.

Mesencephalic preparation. A surgical preparation in which the spinal cord is cut at the midbrain, essentially separating higher centers from the spinal cord.

Motor program. An abstract representation that, when initiated, results in the production of a coordinated movement sequence.

Preprogramming. The process of preparing the motor program for initiation, usually studied with RT methods.

Reflex-reversal phenomenon. The phenomenon by which a given stimulus can produce two different reflexive responses depending on the location of the limb in a movement.

Response-chaining hypothesis. A movement-control theory whereby each element in a sequence is triggered by the response-produced feedback from the previous element.

Spinal generators. Mechanisms in the spinal cord capable of providing oscillatory behavior thought to be involved in the control of locomotion.

CHAPTER **8**

Motor Programs

In Chapters 6 and 7, I focused on the many separate control processes that have been conceptualized, studied, and argued to be a part of the mechanisms that underlie motor behavior. The mechanisms were quite varied, and each seemed to have a particular kind of task or time within a task when it was the most operational. In some situations, a given mechanism might not be involved at all. In Chapter 8, I consider some of these mechanisms in more detail and focus on those that can be classified as open-loop mechanisms. The chapter is primarily about the laws and principles that have been formulated about these complex structures called *motor programs*.

First, it will be helpful to review some of the evidence leading to the belief that certain kinds of movements can be controlled by motor programs. The three lines of evidence I will review state: (a) that the processing time for feedback is quite long, (b) that the movements can be planned in advance, and (c) that deafferented animals can perform skilled movements.

RATIONALE FOR THE MOTOR PROGRAM CONCEPT

Limitations in Feedback Processing

One of the original ideas supporting motor programs was that the information-processing stages were too slow to allow the presentation and detection of error and the execution of a movement correction during a rapid action. As discussed in Chapter 7, the amount of time required to initiate a correction was essentially one RT, and a rapid movement could be completed before the first correction could even begin to be produced. In addition, the corrective movement itself takes time, as the limbs have a great deal of inertia and momentum. For these reasons many people have suggested that rapid movements are planned in advance and carried out without further involvement of the stages of information processing. And movement *time* seems to be the critical determinant of whether or not a movement will be programmed (Schmidt, 1969, 1972c; Schmidt & Russell, 1972).

Advance Planning

A second line of evidence has shown that certain rapid actions can be planned in advance and that such advance planning requires time and attention before the movement starts. A long line of research begun by Henry and Rogers (1960) showed that the RT to a movement increased as the movement increased in complexity. For example, a simple finger-lift had the shortest RT; a longer RT was found for a response in which the arm had to be moved to grasp a ball; and the longest RT was found for a movement containing reversals in direction. Henry's and Rogers' interpretation—which is the same basic interpretation of these data today, some 20 years later—is that the most complex movement had the most complicated motor program, requiring more time for the motor system to ready it for action. And this preparation occurred before the movement began.

Deafferentation Studies

Various investigators have used a number of techniques that eliminate or greatly reduce the feedback from the responding limbs. Surgical deafferentation (e.g., Taub, 1976), injecting various local anesthetics near a nerve (e.g., Smith, Roberts, & Atkins, 1972), or placing an inflated blood-pressure cuff on the arm (Laszlo, 1967) are some of the techniques. Without sensory information from the moving limb, animals and humans can perform many responses nearly normally, although some decrement occurs in most skills and serious decrements develop in skills requiring fine control in the fingers. The interpretation has been that feedback from the responding limb is not essential for movement control and that some central mechanism (the motor program) is responsible for the movement that is produced in such situations.

Research with very simple species has revealed the existence of spinal pattern generators, programs that are capable of activating one group of muscles after another to produce a patterned sequence of activity that can be used in gait, for example. We can be reasonably assured that such central programs do exist, as least for innate, genetically defined movements such as walking. There is less certainty that analogous programs exist for learned actions such as throwing or kicking.

FEEDBACK AND MOTOR PROGRAMS

Early Definitions of Motor Programs

The above arguments have led to the idea of a motor program as a prestructured set of central muscle commands that is capable of carrying out movement without much involvement from feedback. The original notion, which dates back to original thinking about motor programs by James (1890), Lashley (1917), and more recently to Henry and Rogers (1960), and Keele (1968), views movements as being carried out by these commands, with no possibility of involvement from peripheral feedback until the central information-processing mechanisms have time to produce some required modification.

But I have already presented evidence that such a view cannot be correct, or at least that it is oversimplified, for many examples can be cited whereby feedback processes seem to interact with open-loop processes in the production of movement. (The last section in Chapter 7 was devoted to this issue.) A more reasonable approach to motor programming is to ask how the sensory processes operate together with the open-loop processes to produce skilled actions. The next sections deal with various functions of feedback in movement control. These functions operate before a movement, after a movement, and during a movement.

Functions of Feedback

Prior to the Movement

One of the major roles of feedback is probably to provide information about the initial state of the motor system prior to the action. At the most simple level, I must know whether I am standing with my left or right foot forward in order to initiate a walking pattern (Keele, 1973). The spinal frog (Figure 7-9) requires sensory information from the forelimb in order to direct the hindlimb to the elbow during the "wiping response" (Chapter 7). Such information is presumably provided by feedback from the various proprioceptors, and it would seem to be critical for the selection of the proper action. Such processes were argued in Chapters 3 and 5 to be very important for open skills, when the nature of the environment is unpredictable and/or constantly changing.

Some theories of movement control seem to require that the initial positions of the limbs be sensed by the motor system before the programming can occur (e.g., the impulse-timing view discussed in Chapter 7). But the evidence on this issue has been contradictory and difficult to interpret. On the one hand, Bizzi et al.'s work on the mass-spring model (see Chapter 7) using unidirectional, single-joint movements shows that deafferented monkeys moved to the correct target position even though the limb's initial position was shifted either toward or away from the target. The interpretation was that the motor system programmed a movement endpoint and that

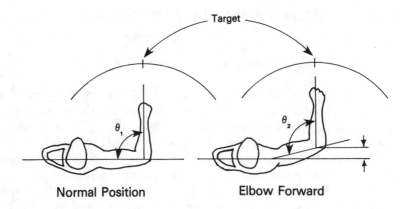

Figure 8-1. In pointing to a target, the equilibrium point of the elbow is dependent on the angle at the shoulder (from Polit & Bizzi, 1979).

this endpoint was achieved by purely mechanical characteristics of the spring-like muscles. Thus, this evidence suggests that the system can program a joint position without any information about where the joint was before the movement began. Recent data on eye movements suggest the same thing (Mays & Sparks, 1980).

But various lines of evidence say that it does not always work in this way. Our golden retriever, Max, when in a standing position, responds flawlessly to the command "sit," but if he is lying down when the same command is issued he does not know what to do. His response is to try to get even lower to the ground, and he never sits. The point is that the command to sit produces action contingent on his initial position. It does not appear that the sitting position (as an equilibrium point) was generated by the command to sit. Rather, an action was called up that was meaningful only if Max was standing.

More scientifically based evidence can be cited as well. Polit and Bizzi (1979), using deafferented monkeys, showed that when the initial position of the shoulder changed prior to the elbow action, a systematic error occurred in pointing to the target position. This is understandable from Figure 8-1, because changing the shoulder as shown necessarily affects the elbow angle necessary to point to target in a given position in space. If the monkey programmed a given elbow joint angle, then the mass-spring mechanism would achieve that angle, and the arm would not be pointing to the proper target. These monkeys did not learn to point to the target, even after considerable practice. By contrast, normal, intact monkeys learned in a few trials to compensate for the shfts in the shoulder position. The interpretation is that the intact animals had feedback from the shoulder joint and could adjust the angle at the elbow to compensate for the felt change in the shoulder angle. Thus, these data say that to point to a position in space, feedback about the initial positions of the joints is required if the environment is not perfectly predictable.

Another role of feedback involves what has been called *functional tuning* by a number of authors (Fitch, Turvey, & Tuller, in press; Turvey, 1977).

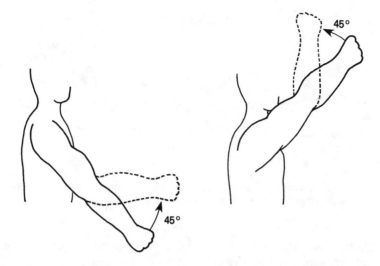

Figure 8-2. Two 45° elbow-flexion movements that appear to require different commands for the action and different forces at their endpoints because of the effects of gravity.

Recall (Figure 6-17) that the spinal apparatus and resulting limb strength could be affected by changing the head position, much as would be expected from the idea that the tonic-neck reflex was involved in the action (Hellebrandt et al., 1956). Here, feedback from the neck presumably adjusts the spinal mechanisms prior to action, thereby facilitating or inhibiting them.

But a more compelling reason for assuming that pre-response tuning must occur is related to some simple facts about the nature of the motor apparatus. In Figure 8-2 are two diagrams of a hypothetical rapid movement. In both cases, the movement involves flexion of the elbow a distance of 45°, beginning with the arm straight. These two situations differ only in the initial orientation of the limbs with respect to gravity. In the situation on the left, the upper arm is positioned 45° to the vertical, so that a flexion of the elbow 45° will result in the forearm's being horizontal at the end. In the second case, the upper arm is 45° above horizontal, so that a 45° flexion movement will result in the forearm's being vertical at the end. The same command signal delivered to the biceps muscle group will not "work" in these two situations for two reasons. First, a force is required to hold the forearm against gravity at the target position in the first situation, but not in the second. Second, increased force is required to move the forearm against gravity in the first example relative to the second. A logical conclusion from this simple example is that the motor system must know where the shoulder position is prior to the action in order that the command to the elbow flexors produces the required 45° movement. Presumably, feedback provides this information prior to movement, and this information is somehow integrated in generating the command to the muscle as did the frog in Figure 7-9. How this happens is a mystery at present, but that it happens seems to be relatively clear.

Consider another simple example, shown in Figure 8-3, viewed from the top. The movement is again a 45° flexion of the elbow joint, but the dif-

Top View

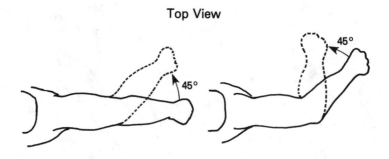

Figure 8-3. Two 45° horizontal movements require different commands because the different initial lengths of the elbow flexors result in different initial forces.

ference in the two cases is the initial angle of the elbow. Assume that the movements are supported by a lever in the horizontal plane, so that gravity is not involved. Notice that the initial length of the biceps muscle is different in these two cases. From Figures 7-10 through 7-13 in Chapter 7, evidence was provided that the tension developed from a given command signal depends on the initial length of the muscle; the length-tension diagram was a description of this relationship. Therefore, the same motor command to the muscle in these two situations will result in more tension being produced in the first case (left) than in the second (right).

But we are all capable of producing these two actions with nearly identical speeds if we try. Thus, the motor system takes into account the length-tension relationship in the biceps in determining the command for action. How it does this is an interesting question, but feedback from the responding muscles was probably involved, because seemingly this is the only way the system could have known about the initial muscle length.

Here is another complicating factor for the motor system to have to cope with in producing a movement. Figure 8-4 is a schematic diagram of the muscle attachments involved in a simple movement. This time imagine that the movement is an extension movement in which the elbow is to be moved through 45°. Notice that the triceps muscle, which is the primary elbow extensor, is attached to the humerus in two places (internal and external heads) and to the scapula of the shoulder area (the long head). Thus, the triceps muscle performs two actions when it contracts: it extends the elbow and it tends to extend the shoulder joint, pulling the humerus back. Therefore, when the triceps is contracting to produce the 45° movement, one of the muscles that flexes the shoulder must contract so that the shoulder joint is stabilized and only the elbow moves. Thus, during this simple extension movement, the motor system must "know" that there is a two-jointed muscle involved and produce some compensatory stabilization. The amount of stabilization will be dependent on the shoulder angle, because of the length-tension relations discussed in the previous paragraphs.

The picture that emerges from these observations is that our "simple" 45° movement of the elbow joint is not really all that simple in terms of the motor system. These and similar problems have been considered in the areas

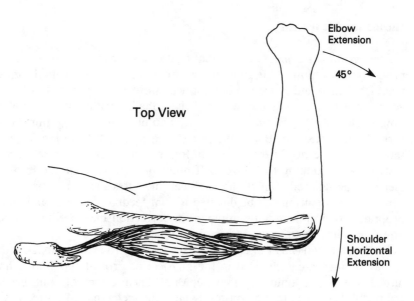

Figure 8-4. Complexity in a 45° elbow extension movement caused by the fact that the triceps muscle both (a) extends the elbow and (b) horizontally extends the shoulder.

of robotics and engineering, where artificial limbs and "robots" must produce certain functions regardless of the initial locations or their initial states. The conclusion from this kind of work is that the computer must do a very large amount of computation very quickly for the movements to resemble human motion. As if this were not enough, even more complicated aspects of the muscle need to be considered by the motor system, such as the nonlinear relationship between the muscle force and limb velocity, and other aspects of the contraction process that make the motor system very difficult to predict and control (Partridge, 1979). Yet, our nervous system controls our limbs beautifully in these "simple" situations. How it does is exciting to ponder.

Following the Movement

After (and during) a movement, extensive feedback is delivered to the central nervous system. Such information can be evaluated, presumably, by the stages of information processing to determine the nature of the movement that was just made. Whether or not the move achieved the environmental goal, as well as its smoothness, its level of force or effort, or its form or style, are derived from feedback. A major role for such information is in the adjustment of the movement on the subsequent trial, perhaps to reduce the errors that were made on the previous trial. As such, this information has a considerable relevance to the learning process. I will discuss this issue thoroughly in the final third of the textbook, but mention it here in relation to the functions of feedback.

During the Movement

Feedback monitoring. One role that feedback seems to have in movement production is a monitoring function, whereby the feedback from the movement is taken in and processed but not necessarily used in the control of the action unless something goes wrong. It is probable that a long string of actions dealing with finger movements in piano playing are programmed and carried out open-loop. But at the same time, feedback from the fingers is returned to the central nervous system for analysis, as if the central nervous system were "looking for" errors. If no errors appear, then the feedback seems to be ignored. But if the feedback indicates that an error has occurred, then attention can be directed to that feedback source, and an appropriate correction may be initiated. A correction may not be initiated, however, when the movement has already been completed.

Feedback involvement in control. A second way to view feedback is that it may be intricately involved in the physical control of the limb. I have already mentioned a number of examples of this in Chapter 6. But, briefly, the possibility exists that a constantly changing reference of correctness is specified by the gamma motoneurons to the muscle spindles and that their actions result in a continuous set of corrections to keep the movement on the proper course. The feedback could be involved in the determination of the end location of a movement if the reference of correctness were set for this position. And in repetitive movements, the feedback from early segments of the sequence can provide adjustments for the later segments.

Integrating Feedback and Motor Program Concepts

Various theoretical statements about motor control processes have attempted to integrate these ideas about the role of feedback with the concepts presented in Chapter 7 about open-loop processes. These ideas are presented in the next sections. The first task will be to define two distinct types of errors that the motor system can make, each of which will be dealt with by feedback in distinctly different ways.

TWO KINDS OF ERRORS

Goals in Motor Responding

When a person makes a rapid movement, he or she really has two goals (Schmidt, 1976a). First, there is an environmentally defined goal, such as putting a basketball through a basket, keeping the car in the center of the lane, or doing a somersault from a diving board. A second goal can be defined in terms of the muscular activities required to produce the desired outcomes in the environment. For example, I must contract the muscles in the arm and torso in one of a limited number of ways in order for the ball to go through the basket, and only certain patterns of muscular activity will result in a somersault. Essentially, how to achieve this subgoal is the problem facing the motor performer. It is often perfectly clear what the overall goal is (put the ball in the basket), but it is not clear how to contract the muscles so that the environmental goal is achieved. Thus, the performer must select a pattern of muscular contractions that will achieve this particular environmental goal.

One way to think of this subgoal is as a spatial-temporal pattern of action. That is, what the performer produces is a pattern of muscular activity that appears to be structured in terms of both space and time. Thus, such a pattern of action will determine where a particular part of the body will be at a particular time after the response starts. If this spatial-temporal pattern (the subgoal) is produced accurately, then the environmental goal will have been achieved. Of course a number of different patterns of action will result in the overall goal of shooting a basket, but each of these must be produced accurately for the overall goal to be achieved.

Errors in Response Selection

Given the assumptions about the spatial-temporal goal, the first kind of error that the person might produce can be defined: an error in *response selection*. This kind of failure to achieve the environmental goal results from the performer's choice of response. This can happen in a number of ways. First, the person can produce the wrong pattern of action; the person could move right when a move left was appropriate, or the person could move when it might be important to stand still. Second, an error in selection can occur if the person chooses an appropriate movement (e.g., a batswing pattern when a batswing is required), but the spatial-temporal pattern defined might be slightly incorrect. For example, the batswing could be too high or too low, or it could be too early or too late. Because all of these decisions about where to swing and when, as well as all of the contractions that occur in the swing, must be defined in advance, the performer will have made an error because he selected the wrong pattern to produce. Another way to see this is that, if the person had produced a pattern with a little higher bat location and a slightly earlier swing, then the results could have been a home run instead of a strike.

How does a person make a correction for an error in response selection? According to the evidence presented in earlier chapters, the person must issue a new motor program, as the "old" one will not achieve the goal in the environment. Hence, the person must enter the information-processing stages, a new program must be selected in the response-selection stage, and it must be programmed in the response-programming stage. These processes are very slow, they will require about one RT, and they will require attention (review Chapter 6). The result is that a new pattern of action in a rapid motor skill usually cannot be selected before the movement has been completed, and the movement will be in error. If the movement has a somewhat longer MT, then it is possible that a correction for an error in selection can occur. But such corrections, to be effective in achieving a new spatial-temporal pattern, must have a considerable time in which to be produced.

These ideas can be stated as a principle: When a new stimulus is presented indicating that an existing pattern of action will not achieve the environmental goal, a different pattern of action must be selected. This involves attention, the stages of information processing, and considerable time. It involves correcting an error in response selection.

Errors in Response Execution

An error in execution is fundamentally different from an error in selection (Schmidt, 1976a). An error in response execution can occur if the person produces a program of action that is appropriate for the environment, but some unexpected event occurs that disrupts the movement. One way this could happen is if the contractions specified by the motor program are not quite achieved by the muscles, perhaps because of inconsistencies in the system that determines which (and how many) motor units are to be activated. Or in a tennis game on a windy day, a perfectly programmed and timed swing will be slowed by an unexpected puff of wind. When picking up a milk carton that I thought was nearly full, but which really was nearly empty, I smashed the carton into the top shelf of the refrigerator.

These influences do not make the originally intended movement pattern incorrect, as some compensation that will achieve this originally planned spatial-temporal goal will still result in the environmental goal's being achieved. Thus, the correction for an error in response execution may not require a new motor program, as the original pattern of action defined by the "old" program will be correct if the motor system can compensate for the unexpected environmental influences. This implies that because the system does not have to select a new motor program, the correction for an error in execution does not require the stages of information processing, does not require attention, and will be far more rapid than correcting for an error in response selection.

What is the evidence for this second kind of correction, and is the correction for error in execution fundamentally different than that for an error in selection? Consider the example presented in Chapter 6 (Figure 6-12) from Dewhurst (1967). Recall that the subject was instructed to hold the limb at right angles and to attempt to compensate for any added or subtracted weight that might be applied to the hand. When weight was suddenly changed, a correction followed in the biceps EMG within about 30 msec, and a more sustained correction followed in about 50 to 80 msec which served to move the limb back to the originally defined location. First, the corrections were far faster than can be explained by the production of a new program of action, hence it seems reasonable to believe that the original program of action was in some way modified. More importantly, the person did not have to select a new program of action to compensate for the added weight, as the "old" spatial-temporal goal was still appropriate. The goal before the weight was added was "Hold the limb at right angles," and the goal afterward was the same; the subject seemed only to require additional muscular tension in order to continue with the "old" goal. Thus, it appears that the corrections made served the purpose of maintaining the original pattern of action, and they did not result in the generation of a new one. Because a new program did not have to be initiated, the corrections had a far shorter latency than would be expected if a new pattern would have had to be produced.

What about the role of attention in corrections for errors in selection? For evidence on this point, refer to the discussion of Henry (1953; Figure 6-13 and Table 6-1 in Chapter 6). The subject was involved in a task in which the limb was to push against a "pad" so that the position of the pad remained constant in the face of changing tension produced against it by the apparatus (see Figure 6-13). Henry found that the size of a change in force required for the subject's conscious awareness of a change was .559 dynes, while the size of a change in force required for an adjustment of the tension in the limb to maintain constant position was only .029 dynes. That is, the person was probably responding to changes in position of the limbs that were too small to be detected consciously. In terms of errors in response execution versus selection, the person did not have to select a new program when the force changed, because the original program that defined the constant position was still acceptable. Force changes were required, however, to hold the limb in this constant position; such changes appeared not to require attention; and they appeared to be able to compensate for very small force changes indeed.

From Chapter 6, evidence indicates that these corrections were based on closed-loop, reflex-based processes, especially related to the muscle spindle; and some of the neurological mechanisms thought to be responsible for these compensations were described. Seen in this way, such processes can be thought of as correcting for changes in the forces required to ensure that a given pattern of activity (already programmed) is carried out faithfully. Thus, corrections for an error in execution can apparently occur during a higher-order program of action, all without interrupting the outflow of commands from the program, but with a slight change in the tensions required at the spinal level to keep the movement "on track." Because the mechanisms are reflex-based, the corrections are very rapid, and they seem not to require attention.

Finally, what is the evidence that the corrections for errors in execution tend to keep the movement "on track"? The theory holds that gamma motoneurons (review Chapter 6, Figure 6-14 and related text) can be controlled somewhat independently from the alpha motoneurons that control the extrafusal fibers and that the gamma motoneurons can change the bias on the muscle spindles' sensory region. If so, then it is reasonable to believe that one role of the gamma motoneuron is to control the tension on the sensory region of the spindle as the limb moves, so that at each moment in time the output of the Ia afferent will reflect the position of the limb with respect to some "desired" position of the limb. Another way to say this is that at any moment in time one can regard the limb's position as having its own "reference of correctness" defined by the drive to the intrafusal fibers (via the gamma motoneurons). If, for some reason (e.g., added weight during a movement), the limb is lagging behind the position that the spindle "wants" it to be in, increased Ia activity, increased tension in that muscle, and a correction that speeds up the limb will take place. The opposite happens if

Table 8-1

Characteristics of corrections for errors in execution and selection (adapted from Schmidt, 1976a, in press-a)

Characteristic	Selection	Execution
1. Latency of correction?	120-200 msec	30-50 msec
2. Old Spatial-Temporal goal OK?	No	Yes
3. New program selected?	Yes	No*
4. Attention required?	Yes	No
5. More than one at a time?	No	Yes
6. Hick's law apply?	Yes	No?

*Provided that the deviation from the Spatial-Temporal goal is not very large.

weight is less than expected (e.g., the empty milk carton).

Such a theory of movement control would predict that regardless of when or where in the movement the changed load is applied there will be a correction with a latency of 30 to 50 msec. Recall that, using back-and-forth thumb movements, Merton (1972) showed that a resistance to the motion presented anywhere in the movement's trajectory resulted in an increase in the EMG, with a latency of from 30 to 50 msec (see Chapter 6 for more evidence). Such evidence supports the view that the spindle is a mechanism that can be a length detector at each moment throughout a movement and that the deviations from the length defined at any moment in time can result in corrections with very short latency and probably without attention. (These corrections do not, however, result in very large changes in the actual trajectory of the limb.) The corrections are, to my thinking, classified as errors in execution (Schmidt, 1976a, 1982a).

Execution versus Selection Errors

In Table 8-1, some of the fundamental characteristics of these two kinds of errors are listed so that their differences can be seen more easily. These differences are important, because without a systematic and testable distinction between these two categories of error it would make little sense to think of them as separate.

Latencies

As previously discussed, correcting for an error in selection seems to require one RT, or at least 120 to 200 msec. In contrast, correcting for an error in execution may require as little as 30 msec for a correction to be initiated, although other corrections may take as long as 80 to 120 msec, depending on the level in the motor system at which the correction is mediated.

Spatial-Temporal Goal

In correcting for an error in selection, a new spatial-temporal goal must be established, because the previous goal was inadequate to achieve the overall goal in the environment. The correction for an error in execution, on the other hand, maintains the spatial-temporal goal that was programmed earlier and merely alters the forces applied so that the original trajectory is achieved. Recently, Cooke (1980) has argued that the muscle spindles are responsible for the re-acquisition of a given trajectory after a perturbation.

The ability of the gamma system to correct for disturbances is related to the "gain" of the gamma loop. Gain usually refers to the amplification of a system; a car radio has a great deal of gain in changing the very weak radio waves into powerful mechanical vibrations of the speakers. With respect to the gamma loop, gain refers to the amount of tension that is produced in the extrafusal fibers in relation to the size of the signal from the stretched muscle through the Ia afferents. The gain of the gamma loop is quite low, so that even when the muscle is stretched considerably from a large movement perturbation, the resulting increase in tension is usually quite modest. In these cases, the gamma loop cannot produce an adequate correction for the error in execution, and some higher-level process must be involved in order to achieve the extra tension. Such processes could involve the trans-cortical (or long-loop) reflex or even a total reprogramming of the movement to achieve the extra speed of contraction (i.e., a correction for an error in selection). The main point is that definite limits seem to exist on the size of the perturbation that can be corrected by these reflexive mechanisms. (See Houk, 1979, for a more complete treatment of this question.)

Same versus Different Program

Third, the selection of a new program of action is required for the correction for an error in selection. For the error in execution (provided that the perturbation is small), the original program is still acceptable, but modifications in muscular output must be made so that the movement is back "on track."

Role of Attention

Fourth, what is the role of attention? For the correction of an error in selection, a new program is required. I have repeatedly emphasized that the selection of a new program requires the stages of information processing and attention. For an error in execution, though, the stages of information processing are presumably not required, and attention is not allocated. Henry's (1953) data tended to support this point of view when he apparently showed that people could correct for errors in execution without awareness.

Are Corrections Simultaneous?

The next two characteristics of error corrections are not based on evidence but are logical extensions of the basic theory. They could be regarded as predictions that could be tested in future experiments. Can a correction for more than one error in selection be done at the same time? My analysis and some data reviewed in Chapter 5 (see "Psychological Refractoriness") indicate that only one correction for an error in selection can occur at a time, as each correction requires the initiation of a new program. (I argued earlier that only one program can be selected and initiated at a time.)

For an error in execution, however, there is reason to suspect that a large number of corrections could be occurring at the same time, some in the arms, some in the legs, etc. In fact, this is a common view of postural control. As you sit reading these pages, you are maintaining a posture appropriate to reading, and your motor system is probably making hundreds of modifications in your posture to ensure that you are in a stable, upright position. Because these corrections do not require attention and the stages of processing, being handled at lower spinal levels through reflexes, they may not interfere with each other or with your reading at all. The experiments have not been done on this issue, though, and judgment must be reserved until the data are in.

Hick's Law

Finally, does Hick's (1952) law apply to these corrections? Remember that if the number of possible actions the person could make when a stimulus comes on is increased, RT is increased linearly as a function of the Log_2 (N), where N is the number of stimulus-response alternatives (see Chapter 4 for the complete discussion). By an extension of this argument, because the stages of processing are involved in correcting errors in selection, increasing the number of possible corrections required would increase the latency of a correction by an amount defined by Hick's law. The corrections for errors in execution, however, should not follow Hick's law, because the stages of processing are not involved and the system could presumably correct for one of two alternate errors in execution just as quickly as it could with one alternative. Crago, Houk, and Hasan's (1976) experiments appear to contradict this later generalization, but other interpretations of their data are possible (see "Triggered Reactions" in Chapter 6).

Other Reflex Involvements

Finally, other kinds of reflex-based compensations can occur during programmed action that cannot be simply corrections for a predetermined spatial-temporal pattern. The best example is the reflex-reversal phenomenon (Forssberg, Grillner, & Rossignol, 1975) in which the cat's reaction to a tap on the top of the foot during walking is different depending on when in the step cycle the tap is applied (see Chapter 6). Also, I should emphasize that the distinction between errors in execution and selection, and between their correction processes, is largely theoretical and quite tentative. Nevertheless, I think it is a useful distinction, because it seems to provide a basis for understanding the role of feedback in the production of motor programs. As with any theory, the structure provides order to the various experimental data in the literature, but more experimental tests must be conducted before the idea can be considered correct.

MOTOR PROGRAMS REDEFINED

From the previous sections, it seems reasonable to postulate the idea of an open-loop mechanism that is structured before the movement is initiated. The evidence for such a structure is considerable. Solid evidence for motor programs also comes from the gait literature concerning pattern generators (see Chapter 6). The findings from this work point strongly to centrally structured plans of action that can control the limbs without much involvement from feedback from the periphery.

But it no longer makes sense to conclude, as a number of us have (Keele, 1968; Schmidt, 1975b, 1976a; Schmidt & Russell, 1972), that the motor program is a centrally stored structure that carries out responses without *any* involvement of peripheral feedback. Substantial evidence suggests that feedback from the responding limb can, through a variety of mechanisms, help to keep the movement "on track" in the face of unexpected perturbations. And reflexes can modify the movement pattern in cases such as the tap on the top of the cat's foot (see Chapter 7), when the reflex interaction was different at different portions of the cat's stepping cycle. There is evidence (Merton, 1972) that the feedback from the touch receptors in the skin can modify the way in which the gamma loop functions; the feedback from the skin may modify the gain of the spindle loop. Thus, for all these reasons and many more, it does not make sense to claim that motor programs operate without feedback.

Levels of Control

A few years ago, I (Schmidt, 1976a) suggested that the motor program should be defined as a central structure capable of defining a movement pattern, but that the involvement of feedback should be incorporated into the definition of the motor program. I argued that motor programs can operate while corrections for errors in execution are being made. In terms of the ideas about embedded closed- and open-loop systems presented early in Chapter 6, a higher-order, open-loop movement program has embedded within it a closed-loop set of processes that serve to keep the limbs "on track," correcting for errors in execution. But when a signal appears in the environment suggesting that an ongoing pattern of action should be stopped and a different one adopted, the system must produce a correction for an error in selection which involves the sluggish stages of processing and a new motor program.

These thoughts lead to a modified definition of motor program, one that is in keeping with the literature on feedback process yet retains the essential feature of the open-loop concept: The motor program is an abstract representation of action that when activated produces movement without regard to sensory information indicating errors in selection. Once the program has been initiated, the pattern of action is carried out for at least one RT even if the environmental information indicates that an error in selection has been made. Yet, during the program's execution, countless corrections for minor errors can be executed that serve to ensure that the movement is carried out faithfully. Grillner (1975, p.297) has said essentially the same thing with respect to the control of gait:

> Perhaps it is useful to regard the relevant reflexes as *prepared* (emphasis mine) to operate but without any effect as long as the movement proceeds according to the set central program. At the same instant when the locomotor movements are disturbed (small hole, a slippery surface, etc.) the reflexes come into operation to compensate.

Others (e.g., Smith, 1978) suggest that the peripheral mechanisms have a slightly stronger role than Grillner states, this role relating to tuning of the spinal cord (see Chapter 6), making the movements smooth and effortless, and providing additional flexibility in the fact of very small unpredictable variations in the environmental conditons. These factors do not dull the argument that the central program determines the pattern of action, which is carried out with the "help" of the reflex mechanisms.

Programs and Coordinative Structures

I should mention again that this idea is similar in some ways to the coordinative concept structure discussed by Greene (1972), Fitch, Turvey, and Tuller (in press), and Turvey (1977). In both concepts, the many degrees of freedom in the responding musculature are reduced by a structure or organization (a coordinative structure or a motor program) that constrains the limbs to act as a single unit. Also, both notions involve the tuning of spinal centers from higher centers or by sensory input, corrections for what I call errors in execution, and freedom of the executive level from the details of what occurs at lower levels in the motor system.

Multi-Level Hierarchical Control

These ideas are both similar to other aspects of Greene's (1972) point of view, which emphasizes the hierarchical nature of motor control. He suggested that at the highest levels of the system the global aspects of the movement are represented in the form of a goal (shoot a basket). The control is passed down through progressively lower levels until all of the particular decisions about which motor units are to fire and which are defined in the muscles. The higher levels in the system do not have any direct control over muscle contractions—they only have control over adjacent levels of control that eventually result in those contractions. This idea is related to the motor program view, in which only two levels exist—an executive and a program or effector. Greene's view suggests that there are more than these two levels.

Along these lines, the highest level that specifies what Greene called a "ballpark" response, which would result in any of a number of actions that were "in the right ballpark" for the goal to be achieved. As the system passes control to lower levels, the individual details of the actions are defined by the initial conditions of the limbs, the posture of the performer, the relations with respect to gravity, and a host of other factors of which the highest level of the system is not aware. These lower functions then determine the ultimate movement that will result on the basis of these lower-level interactions with feedback, tuning, and other factors. In short, the "ballpark" response becomes increasingly well specified at each lower level in the motor system.

SOME PROBLEMS WITH THE MOTOR PROGRAM NOTION

The advantage of the motor program notion as a theory of movement control is that it provides order to a large number of separate findings in the area, such as the inability to use certain kinds of feedback, and the kinds of corrections that can and cannot be made. But the ideas about programs that have been stated so far have other logical drawbacks that must be considered. The next section deals with two of the most important: the storage problem and the novelty problem.

The Storage Problem

Given that the animal can produce a motor program "on command" and initiate it, how many such programs must the organism have at its disposal in order to move as it does? Remember that a motor program is thought to result in commands to muscles that define only a particular pattern of action. In this view, if the pattern is to be changed (e.g., throwing overhand versus sidearm), then a totally new program must be produced. Imagine all of the ways to produce a throwing action, each of which has a separate program.

MacNeilage (1970) has pointed out this problem in the context of speech production. According to programming theories of speech, each sound (called a *phoneme*) that the system can produce is presumably governed by a separate program, and in order to speak I simply string together these separate programs in a way that follows the "rules" of intelligible speech. This solution seemed to be a good one, as there are only about forty-four sounds in English, which should require only forty-four programs. The difficulty was that the actions of the musculature of the mouth, jaw, tongue, etc., for a sound are different depending on the sound that precedes it. That is, to make the sound of a "t," the musculature must make two different movements depending on whether the word is "eat" or "boat." The movements of the tongue in the space of the mouth involved in reaching the position on the hard palate (the "roof" of the mouth) are obviously different, as you can easily discover for yourself when you say these two words and note the actions of your own tongue. Thus, the 44 programs for tongue movement for the various sounds must now be multiplied by the number of possible sounds that could precede it. It can also be shown that the movements of the vocal musculature depend on the sound that follows the sound in question. All of this led MacNeilage to estimate that a very large number of programs must be stored in memory for us to speak as we do. Considering all of the various accents, inflections, and combinations, as well as any foreign language sounds, he estimated that something like 100,000 programs are required for speech alone.

Where does the motor system store all of these programs? Or does the system store them at all? We do not know that the motor system cannot store 100,000 programs for speaking, of course, as the long-term memory has a very large capacity. But when I consider the number of ways in which we move other than speech, and the interaction of previous states and following states for each of these movements, there would have to be a nearly countless number of programs in long-term memory.

This postulation seems unwise for several reasons. First, many mechanical or electronic control systems have this storage problem, and it is crippling to them; examples are libraries that have to cope with tons of paper and computer systems that have to store programs for every kind of computation. They simply run out of room. A second reason that such a postulation seems unwise is related to the belief that our motor system evolved in such a way that it was simple to operate and efficient in terms of storage. To store a complex program for every movement is not a simple and elegant way for a system to have developed (e.g., Schmidt, 1975b; Turvey, 1977). Is there a better way to conceptualize the storage of programs?

The Novelty Problem

The next concern about motor programming is related to the storage problem, but it takes a slightly different form. The basic issue is how we make new movements. Consider a movement like this: begin in a standing position, jump up from both feet, touching your head with the right hand and your leg with your left hand before you land. Certainly, most of us could do this on the first try. If you had never done that particular movement before and the action requires a program for its execution, where does the program come from? It is difficult to assume that the program was genetically defined (as walking might be), because such an action does not seem essential for survival. And you could not have learned it through practice, as this was the first time that you produced this action. A logical dilemma arises about motor programming for novel responses.

The same sort of problem exists for more common skills. If you were to study a series of fifty shots in tennis, examining the fine details of the feet, hands, and body, you would find that no two of the movements were exactly the same. This feature is compounded by the fact that the ball never has exactly the same velocity, same location on the court, or the same height. Therefore, it is unlikely that any two tennis strokes can be exactly the same. If no two shots are exactly the same, then the programs must also be different. Thus, according to this analysis at least, every shot is "novel," in the sense that it has never been produced in exactly that way before. When I make a movement, I do not merely repeat a response that has been learned earlier.

On the other hand, a given tennis stroke is certainly very similar to strokes I have made previously. For example, I have a certain (but very odd) style of hitting a tennis ball that is characteristic of me and no one else. And your favorite performer's style is easily recognized. Thus, it is not fair to say that every tennis stroke is absolutely new, as considerable practice and experience have led to the production of that action, and this experience tends to make the actions somewhat similar.

Writing almost a half century ago, Bartlett (1932) made the following observation about tennis strokes:

> When I make the stroke I do not, as a matter of fact, produce something absolutely new, and I never repeat something old (p.202).

His point summarizes the issues in this section very well. When making a stroke, I do not make a movement that is absolutely new, as that movement will depend on my past learning about tennis strokes. But I do not make an old response either, as any particular movement will be slightly different from all of the others I have made. In this sense, the tennis stroke is considered as novel.

One weakness of the earlier ideas about motor programming is that they do not explain how the individual can produce a novel movement or how a movement such as a particular tennis stroke is somehow slightly different than all earlier ones. If our theories about movement programs are to have an application to everyday motor behavior, then they must be able to explain these phenomena.

The Need for Revision

These two rather persistent problems—the storage problem and the novelty problem—must be seen as rather severe limitations for the motor programming idea as it has been stated previously. One solution has been to introduce a modification to the fundamental programming notion, which retains all of the attractive aspects of the programming idea that have already been discussed but which also provides a solution to the two problems mentioned here. This kind of thinking led to the idea that the motor program should be considered as *generalized*.

GENERALIZED MOTOR PROGRAMS

The idea of a *generalized motor program* is that a motor program for a particular kind of action is stored in memory and that a unique pattern of activity will result if the program is executed. However, in order to execute the program, certain parameters must be supplied to the program which define exactly how the motor program is to be executed on that particular trial. Because the program's output in terms of movements of the limbs can be altered somewhat according to the parameters chosen on a particular trial, the program is said to be generalized. Before describing how such a system may operate, it will be helpful to consider an example of a generalized program for another field of study.

An Example from Computer Science

Perhaps the best example of a generalized program comes from computer science (see Schmidt, 1975b, 1976a). In this field, many different "packages" of statistical programs do common statistical procedures. Consider a program that calculates means and standard deviations. Such a program is generalized so that it can produce output for various numbers of subjects and for various numbers of scores per subject. In order to run the program, I must specify certain parameters, which in this case include the number of subjects to be used and the number of scores per subject to be analyzed. Once specified, the program is executed for this particular subject-score combination.

How does this kind of program solve the storage and novelty problems? First, the storage problem is reduced, because, for this class of computing problem, there is the need for only one program to be stored in the system; and this one program can handle a wide variety of different combinations of number of subjects and number of scores. For example, if the number of subjects can range from 1 to 100,000 and the number of scores can range from 1 to 1,000, there is the potential to run this program in 100,000 x 1,000 different ways—100,000,000 combinations! Thus, generalized programs are capable of a variety of different outputs with just one stored program. Massive storage space in the computer system is saved.

With respect to the novelty problem, notice that the program for means and standard deviations can produce results for combinations of subjects and scores that it has never before been "asked" to produce. One simply specifies the proper parameters, and the program is executed beautifully, without ever having done it previously. In this sense, the generalized program provides one kind of solution to our novelty problem.

Given this example, I turn now to analysis of the evidence from motor skills in humans. I will consider why it makes sense to speak of generalized motor programs, and what some of the parameters for these programs might be.

Invariant Features

I have said before that motor programs are thought to be responsible for the production of a pattern of action, expressed in both space and time. When these patterns of action are examined carefully, it can be seen that various aspects of them are easy to change, while other aspects are almost completely fixed from response to response. It is not always clear from watching a movement which of the aspects of the movement are fixed and which are easily changed; but examining the movement in certain ways or

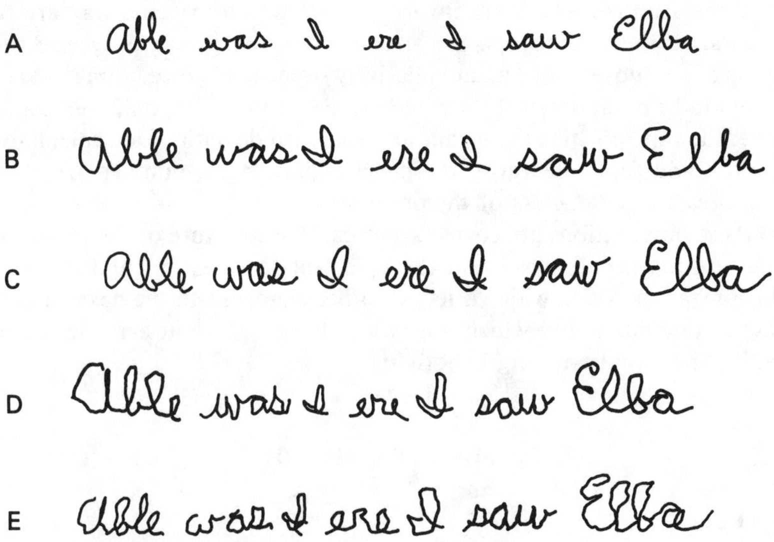

A   *Able was I ere I saw Elba*

B   *Able was I ere I saw Elba*

C   *Able was I ere I saw Elba*

D   *Able was I ere I saw Elba*

E   *Able was I ere I saw Elba*

Figure 8-5. Invariant features in writing. (In A, writing is with the right (dominant) hand; in B, writing is with the right arm, with wrist immobilized; in C, writing is with the left hand; in D, the pen was gripped in the teeth; and in E, the pen was taped to the foot) (from Raibert, 1977).

with certain theoretical biases can reveal these features.

Consider an example of one of our most common movement patterns—handwriting. Raibert (1977) has recently published some records of his own handwriting, where the sentence "Able was I ere I saw Elba" is written in various ways. The top line in Figure 8-5 is Raibert's usual handwriting with the right hand. Line B is the same sentence written with the right arm with the wrist and hand immobilized. Line C is the same sentence written with the left hand. For Line D the pen was gripped in the teeth. And for Line E the pen was taped to the foot. Merton (1972) has also published examples like this for check-sized and blackboard-sized handwriting; the conclusions are the same.

These lines of writing are obviously different in various ways. First, they are of different sizes, with the various lines of handwriting being photographically reduced or enlarged so that they can be compared in the figure. Next, increase in "shakiness" is seen from the top to the bottom of the figure. Notice also that the muscles and limbs with which these patterns were produced were different. The speed with which the sentence was produced was probably not the same either.

But in many ways, these lines of writing show remarkable similarities. A certain "style" is seen in all of them, such as the curious little curl at the top of the "E" in Elba and the common horizontal portion of the "I." Some aspects of these lines of writing appear to be invariant, even when the limb used or the size or speed of the writing changes. What is invariant is the spatial-temporal pattern, or the shapes of the letters.

This observation suggests that something in the performer's memory is common to all the lines of writing. Some abstract structure expressed itself regardless of the variations in limb or muscles used, speed, or size. I argue that those features which are invariant, and which in some way are fundamental to these sentences, are structured in the motor program; those aspects of the movement that are relatively superficial (speed, limb used) are thought to be parameters of the program. Remember the computer example above: the way in which the means and standard deviations are calculated is invariant and fundamental to the program, while the number of subjects and scores are parameters of the program.

If these observations are correct, how can the structure of the motor program be conceptualized so that the invariant features of handwriting are held constant across a wide variety of other changes? In the next section, I consider one possibility which appears to have abundant evidence to support it—the impulse-timing hypothesis.

Impulse-Timing Hypothesis

Impulses

One straightforward viewpoint about the structure of motor programs is the *impulse-timing hypothesis*, discussed earlier with respect to the control of gait and other tasks. The fundamental idea is that the motor program provides pulses of motoneuron activity to the relevant musculature. These pulses produce contractions in the muscles which can be seen in records of EMG or in records of force produced. The pattern of innervation produces patterns of force in the muscles. The amount of force produced is related in a complex way to the amount of neurological activity, and the duration of the force and its temporal onset are determined by the duration of the neurological activity and the time of its occurrence. A motor program tells the muscles when to turn on, how much, and when to turn off. That is, the motor program ultimately controls force and time.[1]

The combination of force and time is called an *impulse*. It is a common principle in physics that the amount of movement produced in a limb is a product of the force(s) acting on it and the time over which the force acts; this product of force and time is called the impulse. Therefore, the impulse-timing hypothesis really means that the motor program controls impulses—bursts of force spread out over time to the proper muscles.

In Figure 8-6 are three hypothetical, idealized records of the forces produced by a muscle over the time that this muscle is acting on the limb. At each moment of the contraction, the muscle is producing a different force against the bone (it could have produced a constant force in some other situation, of course), and the resulting curve in Figure 8-6 is called the *force-time curve*—a record of the force produced over time. The impulse is the shaded *area* under the force-time curve. From mathematics, this area is frequently called the *integral*, or a *force-time integral*.

---

[1]Programs may control other processes as well, such as the focus of attention, or the involvement of certain reflexes. But the control of force and time is seen as its major role.

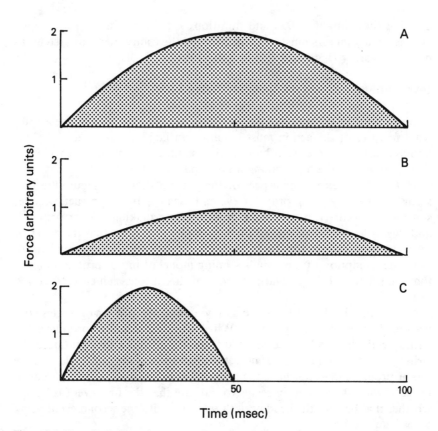

Figure 8-6. Hypothetical impulses seen as the area under force-time curves. (Impulses B and C have half the size as A, but B is achieved by halving the force with time constant, and C is achieved by halving the time with force constant.)

In the figure notice that the impulse (the area) can be changed by changing the amplitude of the force for a given amount of time (Case B), or by changing the duration of the impulse for a given amplitude (Case C), or both. From physics the velocity of the limb after the impulse has ended its action will be directly related to the size of the impulse. Thus, Impulses B and C in Figure 8-6 would theoretically produce the same velocity at the end of their respective actions (because their areas are equal). And the velocity of the limb with Impulse A would be twice as large as for the other two, as its area is twice as large. In this view, the motor program controls a feature of muscular contraction that is known to be a direct cause of movement—impulses.

If it is correct that the motor program is capable of determining an impulse, it is reasonable to assume that the motor program is capable of producing a group of impulses, each one in a different muscle group and each one at a different time. The idea is that the motor program can define an impulse in one muscle group, then in another muscle group, and so on, resulting in a pattern of activity that produces a skilled movement. Remember, producing impulses in muscles is really nothing more than defining the time of onset and offset of the relevant contractions, as well as their forces. Once these are defined, the movement is defined. Even so, defining these impulse sizes and durations should not be seen as simple, because many factors must be considered by the central nervous system, as discussed earlier (Figures 8-2, 8-3, 8-4).

Invariant Features and the Impulse-Timing View

Given a model of impulses that are patterned in time to produce a skill, what features of the action must remain invariant? What aspects of these impulses are the same from handwriting sample to sample, and which of them can vary while maintaining a given pattern of activity?

Order of elements. One aspect of the pattern shown in Figure 8-6 that seems not to vary is the order of events (Lashley, 1951). In each sample, some event occurred before some other event in making a letter or word, and this order was fixed for all of the samples. I assume that the order of muscular contractions for this inflexible order of events is in general fixed. A basic assumption of the impulse-timing model of motor programming is that the program has an invariant order of the various elements structured in it.

Notice that this is not the same as saying that the order of muscles contracting is fixed in the program. Why? The muscles that produced the writing with the head are certainly different than those that produced the writing with the foot or hand, and yet the pattern was the same. Clearly, the motor program does not have the order of muscles in it; rather it seems to order *actions*. The program seems to indicate that the first event is "up," whether that be with the head or with the foot, with the second event being across, and so on.

Phasing. A second aspect of the program that is thought to be invariant is the temporal structure of the contractions, usually termed *phasing*. The temporal structure of a series of events (in this case, a series of actions) can be measured in various ways, but one of the most common is to evaluate the structure in terms of relative time. In Figure 8-7 are hypothetical examples of records taken from two similar actions. This particular record has EMGs in it, but the record could have been defined in terms of movements of the limbs, the forces produced, or other characteristics that "capture" in some way the nature of the movement produced. The muscles whose EMGs are shown were chosen because they act at different times in the movement sequence. The sequence begins with a strong burst of EMG from Muscle 1, then Muscle 1 appears to be turned off and Muscles 2 and 3 are activated, with Muscle 2 ceasing its activity before Muscle 3. How can this temporal pattern of events in these three participating muscles be described?

One method is to measure the durations of the various elements within the sequence. Shown in the figure are two similar movements, but one of them has a longer MT (Movement 2) than the other (Movement 1). If these two records are evaluated with respect to the durations of the relevant contractions (EMGs), the Interval a can be defined as the duration of the contraction of the muscles in the entire action, Interval b is the duration of contraction of Muscle 1, Interval c is the duration of contraction of Muscle 2, and Interval d is the duration of contraction of Muscle 3. One way to evaluate the temporal structure of these events is to produce ratios of these

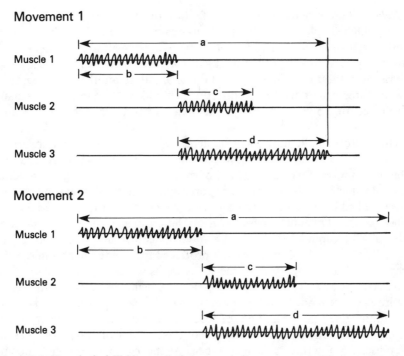

Figure 8-7. Hypothetical EMG records from two similar movements differing only in MT. (Phasing is defined by the ratios of the EMG durations among various muscles, e.g., b/c, c/a, etc.)

various times. This sequence for Movement 1 has a ratio of Interval *c* to Interval *d* of 1:2, or .50. That is, Interval *d* is twice as long as Interval *c*. Also, Interval *b* is one and one-half times as long as Interval *c*, making their ratio 1.5:1, or 1.5. Similar ratios can be made for any two intervals in the sequence.

A common ratio is that of an element in the sequence to the overall length of the sequence. For example, in this sequence the ratio of Interval *d* to the overall length of the sequence (Interval *a*) appears to be about .60; thus, Muscle 3 is contracting for about 60 percent of the entire MT.

The fundamental idea of these ratios is this: The temporal structure is measured by (or characterized by) the values of these ratios. If all the ratios are the same in two separate movements, then the temporal structures are the same. Thus, any two movements with the same order of contractions (perhaps that shown in Figure 8-7) and the same ratios of muscle action to total MT (e.g., .45, .30, and .60 for Muscles 1, 2, and 3) have the same temporal structure. Further, these two movements are assumed to be produced by the same motor program.

Movements 1 and 2 in Figure 8-7 have this characteristic. The proportion of total MT for each muscle is about the same in the two movements, even though the amount of time that each muscle is contracting is different for the two movements. Movements 1 and 2 are thought to be governed by the same motor program, because their temporal structure is the same. If two movements have different temporal structures, then they are governed by different motor programs.

Relative force. A third important feature of motor programs is *relative force*, which simply means that the amounts of force produced by any two muscles remain in constant proportion from movement to movement. If in Movement 1, Muscle 1 produced 2 kg of force and Muscle 2 produced 4 kg, the ratios of these two forces would be 1:2, or .50. In another movement using the same program, these proportions should be the same, but perhaps with forces of 2.5 kg for Muscle 1 and 5 kg for Muscle 2. The ratio remains 1:2, or .50.

This feature of the movement sequence would seem to remain invariant for the patterns of handwriting in the examples in Figure 8-5. This can be seen in two ways. First, in this kind of model, the height of a given letter is determined in part by the amount of force applied to the limb during the impulse applied by the motor program. But the heights of the letters remain in almost constant proportion as the various letters in a given sentence are considered. The capital "I" is always about twice the height of the "s" in "was," for example. The forces that produced these letter heights may have been in constant proportion in the sequence as well.

A second way to view relative force is to remember that the sentences in Figure 8-5 were made by different limbs, yet the pattern was the same. It is easy to imagine that the amount of force produced in the muscles of the leg during this action was much larger than the amount of force produced in the muscles of the fingers. This is so because the leg is a large segment compared to the finger, and the muscles that drive it are larger and more forceful in their contraction. Yet, because the patterns of writing were essentially the same, the logical conclusion is that the relationship between the amounts of force produced by the various muscles in the leg action were the same as the corresponding relationships for the finger action. That is, the relative force was the same in these two actions. Like the relative timing (or phasing), I think that this means that relative force may be structured "in" the motor program as an invariant feature. It is difficult to explain these elements of the different writing samples without this assumption about motor programs.

The Phonograph Record Analogy

It is sometimes helpful in understanding motor control theories to consider a *model* with many of the same features as the theory. My favorite model for the generalized motor program is the standard phonograph record. On the record, structured as invariant features, are three things. First is the order of the events, specifying that the drum beat comes before the guitar, and so on. Next is the phasing structured in the record. Think of phasing as a kind of rhythm, so that the time between any two events on the record divided by the total record time is a constant. For phonograph records, the ratios between the time of occurrence, or the durations, of any two events on the record are always fixed. Also, the relative force is fixed. That is, the first drum beat is always twice as loud as the second one. Finally, the actual muscles which produce the action (here, the particular speakers that will be driven) are certainly not on the record, because the record can be played on two different stereo systems in different homes.

What is on the record is a code that is translated into sound when the record is played on a given stereo system. It is helpful to visualize motor programs as records, because in many ways they behave the same, which allows me to visualize the motor program more vividly.

But we know that the record can be played in various ways to produce different sounds. It can be played rapidly or slowly, loudly or softly, with the treble or bass turned up, and so on. Yet, the raspy voice of Bob Dylan is still recognized, because the pattern of the sounds produced is invariant, even though some of the superficial features of the pattern may have varied. In the next section, I discuss some of these more superficial features of movements. These aspects of the movement are considered to be *parameters*.

Parameters of Generalized Motor Programs

Overall Duration Parameters

Learned Sequences. Of all the parameters mentioned here, the evidence supports an overall duration parameter more strongly than any other. Basically, the idea is that the motor program contains phasing and sequencing information but that this sequence can be run slowly or rapidly by assigning a different overall duration parameter, just as the speed of the phonograph's turntable speeds up the entire sequence of sounds as a unit.

Initial evidence for an overall duration parameter was found in an unpublished study by Armstrong (Note 11). Subjects were asked to learn an arm movement during which a lever had to be moved through a particular spatial-temporal pattern. Figure 8-8 shows a tracing of the position of the lever as a function of time in the 4.0 sec movement. Armstrong noticed, though, that when the subject made the movement too rapidly, the entire se-

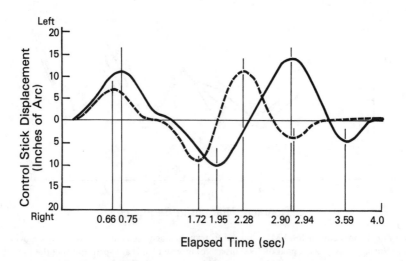

Figure 8-8. The position-time record of an arm-movement task, showing the correct move and a move in which the overall MT was too short (from Armstrong, Note 11).

quence was made too rapidly, as if the movement were sped up as a unit. It was as if the entire movement record was "contracted," so that all parts of the movement were shortened in the same proportion. Although Armstrong did not compute the proportions suggested in Figure 8-7, a critical test of the idea is that the time between Peak 1 and Peak 2 divided by the time for the entire movement is about the same in the two movements shown in Figure 8-8. Such findings gave initial insight into the possibility of an underlying generalized motor program, with an overall speed parameter that retained the invariant phasing in the movement pattern (see Pew, 1974, for an early discussion of this work).

Following Armstrong's (Note 11) and Pew's (1974) suggestions, Summers (1977) and Shapiro (1977, 1978) attempted to show similar findings in tasks in which the experimenter could instruct the subject to change the overall speed intentionally, rather than incidentally as Armstrong had done. Shapiro's paradigm involved practice at a task in which precise spatial-temporal patterning of pronation/supination of the wrist was required. Thus, the subjects, to be successful, had to make a series of actions defined in both space and time. The pattern of action for Shapiro's (1978) study is shown in Figure 8-9. The proportion of the total MT (which was 1600 msec) occupied by each of the seven wrist-twist movements is plotted as the line having data points marked with an X. After a considerable practice, Shapiro asked her subjects to speed up the movement but to keep the pattern the same; the pattern of proportions for these "compressed" trials is shown as the line with open circles in Figure 8-9. Notice that the proportions of time from segment to segment were almost exactly the same for the nor-

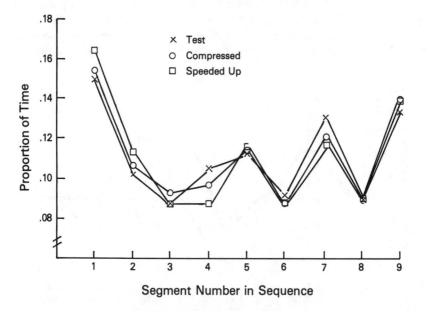

Figure 8-9. Proportion of total MT required to traverse each segment in a wrist-twist movement. (Normal trials have a goal of 1600 msec; compressed trials are sped up using the same phasing; speeded-up trials are sped up while subjects attempted to ignore the earlier-learned phasing.) (from Shapiro, 1977).

mal trials and the "compressed" trials, but the MT in the latter trials was decreased to 1300 msec, on the average. Essentially, Shapiro showed that the subjects could decrease the time of this well-learned movement sequence as a unit, keeping the phasing in the movement (defined by the proportions of time for each of the movement segments) constant. This again suggests that a movement duration parameter can be applied to some fundamental program so that the given pattern can be sped up as a unit.

Even more remarkable was another finding that both Summers (1977) and Shapiro (1977, 1978) obtained. They asked their subjects to make the movement as rapidly as possible and to ignore the phasing that they had learned in the earlier practice trials. That is, they instructed subjects to make the same movement sequences, but with some different phasing. Subjects were able to speed up the movements, but they were apparently unable to do so with a different phasing. In Figure 8-9, the line with open squares represents these speeded-up trials; again, the pattern of proportions was almost identical to that for the normal trials. The interpretation is that the person had developed a movement pattern (containing phasing and sequencing) and that when the person was asked to produce a different phasing, the person was apparently unable to do so.[2] Rather, the action was more rapid in time, but the original phasing remained. Shapiro's data suggest that phasing and sequencing are closely linked components of a movement program and that, again, a movement-duration parameter can be applied in order to change the overall time of a pattern with this previously learned phasing. Recently, Carter and Shapiro (Note 1) have shown that phasing, measured in terms of EMGs to the relevant muscles, is maintained when the duration of a learned sequence is decreased.

There are other examples. Terzuolo and Viviani (1979) studied the typing of various words, examining the phasing characteristics. Figure 8-10 is a diagram showing the word *trouble*. In the top portion, the time of occurrence of the various letters is plotted for twenty-seven different movement trials; the words are presented in the same order that they occurred in the experimental session, and no recognizable pattern of phasing appears in them. In the middle section of the figure, though, the words have been reordered so that the word with the shortest overall MT (845 msec) is at the top, and the word with the longest MT (1218 msec) is at the bottom. Notice that the onset times of the various letters "line up" on the sloped lines, as if the longest words were simply "stretched" versions of the shortest ones. And, in the bottom section of the curve are the same words, but the time of occurrence of each letter is given as a proportion of the total MT. Also notice that the relative time of occurrence of a given letter in the word *trouble* is almost constant from attempt to attempt. Similar findings have been produced by Shaffer (1980) in the study of typing and piano playing. All of these data support the notion that a given overall sequence can be sped up or slowed down as a unit while maintaining the constant phasing in the se-

---

[2]Researchers should be careful with this conclusion, though, as all we really know is that the subject *did* not use different phasing, rather than that the subject *could* not. Instructional sets, for example, may have prevented the subjects from producing a different phasing pattern.

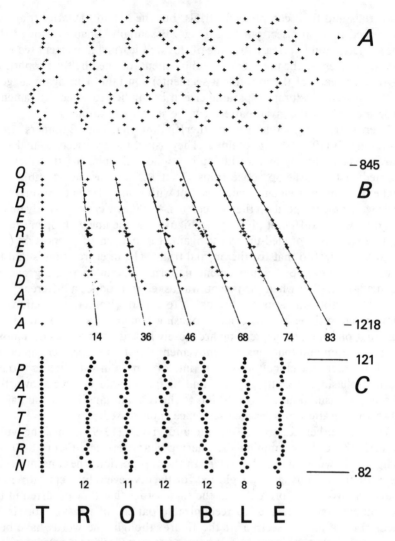

Figure 8-10. Temporal structure in typing the word "trouble." (Top, words are shown in the same order in which they were originally typed; center, words are ordered in terms of their overall movement time; bottom, the letter durations are expressed as proportions of overall movement time.) (from Terzuolo & Viviani, 1979).

quence. These data indicate that all of the words in Figure 8-10 were produced by the same motor program but with a different duration parameter. (See Shapiro & Schmidt, in press, for a review of this work.)

Control of Gait. Some evidence in the control of gait has been taken to mean that the idea of the generalized motor program, with invariant phasing, is not correct; yet, I do not believe that this evidence has been interpreted properly. For example, a set of findings discussed in a number of separate reviews (e.g., Grillner, 1975; Tuller, Fitch, & Turvey, in press) comes from work of Goslow, Reinking, and Stuart (1973). The durations of the swing phase (during which a given foot is not in contact with the ground and is swinging forward) and the stance phase (during which the foot is in contact with the ground) were each plotted as a function of the speed of a

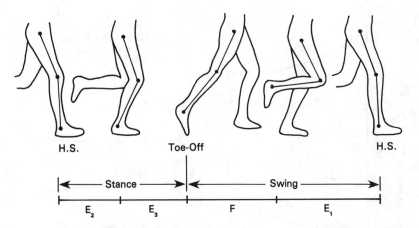

Figure 8-11. The Philippson step cycle. (H.S. = heel strike; F is the interval from the beginning of swing to maximum knee flexion; E_1 is the interval from maximum knee flexion to heel strike; E_2 is the interval from heel strike to maximum knee flexion (Yield phase); and E_3 is the interval from maximum flexion to the beginning of the swing; the "swing phase" is $F + E_1$, and the "stance" phase is $E_2 + E_3$.) (from Shapiro, Zernicke, Gregor, & Diestal, 1981).

cat's locomotion on a treadmill (see Figure 8-11). Goslow et al. showed that the time for the stance phase decreased as the movement speed increased (that is, as the time per step cycle decreased), as might be expected from the previous section. Yet, at the same time, the duration of the *swing* phase did not appear to change at all. Of course, the finding that the time for one phase of the step cycle decreased while the time for some other phase stayed the same means that the ratios varied, which is strong contradiction to the notion that phasing is invariant in these sequences.

The problem with the data of Goslow et al. (1973) is that the animals crossed a number of different gaits in changing the overall running speed. For the cats in the Goslow et al. study, the speed changed from about .75 m/sec to over 7 m/sec (a tenfold increase), which is probably equivalent to the cats' changing from a very slow walk to a trot and perhaps finally to a gallop. It is reasonable to expect that the phasing characteristics would change when the gait changes, since the idea is that a given gait is controlled by a given motor program.

What was needed was a study of a given gait, examining the durations of, and ratios among, the various phases of the step cycle. Shapiro, Zernicke, Gregor, and Diestal (1981) did just this in humans. They filmed subjects ambulating on a treadmill, gradually increasing speed to produce gaits ranging from a very slow walk to a moderate jog. They presented their results in terms of the Philippson (1905) step cycle, whereby the movement of the leg is divided into four distinct phases, as shown in Figure 8-11. Beginning at the left, the phase from the heel strike (H.S.) until the knee is maximally flexed is termed the *second extension phase* (E_2), and is the time over which the knee extensors are yielding under the weight just applied to them. Next, the knee begins a powerful extension to thrust the body forward, and this phase from maximum knee flexion to the moment the toe leaves the surface ("toe-off") is termed E_3. Together, E_2 and E_3 are termed the *stance phase*, during which the foot is in contact with the surface. After toe-off, the knee begins

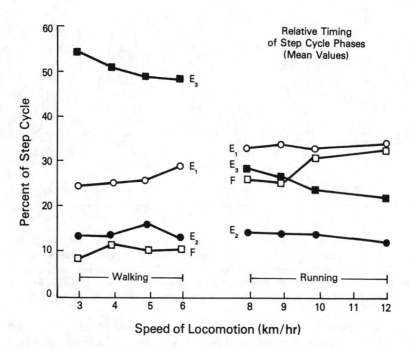

Figure 8-12. The proportion of time in the four Phillipson phases as a function of speed of walking and jogging. (The invariance of proportions for walking and for jogging give evidence of walking and jogging programs respectively.) (from Shapiro, Zernicke, Gregor, & Diestal, 1981).

to flex to swing the foot forward, and the time from toe-off until maximum knee flexion is termed the *flexion phase* (F). After maximum flexion, the knee begins to extend again in preparation for heel strike, with this phase being termed the *first extension phase* (E_1). Thus, F and E_1 make up what has been termed the *swing phase* in gait.

In Figure 8-12, Shapiro et al. plotted the proportion of the total cycle time for each of the Philippson phases for the various treadmill speeds. For example, they measured the duration of each of the phases at the different treadmill speeds, and the proportion of time for a given phase (say E_1) was the time of E_1 divided by the total time for a step cycle at that treadmill speed. As the treadmill speed increased, almost no change occurred in any of the proportions of the step cycle until about 7 km/hr. Then, however, a considerable shift in these proportions occurred, and no important changes in them were seen as the treadmill speed increased further. The periods of relative constancy in the proportions represent increases in speed within a gait. The abrupt shift in the values of the proportions to new values represents the shift from one gait (walking) to another (jogging). These data show that the walking pattern (or program) appears to be generalized across different walking speeds, so that we can walk faster or slower by applying an overall speed parameter, keeping the phasing constant.

Overall Force Parameter

A second proposed parameter for the generalized motor program is an overall force parameter which modulates the amounts of force produced by the participating muscles. Remember that the generalized motor program is thought to contain phasing and sequencing of actions resulting in impulses. The force parameter is involved with determining how forcefully the relevant muscles will contract when they are called into play by the program. The evidence is weak that such a parameter is actually present, but logically a force parameter must be included in the model. For example, in the Detroit post office a conveyer belt carries small packages to a person at the end. The person's job is to pick up the package and, with a "set shot" that would be considered good form in the National Basketball Association, cast the package into one of about fifteen equidistant bins for later delivery. This highly modernized and sophisticated package-sorting system requires a number of processes on the part of the performer. First, because the bins are equal distances from the person, the final velocity (as the package leaves the hand) of each of the packages should be approximately the same in order for each package to reach its bin. That is, the motor program for the "set shot" must move the limb and package at a speed that is the same regardless of the weight of the package to be tossed. Thus, tossing the packages with a constant velocity at release means that the duration parameter is held constant. But a package with a larger mass will require that more force be applied to it at a given duration to achieve the desired terminal velocity. Thus, the performer must choose a force parameter that can be applied to the generalized "set shot" program. Presumably, the person would pick up the package, "heft" it to determine its mass, and then select a force parameter for the generalized program that will achieve the proper goal. When the force and duration parameters have been selected (the duration parameter could be the same on each trial), the program can be run. Thus, the tossing program with predetermined phasing is run with different amounts of overall force on various trials. This explains how a given pattern is executed with a constant duration and different force requirements.

Another example that supports the concept of an overall force parameter comes from Hollerbach (1978). Figure 8-13 shows the acceleration tracings from a subject writing the word *hell* two times, one word twice the size of the other. The accelerations are, of course, directly proportional to the forces that the muscles are producing during the action. What is important about the tracings is that they have the same temporal pattern; the peaks and valleys appear to occur at the same places in the two tracings. Yet the accelerations in the tracing for the larger word are uniformly larger than those for the smaller word, and it appears that the forces applied to the pen were simply increased while maintaining the original temporal pattern. Of course, increasing the force leads to increased distance that the pen travels; hence, the word is larger with the same spatial-temporal pattern. Similar interpretations can be made from a study of handwriting by Denier van der Gon and Thuring (1965) who showed that when the friction of the pen on the writing surface was increased, a systematic decrease in the writing size resulted; but there was no change in the pattern of letters produced. Increasing friction, of course, can have the same effect on the movement as decreasing the muscular force applied to the pen. Both retain the essential

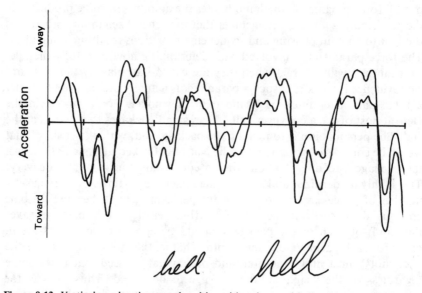

Figure 8-13. Vertical accelerations produced in writing the word hell, with one word having twice the amplitude as the other. (The tracings show a remarkable degree of temporal agreement, with systematic differences in amplitude of acceleration.) (from Hollerbach, 1978).

pattern of writing.

The previous examples consider that the overall force parameter applies to all the participating muscles proportionally, maintaining the relative forces applied to the limb, as discussed above. This concept is very much like the overall duration parameter, which is applied to the sequence as a unit. This assumption may prove too restrictive, though, so a second version of this model is possible. This view implies that the force parameter can be applied to various actions in the sequence selectivity, without other actions in the body being affected. For example, carrying a heavy backpack would seem to require that more force be applied to the muscles that operate against gravity in walking, but the muscles that cause the foot to move through the air in the swing phase would not need to have extra force applied to them. Perhaps we humans can select a force parameter that applies only to those aspects of the program that require extra force. This idea has the disadvantage of requiring the motor system to do more "computing" in order to move, with the selection of force parameters being required, each for various portions of a walking program. It is far simpler theoretically to have the person select one force parameter that governs the entire response.

Thus, an overall force parameter seems to be required to explain how we can produce a given pattern of action at a constant speed but with variable force production. Whether this parameter governs all muscles in the movement proportionally, or whether it can be applied to various muscles selectively, is yet to be determined.

Duration and Force Parameters

There is a further argument with respect to the necessity for a force parameter, but it is less obvious than the one just given. Consider a movement which begins with your elbow straight, flex it to 90°, then extend it to the straight position again, such that the overall movement time is 300 msec. The motor program presumably determines the phasing of the biceps, the cessation of the biceps and the initiation of triceps (for the reversal), and the contraction of the biceps to bring the movement to a stop. Now consider what would happen if you simply decreased the duration parameter of the program without changing a force parameter. Selecting a more rapid duration parameter would cause the program to move through the biceps-triceps-biceps sequence more rapidly while keeping the forces produced by these muscles constant. What will happen to the movement? Because the impulses (the "product" of force and time) will be smaller, the limb will not have moved as far in the time allowed for biceps activity, and thus the movement will reverse itself short of the 90° position. Increasing a duration parameter while holding a force parameter constant results in an inappropriate movement in terms of its extent.

One possible remedy is to choose the duration parameter so that the overall MT is correct, and then to choose an overall force parameter that will be sufficient for the limb to actually move to 90° before reversing itself. If the force parameter is too large, the movement will go too far in the proper time; if the force parameter is too small, the movement will not go far enough. Thus, with this view, movement distance for a given program is determined by a complex combination of duration and force parameters.

Clearly, duration and force parameters must compliment each other. That is, the selection of the force and speed parameters are not independent, as the particular value of the force parameter seems to depend heavily on the particular duration parameter chosen. The two parameters may be selected in independent stages of information processing, but the values actually chosen are highly dependent on each other in this model.

Muscle Selection Parameter

In the analysis of the handwriting examples shown in Figure 8-5 (from Raibert, 1977) and also from Merton (1972), I argued that the muscles for the particular action could not be structured "in" the motor program, because the same program produced movements in entirely different limbs. Thus, the motor program is seen as quite abstract, with additional specifications about which joints are to produce the action and which muscles are to be involved. In this case, it is reasonable to think of the specification of muscles (or joints) as another parameter of the motor program.

Coordination of the two hands. Here is an amusing experiment. You will need a blackboard and two pieces of chalk. First, try to write your first name with your nondominant hand, but backwards, moving in the opposite direction that you would if you were writing it normally (producing a mirror image of your normal name). You will find that it is very difficult to do, and that the pattern is barely legible. Now do the "same" task again, but do it simultaneously with the dominant hand. That is, perform the backwards writing with the nondominant hand at the same time that you do it normally with the dominant hand. Notice that the left-hand writing is now much smoother and that the patterns that are produced are similar for the two hands. And, as you perform the two-hand task, notice how the two limbs seem to be "locked" together, as if they were controlled by the same structure. Even though the left-hand writing is somewhat more uncontrolled than the right, a characteristic pattern still emerges—the same loops, straight parts, and so on. This is an example of a phenomenon noticed over seventy-five years ago by Woodworth (1903). He said,

> It is common knowledge that movements with the left and right hands are easy to execute simultaneously. We need hardly try at all for them to be nearly the same (p.97).

How do the two hands become linked together? One interpretation is that the motor programs for writing—usually directed to the muscles in the dominant hand—were simply coupled to the "same" muscles of the non-dominant hand at the same time. This interpretation holds that the selection of the muscles is a parameter that can be applied to a more fundamental and abstract motor program for signing your name.[3] Even though this kind of evidence and interpretation are fairly convincing, more formal evidence about muscle selection parameters must be obtained.

Kelso, Southard, and Goodman (1979) had subjects make two-handed aiming movements to separate targets. In one condition, the right hand had to move as quickly as possible a short distance to a large target on the right, while the left hand had to move a large distance to a small target on the left. As discussed in Chapter 9, strong determiners of the time required to make these moves are the movement distance and the size of the target to which the limb is aimed, according to Fitts' (1954) law. Fitts' law predicts that because the right hand has a shorter distance and a larger target, the time for the right hand should be far less than the time for the left. (When the moves are done in isolation, one at a time, this result occurred.) Which hand arrives first to its respective target when the subject is instructed to move both hands at the same time?

Kelso et al. found that rather than arriving at markedly different times as Fitts' law (and common sense) would predict, the two hands arrived at their respective targets almost simultaneously. Moreover, the two hands appeared to the "locked" together, in that the time of maximum height of the hand, the time for peak acceleration, the shapes of the trajectories, etc., were remarkably similar for the two hands.

In another situation, when the two hands moved the same distance to the same sized target, Kelso et al. placed a cardboard barrier between the starting location and the left-hand target only, so that the left hand had to move with a trajectory of approximately twice the height to clear the barrier. The results of this procedure are shown in Figure 8-14. Even though the right hand did not have this barrier, when the two hands were moved to their respective targets at the same time, the right hand moved over its "barrier" just as the left hand did. Again, the two hands appeared to be strongly "locked" together, and this effect persisted for 10 to 20 trials, although a

---

[3]This kind of analysis does not, however, explain why I cannot simply link the program for writing with the right hand to the muscles with the left hand when it is performed alone. Perhaps, with a great deal of practice I can.

TRAJECTORIES (HURDLE ON LEFT ONLY)

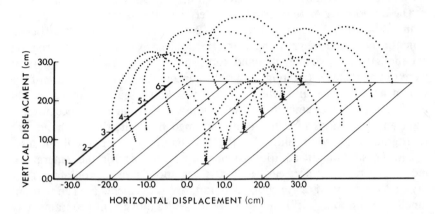

Figure 8-14. A subject producing a two-handed aiming movement. (One hand moves over a barrier and the other hand mimics it even though no barrier is present; from Kelso, Goodman, & Putnam, Note 12.)

systematically lower trajectory in the right hand occurred over trials.

Kelso et al. (Note 12) and our group (Schmidt et al., 1979) interpreted these findings to mean that a single structure was controlling both hands. Certain features of the movements—predominantly the phasing characteristics of the two limbs—appeared to be invariant across the two hands. Other features, however, such as the distance the limbs traveled, appeared to be easily changed between the two hands, and we (Schmidt et al.) interpreted this to mean that distance was determined by parameters to the two limbs (an overall force parameter) that were selected differently for the right and left hands. (Other interpretations of these data are possible, though, such as that provided by Marteniuk & MacKenzie, 1980.)

Perturbing one of the two hands. Additional evidence that the two hands are controlled by the same program comes from McGown and Schmidt (Note 13). They used a task much like that of Kelso et al., except that different goal MTs (100, 150, 200, or 250 msec) were used, with both hands having the same distance and MT goal. Subjects released the two styli after each trial and grasped them after the experimenter had placed them both in special holders that prevented their movement until the test movement began. Occasionally, the experimenter would switch the normally light (52 gram) stylus with one much heavier (454 grams) for the right hand only, and the subject could not detect this switch until after the movement began. From previous research (e.g., Schmidt, 1980) we knew that the unexpected heavier stylus would slow the right hand. The question in this experiment was what would happen to the left hand when the right hand was so perturbed.

When the MTs were 100, 150, or 200 msec, the slowing of the right hand had almost no effect at all (average change = 4 msec) on the arrival time of the left hand at its target. The left hand produced an action that was preprogrammed, and the perturbation of the body's right side had no effect at all on it. But, when the goal MT was 250 msec, then the left hand slowed down so that the right and left hands arrived at their respective targets simultaneously! (Right hand movement time = 279 msec, left = 282 msec.)

These findings can be interpreted in terms of the generalized motor program. When the MTs were short (100 to 200 msec), there was not sufficient time for the added weight to have an effect on the execution of the program for the left hand, so the left hand and probably the right hand programs were run as planned (although the right hand moved slower because of the weight added to it). But when the MT was 250 msec, the added weight resulted in a reprogramming of the actions in the right hand; because the right and left hands tend to be programmed together, the left hand was reprogrammed also, resulting in the two hands' moving simultaneously again. These data, in addition to providing support for the generalized motor program, support earlier discussions about motor programs. They say that when the MTs are short, programmed movements are run without much interruption. But if the MTs are long, the movement programs may be changed with the production of some new pattern of action.

One-handed movements. Shapiro (Note 14) used a wrist-twist task described earlier, having subjects practice this sequence with the right hand for five days; the pattern (proportions) for this task was shown earlier in Figure 8-15. After the five days of practice she asked the subjects to make the same movements with the left hand, which had never been used for this pattern before. She found a pattern of activity shown in Figure 8-15, where the well-practiced right-hand pattern is shown by the open circles and the novel left-hand pattern is shown by the closed circles. The two patterns are nearly identical, and the case can be made that the program that was generated by practice with the right hand had different muscles and joints applied to it so that it could be produced in the left hand. Such evidence supports the idea that bilateral transfer (Chapters 11 and 12) is so easily accomplished; the program used for one limb is simply used with another set of muscles.

Klapp (1977b), using a RT paradigm and methods described in Chapter 5,

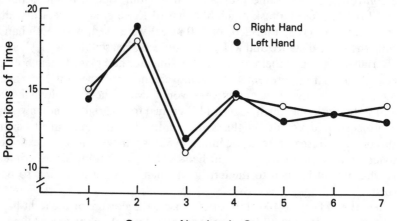

Figure 8-15. Proportions of total MT required to traverse various movement segments in a wrist-twist task (The pattern is similar for the practiced right hand and for the unpracticed left hand.) (from Shapiro, Note 14).

has also provided evidence that muscle selection is a parameter of the program. You may recall that the Morse code *dit* had a shorter RT than the *dah*, the major difference being that the *dah* had a longer hold component inserted between the key press and release. Because the phasing of the press-hold-release is different for the *dit* and the *dah*, the motor programs are assumed to be different as well.

In Klapp's Experiment 1, subjects did not know which program—*dit* or *dah*—they were going to have to make until the stimulus came on. But in one condition they did know which finger was going to be used, while in another condition they did not. Klapp found that when the finger to be used was known in advance, RT was shorter than when the finger was not known in advance. This finding might mean that the selection of the finger to be used came before the stimulus, whereas the selection of the program came after the stimulus. It also means that the program did not have the muscles specified, because the finger was selected before the subject even knew which program was going to have to be produced.

To summarize, substantial indirect evidence leads to the conclusion that the motor program is an abstract structure which does not have muscle information "in" it, containing only phasing and relative force. At the appropriate time presumably the person must select which muscles or limbs are going to be used in the movement, and the same pattern of action can be carried out in many different parts of the body, as seen in the handwriting examples. Such findings and thinking about muscle selection parameters have been valuable in coming to an understanding of the abstract nature of motor programs.

Other Parameters

Research on motor programs and parameters has only begun, and it is likely that additional parameters could be discovered. One of these might be *spatial parameter*. Consider throwing a ball overarm versus sidearm. It is possible that the patterning of activity (phasing and relative force) is the same for these two actions, but that they differ only in terms of the angle of the arm with respect to the torso. Thus, a spatial parameter could perhaps be applied to a movement to define a large number of throwing movements differing only in the position of one of the limbs. The evidence for such a supposition could come from an experiment in which the phasing and relative forces for two such throws are found to be the same but the angle of the arm is different. But this research has not been done. Other parameters probably could be defined, but none have very strong evidence at this time.

The Phonograph Record Analogy (Again)

Earlier I discussed the possibility that a motor program is analogous to a phonograph record, with order information, phasing, and relative force structured "in" it to define a given pattern. To complete the analogy, add the ideas about parameters just discussed. The overall duration parameter is analogous to the speed of the turntable. When the record turns more rapidly, the overall time of the record's activity decreases, but the phasing of sounds remains invariant. Next, the overall force parameter can be thought of as the volume control, whereby the same pattern of action can be produced either loudly or softly. This is very much like writing in very small letters or in very large letters with the pattern of the writing remaining the same. Muscle selection parameters are analogous to the operation of speakers. In my own stereo system, I have one set of large speakers in the living room and a set of small speakers in the den. I can, with the selection of a switch, have in operation one set or the other or both. If the speaker is analogous to a muscle, this is an example in which the same pattern is produced in two different "muscles."

Changing Parameters and Programs

Some additional evidence supporting the generalized motor program comes from experiments in which some aspect of the movement has to be changed during the movement. For example, Quinn and Sherwood (Note 15) had subjects make elbow flexion or extension movements, following through past a switch near the end, such that the time from the beginning to the switch was 400 msec. Occasionally, a signal would come on that instructed the subject to either (a) move faster or (b) reverse the movement, administered in different blocks of trials. Earlier evidence (Gottsdanker, 1973; Vince & Welford, 1967) suggested that speeding up a movement could be done more quickly than reversing it. Theoretically, when the movement has to be reversed, the subject has to stop running a given program and initiate a different program with new phasing that would reverse the limb's direction. In this case, the subject would have to select a new program plus the parameters for it before the reversal could be initiated. When the movement had only to be sped up, on the other hand, the performer can continue to run the same motor program and simply supply a different parameter to it. Here, a change probably would occur in the overall force parameter and/or in the movement duration parameter. Quinn and Sherwood found that the time to increase the speed of the movement, measured from the stimulus until the first increase in the agonist EMG, was about 100 msec shorter than the time to reverse the movement, supporting this hypothesis.

Other Theories Using Generalized Motor Programs

Handwriting

A number of other points of view use some invariant structure (like a motor program) combined with parameters to produce flexible movements. One of these views was proposed by Denier van der Gon, Thuring, and Strackee (1962), Denier van der Gon and Thuring (1965), and later by Vredenbregt and Koster (1971) and was directed at explaining handwriting as shown in Figure 8-16. Time is represented across the horizontal dimension. On the four lines of the figure are the forces applied by four muscle groups controlling the movements of the fingers—one for up movements, one for down, one for right, and one for left, as indicated by the arrows. A

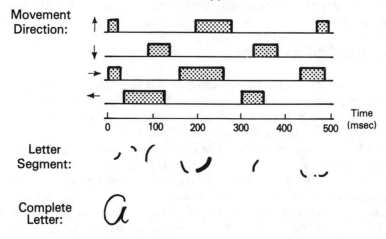

Figure 8-16. An impulse-timing model for handwriting. (Pulses of force with fixed amplitude indicated by solid bars are sufficient to produce trajectories resembling script.) (from Vredenbregt & Koster, 1971).

box drawn on the line means that this muscle group is active for the period of time indicated.

Their model assumes that the amount of force produced by a given pulse is constant and that the only way that the pattern can be modulated is to change the times of occurrence of, or the durations of, the pulses of force. For example, the first events are two simultaneous pulses, one upward and one to the right, resulting in the upward beginning of the letter "a" shown at the bottom of the figure. Next, these pulses are turned off, to be replaced by a leftward pulse that carries the pen along the top portion of the "a," and then a downward force is added that causes the path to slant downward to the left. Then a rightward pulse at about 150 msec is coupled with an upward force at about 200 msec, which results in the bottom of the "a" and the half stroke upward. In a similar fashion, the remainder of the letter is produced by combinations of forces applied just at the proper time. Denier van der Gon et al. and Vredenbregt and Koster showed with a mechanical limb that writing could be simulated by properly adjusting the temporal locations and the durations of these pulses of force (see also Wing, 1978).

These kinds of experiments are interesting for a number of reasons. First, complex trajectories of the limbs can be simulated with very simple pulses of force, presumably adjusted in duration and temporal location by the motor program in the human. Next, this is really an impulse-timing model, but the amplitude of the pulse cannot be adjusted. These amplitudes can be adjusted based on records of EMGs taken in tasks like these, but it is interesting to note how much movement complexity can be produced by changing only the temporal aspects of the program. Such a model does not, of course, prove that humans actually write in this way, but the ability to simulate handwriting suggests that motor programs for complex activities may be structured in terms of impulse-timing mechanisms. Finally, although these authors do not really say so, the possiblity exists that the amplitudes of the pulses could be increased together to make the writing larger, while the speed of traversing through the sequence of pulses could be changed to make the writing more slow or rapid (analogous to the overall force and movement duration parameters, respectively).

Simple Rapid Movements

Considering much less complicated movements than handwriting, a number of possible variations in the theory of the generalized motor program are possible. For rapid movements, such as a 150 msec elbow flexion to a new position, the generalized motor program idea suggests that the amplitude of the movement (time fixed) could be increased by increasing the size of the overall force parameter, so that the impulse drives the limb farther in the time that it is activated by the motor program. To decrease the MT, the movement duration parameter could be decreased together with an increase in the overall force parameter. This idea has been suggested by Schmidt et al. (1979), although they presented no substantiating evidence. Wallace (Note 16) showed, however, that when the MT was increased in this kind of task the bursts of EMGs tended to increase more or less proportionally, so that phasing of EMGs tended to remain constant when MT was changed.

An alternative viewpoint was presented by Ghez and Vicario (1978) in a study of rapid positioning responses in cats. They suggested that a rapid burst of agonist EMG is primarily responsible for "throwing" the limb in motion in the direction of the target. This burst, at least in this movement task in cats, appeared to be fixed in duration, regardless of the overall duration of the movement that was to be produced. Then, some secondary process, such as the *equilibrium achievement* associated with the mass-spring model (Chapter 7) might take over to clamp the limb in place at the target. Thus, in this model one process determines where the limb goes (equilibrium-point achievement), and another process determines how rapidly it goes there (the amplitude of the initial EMG burst).

These findings, particularly with the constant duration EMG burst in spite of changes in the overall movement duration, suggest that phasing is not invariant in these actions; and they are therefore contrary to the ideas presented earlier about the generalized motor program. As well, the finding of a constant duration initial burst does not agree with the findings by Wallace (Note 16) in humans. It is certainly possible that the structures of the movements in cats and humans were different because of a situational variable, such as instructions or the "set" under which the subjects were responding. Certainly, more work is needed in this area of rapid-limb-movement programming.

NATURE OF MOTOR PROGRAM REPRESENTATIONS

Impulse Timing versus Point-to-Point Computation

The impulse-timing models mentioned in the previous sections point out one additional aspect of the motor programming process that needs to be emphasized. The representation in the program, for these theories, was a series of pulses of innervation, delivered to the proper musculature at the proper time and graded so that the resulting forces produced in the musculature would be adjusted in terms of the amount of force produced and the duration of the contraction. Seen in this way, the motor program's code or structure—being nothing but a series of pulses—does not resemble at all the nature of the movement to be produced. Look at Figure 8-16 again. Here, the pattern of actions in the muscles is quite different from the pattern of actions produced by the muscular system (i.e., a script "a").

Contrast this kind of model with the idea of point-to-point computation mentioned in Chapter 6. Recall that, for some mechanical control systems, one way to control the movement's trajectory was to store or compute the coordinates (or the locations in space, the joint angles, or the muscle lengths, etc.) that should exist for each moment in time. This is very much like filming a tennis stroke, measuring the locations of the limbs at each millisecond of the action, and then storing this collection of coordinates in a memory system. When the action is to be reproduced, the motor system would be programmed to go to the first position, then the next position, and so on until all of the positions had been achieved. Achieving these positions in the proper order and speed means that the limbs would go through the proper pattern in space in time, and thus the action of hitting a tennis ball could be produced.

As mentioned previously, this kind of control mode is very difficult to handle from the point of view of the engineer, because so much computation has to be done for the limbs go to the proper place; and much storage of the individual positions of the limbs is required in some systems. For these reasons, people designing such systems have not favored the point-to-point computation method of control. For the same reasons, most motor control scientists feel that such mechanisms are too complicated to explain skilled movements in humans. Other, more simple, methods have been sought, such as the impulse-timing model discussed in the previous sections and the mass-spring model discussed in Chapter 7.

The major point to be made about these latter models is that they are designed to interact with the physical system that they are intended to control. This is not necessarily the case with many point-to-point computation methods, where it does not matter what kind of system is being controlled; the program is designed to have the system achieve a series of locations in space that result in a pattern. With the impulse-timing and mass-spring mechanisms, though, the system is given a pulse of force (acceleration), and the trajectory that results is determined by the physical characteristics of the system, such as the moment of inertia of the limbs, the effects of gravity, the friction in the joints, or the stiffness of the muscles. It is important to note that all of the details of the movement are not represented in the program (Bernstein, 1967; Turvey, 1977). A simple example will help to make this clear.

Consider a father pushing his daughter on a swing in the park.[4] Think of

---

[4]Thanks are due to J.A. Scott Kelso for this example.

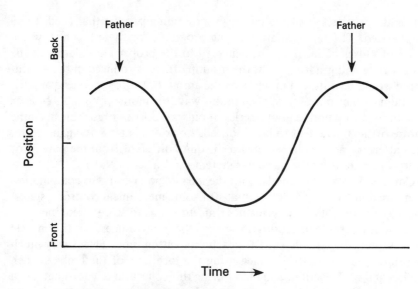

Figure 8-17. The position of a swing as a function of time. (A pulse of force added at the back of the swing is sufficient to maintain the trajectory.)

the father as the program that is capable of affecting the swing, and the swing and daughter as the limb system in the human. First, the father provides a pulse of force to the swing when it is at the back end of its travel, timing the force so that it is applied after the swing has achieved its farthest backward travel, as shown in Figure 8-17. Then the swing moves forward, propelled by the forces from gravity and the father, eventually decelerating near the front of the swing until it is finally stopped by gravity. Then gravity "pulls" it backward again, eventually to reach the father where it is pushed again, and so on. The swing has a trajectory that can be described in any of a number of ways, one of which is shown in Figure 8-17. This trajectory is relatively complex, in that there is a period of acceleration until the center, a period of deceleration, a reversal at a relatively fixed location, and then the same (or a similar) pattern of acceleration toward the father again. Is all of this detail structured "in" the motor program? Of course not. All that was structured "in" the program that produced this complex trajectory was a simple pulse of force, produced at the proper time and with the proper intensity. The complex trajectory was achieved by the interaction of the physical system with the program's input to it.

Program Interactions with the Physical Environment

With but a small shift in focus, this example tells us a great deal about how motor systems might operate. Our motor programs might be quite simple—perhaps pulses of innervation phased in time as I have suggested—yet the movement trajectories that are produced in the limbs could be quite complex. First, the pulse of force is applied to a physical system, the system of levers and tendons and joints that make up our skeletal muscular system. And this physical system acts in ways that are defined by the well-known principles of mechanics, being subject to gravity, friction, and a host of other factors.

Second, the pulse of innervation that results in force does not produce force in exact proportion to the amount of input; in other words, the motor system is nonlinear in many ways. If a system is nonlinear, its output is not directly proportional to the amount of the input. In the case of muscle, for example, doubling the amount of drive to it through the alpha motoneurons does not produce exactly twice as much force. And a delay in the rate of force build-up occurs that is not linearly related to the amount of force to be produced. Different forces are produced for different muscles, for the same muscle in different positions, and even for the same muscle innervated at different times within a movement. Finally, the amount of force produced by a muscle will be dependent on the velocity with which the muscle is shortening, with less force resulting when the muscle is shortening quickly than when it is shortening slowly, given the same alpha motoneuron drive (Partridge, 1979).

As a result of this thinking, largely motivated by the early writings of Bernstein (translated in 1967) and more recently by the workers at Haskins Laboratory (e.g., Turvey, 1977; Kelso et al., 1980a, 1980b; Kugler et al., 1980), a strong emphasis has been given to the understanding of how the physical structure of the motor apparatus interacts with the motor programming mechanisms to produce controlled actions. One direction this work has taken has been to consider simple motor programs that will produce complex motor behaviors. The analogy, of course, is the very simple "program" for pushing the swing, which results in the relatively more complex swing-movement pattern. Essentially, how does the motor system move a physical system in a gravitational environment, and do so in the simplest way possible?

Trajectory Control in Handwriting: An Example

The Denier van der Gon and Thuring (1965) and Vredenbregt and Koster (1971) models for handwriting are examples in which the properties of the physical system are exploited by the motor system to produce handwriting. While this kind of system is far more simple than a point-to-point computational method for producing the same letter, even simpler ways exist to consider the production of handwriting. The following example is from the work of Hollerbach (1978, 1981), who has considered handwriting from a quite different viewpoint.

Hollerbach attempted to simulate handwriting by using some simple and well-known properties of the motor apparatus. The most fundamental of these properties is that the muscles act like "complicated springs." (Review the section on mass-spring mechanisms in Chapter 7, as well as the ideas about length-tension relationships. The conclusion was that an innervated muscle can be regarded as a kind of "complicated spring.") One feature of springs is that they oscillate when set in motion. Take a rubber band (a rubber version of a spring), tie a small weight to one end, and drape the other end over your desk lamp. Give the weight a slight tug downward and let go.

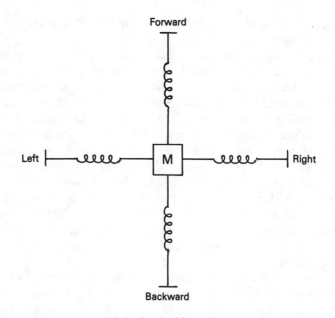

Figure 8-18. A mass-spring model for handwriting. (The forward-backward and right-left spring pairs oscillate to produce writing-like patterns.) (from Hollerbach, 1978).

The weight will oscillate up and down, gradually decreasing its amplitude of oscillation because of friction and finally coming to rest at an equilibrium point where the tension in the spring is equal and opposite to that produced on the weight by gravity. Also, the time per cycle is the same throughout, and only the amplitude of the cycle changes with time. How can thinking about muscles with properties more or less like this weight and rubber band help in understanding how the motor system produces handwriting?

Hollerbach (1978) conceptualized the muscles that make up the finger movements as springs, as shown in Figure 8-13. Here, muscles or groups of muscles move the finger up (toward the top of the page placed horizontally), down, left, and right, each group capable of being controlled independently. What happens if the system shown in Figure 8-18 is put in motion? The system begins to oscillate purely because of the physical interactions of the springs and the mass that it is to move. If the mass is thrown in a diagonal direction and then released, it will oscillate in a circle. And if the up-down and right-left springs are of different stiffness, the pattern can be made into an oval (a cycloid). (Remember, stiffness—the resistance to elongation—can be increased by contracting the muscle "harder.") All that is required to keep the mass oscillating is an occasional pulse of force delivered at the proper time in the sequence, just like the pulse of force that the father delivered to his daughter on the swing.

Next, imagine that the paper is translated leftward under this oscillating spring system. What will the resulting trajectory of the mass be when it is traced on the paper? Perhaps you can see that the resulting trajectory will be a series of loops. In handwriting, these loops would be recognized as a series of script "e"s, such as those shown in Figure 8-19. If the pattern of the force application is changed very slightly, a set of loops that forms the let-

Figure 8-19. Handwriting synthesized from the mass-spring model (from Hollerbach, 1978).

ters *e u n e* can be formed as shown. Hollerbach goes on to show how this kind of model can account for other letters, but more detail at this point would be beyond the scope of this discussion.

The important point is this: By considering the well-known property of muscle to behave like a complicated spring and by designing a motor program to exploit this feature of the motor apparatus, a complex trajectory can be achieved with a minimum of complexity in the program itself. Compare the three models that I have discussed here. A point-to-point computation model would require a set of coordinates for each of the locations in the set of "e"s—a very complex programming method indeed. An impulse-timing model forms the "e"s by "nudging" the fingers around the path defined by the series of letters—a simpler, but still complex way. In Hollerbach's model the trajectory of the letters is formed by the purely mechanical properties of the muscular system, with only a small pulse of force—perhaps only at the downward end of the cycle—necessary to produce this action.

The point is not that this may be the way we write. Rather, the point is that effective ways of thinking about how the motor program works can be developed by considering elementary physical properties of the muscular apparatus and by matching these characteristics with motor programming models that are very simple and highly compatible with these physical features. This kind of thinking solves a large number of theoretical problems that have faced motor control scientists for a long time. Finally, it is probably not necessary to believe that writing movements are handled only by springlike oscillations of the muscles in the fingers and wrist. Another view that leads to the same result as Hollerbach's considers that the spinal generators oscillate in some rhythmic on-off pattern and that the muscles of the fingers are turned on and off in the same sort of rhythm as Hollerbach showed. This view, of course, is closely related to the impulse-timing model for the control of gait discussed earlier. Perhaps a model that uses both of these mechanisms—oscillation in the spinal generators and oscillation in the muscles and limbs themselves—will turn out to be the best explanation of these complex skills.

SUMMARY

Motor control scientists have three reasons for believing that movements are controlled by programs: (a) the slowness of the information-processing stages, (b) the evidence for planning movements in advance, and (c) the findings that deafferented animals and humans show only slight decrements in skill. This is not to say that feedback is not used in movement. Feedback is used (a) before the movement as information about initial position, or perhaps to tune the spinal apparatus, (b) after the movement to determine the success of the response and contribute to motor learning, or (c) during the movement, either "monitored" for the presence of error or used directly in the control of movements reflexively.

The earlier definition of motor programs as structures that carry out movements in the absence of feedback was found to be inadequate to account for the evidence about feedback utilization during movement. As well, problems were associated with the requirement for storage of many different motor programs (the *storage problem*) as well as with how the motor program could create a novel action (the *novelty problem*). For these reasons, the motor program is thought of as *generalized*, containing an abstract code about the *order* of events, the *phasing* (or temporal structure) of the events, and the *relative force* with which the events are to be produced.

These generalized motor programs require *parameters* in order to specify how the movement is to be expressed. Such parameters are the *overall duration* of the movement, the *overall force* of the contractions, the *muscle* (or limb) that is used to make the movements, as well as others. With such a model, many different movements can be made with the same program (reducing the storage problem), and novel movements can be produced by selecting parameters that have not been used previously (reducing the novelty problem).

In considering what is represented in the motor program, various possibilities exist. Point-to-point computation models, in which each point in the trajectory of a movement is represented and achieved by the motor system in the response, are far too complex and cumbersome for human motor control. Impulse-timing models, in which the forces, onset times, and durations of the contractions are programmed, are less complex. And there is substantial evidence that movements are controlled in this way. Even simpler models exploit the mechanical properties of the limbs and physical environment—particularly in relation to their spring-like and oscillatory properties—and simple and elegant models of handwriting have been proposed using these ideas. A major conclusion is that not all of the limb's movement is represented in the motor program.

GLOSSARY

Error in execution. An error in which the planned spatial-temporal goal of a movement is appropriate, but the movement deviates from the desired path because of factors occurring during execution.

Error in selection. An error in which the planned spatial-temporal goal is inappropriate given the nature of the environment.

Gain. The relationship between the amount of input to a system and the output produced by it; usually expressed as a ratio.

Generalized motor program. A motor program whose expression can be varied depending on the choice of certain parameters.

Impulse. From physics, the aggregate of forces applied over time; the area under a force-time curve, or the force-time integral.

Impulse-timing hypothesis. A theory of motor programming in which the program controls the application of force, as well as the timing and duration of the forces, produced in the muscles.

Invariant features. Aspects of movements that appear to be fixed (or invariant) even though other, more superficial features can change; contained "in" motor programs.

Motor program. An abstract code or structure that, when executed, results in movement that is carried out in the absence of feedback about errors in selection.

Muscle selection. A parameter of the generalized motor program related to the selection of the muscles or limbs that will be used in the response.

Novelty problem. A problem with early motor program definitions that prevented the generation of movements that had not been produced previously.

Order of elements. An invariant feature of motor programs in which the order of actions is fixed.

Overall duration parameter. A parameter of the generalized motor program that defines the overall duration of the program's action; often called a "speed" parameter.

Overall force parameter. A parameter of the generalized motor program that defines the amount of force with which all of the participating muscles will contract in the action.

Parameter. A value that is specified to the generalized motor program that defines the particular expression of the pattern of activity.

Phasing. The temporal structure of a sequence, usually measured by the ratios of element durations and the overall movement duration.

Point-to-point computation. Models of limb control in which the coordinates of each point in a limb's trajectory are achieved sequentially by the motor system at the time of response execution.

Relative force. An invariant feature of the motor program that defines the relationships between the forces produced in the various actions in a movement.

Sequencing. An invariant feature of motor programs in which the order of actions is fixed.

Spatial-temporal goal. A subgoal for the performer in which a pattern of limb movement defined in terms of both space and time is selected; the major product of running a motor program.

Storage problem. A problem with early notions of motor programming in which the number of necessary programs was so large that their storage in the central nervous system seemed impossible.

CHAPTER 9

Laws of
Simple Movement

In this chapter, I turn from an examination of the fundamental mechanisms for the control of movements to an examination of broader aspects of movement behavior. The concern is with the fundamental relationships among various movement variables, and secondarily with the processes that underlie these relationships in the central nervous system.

Such fundamental principles—or laws, as they are usually termed (Chapter 2)—are critical to any science, as they describe the relationships of the objects under study about which scientists will theorize. As such, the basic laws in motor behavior may be seen as analogous to the fundamental principles of physics. The laws relating the mass, velocity, and acceleration of objects when forces are applied to them (the principles of mechanics), for example, have served as the cornerstone of the physical sciences, and hence they deserve a special status. In the same way, the field of motor behavior has analogous principles that are somehow fundamental to all the rest. These describe the relationship between the distance or speed that a limb moves and its resulting accuracy, the relationship between the distance a limb moves and the time it takes to make the move, and so on.

These principles are not nearly as many in number, nor are they as precisely stated, as their counterparts in the physical sciences. First, the motor control principles have been far more difficult to discover, based as they are on the data from biological systems that are more variable and complex than the physical systems. The relationships are not as obvious and often have to be "teased out" of background "noise" in a set of data by various statistical techniques. The situation is complicated further by individual differences (Chapter 10)—the fact that different individuals are different from each other. Physicists do not have this problem as one mass tends to behave just like any other.

Second, the early principles of physics are more precisely stated, perhaps, because their simplicity and elegance was relatively easy to describe even with little equipment. On the other hand, the motor behavior laws tend to be more complicated, probably because the central nervous system is far more complicated than is the physical world of mass and acceleration. Even so, some very simple relationships are emerging which are basic to the understanding of a large number of even more complex separate movement relationships. Do not expect a set of laws and principles to be presented that describe in totality the relationships among fundamental aspects of movements. What exists is a smaller set of statements, more limited in generality. The motor control field is far younger than physics, and with time the list should grow.

The discussion begins with the speed-accuracy relationship, which has been evident in general terms for centuries. It is not surprising that people began to wonder about it early in our history, because it is one of the most obvious features of motor functioning.

SPEED-ACCURACY RELATIONSHIPS

Everybody knows that as we move more rapidly, we become more in-accurate in terms of the goal we are trying to achieve. It probably was obvious to early man with respect to the accuracy needed in the making of objects with tools, and the addage "haste makes waste" has been a long-standing viewpoint about skills.

Early Research

Probably the first attempt to study scientifically this relationship between a movement's speed and its accuracy came from Woodworth, who in 1899 published a voluminous manuscript full of experiments on movement control. This work was far ahead of its time, in terms of both the ideas and the techniques that were used. For example, Woodworth (p. 41) proposed that aiming movements are made up of an *initial adjustment* that carries the limb toward the target in an open-loop fashion and *current* or *contemporary control* based on feedback that causes the limb to "home in on" the target. This distinction, with some qualifications, exists today (Chapter 8). As well, at the time his experiments were conducted, sophisticated electronic recording apparatus was not yet available, and methods had to be used that were practical and yet provided the precision necessary to answer the questions.

Woodworth used simple repetitive line-drawing movements to a target, varying the speed of the moves by changing the setting of a metronome that triggered the start of each. Studies were done with various distances, with the right and left hands, and with the eyes closed and opened in an attempt to uncover some of the fundamental relationships between speed and accuracy. Generally, Woodworth found that accuracy decreased as the movement speed increased, that the left hand was less accurate than the right hand, and that the decrement in accuracy with increased speed was greater when the eyes were open than when the eyes were closed. These last findings related to vision are strikingly similar to the results of the more recent vision experiments done by Keele and Posner (1968) and by Hawkins, Zelaznik, and Kisselburgh (Note 7) discussed in Chapter 7. Most of the other results have not, in general terms at least, been contradicted since. It was not until fifty-five years later that the next major contribution to the understanding of speed-accuracy relationships was made, this being the presentation of a formal mathematical relationship between speed and accuracy by Fitts (1954).

Fitts' Law

In 1954 Fitts conducted a systematic analysis of the relationship between speed and accuracy that has stood nearly unmodified for over a quarter of a century. In the *Fitts paradigm* (or *Fitts task*), a person is to tap a handheld stylus alternately between two target plates as rapidly as possible for a 20-sec trial. The two targets are usually rectangular and oriented as shown in Figure 9-1, with the long dimension perpendicular to the line between the two targets. Both the width of the targets (W) and the amplitude of the movement between them (A) can be altered from condition to condition, producing a large number of possible combinations of A and W. The task is scored as the number of taps (regardless of whether they are correct) in 20 sec, but subjects are cautioned to make no more than about 5 percent errors in their movements. A more general view of the experimental set-up is shown in Figure 9-2.

Fitts found that the relationship between the amplitude (A) of the movement, the target width (W), and the resulting average movement time (MT) was given by the following equation:

$$\overline{MT} = a + b[\text{Log}_2 (2A/W)], \qquad (9\text{-}1)$$

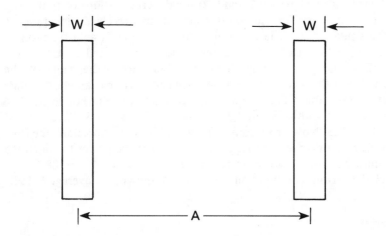

Figure 9-1. The Fitts paradigm. (The performer taps a stylus alternately between two targets of width W separated by a distance A.)

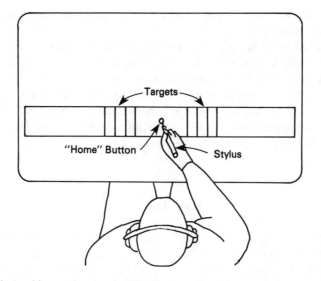

Figure 9-2. A subject performing the Fitts tapping task (from Fitts, 1964).

where MT is the average[1] movement time for a series of taps, computed as the trial duration (20 sec) divided by the number of taps completed in that time. For example, a 20-sec trial duration divided by, say, 50 taps in the trial yields $20/50 = .40$ sec/tap, or 400 msec/tap as the average MT.

The form of the Fitts equation is linear. The average MT is linearly related to the quantity $Log_2(2A/W)$. The equation has the general form MT $= a + bX$, where $Log_2(2A/W)$ is thought of as X, and a and b are empirical constants. (Review the section on linear empirical equations in Chapter 3 and the discussion of linear empirical equations in relation to Hick's law in Chapter 4.) Therefore, a graph in which average MT is plotted against $Log_2(2A/W)$ should be linear.

In Figure 9-3 are the data from Fitts' original experiment. The values of A and W were varied experimentally by changing the arrangement of the target board (as in Figures 9-1 and 9-2) for different groups of trials, and the resulting MTs were measured after subjects had received some practice at the particular tasks. The figure has the average MTs as a function of $Log_2(2A/W)$, where each of the latter values is computed by taking the values of A and W, dividing them, and looking up the value of the $Log_2(2A/W)$ in the Table of Logs (see Appendix). For example, the data point at the far right of Figure 9-3 has a target amplitude (A) of 16 in. (40.6 cm) and a target width (W) of ¼ in. (.64 cm). Thus, the value $2A/W = 2\cdot(16)/.25 = 128$. Now, from consulting the table in the Appendix, the Log_2 $(128) = 7.0$. (Remember, the Log_2 of a number is the power to which the base 2 must be raised in order to reach the number; i.e., $2^7 = 128$.)

So for the various combinations of A and W shown, the average MTs lie

---

[1]A horizontal bar placed over a symbol usually means the average of that symbol; thus $\overline{MT}$ = average MT.

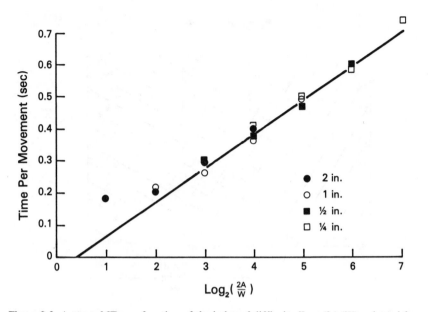

Figure 9-3. Average MT as a function of the index of difficulty [$\text{Log}_2(2A/W)$; adapted from Fitts, 1954].

nearly on a straight line, except perhaps for the first three data points where the movements were very rapid. Notice, for example, that two conditions for which the $\text{Log}_2(2A/W) = 6$ have target widths of ½ and ¼ in, and amplitudes of 16 and 8 in, respectively. Yet these two conditions had virtually identical MTs. You can see similar situations with the other data points plotted under a given value of $\text{Log}_2(2A/W)$, such as 3, 4, and 5.

Interpretation

What does it mean that the $\text{Log}_2(2A/W)$ plots linearly with the average MT in the Fitts task? First, notice that the value of $\text{Log}_2(2A/W)$ seems to determine how much time was required for each of these movements, so this value seems to be related in some way to how difficult the particular combination of A and W was for the subject. For this reason, Fitts called this value the *index of difficulty (ID)*. Thus, in Fitts' terms, the "difficulty" of a movement was jointly related to the distance that the limb moved as well as to the narrowness of the target at which it was aimed.

In fact, the relationship is even more restrictive than this, as the "difficulty" of the movement is theoretically the same for any combination of A and W that has the same ratio. Doubling A and doubling W at the same time results in a value of 2A/W that is the same (try it for yourself), and hence the same value of $\text{Log}_2(2A/W)$ has the same predicted average MT. Another way to say this is that the average movement time is linearly related to the ID, where ID $= \text{Log}_2(2A/W)$; MT $= a + b(\text{ID})$.

Next, the values a and b are the empirical constants, and they are required in order that the mathematical equation of the line actually fits the observed data from the experimental setting. (Review "Empirical Equations" in Chapter 3 for a discussion of empirical constants, their computation, and

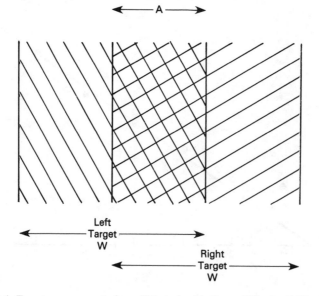

Figure 9-4. Target arrangements for a Fitts task with "zero difficulty." (The left and right target are overlapped.)

their general meaning.) Briefly, the first constant a is the intercept, referring to the value of MT where the line of best fit crosses the MT axis. Here, the intercept is the value of MT when the ID is zero. But what does it mean to say that a movement has "zero difficulty"? This has been a serious problem for the understanding of the ideas surrounding the Fitts task (see Welford, 1968, for a more thorough treatment). For the purposes of this discussion, a movement with "zero difficulty" is one with a ratio of 2A/W of 1.0 (because $\text{Log}_2(1) = 0$). Therefore, the intercept refers to the situation in which the amplitude is one-half the target width, the rather strange situation shown in Figure 9-4. Here, the targets are actually overlapping, so that the subject's task to tap alternately from one target to another involves tapping up and down as quickly as possible.

The slope constant b, on the other hand, is far more straightforward in its interpretation. The slope of any linear (X-Y) relationship means the amount of change in Y associated with increasing the value of X by one unit. Here, the slope refers to the added MT caused by increasing the ID by one unit. In this sense, the slope refers to the sensitivity of the limb movement system to changes in the ID. This can be seen more easily in Figure 9-5 from Langolf, Chaffin, and Foulke (1976), where the results from a number of different movement situations using the Fitts task are plotted. Notice that the slope increased progressively as the limb used is changed from the finger, to the wrist, to the arm. Although the interpretation of this effect is not perfectly clear, the data suggest that the larger and more cumbersome limbs (the arms) are more sensitive to the changes in the ID than are the fingers, that can be controlled more precisely. Finally, even though the slopes and the MT values are different for these various limbs, Fitts' law still holds for any one of them; that is, the average MT for any given limb still plots linearly with the ID.

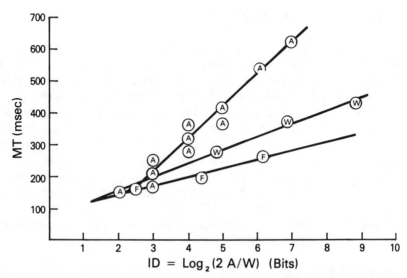

Figure 9-5. The Fitts relationship holds for finger (F), wrist (W), and arm (A) movements, but with systematically different slopes (from Langolf, Chaffin, & Foulke, 1976).

Next, why is a Log term in the equation, and why is the Log given to the base 2? When the idea was originally published, the interpretation was in keeping with a dominant theme of the day—information processing. Recall the discussion of Hick's law of choice RT in Chapter 5; the equation of that relationship also had a Log_2 term. The $Log_2(N)$, in which N was the number of equally likely stimulus-response alternatives, was a measure of the amount of information (in bits) required to resolve the uncertainty about N alternatives. The Log_2 term in Fitts' law can be seen in a similar way, where 2A/W is related to the number of possible movements and the $Log_2(2A/W)$ is the information required (in bits) to resolve the uncertainty among them. This notion is quite abstract, and I will not go into the argument in any detail here. (The interested reader should consult Fitts, 1954, for the original argument.)

Generally speaking, the original interpretation of Fitts' law was that the system is a processor of information and that when the movement is made more "difficult" by either increasing the amplitude or decreasing the target width, more information has to be processed in order to generate a movement that will arrive at the target. Because the amount of information that the human can process per unit time (i.e, the rate of processing in bits/sec) is limited (Chapter 5), the individual compensates for a difficult combination of A and W by increasing the MT, thereby enabling the completion of the necessary processing. According to Fitts, this is why making the movement more difficult requires more movement time.[2]

---

[2]Stuart Klapp in a personal communication has pointed out that the use of the base-2 Log is purely arbitrary and that any other base (e.g., e or 10) could have been used with equally good mathematical fits. The use of the base 2 makes it appear that Fitts' law necessarily has relevance to the information-processing ideas presented earlier, as these notions use the Log_2 as a measure of information (bits). However, other noninformational theoretical explanations for Fitts' law are both possible and preferable (see Keele, 1968, in press). I will present these alternatives later in this chapter.

The Speed-Accuracy Trade-Off

Fitts' law implies an inverse relationship between the difficulty of a movement and the speed with which it can be performed. Increasing the difficulty (ID) decreases the speed (i.e., increases the MT). One way to think about this is that the individual in some way "trades off" speed against accuracy, and this trade-off is done so that, in Fitts' terms, the rate of information processing is held constant. In addition to this strict interpretation in terms of the constancy of information processing, people presumably have some control over their mode of responding, so that they can move very quickly at the expense of accuracy or very accurately at the expense of speed. In this way, the Fitts idea has been fundamental in describing the *speed-accuracy trade-off*, or the performer's capability to change the control processes so that speed and accuracy are kept in some balance. Fitts' law describes the nature of this balance, seemingly very well.

Evidence for Fitts' Law

Since the Fitts principle was published, investigators have studied this relationship in a variety of contexts. This work has been directed toward the generality of the relationship to other situations, to other subject populations, and to other tasks.

Generality of Fitts' law. The Fitts principle has impressive generality. For example, the relationship holds well for adults as well as children, for retarded persons as well as "normals," in the foot, arm, hand, and fingers; underwater and in the air; and for movements so small they must be viewed under magnification as well as for large movements (see Schmidt, Zelaznik, & Frank, 1978, for a review). Fitts' law has predicted MT quite well. Slight modifications to the basic equation have been tried in an attempt to achieve a somewhat better fit of the experimental data to the values predicted by the equation, but little or no additional accuracy in prediction has been achieved (see Welford, 1968, Chapter 5).

Other movement tasks. The Fitts task is a rather strange movement situation, and many have felt that the particular configuration of alternate tapping is not very representative of many real-life tasks (e.g., Schmidt et al., 1978). Can the fundamental principle of Fitts' law be applied to other, more "natural" movement situations? Fitts and Peterson (1964) showed that the principle applied to a single-aiming task in which a stylus is aimed at a target in a single, discrete move. The amplitude (A) of the movement was the distance to the target, and W was the target width; the person's task was to move as quickly and accurately as possible to the target. In discrete moves, people appear to trade off speed for accuracy in much the same way as they do for continuous, cyclical movements.

In addition, the Fitts paradigm has been extended to movements other than tapping. In one modification, Fitts' (1954) subjects placed discs over pegs, where A was the distance between the pegs and W was the clearance (or tolerance) between the size of the hole in the disc and the diameter of the peg. Defined in this way, the Fitts equation seemed to predict MT very well. Also, tasks have been used in which pegs had to be fit into holes with varying tolerances, sometimes under microscopic conditions (Langolf et al.,

1976); the Fitts relationship appears to hold in these cases as well. The principle also holds for aiming a pointer at a target (e.g., Knight & Dagnall, 1967) or for controlling the movements of a dot on an oscilloscope screen with a handheld lever (Jagacinski, Hartzell, Ward, & Bishop, 1978).

Importance of Fitts' Law

It may not be obvious why so much attention has been paid to a single principle of motor performance. There appear to be two reasons. First, human motor behavior is obviously complex and difficult to understand. Because the system is so complex, it is difficult to provide precise mathematical descriptions of behavior that are generally applicable. Yet the Fitts principle does just that, and Fitts created it when almost no precise mathematical work was being done in motor behavior upon which to base his thinking. Second, the principle appears to relate to many different situations and for a number of variations of the original Fitts task. As such, the principle appears to represent some fundamental relationship that governs many kinds of motor behavior. Finally, since the publication of Fitts' law, no investigations have shown it to be incorrect, and only a few other studies provide alternative ways of dealing with the relations between speed and accuracy (e.g., Beggs & Howarth, 1972; Howarth, Beggs, & Bowden, 1971). I will discuss these more modern versions in a later section.

Interpretations of the Speed-Accuracy Trade-Off

As discussed in Chapter 2, one of the major goals of science is to provide an explanation or understanding of the various lawful phenomena that are established by empirical (i.e., data-gathering) methods in the laboratory. One of the most powerful motivations for scientists working toward an explanation is the existence of a well-established principle or *law*—one that has survived the "test of time" and been shown to be applicable to a wide variety of situations or kinds of subjects. Fitts' law certainly meets these criteria. Thus, one natural outgrowth of the work on Fitts' law was an attempt to understand the movement control processes which produced the particular relations shown. That is, people began theorizing about it. I have already mentioned theorizing in relation to information theory, whereby the index of difficulty was taken by Fitts (1954) to be a measure of the amount of information needed to resolve the uncertainty about the movement. Another approach was provided by Crossman and Goodeve (Note 8), when they proposed that Fitts' law could be explained by feedback correction processes.

The Crossman-Goodeve Theory

In 1963 Crossman and Goodeve presented an idea based on feedback control in movement which showed (with a number of assumptions) that Fitts' law could be derived mathematically without having to resort to ideas about information as Fitts (1954) had done. This derivation and associated argument was produced in a more accessible form some years later by Keele (1968).

Crossman and Goodeve assumed that the movement toward a target is made up of two kinds of processes—much as Woodworth (1899) had said fifty years earlier, except that the open-loop, distance-covering phase and the feedback-controlled "homing in" phase were thought to operate in rapid alternation during a movement to the target. This mode of control was termed *intermittent* in Chapter 6. The open-loop, distance-covering phase would operate for a fixed period of time, and it would have a spatial accuracy that was proportional to the distance that it had covered in that time. Then, feedback processes would evaluate the size and direction of the error and issue a second open-loop movement that would serve as a correction. This second movement would have an accuracy proportional to its much shorter distance; its error would be evaluated; another correction would be made; and so on until the movement landed on the target. Thus, the model is based on rapid alternation between open-loop movement processes and closed-loop corrective processes during the course of the movement. The MT, which is the critical variable in the Fitts equation, was thought to be based on the number of corrective processes that had to be made to achieve the target.

The number of corrections, and hence the MT, should be related to the amplitude and target width. With greater amplitude, the first open-loop movement would be longer and hence would have more error, requiring more subsequent corrections to achieve a target of a given size. If the target width were smaller, more corrections would be required for the movement to land on the target. Combining both of these factors resulted in a mathematical derivation of Fitts' law based on processes involving feedback, error detection, and error correction. Keele (1968) used this basic idea but added to it the assumptions (based on data from his own experiments) that the time between corrections be fixed at 190 msec and that the error in each movement be about 1/7 of the total distance moved in each correction. Keele argued that each of the corrections was processed in the stages of information processing, requiring attention, and that these movements were made up of a string of such corrections leading to the target.

Criticisms of the Crossman-Goodeve Theory

Certainly the major drawback to the theory that these rapid tapping movements were composed of a series of successive feedback-based corrections is related to the problems that humans have in processing information rapidly enough to be useful in rapid movement. This was the major theme of Chapter 5, and it is one of the most fundamental reasons for believing that rapid movements must be planned in advance through motor programs. Also, a problem is raised in relation to the psychological refractory period (PRP): Even though one such correction might be able to be made in 190 msec, it is doubtful that the second and third corrections could also be made this quickly (review PRP effects, Chapter 5). These and other criticisms of the Crossman-Goodeve theory have been discussed in more detail by Schmidt et al. (1978, 1979).

Perhaps the most persuasive argument against the Crossman-Goodeve theory was based on biomechanical records of subjects' movement trajectories in these aiming responses (Langolf et al., 1976). Breaks between one open-loop segment and the next could be seen as sudden changes in the position or velocity of the limb. Generally, most of the movements studied had one correction (a very few had two), and some had no visible corrections at all, even with MTs of 700 msec. These findings fail to support the hypothesis that a correction occurs every 190 msec in these actions.

Other hypotheses were sought that could explain the data more effectively. Schmidt et al. (1978, 1979) assumed that the impulses which produce action are "noisy" and that the amount of noise or variability increases as the amount of force increases. This *impulse-variability* model holds that when the distance is increased more force must be produced, leading to greater variability in the movement trajectory, causing the subject to miss the target. The response by the subject, then, is to slow down, increasing MT. Also, when the target size is decreased, the performer should slow down so that the variability in force is reduced, leading to more accurate endpoints in the open-loop movements. The impulse-variability model leads to the speed-accuracy trade-off, because greater distances and smaller targets should lead to systematically slower MTs, as Fitts found. While this kind of idea can explain Fitts' law in general terms, it cannot predict the relation mathematically, and this has been seen as a drawback. I will discuss the impulse-variability model later in this chapter.

Exceptions to the Speed-Accuracy Trade-Off

Certainly the view that when we do things faster, we do them less precisely or accurately is widespread, with considerable evidence to support it. Yet, some instances can be cited for which the speed-accuracy trade-off appears incorrect. I will deal with these next.

Timing Tasks

Many motor tasks require anticipation and timing, such as hitting a baseball. The individual must monitor the environmental situations (the flight of the ball) and decide when to swing so that the bat arrives at the plate at the same time as the ball does. Earlier I mentioned that these tasks require *receptor anticipation* of the ball flight, as well as *effector anticipation* of one's internal processes and MT. Errors in timing result if the bat arrives earlier or later than the ball. What is the effect of increasing the speed (decreasing the MT) of the limb or bat, while keeping the movement distance constant, on errors in timing?

Some years ago, I (Schmidt, 1967, 1969c) asked subjects to move a slide along a trackway so that it would "intercept" a target that was moving rapidly at right angles to the trackway (see Figure 9-6). The task was to move the slide so that a pointer attached to it would arrive at the coincidence point at the same time that the moving target did, but with a follow-

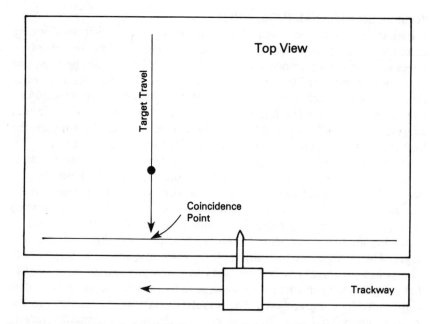

Figure 9-6. A coincident-timing task. (A target on a belt moves directly toward the subject, who attempts to move the pointer so that the two "coincide" at the coincidence-point; adapted from Schmidt, 1967).

through permitted. Accuracy in this task was scored in terms of errors in time—either early or late with respect to the target arrival. In two of the conditions, I asked subjects to make a movement that was of "maximal" speed or of "moderate" speed. There were four movement distances (15, 30, 45, and 60 cm), and the "maximal-moderate" instruction was used with each.

In Table 9-1, the absolute errors in timing are given as a function of the movement distance and the movement speed instruction. Overall, as the movement instruction was changed, the MT naturally changed as well, with the "moderate" instruction having a longer MT than the "maximal" instruction. Notice, however, that the absolute error in timing (for any movement distance) was uniformly smaller (20 percent on the average) for the "maximal" instruction than for the "moderate" instruction. Thus, when the person was performing the task more "violently," with a smaller MT and larger movement velocity, the timing accuracy in these conditions increased. Such findings seemingly contradict the notion of the speed-accuracy trade-off.

At least two explanations are possible for these effects. First, when the person moved the handle more rapidly (from the same starting point), the movement was initiated when the target was closer to the coincidence point than was the case when the movement was slower. That is, the subject waited longer before initiating the rapid movement. This may have provided the person with a better estimate of when the target would arrive at the coincidence point—i.e., better receptor anticipation—which would permit a better estimate of when the person should initiate the movement.

A second explanation is that the rapid movements were more consistent

Table 9-1

**Movement time, absolute error in timing, and variable error in movement time as a function of movement distance and instructions in a timing task
(adapted from Schmidt, 1967, 1969b, 1969c)**

| Movement Distance | Movement Instructions | | | | | |
| | Maximal | | | Moderate | | |
	MT	AE	MT VE	MT	AE	MT VE
15 cm	76	20	3	139	24	9
30 cm	123	23	7	209	27	13
45 cm	144	25	7	253	30	12
60 cm	206	28	9	274	41	13
Averages	137	24.0	6.5	219	30.5	11.7

Note: MT = movement time, AE = absolute error, MT VE = variable error of MT, all times are in milliseconds.

than the slower ones. The variable error (the within-subject standard deviation—see Chapter 3) of the MTs (see Table 9-1) was approximately 44 percent smaller for the rapid movements than for the slower ones. This suggests that a second feature of fast movements is more temporal stability from trial to trial than for slower ones. This can be seen as an advantage for effector antcipation, because the person can predict with greater accuracy when the limb will arrive at the target if the movement is rapid since the trial-to-trial variability in the movement's travel time is smaller. So, it is possible that the effects in Table 9-1 could have been caused by increased receptor anticipation and/or increased effector anticipation as the MT was decreased. Some subsequent experiments have helped to decide between these two views.

Temporal Consistency and Movement Time

Newell, Hoshizaki, Carlton, and Halbert (1979) performed a number of experiments on the temporal consistency of movement, and they provided perhaps the best documentation of the effects of MT. They used the ballistic-timing task, in which the subject moved a slide along a trackway; the initial movement started a timer and passing by a switch along the trackway stopped it, with the major dependent variable being the MT. The person could follow through past the end switch, the experimenters only interest being in the interval between switch activations. They used a number of MTs (ranging from 100 to 1000 msec) and a number of movement distances (ranging from .75 to 15 cm) presented in various combinations. They were particularly interested in the effect of making the movement more rapid, while holding constant the physical length of the movement.

Table 9-2

Errors in timing as a function of movement distance and movement time (from Newell, Hoshizaki, Carlton, & Halbert, 1979)

Distance (cm)	Movement Time					
	100		500		1000	
	5	15	5	15	5	15
Velocity	50	150	10	30	5	15
VE_t(msec)	10.8	9.0	74.6	42.8	125.7	91.2
VE/MT %	10.8	9.0	14.9	8.6	12.6	9.1

Note: The t subscript is excluded in the VE/MT % values to simplify the expression. Velocities are in cm/sec.

The primary variable of interest was the variable error in timing (VE_t), or the within-subject standard deviation of the MTs about the subject's own mean, taken to be a measure of movement consistency. The VE_t values from Experiment 1 are provided in Table 9-2 for different values of MT. Consider first the VE_t for the 5 cm movements. The inconsistency in movement timing increased markedly as the MT increased from 100 to 1000 msec (VE_t increased from 10.8 to 125.7 msec). Next, for the 15 cm movements, the effect was essentially the same, with VE_t increasing from 9.0 to 91.2 msec as the MT increased from 100 to 1000 msec. Thus, it appears that this is another exception to the speed-accuracy trade-off; the same distance with a smaller MT produced increased movement consistency in terms of timing errors.

An even more interesting feature of these findings is the suggestion that the timing error is directly related to the MT. In the fourth line of Table 9-2 are the VE_t divided by the MTs, multiplied by 100 to convert them to percentage values. If the VE_t is proportional to movement time, then the VE/MT % values will be the same for any movement time from 100 to 1000 msec. Indeed, this is essentially what happened, as the VE/MT % values were 10.8, 14.9, and 12.6 percent for the 5-cm movements. The corresponding values were 9.0, 8.6, and 9.1 percent for the 15-cm movements. Thus, the VE_t was approximately 9 to 15 percent of the MT produced by the subjects.

Schmidt et al. (1979) and Sherwood and Schmidt (1980) have provided a theoretical explanation for this phenomenon, which I will discuss in a later section in this chapter. For now, this effect of MT can perhaps be thought of as stemming from the generally held view that short intervals of time are "easier" to estimate or produce than are long intervals of time.

To illustrate, do this simple experiment. First, take a stop watch and estimate ½ sec (500 msec) without looking by pressing the button and releasing it at the appropriate time. Record the actual time for each of ten trials. Estimate your VE_t in timing this 500-msec interval by calculating the absolute error (AE) in time (the average difference between your time on each trial and the 500-msec target time). Now, do the same task again, with a target interval of 1 sec (1000 msec). You should find that the shorter interval is much "easier" to produce accurately, in that you are much closer, on the average, to the target interval with the 500-msec task than with the 1000-msec task. And, if you calculated the AEs for your performances, your AE for the 1000-msec task should be roughly twice that for the 500-msec task. The processes that are responsible for determining the duration of the intervals that you produced are variable, and they seem to be variable in direct proportion to the amount of time that is to be produced. Because the movements in the Newell et al. (1979) experiments were, in effect, based on processes that take time, it is reasonable to assume that they are going to be variable in time in about direct proportion to the amount of time that they occupy. This is basically what Newell et al. found (see Table 9-12) (see also, Newell, 1980).

Generally speaking, there has been considerable evidence that the VE_t (or inconsistency) in producing some interval of time tends to be a nearly constant proportion of the amount of time to be produced, at least within broad limits. For example, Michon (1967) has found essentially this effect with rhythmic tapping at different rates, Gottsdanker (Note 17) has found this effect for RT (where subjects with long RTs had greater within-subject VE_t of their own RTs), and we (Schmidt et al., 1979) have found these effects for aiming tasks in which the MTs were controlled. This well-documented behavioral law is an apparent exception to the general principle that speed is traded off for accuracy. Here, increasing the speed (by decreasing the MT) produces increases in accuracy in timing.

Temporal Consistency of Muscular Action

The idea that a movement duration becomes more consistent as the MT decreases implies that the durations of the particular muscular actions causing them become more consistent as well. We (i.e., Schmidt et al. 1978, 1979) studied this problem by having subjects make rhythmic back-and-forth movements of a lever in time to a metronome. We measured the forces the subject exerted (and their timing) with a strain gauge on the handle and recorded them on stripchart paper for later analysis. There were four different MTs (200, 300, 400, and 500 msec per movement), and the concern was the variability in the duration of the impulse that was produced by muscular action during these movements.

The results of this experiment are in Figure 9-7, where the within-subject variability in impulse duration is plotted against the MT imposed by the metronome. A strong linear relation was found between these two variables, suggesting that as the MTs become longer the variability in the duration of muscular action becomes larger, in direct proportion. This evidence is certainly in keeping with the data presented in the previous section about movement durations as a whole.

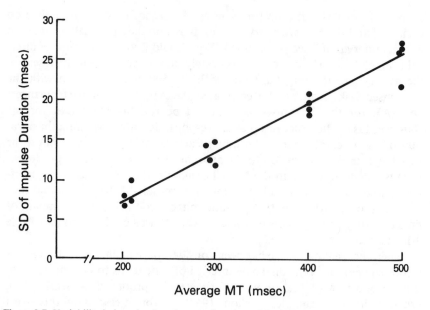

Figure 9-7. Variability in impulse duration as a function of the MT (from Schmidt, Zelaznik, & Frank, 1978).

Temporal Consistency and Movement Velocity

The MT is not the only factor that strongly affects the VE_t in timing; the movement's velocity (i.e., the movement distance divided by the MT—in cm/sec, miles/hour, or furlongs/fortnight) has a very strong effect as well. Return to Table 9-2 (Newell et al., 1979) and consider the VE_t for the various values of movement distance—either 5 or 15 cm. Notice that for a given MT (e.g., 100 msec), the movement with the smaller movement distance, and hence the lower movement velocity, has a slightly higher VE_t in timing (10.8 msec for the 5-cm movement, and 9.0 msec for the 15-cm movement). This effect is even stronger for the 500-msec and 1000-msec movements in the same table; the movement with the higher velocity had a smaller timing error, even when the MT is held constant.

Another way to express this effect is to examine the VE/MT % values presented in the bottom line of Table 9-2. Because the division by MT theoretically "cancels out" the effects of MT per se on the timing error (these two variables are proportional), any changes in VE/MT % as a function of movement velocity must be due to something other than MT. Here, the movements with the longer movement distance (and hence the greater movement velocity) have smaller VE/MT % values. For the three MTs, these values were just about 9 percent for the 15-cm movements and from 10 to 14 percent for the 5-cm movements. Increasing movement velocity made the movements more consistent.

Newell, Carlton, Carlton, and Halbert (1980) have studied these velocity effects more thoroughly than Newell et al. (1979) did in the earlier paper (see Newell, 1980, for a review). Various movement distances (ranging from 1.5 to 67.5 cm) and MTs (ranging from 100 to 600 msec) were used in combination, producing a set of velocity values that ranged from 5cm/sec to 225

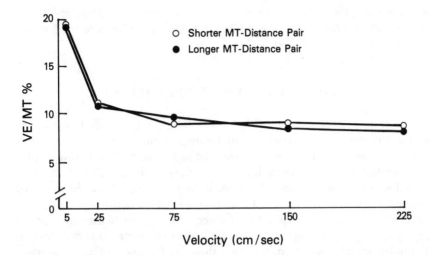

Figure 9-8. Variable error in timing (expressed as VE/MT%) as a function of the movement velocity. (Dividing VE by MT theoretically "cancels out" the effect of MT on errors; from Newell, Carlton, Carlton, & Halbert, 1980; the VE values were supplied in a personal communication with Karl Newell, and do not appear in the published report.)

cm/sec. The timing consistency (VE_t) was studied as a function of these variations in velocity, and I have converted these data to the VE/MT % measure so that it can be compared to the findings in the previous section. The Newell et al. (1980, Exp. 3) data are shown in Figure 9-8, where the VE/MT % is plotted against movement velocity. (Remember, the interpretation of the VE/MT % measure is the effect of velocity with the effects of MT "cancelled out" by division; or these conditions can be thought to have the "same" MT, because the effects of MT are nullified by division.) Here, as the velocity increased, the errors in timing decreased markedly. The decrease was sharp at low velocities and became more gradual with further increases in velocity.

I will discuss the possible interpretation of this velocity effect in a later section of this chapter, as understanding the issues requires some additional background. But for now consider this as yet another exception to the speed-accuracy trade-off. Even with a fixed MT, increasing the velocity of the movement by making the movement length greater produces an increase in timing accuracy—not a decrease as would be expected. These findings, as well as the findings for the effects of MT, do not, of course, negate all of the work that supports a speed-accuracy trade-off. Rather, it provides a limitation (or boundary condition) on the speed-accuracy principle, showing that it is not the universal law it was once thought to be.

An interesting application of these findings is that as the batter swings "harder," with a smaller MT and/or a larger movement distance, the errors that he or she will make in timing should tend to decrease, not increase. Note that this evidence is limited to errors in timing and does not speak to the issues concerning errors in spatial accuracy. It is certainly possible that increasing the velocity could decrease accuracy in the spatial aspects of the task, while at the same time increase the accuracy in the temporal aspects of the task. I will consider this issue in a later section of this chapter. It turns out, however, that many of these effects can be understood by considering the variability in forces that are applied to limbs during impulse production, and this issue is treated next.

FORCE-VARIABILITY PRINCIPLES

This section is concerned with factors that produce variability in the amount of force that is generated by the innervation from the motor program. This turns out to be an important issue for the understanding of processes underlying skillful behavior. All that the muscles can do to bones is to exert force on them, with this application being adjustable in terms of amount of force or in terms of the temporal onset and duration of that force. (Complex patterns of force produced during a particular contraction are presumably also under the control of the motor system.) If the innervation to the muscles is preprogrammed, then any factors making the amount of force that results from this innervation deviate from the intended amount of force will cause the movement to deviate from its intended path or fail to meet its environmental goal. To put it more simply, forces produce movements, and variability in forces produce variability in movements. When the muscles and limbs do not act as we intend them to because of this variability, it is usually considered to be a lack of skill.

The initial examination of force variability by members of our laboratory group (Schmidt et al., 1978, 1979) was motivated by attempts to understand how variability in forces called up by the motor program could be related to the accuracy (or, more precisely, the inconsistency) of the movement that resulted. In other words, does a relationship exist between (a) the nature of the movement (e.g., the MT, the movement distance, the load applied to the movement), (b) the variability of the forces applied to the limbs by the muscles, and (c) the resulting accuracy of that movement in terms of some environmental goal? This section deals with these basic questions.

Relationship between Force and Force Variability

Initially we (Schmidt et al, 1978, 1979) asked what the relationship might be between the amount of force that was produced and the resulting variability in that force. Why did an aiming movement with twice the amplitude (MT constant) have approximately twice the error in hitting a target (e.g., Woodworth, 1899)? In order to produce a movement of twice the amplitude, the generalized motor program might remain the same, but the overall force (or gain) parameter might be increased so that the limb would travel twice the distance in the same MT (see Chapter 8). Could it be that when the forces in the limb are increased in order to travel farther, the variability in this force is increased as well, making the output of the movement twice as variable? We thought so.

Mid-Range Force Values

Two initial experiments provided a fundamental relationship between force and force variability. We had subjects produce quick "shots" of force against an immovable handle. Attached to the handle was a strain gauge that sensed the amount of force applied; this information was sent to a recorder, as well as to an oscilloscope so that the subject could see the forces. A zero-force level was indicated at the bottom of the oscilloscope screen, and increasing force applied to the handle would result in the dot moving upward on the screen. Either five or six targets on the screen were used in separate experiments, and subjects attempted to produce ballistic "shots" of force that would have the peak force exactly at the target. The force production was very rapid and probably did not allow for the modification of the force on a particular contraction by visual feedback. Subjects produced a long series of contractions (e.g., 25), attempting to produce the same force on each trial. We measured the peak force and the within-subject variability (VE) of the peak forces, separately for each of the amounts of force that the subject was asked to produce in the different series of trials.

Typical results are in Figure 9-9, where the VE in peak force is plotted as a function of the amount of force that the subjects were asked to produce. A clear linear relationship between force and its variability was found. From a number of other experiments, force and force variability are linearly related in situations where the forces are much smaller than indicated in Figure 9-9 (40 gm elbow flexion measured at the wrist) and where they are as large as 65 percent of the subject's maximum (Schmidt et al., 1978, 1979; Sherwood & Schmidt, 1980). These data certainly supported our suspicion that as the amount of force was increased in order to, for example, move farther in the same MT, the variability in the force would increase in nearly direct proportion, probably leading to variability in the movement out-

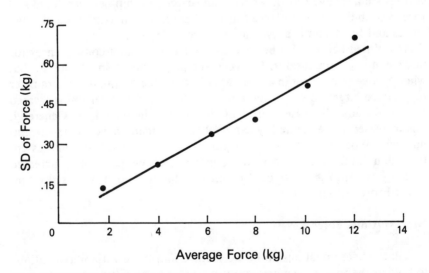

Figure 9-9. Variability in peak static force as a function of the amount of force to be produced (from Schmidt, Zelaznik, & Frank, 1978).

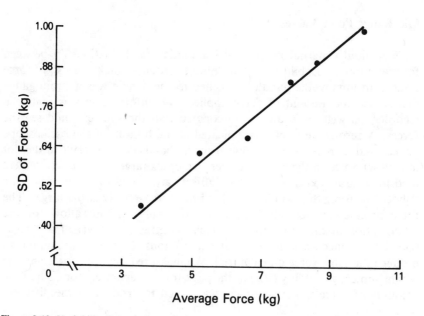

Figure 9-10. Variability in peak dynamic force as a function of the amount of force produced (from Sherwood & Schmidt, 1980).

come—in this case, hitting the target with accuracy.

These results were produced using isometric contractions, and one wonders if they apply to "real" movements, when the forces are applied by muscles that are actually shortening in length. Sherwood and Schmidt (1980) studied the forces that were applied to a handle during a ballistic-timing task with MT held constant. We studied the relationship between force and force variability as the load on the limb was increased. From Figure 9-10, the force and force variability were again strongly linearly related, with a function that resembled that in Figure 9-9. Overall, these various studies have shown a strong linear relationship between force and force variability for both large (up to 65 percent of maximum) and small forces and for dynamic as well as static contractions.

As I hinted before, this behavioral law has important consequences for understanding human skills. If it is correct, as discussed in Chapter 8, that when I move twice as far in a given MT, I adjust the overall force parameter to produce larger forces in the participating muscles, then this increased force will lead to increased variability in force at the same time. Generally, this increased force variability can explain why many have found—beginning with Woodworth (1899)—that doubling a movement's distance essentially doubles the spatial error in the movement's endpoint. The increased spatial error then is the "cost" of moving faster, and it is caused by increased force variability.

Near-Maximal Force Levels

Will the linear relationship between force and force variability continue to hold as the forces are increased even further? This is an important question, as many of the skills performed by athletes have very high force re-

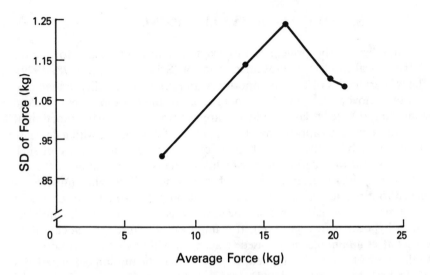

Figure 9-11. Variability in peak dynamic force as a function of force produced including near-maximal force values (from Sherwood & Schmidt, 1980).

quirements, such as the forces in the quadriceps muscles generated during a football punt for distance. With such large forces, one might expect that there would be no "room" for variability near the performer's maximum. If the subject actually did produce the theoretical maximum on every trial, there would be no variability (because the standard deviation of a set of constant values is zero). Thus, as the maximum force is approached, there would be a point of maximum force variability (perhaps near the middle of the range in force capability) and a gradual decline in force variability (i.e., more consistency) as the forces were increased further. With this reasoning, an inverted-U function should exist between force variability and force across the total range of forces available to humans.

In Figure 9-11 are the data from Experiment 4 of Sherwood and Schmidt (1980), in which the forces were increased to very near the subjects' maxima. The figure shows the variability in peak force as a function of the level of force produced, as before. But in this case a distinct peak occurred in force variability, with a strong tendency for decreasing force variability as the forces were increased further. The peak force variability occurred, on the average, at about 65 percent of maximum force for these subjects, with the largest force being about 92 percent of maximum. A major implication of this finding is that as the movement becomes more violent because of the subject's attempts to produce very rapid actions, movements become more consistent in their spatial and/or temporal output. This could be so because the forces that are being produced are near maximum where, according to Figure 9-11, the forces are becoming quite consistent, so that the resulting movements could be both very rapid and spatially consistent. I will discuss evidence for this notion later; but this could represent yet another violation of the speed-accuracy trade-off.

IMPULSE-VARIABILITY PRINCIPLES

A number of the principles just examined form the basis for simple mathematical models of movement control (Schmidt et al., 1978, 1979). The two principles of critical importance are: (a) the variability in the duration of a movement is directly proportional to the duration (velocity constant), and (b) the variability in force applied was an increasing function of the force applied to approximately 65 percent of maximum, with a decrease in force variability thereafter. The reason that these principles are of such interest is that they define the variability in the two dimensions of the *impulse*—the primary determinant of what the limb will do when muscles attached to it are activated. The notion of the impulse—the forces produced over time—has been discussed in the past few chapters (review the impulse-timing hypothesis in Chapter 8). It is important because the velocity of an object after an impulse has ceased to act on it will be directly proportional to the size of the impulse applied. It appears that the motion characteristics of the limb are directly related to the nature of the impulses acting on it. This is a major assumption of the impulse-timing hypothesis.

Notice that two separate determinants of the size of an impulse can be identified: the amount of force applied over the interval and the duration of the interval over which force is applied. From physics, these two aspects of the force-time curve have essentially the same effects on the limb's velocity. That is, if I double an impulse by doubling its force, holding the duration of the action constant, I will produce the same doubled velocity as if I doubled the duration of the impulse, holding the level of force constant. This is so because it is the area under the force-time curve that is important, and the area can be doubled by doubling either the force (duration constant) or the duration (force constant). Review Figure 8-6 and related text.

Now I will return to the ideas about force variability and time variability and their relevance to impulses. If impulses are critical determinants of action, then variability in the impulse should lead to variability in the action produced, and thus to a lack of skill. One can divide the variability in impulses into two components: the variability in the forces applied and the variability in the duration over which the forces are applied. The major point is that the variability in the impulse is determined by a combination of variability in force and variability in time. These sources of variability have been related in the previous sections to the nature of the movement produced.

Accuracy in Aiming Responses

How can these ideas about force variability and time variability components of impulse variability be used to explain some interesting features of human movement behavior? To answer this question, consider one kind of motor behavior that has been studied a great deal—the single-aiming response. The subject moves a handheld stylus from a starting position to a target a few centimeters away. In our version of this response (Schmidt et al., 1978, 1979), we measure MT as well as the accuracy in hitting the target.

We attempt to have the person move at a given time by providing knowledge of results about MT after each trial. The most important dependent variable is the effective target width (W_e), or the within-subject variability of the movement endpoints about the subject's own mean. W_e is really the variable error (VE) in producing movements of a given length (see Chapter 3, "Variable Error").

With the assumptions from the impulse-timing hypothesis and the ideas of the generalized motor program concept, we analyzed the motor control processes in these movements done with a rapid MT (say, 150 msec). First, the motor program will activate the agonist muscle group to produce an impulse for acceleration toward the target; this impulse will be switched off by the motor program approximately at the movement's midpoint (see Figure 7-2). At the same time, there must be an impulse upward to give the movement some "altitude" off the table top, and we assumed that this impulse is stopped at about the movement's midpoint as well. (Exactly when these impulses cease acting is not critical to the argument.)

Then, in the second half of the movement, the limb is decelerated as the subject attempts to bring it to a stop at the target. The limb is moved downward from its peak height, and the antagonist muscles are contracted to brake the movement's horizontal velocity. Schmidt et al. (1979) have shown that the stylus more or less "collides with" the target; striking the target surface provides a great deal of deceleration for the horizontal (and vertical) velocity. When these actions of acceleration followed by deceleration are coupled together in rapid succession (presumably by the motor program), the movement produces a trajectory that resembles the "typical" pathway as shown in Figure 9-12.

What happens to this kind of movement when the muscular impulses are variable from trial to trial, as they are? Suppose that, on a given movement, the motor program calls up too much force for the initial agonist burst. Because the velocity (after the initial impulse has been terminated) will be directly proportional to the size of the impulse, velocity in this particular movement will be too large. If the limb is traveling too rapidly at about the midpoint (where the initial impulse is switched off), the preprogrammed antagonist impulse will be insufficient to stop the limb in the same position, and the movement will overshoot the target. By similar reasoning, if the initial impulse is too small because of insufficient forces being developed, the

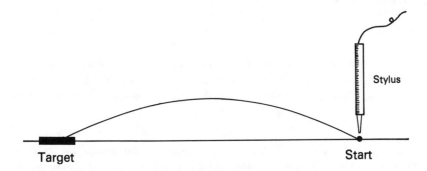

Figure 9-12. Stylus and target arrangement for single-aiming movements.

limb will drop to the target surface short of its mark. Thus, the variability in the muscular impulse to start this action is going to be a primary determinant of the amount of variability in where the stylus lands. That is, variability in the muscular impulses will be a major determinant of accuracy, W_e. This issue will be examined in more detail in the next sections.

Effect of Movement Amplitude

Consider what happens to this movement system as the person is asked to move twice as far in the same movement time. According to the idea of the generalized motor program, the movement duration parameter must remain fixed, but the overall force parameter will increase so that the forces produced will be twice as large as they are for the shorter movement. From the earlier section on force and force variability, as the amount of force produced is doubled, a doubling in the amount of variability in force is produced.[3] Because the duration of the initial impulse is assumed to remain constant (because the duration parameter remained constant), the increased variability in force will directly affect the variability in the initial agonist impulse, essentially doubling it. Then when the variability in the initial impulse is doubled, according to the analysis above, a doubling in the variability should occur in terms of where the stylus lands; that is, W_e should nearly double as well. This leads to the conclusion that the accuracy of the movement, W_e, should be linearly related to (and nearly proportional to) the amplitude of the movement. In simpler terms, doubling the amplitude of the movement nearly doubles the variability in the movement endpoint. Of course, this increased variability in the movement endpoint makes a small target very difficult to hit consistently. This can account for the finding, dating back to the time of Woodworth (1899), that the movement error tends to be linearly related to the movement length, especially if the movements are rapid.

Equation 9-2 summarizes this prediction,

$$W_e = a + b(A), \tag{9-2}$$

where a and b are empirical constants, and A is the amplitude of the movement. This is a linear equation, stating essentially that W_e is linearly related to A, with slope b and intercept a. (See earlier discussions of these empirical equations in Chapter 3.)

Effect of Movement Time

Next consider the effect of MT on the accuracy W_e. When the MT is decreased from, say, 200 msec to 100 msec, the notion of the generalized motor program would require that the duration parameter be decreased so

---

[3]This analysis assumes that the amount of force produced is less than 65 percent of the subject's maximum force—the point at which force and force variability are no longer linearly related. See Figure 9-11.

that the entire sequence of muscular actions runs off more rapidly. As well, the overall force parameter would have to be increased at the same time, as discussed in Chapter 8. So changing the speed of the movement seems to require a more complex set of adjustments than does changing the amplitude.

Changes in duration. What is the effect of increasing the duration parameter on the accuracy of the movement? Changing this parameter will have effects on the temporal dimension of the impulse. According to the earlier analysis of the effect of MT on the variability in impulse timing (Figure 9-7), the variability in the duration of the motor impulse is directly related to the duration of the impulse. That is, decreasing the MT should make the variability in the duration of the impulse smaller. As a principle, the variability in the temporal dimension of the impulse will be directly proportional to the MT:

$$\text{Impulse Variability (temporal)} = a + b\,(MT). \qquad (9\text{-}3)$$

Because the impulse variability affects the consistency of the movement, it is interesting to note that this equation states that MT has a component such that decreasing the MT makes the movement more consistent (i.e., temporally). However, this equation neglects the effects of concomitant variations in the forces that are produced as the duration of the movement changes.

Changes in forces. Equation 9-3 cannot represent the entire effect of MT, as it is obvious that increases in muscular forces must occur when the MT is decreased. Also, increased forces mean increased variability in force applied, according to the data presented in Figures 9-9 and 9-10. (As before, this kind of thinking depends on the forces remaining below about 65 percent of the subject's maximum force, as the relationship is no longer linear past this point, as shown in Figure 9-11.)

It is possible to estimate how much force increase would be required if the MT were halved. Holding the movement amplitude constant, halving the MT requires the velocity of the movement to be doubled; the limb travels the same distance in half the time, hence twice the velocity. From earlier analyses, the velocity of the limb after the impulse has stopped acting will be proportional to the size of the impulse, so the impulse will have to be doubled also. But notice that the impulse in the rapid movement has only half the time over which to act. So, in order that the impulse be doubled, the amplitude of the impulse must be quadrupled while the duration of the impulse is halved; the net result is that the fourfold increase in the amplitude and the halving of the duration produce a doubling in the size of the impulse. Thus, halving MT should essentially produce four times the impulse amplitude and, by Figures 9-9 and 9-10, essentially four times the variability in muscular forces. As a principle, the variability in the force dimension of the impulse is nearly inversely proportional to the square of the MT:

$$\text{Impulse Variability (Force)} = a + b\left(\frac{1}{MT^2}\right). \qquad (9\text{-}4)$$

Changes in force and time. Equations 9-3 and 9-4 provide descriptions for the variability in the impulses as MTs are changed. Equation 9-3 says that as the MT is shortened the temporal dimension of the impulse decreases. Equation 9-4 says that as the MT is shortened, the force dimension of the impulse increases. Thus, when the MT is shortened, two opposite effects occur on the impulse variability: a decreased variability in time and an increased variability in force. These two effects can be combined to form a single expression that describes the relationship between MT and total impulse variability (i.e., considering variations in both force and time).

$$\text{Impulse Variability (Total)} = a + b\left(\frac{MT}{MT^2}\right) = a + b\left(\frac{1}{MT}\right). \quad (9\text{-}5)$$

Equation 9-5 states that the total variability of the impulse will be related to the reciprocal of MT or, in other words, inversely related to MT.

The idea that variations in the impulse lead to proportional variations in the movement endpoint shows how MT is theoretically related to movement endpoint variability, W_e. W_e should be linearly related to the reciprocal of the MT, provided that movement amplitude is held constant.

$$W_e = a + b\left(\frac{1}{MT}\right). \quad (9\text{-}6)$$

Effects of Movement Amplitude and Movement Time

The effects of MT just discussed can be combined with the effect of movement amplitude (from a prior section) to provide a more general statement of the relationship between combinations of these variables on movement endpoint accuracy. That is, knowing the separate effects of movement amplitude and MT on W_e, predictions can be made for W_e for any specific combination of amplitude and MT. Combining Equations 9-2 and 9-6 gives a generalized statement of these combined effects:

$$W_e = a + b\left(\frac{A}{MT}\right). \quad (9\text{-}7)$$

Effective target width should be linearly related to the ratio of the amplitude of the movement divided by the MT. This equation states that increasing the movement amplitude or decreasing the MT will produce increases in error (W_e) in the movement's endpoint. Or the equation states that any combination of movement amplitude and MT that yields the same ratio of A and MT will yield the same W_e. This is similar to, but obviously not the same as, the Fitts equation, where the MT was theoretically constant for any constant ratio of A and W (review the section on Fitts' law).

Notice that the term A/MT is a measure of the movement's average velocity. The numerator is a measure of distance traveled, and the denominator is a measure of the time required to travel it. This is expressable in cm/sec. In simpler terms, the model says that the movement endpoint variability is linearly related to the movement's average velocity. Thus, the velocity of the movement, according to this kind of thinking, is thought to be a primary determinant of the "difficulty" of the movement. In terms of aiming responses, at least, increasing the average velocity increases "difficulty," which can be influenced by increasing the movement amplitude and/or by decreasing the MT.

Tests of the Impulse-Variability Model

Tests can be made of the extent to which the model in Equation 9-7 is correct. Certainly the most obvious prediction is the statement of the model itself: the W_e in a series of aiming movements should be linearly related to the ratio of the movement amplitude and the MT. Thus, if various movement conditions are used, each with a different movement amplitude and MT, the resulting W_es should plot linearly with the ratio of the amplitude and the MT.

Schmidt et al. (1978, 1979) have provided just such a test of this model. Subjects produced single-aiming movements to a target. The distance from the starting position to the target (A) was either 10, 20, or 30 cm; and the MT was either 140, 170, or 200 msec. Thus, nine A/MT combinations were formed. MT was "controlled" by giving knowledge of results after each movement to inform the subject as to whether the response was too fast or too slow, and we only used data from those movements that had the proper MT (i.e., that were within 15 percent of the correct MT). Using these trials, we measured the variability in movement endpoint.

From the statement of the model, the most important measure of accuracy is the W_e for extent, or the VEs of the movement endpoints measured parallel to the overall movement direction. The plot of the W_e for extent for the various combinations of A/MT is given in Figure 9-13. The relationship between W_e-extent and the values of A/MT is essentially linear, with nearly all of the points falling close to the line of best fit. The

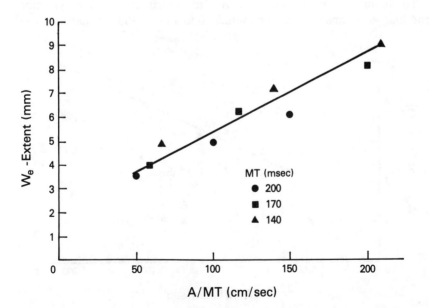

Figure 9-13. Effective target width (W_e-extent) as a function of the average velocity (A/MT) (from Schmidt, Zelaznik, Hawkins, Frank, & Quinn, 1979).

equation of the line in Figure 9-13 is

$$W_e = 2.12 + .033(A/MT), \tag{9-8}$$

where the value of a (the intercept) was 2.12 mm, and the value of b (the slope) was .033. Notice that for very different amplitudes and movement times, but for which the ratio of A and MT is about the same, the W_e-extent was also about the same.

We also considered the relationship between the errors measured in the dimension perpendicular and the overall movement direction (called W_e-direction), which represents variations in the aiming component of the movement. Effects of A and MT on this variable are not derivable from the basic model, but it is interesting to consider their effects on this aspect of accuracy. A plot of these W_e-direction values against the values of A/MT is shown in Figure 9-14. Here again, the ratio of A/MT and the W_e-direction measures were related linearly, with all of the data points falling close to the line of best fit. Here, though, the errors were about half the size of the W_e-extent errors, suggesting that the person tends to produce an elliptical pattern of responses about the target, with the long axis of the elipse falling in line with the overall movement direction. For the line in Figure 9-14, the equation was:

$$W_e = 1.20 + .018 \, (A/MT). \tag{9-9}$$

Notice that the intercept (1.20 mm) and the slope (.018) were both substantially smaller than they were with extent errors (Equation 9-8), but that the relationship between the movement's average velocity and the resulting errors was linear for the two kinds of errors.

To summarize, we assumed that the movement is totally programmed and that variations in a speed parameter and an overall force parameter are

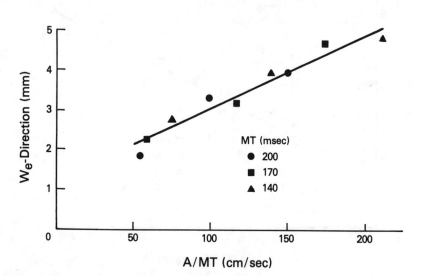

Figure 9-14. Effective target width (W_e-direction) as a function of the average velocity (A/MT) (from Schmidt, Zelaznik, Hawkins, Frank, & Quinn, 1979).

responsible for modulations in the MT and movement amplitude, respectively. Combining these ideas with the fact that force and force variability are related linearly, as are impulse duration and its variability, we arrived at a simple equation that relates errors in movement to the movement amplitude and the MT. Experiments on aiming movements with various amplitudes and MTs produce effects which are predicted by the model. Average velocity appears to be a major determinant of the "difficulty" of a movement, as measured by the error involved in hitting a target.

Relationship to Fitts' Law

The variables in Fitts' law are very similar to those presented in Equation 9-7. Two are identical: movement amplitude and MT. The third, movement accuracy, is defined as variations in produced movement endpoint in our model (W_e) and as the objective width of the target to which the subject aims (W) in Fitts' law. Both W_e and W represent the accuracy demands of the movement. If the variables in these two laws are so similar, what are the connections between the A/MT model and Fitts' law?

First, it should be noted that the paradigms in these two situations are quite different. Recall that the Fitts' equation was based on repetitive movements back and forth between two targets, the moves being made at the highest speed that was consistent with achieving the proper proportion of "hits." The principle also holds for single-aiming movements under the instruction to "move to the target as quickly as possible" (Fitts & Peterson, 1964). In the A/MT model, though, the instruction is to move as accurately as possible but in the proper MT. Thus, while MT is the dependent measure in the Fitts equation, it is an independent variable in the A/MT model. Treating MT as an independent variable is consistent with the ideas about programming expressed in the previous two chapters. I believe that the subject determines the MT in advance (perhaps by the selection of a movement duration parameter for the generalized motor program), and the movement accuracy is the result of this selection. Thus, the variability in the movement is the "price" the subject has to pay for the selection of a certain MT, the "price" usually being higher if the MT is shorter.

Second, the mathematical statements of the two principles are quite different. Even though they have the same variables (A, MT, and W or W_e), they are by no means the same, as Fitts' law uses a Log_2 term and the A/MT equation does not. And the data, as we have found, do not fit both equations at the same time. For single-aiming responses, the data fit the A/MT equation better; and for the Fitts reciprocal-tapping paradigm, the data fit the Fitts equation better. The two equations are quite different statements of the relationships between the same movement variables. Why?

At this stage, it is not certain. However, the A/MT relationship (Schmidt et al., 1979) seems to hold for movements that are less than 200 msec in duration, while the Fitts equation seems to hold for movements that are 150 msec to 900 msec in duration. Remember that a consistent theme in the previous chapters is that movements with short MTs do not have sufficient time for movement corrections (based on the information-processing stages) to occur, and thus they are thought to be programmed before the movement is initiated and run off as a unit. Perhaps this is the basis for the distinction for the A/MT and Fitts' equations. I suspect that the A/MT principle is most applicable for those movements that are preprogrammed, while the Fitts equation is more applicable for those movements that have a correction or a series of corrections in them to achieve a target. In this view, then, these two laws are not "competitors" in the sense stated in Chapter 2. Rather, the two equations can be seen as explaining the relationships equally well, each for different kinds of movements.

It might seem that the A/MT principle holds for fast movements and the Fitts equation holds for slow ones, but this is probably too simple a generalization. I think that the distinction between the two principles is related to whether the movement is programmed, rather than to the movement time per se. Remember that there are many examples of programs for controlling movements with long MTs—some of them as long as 1300 msec (Shapiro, 1977, 1978; review the section on the duration parameter in Chapter 8). Recall also that in order for a long-duration movement to be governed by a motor program, the person has to have a well-defined and "effective" motor program (either genetically defined or resulting from a great deal of practice). Also, it is probable that the conditions surrounding the movement have to be conducive to programming: errors in movement might not be very "costly" to the person, the person's attention could be required to perform some other important secondary task, and/or the person might be bored or tired so that attention is not directed to the movement.

As a result, it could be expected that for movements with long MTs, but which are nevertheless totally preprogrammed, the A/MT equation would hold. That is, even with long MTs, movement accuracy will be linearly related to the movement's average velocity. Some initial experiments to test this idea by Zelaznik, Shapiro, and McColsky (1981) showed that when attention is occupied by a probe-RT task done simultaneously with the aiming movements, the A/MT relationship appears to hold even for movements with durations as long as 500 msec (see also Schmidt, 1980). It is probably too early to tell whether this idea is correct. In any case, it is certainly consistent with the view of the generalized motor program presented earlier.

If this view is correct, then what kinds of movements would have their accuracy governed by the A/MT equation? First, any movement with a MT of less than about 200 msec would be so governed. Second, any movement that is programmed but has a MT longer than 200 msec would be expected to be governed by this equation. Also, if it is correct that the person can direct attention to only one body segment at a time, then the accuracy of any body segment involved in a skill (e.g., pole vaulting) that is not attended to will probably be governed by this equation. It could be that the A/MT relationship is far more general than the Fitts equation, for the A/MT relationship will govern most of the limbs' movement accuracies, with the Fitts equation governing only the one limb (if any) that is attended to during a complex movement. These points are mainly conjecture, however, and more work must be done on these questions to obtain firm answers.

SOME IMPLICATIONS AND APPLICATIONS

In the previous sections I have outlined what I think are some fundamental principles of simple limb movement that have been given empirical support in variety of experimental settings. In the next section I present some of the extensions, implications, or applications of these basic principles. Some are quite surprising and not at all what would be expected from "common-sense" analyses of movement skills.

Effect of Mass to Be Moved

A common feature of many industrial and sport situations is the need to move a mass from one place to another in some controlled way. In many cases, this mass is simply the limb, but in others the need may be to move objects such as boxing gloves, beer mugs, or steering wheels. Often we have direct control over the mass of these objects (e.g., the person can choose a heavier or lighter baseball bat), and it is important to know if the amount of mass has relevance for the eventual level of skill that emerges.

Tracking and Positioning Responses

In earlier research, the effect of mass was evaluated for a variety of tasks, such as tracking and positioning responses. Much of this research was done in the context of attempting to understand "control dynamics," or the particular way in which control systems (e.g., steering mechanisms in a car, or the "feel" of the control stick in aircraft) could be designed to maximize the ease with which people could perform and learn the tasks. Many variables were manipulated, such as spring-like resistance on a control, the mass of the control (inertial resistance), the relationship of the movements of the control to the movements of the vehicle (*control-display relationships*), and so on. Summaries of this work suggest that none of these variables has particularly strong effects on tracking or positioning accuracy (e.g., Bahrick, 1957). True, some of the variables do produce slightly more effective tracking or positioning performance, but the effects appear to be inconsistent from task to task and it is difficult to generalize about the effects of these variables.

A major interpretation (and sometimes a motivation) of this work was that these changes in the control dynamics altered the way in which the control "feels" to the responder. The underlying theory was that of the closed-loop control system (Chapter 6). According to this view of tracking behavior, feedback—including that received from the responding limb through the movements of the control mechanisms—should be an important factor in the control of this kind of task. Thus, the prediction for such a model was that increased "feel" from the controls of a tracking task should improve the overall performance. Most of the research on this question, however, has failed to demonstrate much of an effect for these control dynamics variables, suggesting that feedback (from the responding limb) is not critical for tracking tasks. Also, remember that the deafferentation work (Chapter 7) showed essentially that feedback from the responding limb was not essential for motor control, although it aided it in some instances.

When engaged in a tracking task, such as steering a car, the primary feedback source appears to be vision. Using visual feedback, we might expect to perform effectively with a wide variety of "feels" in the control systems; for instance, we can steer a car with power steering, a car without power steering, a sports car, and a truck with about equal accuracy in normal driving situations. This is clearly oversimplified, as there are certainly configurations of steering controls that are more effective for racing cars, for example. But I do not think that these changes have much to do with the "feel" of the control, although such variables obviously have effects on comfort and effort.

Rapid Ballistic Responses—Timing Errors

A major conclusion of the literature discussed above is that the power of visual feedback is sufficient to override any changes in the control dynamics (truck vs. sports car) produced by changes in the mass, spring-tension, etc. But what about tasks in which visual feedback cannot have an effect because the movement is too rapid, such as batting a baseball? Here, the mass and other physical characteristics of the objects to be moved (e.g., the length of the bat, its moment of inertia) could possibly have effects on the accuracy with which the motor system could move it. If these events are programmed, then one can perhaps evaluate the effect of mass, for example, by considering its effects on the variability of the muscular impulses that produce the movements. Knowing what effect mass has on impulse variability could perhaps aid in evaluating the effect of mass on movement accuracy in these tasks.

To do this, return to Figure 9-11, which shows the relationship between the amount of (peak) force produced and the variability in that force. When the force is below about 65 percent of the subject's maximum, an increasing linear relationship exists between the force produced and the variability in that force. And, when the force exceeds about 65 percent of maximum, the variability peaks, with increased force producing decreased force variability thereafter. As force is increased further, one would expect force variability to approach zero, as force variability should be small when the forces are all close to the subject's own maximum force. I will consider the rising and falling portions of the curve in turn.

Small to moderate forces. Imagine swinging a baseball bat, which is done with a constant MT, but with various bats of differing mass. Naturally, as the weight of the bat is increased, an increase in muscular force must be applied so that the MT (or bat velocity) remains constant. If this force remains below about 65 percent of the batter's maximum, where the force and force variability are almost proportional, impulse variability should increase as the mass of the bat is increased. That is, with increased bat weight, the muscular activity would be progressively "noisier." Another effect, however, is evident when the mass is increased; the inertia of the system (limb plus bat) is increased, so the limb system becomes more resistant to the effects of variability in muscular impulse. Just as a very light object can be affected greatly by the small variations in forces operating against it and a heavier object will be relatively insensitive to these same forces, increasing the mass of the limb system makes the limb and bat more insensitive to the variations in the muscular impulses acting on it. It turns out that the increases in variability of muscular action caused by increased bat weight are nearly compensated for by the changes in the inertia of the system to be moved. The net result is that the increased mass of the bat should produce small decreases in movement errors.

This is a curious prediction, because it seems to run counter to common sense. But it comes directly from the impulse-variability notion. The reason for the prediction of a small decrease in error with increased mass is based on the fact that force and force variability are not quite proportionally related to each other; proportionality means that the "line of best fit" passes through the origin, and as in Figures 9-9, 9-10, and 9-11 a small non-zero intercept results. So, as the mass on the system is increased, the percentage change in inertia (the "resistance" to variability effects) is always slightly greater than the percentage change in force variability. Check it for yourself. In Figure 9-9, if the mass of the limb and lever are increased so that 5 times the force is needed (e.g., from 2 kg to 10 kg in the figure), only 3.8 times as much force variability is produced (from .14 to .53, or .39 kg).

Data from various experiments tend to support this kind of prediction. Schmidt et al. (1979) showed a very slight (4 percent) advantage for mass applied to a lever in a ballistic-timing task when the movements were 200 msec, but the effect was absent at a 100-msec MT. Sherwood and Schmidt (1980), using six different masses in a ballistic-timing task, found slight decreases in VE_t with increased mass (Figure 9-15). And, Newell, Carlton, and Carlton (in press) reported similar findings, showing a gain in accuracy as the mass was increased. These results, then, tend to support the impulse-variability model, but only if the non-zero intercept in the force/force variability relationship is taken into account.[4]

The implication of these findings is that increasing the mass of the bat in baseball will have a slightly positive effect on timing accuracy (assuming MT to be constant) and will have a strong positive effect on the action of the ball if it is hit. Hitting a ball with a heavier bat causes the ball to go faster and farther, which is certainly important to the game.

Near-maximal forces. What if the mass is larger, so that the forces required to move it in the proper MT are near the subject's maximal force capability? From Figure 9-11 and from the previous section, as the mass continues to increase, the force increases and the force variability reaches a peak (at about 65 percent of maximum) and decreases thereafter. That is, the force will become more consistent as the forces increase from 65 percent toward maximum. From the previous arguments, as the mass increases, the

---

[4]In the original paper, Schmidt et al. (1979) did not take this non-zero intercept into account, and the predictions reported there are different in this regard from the predictions in this section.

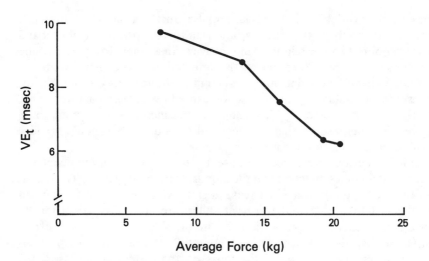

Figure 9-15. Variable error in timing (VE_t) in a ballistic-timing task as a function of force produced (from Sherwood & Schmidt, 1980).

inertia (or the resistance to force variability) continues to increase. Hence, there is a continued increase in resistance to variability (inertia) and a decrease in the amount of muscular variability, resulting in the prediction that increased mass will lead to a substantial *decrease* in timing variability.

Sherwood and I (1980, Experiment 4) examined this question in a ballistic-timing task, where we adjusted the masses to be added to the lever, up to the point that they required nearly maximal contractions from our subjects in order that the movement be made in the proper (constant) MT of 150 msec. A plot of the variable error in timing (VE_t) as a function of the amount of added mass is given in Figure 9-15. As the mass, and hence the forces applied to the lever, were increased in these violent responses, a substantial decrease in VE_t resulted. This finding is also predictable from the impulse-variability model, and it is another example of a situation in which the usual speed-accuracy trade-off notion does not appear to hold.

Some interesting implications of these findings can be made for baseball, racquetball, and other games in which an implement is moved rapidly to strike a ball. The mass of the objects to be moved can be increased to the point that the contractions necessary to maintain MT are nearly maximal, and the temporal consistency will (in these cases, at least) increase, not decrease. I have not, to this point, discussed what effects such a heavy bat might have on the spatial consistency of the movement, and this is the main question for the next sections.

Rapid Ballistic Responses—Spatial Errors

In a task like hitting a baseball, timing the swing properly is obviously important, as swinging too early can result in the ball's being "pulled" (hit to the left side for a right-handed batter) or even missed. But timing accuracy is not the only factor involved in hitting successfully, because swinging in the wrong place (too high or too low), even with the proper timing accuracy, will result in a missed ball. How do these effects of mass and force variabili-

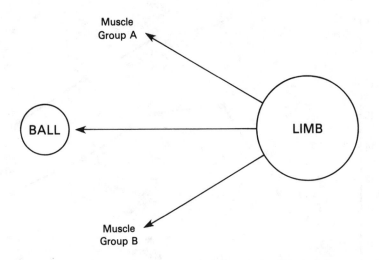

Figure 9-16. The limb conceptualized as a mass moved by two forces (muscles) operating in different directions.

ty determine the spatial accuracy of a response?

Think of a baseball swing (or a pitch or dart throw, etc.) as made up of a number of muscle groups acting on a bone or bones in coordination. This picture can be simplified by the diagram presented in Figure 9-16. The mass (the bat and limb) is being moved by two muscle groups (A and B) that act together to produce some motion in the direction of the arrow toward the ball. Any variation in the force which Group A or Group B produces will produce changes in the direction of the limb's travel and, hence, will affect how "squarely" the ball will be hit or whether it will be hit at all. Now consider what happens to this model in Figure 9-16 when the mass of the bat is increased, holding the MT constant.

If Muscle Groups A and B are contracting with less than 65 percent of maximum, then increasing the mass of the bat will cause increased force output in both of them, and the force variability will increase in both muscle groups as the mass is increased. This should result in progressively larger variations in the direction the bat travels and, hence, progressively lower probability that the ball will be hit successfully. But what if the forces in the two muscle groups are larger, perhaps greater than about 65 percent of maximum? Here, with increased mass of the bat, there would be (by the data from Figure 9-11) a decrease in the force variability in these muscle groups, resulting in increased consistency in the direction that the bat travels. If this is the case, as the bat becomes heavier and heavier (again, with the MT remaining constant), the probability of hitting the ball should increase progressively; that is, less spatial error should occur with near-maximal contractions.

Sherwood and I (Schmidt & Sherwood, in press) did an experiment that seems to show just that. We had subjects hold a handle with a pointer attached. With the elbow straight, subjects made a horizontal, forward arm-swing movement to attempt to hit a target. Moreover, they were to do the movement in as close to 200 msec as possible. Figure 9-17 shows the effect of the amount of mass added to the handle on the spatial accuracy (in the

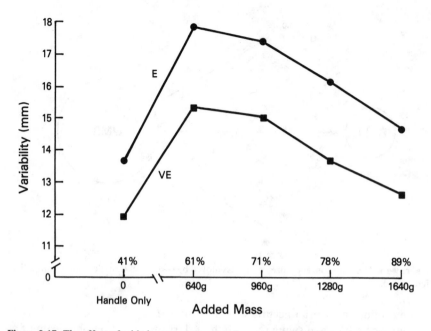

Figure 9-17. The effect of added mass on the spatial accuracy of a 200-msec arm-swing movement (from Schmidt & Sherwood, in press).

vertical dimension) in hitting the target, measured as VE and E. As the mass was added to the unloaded handle, there was at first an increase in spatial errors. But the function soon peaked, so that the errors decreased with further increases in mass. Even at the highest level of mass in the study, which resulted in about 89 percent of maximum torque for these subjects, the high levels of mass were associated with very accurate responding. Thus, the findings of a peak in spatial inconsistency is in keeping with the ideas presented in Figure 9-16 and with the data on force variability at forceful contractions presented in Figure 9-11.

Obviously, more work needs to be done on this issue. But these data suggest that as the mass of the objects become very large, so that the strength of contraction of the involved musculature needs to be near the subject's maximum in order to move at a rapid velocity, progressively more and more spatial consistency results. Perhaps this can explain why batters who use very large bats and have a very rapid MT can still be accurate enough to have high batting averages.

Effect of Velocity

If spatial accuracy can be increased by adding mass to the bat in near maximal contractions, then it also follows from the theory that spatial accuracy can be increased by increasing the velocity of the movement with bat weight held constant (provided that the level of contraction is greater than about 65 percent of maximum force). This is again counter to common sense, as many of us learned that to be accurate in, say, batting we should

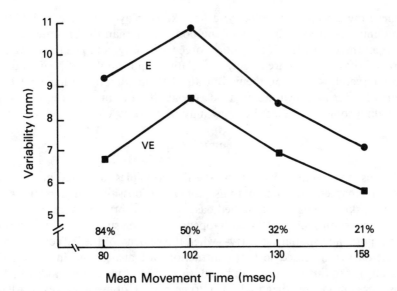

Figure 9-18. The effect of movement time on the spatial accuracy in a horizontal arm-swing movement (from Schmidt & Sherwood, in press).

not swing "hard" but should attempt to merely "make contact" with the ball.

Schmidt and Sherwood (in press) investigated this question directly with their arm-swing paradigm mentioned above. Here, though, the mass applied to the limb was held constant, and the MT was varied so that their values spanned the point at which peak variability in force had been found (i.e., about 65 percent of maximum). In Figure 9-18 are the VE and E scores representing accuracy in the (vertical) spatial dimension as a function of the various MTs. As MT was decreased from 158 msec, a systematic increase in error occurred. But as MT was decreased further, the error functions peaked and a decrease in error was found as the MT was decreased to 80 msec. It is interesting that the amount of error when the MT was very short and required 84 percent of the subject's maximum was comparable to that in a very slow response (130 msec). These data provide considerable support for the impulse-variability model and provide another interesting exception to the notion of the speed-accuracy trade-off.

These findings, if they can be shown to be general, lead to some interesting potential applications in various sport situations. Perhaps telling a baseball player to swing slowly to "make contact" would actually result in less spatial accuracy than telling the player to swing "hard." Or, in place-kicking in American football or rugby, if a kicker has to make a short kick, the accuracy in making the point might be increased by kicking the ball nearly maximally, rather than with just enough force for the ball to travel the required distance. Findings from Zernicke's and Roberts' (1978) biomechanical study of soccer kickers at different foot velocities showed this increased spatial consistency as foot velocity approached the subject's maximum. I have a hunch that expert dart players throw by using as few muscles as possible, with these muscles contracting nearly maximally to achieve the desired dart velocity; a less skilled player, I argue, would use more muscles in various parts of the body other than the arm and would contract these with less force, more force variability, and less throwing accuracy. These notions are largely speculation, and should not be used until more research is done on them. But all of them come from logical extensions of what is known about force variability and motor programming, providing some assurance that they may be correct.

Summing Up

In this final section, I want to take the principles presented in this and previous chapters and attempt to use as many as possible in understanding a complex skill like batting a pitched baseball. These principles can be used if I ask a question such as, "What happens to batting success—both in terms of temporal and spatial accuracy—when the velocity of the bat (or the mass of the bat) is increased so that contractions are at near-maximal levels?" The answer to this question can be considered in terms of the kinds of processes or components that are known to be important in such actions. All of these have been discussed before in the previous five chapters, but I find it useful to discuss them together here so that they can be more effectively understood and interrelated. I have chosen hitting a baseball because it is familiar to most people and it involves a wide variety of perceptual and motor processes (see also Whiting, 1972).

I will review some basic facts about the skill of hitting a baseball. In Figure 9-19, I have collected some results from a number of studies reported earlier and from Hubbard and Seng (1954). Essentially, it requires about 460 msec for a ball (at 89 mph) to travel from the pitcher to the plate. Hubbard and Seng found that the MT of the bat (the time from the first movement of the bat until it reached the plate) was about 160 msec, so that the bat started moving 160 msec before the ball reached the plate; this is equivalent to about 21 ft. (6.4 m) of ball travel. Further, I argued in Chapter 7 that the decisions to make this action had to have been terminated at about 168 msec before the bat started moving (Slater-Hammel, 1960). This means that all of the decisions about the nature of the swing had to be made before the ball was 328 (168 + 160) msec from the plate; this is equivalent to about 43 ft. (13.1 m) of ball travel and more than half the total distance of 60.5 ft. (18.4 m). Presumably, the time from the release of the ball by the pitcher until the batter "instructs himself" to hit the ball is occupied by perceptual processes involved in deciding where (or whether or not) the ball will cross over the plate, how rapidly it is traveling, its trajectory, and so on.

With this review, what would happen if the batter were to speed up the batswing 20 msec from 160 msec to 140 msec? Consider first the effect of this change on the nature of the decision processes prior to swinging.

Decision Processes

As the person is watching the ball fly toward the plate, it seems reasonable to assume that the most important aspects of the ball's flight are those that are closest to the batter. But notice that by speeding up the bat-

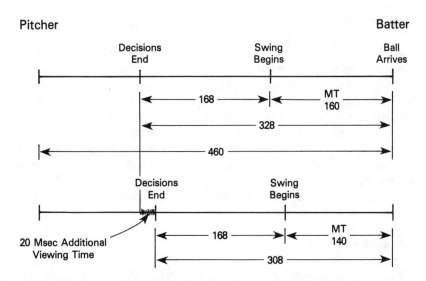

Figure 9-19. A timeline showing the critical events in hitting a pitched baseball. (The top example has a 160-msec MT, and the bottom example has a 140-msec MT.)

swing to 140 msec instead of 160 msec (see Figure 9-19), the batter is allowed to view the ball for 20 msec longer. More importantly, that 20 msec is during the time that the ball is as close as possible to the batter before the ultimate decision has to be made. In this way, the batter should be able to make more effective choices for the upcoming swing, because the ball is viewed closer to the plate.

Batswing Initiation Time

Next, consider the effect of swinging faster on the timing of the batswing initiation. Remember from the discussions about anticipation in Chapter 5 that in order for the bat to arrive at the plate at the proper time (relative to the ball, of course), the batter must be able to anticipate the processes that will intervene between the final "go" signal and the end of the movement. This is called *effector anticipation*. In the present example (Figure 9-19), the relevant interval that must be timed is the one that begins with the label "Decisions End" and ends when the bat reaches the plate. When the MT is 160 msec, this interval is estimated as 328 msec, and it is 308 msec when the MT is 140 msec. Because this interval must be timed and because the accuracy in timing an interval is poorer as the interval increases, better effector anticipation should occur when the batswing is 140 msec rather than 160 msec, and less variability in when the swing is initiated should result. Using a laboratory task resembling batting (Figure 9-6), I found that when the MT was decreased, the variability in when the batswing was initiated was decreased as well (Schmidt, 1969b). Thus, another advantage of swinging more rapidly relates to timing the onset of the swing so that the end of the swing is coincident with the ball's arrival at the plate.

Movement Time

A third advantage of swinging more rapidly is that the MT itself is more consistent as the movement time is shorter. As reported earlier in this chapter, in a number of studies (e.g., Newell et al., 1979, 1980; Schmidt et al., 1979) the authors have found a decreased MT variability as the MT is decreased. Newell et al. (1979, 1980) found an effect of movement velocity that is essentially independent of MT, so that swinging both faster (degrees/second) and with less MT (seconds) both produce increased consistency in the MT. So when the batter swings harder, the movements become more temporally consistent. Because decreasing the MT increases the temporal consistency of the movement, the swing becomes more predictable and increases the capability for effector anticipation.

Timing the Ball Contact

The combination of increased consistency in when the batswing is initiated and the increased consistency in the duration of the batswing itself should lead to increased consistency in when the bat arrives at the plate. For a given level of receptor anticipation (about the ball's flight pattern), increases in the swing speed should therefore result in increased timing accuracy in terms of the arrival of the bat at the plate in relation to the time of the ball's arrival. In the laboratory "batting" task mentioned previously (Figure 9-6), I (Schmidt, 1969b) found that the temporal accuracy of meeting the "ball" was greater when the MT was shorter (see Table 9-1). Such effects should also occur if the mass of the bat is increased (beyond contraction levels of about 65 percent of the subject's maximum) with a constant MT, because the increased mass also tends to make the movements more consistent (see Figure 9-15; Sherwood & Schmidt, 1980).

Spatial Accuracy

If the levels of muscle contraction in the batswing are above about 65 percent of the batter's maximum, then increased swing speed or increased bat mass with a constant swing speed both produce increases in the spatial accuracy of the swing. This is because with increased levels of contraction increased consistency occurs in force production, which results in increased consistency in where the limbs go during the action. In this way, the limbs tend to "do what the program tells them to do" more effectively, and the probability that the bat actually meets the ball to which it is aimed should increase. These kinds of effects have been shown for laboratory tasks (Schmidt & Sherwood, in press), as well as in more sport-related responses (Zernicke & Roberts, 1978).

Combined Effects

The foregoing sections indicate that the effect of swinging more rapidly at the ball in a baseball situation (provided that the contraction levels are greater than about 65 percent of maximum) is very much contrary to the kinds of effects expected from a common sense analysis of batting. Speeding up the swing (a) increases time for analysis of ball flight, (b) increases the timing consistency of the batswing initiation time, (c) increases the consistency of the MT (the latter two of which combine to increase the timing consistency in hitting the ball), and (d) increases the spatial consistency in the bat's trajectory. Increased mass of the bat (MT constant) could have the same effects on all but the first of these factors.

These principles are based on a few fundamental findings about time and force variability (those in Figures 9-7, 9-9, 9-10, and 9-11) and the use of simple laws of physics involved with motion characteristics. In addition to the usefulness of these ideas for understanding various sport (e.g., batting) or industrial situations or for generating future research findings to apply to other settings, these principles illustrate an additional, more general point: Theories, far from being esoteric exercises with very little practical reality, can serve as useful tools for generating new principles before they are found empirically, and they can lead to many possibilities for application if the principles are understood properly. This is really the same point I tried to make in Chapter 2. As Kerlinger (1973, p.10) has said, "There is nothing more practical than a good theory."

SUMMARY

One of the earliest relationships about motor skills was the speed-accuracy trade-off, suggesting that humans tend to trade off speed of movements with their accuracy. A formal mathematical statement of this relationship was proposed over twenty-five years ago by Fitts, and is called Fitts' law in his honor. It says that in reciprocal movements, the average MT is linearly related to the Log_2 of the ratio of the movement amplitude and the target width. This principle holds for a wide variety of movement situations, and types of subjects, and it must be considered one of the cornerstones of motor control.

Early explanations for Fitts' law were based on intermittent control models, in which the commands for action were produced alternately with the analysis of feedback to determine movement corrections. One view of this process by Crossman and Goodeve enjoyed a great deal of popularity, but recent evidence suggests that it may be incorrect. More acceptable views of movement control are that the movement is handled by an open-loop, distance-covering phase and (if corrected at all) a "homing-in" phase at the end, with the distance-covering phase being increased in its inconsistency as the forces applied to the limb are increased.

An analysis of laws of movement timing show that as the MT is decreased, an increase occurs in MT consistency. This is in addition to the effect of movement velocity, in which movement consistency is increased as velocity is increased. Both of these effects combined imply that more rapid movements in timing tasks lead to increased temporal consistency, contrary to the ideas about the speed-accuracy trade-off.

Force and force variability are strongly related to each other, with the relationship being essentially linear until forces of about 65 percent of the subject's maximum are achieved. The force variability decreases with further increases in force toward the subject's maximum. The laws about MT variability and force variability have been combined into a model for rapid limb accuracy: the prediction is that the spatial accuracy in aiming movements is linearly related to the ratio of the movement amplitude and the MT (A/MT), or average velocity.

The various principles of movement control can be combined to produce interesting and useful predictions about common, complex skills such as batting. Increasing the velocity of a swing or the mass of the bat increases both temporal and spatial accuracy. These predictions appear to be borne out by recent evidence from laboratory and sport tasks.

GLOSSARY

Average velocity. The speed of a movement, or the movement distance divided by the movement time; expressed in centimeters/second.

Control dynamics. The mechanical characteristics of the levers, handwheels, etc., in control systems; affected by variables such as spring tension, inertia, etc., that change the "feel" of the control.

Crossman-Goodeve theory. A theory of the Fitts relationship that assumed a series of constant-duration movements, each interspersed with feedback-based corrections; an intermittent control theory of rapid movement.

Current or *contemporary control.* Woodworth's idea that the latter portions of a movement were controlled by a feedback-based "homing in" process that allowed a target to be achieved.

Difficulty. Depending on the particular paradigm, either the ratio of the amplitude to the target width (Fitts, 1954) or the ratio of the movement amplitude to MT (Schmidt et al., 1978, 1979).

Dynamic contractions. Muscle contractions in which the muscle is changing length as it is producing force; sometimes called isotonic contractions.

Effective target width. The size of the target area that the performer actually uses in a series of aiming movements, calculated as the VE of the movement endpoints; abbreviated W_e.

Fitts' law. Fitts' (1954) mathematical relationship of the speed-accuracy trade-off in which the average MT equals $a + bLog_2(2A/W)$.

Force variability. The within-subject variability in a series of forces produced either in static or in dynamic contractions.

Impulse-variability theory. A theory of rapid actions in which the variability in the muscular impulses leads directly to the variations in movement endpoint.

Index of difficulty. In Fitts' law, the $Log_2(2A/W)$, or the theoretical "difficulty" of a movement; abbreviated ID.

Initial adjustment. In Woodworth's terms, the initial open-loop portion of an aiming movement.

Moment of inertia. A physical quantity defining a segment's resistance to rotational forces; the mass of the segment times the square of the distance of the center of the mass from the point of rotation.

Speed-accuracy trade-off. The general principle describing a person's tendency to decrease the accuracy of a movement when the speed of it is increased.

Static contraction. Contractions in which the muscle is not changing length as it is producing force; sometimes called isometric contractions.

Temporal variability. The inconsistency of some events with respect to time.

Variable error in timing. Abbreviated VE_t, the within-subject standard deviation of the duration of some process or event.

Velocity effect. The finding from Newell et al. that the movement timing consistency increases with increases in velocity.

CHAPTER 10

Individual Differences and Capabilities

Why is one person a better gymnast than another, even after the same amount of practice? What are the abilities or aptitudes that contribute to success as a skilled woodworker? How many basic motor capabilities do humans possess, what are they, and how can they be measured? These are just some of the questions considered in this chapter on individual differences—that is, the factors that make individuals different from each other.

The approach to motor behavior represented by this chapter is a marked departure from the approaches in the earlier chapters. The fundamental distinction is this: With the earlier approach, which is typically termed the *experimental* approach to motor behavior, the concern was for the effect of certain independent variables on certain other dependent variables. Procedures called *experiments* were used to examine these effects as they were revealed by the changes in the average behavior of a group of subjects. With the *differential* approach discussed in this chapter, however, the concern is for how the individuals within a group are different from each other, not for the averaged performance of the group. Because these two scientific traditions are so different in method and goal, they are usually treated as separate points of view. I will examine some of the differences between these two approaches more closely in the next section.

EXPERIMENTAL VERSUS DIFFERENTIAL APPROACHES

Scientific Goals

Experimental Approach

The most obvious difference between the experimental and differential approaches is in terms of the goals of these two traditions. The experimental approach is primarily concerned with understanding the effects of certain independent variables (e.g., a lighted environment when moving) on some dependent variable (e.g., the accuracy of the movement). In this example, the concern is for how visual processes work in (all) humans to aid movement accuracy. A fundamental belief is that humans are not really very different from each other (especially when contrasting human-to-human differences with human-to-giraffe differences), so by treating the subjects in a group alike, the behavior of all humans (or of a "typical" human) can be estimated by considering the effect of the light on the average accuracy of the subjects. By experimenting (see Chapter 1), the researcher can hope to arrive at statements such as, "Removing vision tends to decrease accuracy in movements with long MT," as Keele and Posner (1968), as just one example, did.

In these kinds of experiments, little concern is shown for one individual in the group who may have more trouble with reduced vision than another individual. Almost no interest is shown in the possibility that one person might use a different strategy than another, or have more skill than another. These factors are usually averaged out and never seen in the group data. In fact, if some individual differs "too much" from the mean behavior level of the group, common experimental practice is to remove that person from consideration. Thus, variations among people are considered "noise," or a nuisance, in an experiment, and many methods are employed to eliminate or control such between-subjects variations.

Differential Approach

The differential, or individual-differences, approach, on the other hand, is concerned with understanding very different aspects of behavior and uses very different methods and assumptions to arrive at solutions. As mentioned above, the primary focus is on the differences between or among individuals. Thus, the things that the experimentalist considers "noise" in experiments are the very things that the differentialist considers interesting and worthy of study! Generally, the differential approach is concerned with two basic issues.

First, concern is shown for the nature of the underlying *abilities* (or *capabilities*), for how these abilities are of different "strengths" in different people because of genetic variations or experience, and for how these abilities are related. For example, are abilities concerned with strength related to the abilities involved with accuracy in motion? Does high strength ability imply that the person will have low accuracy ability? A second problem, closely related to the first, is concerned with *prediction*, or the estimation of performance in one situation based on measurements taken in some other situation. For example, how do intelligence test scores relate to success in graduate school? Or how does height relate to success in gymnastics?

The differential approach deviates from the experimental approach because it is concerned with attempts to explain and predict differences among people, rather than to general phenomena that occur in the average person. As might be expected, such differences in goals naturally create differences between the points of view of the differentialists and the experimentalists. Indeed, such differences have become so great that the two groups of psychologists are almost totally separated, with separate methods of doing research, statistical designs, goals, textbooks, and scientific journals. These differences have been described, and decried, by Cronbach (1957) in his article entitled "The two disciplines of scientific psychology." There have been attempts to bring these camps closer together (e.g., Underwood, 1975), but resistance to amalgamation is strong and little progress has been made.

Scientific Methodologies

The experimentalist and the differentialist answer their respective questions quite differently. While I have devoted considerable space to the experimental approach (see Chapter 2, and 4 through 9), a brief review of its characteristics will help to contrast it with the differential approach.

Experimental Methods

Essentially, the "true" experiment involves the manipulation (or artificial variation) of some independent variable, while holding all other (or at least most other) variables constant. This can be done by administering one level of the independent variable to one group of people, and another level to another group and noting the differences in terms of some dependent variable. Sometimes only one group of people is used; but one level of the independent variable is administered to the group at one time and the other level is administered at another time, with differences between the two times (in terms of the dependent variable) being the chief comparison of interest.[1] I have discussed many examples of both of these designs in previous chapters.

In such experiments, the critical comparison is between the means of groups of people (or of a single group tested under two different conditions). Typically no regard is given for the variations among people within the group, except for the usual reporting of statistics that describe

---

[1]The former experimental designs are called "between-subjects designs," whereas the latter are called "within-subjects designs."

the extent to which people differed. In any case, such dispersion statistics are rarely the primary concern in experiments; rather, they are included to be certain that the variations among people were not so large as to obscure or change the conclusions drawn about the differences between means. Finally, the conclusions that come from these experiments are usually stated in cause-effect terms; thus, the variations in the independent variable *caused* the changes in the dependent variable. As such, experimental methods provide relatively powerful ways of coming to an understanding of one's scientific area.

Differential Methods

The differential methods are starkly different from those described above, relying substantially on correlational (or associational) techniques, whereby the *relationships* between or among variables are studied. In its simplest form the differential approach uses one group of people and at least two tests measured on each individual. (Remember that the experimental method uses at least two groups of people and one test, or dependent variable[2].) The primary concern is the extent to which one test (e.g., height) relates to another test (e.g., accuracy) in the same people, with the nature of the relationship being determined by the size and sign of a statistic called the *correlation coefficient* (discussed in a subsequent section). With these correlational methods, the relationship between the two tests, or among the groups of tests if more than two are used, is the chief concern. Sometimes the relationship is computed between a group of tests (called a "battery") and some other single measure. An example is the relationship between a fitness battery (consisting of five subtests) and some other measure, such as probability of becoming a successful fire fighter.

A second major method of individual differences research uses essentially the same logic, but the appearance of the procedures may make the unwary student think that the methods are experimental. Consider a study to determine the relationship between age and capability to throw. Typically, the researcher chooses one group of people at one age and another group at another age and compares the group means on some "dependent" variable, such as throwing accuracy. This appears to be an experiment, because there are two groups and one dependent variable and the focus is on the group means. But it is not really an experiment (see the section on pseudo-experiments in Chapter 2) because the level of the independent variable (age) is not manipulated by the experimenter; that is, the age of the people in the group was already established when the subjects were chosen, and such a procedure is merely a study of the relationship between age and throwing accuracy. Such variables are usually called *individual difference variables*, and examples are race, sex, musical background, country of birth, etc. Thus, the study of which individual difference variables are related to certain kinds of performances is a primary concern of the dif-

---

[2]There are exceptions to this simple contrast in so-called multivariate experimental methods, but this simple generalization will do for our purposes here.

ferential approach. Indeed, textbooks have been written about age, race, and sex as individual difference variables (e.g., Osborne, Noble, & Weyl, 1978).

With the differential approach, conclusions about the results tend to be phrased in considerably different language from that of the experimental approach. Whereas in experiments one is often "permitted" to conclude that the independent variable caused changes in the dependent variable (because other variables are held constant or "controlled"), with differential studies causation can seldom be inferred logically. The major reason is that in studying the relationship between height and throwing accuracy, for example, many other things may differ. For example, a person's weight is usually associated with height, so one cannot be certain that a relationship between height and accuracy is really not due to the relation between weight and accuracy. Also, taller people are usually older (considering children), and one could easily confuse the height-accuracy dependency with an age-accuracy dependency. The primary limitation in these studies is that the level of the variable of concern is not manipulated (artificially determined by the experimenter). Rather, the variable is allowed to vary naturally, and the scientist measures its value and attempts to understand how it relates to some other variable that is also varying naturally. Such procedures are often called *natural experiments*, and a good recent example is the study of variables associated with the eruption of Mt. St. Helens in Washington state. Certainly, variables leading to an eruption cannot be manipulated experimentally, and the differential approach is used.

Differential and Experimental Combinations

A recent shift in emphasis in individual differences work is to combine experimental and differential methods. For example, suppose I use two groups of subjects (randomly divided) and expose one to stress (e.g., noise) while leaving the other in quiet environment. Then, while the noise treatment is in effect, I could measure behavior on two other variables, such as success on a motor task and amount of eye movement, noting the relationship between eye movement and task success separately for the two groups. With such procedures, I can evaluate hypotheses about the effects of stress on the dependence of task success on eye movements. Situations analogous to this have been advocated by Fleishman (1965, p.170) in conjunction with testing hypotheses about the nature of differences among people. As such, these techniques represent blends of the experimental and differential approaches—a welcome trend given the level of disagreement between the rival factions that is usually seen.

On Humanism

Many students receive the impression from this kind of discussion that the differential approach, with its apparent "concern for the individual," is more humanistic than the "cold, hard," experimental approach that treats everyone alike and averages people together as though they were simply numbers. In a small sense, this is correct. But in another way the differential approach is even less humanistic than its experimental counterpart. Suppose that I am interested in the relationship between height and success at basketball and I find with differential methods that greater height is related to increased success at basketball. Such knowledge apparently allows me to discriminate between people of various heights. That is, regardless of one's real ability, I can, on the basis of this relationship between height and skill, decide that no person under 5'9" (175 cm) shall play on my team. If that does not sound so bad, then consider this analogous situation. I find that, on the average, females have less electrical knowledge than males and thus conclude that women should never be hired as telephone installers. It works the other way too, as males under the age of 25 (regardless of their real driving ability) are charged higher auto insurance rates than are females, largely because of the relationship between sex and the number of accidents among people between 16 and 25. The point is that the individual differences approach can be more anti-humanistic than the experimental method, which simply and coldly ignores the fact that people are different.

I will return to some of these issues later when I discuss the problem of prediction. But first, in order to understand the research on individual differences, I must explain some of the statistical methods that are used in this research.

CORRELATIONAL METHODS

An important statistical tool used in research on individual differences is the *correlation coefficient*. In fact, the correlation is the "language" of individual differences research. The correlation is a measure of the degree of *association* between two tests. The usual situation is to have a relatively large group of subjects (say, 50), with two different tests administered to each person (e.g., RT and MT). These two tests can be motor or verbal in nature, and they can have the same or markedly different scoring systems. In some situations, the test may be simply the level of a dichotomous (i.e., two-state) variable, such as sex (here, males could be given a score of zero, females a score of one), or it may be whether or not one had played competitive basketball. The next section describes some of the ways that these data are treated.

Scattergrams

One of the ways that this data can be described is by a special kind of graph called a *scattergram*. Here, the two axes are the scales of the two tests, respectively, and each of the subjects is represented as a dot, located according to the scores on the two tests. Consider the data shown in Table 10-1, which have been plotted on the scattergram in Figure 10-1. The data are hypothetical scores that might be obtained on a common playground and consist of age (in years) and the time for a 100-m dash (in seconds). In Figure 10-1, the scores for these 10 people are plotted, so that each of the 10

Table 10-1

Hypothetical data for age (in years) and 100-meter dash performance (both in seconds and in kilometers per hour)

		100-meter dash	
Subjects	Age	Time	Average Speed
1	13.1	13.5	26.6
2	11.6	12.8	28.1
3	12.2	12.0	30.0
4	16.1	10.5	34.3
5	9.2	16.1	22.4
6	8.5	15.2	23.7
7	8.1	16.0	22.5
8	11.3	14.1	25.5
9	12.2	13.0	27.7
10	7.3	18.0	20.0

Note: Speed data were computed from the time data.

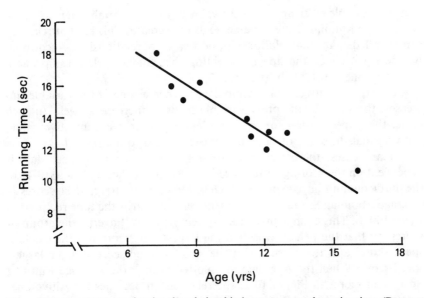

Figure 10-1. A scattergram showing the relationship between age and running time. (Data are from Table 10-1, and each dot represents one of the 10 subjects.)

dots on the graph represents each person's joint scores on the two tests.

A relationship apparently exists between the score on the age variable and the score on the running test, indicating that as the age score becomes larger the number of seconds on the running test tends to become smaller. There are some individual exceptions to this basic statement, as Subject 1 (13.1 yr) had a larger running time than Subject 2 (11.6 yr). Of course, these variables would not be related to each other perfectly and instances would arise when a younger child would be able to complete the 100-m test in less time than an older child. But, in general, the 10 subjects showed a relationship between these two variables.

Notice also that in Figure 10-1, the points suggest that a line could be drawn through them, perhaps representing the "direction" in which the "cloud" of points is oriented. The "line of best fit" in correlations is called a *regression line*. Such a point can be located "by eye," but techniques called *regression analysis* allow one to "fit" the line to the points according to one of a number of mathematical criteria. Once established, the line's empirical equation can be described in earlier sections (see Chapter 3, "Empirical Equations"). The equation is of the form

$$Y = a + b (X), \qquad (10\text{-}1)$$

where here the value Y is Running Time, X is Age, a is the intercept, and b is the slope of the line. Thus, the best estimate, based on the data at hand, of the hypothetical relationship between age and 100-m time is given by Equation 10-1, where $a = 27.18$ and $b = -1.19$.

Direction of the Relationship

In the example given above, as the value of the Age variable increases, the value of the Running Time variable tends to decrease. This kind of relationship is called an *inverse* relationship, or a *negative* relationship. Accordingly, the equation of the line representing this kind of relationship has a negative slope constant (b) (Chapter 3).

A direct, or positive, relationship occurs when as one of the variables increases, the value of the other variable tends to increase as well. In such cases, the slope constant of the regression equation has a positive value, showing that the "line of best fit" slopes upward to the right.

In many cases, the direction of the relationship shown in such data is dependent on the scoring system used. Consider the data in Table 10-1. In the third column I have expressed each of the subject's 100-m dash scores as Average[3] Running Speed (kilometers/hr) rather than as the time required to travel 100 m. This change in scoring system tends to "invert" the group of scores, so that the person who had the largest time score has the smallest speed score, and the person with the smallest time score has the largest speed score. When the Age data are plotted against the Average Running Speed and scores in Figure 10-2, the relationship becomes a positive one, with increases in Age tending to be associated with greater Average Running Speed. The empirical equation can be fit just as above, but now the slope constant b has a positive value rather than a negative one. Thus, nothing makes a positive relationship any "better" than a negative one; the sign of the relationship simply indicates the direction that the "line of best fit" is sloped, and it can be altered by a simple change in the scoring system. There

---

[3]The term *average* refers to the average speed that a person ran in the test expressed as the total distance traveled divided by the time required to travel it. "Average" does not mean the average of a number of people in this instance.

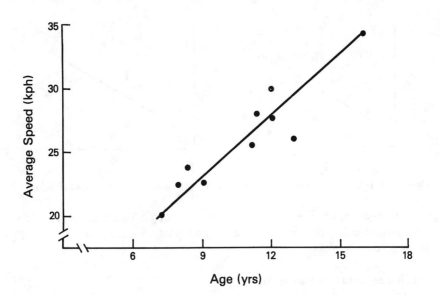

Figure 10-2. A scattergram showing the relationship between age and running speed. (Data are from Table 10-1, where speed is computed from running time; each dot represents one of the 10 subjects.)

are, of course, numerous examples of both directions of slope in the motor control literature.

Strength of the Relationship

A second characteristic of these relationships between variables is *strength*. By strength, I mean the extent to which the relationship is perfectly linear, or the extent to which all of the subjects' points fall exactly on the line of best fit.[4] Figure 10-3 shows two scattergrams that represent relationships of different strengths. In the plot to the left, the relationship can be considered to be quite strong, as nearly all of the points seem to fall close to the line of best fit. In the plot to the right, however, the relationship is not very strong, as the points tend to fall away from the line of best fit. Alternatively, one could say that the line does not fit the data very well in this last example. An example of two variables that might be strongly related are children's Age and Weight, as older children tend to be larger, thus heavier. An example of a relationship that is weak might be one between Weight and Running Speed, whereas the weight of a child would not have much relationship to the speed with which he or she could run.

Direction versus Strength of Relationships

These two aspects of relationships are the primary ones that are used to

---

[4]There could, as well, be perfectly *nonlinear* relationships, whereby all of the subjects' scores fall exactly on a curved "line." Such examples are beyond the scope of this discussion.

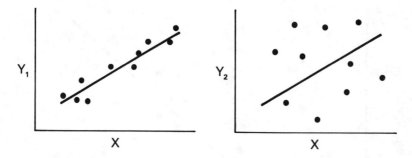

Figure 10-3. Hypothetical scattergrams for a strong (left) and a weak (right) relationship.

describe them in the literature. They are separate, in that a strong relation-ship can be either positive or negative and a negative relationship can be either strong or weak.

Predicting from a Relationship

One of the most important reasons that scientists want to know the nature of the relationship between two variables is for the purpose of *prediction*. For example, if I know that the relationship between Age and Running Time was found to be that described in Figure 10-1, then on a new group of playground children I can perhaps estimate (or predict) the 100-m time given the age of a person not in the original data set, without actually measuring running time. That is, knowing that the next person has an age of 11.6 yr, I can predict that his or her running time will be approximately 13.4 sec (work this out from the scatterplot). Such procedures are used extensive-ly in everyday situations, such as in predicting the probability of having an automobile accident from one's age, or predicting success in graduate school from achievement test scores.

As the strength of the relationship increases, the predictability of one variable from the other increases as well. When the relationship is perfect and all of the individual data points fall exactly on the regression line, perfect predictions can be made. That is, no error is made in predicting from a relationship in which all of the points fall exactly on the line of best fit. When the data are related less perfectly, such as in the examples shown on the right-hand side of Figure 10-3, then considerable error is made in predicting the Y variable from the X variable. Thus, the strength of the rela-tionship—but not the direction—is the primary determinant of the extent to which it can be used to predict.

Correlations

These concepts of strength and direction of relationships taken from data on human subjects can be quantified using a statistic called the *correlation coefficient*. The correlation, abbreviated *r*, can only take on values that range from + 1.0 through zero to − 1.0. The two aspects of the correlation to be concerned about are the sign of the correlation and its absolute size.

Sign of Correlation

The sign of the correlation indicates the direction of the relationship, exactly as described in the previous sections. That is, if the correlation between Height and Weight was $+.80$, then the slope of the regression line of these two scores in a scatterplot would be sloped upward and to the right. A correlation of $-.30$ between Weight and Running Time indicates that the line is sloped negatively.

Size of Correlation

The absolute size of the correlation indicates the strength of the relationship and, hence, is critical for evaluating the extent to which one can use the relationship for predictive purposes. In Figure 10-4 are five hypothetical examples of correlations and the associated scatterplots. Both a $+.90$ and a $-.90$ are near-perfect relationships, as all of the data points fall almost exactly on the lines, although the lines are sloped in opposite directions in these two examples. Correlations of $+.50$ and $-.50$ are moderate in

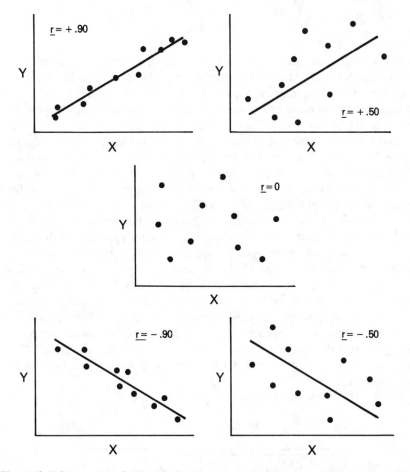

Figure 10-4. Scattergrams for hypothetical data showing high, moderate, and low relationships.

strength, and the points fall considerably away from the lines of best fit. A correlation of zero is weakest in terms of the strength of the relationship, indicating that no predictive capability is possible between these two variables.

Computation of the Correlation

For our purposes, the most important aspects of the correlations are the interpretations based on them as reported in various studies, but it is important to be able to compute a correlation as well. In any case, the process is relatively easy with today's hand calculators. Most of the values needed to compute them are determined with techniques used in the computation of variable error in Chapter 3.

The correlation coefficient (r_{xy}) between tests X and Y is given by the following formula:

$$r_{xy} = \frac{\Sigma XY - \dfrac{\Sigma X \cdot \Sigma Y}{n}}{\sqrt{\left[\Sigma X^2 - \dfrac{(\Sigma X)^2}{n}\right]\left[\Sigma Y^2 - \dfrac{(\Sigma Y)^2}{n}\right]}} \qquad (10\text{-}2)$$

where n is the number of cases and the Σ sign indicates summation as before (Chapter 3). At first glance, this formula appears to be very complicated; but it really requires you to compute only five values from a set of data and combine them according to the rules of arithmetic expressed in the formula. These five are: ΣXY, ΣX^2, ΣY^2, ΣX, and ΣY.

Consider the calculation of the correlation using the hypothetical data in Table 10-2. Here, there are two tests, X and Y, and five subjects. In doing these calculations on your own, you would have, as a start, only the data in the table in Columns X and Y as your "raw" scores. Examining the formula for the correlation (Equation 10-2) and the previous paragraph, the five "ingredients" for the correlation, listed again at the bottom of Table 10-2, must be calculated first. ΣX and ΣY are simply the sum of the X and Y scores, respectively; these values are 26 and 29 in this example. Next, ΣX^2, which is the sum of all the squared X values, is obtained by first squaring each X score and then adding the squared values for the five subjects; the total for ΣX^2 in this example is 150. ΣY^2 is calculated in the same way, except the Y scores are used; the sum there is 213. Finally, the value ΣXY is the sum of "cross products," or the sum of the products of X and Y. Notice that the entry for Subject 1 (48) is the product of that subject's X (6) and Y (8) score. The sum of these values is 176. Finally, n is the number of subjects (5).

By inserting these obtained values, the formula becomes

$$r_{xy} = \frac{176 - \dfrac{(26)\,(29)}{5}}{\sqrt{\left[150 - \dfrac{(26)^2}{5}\right]\left[213 - \dfrac{(29)^2}{5}\right]}} = \frac{25.2}{\sqrt{(14.8)\,(44.8)}} = +.979$$

$$(10\text{-}3)$$

Table 10-2

Hypothetical data for five subjects on two tests X and Y (The values needed for the correlation coefficient are shown at the bottom of each column.)

Subjects	X	X^2	Y	Y^2	$X \cdot Y$
1	6	36	8	64	48
2	4	16	3	9	12
3	8	64	10	100	80
4	5	25	6	36	30
5	3	9	2	4	6
Sums	26	150	29	213	176
	ΣX	ΣX^2	ΣY	ΣY^2	$\Sigma X \cdot Y$

Thus, the correlation between X and Y in this example is +.979, a very strong positive relationship. I performed these calculations in 5 min with a simple hand calculator. Of course, with the advent of computers and automatic data analyses, scientists don't have to do these by hand any longer, but it is still important to have done one of them at some point.

Interpreting the Correlation

As mentioned before, there are two aspects of the correlation to consider: the sign and the absolute size. I have already mentioned that the sign tells the direction of the relationship; in the present example, the slope of the regression line is positive. The size of the correlation, here .979, indicates the strength of the relationship. A convenient method for estimating this strength of relationship is to square the correlation coefficient, multiplying by 100 to convert it into a percentage score. In the example, $.979^2 \times 100 = .958 \times 100$ or 95.8%. Here, one could say that the two tests X and Y have approximately 95.8% of their "variance in common" with each other. It is beyond the scope of this discussion to go further with this interpretation, but consider that the correlation squared indicates the extent to which the two correlated tests can be considered to measure the same things and also gives a measure of the usefulness of the relationship for predictive purposes.

Notice that this fits nicely with the earlier discussion of the strength and direction of relationships. The percentage in common for two tests that correlate +.90 or two others that correlate −.90 are the same (i.e., $-.90^2 \times 100 = 81\%$), indicating that the strength of the relationship is not concerned with the sign. The strength of the relation is 100% if the correlation is either +1.0 or −1.0 ($1.0^2 \times 100 = 100\%$), and the percentage in common is zero if and only if the correlation is zero ($.00^2 \times 100 = 00.0\%$). Finally, notice that for two tests to have 50% in common with each other the correlation between them must be .707 (i.e., $.707^2 \times 100 = 50\%$). Thus, the strength of the relationship (the percentage in common) between two tests is not related to the sign of the *r* and is totally concerned with the absolute value of the correlation, with the strength increasing markedly as

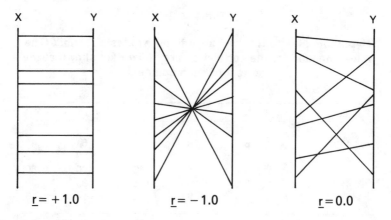

Figure 10-5. Laddergraphs as alternative ways of visualizing relationships between two variables. (Each subject has a score on X and Y and is represented by two dots and a line between them.)

the correlation approaches either +1.0 or −1.0 and having minimum strength when the correlation is around zero.

Laddergraphs

To make the task of understanding research using correlations more concrete and understandable, consider one more method for describing the nature of relationships. Consider two tests, X and Y, and orient the X and Y scales vertically as I have done in Figure 10-5. To do this, place the mean of X and the mean of Y opposite each other and "stretch" or "compress" one or both of the scales so that the highest and lowest X and Y scores are about opposite each other. Next, let each subject be represented by a point on the X scale and a point on the Y scale, together with a line drawn between them. If all subjects are placed on the laddergraph in this way, we can visualize the nature of the relationship that is expressed numerically by the correlation coefficient.

What if the correlation is 1.0? The laddergraph's "rungs" (the subjects) would be parallel to each other. The amount of distance between two adjacent subjects on the X scale is proportional to the amount of distance between those subjects on the Y scale. If the correlation is −1.0, we have the same thing, but one of the scales is simply "turned upside down." This can be visualized if the scales are broomsticks and the lines representing subjects are rubberbands; turning one of the scales upside down results in a laddergraph in which the spaces between subjects are still proportional but the lines cross at a single point. When the correlation drops toward zero (from either +1.0 or from −1.0), there is more and more randomness involved in the locations of the lines, to the point that a correlation of zero produces a laddergraph that looks like uncooked spaghetti noodles dropped on the floor. Some of these laddergraphs are shown in Figure 10-5.

These laddergraphs are seldom used in research, as investigators usually summarize the nature of the relationship by the sign and size of the correlation coefficient. But they do point out one important fact about the nature of the correlations. A high correlation (close to either $+1.0$ or -1.0) means that the order of the subjects on one of the variables tends to be the same as the order of the subjects on the other variable (although the order is turned "upside down" for a negative correlation). When the correlation is close to zero, the ordering of subjects on one variable is completely unrelated to the ordering of subjects on the other.

Reliability

One additional aspect of the measurement of individual differences must be mentioned. This has to do with the concept of *reliability*. People can differ from each other in at least two fundamental ways. First, you and I might be fundamentally and consistently different from each other in some stable characteristic such as height. Such differences between us will be enduring and constant across both time and testing conditions. But we might also be different in other ways that seem to result from chance effects or variability in our behaviors. If I make a pool shot and you do not on one trial, we might not be willing to say with such certainty that you and I are different in poolshooting capability, as on the next shot you might make the shot and I might not. Two people's being different from each other on some measure of performance does not necessarily indicate that these differences are stable and enduring. The stable, enduring differences among people are the subject of this chapter on individual differences. In fact, the definition of individual differences is *the stable, enduring, and underlying differences among people* (Henry, 1959).

The reliability coefficient provides a way to evaluate the extent to which the differences among people on some test are due to individual differences (stable, enduring differences) or to chance or transitory effects. The reliability coefficient is really another use of the correlation, but in this instance the concern is with the correlation of a test "with itself." This is not really nonsense as it might sound, as the example that follows will demonstrate.

Computation

Assume that five subjects each perform six trials on a RT task, so that the "raw" data are the 10 scores for each of the five subjects as shown in Table 10-3. To compute the reliability, the scores for a single test are divided into "halves" according to one of a number of different methods. One common method is called the "odd-even" method; the sum of (or average of) the odd-numbered trials is computed as a separate score from the sum of the even-numbered trials. Thus, in Table 10-3, the first value under the column headed "odd" (i.e., 619) is the sum of Trials 1, 3, and 5 for Subject 1. The first value under "even" is the sum of Trials 2, 4, and 6 for that person. The extent to which the odd and even sums tend to deviate from each other is a measure of the amount by which there are random variations in the individual trial data. Indeed, if there were no variation at all, then the sum of the odds and evens would be exactly the same for a given subject.

Table 10-3

Hypothetical reaction-time data for five subjects over six trials. (Reliability is based on the correlation between the sum of the odd and even trials.)

	Trials						Sums	
Subjects	1	2	3	4	5	6	Odd	Even
1	196	205	208	194	215	209	619	608
2	220	225	213	215	219	222	652	662
3	246	248	250	225	228	219	724	692
4	200	210	211	213	220	211	631	634
5	262	265	248	270	235	263	745	798

Next, the correlation coefficient is computed between the odd and even scores. For each subject there are two scores—the sum of the odds and the sum of the evens—the essential "ingredients" to compute a correlation between the two sets of scores, as done in the previous section. The only difference is that these two "tests" are both RT, but are measured on different sets of trials. In doing the computations, the correlation between the odd and even trials, which is what is typically called the *reliability coefficient*, worked out to be +.916.

Interpretation

Reliabilities can, theoretically, take on any value between +1.0 and −1.0, because they are computed with the correlation coefficient. But in practical situations, the reliability seldom is negative and usually ranges from .00 to +1.0. The reliability of a test can be interpreted in various ways. One is to consider the reliability coefficient as a proportion which when multiplied by 100 to change it to a percentage (91.6% in the present example). The observed variation among people is made up of (a) differences among people in their stable, enduring traits (termed *individual differences*) and (b) random (or other) fluctuations that tend to make people appear to be different from each other. If so, the reliability is the proportion of the observed variability (all sources of variability combined) that is accounted for by individual differences. In the present example, individual differences account for about 91.6% of the variability, with other variations accounting for about 8.4%. When the reliability is quite low (e.g., .2), then only 20% of the variation is accounted for by individual differences, with about 80% of the variation being due to random (and other) variations.

As mentioned earlier, the primary concern of individual differences research is in the relationship between pairs of tests. Statistically, the size of the correlation between two tests is limited by the reliability of either (or both) of the tests being correlated. Therefore, in evaluating the size of the correlation between two tests, one must be certain that the reliability of each of the tests being correlated is reasonably high—ideally .80 or higher.[5]

Finally, the reliability coefficient represents a measure of the "stability" of the test under different applications. More properly, it represents the stability of the subjects' performances on the test, as the test itself usually cannot be considered as being either stable or unstable. One might expect that as the number of trials administered to each subject is increased, the mean performance of the subjects would become more stable and the reliability coefficient would increase. A measure of RT based on 100 trials is far more reliable than one based on only one trial, since with the former measure the nonsystematic variations would have been "averaged out" to some extent, resulting in a better measure of the subject's "true" capability to react. Accordingly, the number of included trials that make up a test is a strong determinant of the reliability of the test, to the point that if the number of trials is increased enough, the reliability can actually be brought to 1.0 (e.g., Gullicksen, 1950). As easy as this is to do (usually), there is seldom a good excuse for a test with low reliability.

ABILITIES

Probably the most important topic in the area of individual differences is *abilities*. In this section, I will begin by providing a definition of the concept of ability, after which I will turn to some of the research indicating the structure of abilities.

Abilities Defined

The term *ability* which is often used interchangeably with the terms *capability*, and *aptitude*, usually refers to a hypothetical construct (see Chapter 2) that underlies (or supports) performance in a number of tasks or activities. An ability is usually thought to be a relatively stable characteristic or trait that contributes to performance in certain ways. These traits are usually thought of as being either genetically determined through the relatively automatic processes in growth and maturation, and they are not easily modifiable by practice or experience. Abilities represent the collection of "equipment" that one has at his or her disposal that determine whether or not a given motor task can be performed either poorly or well.

Abilities are usually inferred from patterns of performance on groups of tasks, largely using correlations as the primary method of measurement. For example, suppose I find that for a group of individuals those people who perform well on Task A also perform well on Task B. I also find that those people who perform poorly on Task A also perform poorly on Task B. This pattern of findings is what one would expect if Tasks A and B were

---

[5]The limiting factor is that the correlation between Test X and Test Y is theoretically less than the square root of the reliability of either Test X or Test Y; that is $r_{xy} \leqslant \sqrt{r_{xx}}$, or $r_{xy} \leqslant \sqrt{r_{yy}}$. See Gullicksen (1950).

related, or correlated statistically. If two tasks are related, then it is possible to infer that they are related because of some underlying property or process that is included in both tasks. The differential motor behavior scientist is interested in the possibility that the underlying properties common to these two tasks are abilities, or enduring, stable traits that contribute to these two tasks. For example, if Task A is a sprint start RT in swimming while Task B is a sprint start RT in running, a correlation between these two tasks might mean that both tasks have a reaction speed as an underlying ability. The tasks are different, but they both have at least one underlying similarity.

Abilities versus Skill

Another way to understand the concept of abilities is to distinguish it from the notion of skill. While often these two terms are used interchangeable in casual conversations, these terms should be separated when thinking about individual differences. An ability is a relatively stable, underlying trait that is largely unmodifiable by practice on a particular task or activity. Skills, of course, can easily be modified by practice or experience (the last section in this book deals with these changes with practice—called motor learning). Thus, abilities are underlying capabilities that support certain skills. For example, the capability to react quickly may underlie a number of specific skills such as sprint starts in swimming or in track. Think of a given skill as being "composed of" a number of different abilities. Thus, the skill of driving a car may be made up of various abilities, such as those involved in vision, an ability to switch attention from one event to another, an ability to anticipate, and so on.

Abilities as Limiting Factors

Abilities can also be conceptualized as representing limitations on performance, or as defining a person's potential for success in a particular activity. Thus, I will never become a professional basketball player regardless of the amount of time and effort I devote to it, because I do not possess the requisite abilities for the game (one of them being height). Two individuals could have the same skill level, but one of them could have far greater potential because he or she has greater abilities for the skill in question. The other person is likely to be frustrated by attempts to improve beyond the level defined by his or her underlying capabilities.

Varieties of Abilities

Abilities as underlying capabilities can be thought of in many forms. One form that is common to many sports is body configuration. For example, the ability (or trait, if you prefer) of height is important to basketball, small people rarely succeed in American football, and large people rarely succeed in gymnastics. Such characteristics are surely genetically defined and are, for the most part, relatively difficult to modify by training or practice. Another variety of ability is related to certain emotional or personality characteristics. For example, it may be that certain personalities are more amenable to team sports than to individual sports, that some personality types are more accepting of violent body contact, and so on. Finally, the abilities that I will be most concerned with here could be called "motor abilities." They are the underlying characteristics that tend to contribute to success in moving the limbs in particular ways, and some which will be discussed in a subsequent section are Reaction Time, Movement Speed, Manual Dexterity, and Rate Control (or anticipation). These abilities are often not as easy to measure or isolate for study as are abilities having to do with body configuration, but they are no less important for understanding why certain people become more effective race car drivers than others, for example.

The Structure of Motor Abilities

How many abilities related to motor skills are there? What are they, and how can they be measured? These questions have been asked for many years, and the answers have changed systematically as more effective techniques have been developed for studying abilities. First, consider some of the earlier thinking about motor (and cognitive) abilities that led to present-day beliefs.

General Motor Ability

An early notion about motor abilities—one which is still present to a great extent among people who are not familiar with the research—was the idea that all motor responding was based on a single, all-encompassing ability. This idea goes by different names, such as "athletic ability," "coordination," "motor ability," a more formal label of "general motor ability." All of these terms imply essentially the same thing. According to this idea, we are structured so that a single capability to move can be defined, with this capability having relevance to any motor task in which we choose to engage. That is, if a person had a strong general motor ability, then that person would be expected to succeed in any motor task. These ideas, which were generated in the 1930s, were no doubt supported by the common observations (on playgrounds, in athletics, etc.) that certain individuals could (or so it seemed) do anything they tried (so called "all-around athletes"), while other individuals could not do well at any motor task they tried. Given these casual observations, it seemed natural to postulate an underlying factor that tended to make all of the various tasks in athletics related to each other: a general athletic (or motor) ability.

This idea of general motor ability was probably led by the analogous research on cognitive abilities that was prevalent in the 1930s. It is beyond the scope of this chapter to go into much detail, but one important concept that emerged from this work was that of *intelligence*. It was during this period that the measures of IQ (intelligence quotient) were developed, and educators and parents became strong believers in the predictive power of IQ tests as measures of a child's capacity for "success" in society. IQ was designed as a measure of the hypothesized general mental ability; the idea was that this single mental ability was important for success in almost any mental activity in which the person engaged. For this reason, IQ tests were heavily used in educational settings for dividing children into academic ability groupings, for determining whether or not a child should be held back or "skipped" in grade level, and for entrance to college or special programs.

In the 1950s and 1960s, however, the concepts of general intellectual ability and general motor ability both came under serious attack. With respect to motor skills, the threat came from essentially two major sources: (a) the work on individual differences conducted by Henry and his students at Berkeley and (b) the research program related to individual differences in pilotry and similar tasks conducted by Fleishman and his associates through the U.S. Air Force. These two important programs, while they are quite different in terms of the methods and the interpretations, had strong impacts on the concept of general motor ability.

Predictions from the General Motor Ability Notion

The hypothesis of a general motor ability can be considered in the same way as any other hypothesis about motor skills. Predictions must be supported in laboratory situations; if they are not, scientists will tend to reject these hypotheses in favor of others whose predictions are more effectively supported. The general motor ability hypothesis has one important prediction that has been tested a great deal, and which relates to the sizes of the correlations between tests of various skills.

The logic goes like this. Take a group of individuals and test them on Task A; after a great deal of practice the people tend to order themselves on this task from "best" to "worst." According to the general motor ability hypothesis, the "best" people are where they are on the task because of a strong general motor ability; conversely, the "worst" people are where they are because of a weak general motor ability. Thus, the performance on this task can be taken as a measure of the strengths of these subjects' general motor ability.

Now, suppose that these same people are tested on Task B; Task B can be either similar or vastly different from A—it does not matter for the theory. How should these people tend to be ordered on Task B, given their order on Task A? The argument is that because the individuals "best" on Task A are in this position because of a strong general motor abilty and because the general motor ability applies to all motor tasks, then these same individuals should be "best" at Task B. Similarly, the individuals "worst" at Task A should be "worst" at Task B as well.

This kind of prediction can be seen by the laddergraph shown in Figure 10-6, where the hypothetical subjects on these two tasks tend to be ordered similarly. Remembering the discussion of graphical and statistical methods for measuring the degree of relationships between two tasks, a laddergraph such as that shown in Figure 10-6 implies that the correlation between Tasks A and B should tend toward 1.0, regardless of what tasks A and B actually involve. Thus, the major prediction of the general motor ability hypothesis is that any motor tasks A and B should correlate highly with each other. If

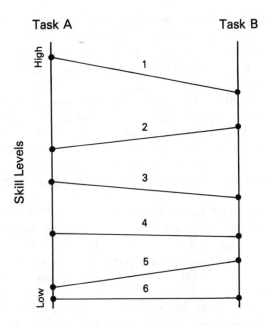

Figure 10-6. Predictions from the general motor ability hypothesis, displayed as a laddergraph. (The order of performers on Task A is predicted to be similar to that on Task B.)

the correlation between tasks is small, however, this would be evidence counter to predictions. And should this pattern of low correlations happen in general (in a wide variety of separate studies), then considerable doubt would be cast on the general motor ability hypothesis. With that introduction, I will turn to an examination of the correlations among tasks that have been found in the literature.

Correlations among Skills

Perhaps 30 to 50 separate investigations in the published literature are concerned with the correlations among well-practiced skills. I will mention but three of them to provide a general idea of how this work is done. One example from the Berkeley laboratory is by Bachman (1961). A group of 320 people practiced two motor tasks that supposedly involved balancing in some way. One of these, the Bachman ladder task (see Figure 3-11, page 77), involved the subject's climbing a free-standing ladder. The subject stood on a gymnastics mat and began climbing until the ladder toppled over. When it did, the subject quickly picked it up to begin climbing again, and so on. The score was the number of rungs climbed (with skipped rungs subtracted) in a 30-sec trial. Subjects had 10 trials, and their ability level on this task was taken as the average performance on the last two trials.

The second task that Bachman's subjects performed was the stabilometer (see Figure 3-8, page 72). This apparatus was an unstable balancing board on which the subject stood, pivoted so that the board could tip in the frontal plane; that is, the board tended to tip so that the right foot would move down as the left foot would move up, similar to standing, facing forward, in a rocking canoe. By appropriate action, the subject could halt the rocking and keep the board still, but a great deal of practice was required to learn to do this. The task was scored in "movement units," or the amount of movement of the board that occurred in a 30-sec trial. The subject performed 10 trials, and ability was estimated as the average of the last two trials, similar to the performance measure for the ladder.

It should be noted that the stabilometer has a scoring system for which larger scores are "worse," whereas the Bachman ladder task has a scoring system for which larger scores are "better." This is no problem, as the general motor ability hypothesis predicts that "good" subjects on the ladder (high scores) should also be "good" on the stabilometer (low scores); thus, the prediction is that the correlation should be large in absolute value, but negative.

Bachman (1961) found that for various subgroups of his subjects (defined by age and sex) the correlations between success on the ladder and success on the stabilometer ranged from $+.25$ to $-.15$, with most correlations being very close to zero. Thus, the low relationships between the ladder and stabilometer tasks did not permit predictions of success on one from the score on the other. The lowness of the correlations can be emphasized considering that, by taking the largest correlation ($+.25$) and squaring it to determine the percentage in common between these two tasks gives $.25^2 \times 100 = 6.25\%$ in common. About 94% of the abilities in these tasks were specific to each task and not shared by the other.

Consider another study. Lotter (1960) had subjects perform striking and kicking movements with the hand and foot, respectively, in a RT setting. The arm movement involved a forward-downward movement to hit a suspended tennis ball as quickly as possible (for left and right hands separately); and the leg movement involved kicking a small plate with a movement resembling a place-kick in American football (again, for right and left legs), thus six possible pairs of tasks between which a correlation could be computed. The arm-arm correlation was .58, and the leg-leg correlation was .64. These correlations were considerably higher than those found by Bachman (1961), but these correlations are based on the same task done with limbs on opposite sides of the body. The correlations between arm and leg, with both on the same side of the body or on opposite sides (i.e., left arm vs. right leg), were lower: .24, .36, .23, and .18. Using the rule for computing the percentage in common, the same tasks on opposite sides of the body had approximately 37% in common, whereas the different tasks (arm vs. leg) had approximately 6.3% in common, based on the averaged correlations. Even though these activities all involved rapid striking activity, they were apparently different enough in terms of their underlying abilities that they did not correlate very highly with each other. It is interesting to wonder if the arm-arm and leg-leg correlations were so much higher than the others because these pairs used the same motor program while others did not, such as with the two-hand writing tasks discussed in Chapter 8. In any case, Lotter's data are not supportive of the general motor ability hypothesis.

In another example, Parker and Fleishman (1960) had 203 subjects perform a battery of 50 tests in conjunction with an armed services testing program. This produced a 50 × 50 correlation matrix, whereby every test is correlated with every other test and the resulting correlations are placed in a large table, or matrix. Scanning through 1,225 correlations presented in Parker and Fleishman's Appendix D, the majority of these tests correlated about .40 or lower with each other; only rarely was there a correlation of .50 or higher, and the highest correlation was .85 between tests that were practically identical. Thus, from this and other batteries of tests that have been studied the general pattern is low correlations, with a few high ones when the tasks are practically identical (e.g., walking a 2-meter balance beam versus a 4-meter balance beam, with the same beam being used in each).

Many more studies have been done, but the point has been made by now; generally, low correlations are found among different skills. This pattern does not support the notion of a general motor ability or even of general motor subabilities such as general athletic ability. Notice also that there did not appear to be a general balancing ability, since Bachman's (1961) two balancing tasks (the ladder and stabilometer) did not correlate with each other. Also, there did not appear to be a general hitting ability, as seen by the fact that Lotter's (1960) striking tasks correlated very poorly. The various motor tasks that humans perform, based on this evidence at least, appear to be supported by a collection of relatively independent abilities with a different pattern of abilities being required for each different task that one might attempt. One such idea about motor abilities was proposed by Henry (1958-1968; 1961), largely as a result of the patterns of correlations like those presented here.

Henry's Specificity Hypothesis

In the late 1950s, Henry (1958-1968) proposed the idea, in direct contradiction to the general motor ability hypothesis, that motor abilities are specific to a particular task. Essentially, there were three aspects of this hypothesis. First, he thought that the number of motor abilities that we have is very large, perhaps numbering in the thousands. Second, he believed that these abilities were independent, so that the strength of one particular ability is unrelated to the strength of any other ability. One way to think of this is that we have a large collection of abilities, some of which are "good," some of which are "weak," and others of which are "average." Third, each task or skill that we perform depends upon a large number of these abilities. When the task is changed, the particular collection of abilities that support the performance must change to meet the demands of the new task.

Probably the most important prediction of the specificity hypothesis is that two tasks, even if they appear to be quite similar (such as throwing a baseball and throwing a football), will tend to correlate nearly zero with each other. This is because the group of abilities that underlies these two tasks are, according to this view, two distinct collections with nearly no shared abilities. Also, because the collection of abilities for one task and those for another task are independent of each other, this leads to the expectation that the correlation among skills should be zero, or at least very low. The evidence tends to support such a viewpoint.

Also, the Henry hypothesis predicts that transfer among skills should be quite low. Transfer is defined as the attainment (or loss) of proficiency in one task as a result of practice or experience at some other task (Chapter 11). If the two tasks have no abilities in common, then no element practiced in one of them would contribute to (or transfer to) the other. Generally, the transfer literature supports Henry's hypothesis, showing essentially that motor transfer is generally low and positive (Chapter 12). I will deal with this evidence when I discuss some phenomena about motor learning in the last third of the book.

Factor-Analytic Studies

A second major research thrust that tended to argue against the general motor ability hypothesis was the factor-analytic method; so-called because it used a statistical tool termed *factor analysis*. Various investigators have used this general method, but certainly the most active of them was Fleishman (1964, 1965, 1967; see Fleishman & Bartlett, 1969, for reviews). After a brief discussion of the factor-analytic method, some of the major findings from this body of research will be presented.

Factor analysis. Factor analysis is a complex statistical method based on correlations, but an understanding of the technical aspects of this method is not necessary in order to appreciate the kinds of knowledge that it has generated. The essential details are these. Typically, a large number of people (e.g., 100 to 200) perform each of a smaller number of tests (e.g., 50). (Examining 200 people on each of 50 tests is a mammoth undertaking in terms of testing time.) Factor analysis groups the tests into *clusters*, or *factors*, so that the number of factors is considerably less than the number of original tests (e.g., 10 or so, depending on a number of other considerations). These tests that make up a particular cluster or factor have the property of showing relatively high correlations with each other, whereas two tests that are members of different factors tend to show low correlations.

This perhaps will be clearer by considering the diagram in Figure 10-7. Say there were 20 tests and the factor analysis grouped them into five clusters, or factors, each represented by the squares. The circled numbers within the squares refer to the test numbers (which are, of course, purely arbitrary), and the numbers on the lines joining two tests represent the correlation between the two indicated tests. For clarity, not all of the 20 tests are included.

Notice that for Factor I the tests that are included tend to show relatively high correlations with each other (.52, .49, and .65), indicating that these tests, to some extent, tend to be measures of some underlying ability or abilities. Notice also that in Factor II the tests also tend to correlate with each other (.60, .48, and .50), and they tend to measure some ability. However, a test in Factor I (e.g., Test 9) does not correlate well ($r = .06$) with any test in Factor II (e.g., Test 13). Also, Test 6 (in Factor II) and Test 2 (in Factor III) do not correlate well with each other ($r = .10$). The interpretation is that the tests within a factor tend to measure some basic ability or abilities, while each of the factors itself tends to represent a different ability. In this way the factor-analytic technique seems to allow the division of a large group of tests into a smaller group of factors, each of which is thought

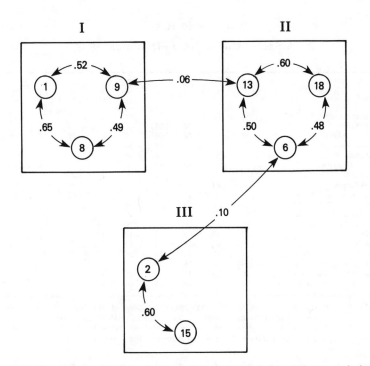

Figure 10-7. Three clusters (the boxes) of tests that would result from a factor analysis. [Correlations between tests (shown as circles) within a cluster are higher than correlations between tests in different clusters.]

to represent a separate ability or abilities.

Naming abilities. The next step in the factor analyst's job is to determine what abilities the factors represent. Assume that the person has tested 200 people on each of 18 tests and has performed a factor analysis. The result of this effort is a table called a *factor matrix*, and an example from one of Fleishman's (1957) studies is included in Table 10-4. Across the top of the table are the nine factors that emerged in the analysis, analogous to the clusters or groupings of tests in Figure 10-7. Down the left side of the table are the tests that were administered to the large group of subjects, ordered arbitrarily. The numbers in the body of the table are called the *factor loadings* and actually provide the most interesting aspects of the analysis. These factor loadings indicate the extent to which the test in question is a "measure of" the ability or factor in that column; or the factor loading is often thought of as the correlation between the test and the ability that it represents.[6] For example, consider Test 2 (Reaction Time). This test has a high loading (.60) on Factor I but a relatively small loading on Factor II (.15). On the other hand, Test 4 (Pattern Comprehension) has a high loading on Factor II (.66) but a very small loading on Factor I (.12). Thus, it

---

[6]This is somewhat misleading to students. Such a correlation cannot ever be measured directly, since the factor cannot be measured directly. Perhaps it is best to think of it as the correlation between the test and the factor if it could actually be measured.

Table 10-4

A Factor Matrix (from Fleishman, 1957)

| | Factors | | | | | | | | | |
Variable	I	II	III	IV	V	VI	VII	VIII	IX	h²
1. Instrument Comprehension	18	22	18	13	54	02	15	−01	20	48
2. Reaction Time	60	−15	03	−03	08	07	16	−07	−09	43
3. Rate of Movement	43	19	−02	−06	09	09	22	−01	14	31
4. Pattern Comprehension	12	66	18	07	34	26	11	−07	08	69
5. Mechanical Principles	03	53	22	52	09	07	06	12	05	63
6. General Mechanics	05	19	12	65	14	02	11	−03	10	52
7. Speed of Identification	27	44	44	17	21	27	01	00	00	61
8. Visual Pursuit	14	23	38	05	25	23	10	16	17	40
9. Complex Coord. Trials 1-5	05	35	21	26	35	38	42	22	04	73
10. Complex Coord. Trials 12-16	23	16	23	21	19	47	46	41	22	86
11. Complex Coord. Trials 49-53	42	13	−03	22	19	38	47	52	−07	92
12. Complex Coord. Trials 60-64	43	12	01	20	19	34	40	58	06	89
13. Rotary Pursuit	28	15	15	15	13	16	55	01	00	49
14. Plane Control	16	07	−06	28	20	33	31	−11	20	41
15. Kinesthetic Coordination	−01	−16	15	28	16	35	09	11	00	29
16. Undimensional Matching	14	16	34	14	08	19	45	14	06	45
17. Two-Hand Matching	16	21	14	15	−01	70	08	02	15	63
18. Discrimination Reaction Time	28	24	23	20	46	40	04	−16	00	63

Note: Decimals omitted. Factors are identified as follows: I—Speed of Arm Movement; II—Visualization; III—Perceptual Speed; IV—Mechanical Experience; V—Spatial Orientation; VI—Response Orientation; VII—Fine Control Sensitivity; VIII—Complex Coordination "Within-Task" factor; IX—Residual Factor; h² is called the communality, and is the sum of the squared factor loadings for that test (e.g., $.18^2 + .22^2 + \ldots + .20^2 = .48$)

can be said that Reaction Time is a measure of Factor I (but not of Factor II), whereas Pattern Comprehension is a measure of Factor II (but not of Factor I). Had I displayed these factors as clusters as in Figure 10-7, Reaction Time and Pattern Comprehension would have been represented as members of different clusters.

It is through the values of the factor loadings in these factor matrices that the scientist comes to understand the structure of the abilities that underlie the various tests studied. Return to Table 10-4, where these loadings are presented for Fleishman's data. Consider Factor IV first, as the point is made clearly in this case. Scan the factor loadings for Factor IV, noting which ones are high and ignoring the low ones. You will find that all of the loadings are less than .30 except for two—a .52 for the Mechanical Principles test and a .65 for General Mechanics. On this basis, the scientist would be tempted to believe that Factor IV has something to do with the performers' knowledge of mechanical principles and to name this factor accordingly. Fleishman named Factor IV "Mechanical Experience." Now look at Factor II. The tests that have high loadings on Factor II are Pattern Comprehension (loading = .66), Mechanical Principles (loading = .53), and perhaps Speed of Identification (loading = .44). On this basis, Fleishman named this factor "Visualization." In some cases (Factor IV) the name of the factor is nearly obvious by examining the nature of the tests that "load on" it. In other cases (such as with Factor II), the name of the factor is not so obvious. It may require a number of different factor analyses, all of which use some of the same tests, to identify a particular factor.

Notice that a given test can load on two factors at the same time. An example is Test 5 (Mechanical Principles), which loads on both Factor II (loading = .53) and Factor IV (loading = .52). What does this mean? One interpretation is that this test is made up of at least two abilities (Visualization, Mechanical Experience) and that it measures both of these abilities at the same time. This is in keeping with the idea that any given performance or skill (e.g., Test 5) can be thought of as being made up of many abilities. Other patterns can be seen across the factor loadings shown in Table 10-4, such as with Test 7 (Speed of Identification).

Finally, notice that the pattern of factor loadings is different for the different factors. That is, the tests that load highly on one factor are typically not the same tests that load highly on the other factors. Each of the factors seems to have its own "personality" in terms of which tests have high loadings and which tests have low loadings. Compare Factors I and II, for example. Here, the tests with the highest loadings on one are loaded very low on the other. This observation is really the same as that in Figure 10-7, where each of the factors was thought to represent a separate ability or group of abilities. Since each of the factors is separate, it is logical that the tests that measure these separate factors will be separate as well.

Through such techniques, Fleishman and his colleagues, together with a few others, have provided a series of hypothesized underlying abilities that seem to be relevant to various aspects of motor behavior. In the next section, some of these abilities are outlined to give a "flavor" of the nature of this work.

Factor Analytically Defined Motor Abilities

The following list of abilities has been determined in a number of separate studies. This list is not exhaustive, and it is merely intended to provide an idea of the kind of abilities that have been produced by these methods. They all come from Fleishman's work (e.g., Fleishman, 1964, 1965, 1967; Parker & Fleishman, 1960) and bear the names given by him. After each I have provided an example of a "real-world" task in which this ability might be used; these are based largely on conjecture on my part.

Control Precision. This ability underlies the production of responses for which the outcomes must be rapid and precise, but the motions are made with relatively large body segments. Example: golf drive.

Multi-limb Coordination. This ability underlies tasks for which a number of limb segments must be coordinated while moved simultaneously, such as the two hands, the two feet, or the hands and feet. Examples: juggling, playing a piano.

Response Orientation. This ability underlies tasks for which rapid directional discriminations among alternative movement patterns must be made, and it is apparently related to the ability to select a correct movement under choice RT situations. Example: defensive lineman in American football.

Reaction Time. This ability underlies tasks for which there is one stimulus and one response, and the subject must react as quickly as possible after a stimulus in simple RT situations. Example: sprint start in swimming.

Speed of Arm Movement. This ability underlies tasks for which the limb must be moved from one place to another very quickly and the measure of performance is MT. Example: Muhammad Ali's left jab.

Rate Control (Timing). This ability underlies tasks for which the movement speed of the limbs must be adjusted to the movements of the environment so that the person's limbs are timed correctly. Example: tracking tasks.

Manual Dexterity. This ability underlies tasks for which relatively large objects are manipulated, primarily with the hands and arms. Example: carpentry.

Finger Dexterity. This ability underlies tasks for which small objects are manipulated, primarily with the fingers. Example: repairing a wristwatch.

Postural Discrimination. This ability underlies tasks for which subjects must respond to changes in postural cues in the absence of vision in making precise bodily adjustments. Example: walking in the dark.

Response Integration. This ability underlies tasks for which the person must utilize and apply sensory cues from several sources into a single, integrated response. Example: basketball.

Arm-Hand Steadiness. This ability underlies tasks in which the person must be quiet and steady. Example: riflery, archery.

Wrist-Finger Speed. This ability underlies tasks for which alternating movements (e.g., tapping) must be made as quickly as possible and seems to represent the rapid coordination of the muscles required for up and down movements of the fingers and wrist. Example: piano trills.

Aiming. This ability underlies tasks for which the subject must aim a stylus or a pencil at a target, attempting to hit it with very quick movements. Example: dart throwing, Muhammad Ali's left jab.

Physical proficiency abilities. In addition to the abilities listed above that are thought to exist within the movement control area, other abilities have to do with activities that seem to depend on physical or structural aspects of the body. Some of these outlined by Fleishman (1964) are: Extent (static) Flexibility, Dynamic Flexibility, Static Strength, Dynamic Strength, Trunk Strength, Explosive Strength, Gross Body Coordination, Gross Body Equilibrium, and Stamina (Cardiovascular Endurance). These nine abilities can be thought of as underlying dimensions of physical fitness or physical proficiency, and they appear to be separate from the skills-oriented abilities presented earlier. For more information on these abilities, see Fleishman's (1964) book entitled *The Structure and Measurement of Physical Fitness*.

Role of the Factors in Skills

Some interesting features of this list of hypothesized factors should be mentioned. First, if some individual has a strong ability with respect to Arm-Hand Steadiness, the strength of any other ability (say Reaction Time) could be high, low, or intermediate. With this observation, it is interesting to consider that a number of factors represent what is often called "quickness." For example, Response Orientation represents a RT situation for which there is more than one stimulus-response alternative (i.e., choice RT). Reaction Time refers to RT tasks for which there is only one stimulus-response alternative (i.e., simple RT), and Movement Time refers to the abilities necessary to move the limb quickly once the action has been started. Interestingly, "quickness" is not really represented as a single ability; rather, it seems to be defined by different abilities depending on the environmental situation (one, or more than one, stimulus-response alternative) or on what part of the action is measured (the RT or the MT). Henry (1961) and many others have shown essentially zero correlations between RT and MT, suggesting that they are based on separate abilities.

Also, note that Manual Dexterity and Finger Dexterity are separate abilities. Both use the hands, but for different sized objects. If this is correct, then what does it mean to say that a person "has good hands"? To answer this question adequately, I would have to know about at least two different abilities. As well, the issues about "good hands" can be seen in a slightly different way. Most of the abilities defined in the previous section (with the exception of the physical proficiency abilities) are defined with tasks that use the hands for manipulations of various controls in various ways defined by the task. Yet, depending on the ways in which the hands are used (e.g., to react quickly, to move quickly, to move in conjunction with another hand, to move in time to some external object, to move accurately, and so on), different abilities are involved. Clearly, the structure of human motor abilities is far more complicated than common sense would lead us to believe. And it seems to be a gross oversimplification to make a statement such as "John is good with his hands." In order for this statement to make any sense, it must be combined with information about how John is to use his hands, and then he may or may not be "good" in the various ways specified.

Skills have complex structures. It should be pointed out that these abilities are but a few of many that probably underlie most complex activities. There are many abilities involved in playing basketball, such as those involved in tracking a ball to be caught, maintaining attention toward the basket when an opponent tries to be distracting, switching attention from one source to another (e.g., from a player who is guarded to one who is not, so that a pass can be made), and producing accurate but forceful muscular contractions in shooting. I have no idea if these possible abilities will be shown to be separate and independent, but research is currently under way to investigate these kinds of abilities in fast games (e.g., Keele, Note 3). Knowing about the nature of abilities underlying games such as basketball would provide a much more effective way to predict success in the game from measures of these abilities, as well as generate a better understanding of the structure of human abilities in general, perhaps for use in other situations in industry, sport, and the military.

The structures are variable. A second, allied point is that the particular collection, or pattern, of these abilities appears to change markedly as only minor changes in the task or situation are imposed on the performer. For example, the employment of a choice RT ability or a different simple RT ability depends on the number of stimulus-response alternatives presented to the subject; changing the situation from a simple to choice RT situation presumably results in the "abandonment" of one ability in favor of another.

This concept has been shown more formally in some of Fleishman's work in which the nature of the control-display relations was varied experimentally. In this work, the task always remained the same with respect to the movements made, but the way in which the movement was signalled from the display was changed. The situation was somewhat analogous to driving a car from a seat that can be oriented in any direction with respect to the car's direction of travel. As the directional orientation was altered, systematically different abilities were brought into play while others were dropped; still others remained constant. This notion underlines the problem in trying to measure abilities in one situation, hoping to apply these measures for prediction of success in a similar, but not quite identical, situation. If the task has changed much at all, then it is likely that different abilities will be used in the two situations, leading to false estimates of the nature of abilities in one task based on measures in the other. The use of abilities by subjects appears to be highly varied, which makes understanding them very difficult indeed.

Abilities and information processing. Finally, it has been tempting to try to align the understanding of human abilities defined by factor-analytic methods with the experimental research described in the first sections of this book. Fleishman and Bartlett (1969) discuss the hypothesis that the factor analytically defined abilities are measures of separate ways that the humans process information, with each of these information-processing mechanisms being essentially independent. In some situations, this connection is easy to imagine; for example, the simple and choice RT abilities could be differentiated on the basis that the choice situation involves the information processes related to resolving uncertainty (as in Hick's law, Chapter 5), while the simple situation involves the prestructuring of a motor program. Similarly, abilities like Rate Control (or anticipation, timing) involve the processes related to the analysis of incoming sensory information.

But in other cases the connection is not so easily made. It is difficult to see how abilities like Aiming can represent a fundamental information-processing mechanism. Perhaps it is more reasonable to think that these abilities represent "real" mechanisms in the human motor system, only some of which have to do with the processing of information in the sense in which Fleishman and Bartlett (1969) think of it. For example, some abilities could be related to the amount of variability produced during a muscular action (see Chapter 9, force-variability relations) or to the actual structure of the neurological tissues in the cord and other areas in the central nervous system. These are issues that should occupy individual differences researchers in the future.

Criticisms of the Abilities Approach

It would not be fair to end this section without mentioning that the abilities approach, primarily that using factor analytic methods, has not been without its critics. One problem is methodological. There are many varieties of factor analysis and of other techniques (called "rotations") that are applied to factor-analytic outcomes to aid in interpretation. Arbitrary choices about the way in which the same data are analyzed can change the nature of the factors that emerge from these analyses and thus alter the interpretation in terms of the abilities that the scientist is trying to understand.

Next, Fleishman's work has been criticized—unfairly, in my opinion—for being limited in scope. Remember that his work deals primarily with young men in the armed services. Rarely are women used, children are never included, nor are older people. Thus, the studies suffer some limitation in generalizability. But it should also be recognized that these studies are difficult to perform, with a great deal of effort and expense required for just one. Remember also that Fleishman's research support has come primarily from the armed forces, where a major concern was the understanding of the abilities involved in pilotry. It is natural that these studies used adult men only, as they were done in the 1950s and 1960s when women played less important roles in the armed services than they do at present.

Finally, the abilities that have emerged from these studies have been based on skills for which the person is typically seated and using the hands (occasionally the feet as well), and for which the performance is noncompetitive. These kinds of performances are but one kind of action involved in the total spectrum of motor activity, and the abilities that emerged from these studies probably are somewhat limited as a result. After all, if no task requiring Ability A was included in the original battery of tests to be factor analyzed, then Ability A could never emerge. A large number of abilities that are important for other kinds of tasks have undoubtedly been missed as a result. These are problems for the future, but it should be clear that Fleishman has provided a major contribution by defining the methods and demonstrating how to make the next step.

Superabilities

The model of abilities used with the factor-analytic approach assumes that the underlying abilities are independent (although some models do not make this strict assumption). However, recent evidence from Eysenck (Note 18) in the realm of intellectual abilities leads to the possibility that this structure is too simple to account for the kinds of data that have been collected. The primary difficulty with the idea of strictly independent abilities is that when a pattern of intercorrelations from a battery of intellectual (or motor) tasks is studied, a systematic tendency develops for the tests to all correlate with each other to some small degree. One explanation for this is that all of the tests depend on a weak superability that "resides above" all of the smaller abilities discussed so far.[7] In the area of intellectual abilities, the superability can be thought of as "general intelligence," an ability that seems to have relevance to any intellectual task that the subject is asked to perform. But this superability is not thought to account for very much performance variance, with far more being accounted for by the separate abilities that relate to particular kinds of capability that might be applicable for a limited number of tasks (e.g., spatial relations, abstract reasoning, etc.).

It is certainly possible that similar models will be applicable for motor

---

[7]The prefix *super-* refers to the ability's higher position with respect to the others, not to its strength.

tasks. One reason is that in large batteries of motor tasks, the performances tend to correlate to a small extent with each other, just as intellectual performances appear to do. Thus, it may be that a superability can be thought of as "residing above" the specific motor abilities that Fleishman and his colleagues have discovered. But this superability cannot be very powerful (i.e., account for a great deal of performance variance), as such a superability would demand that the correlations between motor tasks be quite substantial, which they clearly are not. In this limited way, it could well be that the concept of the general motor ability as a superability might have some merit after all, contrary to the conclusion I drew in previous sections. However, I do not want to convey the impression that general motor ability, as a unitary ability that was thought (40 years ago) to be a strong determiner of all motor tasks, should be brought back as a useful concept. My point is that some very weak general capacity to move might be necessary to account for the very small correlations that are typically observed among motor tasks. I am certainly not advocating the resurrection of tests of general motor ability.

These kinds of ideas are related to a notion of motor abilities presented by Cratty (1966). This framework, with the addition of some other ideas, is diagrammed in Figure 10-8. At the top of this hierarchical structure is the superability, for want of a better term called "general motor ability." This ability could have a number of separate but related components, such as the

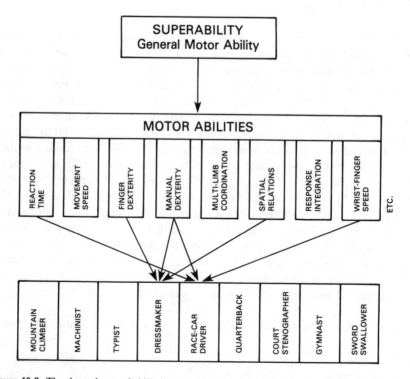

Figure 10-8. The dependence of skills in various tasks on hypothesized motor abilities and a superability.

overall motivational level, the level of general intelligence, certain physiological factors such as the state of health or fitness, and so on. At a level under the superability are the individual motor abilities that have been discovered by Fleishman and his colleagues and which have been discussed in the previous sections. Some of these are Reaction Time, Movement Speed, Finger Dexterity, and so on (not all of these are given in the figure of course). At the bottom of the hierarchy are the various skills, tasks, or occupations that people can perform. Each is based on a small subset of the motor abilities, such as the dressmaker whose performance might be based on Finger Dexterity, Manual Dexterity, and Spatial Relations. Each of these skills is thought to be based on its own performance factors, the most important of which are related to that task, such as practice, experience with similar tasks, and so on. It is also based, to some extent, on the strength of the superability.

The "All-Around" Athlete

The foregoing sections should provide a number of important generalizations about the structure of human motor abilities. Skills tend to be quite specific, and they do not correlate well with each other unless the skills are practically identical. The interpretation is that the abilities underlying these tests are independent and relatively large in number and that a general motor ability, if it exists at all, is relatively minor in terms of understanding the relationships among tasks.

Students are generally bothered that these findings and conclusions do not agree very well with their common observations that some children appear to be able to do well in all sports while others do well in none. Such casual observations seem to suggest that a general motor ability should be given more credibility than I have suggested. So how can these common observations be explained in the light of the evidence presented about human abilities? A number of forces seem to operate with children's motor behavior to provide a tentative explanation for these observations.

Parental encouragement. It seems logical that some children receive a great deal of encouragement for participation in sports of all kinds, while other children receive almost none. If so, it might be expected that those children who have been encouraged and rewarded for participation will have greater skill at the common sports than those children who have not been so encouraged, making the sports appear to be dependent on the same underlying ability. Increased participation might be related to a general motivational component.

Body configuration and maturation. One feature of playground sports is that, for the most part, large, strong, mature children are more effective than are small, weak, and immature children. If a child is large or is physically mature early, he or she might enjoy an advantage at all sports and be more inclined to practice them on the playground.

Personality characteristics. It is possible that certain personalities do not enjoy affiliation and cooperation as is usually required for playground sports. If so, it might be expected that these children would not care to participate in any of these activities, leaving them with a decrement in skill that becomes increasingly difficult to overcome as the age and skills of the other children increase.

Summary. These notions have not been well established, but they do represent one way that the abilities research and the common observations about children can be brought together. Thus, according to this view, "all-around athletes" develop from, in large part, the patterns of prior experiences, resulting in learning and socialization that tend toward participation in all sports. A kind of "rich-get-richer" phenomenon develops, whereby a little experience and encouragement tends to lead to more experiences and more skill, which leads to more involvement, and so on. Children without the first signs of success will perhaps tend to avoid sports. This thinking suggests that it would be an oversimplification, and perhaps a grave mistake, to ignore children who do not perform well in sports when instigating a new activity on the grounds that they do not have the requisite general motor ability. It's not that simple.

Finally, there probably are some true "all-around athletes" who behave as though they have a very large general motor ability. Perhaps these people have, by chance occurrences involved in genetics and prior experiences, many of the requisite abilities for a wide variety of sports and physical activities. These examples can be seen, perhaps, in decathalon athletes and on television programs like "The Superstars," where athletes compete successfully in a wide variety of sports not directly related to their major sport. It appears that these individuals are very rare indeed. It would probably be a mistake to interpret the apparent generality of the pattern of their motor capabilities as indicating that a general motor ability exists for people of more average overall capabilities. A number of other hypotheses—explained in the previous sections—can handle these effects just as easily and are more in keeping with the research evidence on human motor abilities.

TAXONOMIES

A *taxonomy* is a classification scheme that can be used to assign items in a set into various categories. I have already discussed a few of these classification methods in Chapter 3, such as open versus closed skills and continuous versus discrete skills. More elaborate systems for classification are now being developed, based on the underlying structure of the abilities involved in motor tasks.

The basic notion is that one of the ways to classify tasks is in terms of the pattern of abilities that underlie them, rather than the more superficial and obvious characteristics such as, for example, whether the performance is discrete or continuous. For example, performing on the pommel horse in gymnastics might be made up of Strength, Rate Control, and Multi-Limb Coordination, with each contributing a certain proportion to the performance. These descriptions of tasks in terms of their abilities are just beginning to be done. Again, the primary worker in this area has been Fleishman (see Fleishman & Stephenson, 1970, for a more complete description).

These descriptions can be made in a number of ways and two of them are mentioned here. In one way, the scientist uses factor-analytic techniques, and in another the procedure is called *task analysis*.

Factor-Analytic Classifications

With this method, after a great deal of experience with the various motor tasks in previous factor analyses, the scientist sees that certain tests seem always to result in the emergence of certain factors or abilities. A good example is the various tests of rapid movement which, when included in factor analyses, typically produce a factor that is labeled Movement Speed. Such stable findings lead to the establishment of a particular MT test as the "best" measure of the ability of Movement Speed, with the "best" test being defined in terms of ease of administration, the size of the loadings, etc. These tests are often elevated to the status of *reference tests*, or the generally agreed-upon measures of a particular motor ability.

Now, if this reference test is included in another, subsequent factor analysis, in which tests for an entirely different activity (e.g., pilotry) are included, the structure of this task can be understood somewhat by noting the extent to which it loads on the Movement Speed ability defined by the reference test. If high loadings on the Movement Speed ability are obtained, then we can say that the new activity has a Movement Speed component. By including other reference tests at the same time, each representing a different predetermined ability, the abilities represented in this new activity can be pinpointed.

A good example is provided in the factor matrix shown in Table 10-4, in the previous section (page 404). Tests 1 through 8 are tests of various kinds of skills, such as Instrument Comprehension, Reaction Time, and so on. These eight tests are the reference tests, items that had been studied extensively so that their underlying abilities were understood. Now notice that Tests 9 through 12 are all based on the same apparatus, one called the Complex Coordination Task (see Figure 3-8), in which the person manipulates the forward-backward and left-right movements of an aircraft-type "joystick," as well as the left-right movement of foot pedals, to respond to a pattern of lights presented on a display. The difference between these tests is that they represent different stages in practice (Trials 1 through 5, 12 through 16, and so on). The question is what are the underlying abilities in the Complex Coordination Task. (The tests numbered 13 through 18 are also under investigation in the same way, but I will not be concerned with these issues here.)

What abilities underlie the Complex Coordination Task? For simplicity, consider the final performance, Trials 60 through 64 (Test 12). The highest factor loadings for this test are on Factor I (.43) and Factor VIII (.58). These factors were named, according to procedures described earlier, Speed of Arm Movement and Complex Coordination, respectively.[8] We could say

---

[8]The Factor VIII here is a factor that is strictly limited to the particular task in question, and does not provide much new information about the underlying abilities. This is somewhat like saying that skill in driving a car is dependent on the ability to drive a car. It is very different from saying that driving a car is related to visual acuity, for example.

that the Complex Coordination Task is heavily based on limb speed. It is also dependent to some extent on Factor VII (loading = .40) and Factor VI (loading = .34), which are labeled Fine Control Sensitivity and Response Orientation (i.e., choice RT), respectively. The Complex Coordination Task does not seem to depend on Factors II and III at all, which are labeled Visualization and Perceptual Speed. Thus, from such a procedure, an estimate of the nature of this task in terms of the abilities that underlie it can be formed: The Complex Coordination Task is made up of (a) Speed of Arm Movement, (b) Fine Control Sensitivity, and (c) Response Orientation, with minor contributions from other abilities.

In theory, this procedure can be applied to any new task in order to understand its underlying abilities. Let's say that I choose the game of golf. I could use a large number (e.g., 50) of well-practiced and skilled golfers and administer to them reference tests, perhaps the eight tests mentioned above. (I might wish to use somewhat different tests if I have reason to believe that some factor definitely is, or definitely is not, involved in golf.) Then, I administer a golf performance test and analyze the reference tests and the golf test with factor analysis. The nature of the loadings that emerges will give a surprisingly good indication of the nature of the abilities involved in golf.

This is not as simple as I have perhaps made it sound. A major problem is having "good," well-understood, reference tests in the first place. Fleishman's work has provided a start in this direction, but limitations exist to the applicability of this work, as I have discussed earlier. And many abilities that might be involved in golf may not be uncovered, as they may not be represented by any of the reference tests. But with progressive additions to knowledge about the underlying abilities, the reference tests will become more effective and greater in number, making the task of discovering new tests easier in the future. This method has a great deal of potential for practical application for new jobs for which the nature of the abilities underlying it need to be known.

Task Analysis

A considerably easier, but less effective, way to determine the nature of underlying abilities is through a series of procedures that together have been termed *task analysis*. The essential idea is to "analyze" (i.e., "break down") the task to consider what kinds of abilities might be involved in it. For example, one might say that a soccer goalie has to be able to move quickly, to react quickly, to remain alert, to be relatively tall, and so on. Each of these features suggests that a known ability might be involved, giving a partial picture of the structure of the underlying abilities.

A second way that these analyses can be done is somewhat more formal and more effective in that the performers themselves are guided in giving the answers needed to understand the underlying abilities. Consider the flow chart in Figure 10-9, taken from Fleishman and Stephenson (1970; Fleishman, 1975). Consider a skill such as the throwing task involved in being a shortstop in baseball. Begin at the top of the chart, asking whether or

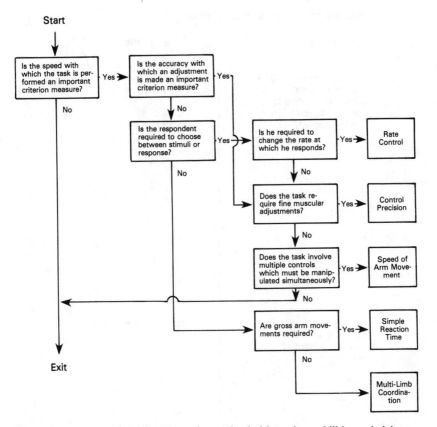

Figure 10-9. A binary flow diagram used to make decisions about abilities underlying particular tasks (adapted from Fleishman & Stephenson, 1970).

not speed is important to performance. It is, so move to the right and ask whether accuracy is important also. Follow the arrow dictated by that decision. If baseball players or coaches are asked to evaluate throwing with such procedures, researchers can come to a tentative understanding of the kinds of abilities required for this action. I would probably come to the decision that this task involves Control Precision, because speed, accuracy, and fine control are all needed for success. These methods are only in the beginning stages of development, and problems obviously exist, such as ambiguity in coming to decisions involved in each particular box.

A related method, used by Farina and Wheaton (1970, 1973) and Fleishman (1975), is to devise a scale such as that shown in Figure 10-10. In this case, expert performers are again asked about their tasks, but here the subject is given a scale with certain "anchor points" on it. In the figure, the performer is asked to rate how regular (or predictable) the stimuli involved in a particular job are. The "anchors" are other tasks with which the person is already familiar, such as looking at a picture, receiving Morse code, and so on. Each has a relatively well-understood "location" on the rater's own dimension of regularity. Then the person is asked to rate some performance in which he or she is an expert, such as fielding ground balls in baseball, and to mark the scale in terms of this characteristic for the task in question. I would mark this scale at about "4" for baseball, as the balls do vary in

Rate the present task on this dimension.

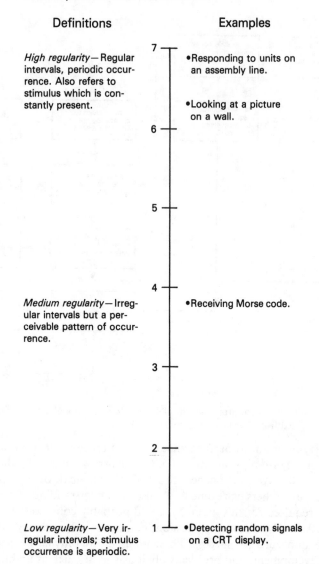

Figure 10-10. A task-characteristic scale for estimating the extent to which a given factor is involved in a particular task (adapted from Farina & Wheaton, 1970).

speed and direction but in relatively predictable and limited ways. You might give it a different value.

Through a series of such scales, each describing a particular ability that is suspected to underlie the task, one can estimate which abilities seem to be most involved and which seem to be least involved. While this method is relatively imprecise, it seems to provide an easy way to approximate the abilities that underlie performance on a particular task or job.

Applications of Taxonomies

The primary reason for classifying tasks according to abilities involved is to be able to predict success among people who have never experienced the task in question. Thus, if I know what abilities are represented in a particular skill or job (through the techniques described in this section), then I can possibly measure these abilities in people and choose individuals whose pattern of abilities most closely matches the pattern of abilities required for the job. Of course, I cannot even begin to do this if I do not know something of the abilities that are important in the job or skill, so the techniques involved in this section are an important part of the prediction process.

PREDICTION

A second major aspect of the work on individual differences is the problem of *prediction*. This area of work is closely related to, and even depends on, the work on abilities that I have just discussed. The fundamental problem is to be able to say (or predict) with some degree of accuracy what a person's score or level of skill will be on one task as a result of information about that person's skill on some other task.

These problems exist everywhere in the practical world. For example, insurance companies attempt to predict the probability that you will have a heart attack based on information that you supply on an application form, such as age, occupation, sex, and so on. Also, my university attempts to predict success in graduate school from tests that supposedly measure certain intellectual abilities (e.g., the Graduate Record Examination). More important to motor skills is the need to predict success in jobs or occupations on the basis of abilities testing, using such predictions as a basis for hiring procedures. Professional football teams attempt to predict success from various measures of body composition and motor performance measures.

Prediction in this sense implies the concept of *futurity*—prediction of some event or behavior before it happens. While this is the primary kind of application of individual differences work, it is not the only way that the idea of prediction is used. A second way involves the study of which tests best "predict" (or are correlated with) some other score that I already have in hand. Such techniques are intimately involved in the development of test batteries, and some of these procedures are described in the next section.

Test Battery Development: An Example

Suppose that I am a personnel director for a large company, and I want to predict success in some particular job in the company. In many jobs, this is easy. If I know the relevant skills, I can simply measure whether an applicant has these skills. For example, in order to be a secretary, one must type with a particular speed and accuracy, be able to run various office machines, and so on. But a problem arises when one wants to hire people for a job for which the applicants have had no previous experience. Common examples involve signing on applicants into a flight-training program in the Air Force or hiring a person to perform a particular job on an assembly line which only exists in my company. The problem is to determine by whatever means I can whether or not the applicant has the necessary abilities to do this job when he or she is eventually trained to do it, as no applicant would be expected to have the particular skill without prior experience.

Such a problem suggests a number of possible procedures that could be used. First, I could do some research, perhaps like that suggested in the previous sections, to find out what kinds of abilities are represented by the job in question. Along with this would be the discovery of the best ways to measure these abilities, such as with the use of established reference tests, tests I develop, and so on. Then with these measurement techniques, I can estimate the level of the important abilities in each applicant for the job, finally selecting that person whose pattern of abilities seems to match the requirements for the job most effectively. An example that I worked on a few years ago will perhaps make these kinds of procedures more clear.

Posing the Problem

Dick Pew and I (Schmidt & Pew, Note 19) were asked to design a battery of tests to predict success in becoming a dental technician. In this occupation, the primary task is to make appliances for the mouth, such as crowns, bridges, artificial teeth, etc., according to a dentist's prescription. The job involves the use of the fingers and hands in the manipulation of tools and various materials, such as gold, plastics, wax, etc. The employees usually perform their tasks seated at a workbench, and the job is relatively sedentary. There is, however, a great deal of manipulation of the hands and fingers required; shaping materials as a sculptor might is a common subtask. The major problem was that the particular firm for which we worked had a turnover rate of 80% per year. The employees simply could not, or would not, continue the job for very long, even though the pay was quite good. The management suspected that they were not hiring people with the proper abilities.

Task Analysis

A next step in developing a test battery was to evaluate just what employees had to do on the job. A description of the job in terms like those in the previous paragraph resulted from this analysis. We then asked what kinds of abilities might be required in these particular skills. Earlier work on abilities provided a number of possibilities, such as Manual Dexterity, Finger Dexterity, Steadiness, and so forth. Thus, the first tests included in our preliminary battery were reference tests of the abilities that we guessed were involved in the job. A second group of tests were called *face valid tests*, in that the performances involved in the tests were closely related to the actual performance on the job. For example, we had perceptual tests in which the subjects had to choose which of four model teeth most closely matched a reference tooth in size and color; another involved matching two-dimensional pictures of teeth with three-dimensional models.

A third group of tests was thought to relate to fundamental mechanisms in motor control and learning, many of which I have discussed in detail in Chapters 4 through 9. For example, we were interested in the consistency of muscular impulses as a possible mechanism in the precision of programmed shaping movements. We made up a test called Velocity Production, for which rapid, ballistic movements of the fingers and a stylus, with a goal MT of 100 msec, were required. We also used the Fitts tapping task, as various authors have felt that this task measures the rate of information processing involved in making movement corrections. A ballistic-aiming task of a stylus to a target, using primarily the hands and fingers, measured the con-sistency of programmed output. Thus, this part of the project involved a great deal of "brainstorming" in seminar sessions, where we would think up abilities that might be involved in the job and ways that we might measure these abilities (either through established methods or by a method we could create). This part of the process was a great deal of fun.

Predictor Variables

The result of this process was 24 *predictor tests*, so-called because we were going to attempt to predict success on the job from these tests taken in various combinations. Note that this is an example in which the idea of prediction does not imply futurity, as we were attempting to develop ways for combining these predictor tests so that the success on the job of employees who were already there could be predicted. (Of course, having established this optimum combination, management would use this battery to predict success for future applicants that had not been trained in the skills.) These 24 predictor tests, about equally divided among the three categories described above (reference tests, face-valid tests, and tests of underlying processes), were then administered to 44 of the present employees, all of whom had had at least one successful year on the job. Ad-ministering all of these tests to all of those people was not a lot of fun, in contrast to the earlier stage.

Criterion Variable

Probably the most critical aspect of the project was the development of a *criterion score*. This score was the best estimate of the employee's level of skill on the job, and it might take many forms. In this instance we asked the supervisors to rank the employees from "most skilled" to "least skilled" and to do this in a group session where each employee was discussed in terms of his or her skill and a consensus was achieved about the final order-ing. It was this rank that we attempted to predict with the battery of tests. In other occupations, the criterion score might be one's yearly production level, quality of play in a sport as judged from game films, peer ratings of performance on the job, or any other measure providing a "best" estimate of success.

The criterion score is what one is really trying to predict. Alternatively, if one could have some advance information about the applicant's criterion score before hiring, the task of hiring (or not hiring) people would be trivial. I would simply hire the person with the highest criterion score. The problem is that this criterion score is not available for new applicants, as they have had no training on the job, so we must estimate it (or predict it) from tests of the abilities that underlie the job or sport.

Validation

At this stage we had 24 tests measured on each of the employees, with one additional test being the criterion ranking of job success. The task now was to determine which of the 24 predictor tests was the most valid (or useful) in predicting the criterion. This was done in two ways. First, the correlation between each of the predictor tests and the criterion was computed. We decided that we would not use any test that correlated less than .15 with the criterion as such a test would have so little in common ($.15^2$ x 100 = 2.25%) that it would probably not be worthwhile to include it in a test battery. This preliminary screening of tests resulted in 14 tests that correlated .15 or greater with the criterion. This pattern of low correlations, even when we chose the tests because we thought they would correlate with success on the job, was not surprising given the evidence about specificity of skills.

Next, the process involved deciding which of these tests, and in what combination, were most effective in predicting the criterion score. One problem is that two of these tests, both of which correlate, say, .40 with the criterion score might correlate .60 with each other. Thus, it is likely that these two tests tend to measure the same ability and hence are redundant in predicting the criterion score, so that including one would be as effective as including both. Decisions like this are based on a statistical procedure called *multiple correlation*.

Multiple Correlation

Multiple correlation methods are very similar to "regular" correlation measures, except that the multiple correlation (abbreviated R) is the correlation between the criterion score and a weighted combination of the predictor scores. Imagine combining the predictor scores [for example, (1.0 × Test 1) plus (2.5 × Test 2) plus (8.0 × Test 9) plus (5.5 × Test 24)] to form a single sum for each subject. If we correlated this weighted sum (a single score) with the criterion score (another single score) with traditional correlation as described earlier, we would have a kind of multiple R. The only difference is that inherent in the multiple correlation procedures is the automatic determination of the weights in the sum, so that the correlation between the weighted sum and the criterion score is maximal. That is, the multiple correlation technique automatically adjusts the weights so as to achieve a maximum correlation between the predictors and the criterion, and thus it "decides" which of the predictors are most and least effective in predicting the criterion and in what combination.[9] This procedure produces what is called a *regression equation*, which is the specification of the weights and the variables that best predict the criterion score, the employees ranking. In our case, this equation had the form

$$\text{RANK} = .589(\text{BA}) + .422(\text{TL}) + .560(\text{SS}) + .297 (\text{RL}), \qquad (10\text{-}2)$$

where the abbreviations (BA, TL, SS, and RL) are our predictor test names: Ballistic Aiming, Tapping (Left Hand), Spatial Scaling, and Rotated Letters, respectively.

The final step was the determination of the test battery that will be used to predict success with new applicants. It should be recognized that the prediction would be best if we were to use all 14 tests, but the time involved in measuring 14 tests performances on every new applicant would not be worth the effort. Thus, there is a trade-off between the number of tests and the size of the multiple R. Adding tests systematically raises the R, but with each added test the multiple R is raised by a smaller and smaller amount, eventually to the point that adding another test will not be useful. The battery that we decided to use involved four tests. For these four tests, the multiple R (adjusted[10]) was .50. Think of this R in the same way as a traditional correlation. We had accounted for about $.50^2 \times 100 = 25\%$ of the variance in the criterion score with the various predictors. Thus, about 75% of the abilities that were important for this job were not included in our battery of tests.

Applicability

This particular example of prediction of success in dental technicians is one of many examples that could have been given. Each would have demonstrated the same major methods. The general steps are (a) analyzing tasks, (b) generating a tentative battery of predictors, and (c) evaluating the battery by multiple-correlation methods to establish a battery that predicts the criterion reasonably well. The method can be applied to a variety of situations with only slight modifications. The techniques are relatively time consuming and expensive (because of testing time), but various ways of cutting costs with minimal reductions in effectiveness can be employed. The area of industrial personnel selection has used these techniques for years, and the armed services have employed them in pilot selection programs. But the area of sport has just begun to discover them. A few professional football teams use batteries of tests that have been developed in ways like those described here, but this is more the exception than the rule. Other professional sports could use such techniques, and certainly the Olympic efforts could benefit by being able to predict which children have the requisite abilities before training in the particular sport is undertaken.

---

[9]The number of subjects should be approximately 3 to 5 times the number of tests. Here, the number of subjects (44) was minimal given the number of tests (14) used.

[10]For reasons that we need not go into here, the multiple R must be adjusted according to the number of tests in the set in relation to the number of subjects in the set.

Some Efforts at Prediction of Skill

Using the basic methods described in the previous section, attempts have been made to develop batteries of tests that would predict success in various situations in the military, in industry, and in professional sports. Clearly the most systematic and large-scale effort in this regard has been the attempt to develop prediction batteries for U.S. Air Force and Navy pilots. Here, the problem is very serious, as the Air Force and the Navy cannot afford to train a large group of unselected recruits to determine who will and who will not "make it." There is a strong possibility of accidents, the loss of very expensive equipment, and even the loss of life if the "wrong" people are included in the training. For these reasons primarily a great deal of research was directed toward the problem, mostly in the post-World War II years, the 1940s and 1950s.

Fleishman has been one of the most active researchers in this area; in fact, most of the knowledge about motor abilities that I discussed earlier in this chapter comes indirectly from the Air Force and Navy pilot training programs. Some of the important findings are presented in the next section. For more information on these programs of research, see Fleishman (1956) or Adams (1956).

Prediction of Pilot Success

In this research the criterion score—the score that is the "best" measure of the behavior to be predicted—is usually a measure of success in Flight School. This is, in itself, a complex score, consisting of instructors' ratings of flying skills, performances on a wide variety of knowledge tests, evaluations based on "leadership" qualities, and various subjective evaluations of personality. Typically, this research is done by using a large group of pilot trainees (selected by previous methods), measuring a variety of motor and perceptual tests (the predictors) as well as the criterion score of success in Flight School, and then using multiple-correlation methods to determine which of the predictors, and in what combination, are the most useful for predicting success in Flight School. About 10 tests have been so identified, and they are described below.

Two of the tests closely resemble the task of controlling an airplane. The Complex Coordination Test (Figure 3-8) involves manipulation of a joystick and foot pedals to control a three-dimensional display. The Rudder Control Test involves controlling the direction of a cockpit-like structure with foot pedals. These tests have validity coefficients—that is, correlations with the criterion score of $r = .45$ and .40, respectively.

Other tests are used that do not resemble the task of pilotry so obviously. One is the Pursuit Rotor (Figure 3-8), in which the person attempts to follow a rotating target with a handheld stylus; its validity is .30. A Pursuit Confusion Test, in which a target is tracked in a diamond-shaped pattern, correlates .30 with the criterion. A Two-Hand Coordination Test (Figure 3-8), in which the two hands control perpendicular movements of a pointer to follow a target, correlates .30 with the criterion. And a Direction Control Test, in which the proper movement must be selected quickly in response to a signal, correlates .34 with the criterion.

Notice that none of the predictor tests correlates, by itself, very highly with the criterion measure, the highest being .45. Remember that this means that at most about 20% ($.45^2 \times 100 = 20.25\%$) of the abilities are common between the "best" test and the criterion score. However, when these tests are combined to form a battery of tests, Fleishman found that four of the tests combined predicted the criterion score about as well as a much more time-consuming battery of 14 paper-and-pencil tests that had been previously used in pilot selection. When the psychomotor tests were added to the printed tests to form a larger battery, the multiple R increased from the previous value of .47 to .57. In some cases, the total battery of printed and psychomotor tests correlated .70 with the criterion score. This is about the highest level of prediction that can be claimed in the Air Force program.

One has to be impressed that, despite the amounts of money, time, and effort devoted to this program, the prediction of pilot success is quite poor. Remember that a multiple R of .70, which is the highest value reported in this research, means that less than half of the relevant abilities in pilotry have been "captured" by the battery of tests (i.e., $.70^2 \times 100 = 49\%$). There is still a long way to go to predict success effectively. The next half of the problem is the toughest of all, as the obviously involved and easily measured abilties have already been identified.

The situation described above is similar for a wide variety of situations where prediction of success is attempted from batteries of tests. For example, in our research (Schmidt & Pew, Note 19) we found a multiple R of .50 (corrected) for prediction of success in becoming a dental technician, and similarly low multiple Rs have been found in a number of different situations. Why is the prediction of success so difficult, even though large amounts of energy have been devoted to the solution of the problem?

Reasons for the Lack of Predictability

Certainly the most important problem is that human motor abilities are not understood very well. With the exception of Fleishman's and others' work, research on individual differences has not been extensive. As a result, the abilities that have been discovered are quite tentative, they are not well understood, and they are limited in scope to capabilities having the strongest relationships to tasks using the hands. Certainly if the structure of abilities were better understood, researchers would be in a far stronger position to predict success in various occupations and sports.

A related problem is that even though a person may have a solid hunch about which abilities might be involved in a particular activity, the research necessary to develop effective tests of these abilities has not been done. The development of tests is a long, time-consuming process in which the nature of instructions, the scoring procedures, and the configuration of the apparatus are constantly adjusted, with each adjustment producing (hopefully) progressively higher correlations between the test and the criterion score. And this work requires many subjects, as correlations are most meaningful and stable when they are computed with large samples. All of this makes the development of tests a difficult task indeed.

A third problem, also related to the above, is that the number of human abilities appears to be quite large. The number of abilities that will underlie a particular job, such as pilotry, will be quite large as well. Thus, in order to predict success in the activity, we must somehow obtain a measure of the majority of these underlying abilities. Of course, when we do not know what these abilities are or how to measure them the result is only moderate success in predicting performance in these industrial and military settings.

The problems in prediction are many, yet this kind of research is important for many reasons. Individuals will naturally be happier if they can be directed toward occupations for which they have the requisite abilities and away from occupations for which they are not suited. Also, efficiency of the institution will be increased and accidents will be reduced. The payoff clearly seems worth the price.

INDIVIDUAL DIFFERENCE VARIABLES

This final section about individual differences describes some research and findings about certain kinds of individual difference variables and how they are related to skilled performance. An individual difference variable, sometimes called an *organismic variable*, is usually some definable trait that can be measured in people, such as age, height, weight, sex, skin color, number of brothers and sisters, and so on. It has been of some interest to determine what relationships these variables have on the performance of certain kinds of skills. Such questions as "Do men out perform women on tests of pursuit tracking?" or "How much does movement speed decline as age increases beyond 40?" are all tied to this general way of studying individual differences.

The studies that are done to examine individual difference variables can be termed *pseudo-experiments* (see Chapter 2, and the early sections of this chapter), largely because they appear to be "true" experiments but really are not. That is, subjects are typically classified in one of a number of categories, such as male-female, old-young, or athlete-nonathlete. Then, the "effect" of this classification is examined by seeing how one subgrouping differs on the average from the other subgrouping. There can be more than two subgroupings, of course, such as short, medium, and tall people, or each of the 10-year categories from 20 to 80 years of age. The important point to remember in these studies is that the interpretation of any differences between the average performance of the various subgroups is usually stated in the form in which differences between the subgroupings are related to changes in the dependent variable studied (e.g., sex is related to skill in the pursuit rotor). However, it is not logically correct to infer that the differential sexes of the two groups of subjects necessarily was the cause of the differences in performance. Any number of factors related to (correlated with) a person's sex could just as easily be the cause. Sex effects could be caused by associated differences in body weight, height, strength, amount of previous movement experience, and a host of other factors.

Varieties of Individual Difference Variables

As mentioned before, there are countless ways to classify people and then to measure the differences between groups of people under different levels of these classifications. Space does not permit a discussion of many of these individual difference variables, so I will concentrate on those that have had the most study and have the most interest and relevance for understanding human skilled performances. The discussion will focus on three important variables: age, sex, and intelligence. Others, such as race or country of national origin, sociological variables such as number of siblings and birth order, and body configuration such as height, eye color, weight, percentage of fat, and fitness have obvious importance but will not be dealt with here. For more on these kinds of variables, see Noble (1978) or Singer (1975).

Effects of Age on Skilled Performance

The study of the effects of age has traditionally been divided into two separate age spans. First, there are studies of what is called *motor development*, or the study of the child as he or she matures and gains experience. A second category of studies is related to aging effects, or the processes related to the effects of age on performance in individuals past puberty or in the upper age categories. The kinds of changes that occur in skills during these two age spans are markedly different, even though the variable of interest—age—is the same in both cases.

Motor development. The field of motor development is a relatively new and active one within the area of motor behavior, and this brief review of the essential findings cannot possibly do justice to this kind of work. Certainly one major finding that emerges from all this work is that as age progresses to about the eighteenth year, large and progressive improvements occur in just about every conceivable measure of skilled motor behavior. These improvements can be divided into categories related to fitness and strength, capacities to anticipate and predict, ability to process information from complex displays, speed of decision and movement, accuracy in fine control tasks, and so on. We could probably make the case that most of the laboratory and real-life tasks that are studied in some way involve the various abilities discussed in earlier sections in this chapter. And these abilities appear to develop, either through maturation or experience or both, with increasing age up to about 18 years. So, it is not surprising at all that older children typically outperform, on the average, younger children.

One of the common hypotheses in the motor development literature today is the idea that as humans become older (up to about 18 years of age), they increase the capacities for processing of information (e.g., Thomas, 1980). Certainly this theme is important for adults (see Chapters 4 and 5), and it is an important idea in the individual differences work as well. Fleishman and Bartlett (1969) feel that abilities are in some way related to the various ways in which humans process information. Thus, in the performance of skills, children appear to be relatively deficient in the rate and amount of information that they can handle. Thus, children appear to have smaller capacities to hold information in short-term memory, shorter attention spans, and perhaps less effective mechanisms for processing information necessary for movement (e.g., feedback or environmental cues).

The idea that children are in general less skilled than adults implies that children are less consistent in their behaviors than are adults, as the primary measure of skillfulness is consistency of action, such as variable error or absolute error (see Chapter 3 for a review of these scores). If so, then it is also possible that children will be less consistent in terms of the impulses that are fundamental determinants of the VE in a particular task (see Chapter 9, Impulse Variability). It might be that children, as compared with adults, produce more force variability or more timing variability or both, which contributes to this kind of inconsistency. We know that children are inconsistent in their movement outcomes, but the studies have not been conducted to determine whether or not this is because of the variability in impulses.

Aging effects. One of the fastest growing areas in the behavioral and biological sciences is *gerontology*, or the study of aging. Here, unlike the study of development, the primary concern is with the upper age levels and the associated changes in the motor system that affect movement abilities. One simple generalization is that past the age of about 25 years, a progressive decline occurs in just about every measurable aspect of motor behavior.

One example—numerous others could be given—comes from a study by Hodgkins (1962), who studied age effects in RT and MT. She studied subjects ranging in age from 6 years to 84 years. As can be seen from her data in Figure 10-11, a systematic reduction in RT and MT occurred through the developmental years up to about age 19, followed by a period of relatively stable capability through age 30, following by a systematic slowing in both these variables as age of the subjects increased further. The findings are typical of many other variables that could be studied, such as strength, speed, perceptual skills, anticipation, and so on. For more evidence on other kinds of tasks, see Birren (1964) or Noble (1978).

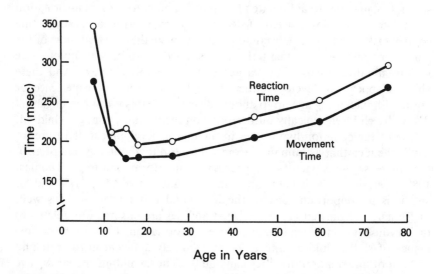

Figure 10-11. Reaction time and movement time as a function of age (from Hodgkins, 1962).

One of the most consistent findings in the aging literature is that people become slower with age. We see such effects on speed not only in tasks for which speed is measured directly (e.g., in Figure 10-11), but in other tasks for which speed is evaluated indirectly. For example, in tasks for which accuracy and speed are required, the overall score will often suffer with increasing age because speed decreases, or there may be a marked shift in the speed-accuracy trade-off, with speed decreasing and accuracy either increasing or held constant. Early thinking about these speed deficits with age was that this slowing was reflective of slowing in neurological activities in the central nervous system, not only those involved in nerve conduction times but also those involved in decision making and other aspects of information processing. Later work has suggested, however, that this slowing need not be related to any slowing in the central nervous sytem, but rather is related to the fact that older people appear to be more "cautious" than younger people. If so, being unwilling to make errors on a task makes one—old or young—appear to be slow. Such issues, among others, are currently the subject of much continued research in aging and human performance.

Sex Effects on Skilled Performance

Investigators have examined the differences between the sexes on nearly every motor task imaginable. Some investigators have been directly concerned with these differences, while others have seen sex differences as incidental findings in studies directed toward other questions.

Certainly one common observation would suggest that men out-perform women in many, if not most, motor tasks. Some of these differences are obvious, such as the different levels of Olympic records for swimming, track and field, etc., for women and men. These casual observations are borne out in looking at the literature, where it has been found that men out-perform women in motor behaviors such as various athletic skills, strength, pursuit tracking, ladder climbing, throwing, jumping, running, and so on (e.g., Singer, 1975; Noble, 1978). It is difficult to know whether or not these differences have to do with sex, per se, as for many of these tasks success is correlated with body size; and it is no surprise that males are generally larger and stronger than females.

It is interesting to consider those tasks for which women out-perform men. Various authors have shown that women perform tasks requiring sensory discrimination (e.g., color discrimination) more effectively and that women are better than men at tasks such as rapid manipulation (card-sorting, dotting, tapping, aiming), when speed and repetition are important (Noble, 1978). Sex effects in favor of women have also been found for the inverted-alphabet task (which involves printing the alphabet upside down and backward as quickly as possible) and for many small-motor responses (see Noble, 1978, for a review).

Rather than simply documenting that males are or are not different from females on some task, a more fruitful approach is to ask what the sources of these effects, if present, may be. In one example of this approach, Laszlo, Bairstow, Ward, and Bancroft (1980) used a task in which subjects had to roll (by hand) pool balls to strike a target a few meters away. When the background, or surrounding environment, was very "quiet" and plain, males and females performed about the same on this task, with males having a slight edge. But when the environment and background were complex, either visually with distracting lines and shapes or auditorially with tape-recorded traffic noise, it apparently had strong detrimental effects on females' performances but no such effects on males'. Is it possible that females found it more difficult to ignore the irrelevant information in the environment than males did? If so, these differences in the ways that males and females appear to handle or process information could have important influences in sport and industrial settings, but at this stage we do not know exactly why these effects occurred. And these findings are probably related to Witkin's (1949) well-known findings of sex differences in handling spatial information; women appear to be more tied to external environmental information (i.e., they are more "field-dependent") than men. (See also Cratty, 1964).

Perhaps we should not take all these sex differences at face value. First of all, one has to wonder how important they are. A great deal of variability exists among both men and women, and the distributions overlap considerably on most tasks. That is, even though men are statistically better at some tasks than women, usually many women in the sample out-perform most of the men in the sample.

Next, it is not clear at all what proportion of sex differences are due to sex per se. As we know, many socially imposed standards of behavior are different for males and females; boys are traditionally praised for playing sports, while girls are traditionally praised for being "feminine" and passive. Our society is beginning to emerge from a time when these effects were probably very strong. Women are participating in physical activities—with social approval from males—to a much greater extent than they did a decade ago (See Falls, 1977, for an example from the Boston Marathon). Next, it is possible that many of the differences in performance between males and females are due to the differential movement experiences of the two sexes. Finally, as mentioned above, well-documented differences exist in body size and strength, which could be major determinants of success in athletic skills. When these factors are not present, the sex differences are considerably less, with women out-performing males at many tasks requiring nearly no strength.

Intelligence and Motor Performance

Intelligence is usually defined as a capacity of the individual to act purposefully, to think rationally, and to deal effectively with the environment. In our society, which stresses activities involving abstract concepts, reasoning, and the acquisition of knowledge and education, the idea of intelligence implies abilities related to cognitive skills, such as might be learned in the classroom. It is, therefore, difficult to define intelligence (some have defined intelligence as "what intelligence tests measure"), and a large variety of different tests are available.

Intelligence (measured as an *intelligence quotient* or IQ) has had a rough time of it lately. First, a dominant theme in the ideas about IQ was that it measured the ability or capacity to learn new facts and concepts. Yet, studies that have measured IQ and the "rate" of learning new verbal materials (see DuBois, 1965) have failed rather consistently to show that IQ predicts the "ease" with which new material is learned. As well, serious social problems have been associated with IQ tests and the strong possibility that the tests are "culturally biased." The IQ tests, like any test, are measures of performance. Such tests, based as they are on word knowledge and verbal proficiency (among other things), are likely to be biased in favor of those people in society who have had the benefit of these teachings in home and in school. The problem in the U.S. has been the most severe with respect to poor, primarily black and Hispanic, people for whom opportunities have not been equal to those of more affluent whites. As a result, it is not clear that the notion of IQ is very meaningful (but see Jensen, 1970, 1978). Yet, it is one of the measures which is still used and discussed in a wide variety of situations.

We might expect that intelligence—whatever it is—would probably be related positively to sucess in skilled activities. One point of view is that we appear to be processors of information when we produce motor skills (Chapters 4 and 5), so more effective information processing as a result of greater IQ would lead to more effective performance. For such reasons, we might expect to see strong differences in motor skills among groups classified according to IQ, or correlations between IQ and performance.

But such relationships have not generally been found. Ryan (1963) found no relationship between academic achievement (presumably related to IQ) and performance on a balancing task (stabilometer). Start (1964) showed that IQ and learning of a novel gymnastics stunt was correlated only .08, suggesting few common abilities between the two tests. Tests of mental abilities and tests of motor abilities are generally related only minimally in children and adults (e.g., Thomas & Chissom, 1972); but Ismail, Kephart, and Cowell (1963) found moderate relationships between motor tests and academic achievement. Also, there are only minor differences between athletes and nonathletes in terms of academic success in high school or college, with some studies showing advantages for athletes and others showing disadvantages. (These differences are difficult to evaluate, however, as there are also differences in what kinds of courses are taken, how many credits per term are taken, and so on.) The possible reasons for the lack of association of IQ with motor skill performance are probably two: (a) intelligence is not very much involved in the production of motor responses, or (b) IQ tests are not good measures of intelligence. I suspect that both viewpoints may be correct.

There are intelligence-related differences in skilled performance when the IQ range examined is extended downward, however. For example, if performances of people with very low IQs (say 60 to 80) is studied, virtually every skill examined is performed with less effectiveness as compared to subjects of "normal" intelligence. There are decrements in strength, speed, accuracy, anticipation, balance, and so on. The study of motor behavior with retarded persons has been quite active lately, and a great deal of work has documented the various ways in which retarded persons are different from so-called "normals" in motor behavior.

While the reasons why deficiencies in IQ are so strongly related to motor behavior have not been well understood, there are various hypotheses. One is the idea that retarded people are generally less active physically (often being institutionalized or in special classes or schools), so that the decrements are perhaps due more to a lack of movement experiences in childhood than to any deficiency in mental functioning. A second idea is that at severely low IQ levels (but not at normal levels), there is a general depression of the functioning of the entire central nervous system, including those parts that are primarily involved with motor control and motor learning. Yet many instances exist of people with low IQs being trained to perform very skillfully on production line tasks where motor performance is critical but decision making is not. Such issues, however, need more research before we can be certain about the retardates' motor performances.

INDIVIDUAL DIFFERENCES AS AN "EXPERIMENTAL" METHOD

To conclude, it is important to mention that the individual differences approach and the experimental approach are not as separated as they may seem, based on the topics discussed earlier in this chapter. As mentioned earlier, certainly the tendency exists on the part of differential and experimental scientists to continue to be separated in method and subject matter, but a few have attempted to bring the fields closer together. One way this has been attempted (see Underwood, 1975) has been to provide tests of theories, which have been most closely related to the experimental tradition, by individual differences methodologies.

Suppose some theory predicts that experimentally (artificially) increasing some independent variable should have a tendency to increase some dependent variable. Ordinarily, a researcher would examine this prediction by taking a group of subjects, manipulating the environment or the setting so as to increase the value of the independent variable, and noting the associated changes in the value of the dependent variable (Chapter 2). This is, of course, the classic experimental method.

But a similar thing can be done with an individual differences approach. Instead of experimentally inducing changes in the independent variable, the researcher could take a large group of subjects and classify them according to their (naturally determined) scores on this independent variable, perhaps into two separate groups. If the theory is correct, then the group classified as highest on the independent variable should out-perform (on the dependent variable) the group classified as low on the independent variable. Or, in a method which is essentially the same, a correlation could be computed between the performance on the independent variable and the performance on the dependent variable; if the theory is correct, then the correlation should not be zero, as some association should exist between the theory's independent and dependent variables.

As an example, O'Brian (1979) tested some of the predictions from impulse-variability theory discussed in the previous chapter (see "Impulse Variability Theory," Chapter 9). In that theory, Schmidt, Zelaznik,

Hawkins, Frank, and Quinn (1979) proposed that the accuracy in hitting a target (the dependent variable) was determined in part by the variability of the muscular forces that were acting on the limb (the independent variable). As an individual differences test of this idea, O'Brian measured the amount of force variability subjects demonstrated on a static test and correlated this value with the measure of accuracy the same subjects had achieved on a stylus-aiming test. If the theory is correct, then the individuals with large force-variabilty scores should also have large error scores on the aiming test, suggesting that these two variables should be correlated. He found that the correlation between these variables was close to zero (average $r = -.05$), providing no support for the theory. Such findings are perhaps not surprising in the light of work by Beggs, Sakstein, and Howarth (1974), who found that estimates of tremor variability were correlated very low across limbs; in addition, Schmidt (1969c) found that within-subject variability tended to be correlated low for various tasks with the same limb, failing to support a notion of general abilities related to within-subject variability.

Some limitations exist to this kind of method, however. First, the procedures—being correlational in nature—are not well suited to the kinds of conclusions about *causality* that are often demanded with experimental tests of theories. Accordingly, when using the individual-differences approach, a person can only conclude that some variable was *related to* (or was not related to) some other, as any other factor correlated with both of the variables (e.g., age, sex, etc.) could have been the causal agent. Second, remember that failures to show relationships between two variables (as O'Brian's data did in the previous paragraph) mean only that the theory was not "supported" (see Chapter 2), not necessarily that the theory is incorrect. This is so because a number of factors could be present that would prevent the theory from being supported in the individual differences context without the theory's being actually incorrect. For example, from earlier in this chapter, motor behaviors are very specific, and tests of different motor behaviors typically do not correlate well. If so, then we might not expect the force-variability variable and the aiming accuracy variable in O'Brian's study to correlate well either. But if they do happen to correlate, then interesting support for the theory is generated. As such, this method has to be seen as having rather limited use in motor skills work; certainly it has not been used much in the past.

SUMMARY

The study of individual differences is concerned with the differences between or among individuals on various tasks or behaviors. This kind of research differs strongly from the experimental approach (Chapters 4 through 9) in which differences between individuals are ignored in order to concentrate on the average performances of larger groups of people affected by certain independent variables. Two major subdivisions of individual differences research can be identified.

Perhaps the major focus is on *abilities*. Abilities are defined as stable, enduring characteristics or traits, probably genetically defined, that underlie certain movement skills or tasks. Since the 1930s, there have been many points of view about the structure of motor abilities. Some convergence has occurred on the idea that humans possess a relatively large number of separate motor abilities (perhaps 50 to 100), that these abilities are independent, and that a given skill or task may have many of these abilities underlying it. Henry's specificity theory and Fleishman's work on factor analytically determined abilities tend to point to this kind of conclusion. Both of these approaches indicate that the idea of a general motor ability, one which defines in a major way the level of proficiency on all motor tasks, is surely not correct.

A second major division of individual differences research is related to *prediction*. In studies of prediction, the relationships between scores on various tests (the *predictors*) are used to predict or estimate the scores on some other test (the *criterion*). A common example is the prediction of an applicant's probable success on the job from various measures of abilities involved in that job. The development of predictive batteries of tests is time consuming, and the effectiveness of such batteries of motor tests in predicting some criterion behavior is disappointingly low, even when a great deal of research funding and effort have been directed toward the problem. The major difficulty is that abilities are not well understood, that many abilities need to be understood, and that not enough research effort has been directed at these important problems.

A large number of individual difference variables have been studied. These variables, such as age, height, sex, country of birth, etc., provide an easy basis for classifying people, so that the performance on some other task can be studied "as a function of" these variables. Three major divisions of this work are (a) the study of age effects, both from the point of view of growth and maturation and from the point of view of older age levels (gerontology), (b) the study of sex effects, and (c) the study of intelligence effects as they relate to motor performance. While such studies provide information about the "effects" of these variables, the results of these studies are often confounded by other variables that are related to these classification variables (e.g., body size being correlated with sex or age).

GLOSSARY

Abilities. Stable characteristics or traits, genetically defined and unmodifiable by practice or experience, that underlie certain skilled performances.

Correlation coefficient. A statistical measure of the degree of linear association between two tests; abbreviated r.

Criterion variable. In studies of prediction, the variable or score that is predicted from the predictor variables; the "best" obtainable measure of the construct that is to be predicted.

Differential approach. That approach to the study of behavior that focuses on individual differences, abilities, and prediction.

Factor analysis. A complex statistical procedure wherein a large number of separate tests are grouped into a smaller number of factors, each of which is thought to represent an underlying ability.

Factor loading. In factor analysis, the statistical values in dicating the extent to which the tests measure the various factors.

General motor ability. An early concept about motor abilities in which a single ability was thought to account for major portions of the individual differences in motor behavior.

Individual differences. Stable differences among individuals on some variable or task.

Intelligence. An ability to act purposefully, to think rationally, and to deal effectively with the environment; often measured with the intelligence quotient, IQ.

Laddergraph. A technique for displaying data in which two test scales are oriented vertically, with an individual's scores joined by a line.

Motor development. A field of study concerning the changes in motor behavior occurring as a result of growth, maturation, and experience.

Multiple regression. A statistical procedure in which the weightings of predictor variables are adjusted so that their sum correlates maximally with some criterion variable.

Prediction. The process in which the score on a criterion variable is estimated from a predictor variable(s) based on an association between them.

Predictor variable. The variable(s) from which a criterion variable is predicted.

Regression line. The "line of best fit" between two variables, whose slope and intercept are determined by regression analysis.

Reliability. The proportion of observed variability among individuals in a test that is accounted for by stable individual differences; the correlation between two administrations of the same test.

Scattergram. A graph on which subjects' scores on two tests are jointly represented as a single data point.

Specificity hypothesis. A theory of the structure of motor abilities in which motor tasks are thought to be composed of many independent abilities.

Superability. A general ability thought to underlie all tasks in a particular domain.

Task analysis. A process of determining the underlying abilities and structure of a task or occupation.

Taxonomy. A system of classification.

MOTOR LEARNING AND MEMORY

This point in the text represents an extreme change in emphasis with respect to the treatment of motor skills. The concern so far has been with skilled performance—often at high levels of proficiency—and the numerous internal processes that make these performances possible. I now shift to a different, but related, problem—the *learning*, or *acquisition*, of skills as a result of practice or experience. The problem is different from the study of skilled performance, because I will be focusing on the *changes in* skill, rather than the nature of skill at some particular level. As such, different methods and logic are needed to understand these performance changes, and in Chapter 11, I document some of the more important ones. Later in this section, I will use these methods to describe some of the laws and principles that have been discovered about motor learning. These chapters also probably provide more opportunity for practical application to teaching situations than did Chapters 4 through 10.

CHAPTER 11

Motor Learning: Fundamental Concepts and Methodology

Learning is a truly critical part of our existence. Think where humans would be if we could not profit by the experiences and practice in which we all engage. You would not be able to read the words on this page, I would not be able to type the words I type now, and I would not be able to speak. In short, we would be simple beings indeed if we were forced to behave in the world equipped only with the skills we inherited. The fact that we can acquire new knowledge and skills has led to a robust interest in the ways in which people learn, the critical variables that determine how people will profit from experience or practice, and the design of instructional programs.

I do not have the space here to do justice to the entire topic of learning. There are examples of learning in all organisms (even the simplest of single-celled organisms), and the learning that man enjoys is the most complex of all. Thus, many forms of human learning will not be discussed here, such as the learning of verbal materials, the learning of concepts, and the learning of interpersonal skills. I will concentrate on the acquisition of motor skills, as defined in Chapter 1. Essentially, the concern will be with the effects of practice and experience on skilled performance, attempting to understand the relevant variables that determine these gains in proficiency. The first step is to develop a more formal definition of motor learning.

MOTOR LEARNING DEFINED

Learning in general, and motor learning as the learning of skilled behaviors in particular, has been defined in a variety of ways by various authors. Four distinct characteristics serve to define it. First, learning is a *process* of acquiring the capability for producing skilled actions. That is, learning is the set of underlying events, occurrences, or changes that happen when people practice allowing them to become skilled at some task. Second, learning is a direct result of practice or experience. Third, learning cannot (at our current level of knowledge) be measured directly, as the processes leading to changes in behavior are internal and are usually not available for direct examination; rather, one must *infer* that learning (the processes) occurred on the basis of the changes in behavior that can be observed. Fourth, learning is assumed to produce relatively permanent changes in skilled behavior; changes in behavior caused by easily reversible alterations in mood, motivation, or internal states (e.g., thirst) will not be thought of as due to learning.

A synthesis of these four aspects produces the following definition: *Motor learning is a set of processes associated with practice or experience leading to relatively permanent changes in skilled behavior.* I discuss these four aspects in more detail next.

Learning Is a Process

In cognitive psychology, a process is a set of events or occurrences that, taken together, lead to some particular behavior. For example, in reading, processes are associated with moving the eyes, in decoding the text, in accessing memory for meaning, and so on. Similarly, motor learning involves processes that contribute to the changes in motor behavior as a result of practice. Thus, the focus is on the changes that occur in the organism that allow it to perform differently after practice.

This is in contrast to a definition of learning that focuses on the behavioral changes as the subject of interest. Many authors define learning as a relatively permanent change in behavior as a result of practice or experience (e.g., Morgan & King, 1971). This definition clearly says that the behavioral change is learning. A more effective definition, at least in my own view, is that motor learning is the set of processes leading to changes in behavior. Thus, learning is not a behavioral change; rather, learning consists of the processes that support such changes (Schmidt, 1971a, 1972a). The importance of this distinction should become clear in subsequent sections.

Motor Learning Is a Direct Result of Practice

The kinds of behavioral changes that I am willing to attribute to motor learning are those that are associated with practice or experience. This restriction on the definition rules out such factors as maturation and growth. Such factors lead to changes in behavior (older children perform a novel task more effectively than younger children, on the average), yet it would be a mistake to conclude that these changes were the result of learning, as improvements in performance can occur without any practice at all. Similar variables, such as changes in strength or endurance, might improve performance on some skilled motor task (e.g., playing soccer), yet it would be incorrect to regard these changes as due to learning.

Motor Learning Is Not Directly Observable

It should be clear that motor learning is usually not directly observable. The processes that underlie changes in skills are probably highly complex events in the central nervous system, such as changes in the ways in which sensory information is organized, or changes in the patterning of muscular action. As such, these changes are rarely directly observable, and a person must infer their existence from changes in motor behavior. This feature of motor learning makes it particularly difficult to study, as experiments must be designed so that the observed changes in behavior allow the logical conclusion that there were associated changes in some internal state.

Learning Produces an Acquired Capability for Responding (Habit)

Another way to talk about learning is that it leads to a *capability* for skilled performance on the motor task. This capability can be thought of as a state within the central nervous system, and the goal of practice is to increase the "strength" or "amount of" this internal state. Often, this internal state is called "habit" (with only minor reference to the usual use of the word), and the goal of the researcher is to obtain an estimate of the "amount" or "strength" of the habit for the task by taking various measurements of skill or performance (e.g., James, 1890; Schmidt, 1971a). The term *capability* is also very important here, as it implies that if the habit is present and "strong," then skilled performance may occur if the conditions are favorable; but, if the conditions are not favorable (e.g., fatigue is present), then skilled performance may not occur. We will see why this distinction is important when we discuss the measurement of learning in a subsequent section.

Motor Learning is Relatively Permanent

Another feature of motor learning is that it is relatively permanent. When you receive practice or experience at some activity, something lasting may occur, something that does not simply pass away in the next few minutes or hours. More dramatically, we could say that when you practice and learn, you will never be the same as you were before. Learning has the effect of changing you (if only slightly) in a relatively permanent way.

With respect to skill learning, this distinction is important because it rules out the changes in skills that can come from a variety of temporary performance factors. For example, skills can improve if the person is in the "right" mood, if motivation is temporarily high, or if certain drugs are administered. Yet each of these changes in behavior will probably vanish when the temporary effects of the mood, etc., "wear off." As such, we should not attribute these changes in behavior to motor learning, because they are not permanent enough.

An analogy may help to make this point more clear. If I cool water, I find that it becomes solid (ice); but I can reverse the effect completely to produce water again simply by warming it. Not so with boiling an egg. Boiling an egg for 10 min will produce changes that are not reversible when the egg is cooled. In this case, some relatively permanent change has been made in the egg.

This analogy applies well to the concept of motor learning and performance. The nature of the water or of the egg can be observed directly, and they both behave in predictable ways when the independent variable of temperature is applied. But beneath the surface is some unobservable change that leads to this change in the nature of the substance; in one case (water), this change is completely reversible and not relatively permanent, while in the other (egg), the change is not reversible. With human learning, then, many analogous variables can be applied to change the observed behavior (skill), but these may or may not change the internal structure of the person in a relatively permanent way. If the effect of some independent variable can appear and disappear as the value of the variable is changed, then this change in behavior cannot be associated with anything relatively permanent, and hence is not thought to be due to learning.

How permanent is "relatively permanent"? This is a vague term, and scientists studying learning are rarely clear about it. Thus, strictly speaking it would be difficult to argue that the effect of a drug that lasted 24 hours was not due to learning, yet the effect of practice that lasted for two weeks was the result of learning. But the intention of this distinction should be clear; learning should have some lasting effect.

Motor Learning Can Be Negative

I have given the impression that motor learning always leads to improvements in performance. There are two problems with this notion. First, the term *improvement* is not value-free, so a change in behavior may be seen as an improvement by one observer, and as a regression in performance by another. Such examples are common in considering changes in movement styles, such as in the high jump or in gymnastics. Generally, scientists try to avoid discussing changes in variables in terms that have their own personal values attached to them.

Even if everyone could agree that a certain change in behavior is an improvement, with the reverse being a worsening, in performance, instances exist in which practice or experience does not lead to improvements in skill but rather to marked decrements. Imagine that you have been learning a dangerous dive from the 10-m tower when suddenly you miss and fall "flat" on your back. It would not be hard to imagine that such an experience would lead to marked fear responses on subsequent attempts, with a disruption of your skill. Or you might decide that diving was not "your thing" any longer after such an experience! This could probably be re-

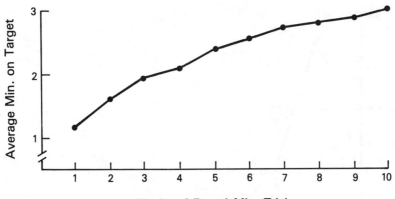

Figure 11-1. A performance curve showing increases in the score with practice (from Fleishman & Rich, 1963).

garded as a negative change in skills.[1]

MEASURING MOTOR LEARNING

Given that motor learning is a set of processes that underlies the changes in behavior resulting from practice or experience, how can such processes be measured in order to understand what variables affect it? It will be helpful to consider a typical motor learning experiment to explain some of the major points in the measurement process.

Motor Learning Experiments

In the most simple of all experiments on learning, a large group of individuals is asked to practice on some motor task, and the experimenter charts their performances as a function of "trials." For example, Figure 11-1 is a graph from Fleishman and Rich (1963) showing the performance on the two-hand coordination task. Subjects had to follow a moving target by movements of two crank handles, one controlling forward-backward direction of a pointer and one controlling right-left movements (see Figure 3-8, page 72, for a drawing). The average time on target (in minutes) for 20 subjects is plotted as a function of successive blocks of four 1-min trials. A clear trend can be seen for the scores to increase with practice, with the increases being somewhat more rapid at first and then leveling off later on.

It is also common that scores may decrease with practice, as shown in Figure 11-2. These data are from Quesada and Schmidt (1970), and are taken from subjects' performances on a timing task. Here, the subject had to operate a switch when a moving pointer became aligned with a stationary

---

[1] But even this conclusion is risky. Couldn't I also argue that such a change was *positive* in that it would lead to increased probability of survival?

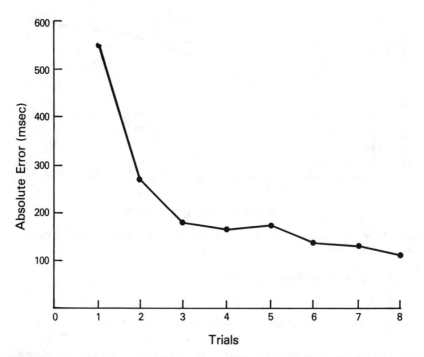

Figure 11-2. A performance curve showing decreases in the score with practice (from Quesada & Schmidt, 1970).

one, and error was the interval between the switch movement and the actual moment of coincidence. Average absolute error decreased rapidly at first,, and more gradual decreases occurred later in practice.

Even though the two curves (Figure 11-1 and 11-2) change in opposite ways with practice, they both represent gains in skill. Such changes almost certainly can be interpreted as caused by motor learning. But, such changes by themselves are rarely of much interest for students of motor behavior, as there is no doubt that practice or experience leads to gains in motor skills. The effect is usually one of the most powerful in the study of motor behavior. In fact, if scientists wish to prevent subjects from learning, they must take very strong precautions.

What is usually of more interest than whether or not learning occurred is whether learning was greater in one condition than in some other condition. Thus, the question of interest is related to the combination of variables which produces the most learning of the motor task. In order to make meaningful inferences about whether or not Condition A produced more learning than Condition B, special procedures are needed to analyze these performance scores in motor learning experiments.

Performance Curves

Graphs such as Figures 11-1 and 11-2 are usually thought to represent the acquired capability for responding (i.e., habit) in the subjects as they practice from trial to trial, and to some extent they probably do. For this reason, such curves are often loosely termed *learning curves*, as it is tempting to regard the changes in performance as reflecting the product of the internal processes of learning. The notion that these curves exactly "mirror" the internal state (the amount of habit) is oversimplified, however, and scientists are very cautious about interpreting the changes in curves like Figures 11-1 and 11-2 as due to motor learning. Some of these considerations are outlined next.

Performance Measures

The first reason that performance curves perhaps should not be thought of as strong measures of habit is that *performance*—not habit—is measured as a function of trials. Because habit cannot be measured directly, any habit that has occurred must be inferred from the changes in performance. Thus, it seems more logical to term such curves *performance curves* rather than learning curves.

Between-Subject Variability

A second problem in making inferences about learning from these performance curves is that they are insensitive to the differences between individuals that occur as a function of practice. Consider how a performance curve is produced. A large number of people (the larger the better, usually) is used. All subjects' first-trial scores are averaged to obtain the data point for Trial 1, all subjects' Trial 2 scores are averaged to obtain the data point for Trial 2, and so on. This averaging procedure has a number of advantages, such as "canceling out" any random (perhaps essentially meaningless) variations in persons' scores due to inattention, errors in measurement, and other factors not directly related to the internal habit changes. But, at the same time, this averaging procedure tends to hide any differences that may have existed between people on a particular trial, or it may hide important trends in improvement with practice.

These effects can be particularly important when studying learning. Consider two hypothetical people whose performances over a number of trials are shown in Figure 11-3. Person 1 has a difficult time improving in the task until late in performance, when finally performance improves markedly. Some would be tempted to say that not much learning occurred early, with marked learning occurring later. But Person 2 seemed to improve in performance early in the sequence, with little change occurring later. It is tempting to say that this person was a "rapid learner" or that a great deal of learning occurred early in the practice sequence.

Now consider what happens if these two subjects' scores are averaged in ways that are typically done for larger groups. In Figure 11-3, the center line is the average of the performances for the two subjects for each of the trials. Now the pattern of improvement with practice is considerably different. It is tempting to say that habit accumulated gradually and consistently. This, of course, would be misleading, as neither of the subjects that produced the average performance curve showed this trend. Thus, it could certainly be that learning does not occur gradually at all, as is evidenced by the in-

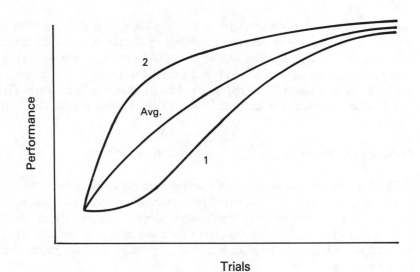

Figure 11-3. Hypothetical performance curves for two individuals together with the curve representing the average of their performances.

dividual performance curves. Rather, it is possible that learning occurs as a sort of "revolution" in the ways in which the subjects attempt the task.

When I was a boy, I attempted repeatedly and without any success for an entire summer to learn a "kip" on the horizontal bar. When finally I tried the skill with a technique that I had not attempted before, suddenly I could do it, and I have been able to do it ever since. There appeared to be no gradual improvement in my skill development at all. If people differ in when they apply the proper technique (I was slow, I think), then these important aspects of the learning process will be obscured with the averaging procedures involved in the generation of performance curves.

Within-Subject Variability

As mentioned above, one of the important aspects of the averaging procedure is the elimination of errors in measurement, and like factors that seem to obscure the "true" habit levels of the people on a particular trial. From Chapter 9, a typical finding was that people inherently vary from trial to trial, even if they are attempting to do the "same" thing for each. But is trial-to-trial variation for a particular person due to some meaningless random fluctuation in the motor system, or is it due to some meaningful change in the way the person attempted the task on a particular trial? This is a difficult question, and no good answer is available at present.

The problem can be illustrated better with an example. Consider the task of free-throw shooting in basketball, when the subjects are relatively inexperienced. Certainly, a great deal of variability exists in this task from trial to trial, and much of this variability does not seem to represent fundamental changes in the ways in which the people attempted the task. If a large group of people is examined on this task, with performance scored as "correct" or "incorrect," each person will have a pattern of scores that shows a large number of apparently randomly ordered hits and misses, with somewhat

Figure 11-4. An averaged performance curve for which probability of success is the dependent measure. (On a particular trial, any given subject can receive only zero or 1.)

more hits as practice continues. And different people will have the hits and misses scattered across the trials differently.

A perfomance curve can be plotted with these data, with the measure for a particular trial being the probability of success on that trial. In Figure 11-4, the data point for Trial 1 will be the total number of hits divided by the total number of attempts (i.e., the number of subjects), or the proportion of subjects that shot successfully on Trial 1; the method is similar for Trial 2. When this is done, the average performance curve usually rises gradually, perhaps moving from .20 to about .40 in 100 trials. From such a curve, it is tempting to conclude that habit again grew slowly as a result of practice. But notice that not a single subject showed this pattern of performance! Indeed, there is no way that a given person could ever achieve a score of .20 on a particular trial, as a single person can only achieve 1.0 (hit) or 0 (miss) on a single trial. Thus, the average performance curve in Figure 11-4 obscures all of the variations that occurred within people across trials and tempts us to make conclusions about the learning process that are perhaps incorrect.

Ceiling and Floor Effects

Ceiling and floor effects are a third kind of problem that leads to erroneous conclusions about learning processes from group performance curves. These effects are present in most of the tasks that are studied in the motor learning area. In most tasks absolute scores exist which no one will exceed. For example, there can be no fewer than zero errors, no less than 0 sec for some timed task, or no more than 30 sec for a time-on-target score in a 30-sec performance trial. Thus, as people approach these ceilings (the limitation in score is from above) or floors (the limitations is from below), the changes in the performance levels of the people doing the task become increasingly insensitive to the changes in habit that may be occurring in the people as they practice. As a person approaches some ceiling or floor, it becomes increasingly "difficult" to improve performances; in gymnastics, for example, it is far "easier" to improve one's score from 6.0 to 6.5 than it is to improve from 9.0 to 9.5, when "perfect" is 10.0.

In addition to these absolute scoring ceilings and floors, psychological or physiological floors and ceilings are present as well. For example, the 4-min mile was at one time a barrier that we thought would remain unbroken. Now, the barrier is considerably lower (3:48.8 at this writing), but I might well argue that no human will ever break a 3-min mile. Will anyone ever pole vault more than 20 ft? Thus, as performers approach these physiological limits, it becomes increasingly more difficult to improve their scores because they are human.

Scoring Sensitivity and the Shape of Performance Curves

The primary problem is that the "rate" of progress (the slope of the performance curve) toward some ceiling is usually quite arbitrary and dependent on the ways in which the task is measured. The rate does not seem directly linked to the habit changes that are underlying this change in behavior. A powerful example of this principle comes from a study by Bahrick, Fitts, and Briggs (1957, "simple task"). Here, the authors studied 25 male subjects on a continuous tracking task for ten 90-sec practice trials. The pattern of the track that the subjects had to follow, as well as the movements of the lever that the subjects made when following it, were recorded for later analysis.

The authors analyzed the single set of performances in three different ways. First, they assumed that the width of the target the subject had to follow was small, 5% of the total width of the screen. (There was, in fact, no target width as far as the subjects were concerned, as all they saw in the performance trials was a thin line that moved on the screen.) By going over the tracking records and examining the number of seconds in a trial during which the subject was in this imaginary 5% target band, the authors obtained a separate measure of the "time on target" for every subject and trial. Then, the data from Trial 1 were averaged for all the subjects to form the Trial 1 data point in Figure 11-5 for the curve marked "5%." The other trials for this target size were obtained in a similar way.

The authors then performed this procedure a second time, scoring the subjects on a different sized target (again, there was no target width as far as the subjects knew). Here, the target width was 15% of the width of the screen, and the subjects were evaluated in terms of the number of seconds out of a trial that the pointer was in this target zone. As the criterion of success was much more lenient (the "target" was wider, therefore "easier" to hit), the time-on-target scores were naturally larger, forming a second performance curve in Figure 11-5 marked "15%." Finally, the procedure was done again, this time with a very wide target that was 30% of the width of the screen. Naturally this criterion was quite "easy," and the time-on-target scores for this target width were quite large. The performance curve for these data is in Figure 11-5 labeled "30%."

The important point about these data is that all three curves are based on the same performances, but the differences between them are produced by the ways in which the experimenter has chosen to evaluate those perfor-

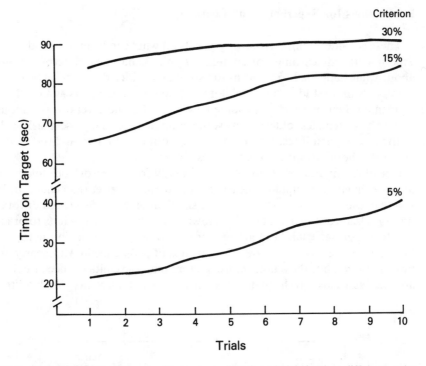

Figure 11-5. Time on target for a tracking task as a function of trials for three different scoring criteria. (The 5% criterion indicates that the target used for scoring was 5% of the screen width, etc.) (from Bahrick, Fitts, & Briggs, 1957).

mances. Thus, but one average pattern of habit change emerges from these subjects—not three as might be inferred from the three curves. But then, how is it that the three different curves have such markedly different shapes? I might conclude (if I did not know that all the data came from the same performances on the same subjects) that habit gains are a positively accelerated (concave upward) function of trials based on the 5% curve, that habit gains are a linear function of trials based on the 15% curve, and that habit gains are a negatively accelerated (concave downward) function of trials based on the 30% curve. This is, of course, nonsense, as but one pattern habit gain emerged (whatever it was), but evidence about this one pattern was obtained in three different ways that gave three different answers about how habit progressed with practice.

The differences are apparently caused by the fact that making the criterion "easier" (moving from 5% to 30% target widths) moves the person through the range from floor to ceiling, where the sensitivity of the scores to amount of habit are different. Thus, the same learning has occurred in all three curves from Trial 1 to Trial 2, but very different amounts of performance improvements are displayed depending on which target zone one chooses to use. So, what *is* the pattern of habit change that occurred with practice? I have no idea, based on these data, and I can conclude (erroneously) anything I choose just by selecting the "right" target width to study. That observation makes the study of learning somewhat scary for me.

Implications for Experiments on Learning

These considerations have strong effects on what can be understood from experiments on learning, often making impossible clear interpretations about what happened to habit in the study. Consider this hypothetical example. I want to study whether children learn more than adults as a result of a given amount of practice at some new task. (I could as easily ask about males versus females, older versus younger adults, etc.) I choose a task such as the rotary pursuit test that is foreign to both the children and the adults and allow both groups to practice these tasks.

One of the findings that emerges consistently from the work on children's motor behavior is that adults nearly always perform better than children. If I were to use a pursuit rotor with a very small target and a fast speed of rotation (a so-called "difficult task"), allowing the children and adults to practice for 50 30-sec trials, I might expect curves that appear as in the top of Figure 11-6. Here, both hypothetical groups of people begin with nearly no time on target, but the adults improve more than the children, because they are relatively closer to hitting the target than the children are. With a little

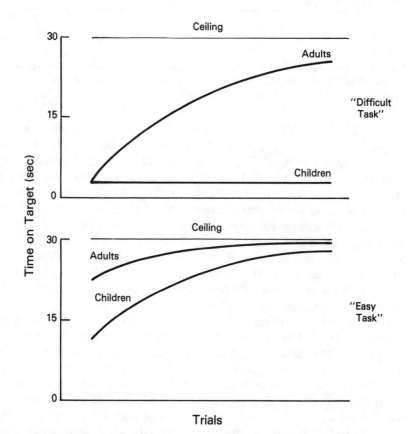

Figure 11-6. Hypothetical performance curves for adults' and children's performances on an "easy" or "difficult" task. [Depending on the scoring criterion, one can (erroneously) conclude that adults learn more than children (top) or that children learn more than adults (bottom)].

practice, their initial advantage in motor control begins to show up in terms of increased time on target, whereas the children show no such effects even though they may be moving slightly closer to the target. I may (erroneously) conclude that the adults learned more than the children because their performance gains were larger.

Now consider what happens if I do the "same" experiment, but with an "easy" version of the rotor task in which the target is large and the speed of rotation is slow. Now the adults begin very near ceiling, and the children are somewhere in the middle range. The adults have little capability to demonstrate continued improvement, whereas the children start in a sensitive area of the scoring range where a little practice produces maximum score gains. In this case, the gains in score are much larger for the children than for the adults. I might (again, erroneously) conclude that the children learned more than the adults.

Notice that these are two identical experiments on adults and children, the only difference being my arbitrary choice of the size of the target and the speed of rotation. Yet, with one of these choices, I could come to the conclusion that adults learn more than children, and with the other that children learn more than adults. This nonsense is caused by the marked differences in the sensitivity of the scoring system to changes in the subjects' behaviors and movement patterns—that is, in the sensitivity to changes in the level of habit of the subjects. The central region of the scoring system (15 sec time-on-target) is very sensitive to changes in the subjects' habit, whereas the regions near the ceiling and floor tend to be relatively insensitive to such changes in habit. In fact, if I wanted to show that children and adults learned the same amount, I could easily choose a scoring criterion so difficult that none of the adults or children could ever achieve the target, or a criterion so easy that all of the subjects could always achieve it. In either case, no improvement for either group would occur, and thus the same amount of learning would be demonstrated. So, given the choice of the sensitivity of the scoring system, I can produce any conclusion I desire about the relative amounts of learning in children and adults.

But games like this are not science, and it does not make much sense to play them. Even so, scientists do not know how to resolve this particular problem, and thus I have no idea whether children learn more than adults, or the reverse. The lesson to be learned here is that such effects are always present in learning studies, and scientists have to be aware of the potential artifacts that they may produce in the conclusions about learning (see also Estes, 1956; Sidman, 1952). Fortunately, experimental designs that minimize this kind of problem are available. Some of these designs are presented in the next section.

DESIGNING EXPERIMENTS ON LEARNING

One of the major goals in the study of motor learning is to understand which independent variables have effects on learning and which do not. That is, scientists want to know which variables are involved in the maximization of learning, which are involved in impairing learning, and which have no effect whatsoever. Clearly, such knowledge is important for developing useful theories of learning, and the implications for practical application in teaching and other learning situations are great as well.

Given the definition of learning and the limitations on the kinds of behavioral changes that scientists are willing to classify as learning changes, how do we go about deciding if a certain variable influences learning or not? One obvious way is to ask two large groups of people to perform and learn a novel motor task. Then we administer one level of the independent variable to one group of people and another level of the independent variable to the other group, then measure the performance levels achieved after considerable practice. The group that has performed "best" at the end of the practice sequence presumably has learned the most. While this approach sounds reasonable, a number of additional aspects need to be considered, as shown in the following example.

Example: Massed Practice and Motor Learning

I could use a large number of independent variables as examples, but I have selected the one called *massing variable* because a great deal of research has been devoted to it. Essentially, *massing* refers to the extent to which trials in a practice sequence are separated by rest periods. If we consider a performance with a 30-sec trial period, a *massed practice* sequence would be one in which relatively little rest (e.g., less than 5 sec) is allowed between the 30-sec trials. A *distributed-practice* sequence would involve rests as long as 30 sec between the 30-sec trials. Thus, the variable of massed versus distributed practice refers to the amount of rest imposed between trials of fixed length. Such variables are clearly of importance to teachers, who need to know how to distribute rest breaks in a practice sequence in order that learning be maximized. I will consider these effects in more detail in Chapter 12.

For now, assume that I want to know what the effects of massed practice (as compared to distributed practice) are on the learning of a novel motor task. One study by Stelmach (1969a) asked such a question. He used 16 30-sec trials on the Bachman ladder task, in which subjects had to climb a free-standing ladder, attempting to maximize the number of rungs climbed in a 30-sec trial. A distributed-practice condition (D) had 30 sec of rest between trials, whereas a massed group (M) had no rest between trials.

The results of this experiment are shown in Figure 11-7, where the number of rungs climbed is plotted against trials for the massed and distributed groups. Both groups began practice at approximately the same level, but the massed group did not appear to improve its performance as much as the distributed group did. By the end of the 16 trials, there was a clear beneficial effect of the distributed practice, with the distributed group having approximately 67% larger scores than the massed group.

Which group learned more? This question is essentially the same as asking "What is the effect of massed practice on learning?" because being able to define which group learned more provides the answer to the question involving the effect of massed practice on learning. At first glance, this ques-

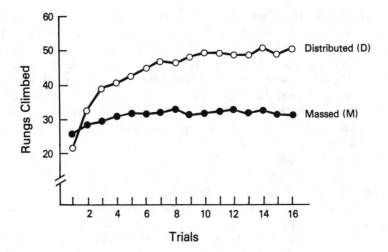

Figure 11-7. Performance on the Bachman ladder task (rungs climbed) over trials for massed (M) and Distributed (D) conditions (from Stelmach, 1969a).

tion seems like asking "Who is buried in Grant's tomb?" as it appears to be perfectly clear that the massed-practice (M) group both (a) performed less well and (b) improved less than the distributed-practice (D) group.

But take another look. I can think of at least two hypotheses to explain why the *M* condition was less effective in performing this task than the *D* condition, and these are listed below:

Hypothesis 1: Group D learned more than Group M. The differences in learning are manifested in the differences in performance, with Group D performing more effectively because of a greater acquired capability for responding. Or massing has interfered with the acquisition of the capability for responding (i.e., habit).

Hypothesis 2: Group D and Group M have learned the same amount, but Group D outperforms Group M because the latter is fatigued temporarily. That is, it is possible that the capability for responding (habit) has been acquired equally by these two groups, but that Group M cannot demonstrate it in terms of performance, because the subjects are temporarily fatigued due to the lack of rest.

You may intuitively feel that one or the other of these two hypotheses is correct. But with the evidence at hand here, there is no way to discriminate between them, and these two hypotheses have to be seen as equally likely to be correct until more evidence can be brought to bear on the question. One method used in these situations involves obtaining an estimate of the "relatively permanent" effects of the massing variable as distinct from the temporary efffects. In these situations, a technique called a *transfer design* is used to great advantage.

Transfer Designs

The problem with the data presented in Figure 11-7 is that it is not known whether the differences between groups are due to the "relatively permanent" effects (i.e., from habit changes) as Hypothesis 1 would have it, or whether the differences are due to temporary effects of fatigue that will disappear as soon as the subjects have had a chance to rest (Hypothesis 2). One way to resolve this uncertainty is to provide an additional test at some later time. If this test were sufficiently separated from the original learning trials, it could be argued that the temporary effects of the fatigue would be dissipated whereas the "relatively permanent" effects would not. Therefore, any differences between groups that remain after this rest period should represent the "relatively permanent" effects of the massing condition, and should provide the basis for deciding about the effects of massing on motor learning. In this situation, since massing is assumed to exert a downward effect on Group M (in Figure 11-7), if Hypothesis 2 is correct, Group M subjects should show a marked gain in performance from the first to the second test and Group D should show little change. However, if Hypothesis 1 is correct, then the two groups should show about the same relative performance levels on the first and second tests, because there would be no temporary effects of massing to be dissipated. Adams and Reynolds (1954) were the first to use this logic, although a small design problem in their study prevents such a clear-cut examination of the two hypotheses presented here. Their experiment is discussed in detail in Chapter 12.

Following the lead from Adams and Reynolds (1954), Stelmach (1969a) (and others) have used such a method to determine the learning effects of massing in the study shown in Figure 11-7. After the initial 16 trials, both groups rested for 4 min, and then both groups switched to a distributed-practice condition for six additional 30-sec trials, with 30-sec rest between trials. The results of this additional test are shown in Figure 11-8, where the original learning trials in Figure 11-7 are included for comparison. The D

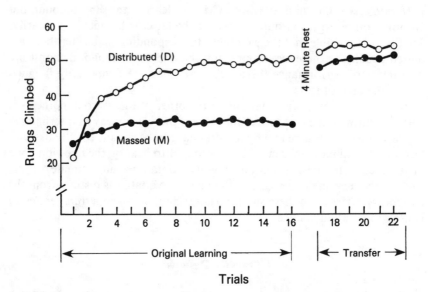

Figure 11-8. Performance on the Bachman ladder task (rungs climbed) in original learning and transfer trials (from Stelmach, 1969a).

group showed almost no change over the 4-min rest period, but the M group showed a marked gain (approximately 50%) in performance. These findings suggest that some temporary effect of massing was present that dissipated over the 4-min rest, allowing performance to improve (this improvement without practice is called *reminiscence*). These data argue against Hypothesis 1 which says that *all* of the difference between Groups D and M on the initial practice trials was due to learning. However, not all of the difference between Groups D and M disappeared on the second test, and thus it is perhaps best to say that some of the difference between Group D and M on the initial practice trials was due to learning but that most of it was due to the temporary fatigue-like effects of massing that can be easily dissipated with rest.

These experimental designs, in which the groups are shifted to a common condition after an initial practice phase to evaluate the "relatively permanent" effects of the independent variables, are called *transfer designs*. They are discussed in the following sections.

Considerations in Transfer Designs

Transfer designs are quite important to the study of motor learning, as they provide a way for various independent variables to be studied with respect to their effects on the learning of motor tasks. Two features of this design are worth mentioning.

Common level of independent variable. First, groups are transferred to a common level of the independent variable. That is, both groups of subjects in the transfer phase practiced the task with the same value of the independent variable. In the massing example above, Stelmach (1969a) shifted the massed-practice subjects to distributed practice, so that the last practice phase was under distributed conditions for *both* groups. This is essential as it is on these trials that one wants to evaluate the "relative amount learned," and it is important that no temporary effects of the independent variable are caused by the test procedure itself. For example, if the test phase were under massed conditions for the massed group and distributed conditions for the distributed group, the possibility would still exist that any differences in performance were due to the temporary effects of massing (e.g., fatigue).

Temporary effects allowed to dissipate. Next, it is important that the temporary effects of the independent variable be allowed to dissipate. Stelmach allowed this by providing a 4-min rest period, during which the temporary effects of fatigue should have largely diminished. However, it could be argued that 4 min is not sufficient for all of the fatigue to have dissipated, and thus it could be that the massed group was still depressed somewhat on the transfer test relative to the distributed group, which could explain why the massed and distributed groups were not quite equal in performance there. In other situations, even 10 min of rest will obviously not be enough. With a variable like heavy physical fatigue, soreness and related muscular effects could last as long as three days. Other variables might have effects that last considerably longer.

Effects of switching conditions. Finally, Dunham (1971, 1976) raised the issue that the massed group was switched to a different level of the independent variable (i.e., to distributed practice), whereas the distributed condition did not switch. He points out that the effect of switching itself could cause decrements in performance. For example, shifting to a new condition could involve some important processes of reorientation to a new situation, which could conceivably detract from the level of skill demonstrated on the first transfer trial (see, e.g., Chapter 15, "Warm-Up Decrement," for evidence on this issue).

The solution suggested by Dunham is a *double transfer design*, in which four groups of subjects are used rather than two. Here, using the massing example again, two of the groups would start the sequence with distributed practice and two with massed practice. When the groups were shifted to different conditions (i.e., after Trial 16 in Figure 11-8), one of the originally distributed groups would shift to massed practice and the other would remain with distributed practice; similarly, one of the originally massed groups would shift to distributed practice, and the other would continue with massed practice. Thus, in this design the effect of the prior massed-practice experience can be evaluated independent of the fact that the group had to switch to a new condition; and the effect of switching, per se, can be evaluated as well. While this kind of design has a great deal of merit, it requires twice the number of subjects as the first design does. It has not been used extensively probably because of this rather "expensive" feature.

Possible Experimental Outcomes

Next, consider some hypothetical independent variable (you can think of your own example) and some of the possible experimental outcomes. Some of the possibilities are shown in Figure 11-9. Consider a task in which the score increases with practice and an independent variable that tends to exert its effects in the direction of making the task scores larger. An example might be motivational instructions on the Bachman ladder. In the top left portion of Figure 11-9 are the original practice curves, showing that the groups with the two levels of the independent variable performed differently on the task. In the right portion of the figure are three possible outcomes when the two groups are shifted to a common level of the independent variable (no motivational instructions) after sufficient rest from the task to dissipate any temporary effects of the independent variable.

In the first situation, the original separation of the two groups is maintained exactly, suggesting that all of the effect of the independent variable was "relatively permanent," so that the variable can be considered as affecting learning of the task. In the second situation, the original separation of the two groups has vanished completely, suggesting that all of the effect to the independent variable was temporary, with none of it due to learning effects. Finally, in the third situation some of the original separation has disappeared upon transfer, but not all of it. Thus, the conclusion would be that the variable in question has a component affecting performance temporarily, but it also has a component affecting learning of the task as well.

The argument is similar with variables that seem to have depressing effects on performance (e.g., fatigue, massing, distraction). This case is

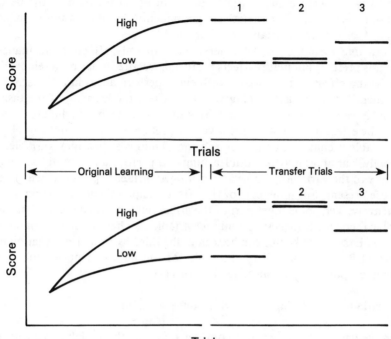

Figure 11-9. Possible outcomes in learning experiments using transfer designs. (In original learning, increasing the independent variable increases the task score (top) or decreases it (bottom); Cases 1, 2, and 3 in the transfer trials are some possible outcomes of transferring to the "low" value of the independent variable.)

shown in the bottom half of Figure 11-9, where the groups are transferred to a common condition (e.g., no fatigue, no distraction) as before. In the first transfer case, the original separation of the groups remained, suggesting that the variable of interest depressed performance "relatively permanently" and that this variable affects the learning of the task. In the second case, the original separation of the groups has disappeared completely, suggesting that the depressing effects of the variable were temporary, with the variable having no effects on the learning of the task. Finally, in the third case some of the original separation between the groups is removed with practice, but some still remains. The interpretation is that the variable had both learning and temporary effects and is basically the same as for Stelmach's (1969a) study in Figure 11-8.

Learning Variables and Performance Variables

Using these experimental designs, it has been possible to classify experimental variables into essentially two categories. One of those categories is that of a *performance variable*. This kind of variable is defined as one which has immediate effects on performance while it is present, but when the level is altered in transfer, the effect is altered as well. A performance variable is thus one that affects performance but not in a "relatively permanent" way. A performance variable does not affect learning of the task, because its effects are not "relatively permanent." Cooling water to make ice is a "performance variable."

A *learning variable*, on the other hand, not only affects performance when it is present, but it also affects performance after it has been removed. That is, the effect of the variable influences performances in a "relatively permanent" way. Thus, learning variables affect the learning of the task. Examples can be seen in the first hypothetical outcome in Figure 11-9, where the effect of the independent variable remains even when the level of the variable is changed; boiling an egg for 10 min is a "learning variable."

Finally, variables may be both learning *and* performance variables. That is, many of the variables that will be examined influence performance when they are present, but some part of the effect dissipates when the variable is taken away. Yet, some other part of the effect remains when the level of the variable is changed, suggesting that the variable also has affected learning in the task. Examples like this can be seen in the third hypothetical situation in Figure 11-9, where not all of the effect of the independent variable has dissipated upon transfer; also, see Figure 11-8.

Implications of Learning and Performance Variables

For theory . In Chapter 13, I consider many of the variables that have been studied in this regard. The attempt has been to discover which of them have important effects on learning, which of them merely affect performance, and which of them do neither or both. One important reason for this issue is that various theories of learning predict that certain variables should have effects on learning. An important example was Hull's (1943) theory (mentioned in Chapter 1), which predicted that massed practice should have negative effects on learning of tasks like the pursuit rotor. That is, after transfer to common distributed conditions, a group with formerly massed practice should perform less well than a group with formerly distributed practice. Early work by Adams and Reynolds (1954; Reynolds and Adams, 1953) produced effects whose interpretations were that massing produced no effects on learning, contrary to the predictions from Hull's theory. As such, these experiments played a large part in the abandonment of Hull's theory during the late 1950s and 1960s (Adams, 1964; but see Noble, 1978, for a different view). [More recent data, such as studies by Stelmach (1969a) and McGown (Note 20), however, have shown small negative effects of massing on learning, which tends to support Hull's theory; these points will be discussed in Chapter 12.] Thus, the outcomes from experiments on learning that use transfer designs can be used to provide critical experimental tests of theories that predict effects of certain independent variables on learning. Many examples of this kind of theory testing are presented in Chapters 12 through 15.

For teaching applications. A second practical outcome is that knowledge about which variables affect performance temporarily and which affect learning allows the production of more effective settings for instruction in various motor tasks in sport, industry, the military, and so on. For example, if I know that a certain variable only affects performance, and it is not important for learning, then I will not have to worry about adjusting the level of this variable in the learning situation. On the other hand, certain variables have powerful effects on the learning of motor tasks. The most powerful of these is knowledge of results (KR)—the information about the performer's movement that is "fed back" to him or her after the movement. In Chapter 13, I discuss evidence showing that, in some circumstances, learning will not occur at all if KR is not present and that changing the ways in which KR is administered has important effects on the amount that subjects will learn. As such, the person who is designing the learning situation must pay close attention to these learning variables, because appropriate choices of how and when learning variables are altered will have important effects on the amount that people will learn.

I find it useful to keep a mental "list" of those variables that affect performance only versus those variables that affect learning; such a "list" helps me to decide how to structure practice settings, in that I can make certain that the variables that matter are handled in such a way that learning is maximized, and I do not then have to worry about those variables that do not matter. Unfortunately, many of the people designing learning situations are not keenly aware of the variables that have the most powerful effects on learning—variables which are usually under their direct control.

SOME ALTERNATIVE METHODS FOR MEASURING LEARNING

Many situations exist in which the measurement of performance, and thus the measurement of learning, does not give good estimates of the "amount" that someone has learned in practice. The problem is often that the performance scores have approached a ceiling or floor over the course of practice. This makes all of the subjects appear to be the same on the task, because all of the scores hover close to the absolute maximum or minimum value on the task. In such situations, attempts to show that a given independent variable has effects on learning will be thwarted because continued practice on the task can result in no changes, as the scores are already minimized.

These problems can occur in at least two different settings. One of these involves simple tasks, for which all subjects perform nearly maximally in only a few practice trials. Here, continued practice can result in no effects on the performance score. A second situation involves more complex tasks, but those for which a great deal of experience has been provided in the past, such as driving a car. Because subjects are so well practiced, little improvement in skills will be evidenced as subjects continue to practice improvements of some kind. The problem again is that subjects are so close to a performance ceiling that no additional improvements can be shown. Other examples are the performance of high-level sports skills or the performance of various highly skilled jobs in industry.

In Chapter 3, I discussed secondary-task methods for the measurement of skills. The problem there is similar to the present one, as the measures of the subject's behaviors in a particular task may not give a good indication of the level of skill that this person possesses. The example I used in Chapter 3 was driving under the influence of fatigue. The accumulations of fatigue from long, uninterrupted stretches of driving were not observed in vehicle control movements at all. However, when subjects were asked to perform a simultaneous secondary task, decrements in this task were observed as a function of the duration of the previous driving, suggesting that there was a decrement in "spare capacity" with increasing levels of fatigue (e.g., Brown, 1962, 1967).

Secondary Tasks and Alternative Learning Measures

The basic notion is that the measurement of performance on a task often does not tell us much about the person's level of learning. Additional practice (at, for example, driving a car) will probably result in some additional learning of the skill even at advanced levels of proficiency, but the experimenter may not be able to see these effects because the subjects are so close to the performance ceiling or floor. By using secondary-task methods, one can often see these changes more clearly. Consider the following example.

Assume that two identical groups of subjects practice a task, and they have reached a performance ceiling. Being at the ceiling could be due to the tasks being relatively simple and easy to learn or it could be that there has been an extensive amount of practice on a relatively complex task like driving; it doesn't matter for the ideas presented here. Figure 11-10 shows some hypothetical curves that could result from such a situation. Now, suppose that one of the groups (A) is told to discontinue the practice sequence, while the other group (B) continues to practice for a large number of additional trials. Group B's curve is shown as a continuation of the earlier performance curve along the ceiling; it must be, as there can be no further improvements in the score after the ceiling has been reached. (This procedure, in which a person practices further after having reached some

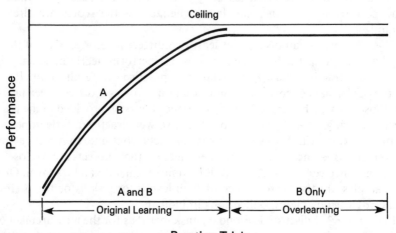

Figure 11-10. Hypothetical performance curves from original learning to a ceiling (Groups A and B) and "overlearning" trials at the ceiling (Group B only).

criterion of success, is often called "overlearning.")

We could ask various questions about this experiment. Did any learning of the task go on during the "overlearning"trials? Which of the two groups had learned more after all the practice had been completed? We might suspect that the continued practice at the ceiling did something to the subjects, but we have no way to make this conclusion from the performance curves in the task, as both groups have the same final score—essentially at the ceiling. I will address these questions using this basic experimental design in the next three sections, so keep the situation indicated in Figure 11-10 in mind. In each case, various methods with so-called "secondary tasks" can be used to answer these questions.

Learning and Attention

One hypothesis about learning which has received a great deal of empirical support (see Chapter 14) is that the attention required to perform a task after a great deal of practice is less than that required in early practice. What if I imposed a secondary task on the Group B subjects during the practice at the ceiling? For example, I could (as Brown, 1962, did) have the subjects do a mental task requiring the detection of a duplicated letter in a stream of auditorially presented letters and measure the extent to which the subjects could improve on this task as they were practicing the main task at the ceiling. Some hypothetical results are presented in Figure 11-11. There might be a continued improvement in the accuracy of the secondary task during the main task "overlearning" trials for which the score was essentially fixed at the ceiling. The improvement in the secondary task would suggest that learning was going on during the "overlearning" trials. Perhaps learning the main task reduced the amount of attention required to perform it at the ceiling, so that more attention could be devoted to the performance

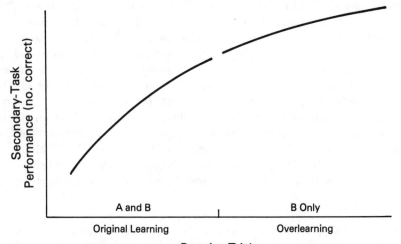

Figure 11-11. Hypothetical data from a secondary task measured during practice trials of task shown in Figure 11-10. (The secondary task score continues to increase even though the main task score is at a ceiling.)

of the secondary task.[2] This technique is essentially the one used by Bahrick and Shelly (1958), and I will examine these findings more closely when I discuss the changes in attention that occur with practice (Chapter 13). This technique has not been used a great deal, but it is useful in situations like this.

Effort and Learning

Closely related to the notion of attention (even equated with it by some—Kahneman, 1973) is the notion of *effort*. As people learn a motor skill, they appear to be able to do the task with less and less physical and mental effort, probably because they learn to perform with more efficient movements or because they process information more efficiently. If so, then a simultaneous measure of physical effort could be used to show that during the overlearning trials in which the subjects are practicing the task at the ceiling, the effort in the task was being reduced simultaneously. Measures like O_2 consumption (assessed by techniques associated with physiology of exercise) or heart rate (also a measure of effort) could be used. If learning is continuing during these overlearning trials and it is associated with less effortful performances that are not measured by the main task scoring system, then we should see physical effort decrease progressively with continued practice on the task. I would interpret such data as showing that the continued practice trials produced some additional learning, and that it was manifested as a decrease in the effort extended in the main task.

Speed of Decision and Learning

Another method is effective in situations in which the main task involves decision making, such as in learning the names of the state capitals or all the cranial nerves. If the task is to respond with the name of the capital when the name of the state is presented, early in the overlearning trials subjects are perhaps barely able to say the name of the city when the stimulus is provided. But later in overlearning, subjects can say the name easily and far more quickly. What if, in addition to measuring whether or not the subject could name the city correctly, I measured the latency with which the subject gave the name (Adams, 1976a)? I would probably see that the latency of the response (which is not yet at a floor) would decrease markedly, even though the accuracy of the response did not change at all (since accuracy performance was at the ceiling). This procedure will not "work" with all motor tasks, but it seems ideally suited to those situations in which accurate decisions have to be made, with the decisions being made more easily and more

---

[2]Of course, I would also have to show that the improvement in the secondary task in Figure 11-11 was not simply due to the practice on *that* task. This could be done by having a control condition which practiced only the secondary task, showing essentially that the improvement in the skill at recognizing the duplicated letters was not changed with practice. If so, then the changes that occurred in Figure 11-11 would be due to the reduced attention required for the main task.

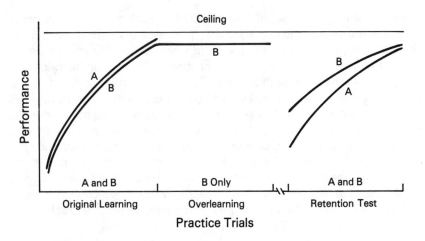

Figure 11-12. Retention as a measure of original learning. (Original learning and overlearning trials are shown at left, with hypothetical scores from a retention test shown at right; the finding that B outperforms A on the retention test indicates B learned during the "overlearning" trials even though no change in task performance could be seen.)

quickly as a result of the practice. If such outcomes occurred, I would conclude that the decreased response latencies indicated that continued learning was going on even though the subjects were at the ceiling, the learning being manifested as increases in *speed* with constant accuracy.

Memory and Learning

Inherent in the notion of learning is the concept of memory (Chapter 15). In fact, most experimental psychologists define learning in terms of memory, saying that something has been learned when a person has a memory of that thing. In this sense, memory and habit are very similar constructs. I can say that I have learned a new word in Spanish if I can remember the word when asked for it later. Similarly, the evidence that I have learned a kip on the horizontal bar is that I can do it again, after the original practice session.

With respect to the problem of overlearning, if the group with overlearning learned while practicing at the ceiling, the two groups should differ on a retention test given some weeks later, perhaps producing a pattern of results something like that shown in Figure 11-12. Here, the group with overlearning trials should outperform the group without these trials on the first retention test trial. Both groups would have lost, in this instance, some of what they had learned in the original session, but the group without the overlearning would be further below the ceiling than the group with the overlearning, leading to the conclusion that a stronger memory (habit) for the task existed in the overlearning condition. Evidence for a stronger habit after a retention interval could indicate that more was learned in the first place. I conclude that learning occurred even when the performance scores did not change in overlearning trials when scores were limited by the ceiling.

Summary of Secondary Methods. All of these methods are consistent with the fundamental notion of learning presented earlier in the chapter.

Namely, learning is the set of internal, unobservable processes that occurs with practice or experience, and these processes underlie the behavioral changes seen when people practice. Even when obvious changes do not occur in the main task, these learning processes can be demonstrated by a variety of other means, such as the decreases in attention or effort applied to a task, the increases in speed with which the task is done, or the improvement in the retention of the task. These techniques highlight the idea that the learning is internal and complex, having many forms in many different situations. Because of this complexity, scientists use various techniques at different times or with different tasks, as the nature of learning processes is probably not the same for various situations. Above all, this section stresses the deficiency in the oversimplified idea that learning is merely a change in behavior of the major task in question. It is obviously much more than that.

ISSUES ABOUT THE "AMOUNT" OF LEARNING

Researchers are often tempted to make statements based on experiments on learning that are phrased in terms of the amount of learning that has occurred as a result of practice. For example, we might wish to say that a group of subjects practicing with massed conditions learned 20% less than a group with distributed conditions. Or you may wish to say that Jim learned twice as much as Jack on this task. Do such statements really have any meaning?

The problem is that habit is a construct that cannot be observed directly. Usually little basis exists for making quantitative statements about it, because it can only be estimated from performance scores. But, you may say that the habit obtained by the person is reflected more or less accurately by the achieved performance score. Not so. Remember the experiment by Bahrick, Fitts, and Briggs (1957) discussed earlier in this chapter? Here, by a simple change in the way in which the task was scored (the change in the strictness of the criterion of success), the authors obtained almost any scores they wanted, and they could easily change the shapes of the performance curves. For example, returning to the data from their experiment in Figure 11-5, I computed that the subjects with the 5% scoring criterion improved 86% as a result of practice, the same subjects improved 29% with the 15% criterion, and they improved 8% with the 30% criterion. How shall I assess the "amount" of habit gain that occurred here? Will I say that it was 8% or 86%? That decision is purely arbitrary, and I would be equally incorrect in saying either. Shall I say that they improved 7 sec in time on target for the 30% criterion, or 19 sec in time on target in the case of the 5% criterion? Again, the choice is arbitrary. Obviously, such methods cannot lead to quantitative statements about the amount that someone or some group has learned.[3]

---

[3]Possible exceptions to this generalization are temporal measures (e.g., RT) as estimators of the duration of mental events. The reason that subtractive logic (Chapter 4) is meaningful is that a proportional relationship is assumed between duration of internal events and the duration of external events that they cause. Such a relationship cannot be assumed for the other performance measures discussed here.

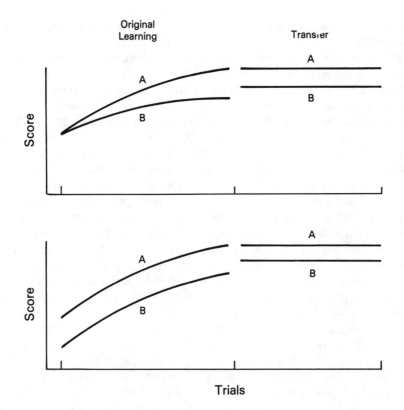

Figure 11-13. Outcomes from an experiment on learning in which the original level of proficiency for the two groups was (top) or was not (bottom) controlled.

About the best one can do is to make statements about the relative amounts that two groups have learned, or about the relative amounts that two people have learned, essentially with statements like "Group A learned more than Group B." The issues are somewhat different for the case where groups are compared against each other versus where individuals are compared against each other, so these two situations will be discussed in turn.

Group Differences

Consider again the transfer paradigm discussed earlier in this chapter. The top of Figure 11-13 is a typical example, where a change in the independent variable tends to increase the scores on the task. Here, the experimenter does not really have any idea about how much learning occurred, but we can make statements about (a) the fact that both groups learned and (b) for however much learning there was, Group A learned more than Group B did. Since the two groups began practice on Trial 1 with the same level of performance, and during the course of practice they progressed to different levels of performance, it seems unavoidable to conclude that B learned less than A in this case. Remember that the test of the relative amount learned should always be on the transfer trials, as it is only there in the sequence that the temporary effects of the independent variable are equated for the two groups.

Consider now the bottom of Figure 11-13, where the two groups began practice at different levels of performance and hence different levels of initial learning. This initial difference could be due to some systematic difference in the nature of the subjects (e.g., males versus females or children versus adults), or it could be due to simple random sampling effects, whereby the groups simply differ by chance. In either case, the two groups learned, but the scientist is in a difficult position with respect to saying which group learned more. Remember, the question is about the amount of change in the internal state (habit) and whether one of the groups gained more of it than the other. You can see that both groups gained about the same amount in terms of the score on the task, but you have no way to know whether the amount of change in the habit was larger or smaller for Group A or Group B. You might want to guess that the habit changed more for Group A than for Group B, because it was "harder" for Group A to change performance, as it was relatively closer to performance ceiling. But such speculations are usually without much basis, and it is better to say you don't know which of the two groups learned more.

The problem is that the differences in the initial level of performance on the task have confounded the interpretations about which of the groups learned more. Thus, in designing these kinds of experiments it is essential, if this question is to be asked of the data, to be certain that the two groups of subjects are equated at the beginning of practice, so that differences in the performance at the end of practice (on the transfer test) can be attributed to changes in the amount learned. This can be done in two ways. First, you can assign subjects to groups so that the groups are forced to be equal on initial performance. This can be done by administering a pretest on the learning task, ranking subjects from highest to lowest on this test, and then assigning the subjects with odd-numbered ranks to one group and those with even-numbered ranks to the other group. In this way the groups are almost exactly equal on the first trial, and the problem is eliminated (other matching techniques are available as well.) The drawback, however, is that the pretest provides some practice on the experimental task, which then reduces the learning that can occur under the different levels of the independent variable. This should not be a real problem with complex tasks, though, as a great deal of improvement is to be seen subsequent to the pretest in these situations.[4]

A second method is to use large groups that are randomly formed from some larger group. In this way the groups will be expected to differ due to chance effects; but if the groups are large (e.g., 25 people per group), then the chance differences in the group means on the motor task should be rela-

---

[4]This procedure has the additional limitation that the first trials on a motor task are usually not strongly related to the last trials in the sequence—i.e., with the final trials on which the relative amount of learning is assessed. Such correlations are frequently as low as .20. If so, then the variable that is matched (initial performance) is not going to influence the "equality" of the groups on the transfer trials to a very strong degree.

tively small. This procedure has the advantage that it does not give the experience on the motor learning task before the independent variable is administered, but it has the disadvantage that chance differences can occur, differences which will make particularly difficult the evaluation of the experimental results in terms of the relative amount learned (e.g., Figure 11-13) (See Schmidt, 1971a, 1972a, for reviews).

Could you "correct for" the initial differences in performance (in, say, the bottom portion of Figure 11-13) by subtracting the initial difference from the differences that occurred in the transfer trials? While this can be done in terms of the arithmetic, such procedures produce nearly meaningless interpretations of the relative amount learned. The problem is that the sensitivity of the scoring system to changes in the internal state of the subject (habit) is different at various places on the performance scale. Thus, subtracting the initial differences in performances (the scores will change a great deal as habit is increased) from the differences in performance at the end of practice (the changes in score will be relatively small as habit is increased) will probably lead to an adjustment that is far too large. Because we have no idea how much too large this adjustment will be and we have no way to find out, such adjustments probably should not be used.

Of course, these adjustments are exactly equivalent to computing "learning scores," or the differences between the initial and final performance for one group, and comparing these differences to the difference between the initial and final performance scores for the other group (Schmidt, 1971a). The use of "learning scores" or "gain scores" is not as prevalent as it was 15 years ago, largely for reasons mentioned in this section.

Individual Differences in Learning

The problem just raised is similar in many respects to comparing the amount learned by one person to the amount learned by another person. This is a common problem in studying individual differences in learning, as sometimes it is of interest to determine whether or not some measure of an abilty correlates with the amount that someone will learn (e.g., Bachman, 1961, and many others). Naturally, in order to compute the correlation, one must achieve a measure of the "amount learned" by each person. But I have just argued that such measures are not meaningful if they are based on the differences between the initial and the final performance.

A second situation in which these kinds of measures are usually taken is in grading procedures. Often, a measure of the student's initial level of proficiency is taken at the beginning of instruction, and then another measure of proficiency is taken after the instruction has been completed; grades are then assigned on the basis of the difference between the initial and final performance levels. Such methods are motivated by the desire to grade on the basis of "amount learned" in the course, with the student achieving the largest *change* in skill deserving the highest grade. There is also the (falsely) humanistic desire to encourage those individuals who do not have the relevant abilities (and, hence, the initial skill levels) to work hard in the practice sessions, even though their final levels of performance might fall far short of those whose abilities are more suited to that activity.

The fundamental problem with this technique is that the difference between initial and final performance is not a good measure of the "amount learned," as discussed earlier. Do you really want to say that the same amount of practice and effort by a person who increases her javelin throw from 30 ft to 130 ft (a 100-ft change) is deserving of a higher grade than a person who increases her throw from 110 ft to 160 ft? (a 50-ft change)? I have no way to determine which of these two performers has learned more, and to judge on the basis of simple difference scores will surely penalize one of the two learners. The problem is that we do not know which of the two performers is penalized, and by how much.

The problem can be addressed in philosophical-educational terms as well. In most aspects of life, we are judged on the basis of what we can do, not on the basis of how much we have improved. My friend received an "A" in physics because she could pass the examinations at the end of the course; no one cared that she was able to pass the examinations on the first day of class because her father taught her physics. Should a person who learned to throw the javelin as a child be penalized in a university class because there is so little performance improvement? I don't think so. The method that is most consistent with other units in the university, on the one hand, and with statistical-logical considerations, on the other hand, is to grade people on the basis of what they can do at the end of a sequence of instruction, regardless of how or where the person achieved the skill. Even if a person was so possessed of the "right" natural abilities that a high skill level could be achieved without any practice at all, in my view that person should receive an "A."

TRANSFER OF LEARNING

I mentioned the notion of transfer of learning earlier in discussing transfer designs, but the issues about transfer really run far deeper than this one application. Transfer is usually defined as the gain (or loss) in the capability for responding (habit) in one task as a result of practice or experience on some other task. Thus, we might ask whether practicing a task like badminton would produce benefits or losses (or neither) for another task such as tennis. If it should turn out that the performance of tennis is more effective after badminton experience than it would have been under no previous badminton experience, then I would say that the skills acquired in badminton have "transferred to" the skills involved in tennis. It is as if something that is learned in the badminton situation can be carried over to (or applied to) the task of playing tennis.

Transfer Experiments

Experiments on the transfer of learning can use a variety of different experimental designs, but we need not consider them all here (see Ellis, 1965, for a complete description). In the simplest of all, assume that there are two

Table 11-1

A Simple Design for an Experiment on Proactive Transfer of Learning

	Transfer Task	Test
Group I	Task A	Task B
Group II	—	Task B

groups of subjects (Groups I and II). In Table 11-1, Group I practices Task A for some arbitrary number of practice trials, after which Group I transfers to Task B for practice in this response. Group II, on the other hand, does not receive Task A at all but merely begins practicing Task B. You can think of Tasks A and B as any two activities; they could be different tasks such as badminton and tennis or they could be two slightly different variations in the *same* task, such as the pursuit rotor under distributed-versus massed-practice conditions. Thus, when the two groups begin practicing Task B, the only systematic difference is whether or not they have had experience on Task A beforehand.

Consider the possible results of such an experiment shown in Figure 11-14. Here, the task of interest is Task B, and the Task A performance is not graphed. In the left portion of Figure 11-14, Group I, which had Task A prior to Task B, performs Task B more effectively than does Group II, which did not have the experience with Task A. Because no other explanation is possible for why these two groups differ, I conclude that experience

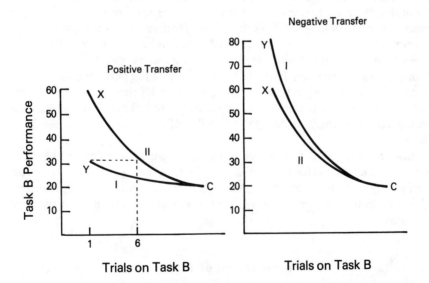

Figure 11-14. Performances on Task B for a group with no prior experience (II) or with prior practice on Task A (I).(If Group I outperforms Group II on initial trials, positive transfer has occurred; if Group II outperforms Group I, then negative transfer has occurred.)

Table 11-2

A Retroactive Transfer Design

Group	Initial Practice	Transfer Task	Retention Test
III	Task B	Task Q	Task B
IV	Task B	—	Task B

on Task A has provided increased habit for Task B and that this habit gain produces about 30 score units on the first Task B trial. When the practice on Task A improves subsequent performance on Task B, we say that *positive transfer* occurred.

You can also imagine that the effect of some other Task Z on Task B might be detrimental. An example is shown on the right in Figure 11-4. Here, Group II performs Task B exactly as on the left in the future, but now Task B performance for Group I is markedly inferior to that of Group II. For the reasons just mentioned, I conclude that experience on Task Z has interferred with Group I's habit for Task B. In this case, *negative transfer* occurred from Task Z to Task B.

In the examples given so far, the transfer is termed *proactive*, because the transfer seemed to work "forward" in time from Task A to Task B. However, we can also consider *retroactive transfer*, i.e., where transfer seems to work "backward" in time. Consider the design shown in Table 11-2. Here, two different treatment groups (Groups III and IV) both perform Task B. Then, Group III performs Task Q while Group IV performs "nothing." Later, both groups return to Task B for a retention test. If the retention performance of Task B is less effective for Group IV than for Group III, we say that positive retroactive transfer occurred from Task Q to Task B; it is as if the Task Q experience "worked backward" to affect the habit already learned on Task B. Alternatively, if the performance of Task B on the retention test is less effective for Group III than for Group IV, we say that negative retroactive transfer (or interference) occurred; here, practicing Task Q seemed to "erode" the habit of the previously learned Task B.

Both retroactive and proactive transfer designs are similar, in that they both consider the performance on the initial trials of Task B in the retention test (or test phase in Table 11-1) to be the critical data indicating transfer. Some measures of these different performances are described in the next sections.

Measurement of Transfer

The "amount" of transfer from one task to another can be assessed in a number of ways, all of which suffer from the basic problem raised earlier in this chapter about the measurement of performance and learning; thus none of these methods will be very satisfactory in actually measuring transfer. Rather, these methods are used to describe the relationships among curves such as those in Figure 11-14 and are helpful in discussing the results of transfer experiments. Some of the major findings of these experiments will be presented later in Chapters 12 and 14.

Percentage Transfer

One method of measuring transfer (see the left portion of Figure 11-14) is to consider the gain in performance as a result of experience on Task A (that is, the numerical difference between Points Y and X in the figure, or 30 score units) as a percentage of the "total amount learned" by Group II in the experiment (that is, the numerical difference between Points X and C, or about 40 score units). Thus, the amount of improvement in Task B by Group II is seen as the total improvement possible in Task B, and thus Group I's experience with Task A has provided 30 out of the possible 40 units of improvement, or 75%. In terms of a more general formula,

$$\text{Percentage Transfer} = \frac{X - Y}{X - C} \times 100, \tag{11-1}$$

in which $X = 60$, $Y = 30$, and $C = 20$ score units. The formula can also be used for negative transfer such as is shown in the right portion of Figure 11-14. Here, the values X and C remain the same, but Y (the initial performance level on Task B by Group I) is larger than it was before (i.e., 80). Being careful to keep the signs of the numbers straight, the numerator of the equation being a negative number (i.e., $A - B$, or $60 - 80$, or -20), transfer is calculated as $-20/40 \times 100 = -50\%$.

Crudely speaking, one can interpret the percentage transfer as the percentage of improvement on Task B as a result of prior practice on Task A. A 100% positive transfer would imply that the performance on the first trial of Task B for Group I would be at the final level of performance (i.e., C) demonstrated by Group II. Transfer of 0% would mean that the two groups are the same in initial performance on Task B (i.e., both at level X). The reason that this measure is inadequate, of course, is that the amount of improvement on Task B (i.e., $X - C$) will depend on the amount of practice provided, on the scoring system used in Task B, on the nature of the subjects, and on countless other arbitrary factors that affect the shapes of "learning curves." But percentage transfer does serve a useful purpose in describing the relationships among the curves; just be careful not to take the finding of 75% transfer too literally, assuming that a 75% transfer of habit occurred. It only describes the outward manifestations (i.e., performance) that result from the habit transfer.

Savings Score

Another, far less frequently used method for describing the amount of transfer is a *savings score*. Here, the savings score represents the amount of practice time "saved" (i.e., reduced) on Task B by having first practiced

Task A. On the left side of Figure 11-14, Group I (which had practiced Task A previously) begins its performance of Task B at a level of performance that is equivalent to that shown by Group II after six trials. It is possible to say that Group I "saved" six trials in the learning of Task B by having first learned Task A. But this is not the whole story, as the "savings" on Task B are almost certainly compensated for by a "loss," because Task A had to be practiced and the practice time on Task A is going to be longer than the amount "saved" on Task B. That is, for learning Task B, usually nothing is as efficient as practicing Task B (but see Chapter 12, "Variability in Practice," for a few exceptions).

But such "savings" begin to have importance when the financial cost of practice is considered. A common example is in learning to fly an airplane, such as a Boeing 747. To actually practice in the 747 would be very costly, so computer-based simulators are frequently used that closely resemble the aircraft cockpit. Here, the time "spent" in the simulator (Task A) is very inexpensive relative to the time "saved" in learning to fly the 747 (Task B), and it is safer as well. In such situations, the effectiveness of a simulator-based training program is often evaluated in terms of financial savings, such savings being the amount of hours saved on Task B (the 747) times the number of dollars per hour of practice on Task B. In the case of the 747, dollar amount of savings can be very large.

SUMMARY

The study of motor learning is considerably different from the study of performance, in that the focus is on the *changes* in performance that occur as a direct result of practice. Motor learning is defined as a set of internal processes associated with practice or experience leading to relatively permanent changes in skilled behavior. Learning leads to a change in an acquired capability for responding, usually termed *habit*. Such a definition must be carefully worded to rule out changes in behavior that are due to maturation or growth, or to momentary fluctuations in performance from temporary factors.

In the typical motor learning experiment, two or more groups of subjects are used, each of which practices a task under a different level of an independent variable. A common method of data analysis involves *performance curves*, or plots of average performance on each trial for a large number of subjects. These curves can hide a great deal of important information about learning, however, such as individual differences in learning or changes in strategies. They tend to characterize motor learning as a slow, constantly growing process requiring continued practice, whereas other evidence suggests that learning is often sudden, insightful, or even "revolutionary." As a result, interpretations about the nature of learning from performance curves must be made carefully.

Learning experiments usually involve what is called a *transfer design*, in which the groups of subjects practicing at different levels of the independent variable are transferred to a common level of that variable. These designs provide for the separation of the relatively permenent effects (due to learning) and the temporary effects of the independent variable. Those independent variables affecting performance "relatively permanently" are called *learning variables*, and those affecting performance only temporarily are called *performance variables*.

In many situations, the performance scores are near a "ceiling" or "floor," where no changes can occur because of task-imposed or biologically imposed limitations on performance. In such situations, a number of secondary-task methods can be used, such as measures of latency, measures of attention or effort, or measures of retention. With all of the methods, it is seldom possible to speak meaningfully about the actual amount that a person or a group has learned.

A variant of the learning experiment is the *transfer* experiment, in which the effect of practicing one task on the performance of some other task is evaluated. Transfer is often measured as a percentage, indicating the proportion of possible improvement in one task that was achieved by practice on some other task. Studies of transfer are important for evaluating training and other instructional programs.

GLOSSARY

Ceiling effect. A limitation, imposed either by the scoring system or by physiological-psychological sources, that places a maximum on the score that a performer can achieve in a task.

Floor effect. A limitation, imposed either by the scoring system or by physiological-psychological limits, that places a minimum on the score that a performer can achieve in a task.

Habit. The acquired capability for responding, an unobservable internal state that underlies skilled performance.

Individual differences in learning. Differences between or among individuals in the amount or rate of acquisition of skills.

Learning. A set of internal processes associated with practice or leading to experience leading to relatively permanent changes in behavior.

Learning curve. A label sometimes applied to the performance curve, in the belief that the changes in performance mirror changes in learning, an acquired capability for motor responding.

Learning score. A difference score, computed as the difference between the initial and final levels of a variable; sometimes used in computing the changes in performance as a result of practice.

Learning variable. An independent variable that affects learning.

Motor learning. A set of internal processes associated with practice or experience leading to relatively permanent changes in motor skill.

Negative transfer. The loss in habit for one task as a result of practice or experience in some other task.

Performance curve. A plot of the average performance of a group of subjects for each of a number of practice trials or blocks of trials.

Performance variable. An independent variable that affects performance only temporarily and does not affect learning of the task.

Positive transfer. The gain in habit in one task as a result of practice or experience on some other task.

Savings score. A statistic used in transfer experiments, representing the "savings" in practice time resulting from experience on some other task.

Secondary-task method. A collection of experimental methods whereby learning on a main task can be estimated by use of simultaneous secondary measures of performance.

Transfer design. An experimental design for measuring learning effects, in which all treatment groups are transferred to a common level of the independent variable.

CHAPTER 12

Conditions of Practice

In the previous chapter, the various research methods and logic that can be used to gain knowledge about the many variables affecting motor learning were discussed. This chapter is about experiments that use the techniques described in Chapter 11, the focus being on the major independent variables that are important for motor learning. There are many such variables, of course, and space limitations prevent a complete treatment of every variable that affects learning. I have limited the discussion to those variables having the largest effects (i.e., those that make the biggest difference) and those that are usually thought to be under the direct control of the teacher or experimenter. As well, I will emphasize those variables for which there is more theoretical interest—i.e., the variables that are included in the predictions from various theories of motor learning. Some of the theoretical implications will be mentioned here, but the majority of the interpretation will wait until theories of motor learning are discussed more formally in Chapter 14.

In addition, the information presented in this chapter will have relatively stronger possibilities for practical application than the information in previous chapters. Because the primary focus will be on those variables affecting learning that are under the direct control of a teacher or instructor, the chapter relates strongly to the design of instructional settings, such as would be involved in teaching or training situations in schools, in industry, or in the military. Thus, the chapter is about that configuration of variables that produces the most effective conditions of practice.

Finally, this chapter should be combined conceptually with Chapter 13, which deals with knowledge of results (KR) and feedback about the response that the person receives after a learning trial. Feedback is one of the most important variables for determining effective conditions of practice, and I have devoted an entire chapter to the topic.

PREPRACTICE CONSIDERATIONS

I begin the discussion of the conditions of practice by considering some of those factors that have been shown to operate before the practice session even begins. Most of these factors concern the preparation of the individual for the upcoming practice sequence.

Motivation for Learning

It is important that individuals be motivated to learn a motor task in order that maximally effective learning occurs. If the potential learner perceives the task as meaningless or undesirable, then learning on the task will probably be minimal. If motivation is too low, *no* learning might occur at all, as individuals would not be sufficiently motivated to practice at all. Aside from this rather obvious conclusion, though, a number of reasonably complex determinants of learning exist as a function of motivational level, some of which are handled in a later section of this chapter. Those aspects of motivation related to prepractice considerations are discussed here.

Making the Task Seem Important

Before beginning the practice session, it is important that the learner see the task as being desirable to learn. Much of this kind of motivation appears already to be established in people, due to culturally derived emphasis on certain activities. But in many cases it is important to show why it would be useful to have a certain skill. A teacher of mine years ago pointed out that the usual all-male games (e.g., tackle football) were fine for playing with other male friends, but a time would come in my life when I might need recreational skills to share with a girlfriend or wife; such an introduction made me realize the importance of learning a number of activities. As well, I considered volleyball to be the silly game I played in fifth grade, until I was shown a movie of Olympic-class volleyball; I was much more interested in learning these skills once I could see them performed in world-class competition. These techniques are easy, and they probably make large differences in the ways learners approach a new skill, and in how well they will learn it. Unfortunately, there is very little experimental evidence on these points.

Goal Setting

Another frequently used motivational technique is *goal setting*, or asking the learners to set goals for themselves before they begin practicing. The goals actually set will be a product of at least two things. First, if individuals are particularly gifted at a number of other skills, then they may feel that there is a good chance of becoming very good in the present skill, so they set the goal higher than another person who has not had such a successful background (see Brame, 1979). Such goals might not be realistic, however; as I pointed out in Chapter 10 it is difficult to predict (even for yourself) success in one skill from knowledge about success in some other. Second, given equal backgrounds and abilities, setting goals higher will perhaps mean that the person intends to "try harder" or practice longer at the task and achieve the resulting gains in the amount learned.

A number of experimenters have shown that if subjects can be convinced to set higher goals for themselves, the result is better performance on the task. For example, Locke and Bryan (1966) had two groups of subjects adopt different goals (standards) before they learned the Complex Coordination Task; subjects had to manipulate a two-dimensional hand control and a foot control simultaneously to control movements of lights on a display. One group was told to "do your best," which is rather typical instruction given in both laboratory and educational settings. Another group was encouraged to adopt a goal that was more difficult.

The results of their study are shown in Figure 12-1. The group of subjects told to "do your best" did not perform the task as effectively as the group that adopted the high standards. Be careful in interpreting these effects as *learning effects*, though, as no transfer design was used; the effects could be due to the *temporary effects* of motivation and not to learning, as we might suspect from the figure. If these are learning effects, then it seems reasonable to suspect that once a different goal has been adopted by the learner, failures to reach that goal during practice are "energizing" in terms of trying harder or practicing longer on the task. On the other hand, it is also possible that setting a goal so high that achievement is not realistically possible might result in discouragement or too much motivation (see Chapter 5), and less learning on the task than would be experienced by no goal setting at all.

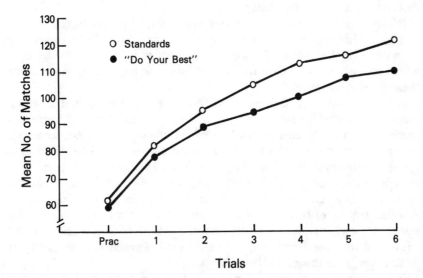

Figure 12-1. The effect of setting a standard for performance of the Mashburn task (from Locke & Bryan, 1966).

Also, if one expects to be able to perform well on a new motor task, performance and learning can be improved relative to expectations of a failure. For example, Brame (1979) gave subjects false feedback (either positive or negative) about their performances on the pursuit rotor task and showed that positive feedback enhanced the subsequent learning of the stabilometer balance task relative to negative feedback. She suggested that the positive feedback indicated to subjects that they would be effective at motor learning, and this led to more effective practice at the subsequent task.

Getting the Idea of the Task

After the learner has become motivated to learn the task, it is important to give the person some sort of "idea" or image or the nature of the task to be learned. There are many ways to do this, of course, such as with films, verbal instructions, demonstrations, and so on. Some of these are discussed in the next sections.

Instructions

Certainly one of the most traditional ways of giving students an initial orientation to the new task is through verbal instructions, usually presented by the teacher or instructor. Instructions can provide useful and important information, such as the initial positions of the limbs in relationship to apparatus or implements used, the stance, what to watch for, and what to do. Perhaps more importantly, an overall "idea" or image of the movement can be conveyed that can serve as a guide for the first attempt. Also, instructions can emphasize the ways to recognize one's own errors; e.g., "After the movement, check to see that your arm is straight." Thus, these kinds of instructions can serve as the beginning of the subject's error-detection mechanism (see Chapter 4).

It certainly seems that instructions are a critical aspect of the learning situation. However, as Newell (in press) has pointed out, little research has been done on the nature of instructions, so there is little knowledge upon which to base our suspicion that instructions are important. But consider the following situation.

A learner comes into a room where a complex piece of laboratory equipment is located which is totally foreign to the subject. The only instruction received from the teacher is "Go!" Imagine the student's bewilderment at trying to figure out what to do. He or she would not know whether to sit on the apparatus, push it around the room, or try to take it apart. Clearly, instructions about how to perform the task, what to do, and what to attempt to achieve as a score will be critical at this stage in the learning process. Another feature of this kind of instruction is that it tells the students what *not* to do; e.g., "Don't sit on it; rather, hold it like this." The students, without instructions, might require a great deal of practice, effort, and time to discover these things on their own.

But as important as instructions are, it is generally believed that instructions are often overused in learning situations. Words alone are relatively crude descriptions of the complex kinds of movements that a learner is attempting to achieve; just try to describe the actions in pole-vaulting, for example. Only the most global, general aspects of the intended movement are going to be transmitted through verbal instructions. Also, a learner can remember only so much about the instructions, and many of these important points will not be assimilated on the first trials of practice. This problem seems even more critical when dealing with children, whose attention span is probably much shorter than those of adults.

One solution is to describe in words those aspects of the skills that are absolutely essential for the first trial or two, making sure that learners achieve them in early practice. Then, as the first important elements are achieved, the learners can be instructed verbally (or with other techniques) as to the next most important aspect(s) to attend to, and so on. In this way, the students are not overloaded with many relatively gross descriptions of action, and progress would seem to be more rapid. The problem is that few investigations have been done on the nature of instructions. We need to know, for example, whether or not the complexity of the instructions should be tailored to the age of the subjects (you would think so), as well as how such instructions should be distributed during the learning sequence. Experimentation in motor learning has been negligent in this respect.

Modeling and Demonstrations

It seems clear that instructions alone are relatively ineffective as aids to learning motor skills and that other techniques can be used along with instructions to greatly facilitate initial performance. One important way to do this is to demonstrate the skill so that the elements of the action can be seen directly by the learners. The learner can then model the action during initial practice. Another variant, of course, is the use of movies, loop-films, videotapes, or even photos of skilled performers. At a superficial level, these procedures seem to be the same, with the demonstrator or model providing essential information about the task to be learned as well as some essential details about technique. But, while widely used, these techniques are not well supported by the experimental evidence.

There is mounting evidence that modeling techniques are important for the acquisition of motor skills, though. For example, Donna Landers (1975) asked three groups to learn the Bachman ladder task, (see Figure 3-11, page 77), for which subjects attempted to climb as high as possible on a specially constructed free-standing ladder. All subjects received tape-recorded verbal instructions, but the groups differed in terms of when an additional, live modeling demonstration was given. One group (Before) was given the demonstration before any practice began, a second group (Middle) was given the demonstration midway through the practice sequence, and the third group (Both) was given the demonstration both before and midway through practice.

The results of Landers' study are shown in Figure 12-2. The two groups given modeling (Before and Both) performed more effectively on the first trial than did the group with only instructions (Middle), showing the benefits of the demonstration. Also, compare the performance of the

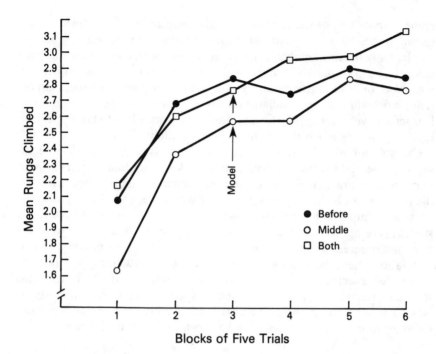

Figure 12-2. Performance on the Bachman ladder task as a function of modeling conditions. [A live demonstration was received prior to practice (Before), during practice indicated by the arrow (Middle), or both at times (Both).] (from Donna Landers, 1975).

Before condition with that of the Both condition that received another demonstration mid-way through the practice session (indicated by the arrow in the figure). The performance was sharply improved, suggesting that the model is important during the practice sequence as well as before it.

Using similar techniques, Landers and Landers (1973) studied modeling effects with subjects of differing initial skill levels on the Bachman ladder task. For the low-skilled subjects, the use of a peer-model was more effective than was the use of a teacher-model. For the high-skilled subjects, however, the reverse was true, with the teacher-model being the more effective. The peer- and teacher-models were selected on the basis of having equal ability, and thus the effect was not due to the teacher-model being the better performer.

These experiments indicate the kind of work on modeling that has been done. Some of these findings are perhaps what we would expect, because it is well known that children mimic adults and other children in many situations. A great deal of children's learning is *observational learning*, without any formal practice at all. Even so, these initial attempts to study modeling in the laboratory pave the way for subsequent experiments that will investigate aspects of modeling that are not so easily predictable. This is an area of research with many unanswered questions, but with practical applications.

Verbal Pretraining

Another prepractice technique for improving the initial performance of the learner is based on giving the person exposure to the stimuli that are going to be experienced in the task when actual practice begins. In this way, the new set of stimuli will not take the person by surprise, their temporal and spatial regularities can be learned, and the performance of the task with the actual stimuli may be more effective when the entire task is put together. Examples might be a batter watching the flight of a curve ball in baseball a number of times before swinging at it, a race car driver walking through a road-racing course before driving it, and so on.

These techniques have generally been studied under the heading of *verbal pretraining*, a somewhat misleading label because the pretraining is not always verbal. A typical experiment would involve the presentation of stimulus information separately before practice, requiring the subject to make verbal (or other) responses to the stimuli; these responses would not be used in the actual performance of the task. For example, the race car driver could be asked to make verbal responses having to do with the direction of a turn and its "tightness" as the race course is traversed.

Adams and Creamer (1962) used a technique like this in a laboratory situation. Subjects were to learn a tracking task that involved moving a lever to follow a stimulus dot in a regular sine-wave pattern, with the dot moving regularly back and forth. Subjects were asked to watch these stimuli and to respond by pressing a button every time the stimulus reversed direction, attempting to anticipate its movement. After considerable experience with this task, subjects were "transferred" to the task in which the same stimuli were used, but now lever movements had to be made with the hand to follow the dot instead of the earlier button press. Subjects who had experienced the verbal pretraining were more accurate in tracking than were subjects who had not had this experience. Similar findings were produced by Trumbo, Ulrich, and Noble (1965) when they had subjects learn to name each stimulus position in a regular series. When subjects had learned to anticipate the order of stimulus positions through this naming activity, they were more effective in responding to those stimuli in a tracking task (see also Schmidt, 1968, for a review).

Thus, on logical grounds as well as on the basis of the evidence, it seems clear that providing subjects with experience about the upcoming stimuli for a task is valuable in having adequate performance on the first few practice trials. Such stimulus presentations should be as realistic as possible, and they should be structured so that the learner attends and responds to them in some way, rather than merely watching passively. With a little ingenuity, these techniques could be modified to fit a wide variety of performance tasks that are to be learned in sport or in industry.

Knowledge of Mechanical Principles

How much should learners know about mechanical principles underlying a particular movement task? Will such knowledge, if provided before the learning of the task begins, be an aid to future performance and learning? Early work on dart throwing to targets submerged under water by Judd (1908) gave some initial indications that such information was useful. Judd showed the learners the principles of refraction, whereby the light rays from the submerged target were bent so that the target was not really where it appeared, and this provided an initial advantage in the task. Practice at the actual task was necessary in order that this knowledge be utilized completely. But, on the other hand, Polanyi (1958) cites an example of a champion cyclist who did not know the mechanical principles involved in the maintenance of balance on the machine, implying that such principles may not be critical for learning the task. This is a complex area, and more work is needed to be able to make definitive statements about these variables. For more on this issue, see Lawther (1968) or Newell (in press) for reviews.

Establishing a Prepractice Reference of Correctness

A number of procedures have been used in skill learning situations that can be interpreted as providing a reference of correctness for the response before any practice has been provided. The reference of correctness, from Chapter 4, is the "heart" of the closed-loop system. It is the structure against which feedback from the movement is compared in order to compute an error in the response. If the response is a very slow one, then the feedback can be used on the next trial after appropriate adjustments to the movement program are made.

One crude way that such references of correctness can be established is through instruction. For example, in giving information about a movement on the still rings in gymnastics, I might say, "You will first feel yourself floating through space and then you will feel a firm, forceful 'tug' at the hands and shoulder joints." This description of a "giant swing" warns the performer about the upcoming sensory feedback from the movement and provides a rough basis for the performer's knowing that he or she did something wrong if this pattern of feedback does not occur in the movement.

But verbal instructions about feedback are quite crude, and more detailed references of correctness can be established by numerous other means. Perhaps the most famous of these is the *Suzuki method* for teaching young children to play the violin (Suzuki, 1969). This method has many facets, but in one application a recorded piece is played to the student repeatedly, establishing a memory about how the properly played music should sound. After much exposure to the correct sound, the student is then allowed to practice. Presumably, as the student attempts to play, he or she compares the sounds actually made against the reference of correctness established by the recorded violin sounds. Deviations from the student's own reference of correctness suggest errors that must be corrected in subsequent attempts. These techniques are reportedly quite successful, and many excellent young violinists have been trained in this way.

Analogous methods have been used by Zelaznik and Spring (1976) and Zelaznik, Shapiro, and Newell (1978) with rapid ballistic timing tasks. Prior to any practice, they provided one group of subjects with the recorded sounds of another subject making the correct movement. After this presentation, this group was able to perform the movement more accurately than another group that had not listened to the sounds. They even showed that the "listening group" could improve slightly in the task without any knowledge of results. The interpretation of these findings is that the listening experience provided the subjects with a reference of correctness, and the reference allowed an evaluation of the auditory feedback produced by the movement and subsequent adjustments on the upcoming trials (see also Wrisberg & Schmidt, 1975). Similar techniques have been tried with auditory feedback in fly casting (Lionvale, cited in Keele & Summers, 1976) and other tasks (Keele, Note 3), but without much success in improving learning.

Overall, the idea of generating a reference of correctness prior to practice appears to be a good one. But more research must be done on this issue before a successful practical application can be made to other motor learning situations.

STRUCTURING THE PRACTICE SESSION

After successfully orienting learners to the motor task, the actual session of practice must be structured so that the amount that is learned is maximized. Seemingly countless variables can affect the way the session is structured; we will consider only several of the more important ones here.

The Most Important: Practice and KR

Certainly two variables dwarf all the others in terms of importance. One is so obvious that it need hardly be mentioned at all—practice. Clearly, more learning will occur if there are more practice trials, other things being equal. A few circumstances exist for which this relationship appears to be incorrect, such as when people practice without any "intention" to learn (but see Dickinson, 1977) or when there is inadequate feedback about performance. But usually more practice leads to more learning. We have evidence of this in high-level sports competition and in industrial tasks, where best performers have devoted an extensive amount of time to their respective activities. Perhaps I do not need to say any more about the variable of trials except this: In structuring the practice session, the number of practice attempts should be maximized.

The second variable of immense importance is knowledge of results (abbreviated KR) and feedback (Chapter 6). KR refers to the information about success in the task that the performer receives after the trial has been completed, and it serves as a basis for corrections on the next trial, leading to more effective performance as trials continue. Without any knowledge of success in the task as practice continues, learning may be drastically reduced—or nonexistent—even though many practice trials are provided. Because of the importance of this variable, substantial research has been done on it, and Chapter 13 is reserved for this issue. KR and feedback are critical for learning, and they must be considered carefully in the design of any learning environment; by contrast, the variables that comprise the remainder of this section are relatively insignificant in their effects on learning.

Massed vs. Distributed Practice

One of the variables teachers have under their control is the scheduling of practice and rest periods. In attempting to study this variable in laboratory settings, experimenters have rather arbitrarily labeled *massed* those practice sessions in which the amount of practice time in a trial is greater than the amount of rest between trials, eventually leading to fatigue in many tasks. For *distributed* practice, on the other hand, the amount of rest between trials equals or exceeds the amount of time in a trial, leading to a somewhat more "restful" practice sequence. In studying the effect of these schedules on motor learning, most of the research on massed *vs.* distributed practice has been used continuous tasks, for which the practice trial might be 20 or 30 sec in duration. I will consider these tasks first and then present some research on a discrete task that appears to have very different results.

Continuous Tasks

During the 1940s and 1950s, many studies investigated the effect of massed and distributed practice on performance. Invariably, the conclusions were the same: The limitation of rest between trials in the massed conditions led to systematically decreased performance compared to the more rested distributed practice. Even though these experiments did not use transfer designs, the conclusions were usually some form of the statement that massed practice interferes with learning, and numerous textbooks adopted this conclusion as a basis for recommendations about the structure of practice sessions.

In Chapter 11, I discussed the limitations of experiments on learning that did not use transfer designs. In this instance, the primary problem is that we cannot be certain whether the massed practice actually interfered with the learning of the task, or whether only a temporary decrement in performance occurred which would disappear when a rest period was provided. That such temporary effects were present in the data was well known at the time; in fact, the recovery in performance following a rest period was given a special name, *reminiscence*, and considerable research was devoted to this recovery phenomenon (see Adams, 1964, for a review). Thus, because at least part of the decrement in performance displayed by the massed group was due to temporary fatigue, not all of the effect could be due to decreases in learning. But how much was due to learning?

A landmark study in this area was by Adams and Reynolds (1954). It was the first study to use a transfer design to evaluate the effects of massed versus distributed practice, and the first to use transfer designs in studying learning. The task was the pursuit rotor, and distributed practice was defined as 30-sec practice trials each followed by a 30-sec rest. Massed practice involved the same trial duration but with only 5-sec rest. One group of subjects (D) received 40 trials under distributed conditions. Four more groups received initial practice for 5, 10, 15, or 20 trials respectively under massed conditions, then rested for 10 min, and then transferred to the distributed-practice condition for the remainder of the 40 practice trials (Groups 5, 10, 15, and 20). Thus, the experiment involved a transfer design, in which the

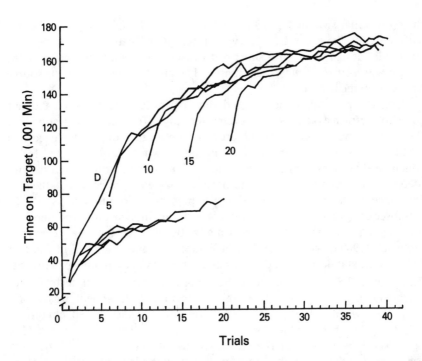

Figure 12-3. Pursuit-rotor performance under massed and distributed practice. (Four groups had various numbers of massed practice trials before a 10-min rest and they shifted to distributed practice.) (from Adams & Reynolds, 1954).

various massed-practice groups were transferred to distributed practice after a rest, so that the relative amount of learning in the earlier trials could be evaluated by the level of performance on the transfer trials.

Adams' and Reynolds' results are shown in Figure 12-3. Notice that as with the earlier studies of massing, marked decrements in performance occurred when the practice was massed. But when the massed subjects were allowed to rest and were then shifted to distributed practice, a large jump in performance level (i.e., *reminiscence*) occurred in every case on the first trial. And the difference between the (formerly) massed and distributed groups disappeared by about the third trial after the shift to distributed practice. Because the performance level on the transfer test is a measure of the relative amount learned and because the formerly massed groups and the distributed group had about equivalent performance on the transfer test, the conclusion is that they learned about the same amount in the practice sequence. Thus, massing was not, in this experiment at least, a variable that affected learning.

Two points need to be made about this conclusion. First, I have indicated that there were no performance differences between the massed and distributed groups on the transfer trials, and from Figure 12-3 you can see that this is not quite correct. The mass-distributed differences were quite large on the first transfer trial and were smaller on the second and third, being essentially eliminated by the fourth. While perhaps these differences should be interpreted as though the group with previously massed practice had learned less than the distributed group, the differences could just as easily exist because the groups that switched had a rest while the distributed group that did not shift did not have a rest. This was not a good feature in Adams' and Reynolds' design, as even a short rest causes a decrement in performance (called *warm-up decrement*; see Chapter 15), and this is probably the source of the decrement here.

Next, the previously massed and the distributed groups often did not come to perform exactly equally even after quite a few trials, suggesting that there was some tendency for the previously massed group to have learned slightly less than the distributed group did. It would probably be safer to conclude that massed practice produced slightly less learning than distributed practice; even so, most of the effect of massed practice was on the performance of the task while massing was present (before the rest).

Subsequent to the Adams-Reynolds experiment, various experimenters investigated the same problem using a transfer design. For example, Stelmach (1969a), whose data are in Figure 11-8 and discussed in Chapter 11, used the stabilometer and Bachman ladder tasks in separate experiments (See Figures 3-8 and 3-11). He found a marked decrement in performance when massing was present, but this performance decrement was nearly eliminated when subjects were transferred to the distributed condition. Whitley (1970) has produced similar results using a foot-operated tracking task. Nearly every one of the recent studies of massed versus distributed practice using the acceptable transfer-design methods has shown that massing is a variable that affects peformance on the task drastically while massing is present but that massing affects learning only slightly as measured by performance on a transfer test in distributed conditions (McGown, Note 20). Thus, the evidence suggests that massing is a powerful performance variable and a relatively weak learning variable.

How can learners practice a task under massed conditions, when performance is clearly inferior to that experienced under distributed conditions, and yet learn just about as much? These effects seem clearly contrary to intuition, as it would seem that fatigue associated with massing would cause people to learn the "wrong" movements. One hypothesis (e.g., Johnson, Note 21) is that the massed practice causes a great deal of variability in the movements that are produced in practice (hence lower skill levels), and that this increased variability in practice somehow leads to stronger learning of the task, which compensates for negative effects of fatigue. In a subsequent section, I provide a great deal of evidence that variability in practice, compared to constant practice (e.g., practicing hitting a baseball with a constant pitch from a machine versus a variable pitch from a human pitcher), can lead to increased learning of the task.

A second hypothesis is that massed practice makes the task more effortful, and this increased "difficulty" causes the learners to process the information about the task at a relatively "deeper" level (i.e., more thoroughly and/or abstractly). I will deal with this issue more directly in Chapters 13 and 14 (see also Chapter 4). Whatever the reason for the effective learning under massed conditions, it is clear that it happens and that we need to be aware of these effects in designing practice sequences.

Discrete Tasks

The evidence about discrete tasks is not as complete as it is for continuous tasks. However, one study by Carron (1967, 1969) does bear on the massing issue with a discrete task, and the results are quite interesting.

Carron used a peg-turn task in which the subject held his hand on a switch; in response to a sound stimulus he moved 44 cm from the switch to grasp a peg in a hole, turned the peg end-for-end to reinsert it into the hole, and then returned to the key again as quickly as possible. This response was discrete and required a MT of from 1,300 to 1,700 msec depending on the level of skill of the performers. Carron had people learn this task under two conditions: distributed (the amount of rest between trials was 5 sec) and massed (the amount of rest between trials was only 300 msec, with a 5-sec rest every 10 trials). There were two days of practice with 60 trials on each day.

Contrary to the findings for the continuous tasks mentioned above, Carron found no effect of the massing conditions on performance of the task on the first day while the massing was present. Thus, massing in this discrete task was not a performance variable. Furthermore, when he tested the subjects 48 hr later as a measure of learning, he found that the massed subjects actually performed slightly faster than the distributed subjects (1,430 versus 1,510 msec), but it is probably more reasonable to say there were no real differences.[1] Because the subjects in the massed and distributed conditions performed equivalently on the transfer test, the conclusion was that they learned approximately equivalent amounts on the first day. Thus, for the discrete peg-turn task massing was neither a performance variable nor a learning variable. I know of no other massing experiments on discrete tasks to which these findings can be compared, so we are left with the conclusion that massing does not seem to have any effect—either learning or performance effects—on discrete tasks.

These differences in findings between the continuous and discrete tasks are quite clear and yet difficult to explain. The subjects in the massed condition, you will remember, had nearly no rest between trials at all (300 msec), and they were clearly hurried in the task; yet they performed and learned the task as effectively as the more leisurely paced distributed subjects did. It is possible that the hurried nature of the massed conditions resulted in more effort being expended with the result being an increased performance that overcame the decrements due to fatigue; but this is purely speculation, and we cannot be sure about the cause at this stage. In any case, it does not seem that massing is a problem for either performance or learning of discrete tasks. This is especially important because many of the tasks that are learned in sport settings are of this general type (e.g., hitting, kicking, throwing, etc.).

---

[1]There was no transfer test, actually, as the Day 2 performance was under the same conditions as Day 1. But this measure—i.e., the average of the first two Day 2 trials—gives an estimate of relative amount learned uncontaminated by fatigue.

Massing and Practice Time

From the foregoing discussions, you may come to the conclusion that one should distribute the practice in learning sessions, because massed practice did not result in more learning, and frequently resulted in slightly less learning, than the distributed-practice condition. But there is another important variable that interacts with massing—the *time* involved in practice. Recall that in the experiments presented so far about massing, the number of practice trials was held constant; and because the amount of time between practice trials was different for the massed and distributed conditions, the overall practice time was allowed to vary. That is, a group receiving massed practice will have a shorter practice session than will an equivalent group with distributed practice. When you remember that the massed groups often learned nearly as much as the distributed practice groups, you might consider that massing is a slightly more efficient way to distribute the practice since it "saves" much time at the "expense" of a little decrement in learning. Perhaps the "saved" time could be devoted to more practice, as more practice will result in more learning.

In many teaching situations, the practice time is fixed, and the instructor has the responsibility for making the most efficient use of that time to maximize the amount of learning. Graw (1968) investigated the structure of the practice session in two parallel experiments, one using the stabilometer (Figure 3-8) and the other using the Bachman ladder task (Figure 3-11). There was a constant 30-min practice period, and Graw used different degrees of massed practice so that the total time for practice plus rest was 30 min. Table 12-1 gives the essential details of the design of each experiment. Five groups (A through E) differed in the amount of rest they were allowed between practice trials; hence, they differed with respect to the number of trials that could be fit into the 30-min period. For example, Group A spent 20% of the 30 min in practice (6 min), with the remainder devoted to rest between trials. On the other hand, Group E devoted 77% of its 30 min to practice (23 min, or about four times the time spent by Group A), with little

Table 12-1

Total practice and rest time, and percentage of time spent in practice, in a study of stabilometer and ladder learning (from Graw, 1968)

Group	Total Practice (min)	Total Rest (min)	% of Time in Practice
A	6	24	20
B	9	21	30
C	12	18	40
D	17	13	57
E	23	7	77

Note: Total session time was 30 min in all groups.

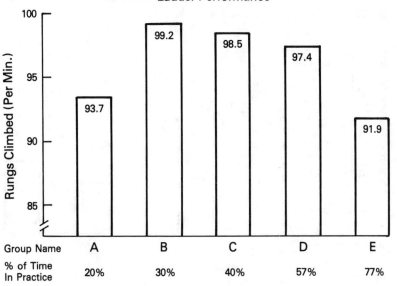

Figure 12-4. Initial Day 2 ladder performance as a function of practice distribution on Day 1. (The percentage of the 30-min practice session spent in actual physical practice was varied.) (from Graw, 1968).

rest between practice trials. Which group learned the most?

Consider first the results from the ladder task shown in Figure 12-4. Here, the average performance on the first transfer trial on Day 2 is given. It seemed clear that Group B (30% of the time in practice) had learned most, closely followed by Groups C (40%) and D (57%). The extreme conditions—Groups A (20%) and E (77%)—clearly learned least in the task. These results say that the most effective practice distribution in this case is reasonably distributed, with from 30% to 57% of the total time spent in practice. Too much rest between trials (Group A) apparently wastes time, whereas too little rest (Group E) is too fatiguing, resulting in less learning.

Next, the analogous scores for the stabilometer task are shown in Figure 12-5. Remember, scores for the stabilometer decrease with practice, and lower scores are "better," just the opposite of the ladder scores in Figure 12-4. For the stabilometer, the most effective performance was from Group D (57% of the time spent in practice), closely followed by Group E (77%). As the amount of rest between trials increased, the amount learned progressively decreased, with the least amount of learning being shown by Group A (20%). Thus, in this task the most effective schedule for practice under these conditions was one in which the practice was quite massed and the amount of rest was small, a pattern that was quite different from that shown by the ladder task in Figure 12-4.

Why should the practice distribution producing the most effective learning be more massed in the stabilometer task than it is in the ladder task? Graw's data do not provide the answer to this question, but one suggestion is related to the energy costs of these two tasks. In the stabilometer task, a very highly skilled performer is hardly moving at all, merely using small ad-

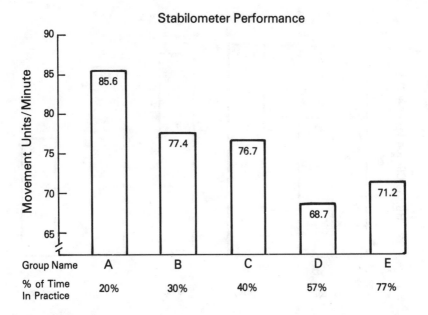

Figure 12-5. Initial Day 2 stabilometer performance as a function of practice distribution on Day 1. (The percentage of the 30-min practice session spent in actual physical practice was varied.) (from Graw, 1968).

justments to balance on the unstable board, and the energy cost of the task appears to decrease with practice. In the Bachman ladder task, however, a highly skilled performer is climbing very high and fast, and the energy costs seems to increase with practice. If so, could it be that the most effective schedule for learning motor skills will be dependent at least in part on the energy cost of the task? This is certainly an appealing hypothesis in this situation.

The implications of Graw's experiments are interesting for the design of learning situations. First, we should recognize that a single, optimal distribution of practice and rest periods does not exist, and that this choice will probably depend on the task that is to be learned. If the task is discrete (e.g., Carron, 1967, 1969), then the practice should be massed as completely as possible, jamming as many practice trials as is practically possible into a practice period. If the task is continuous, then the distribution of practice would seem to depend on such factors as the need for rest, due largely to the way in which the task requires energy as improvements with practice are realized. If the task does not appear to have high energy costs, then we might be safe in massing the practice greatly (e.g., the stabilometer task in Graw's study); and if the task is high in energy cost, such as the Bachman ladder task, then we should probably increase the amount of rest between trials.

Two final points are in order. First, it should be clear that massing has strong effects on performance of many tasks and that the risks of injury in dangerous tasks are going to increase with massed practice. The laboratory tasks used here are not particularly dangerous, but many tasks used in sport (e.g., giant swings on the horizontal bar) and industry (e.g., using a hydraulic paper cutter) have considerably more opportunity for serious injury if errors are made. Thus, caution should be used in applying these massing principles to the design of dangerous learning environments. Second, the measure of the learning to be used for the grading or other evaluation procedures should not be taken on the practice trials. The amount learned, and hence the grade assigned to the performance, should be based on the transfer trials, for which the performance is under rested conditions, because only here is the relative amount of learning demonstrated. In many cases, this requires a test phase on a different day of practice than the original learning session. See also the discussion of grading in Chapter 11.

Scheduling Practice Sessions

A slightly different use of massed and distributed practice is sometimes studied in which the question is related to how many times per day or per week a given segment of instruction should be presented and how long each of these segments should be. A recent study by Baddeley and Longman (1978) employed postal workers who learned to use a typewriter keyboard to control a letter-sorting machine. Four groups of subjects were used, with either a 1-hr or 2-hr session presented either one or two times each day. In Figure 12-6 are the performance curves for these four groups. The initial point in each curve represents the number of hours practiced until all of the keystrokes could be touchtyped correctly, and then the subjects' rates of performance increased rather steadily in all conditions. But there appeared to be a strong performance advantage for the group with the most distributed practice conditions, with 1 hr of practice only once per day. Similarly, the group with the most massed conditions, which had 2 hr of practice twice per day, performed the poorest. While these data suggest the idea that learning is maximized with short practice periods and a small number of practice periods per day, regard these results with caution as no transfer

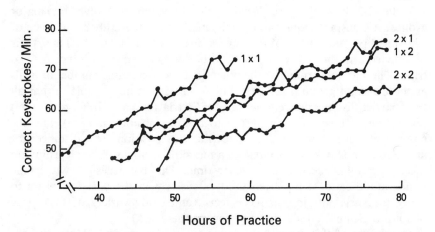

Figure 12-6. Performance in a keyboard task for various practice schedules. (The labels in dicate the number of hours of practice and the number of practice days per week; e.g., 1 × 2 = 1 hr twice a week.) (from Baddeley & Longman, 1978).

design was employed. How would you have designed the study differently?

This aspect of massed and distributed practice has perhaps more relevance for the design of instructional settings than does the earlier work dealing with the temporal spacing of trials within a setting. Yet, by contrast, little research on this question has been completed, and a great deal more needs to be done to understand the relevant variables and how they operate to maximize learning.

Variability in Practice

Another factor shown to affect learning is the amount of variability in a practice sequence. As an example, consider learning to play a particular position in baseball, say shortstop. I could learn to field ground balls in basically two ways. One way to practice might involve the presentation of 100 ground balls delivered from a pitching machine, each being essentially the same with respect to the speed, number of bounces, direction, etc. A second way to practice would be to receive the same number of balls to field, but with every one of them different in its location and direction and in its flight, roll, and bounce characteristics. Which of these ways would produce the most learning with respect to the task of becoming a shortstop on a baseball team? Consider some of the evidence from laboratory tasks that seems to bear on this question.

McCracken and Stelmach (1977) used a task in which subjects were to move the right hand from a starting key to knock over a barrier, moving at such a speed that the time from initial movement to barrier contact was 200 msec. They allowed subjects to follow through past the target, and so the response was essentially the ballistic-timing task that I described earlier (e.g., Schmidt & White, 1972). The task could be changed slightly by changing the locations of the barriers, thereby altering the distance to be moved. In the study, distances of 15, 35, 60, and 65 cm were used in the original practice phase.

Table 12-2 shows the basic design of the study, which involved two major groups. A Constant group was actually made up of four subgroups, each of which had practice at one of the barrier distances for 300 trials. Thus, their experience with the task was limited to but one movement distance for 300 trials. The Variable group, on the other hand, had the same number of trials as the Constant group (i.e., 300), but these trials were variable in that all four barrier distances were practiced for 75 trials of each. In a transfer test phase, the groups were transferred to a novel position (50 cm), and the amount of learning was evaluated for this new position. This distance was also tested on Day 2 (48 hr later) as a measure of how well the learning on the first day had been retained over time. This basic design, with some minor modifications, has been used extensively in the past few years to study the variability-in-practice effects for a wide variety of tasks (see Shapiro & Schmidt, 1982, for a review of this work).

The results of this experiment are shown in Figure 12-7. Here, the absolute errors are plotted for the trials that comprised the end of the original practice phase, as well as for the average of the trials on the two transfer test

Table 12-2

**Experimental design for an experiment on variability in practice
(adapted from McCracken & Stelmach, 1977)**

Group	Original Practice Phase	Transfer Test Phase	
	300 Trials Day 1	Immediate Day 1	Delayed Day 2
Constant			
Subgroup a	15 cm only	50 cm	50 cm
Subgroup b	35 cm only	50 cm	50 cm
Subgroup c	60 cm only	50 cm	50 cm
Subgroup d	65 cm only	50 cm	50 cm
Variable	15, 35, 60, and 65 cm in random order	50 cm	50 cm

phases. Consider first the original practice phase, for which the Constant group had less absolute error than the Variable group. This should not be a surprise, as it has been known for a long time that people can do one thing more effectively than they can do four things. The critical contrast, however, is on the immediate transfer test phase, when the movement was "novel" for both groups. Here, the order of the groups was reversed, with the Variable group now having *less* absolute error than the Constant group.

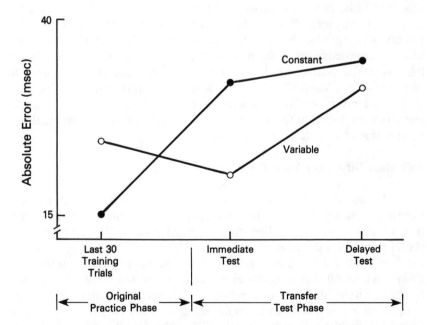

Figure 12-7. Performance in a ballistic timing task as a function of variability in practice conditions (from McCracken & Stelmach, 1977).

This trend persisted into the test phase 48 hr later, but the difference between groups was considerably smaller. Thus, it appeared that variability in practice (during the original practice phase) allowed the subjects to learn the task more effectively, allowing them to perform a new version of the task on the test phase with less error than the Constant group. A number of questions can be raised about this study and its applications. Some of these are considered in the next sections.

Shapiro and Schmidt (1982) reviewed the variability-in-practice literature, emerging with a number of important generalizations. First, if the task is closed, with the environment stable from trial to trial (and within a trial) as defined in Chapter 3, then the literature on adults suggests that variability in practice is about as effective as constant practice in producing learning in the task; at least it is probably not any worse. In a way, the McCracken and Stelmach study represents a contradiction to this generalization, because their task was, according to the definition, closed. Yet in another sense their task can be considered open, in that in the training phase the movement for the Variable groups was not the same from trial to trial, providing somewhat more uncertainty about the movement than is usually the case with perfectly constant closed skills (e.g., with bowling). Also, Wrisberg and Ragsdale (1979) showed similar findings in a task requiring the subject to press a button when a series of "moving" lights arrived at a target—a task that is more or less like timing the arrival of a baseball at the plate, but without the batswing. Variable experience with the velocity of the "moving" lights provided more transfer to a novel speed than constant practice did; however, the transfer-test task was, according to definition, closed because the light speeds were the same on each trial.

But what if the transfer task were truly open, such as the task of playing shortstop in baseball? Here, we might suspect that variability in practice might be even more effective than constant practice, largely because the subject can never plan the movement before the ball is hit and must respond with the knowledge and skill built up over many prior experiences. While this sounds reasonable, and I suspect that it could be shown to be correct in an experiment, I know of no evidence about variability in practice for open skills that supports it. Given the number of skills in daily life that are open, and given the potential for methods involving variability in practice, this is an area that clearly deserves more study.

Individual Difference Variables

The effects of practice variability seem to depend on the nature of the learners. Certainly the most obvious classification is children versus adults. In our recent review of the literature on practice variability, Shapiro and I (1982) found that the advantage for variable versus constant practice was small in adult subjects; but, for children, the advantage was extremely strong. We found that in nearly every study conducted more effective performance on the novel test task occurred when earlier practice was variable as opposed to constant. For example, using a strictly closed throwing skill with young children, Kerr and Booth (1977, 1978) found in two experiments that variable practice was more effective than constant practice when subjects were transferred to a novel version of the task not performed earlier. Even more surprising was the finding that for learning this novel variation of the task, practice at variations of the task approximating the novel task was even more effective than was practicing the novel task itself. In marked contrast to the evidence for adult subjects, the evidence from motor learning studies on children shows that variability in practice is far more effective than constant practice. Practice variability appears to be a powerful variable in children's motor learning.

Another individual difference variable of interest is gender. Wrisberg and Ragsdale (1979), with a task for which the "arrival" of lights at a target was to be anticipated by the subject who was to press a button at the arrival time, found that college women profited from practice variability much more than college men did. In fact, it appeared that male subjects may not have profited at all, with all of the group differences being due to the effects of variability in women subjects. With children, as well, more gain was made by first-grade girls as a result of variability in practice than by first-grade boys (Allen, 1978). Thus, variability in practice tends to be more effective for females than for males, at least in these two studies.

Interpretation: Schema or Rule Learning

Most of the studies on variability in practice have been done in the context of a theory I proposed in 1975 called *schema theory* (Chapter 14). The basic premise is that with practice people develop rules (called *schemas*) about their own motor behavior. Think back to the ideas about the generalized motor program (Chapter 8), for which a set of parameters must be applied to the program in order to perform it. Schema theory proposes that subjects learn a rule in the practice sequence. This rule is a relationship between all the past environmental outcomes that the person produced and the values of the parameters that were used to produce those outcomes. Crudely, the rule is the relationship between what the subject "told the motor system to do" and what the motor system actually accomplished. This rule is maintained in memory and can be used to select a new set of parameters for the next movement situation that involves the same motor program. Knowing the rule and what environmental outcome is to be produced, the person can select the parameters for the program that will produce it. The schema theory is related to variability in practice, because the theory predicts that the generation of the rule will be more effective if the experience that leads to its development is varied rather than constant. I will refer to these experiments on variability in practice in Chapter 14 when schema theory is discussed in more detail.

On less theoretical grounds, it seems to make sense to use variable practice, especially for open skills for which the task is always changing. Considering the skill of being a shortstop again, it would seem important to provide the learner with as much experience as possible about what could *possibly* happen in the task, so that the learner could develop effective ways of coping with each of them as they arise in a game situation. Such experience could not be achieved if the practice were always constant and stereotyped, as with delivering balls without variation from a pitching machine. I suspect that the more open a task is, the more effective will be the variable practice. These techniques are a major theme in most youth-oriented "movement education" programs. [See Chapter 14 or Schmidt (1976b, 1977) for more on this issue.]

Why should variable practice be more effective for children and females? One idea is that children are less experienced at motor responding than older (adult) subjects are, so the rules (schemas) that the children acquire in laboratory settings have already been achieved by the adults in their earlier experiences with motor tasks. Also related to this is the idea that the tasks studied in the laboratory are very simple, and it is possible that the adults already have at their disposal the rules (schemas) necessary to perform the novel tasks, whereas the children must learn some of them in the experimental setting. Here, then, variable practice is more effective for children than for the adults because the children have considerably "more to learn" than the adults.

Regarding the issue of males versus females, one notion is similar to that for children. If females of all ages are, on the average, less experienced in movement behaviors than males, then it may be that females behave as though they are "younger," in a movement sense, than males. Perhaps as a result of some lack of movement experiences, the rules that relate the movement parameters to the movement outcomes (the schemas) are less developed than they are in males, so that the females profit by practice variability in these experiments more than the males do. It is possible that these kinds of observations will have important implications for the development of programs of instruction, but it is a bit early to be certain about it.

Context Effects

Apparently closely related to the findings about variability in practice is a set of findings concerned with what has been called *context effects*. In this work, factors that make the task more "difficult" for the subject have been studied. For example, requiring learners to pronounce nonsense "words" (e.g., XENF) whose letters correspond to individual finger movements makes performance on another version of the finger task more effective (Battig, 1956, 1966). Battig and others have interpreted these findings to mean that *intra*-task (or contextual) interference (the interference between the "word" pronunciations and the finger movements) produces greater *inter*-task transfer, i.e., it increases transfer to other similar motor tasks. Certainly these findings run counter to intuition, as we would expect that transfer to other tasks would be most effective if the first task were learned under the least difficult conditions. Why should it be that naming nonsense letters while performing would contribute to performance on a similar task?

Some of these questions have been investigated more directly by Shea and Morgan (1979). They had subjects learn a motor task in which a tennis ball had to be grasped in a start position, then a series of barriers had to be knocked over in rapid succession, and then the ball had to be placed in a finishing position. The goal was to make the required series of movements to the barriers in minimum time. These responses could be varied by changing the locations and number of the barriers, and before each trial subjects received a "map" indicating where to go.

Shea and Morgan studied the effect of variations in the tasks that the subjects were to learn. One group of subjects performed one of the variations for 18 trials, then switched to the second variation, etc., until all three variations were completed. This Blocked procedure presumably made it easier for the subject to perform the task, as within a block the task was always the same. A second condition (Random) involved a change in the task on every trial; the number of trials (54) and the number of variations (3) were the same as in the first condition, except that on every trial the task was changed. This is analogous to practicing one trial of a tennis forehand, one trial of a tennis serve, one trial of a tennis backhand, and so on, repeating this sequence until 18 trials of each task were practiced. The analogous Blocked condition would practice 18 trials of the tennis forehand, then switch to the serve, and then switch to the backhand without "mixing" them in the practice sequence. Which of these two basic methods would be most effective for learning?

The major results of the Shea and Morgan study are shown in Figure 12-8. Consider first the acquisition trials, in which the two groups of subjects (Blocked and Random) were practicing under different conditions. The Blocked condition showed a clear advantage; the MT on the first trial block was about half as long for the Blocked condition as it was for the Random condition, with the difference persisting throughout the 54 trials. But we cannot know if these differences are due to learning or to performance until the scores are examined under common transfer conditions.

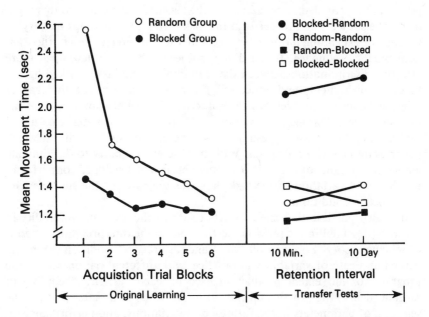

Figure 12-8. Performance on complex movement speed tasks under Random and Blocked presentations. (Relative amount learned is indicated on the transfer test at right.) (from Shea & Morgan, 1979).

These are shown in the right half of the figure, where transfer is measured after retention intervals of 10 min and 10 days.

Examine first only the curves in Figure 12-8 that have the filled and unfilled squares, which represent the transfer test under Blocked conditons. The group that had the earlier practice under the Random conditions (filled squares) performed more rapidly than the group that earlier had practiced under the Blocked conditions (unfilled squares). Thus, there was a reversal in the order of the groups; the treatment that produced the best performance in the acquisition trials (i.e., Blocked) produced the poorer performance in the Blocked transfer test, although the differences were quite small.

Now, focus on the filled and unfilled dots to the right in Figure 12-8. These represent the performance on the transfer test when the conditions were Random. There was a very large advantage for the group that had previously practiced under Random conditions (unfilled circles) compared to the group that had earlier practiced under Blocked conditions. Again, the most effective condition during the acquisition trials (Blocked) was the least effective for learning the task if it was to be performed under Random conditions, and the advantage was very large indeed.

Thus, for both transfer tests (under Random and Blocked conditions) it was more effective to have practiced the task under the more difficult conditions in acquisition (i.e., the Random condition). The practice sequence with the most contextual interference (the Random condition) produced the most effective transfer to a new task. This is certainly counter to intuition. What is happening here?

Shea and Morgan (1979) interpreted these findings in terms of the "levels of processing" concept described in Chapter 4. The idea is that the Random presentation provided interference for the learners. According to this argument, the subjects had to perform the task differently, perhaps by "trying harder" or expending more effort to counteract the interference of the Random practice sequence. By so doing, subjects may have developed more effective discrimination between the variations of the task, worked harder to distinguish them, and processed the relevant aspects of the task at "deeper" conceptual levels. In general terms, this is but another way to say that the subjects learned the task more effectively, but the specific nature of the learning difference is presumably the increase in the "depth" at which the relevant cues are processed. With this increased ability to discriminate among the variants of the task, a stronger basis was developed for performing the novel variation of the task than was the case for the subjects who had Blocked condition.

It is also possible that these effects relate to the ideas on variability in practice presented in the previous section and to the interpretation in terms of schema theory. For example, the Random practice condition can be regarded as a case of variability in practice, with different parameters of the program for movement production used on each variant. According to schema theory, the practice on the variations leads to a better rule for the selection of parameters in the future novel variations, and performance increases as a result. In a way, this is similar to the depth-of-processing idea, in that the development of abstract rules about movement behavior would seem to involve the processing of information about the tasks to "deeper" levels than would the more superficial performance of a task without the formation of such rules.

Whatever the explanation of these curious effects, it is clear they are present and cannot be ignored. As well, these effects have a number of interesting applications for practical learning situations. It may be possible that the traditional method of practicing a given task is less effective for learning than is practicing a different task on each trial; Shea's and Morgan's data seem to suggest this kind of generalization. If correct, we could design a learning environment that deliberately contains intra-task interference; that is, the teacher's task may be to develop learning environments that are purposely more difficult—not less difficult—for the learner. Variability in practice is just one of the ways that this can be done, as mentioned in the previous section.

Fatigue and Learning

Another factor that contributes to the amount learned in a practice session is fatigue, usually developed as a result of practicing the task itself. On one hand, fatigue could result in improper patterns of actions so that the learners practice the "wrong" movements. On the other hand, the earlier discussion about massing (a kind of mental fatigue, together with some physical fatigue) indicated that this was not a particularly important variable for motor learning. On these grounds, we might expect that physical fatigue and massing would have similar effects. As we shall see, the parallel is quite strong.

Many experiments in the 1960s and 1970s investigated the role of physical fatigue in the learning of motor skills. I have cited one of our own studies here, mainly because it seems to be typical of the earlier studies, and it profited by the early experiments in fatigue by reducing some of the design problems present in them. Godwin and I (1971) used a task called the "Sigma task," in which the subjects were to grasp a handle attached to a lever with the right hand, rotate it 350° clockwise until it hit a stop, rotate it 350° counterclockwise until it hit another stop, and then release the handle and move linearly to knock over a barrier. All this was to be done in minimum MT. Subjects learned the task under one of two conditions. The Non-fatigued group learned under "normal" circumstances, having 20 trials, each separated by 45 sec of rest. The Fatigued group, on the other hand, performed on an arm ergometer (a friction-brake cranking device used for inducing fatigue) for 2 min prior to the first practice trial and then for 45 sec between each of the 20 practice trials. The idea was to fatigue the subjects, in this case college women, during the pre-practice phase and to keep them fatigued throughout the remainder of the practice, so that all learning of the motor task would be accomplished under seriously fatigued conditions.

In keeping with the earlier discussions about the transfer designs (Chapter 11), all subjects were evaluated three days later under Nonfatigued conditions to obtain a measure of the relative amount learned on the first day. The results are in Figure 12-9. On Day 1, when the fatigue variable was applied, the Fatigued group had about 400-msec longer MT than the Nonfatigued group, and this effect appeared to remain throughout the practice phase. Certainly fatigue of the arm muscles had a serious negative effect on performance of the task. Did the fatigue affect learning? This question can be answered by considering the transfer trials shown at the right of the figure, where all performance was under Nonfatigued conditions. The group that had Fatigued practice on the first day performed less quickly than the group with Nonfatigued performance on Day 1, but this difference diminished across the 10 practice trials on Day 2. This evidence suggested that fatigue was slightly detrimental to the learning of this task.

These results should be put into perspective before they can be applied to the design of learning sessions. First, while there *was* a decrement in learning for the group that had Fatigued practice on Day 1, notice how severe the treatment was and how small the Day 2 differences were. The Fatigued group engaged in heavy ergometer exercise, which none of the subjects could maintain, and fatigue was intentionally maintained between trials by preventing rest and requiring additional ergometer cranking. These are procedures that we would never consider using in a "real" learning environment. Even so, the groups learned nearly the same amount, and we could estimate from the right half of Figure 12-9 that an additional five practice trials would have brought the fatigued subjects to the final level of performance demonstrated by the nonfatigued subjects. Even in this light, fatigue does not appear to be a critically important variable for learning. Many other studies show essentially the same thing.

An additional point is that fatigue is rapidly dissipated. For example, Clarke and Stull (1969) used a fatigue bout producing a 50% decrement in

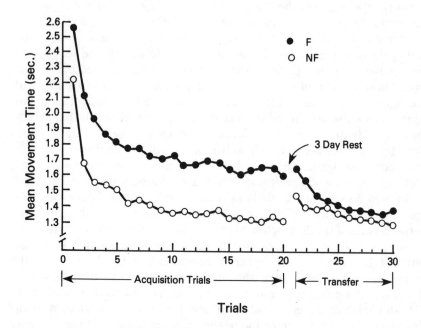

Figure 12-9. Performance on the Sigma movement speed task as a function of conditions of artificially induced fatigue. (Relative amount learned is shown in the transfer test under nonfatigued conditions at the right; from Godwin & Schmidt, 1971.)

strength. After only 60 sec of rest, the subjects were able to produce about 88% of their maximum strength, and recovery was totally complete in about 4 min. This kind of evidence suggests that in practical situations when fatigue may be accumulated as a result of practice or other activities (a) this fatigue will not be critically detrimental to the learning of a task that is attempted and (b) much if not all of the fatigue will have dissipated by the time that practice is under way. Some residual fatigue probably will remain during this practice, but its effects will be so small on the task learning that they can probably be ignored. As with the massing effects, fatigue can cause sloppy performance, so the danger of the task must be taken into account. But overall, one can probably stop worrying about fatigue as a variable that seriously affects learning of the tasks.

These observations create possibilities in practical situations, as we can now be more confident, for example, that learning skills after an exercise bout of heavy intensity will be accomplished as effectively as it would after a period of rest. For example, I would be confident in dividing a large class into two groups, one of which would perform heavy-intensity fitness activities in the first portion of an hour followed by gymnastics in the second (the other subgroup would do the reverse). I feel reasonably assured that the fitness activities would not interfere with the learning of gymnastics, thus allowing much more freedom in terms of scheduling of facilities, etc.

Finally, how is it that learning can occur relatively effectively in subjects when they are highly fatigued? One possibility is that, as with massing, fatigue imposes variability in practice (the variability makes the performance on the fatigued trials less effective) (Johnson, Note 21). As mentioned in the previous section, practice variability can be a positive factor in learning, and perhaps the additional variability "made up for" any loss in learning caused by the fatigue. It is also possible that fatigue caused more intra-task interference, leading to "deeper" processing of task cues. More experimentation is needed before we can be certain about which hypothesis is correct.

Specificity of Learning

In handball a player might practice in various ways, with the major goal being increased skill in a game situation. But, in a game situation, considerable fatigue is usually present, especially later in the game. We could reasonably ask, therefore, if it would be more effective to learn handball when fatigued in order to simulate the game conditions. But the improvement in simulation must be balanced against the fact that fatigue will degrade learning slightly. Similar or analogous situations are present in industrial settings.

Barnett, Ross, Schmidt, and Todd (1973), and Dunham (1976) investigated this problem in laboratory situations. Barnett et al. used the same task as Godwin and Schmidt (1971) did—the Sigma task. The experiment used four groups of subjects, of which two experienced Fatigued (F) practice on Day 1. On Day 2 subjects either continued to practice in the same conditions as on Day 1 or under the opposite fatigue condition. Thus four

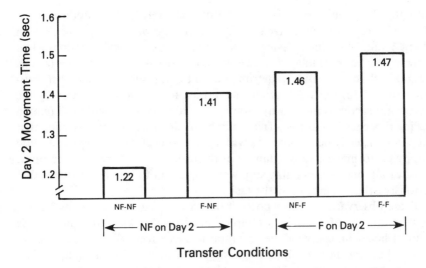

Figure 12-10. Day 2 Sigma task performance under fatigued and nonfatigued conditions as a function of fatigue conditions on Day 1 (from Barnett, Ross, Schmidt, & Todd, 1973).

separate groups were formed: F-F (i.e., Fatigue on Day 1, Fatigue on Day 2), F-NF, NF-F, and NF-NF. According to a specificity of learning perspective, the best way to learn the task to be performed under F conditions on Day 2 would be to practice it under F conditions on Day 1.

The average MTs for the first two Day 2 trials are shown in Figure 12-10. Examine first the two conditions to the left, where the Day 2 performance is under NF conditions. Remembering that lower scores are "better" in this task, the group that had Day 1 practice under F conditions was less effective than the group that had NF practice on Day 1, which is essentially what Godwin and Schmidt (1971) found earlier, as shown in Figure 12-9. But now consider the right portion of the figure, where the performance on Day 2 is under F conditions. The group with F practice on Day 1 was slightly slower than was the group with NF practice on Day 1. It always appeared to be more effective to have practiced the task on Day 1 under rested (NF) conditions, regardless of the task conditions of Day 2. As such, these results do not support the specificity of learning hypothesis, as that view would have predicted that the F-F group would have performed with a smaller MT on Day 2 than the NF-F group. Related to the handball example, you might wish to speculate from this one experiment that practice should be under rested conditions, even for transfer to a game with fatigued playing conditions. Dunham (1976) has found similar results using massing, rather than fatigue, as the variable of interest, with the Bachman ladder-climb as the learning task. Practice under distributed conditions was always slightly better, regardless of whether the transfer conditions were massed or distributed. Similarly, Shea and Morgan (1979), in a study discussed in the previous section, found it was always better to have practiced under the Random condition, regardless of the nature of the conditions in transfer. None of these studies support the specificity of learning hypothesis.

These findings should not be generalized too much, as there exists a wide variety of tasks and variables, not all of which might operate as do the

variables in these situations. For example, it may be more effective to practice football with very loud recorded crowd noises so that players would
have difficulty in hearing the signal counts, as they do in a game. You can
probably think of other examples when duplication of the conditions for a
practice session would be more effective for learning, even though these
conditions might actually interfere with performance at the time. These are
important yet unanswered questions, and the intelligent design of learning
situations would seem to require some of the answers.

Motivation

As I mentioned earlier, motivation is critical for motor learning. An unmotivated person will not practice even a single trial of a task and, hence,
will not learn at all. But will increasing motivation in the usual motor learning situations enhance learning of the task? It seems that teachers and
coaches believe that it would, as one hears a great deal of discussion about
motivating techniques among coaches. There appears to be a similar belief
with respect to individuals in industry (e.g., various incentive programs to
maximize production).

Experiments on Motivation

Numerous experiments have been conducted in the past two decades on
different motivating techniques in relationship to motor learning. In reviewing this literature years ago, I expected to find a nice ordering of techniques,
ranked from most to least effective, with perhaps different techniques being
more effective for certain tasks or for specific kinds of subjects. Instead, the
literature seems to say that motivating techniques, ranging from monetary
incentives, to verbal encouragement, to threats of shock, etc., do not really
do very much for motor learning. When these techniques are compared
(e.g., Nelson, 1962), they seem to have similar effects on performance and
learning, and it is even difficult to see the difference between these techniques and an "unmotivated" control condition given standard instructions
(e.g., "Do your best").

One exception is a study by Fleishman (1958). The task was the Complex
Coordination Test (Figure 3-8), in which the subjects had to control a two-
dimensional hand control and a foot control simultaneously to match positions of lights on a display; the task resembled somewhat the movements involved in flying an airplane. Fleishman used verbal encouragement from the
experimenter (as compared to the usual quiet experimental setting) as a
motivating variable. Figure 12-11 shows the performance curves from this
study. The subjects with initially high skill are plotted separately from subjects with initially low skill. When the motivating techniques were applied
on the sixth trial, there was almost no effect at all for the low-skilled subjects; but a small beneficial effect was shown for the high-skilled subjects.
Apparently, the effects of these kinds of motivating techniques are not
universal across subjects, as the high-skilled subjects are apparently more
receptive to these methods. Also, Locke and Bryan (1966) suggested that

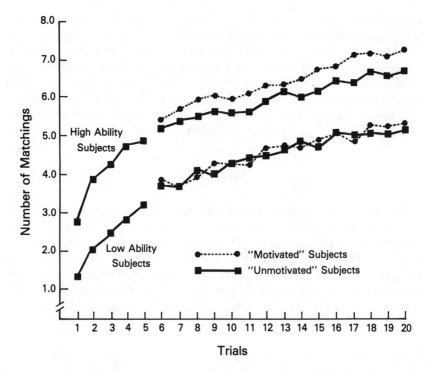

Figure 12-11. The effect of motivating instructions for high and low skilled subjects on performance in the Mashburn task (from Fleishman, 1958).

motivation caused increases in effort applied to the task.

What should we conclude about motivation and motor learning from the Fleishman (1958) study? First, the differences in performance are not very large, and we wonder whether the effort involved in administering the motivating techniques is "worth it" in this case. It appears that an additional four trials under the "unmotivated" practice condition would have made up the performance difference. Second, there is no evidence that motivation is a learning variable because a transfer design was not used. That is, it is certainly possible—even likely— that the motivating techniques had a beneficial effect on performance while they were being used but that these effects might vanish as soon as the subjects are transferred to a non-motivated control condition after a rest. This is a large problem in the studies in the literature on motivation and learning, and transfer designs are seldom used in the assessment of motivational effects on learning. The Fleishman (1958) experiment is interesting and suggestive of some important motivational principles, but, unfortunately, strong conclusions about motivation and learning cannot be drawn from these data.

Why is it that motivational techniques, with but very few exceptions, are so weak in producing changes in motor learning? Is it that motivation is not important for learning? Probably not. Other bodies of literature, such as that dealing with learning in animals, show clearly that increased motivation (in the form of hunger, thirst, etc.) leads to increased rates of learning of tasks that provide rewards which satisfy the motivational drives. Why are the motor learning experiments so different in this regard?

One strong possibility is related to the ways in which learning experiments are typically done in the laboratory. When the subject is asked to participate in an experiment, he or she is faced with an unfamiliar environment, complete with a great deal of formality and the threat of evaluation from the experimenter. As well, there is often a great deal of personal involvement in these motor learning tasks, with the subject becoming very intense about success. Given these conditions, it is not hard to imagine that the subject is already highly motivated before any instructions or experimental treatments are provided. If, then, the experimenter attempts to manipulate this already high motivational level with instructions, rewards, or other techniques, it is possible that motivation cannot be effectively increased further. For this reason, motivating techniques which may be useful are judged as being ineffective in a laboratory investigation. It is a familiar problem: When one brings natural settings into the laboratory for more careful study, they no longer are "natural," and the act of studying the phenomenon may actually prevent its understanding.

It may even be that the motivating instructions and other techniques in the laboratory cause decrements in performance in some subjects and gains in performance in others, with the net result being the essentially zero change (averaged for all subjects) that is seen in the results of experiments. One explanation which I have discussed before involves motivation and the inverted-U hypothesis (Chapter 5). When motivation (or activation, arousal, etc.) is increased, performance increases to an optimum, followed by a decrease in skill as motivation is increased further (e.g., Weinberg & Ragan, 1978; see Figure 5-18, page 173). High levels of motivation may actually interfere with the production of skill. Recall that Weinberg and Hunt (1976) showed a disruption in children's throwing patterns when motivating techniques were applied. (The children were told they were not doing well and to try harder.) Thus, when motivating techniques are used, the induced state in the individual might actually interfere with performance and learning rather than enhance it. Also, this phenomenon seems to depend on the nature of the task studied; the optimal level of motivation for performance of a task requiring fine motor control and accuracy will be lower than the level for a task requiring a great deal of force (see Chapter 5 for a more complete discussion).

To summarize, the objective research evidence, on the surface at least, suggests that motivation is a relatively important variable for learning. But it is likely that many of the effects of motivation are masked by the nature of the experimental procedures. Also, it could be that motivation is highly effective for some subjects and highly disruptive for others. For all these reasons, we must see motivating techniques as being much more complicated than common sense would indicate. The overly simple idea that if some motivation produces learning, then more will produce more learning, is almost certainly not correct.

Behavior Modification Techniques

A slightly different group of techniques for producing changes in performance is called *behavior modification*, or *operant*, techniques. In these situations, certain kinds of behaviors are rewarded, or *reinforced*, when they occur, with the result that the rewarded behavior tends to increase in frequency and the nonrewarded behaviors tend to drop out of the subjects' response patterns. These techniques can easily be shown to operate in animals, as when we "shape" a pet to be "housebroken," or when a pigeon is taught to press a key when a sound occurs to obtain a reward. They are also very powerful determinants of behavior in humans, and B.F. Skinner, certainly the leading proponent of these techniques, believes that our behavior as humans is primarily determined by or past history of reinforcements.

Because these techniques "work" so well in both humans and animals to change behavior, it has been tempting to consider them as methods that could be employed in motor learning (e.g., Rushall & Siedentop, 1972). The idea is that when the learner produces a "good" performance on a learning task, a positive reinforcement is provided; no reinforcement, or even negative reinforcement, may be provided for those trials that are in error. The argument is that if the "bad" responses can be eliminated with negative reinforcement and the "good" responses strengthened, then gradually the individual will produce the more effective action on command. The implication is that this provision of reward is the primary determinant of the motor learning process.

But this conclusion is contradicted by numerous experiments on motor learning. One can think of a "rewarding" statement, such as "Good job," as having at least two components. First, there is a reward or praise component. Second, there is a component that is informational, that informs the individual about what was good and what was not good about the performance in question. The research reviewed in Chapter 13 indicates strongly that it is the informational component that is the more important contributor to motor learning and that a rewarding component is considerably less effective. For this reason, primarily, behavior modification techniques have not been seen as strong contributors to motor learning.

But they do seem to provide two important benefits. First, they seem to contribute to an individual's decisions about which motor response to make in a certain situation (e.g., to throw the ball to first or third base). This can also be seen in the global decisions about whether to play basketball or ice hockey, with the decision being related to an individual's past history or reinforcement in these activities. A person's social actions (e.g., a person's behavior when introduced to someone) are also probably affected seriously by prior reinforcements.

A second aspect of behavior modification techniques is that they seem to provide an important energizing or motivating function. The purpose of the motivation and subsequent rewards would be to cause people to practice even when not directly told to do so. Because practice itself is such a strong determinant of motor learning, any factors that drive people to practice more will surely be related to motor learning, although the relationship will be an indirect, rather than a direct, one.

How can these techniques that work so well as motivators be applied to teaching situations? Rushall and Siedentop (1972) have provided many examples of operant techniques, showing how they can be effective in various sport situations. There seems to be little doubt that with some very simple (and seemingly silly sometimes) procedures, performers and employees can be encouraged to work harder and longer. Such techniques as providing gold stars on a public chart for every 50 miles a distance runner completes, jelly beans for good performances (e.g., Van Rossen, 1968), certificates of completion for a course in beginning swimming, or other forms of recognition have powerful effects. Social approval from one's teacher, coach, peers, or supervisor can have a strong influence. Anyone involved in the design of learning environments should be aware of these powerful motivating techniques and how they can be used.

Social Motivators

Competition. Another class of motivational techniques involves processes that are often discussed by social psycholgists. Most of these stem from the fact that individuals interact with other individuals in various relatively complex ways and that these interactions often provide very strong motivation-like states in people. One of these is the variable of *competition*, in which two learners might be placed in direct conflict with each other, so that the problem is both to master the motor learning task and to defeat one's opponent at the same time. As we might imagine, a variety of factors is at work here, such as threats to self-esteem, the desire to master the task, and so on. Competition can, therefore, be structured to provide strong motivating effects, which probably also have simultaneous effects on level of arousal or activation as well as the effects discussed earlier relative to the inverted-U hypothesis. Thus, it is probably easy to place people in competitive situations which will result in less motor learning than would be the case if the learner were left to practice alone. Obviously this factor will depend on the nature of the task and, especially, on the nature of the learners. Low-skilled individuals and/or individuals who are classified as high-anxious (i.e., people who are generally worried) may be hindered by such competitive techniques. Martens (1975) has provided a review of these findings from a social-psychological point of view.

Coaction. Another form of social effect is termed *coaction*. When two people are asked to perform a task at the same time in close proximity to each other, the performance is often more effective than if these same individuals perform alone. Having another individual seems to improve present performance. It would be tempting to infer that the humans thought that they were competing against each other, but the effects also seem to apply when subjects are told there is no competition, as it does for other species (where competition seems less likely as a consequence of behaving together, as with insects and rodents); see Zajonc (1965) for a review of some of this work and Martens (1975) for a critique of it. It does appear that when the possibility of evaluation is involved, where the coacting individuals are aware of being evaluated, the effects are strongest. Perhaps a competitive element is present in coaction, as Martens has suggested. While it is clear that these coactive effects affect performance, it is not clear that these variables affect learning; it could be that coactive effects disappear as soon as the coactors are removed.

Audience effects. Finally, another class of social motivation is the audience. Subjectively, we all know the kinds of feelings present when we have to perform a task or give a talk before a group, and these feelings seem to be heightened if we are very uncertain of our success in the upcoming task, especially if we are just learning it. There have been many laboratory studies of audience effects (e.g., Bird, 1973; Singer, 1970), and the results are consistent with the idea that audiences are motivating or activating to the learners. Whether this activation will produce beneficial effects or detrimental effects will apparently depend on a number of factors. Audiences seem more effective later in practice than early; audiences are more effective with high-skilled than with low-skilled performers; and audiences are more effective with low- than high-anxious subjects. There are other factors as well (see Martens, 1975; Singer, 1975), but most of these effects are consistent with those seen earlier with other motivational techniques.

Applications. All of these effects seem to have important applications when individuals are performing together. Obviously, an instructional class or training program has this feature, and such effects are certain to be present here. Also, these effects are important for understanding how teams operate, including not only athletic teams but also teams of astronauts and work groups in industry or business (Gill, 1979). Without too much oversimplification, a good understanding of these effects seems possible by resorting to the unifying principle of the inverted-U hypothesis, whereby all of these effects seem motivating or activating, and the effects on performance and learning are determined by the arousal levels defined by the social situation. No doubt it is more complex than this, but we can obtain a useful approximation by considering social effects in this way.

CONDITIONS OF PRACTICE AND TRANSFER

A number of decisions about the design of practice sessions are based heavily on an understanding of transfer of learning—the gain (or loss) in proficiency in one skill as a result of practice on some other (see Chapter 11). In many learning situations, the task actually practiced in a session is not the activity of primary interest, the real concern being for some other task believed to be related to this activity. One example is drills. The instructor does not really care whether the student can perform these drills well or not; rather, the instructor assumes that by practicing the drills, the student will learn something that will transfer to some other task (e.g., performance in a basketball game) that is of major interest. To use drills successfully, one must be certain that experience on the drill transfers to some *criterion task*.

Another example is the common method whereby the task is "broken down" into its components for practice. The assumption is that practice on the parts will transfer to the whole task. Still another example is the use of simulators of various kinds, such as a pitching machine to simulate a "real" pitcher or a simulator to duplicate the cockpit of a Boeing 747. Does practice on these simulators transfer to the criterion behavior? The choices about whether or not to use these methods and, if they are to be used, how they should be structured depends heavily on an understanding of transfer of learning. Some of the principles of motor transfer are considered next.

Basic Principles of Transfer

In examining the literature on transfer of motor learning, many studies using different techniques and tasks have produced many different and sometimes contradictory findings. But two major points emerge. First, the amount of transfer seems to be quite small and positive unless the tasks are practically identical. Second, the amount of transfer depends on the similarity between the two tasks.

Motor Transfer Is Small

When the transfer from one task to a completely different task is studied—sometimes called *inter-task transfer*—we typically find that the transfer is small or negligible. Such evidence comes from studies concerned with attempts to train some behavior or trait in one situation by providing presumably related experiences in different situations. For example, studies by Lindeburg (1949) and Blankenship (1952) have shown that "quickening exercises" (various laboratory tasks that require rapid decision and action) provide no transfer to other tasks that require quickness. This is certainly not surprising in light of what is known about the specificity of motor abilities, as the activities in the quickening exercises probably used different motor abilities than the task to which the exercises were supposed to have contributed. Evidence suggests that such general traits as quickness cannot be improved by the use of different activities involving that trait; and we would not expect that an ability would be improved by practice anyway (see Chapter 10).

What if the tasks are more similar? Here, the transfer among tasks tends to be higher than for the situation above. But the amount of transfer is typically small. For example, Lordahl and Archer (1958) used the pursuit rotor task, with different groups of subjects practicing at 40, 60, or 80 RPM for 30 30-sec trials. All groups then switched to the 60-RPM version of the task for the evaluation of the transfer effects. Here, the group that had 60 RPM in both the training trials and transfer trials was used as the standard against which the transfer in the other two groups was assessed; that is, it served the role of Group II in Figure 11-14. Using the calculation for the percentage transfer introduced in Chapter 11, I computed that the transfer from the 40- and 80-RPM versions of the task to the 60-RPM version was 12% and 31%, respectively. Namikas and Archer (1960), using the same procedures, found somewhat higher transfer ranging from 42% to 64%. Remember that in these experiments the transfer is between the pursuit rotor and itself, with only the speed of rotation changed to define the different "tasks," and it is somewhat surprising that the transfer is so small. Numerous other experiments say essentially the same thing (see Schmidt, 1975a, Chapter 5).

These generally small transfer effects seem to fit with a number of other phenomena that I have discussed already. First, the transfer findings coincide with the ideas about individual differences. In Chapter 10 a conclusion was that motor abilities are both numerous and specific and that even similar tasks appeared to correlate very low with each other. If so, then in transfer experiments when the task is changed in even a small way (e.g., changing the turntable speed of the pursuit rotor), it is likely that different and unrelated abilities are called into play. Fleishman (1965) presented some evidence for this assertion with respect to changed displays in limb-reaction tasks (Chapter 10). Thus, there might be low transfer among even very similar tasks because the abilities are almost completely different.

These findings also fit well with the motor program notion. In Chapter 9, a major idea was that two tasks that appeared to have different phasing (within-task timing) characteristics were assumed to be governed by different programs. If a shift in the speed of rotation of the pursuit rotor, for example, requires the individual to abandon one program in favor of another, then the subjects will be practicing two different programs in the two different variations of the "same" motor task. This is analogous to speeding up a treadmill so that jogging is substituted for walking, each having its own program (e.g., Shapiro, Zernicke, Gregor, & Diestal, 1981). It is difficult to say how wide might be the range of conditions produced by a given motor program, but I suspect that many programs exist and that they are shifted rather freely when the conditions change. Viewed in this way, it is not surprising that tasks do not transfer much to each other.

Transfer Depends on Similarity

A second and related generalization about transfer of motor learning is that transfer depends on the similarity of the two tasks being considered. The idea of similarity is certainly not new, as Thorndike and Woodworth (1901) proposed that transfer depended on the number of "identical elements" that existed in common between two tasks. If one task had elements that were totally different from the elements in another task, then no transfer would be expected. Transfer would be 100% if the two tasks had all their elements in common. The problem with this theory was that it was never specified what an "element" was and how it could be measured, so the theory cannot be tested experimentally. In the previous paragraphs, the implication is that the "elements" could be (a) abilities in common between the two tasks, (b) motor programs that are used for the two tasks, or both. And other possibilities exist.

The theories of transfer have been improved considerably since this early idea. A major contribution was Osgood's (1949) *transfer surface* which provided a description of the amount of transfer of *verbal* learning as a joint function of the similarity of the stimulus elements and the response elements. Recently, Holding (1976) has presented a similar idea for motor responses. In all of these cases, the notion of similarity is a dominant theme, as it always has been. But these recent theories are not completely satisfactory, as a large number of transfer phenomena do not appear to be explained by them. The problem seems to be related to our lack of understanding about what "similarity" is, and what the "elements" are that are supposedly similar in various tasks. Perhaps work with abilities and motor programs will contribute to this area, but it is too early to tell. The conclusion from viewing this literature is that motor transfer is not well understood at all.

Negative Transfer

I have mentioned that transfer is not always positive and that losses can occur in one skill as a result of experience on another. This is called *negative transfer*. In speaking casually with people about motor skills, I am convinced that people generally believe that negative transfer is relatively common and that the skill losses produced by it can be quite large. Almost cliché is the story that tennis lessons in the summer ruined the person's badminton game, presumably because the two tasks are quite similar yet somewhat incompatible (e.g., the wrist action in the two strokes).

But what does the evidence say about negative transfer? First, if you were to search through the literature on transfer of motor learning, you would find that the studies nearly always show low but positive transfer and that negative transfer is seldom the outcome. But negative transfer can be produced if the proper conditions are presented, such as those provided by Lewis, McAllister, and Adams (1951).

Lewis et al. used the Mashburn task, in which a two-dimensional arm control and a foot control were used simultaneously to control the positions of lights on a display (Figure 3-8, page 72). After the subject practiced for a various number of trials (either 10, 30, or 50) with the usual configuration of the task, the subjects were switched to a condition in which the control-display relationships were reversed. For example, in order to move the light on the screen to the left, the lever had to be moved to the right rather than to the left, as had been the case before. All three dimensions of the task (right-left, backward-forward, right foot-left foot) were reversed. This is analogous to driving a car where the "normal" movements of the controls are suddenly backwards (e.g., steering wheel clockwise to turn left, brake pedal released to stop, or learning to back a car and trailer). After either 10, 20, 30, or 50 trials on the task with the reversed control-display relationships, subjects were switched back to the original configuration of the task to see if skill had been lost or gained. This is a retroactive transfer design as shown in Table 11-2, page 468.

In Figure 12-12, the amount of decrease in performance caused by the reversed-task practice (the difference on the main task between the number of matches after and before reversed-task practice) are plotted. A decrement score of zero means that the standard task was performed just as well after the reversed task as before, meaning no negative retroactive transfer occurred; and the amount of negative retroactive transfer increases as the size of the decrement score increases. Transfer was generally negative, and negative transfer increased as the number of reversed task trials increased. This is as you might expect, as the amount of interference from this reversed task should be larger if it is more completely learned. (There was also an effect of the number of original practice trials of the task with standard controls, but it is far from clear what this means; see Schmidt, 1971a, or Chapter 15 for a more complete discussion of this effect.) Thus, this is an example of clear and unmistakable negative retroactive transfer, and similar

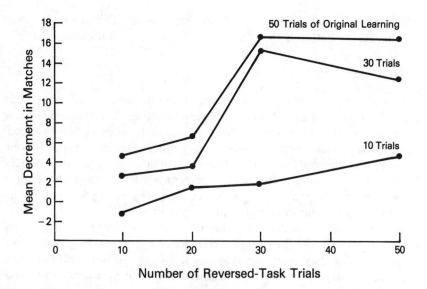

Figure 12-12. Retroactive negative transfer (interference) as a function of amount of practice on the reversed task and the amount of original learning on the standard task (from Lewis, McAllister, & Adams, 1951).

findings have been produced in other studies using similar procedures (see Schmidt, 1971a, 1975a).

What do these studies indicate about negative transfer of motor skills? My position (Schmidt, 1975a) has been that the negative transfer produced was mainly cognitive in nature, and may not have had much to do with motor negative transfer. The conditions probably left the subjects confused about what to do, and it may not have disrupted the motor control processes in the task at all. This argument is not strong, though, as it is difficult to know what the relevant motor and cognitive processes are in such tasks and to come to a decision about which of them were disrupted by the reversed practice. Yet it seems logical to assume that a major portion of the problem for the subjects on returning to the standard task was confusion about what the limbs controlling each of the three dimensions of the task were supposed to do.

Ross (1974) attempted to produce negative transfer in a situation in which it could not be argued that confusion prevailed about what to do, so that any remaining negative transfer would be due to the loss of skill in controlling the limbs. She produced a laboratory analog of the tennis-badminton situation, where the limb movements in the two tasks were identical except for one critical part of the action near the end. Subjects learned one version of the task that required a forceful ending, then learned the alternative task that was the same except for a light touch required at the end. Then she transferred subjects back to the original task with the forceful ending (a retroactive transfer design). Little negative transfer occurred, and what did occur was eliminated in 10 practice trials at the original task. These data supported the idea that the major problem in the Lewis et al. experiment was confusion about the cognitive elements and not a loss of limb control.

Other studies suggest that negative transfer of limb control can be quite large. In a completely different context having to do with the learning of motor programs, Summers (1977) and Shapiro (1977, 1978) had subjects learn complex patterns of movement with a particular experimenter-imposed phasing. These studies are discussed in detail in Chapter 8 (Figure 8-9), but they have relevance for motor negative transfer as well. After the subjects had practiced producing the pattern of action with the proper phasing, they were asked to abandon this phasing and to perform the task as quickly as possible. As I pointed out in Chapter 8 (Figure 8-9), subjects did not produce a different phasing; rather, they produced the original sequence more rapidly with the same phasing. Now, if you see the task with the original phasing as Task A, and the task with a different phasing as Task B, these findings can be interpreted to mean that there was large negative transfer from Task A to Task B. They did not produce Task B at all, and the extensive practice at one pattern apparently made it extremely difficult to transfer to a task with the same sequence but a different temporal pattern. Perhaps this kind of finding will provide a key to understanding negative transfer, and the basis of it will be in the phasing characteristics of the two movements. As a tentative hypothesis, it is possible that negative transfer occurs when the sequencing of two actions is the same but the patterns of phasing are different. This hypothesis could be tested easily in the laboratory.

Finally, it seems reasonable to think that two tasks, each containing a number of "elements," may have some similar elements leading to positive transfer and have other dissimilar elements contributing to negative transfer. Again, the examples from Summers (1977) and Shapiro (1977, 1978) provide some insight. The different phasing in the two actions (the original movement versus the speeded-up movement with different phasing) could have been an element that transferred negatively. At the same time, the *sequencing* is an element that might transfer positively, because the sequencing in the two tasks was identical. Thus, at the same time negative transfer of phasing occurs, positive transfer of sequencing might also occur. Other aspects of the task might not transfer at all—positively or negatively.

This idea can be seen in many tasks in sport, such as handball and racketball, for example. There appear to be many common elements between these two games, such as the angles that the ball bounces off the walls of the court, the strategies of the game, and so on, all of which might lead to positive transfer. Yet, at the same time, other elements of the game would appear to lead to negative transfer, such as the exact positioning of the body just before the shot (this would be different, of course, if the ball were to be hit with the hand versus a racket). The elements of the shot itself might not transfer at all, positively or negatively. The point is that whether or not two tasks transfer positively or negatively might depend on a kind of "balance sheet" that "weighs" the elements that transfer positively against those that transfer negatively. If the positives outweigh the negatives, as they usually do, then the result will be slight positive transfer. This does not represent an adequate theory of transfer, but it may help to conceptualize some of the dynamics that are occurring when two tasks interact.

Figure 12-13. The Link ME-1 Instrument Flight Trainer (photo courtesy of the Singer Co.).

Simulation and Simulators

An important and commonly used method for training people in motor (and cognitive) tasks is through the use of simulators. The main feature is that it provides a practice task that is related to some *criterion task* (the overall goal of the learning process) in some way. For example, pilots may practice procedural skills on ground-based devices that mimic the cockpit of the aircraft, as seen in Figure 12-13. The hope is that the practice of these skills in the simulator will transfer to the actual skills in the airplane (the criterion task).

Nearly countless examples of simulators in various learning situations may be mentioned. At one end of the scale are expensive and highly sophisticated devices that simulate large and complex systems. For example, the simulators for learning to fly are often elaborate, with exact mock-ups of the cockpit area, instrumentation, etc. The pilot-learner is often given televised displays from the windshield showing airport runways approaching; the instrumentation is complete and functioning; and the "feel" of the controls is as similar to the real aircraft as possible. In some simulators even movements of the cockpit as a whole occur to simulate the flight of an airplane in a storm. In these situations, the information displayed on the gauges and dials is produced by the computer, and the learner's responses are monitored by computers as well. There are similar devices to simulate the behavior of a weapons system, and recently there have been developed simulators for controlling the behavior of nuclear power plants. As you might imagine, these devices are expensive to produce and operate.

On the other hand, many simulation devices are relatively simple and inexpensive. Many of us learned to drive by practicing on driver simulators that had not-so-realistic configurations of the automobile's controls, so that the proper motions could be learned before trying them in the real car. Dentists in training practice their skills on plaster-of-Paris models of the jaw, sometimes with the "jaw" on a workbench or even in the position in which it would be if it were the upper jaw of a patient. A simulator can require almost no apparatus, such as when I practice putting on my living room rug, simulating the actual putting green on a golf course.

Simulators provide a number of advantages, as I discussed in Chapter 11. Briefly, these relate to cost and/or time effectiveness, increased safety, and increased convenience of having the simulator for use at any time in any weather. And yet simulators have a number of serious drawbacks. First, the "worth" of any simulation device has to be measured in terms of the amount of transfer that it provides to the criterion task. If the simulator does not provide transfer to the criterion task, the device is essentially useless in terms of the purpose for which it was originally intended. Thus, the evaluation of simulation devices is usually heavily involved with the analysis of the transfer of learning from the device to the criterion task (see Chapter 11).

From the earlier discussion of transfer, one point that consistently emerges is that motor transfer is generally quite low unless the two tasks are so similar as to be practically identical. Thus, it would be easy to assume that a simulation device was producing considerable transfer to the criterion task when it was not producing much at all because the skills involved in the simulation performance were fundamentally different from those involved in the criterion task. From the basic research findings, as well as from the literature on the specificity of skills (Chapter 10), it appears that many simulators will not transfer well to the criterion tasks for which they were designed. Certainly a critical part of simulation is the conduct of a transfer experiment, perhaps with various versions of the simulator, to evaluate the amount of transfer that is actually produced.

To the extent that the simulator and the criterion task are similar—even identical—transfer will increase from one to the other. The recognition of this fact has led the designers of simulation devices to make them very realistic, such as the simulated airplane cockpit that moves as if in a storm. Much effort is devoted to making the controls feel as they do in the aircraft, with proper resistances, feedback, etc., to maximize the similarity. This makes good sense, as the literature on individual differences suggests that only slight modification of the task can cause major shifts in the abilities that underlie them. If differences between simulator and criterion task are too great, it is possible that separate motor control mechanisms might be used, producing no transfer.

Simulation devices are usually excellent for teaching procedural details, the proper order of a sequence of activities, and the like. These aspects of the overall task are important, and considerable time can be "saved" by using simulators at early stages of practice. There is less certainty that the motor elements of the task are so easily simulated, however. It would appear that when complex movements are simulated, even with very complex and expensive simulators, there is a big difference between the behaviors produced on the simulator and those produced on the criterion task, probably because of the difficulty in simulating the dynamics of the controls, providing realistic situations and displays, and so on. Thus, while simulators clearly have their place in the training of procedures, there is good reason to question their utility in terms of the training of movement patterns.

Simulations are often applied rather blindly without regard for the kinds of transfer that are to be produced. Many examples are seen in athletics, where certain kinds of behaviors are simulated in various drill procedures. The use of blocking dummies in American football may be useful in the early stages of learning a play when there are questions about where to go and whom to block, but there would seem to be little utility in using them beyond this point. Players would seem to require practice in blocking other players who do not wish to be blocked; this is, of course, very difficult to simulate. It is difficult to evaluate the effectiveness of these various procedures because we have no research about the transfer of these drills to game situations. But I would guess that many of these procedures are useless. Certainly it would make sense to examine any such drills or simulations very carefully.

Part-Whole Transfer

A very common technique for teaching motor skills is to "break them down" into smaller parts, to eliminate the burden of repeating the simpler parts of the entire task. Also, this would seem to be an effective procedure when the task is very complex and cannot be grasped as a whole. Examples are numerous, such as practicing separately the arm and leg strokes in Red Cross swimming methods, and practicing specific stunts in gymnastics which later become part of a routine.

The ultimate test of whether or not these methods are effective depends on the amount of transfer that can be shown from the practice of the part to the performance of the whole task. It seems obvious that if practice is given on the part, it would certainly transfer highly to the whole task, as these two tasks would seem to have identical elements (the part) in them. The problem with this idea is that practice on the part in isolation may so change the motor programming of the part that it is, for all practical purposes, no longer the same as it is in the context of the total skill. It turns out that the conclusions about whether or not part-whole practice is effective depends on the nature of the task.

Serial Tasks

Seymour (1954) has done extensive research on industrial tasks that are serial in nature. The task consisted of a series of elements to be performed on a lathe. Some of the elements were difficult, requiring a great deal of practice to master, and some were easy and could be accomplished on the first try. Seymour found that if the difficult parts were practiced separately, without any corresponding practice on the less difficult parts, there was considerable transfer of the part to the whole task. One view is that maximum practice time can be devoted to the portions of the task that need the most work, without wasting time on the parts of the task that need little work. This part practice seemed to be an efficient way to practice these kinds of tasks. As well, Adams and Hufford (1962) have found that the practice of a series of discrete acts that were part of the total task of flying an airplane transfered highly to the whole task of flying the aircraft. When the task is strictly serial in nature (with no overlapping of the parts in time) and the overall MT for the total task is long (e.g., a few minutes), the part practice on the more difficult elements is usually highly effective.

Continuous Tasks

In continuous tasks, in which the behavior continues more or less uninterrupted as in walking, steering a car, etc., the parts that can be isolated frequently occur at the same time as other parts. This is, of course, in sharp contrast to the situation in serial tasks, in which the parts are sequentially organized. Also, in continuous tasks the parts must frequently be coordinated with each other, and it might seem that breaking into this pattern of coordination to practice a part might not be very effective, as it is the coordination between these parts that must be learned. Swimming strokes have this characteristic, as the arm strokes, breathing, and kicking actions must be coordinated to form an effective whole.

The evidence about such applied situations is sadly lacking, and we must rely on findings from the laboratory for the answers. For example, Briggs and Brogden (1954) and Briggs and Waters (1958) used a lever-positioning task that required positioning in two dimensions (forward-backward, left-right) simultaneously and continuously, much as the "joystick" in an aircraft would to control the vehicle's motions. They found that transfer on the separate dimensions alone transfered to the whole task. Even so, an important question was whether or not practicing the part in isolation was more effective than practicing the whole task for the same period of time. It is possible that the most effective way to learn such tasks is to practice the whole, unless the task is highly complex or contains rather trivial elements.

Another situation which produces slightly different findings involves those tasks in which the parts interact while they are being performed simultaneously. The most complex example that I can think of involves the operations necessary to take a helicopter from the ground into flight. According to Zavala, Locke, Van Cott, and Fleishman (1965) in their analysis of helicopter pilotry abilities, four separate controls must be handled by the operator. The first is a *cyclic pitch control stick*, which is really a control for two dimensions in one (roll and pitch). It is a stick mounted on the floor of the cockpit in front of the pilot. When moved in a particular direction, it causes the helicopter to tilt in that direction. Thus, it can be used to control roll (side to side) and pitch (nose up or down) simultaneously. Second, a *collective pitch lever* is mounted to the left of the pilot, and up-and-down movements of this lever control the vertical component of the flight. Third, a *throttle* is located as a twist grip on the just-mentioned pitch control; it controls the engine speed, just as the accelerator in an automobile does. Fourth, *anti-torque pedals* under the pilot's feet control the pitch of the small propellor at the tail of the helicopter, thus controlling the direction of the machine and compensating for the torque produced by the overhead rotors.

The problem for the person learning this task is that these components interact strongly. That is, when the throttle control is used to speed up the rotor or the pitch control is adjusted, there is a tendency for the helicopter to turn in the direction opposite the rotation of the rotor. This must be counteracted by an appropriately graded foot-pedal movement to maintain the proper heading. But also, the machine will increase its tendency to roll and will attempt to dive, both of which must be counteracted by the adjustment of the pitch-control stick. Thus, when the lift of the rotors is increased in an attempt to become airborne, three other adjustments must be done simultaneously to prevent the helicopter from turning upside down. The amount of control change in these three dimensions depends on the amount of lift that is imparted to the helicopter in the other two controls. It is said that these control dimensions interact because the setting of one of them will depend on the settings applied to the others.

Thus, the problem of the student helicopter pilot is to learn about this interaction and how to coordinate actions of all the dimensions in a smooth and effortless manner. It would be tempting to take this highly complex task and "break it down" into separate parts. But this breakdown seems to sidestep the most important problem for the learner. Any one of the dimensions can easily be performed separately; but this practice would not be very effective in learning the total task. In general, the limitations of part-to-whole transfer methods will probably depend on the extent to which the parts of the task interact in the whole task. As for the helicopter, it would seem that an effective way to learn the task would be to practice in a ground-based simulator, where all five dimensions would be learned together without the fear of an accident in the actual helicopter.

Discrete Tasks

Can we apply this evidence about part-to-whole transfer to discrete tasks whose MTs are very short (e.g., less than 1 sec)? Probably not, as the evidence gives a different picture in these situations.

For example, Lersten (1968) had subjects learn a hand-movement (rho task) task with two components. A handle was grasped by the subject and rotated in the horizontal plane through $270°$ until it hit a stop, whereupon the subject was to release the handle and move forward to knock over a barrier. This was to be done as quickly as possible (MTs of about 600 msec). Thus a circular component was followed by a linear component, both of which could be practiced and measured separately. Lersten had various groups of subjects practice the circular portion or the linear portion in isolation prior to transferring to the total task. Another group of subjects practiced only the whole task. Lersten found that practice on the circular component alone transfered only about 7% to the performance of the circular phase in the context of the whole task. Other conditions produced no transfer to the whole task. Even more important, he found that the practice on the linear component alone transferred negatively (about -8%) to the performance of the linear component in the context of the whole task. That is, practicing this linear component in isolation produced less learning on the whole task than doing nothing. Overall, the findings seemed to say that practicing these isolated components of the whole task produced essentially negligible transfer to the performance of the whole task.

Sequential parts. How can these findings be explained? First, it seems clear that even though the task Lersten used was "serial" in nature, in that it had a circular component followed by a linear component, this task must be considered as being quite different from the serial tasks used by Seymour (1954). One clear difference is in terms of the overall MT, with Seymour's tasks having durations in the order of minutes and Lersten's task lasting for only about 600 msec. Could it be that these differences are related to the way in which these two kinds of movements are controlled? I think so.

It seems reasonable to assume that Lersten's task was governed by a single motor program containing the instructions for both the circular and linear components, as well as the instructions for the transition between the two (timing the release of the handle, for example). If so, then practicing the circular part in isolation would result in the subject's practicing a different program from that involved in the circular part in the context of the whole skill. It is as if there is a motor program for the circular part in isolation, a second program for the linear part in isolation, and yet a third program for the circular and linear components together—i.e., a program for the whole task. Practicing one program does not help with the other very much, or it might even degrade it slightly. With the serial tasks that Seymour (1954) used, the actions are so widely separated in time that they are not governed by the same program, and this task can be thought of as a series of programs strung together. Practicing one of them in isolation is the same as practicing that program in the context of the total skill, so part-whole transfer is high.

These ideas suggest that the major determinant of whether or not part-whole transfer will "work" will be the extent to which the movement is governed by a single program. With the principles of programming outlined in Chapter 8, it is possible to make an estimate of the number of programs involved in a movement. If the movement is very fast, it will almost certainly be governed by one motor program, and it should be practiced as a whole. Second, if the movement is slower but there is a "break" in the action that is easily adjusted, it is possible that the movement is governed by more than one program. An example is the break between the toss action and the hit action in a tennis serve; the toss seems programmed, but then there is a feedback-based break so that the hit program can be adjusted to the exact location and timing of the toss. A springboard dive is another example; the take-off and tuck are probably programmed, but the timing of the "untuck" movements might be feedback-based, determined by visual or vestibular information. These tasks could probably be split into their component parts for separate practice, and part-to-whole transfer would probably be higher.

Simultaneous parts. A second consideration is when the parts of the task are simultaneous, rather than serial as in Lersten's example. Many examples exist, such as the left and right hands in piano playing or any other task for which one part of the body has to be coordinated with another. Research on these questions is nearly nonexistent, though, and the decisions about part-whole transfer are mostly speculative.

First, it seems from the data presented in Chapters 8 and 9, that two-handed simultaneous movements must be controlled by a single program, with the program containing instructions for both hands. There is the possibility that practicing the movements of one hand in isolation results in the development of a different program than practicing that "same" movement in the context of a total two-handed skill. Bender's (Note 2) data suggested that the program to make a "V" with the right hand was probably different than the program required to make a "V" with the right hand and a gamma with the left hand simultaneously. However, there appear to be contradictions; left-hand piano and typing practice seems to transfer to two-hand performances. The principles underlying coordination of the separate limbs in an action are not well understood and more work is needed, but it seems clear that "breaking down" a task into its components will not always result in large part-to-whole transfer.

Lead-Up Activities

A closely related question for teaching skills concerns the use of so-called "lead-up" activities. In these situations, certain simpler tasks are thought to be in some way fundamental to the learning of more complex tasks, so the simpler tasks are formally taught as a part of the procedure for learning the more complex task. These procedures are often used in gymnastics, where instructors talk of a progression of subtasks leading eventually to the complex goal response. The question, again, can be thought of as transfer from the lead-up task to the goal movement.

What is the effectiveness, if any, of these lead-up activities? On the one hand, such activities might have the disadvantage of being, by necessity, different from the goal action, and the motor transfer from these activities could be very small. Certainly this conclusion is in keeping with the evidence on transfer. But, unfortunately, no effective experiments on lead-up activities can be found, so this conclusion has to be seen as speculative.

On the other hand, lead-ups may have many positive aspects. First, in many tasks (e.g., stunts in gymnastics) there is a strong element of fear. Lead-ups, being simpler and less dangerous, may serve a useful role in eliminating fear responses that can be so crippling in a more complex movement. This fear reduction aspect is borne out in studies of so-called *interactive modeling*, or desensitization techniques, whereby people are taught to eliminate phobic responses (e.g., the fear of snakes, of heights, etc.) by performing lead-up activities that are progressively closer to the target fear (e.g., progressively more "realistic" snakes, eventually leading to an actual snake); see Bandura (1969) or Bandura, Blanchard, and Ritter (1969). These methods "work" to reduce these fear reactions, and perhaps they do the same in skills. Also, many lead-ups are designed with a particular action in mind. In gymnastics, again, the "kipping" action (a forceful but timed extension of the hip) is thought to be involved in a large number of skills, such as the horizontal bar, the parallel bars, in tumbling, and so on. Learning to kip in one simple lead-up activity possibly will transfer to the "same" action in a more complex and dangerous activity. These are just some of the possible positive aspects of lead-ups, and more work needs to be done here also.

MENTAL PRACTICE

One of the most curious phenomena in the motor skills literature is *mental-practice effects*. Here, subjects who are instructed to mentally practice a skill—i.e., to imagine performing it without any associated overt actions—can be shown to produce large positive transfer to skill in the actual task. These techniques, sometimes referred to as *covert rehearsal* techniques, have been studied extensively throughout this century.

One of the most striking examples of mental-practice effects is by Rawlings, Rawlings, Chen, and Yilk (1972), who studied the rotary pursuit test. All groups were introduced to the task on Day 1, and received 25 trials. On Days 2-9 subjects differed in their practice methods. A Physical Practice group practiced 25 trials per day, a No-Practice group received no practice, and a Mental-Practice group practiced the task only by imagining and visualizing the task. On Day 10, all subjects were retested on the task for 25 additional trials; essentially, this is the transfer test on which the relative amount learned in these experimental procedures was evaluated.

The major findings are presented in Figure 12-14, where the performance on the pursuit rotor is graphed for each of the days of the experiment. Notice that there are data points only for Days 1 and 10 for the Mental-Practice and No-Practice groups, as there was no pursuit rotor practice on Days 2-9. The Mental-Practice group improved (learned) considerably over the course of the experiment, almost to the extent that the Physical Practice subjects did. The No-Practice group, which practiced neither mentally nor physically, did not improve much at all in the same period. Other evidence suggests that mental practice can be effective for a variety of movement skills (see Richardson, 1967a, 1967b, for a review of the earlier work on this area, and Singer, 1980, for a more recent treatment). Corbin (1972) even found that distributed mental practice is more effective than massed mental practice.

What is going on here? Earlier I strongly emphasized that in order to

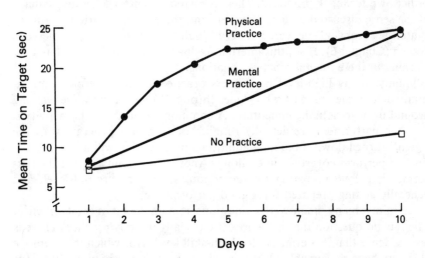

Figure 12-14. Effect of mental practice on pursuit-rotor performance (from Rawlings, Rawlings, Chen, & Yilk, 1972).

learn a movement, one must experience active physical practice of it. The literature, particularly the data from Rawlings et al. (1972), seems to contradict this notion. Certainly a component of mental practice is learning the cognitive elements in the task—that is, learning what to do. Given the requirement of rehearsing mentally, the learner can think about what kinds of things might be tried, the consequences of each action can be predicted to some extent based on previous experiences with similar skills, and the learner can perhaps rule out inappropriate courses of action. This view suggests that not very much motor learning is happening in mental practice, the majority being the rapid learning associated with the cognitive elements of the task. Such a view fits well with some recent data from Minas (1978, 1980), who used a serial throwing task, for which balls of different weights and textures had to be thrown into the proper bins. The main finding was that mental practice contributed to the learning of the sequence (the cognitive element) but did not contribute very much to the learning of the particular throwing actions (motor elements). These cognitive elements are usually present in the early stages of practice, and this fits with the evidence that mental practice is usually more effective in early practice compared to later practice. (See also Schmidt, 1975a, for another discussion of this issue.)

But others feel that there is more to mental practice than this simple view about learning the cognitive elements in a task. One view is that the motor programs for the movements are actually being run off during mental practice, but the learner simply turns down the "gain" of the program so that the contradictions are very small and hardly visible at all. Research on so-called *implicit speech*, whereby subjects are told to imagine speaking a given sentence, can show patterns of EMG activity from the vocal musculature that closely resembles that pattern evoked when speaking. Here, of course, the movements are very small, and no sounds are made by the "speakers." If this hypothesis is correct, then "performing" an action in mental practice may involve the production of small forces, with the person evaluating his or her own feedback produced. There is no movement to generate feedback in the sense discussed earlier, however, and there may be various forms of "internal feedback" delivered at very "high" levels in the central nervous system (Chapter 6). If so, this internal feedback could serve as the basis for learning in these mental-practice situations.

Finally, many high-level performers practice mentally before competition, such as the gymnast who "goes through" the routine while walking around prior to actual competition. A common belief about this activity is that the performers are actually running off a motor program with the "gain" turned down, obtaining additional practice that will help when the time to perform covertly comes along. Another possibility is that the performer is merely preparing for the action, setting the arousal level, and generally getting prepared for a good performance.

Certainly many unanswered questions remain about mental practice. There is no question that it "works," especially in early practice. There is less evidence that it is effective for high-skill levels (for which the cognitive elements have presumably already been learned), but see Suinn (1980) for apparent contradictions. There are important theoretical questions about what is happening in mental practice, but the critical experiments have not been done.

GUIDANCE

Another technique that is frequently used in the teaching of skills involves *guidance*, whereby the learner is in some way guided through the task that is to be learned. Actually, guidance refers to a large variety of separate procedures, ranging from physically pushing and pulling the learner through a sequence, to preventing incorrect responses by physical limitations on the apparatus, or even to the simple act of verbally "talking someone through" a new situation. These guidance procedures tend to prevent the learner from making errors in the task, and hence this issue has been discussed in the theoretical context of the role of errors in learning (see also the discussion on error-free versus error-full learning in Singer, 1980).

In simple terms, the theoretical issues present two opposing views of whether or not guidance should be effective in producing learning of the main task. First, it can be argued that it is important for the learner to avoid making errors, lest he or she learn those error responses and repeat them in the future; guidance procedures can, depending on the particular kinds used, effectively prevent many kinds of errors, and we might argue that these would be good ways to learn from this point of view. This can also help if errors are dangerous or costly.

But, alternatively, we could argue that learning is most effective by trial-and-error, or "discovery" procedures. The learner cannot know that a certain internal command will lead to an ineffective outcome in the environment unless that command has been tried and the outcome experienced. Guidance, under this view, prevents the person from receiving experience about errors, and thus learning might not be as effective as practicing the task under unguided procedures. Also, if the learner cannot make errors, then he or she will not be able to learn how to correct those errors when they are made in the future. As we can see, these opposing viewpoints present a confusing picture to the teacher or instructor who is searching for procedures with which to teach motor skills. What does the evidence say?

Much of the guidance research has been conducted by Holding and his colleagues (Holding, 1970; Holding & Macrae, 1964; Macrae & Holding, 1965). Many tasks have been studied, ranging from simple positioning responses to tracking tasks with relatively complex imputs, and the nature of the guidance has been studied as well. One type of guidance, termed *forced-response guidance*, involves actually forcing the learner through the proper sequence, as when the subject's finger is towed through a finger maze. With another kind of guidance, termed *restriction*, the learner is relatively free to move, but certain movements would be blocked—a far less oppressive method than forced-response guidance. An example is shown in Figure 12-15. Essentially, Holding and Macrae have found that both techniques are effective in teaching various skills, and the effectiveness seems to depend on the nature of the movement studied.

A tracking task was studied by Macrae and Holding (1966), for which the

Figure 12-15. Guidance in learning a gymnastics stunt (from Frey & Keeney, 1964).

rhythmic sine-wave movements of the track were visible as the subject was guided through the proper movements of the control stick to track it. Considerable transfer occurred from this practice to the performance of the task under unguided conditions. The authors suggested that a major advantage of guidance in these situations is that it provides the learner with knowledge about the nature of the task, and it provides a basis for anticipation of the task inputs; this is similar to the effects of verbal pretraining (mentioned earlier), in which the cognitive elements of the task could be learned ahead of time and then applied to the motor task.

Some exceptions exist to the effectiveness of guidance procedures. Armstrong (Note 11; see Figure 8-8) studied various forms of physical guidance in a task for which the learner had to make a four-component forearm movement, with a complex spatial-temporal pattern, in a movement time of either 3 or 4 sec (in separate experiments). This task is considerably different from those used by Holding and colleagues, as there was no visible track to be followed and the movement had to be "memorized"; that is, a motor program had to be formulated that would control the limb in the prescribed trajectory. Armstrong failed to find that any of the guidance procedures he tried were as effective as simply practicing the task.

Why should this be so? One possibility is that, in the Armstrong task, the subject's job is to develop a program of action, and that guidance prevents the subject from gaining a relationship between (a) the commands that are given to the muscles and (b) the results of those commands in terms of movement of the lever in the environment. It may be that the various forms of guidance, preventing as they do the production of movements that are erroneous and off-track, inhibit the learning of the relationship between commands and actions that is critically important in this kind of task. These findings suggest that preventing errors in programmed responses might be harmful to learning.

These various findings permit a number of generalizations, but these are tentative as the evidence is lacking in many of these situations. First, guidance may be more effective in early practice when the task is new and unfamiliar to the learners than in later practice. Much of the apparent contribution of guidance procedures is involved in getting the response "into the ballpark" so that later refinements can be made. Also, guidance may make the stimulus information easier to handle by giving a preview of what is to happen in the task. Second, guidance may be most effective for tasks that are very slow in time (e.g., positioning responses) and/or for tasks that have critical feedback control (e.g., matching some perceived state such as a force or a position). Presumably the guidance gives the learner a good indication of the nature of the state that is to be matched, so that movements may be adjusted to match this state later on. Wrisberg and I (1975) showed that presenting the endpoint in a positioning response was sufficient to allow subjects to learn the active positioning response even when knowledge of results was not provided. Providing the endpoint can be regarded as a kind of guidance that helps to prevent errors.

Direct and indirect lines of evidence, however, suggest that guidance will be less effective for tasks that are rapid and ballistic in nature, and/or for tasks that involve the learning of motor programs (e.g., Armstrong's spatial-temporal pattern). It may be that guidance prevents the subject from developing the set of response commands necessary to produce the effective movements, because the movements are always produced for the learner, sometimes in more restrictive ways than others. It seems critical in these tasks for the learner to experience errors in responding so that the relationships between commands and errors (or movement outcomes) can be established. Thus, except for the effects that occur early in the practice sequence (mentioned above), it may well be that further guidance is nearly a waste of time, preventing the learning of the critical elements of the programmed movements. Guidance appears to act as a "crutch" here.

A final aspect of guidance that is never studied experimentally is the prevention of injury and reduction of fear. In many guidance procedures the individual is guided in performance, with the guidance being relatively "loose" unless the individual produces an error that will result in a serious injury. Gymnasts (see Figure 12-15) use manual assistance and spotting belts regularly to insure that a mistake will not result in a serious fall. Similar aids are used in beginning swimming, where long poles are often used by a partner walking along the pool edge above the learner. If the learner gets into trouble, the pole can be placed over the chest and grasped easily. Such procedures, while they provide a minimum of physical guidance for the actual movements, provide a great deal of confidence for the learners and are probably highly effective in reducing the fear and the resulting disruptions in skill learning. The key feature, it seems to me, is that guidance be minimal, while fear of injury is nearly eliminated. Even so, there remains the problem of the guidance serving as a "crutch," so that when the guidance is removed there is a marked reduction in the skill level.

Gymnasts say that it is difficult to perform a risky new skill "out of the (spotting) belt" for the first time, as the performer knows that now a mistake could cause a serious injury. But it would seem that there is no substitute for practicing the skill on your own as soon as it is safe to do so.

SUMMARY

This chapter discusses the major independent variables that affect the learning of motor skills and, thus, those variables that have an influence on the design of instructional programs. Certain variables affect learning prior to practice. Such methods as motivation for performance, goal-setting, providing instructions, modeling, verbal pretraining, and establishing prepractice references of correctness have all been shown to increase motor learning.

The structure of the practice session itself has been the subject of considerable experimentation. Major factors are (a) the number of practice trials and (b) the knowledge of results provided after each indicating performance. Other factors are massed versus distributed practice; massed practice seems to provide slightly less learning than distributed practice. However, massed practice provides a "saving" in overall practice time that can result in considerable gains in learning certain tasks. Practice sequences in which the task conditions are deliberately varied from trial to trial are slightly more effective than constant-practice conditions for adults and far more effective in children. Variability in practice appears to be more effective for open as opposed to closed skills.

It may be more effective for learning to provide practice that makes the task "difficult" for the learner. By so doing, it appears that the learner processes task cues more "deeply" and learns the task more thoroughly. The fact that fatigue does not appear to produce decrements in learning is perhaps in keeping with this evidence. There is little evidence that the conditions under which the task is learned should simulate those to which the subjects will be eventually transferred, counter to a specificity of learning hypothesis.

Motivation is probably an important factor for learning, but experiments on it do not support this contention, perhaps because of the existing motivational levels of the subjects when they are studied experimentally. Both behavior modification techniques and various social situations can be highly effective motivational methods for certain aspects of skilled performance.

Transfer of learning is involved in the study of conditions of practice. Two basic principles of transfer are (a) that it depends on the similarity between tasks and (b) that motor transfer is usually small but positive. Negative transfer can be produced under certain conditions, but it is probably mostly cognitive in nature. Simulators, drills, part-to-whole procedures, so-called "lead-up" activities, mental practice, and guidance techniques should all be evaluated in terms of transfer of learning to some criterion task.

GLOSSARY

Behavior modification. A class of techniques that use operant procedures to alter human and animal responding.

Coaction. The interaction between two behaving individuals that produces a motivation-like effect on performance.

Component interaction. A characteristic of some tasks in which the adjustment of one component of the task requires an adjustment of some other component.

Distributed practice. A sequence of practice and rest periods in which the practice time is less than the rest time.

Goal setting. A motivational technique in which subjects are encouraged to set performance goals for later practice.

Guidance. A series of techniques in which the behavior of the learner is limited or controlled by various means to prevent errors.

Intra-task interference. The mutually negative effects on performance of certain aspects of a task with other aspects of the same task.

Lead-ups. Certain tasks or activities that are typically presented to prepare learners for some more important goal response.

Massed practice. A sequence of practice and rest periods in which the rest time is less than the practice time.

Mental practice. A practice method in which the performance on the task is imagined or visualized without overt physical practice.

Modeling. A technique for presenting the learning task in which a live demonstration is used.

Operant techniques. Methods for learning in which certain behaviors are reinforced or rewarded, leading to the increase in the probability that they will occur again.

Part-whole methods. The learning technique in which the task is "broken down" into its parts for separate practice.

Schema. A rule, based on practice or experience, between certain aspects of the past responses; e.g., between past commands and response outcomes.

Similarity. A construct in most theories of transfer, indicating the extent to which certain aspects of two responses are the same.

Simulator. A training device in which certain features of the goal response are duplicated, allowing for practice that resembles that in the goal response.

Specificity of learning hypothesis. The hypothesis that the environmental conditions surrounding learning of a movement should simulate those in which the task will eventually be performed.

Suzuki method. A method for teaching violin in which the sounds of the proper techniques are presented prior to physical practice.

Variability in practice. A teaching technique in which the goal response to be made is systematically varied from trial to trial.

Verbal pretraining. The presentation of stimulus or display elements of the task in isolation so that they can be more easily responded to in later whole-task performance.

CHAPTER **13**

Feedback and Knowledge of Results

This chapter deals with one of the more important of the many variables that affect motor learning—the information that is provided to the learner about performance in attempts to learn a skill. This information, which can take many forms in the learning environment or research laboratory, informs the learner about the proficiency of a movement either during or after a response (or both). Knowledge about response proficiency appears to be critical for learning, and the failure to provide such information in some instances prevents learning altogether. The form of this information also is important for learning, and providing more of it, or altering the times at which the information is presented, can affect performance and learning. Not many of the variables studied so far have that kind of powerful influence on learning and performance, and most writers agree that such information is the single most important variable (except, of course, for practice itself) for determining motor learning and performance (e.g., I. Bilodeau, 1966).

Information about performers' movements is often under the control of the teacher or experimenter, and thus can be considered as one of the variables that comprises the conditions of practice discussed in the previous chapter. (Indeed, as mentioned there, this chapter should really be considered as an extension of the previous chapter). Understanding the principles of how such performance information appears to "work" will provide additional bases for the decisions about the design of teaching or training environments.

Finally, the study of feedback information is important for theoretical reasons as well. Any variable that critically affects motor learning must be understood if the learning process is to be understood. Many theories of learning are strongly based on the evidence indicating the ways in which such information is used by the motor system in improving its movement capabilities, and a small part of this chapter is devoted to these theoretical ideas. The evidence in this chapter will provide background information when the various theories of motor learning are discussed in more detail in Chapter 14.

CLASSIFICATIONS AND DEFINITIONS

Consider as the broadest class of information all the various kinds of sensory information that individuals can receive, including all those sources that have to do with the many diverse aspects of our lives. Of course, not all such information is related to our movements, such as the sound of wind in the trees as we walk through a forest. Those sources of information that are involved in our movements can be further classified into (a) those that are available before the action and (b) those that are available during or after the action (see Figure 13-1). Before the action, examples of such information are the position of your limbs, the sight of a ball flying toward you, the nature of the environmental setting, etc. During or after the action, information produced by the movement is received, such as the way the movement felt, sound, looked, etc., as well as the result that the movement produced in the environment (e.g., actions of a ball that is struck). This latter class is usually termed *feedback*, or *response-produced feedback*.

Given the term feedback to mean all of the response-produced information that is received during or after a movement, this class of information can be further subdivided into two broad classes: *intrinsic* feedback and *extrinsic* feedback. This classification system is shown in Figure 13-1.

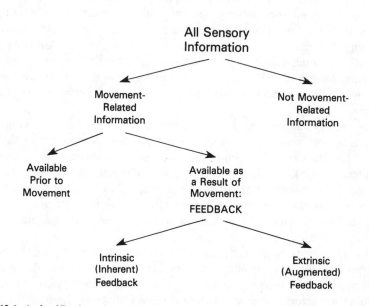

Figure 13-1. A classification of sensory information.

Intrinsic Feedback

People are able to gain information about a wide variety of aspects of their own movements through the various sensory "channels" that are sensitive to movements. These forms of information are inherent in the normal conduct of a particular response. For example, I can know I made an error in a basketball shot because I see that the ball did not go in the basket, or I hear the ball hit the rim, etc. Also, the stinging sensations I receive as I "land" on my back in a pool after a faulty action in a dive informs me that something probably went wrong. Just about every response we can make has associated with it certain of these sources of intrinsic feedback that provide a basis for evaluating those movements. Such feedback is usually rich and varied, containing substantial information about performance.

In many situations this intrinsic feedback requires almost no evaluation; I see that the ball was missed by the bat, or I feel the fall on the ice rink. Thus, errors seem to be signaled immediately and clearly. But other aspects of intrinsic feedback are not so easily recognizable, and perhaps the performer must learn to evaluate these aspects of intrinsic feedback. Examples might be the gymnast learning to sense whether or not the knees are bent during a movement and the race car driver sensing whether or not the engine is running properly during a race. Intrinsic feedback is thought to be compared to a reference of correctness, with this reference acting in conjunction with the feedback to produce an error-detection mechanism that can be learned as a result of practice or experience. Such self-detected errors are often referred to as *subjective reinforcement* (Adams, 1971; Adams & Bray, 1970).[1] Without such a reference of correctness, many forms of intrinsic feedback probably cannot be used to detect errors. I'll return to error detection mechanisms in Chapter 14.

Extrinsic Feedback

In contrast to intrinsic (inherent) feedback, *extrinsic feedback* is information provided about the task which is supplemental to, or augments, intrinsic feedback (Figure 13-1). For example, you can receive information from a buzzer when your car exceeds a certain speed—information that is not normally received in driving a car. Similar devices are used in airplanes to give information about whether or not the airflow over the wing is "stalled" so that it provides no lift. As well, the augmented information could be provided verbally, such as the presentation of one's time after a 100-meter dash or the set of scores after a gymnastics or ice skating routine. You will notice that this information is not strictly verbal in gymnastics and ice skating, but it is in a form that is capable of being verbalized.

Holding (1965; see also Singer, 1980) has described useful dimensions for

---

[1]The use of the term *reinforcement* is unfortunate, as it connotes the idea that the information is being used as a reward, as in behavior modification methods. It might not have this effect at all.

Table 13-1

Dimensions of Extrinsic Feedback

Concurrent Presented during the movement	**Terminal** Presented after the movement
Immediate Presented immediately after the relevant action	**Delayed** Delayed in time from the relevant action
Verbal Presented in a form that is spoken or capable of being spoken	**Nonverbal** Presented in a form that is not capable of being spoken
Accumulated Feedback that represents an accumulation of past performance	**Separate** Feedback that represents each performance separately
Knowledge of Results (KR) Verbalized (or verbalizable) post-response information about the outcome of the response in the environment	**Knowledge of Performance (KP)** Verbalized (or verbalizable) post-response information about the nature of the movement pattern

extrinsic feedback. First, one can distinguish between *concurrent* and *terminal* feedback. Concurrent feedback is delivered during the movement (e.g., the information about engine speed that the racing driver receives from the tachometer), while terminal feedback is postponed until after the movement has been completed (e.g., the gymnast's score). Another aspect of the extrinsic feedback is when it is delivered; it can be either immediate or delayed by some amount of time. The feedback can be verbal (or capable of being verbalized), or it can be nonverbal (e.g., a buzzer indicating that a car is going too fast). Also, the performance can be sampled for a period of time, with the accumulated feedback indicating the average performance for the past few seconds; or the feedback can be separate, representing each moment of the performance (e.g., feedback from a speedometer). Probably other categories could be used as well. See Table 13-1 for a summary of these separate dimensions.

These various dimensions of extrinsic feedback can be thought of as being independent. For example, if the extrinsic feedback is terminal, it could be either verbal or nonverbal in nature; or, if the feedback is concurrent, it might be delayed or immediate. These dimensions, then, should be thought of as separate descriptors of extrinsic feedback which are necessary to define most kinds of feedback commonly used.

Knowledge of Results Defined

One of the important categories of extrinsic feedback is termed *knowledge of results* (KR). Essentially, KR is verbal (or verbalizable), terminal (i.e., post-response) feedback about the movement proficiency, and thus it forms one combination of the various possible dimensions of extrinsic feedback (verbal-terminal) seen in Table 13-1. An example is for the experimenter or teacher to say "You were off target that time" or to present on a screen the symbolic information "Long 12" (meaning that the movement was 12 units too long). KR can be highly specific, or it can be very gross. KR can also have a rewarding component to it, such as "Very good."

Confusion abounds, however, in the motor skills literature about the use of the term KR. I. Bilodeau (1966, 1969) prefers to use the term *information feedback* and perhaps this is a good idea; but her suggestion never took hold. Also, some would use the term KR to refer to all of the information that the person could receive as a result of moving (i.e., extrinsic plus intrinsic information—Holding, 1965), but such a classification is contrary to the normal ways that KR is used in the literature. Sometimes the terms *reward* or *reinforcement* are used in place of KR; but this use is not common, and these terms are more generally used in relationship to behavior modification techniques (e.g., the rat was reinforced for pressing the bar when the buzzer rang). Despite these inconsistencies, the tendency is to use the term KR as I have defined it: verbal, terminal extrinsic feedback.

Knowledge of Performance

An additional variation of KR was presented by Gentile (1972). She coined the term *knowledge of performance* (KP) to mean extrinsic (received from someone else) feedback about the movement itself rather than the outcome of the movement in the environment which is KR as I have defined it. For example, KP refers to verbal, terminal feedback that the batter's stride was too long, while KR refers to the outcome of that stride in terms of hitting the baseball. See Table 13-1 for this additional distinction.

RESEARCH ON FEEDBACK

How do scientists do research to understand feedback and learning? What forms of feedback provide a useful advantage in motor learning, and how are these forms of feedback most effectively presented to the learner? A major problem for such research is that, in most natural situations, it is difficult to control the information received by a performer. For example, there are a wide variety of sources of feedback in the task of shooting a basketball, and it is difficult to know that any one of these channels is (or is not) being used at any one time and how the information is being used. Many researchers in motor behavior alter the environment so that a minimum of feedback information is provided to the subject, and then add back feedback information artificially (in the form of augmented feedback or KR) so that these effects can be studied directly. This technique usually involves experiments with tasks that are highly artificial and quite unsatisfying to some researchers (including myself); but a basic understanding of the functioning of error information can result.

Paradigms for Knowledge of Results Research

The dominant paradigm, or way of gaining knowledge, for understanding the functions of feedback information in learning has been the so-called KR paradigm. Here, the task to be learned is typically very simple; the most common has been the linear-positioning task, for which the person must learn to move a slide or a lever to a given position, usually while blindfolded. Variations of this basic theme are (a) the ballistic-timing task, for which the subject moves a slide or lever through a given distance (with follow-through) in a given amount of time, and/or (b) the force-estimation task, for which the subjects produce a given amount of force on each trial.

These tasks have the advantage that the person cannot effectively evaluate his or her performance outcome without some supplemental information. For example, in the linear-positioning task, when the instruction is to move 20 cm, the person cannot know whether a given attempt to move that distance was correct or not. True, the feedback from the limb is present to signal the movement details, but the person does not have the reference of correctness against which to evaluate that feedback, and hence the person has literally no information about the "success" of the response. (An exception is when the person develops an error detection mechanism prior to practice and then uses this reference as a basis for the evaluation of task feedback, e.g., the Suzuki technique discussed in Chapter 12.)

With this kind of task, one can study the use of feedback or KR by adding it back in a systematic fashion. The most elementary of these experiments might involve the contrast between providing KR and providing no KR at all. A more refined experiment may vary the time of presentation of the KR, vary the way in which the KR is presented (e.g., by a TV screen or an experimenter), or vary the nature of the KR (e.g., general or very precise). In this way, experiments that vary the nature of the feedback given to the learner can be done in the same ways as experiments about any other independent variable. The only difference is that tasks must be used that allow the control of the highly effective intrinsic feedback.

Seldom indicated directly, rather lurking behind the scenes, is the tacit assumption that the provision of KR in these artificial learning situations is fundamentally like the error information a person would normally receive in a more natural setting. Is it correct that the information "You moved 2 cm too far" in a blindfolded linear-positioning movement works fundamentally in the same way as the vision of a shot missing the basket in basketball? Certainly some different processes are involved, but it is entirely possible that the *use* of the error information is the same in both situations, in that it provides a basis for changing the movement on the next response to make it more accurate. If this assumption is correct, then this is a method for coming to an understanding of the way in which intrinsic feedback works to produce learning in natural environments where no KR is present.

The other side of the argument is that such research, using tasks that are so simple and artificial, has little to tell us about the ways in which the rich and varied sources of intrinsic feedback work in more natural settings. Not enough is known about feedback and learning to be able to answer this question at present. For now, the assumption will be that the study of KR is a means to the understanding of intrinsic feedback's operation in natural environments. However, you should be concerned that the principles may not be quite the same in these two situations.

Potential Applications of KR Research

Virtually all of the research done on KR has involved information about movement outcome. That is, the subject receives information about what happened as a result of the movement, such as whether or not the dart hit the bull's-eye, how far the softball went, or how much time was required for a unit of work on an assembly line. The hope is that the information about movement outcome will eventually (in some way) lead to the most effective movement pattern in the subject. Presumably, the learner makes successive adjustments in the movement pattern on the basis of KR so that the outcome becomes closer and closer to achieving the environmental goal.

This use of outcome information may seem odd to those of us who have had extensive practice at some sport or athletic activity. It would seem far more effective to provide information about the *patterns* of movement the person made rather than just the outcome in the environment. For example, a coach might tell a gymnast to "Pull earlier" or to "Pike harder" after a movement, referring to the particular pattern of action that the learner is attempting to produce. Such information about the movement pattern, rather than the outcome of those movements in the environment, is termed *knowledge of performance* (KP), as discussed in the previous section.

Why the focus on KR (movement outcome) when KP (movement pattern) is what will probably be most useful for application to learning situations? Probably the most important reason is that, in experiments on KR, the movement outcome usually can be measured easily, and corrections in it on the next trial can be easily charted. But when the experimenter wants to give KP, there is great difficulty in measuring the pattern of movement and then noting how the pattern changed on the subsequent trial. Until recently, these procedures were tedious (using film analysis, stripchart records, etc.), and motor behavior workers chose not to use them. Now, however, with the advent of laboratory conputers and increased emphasis on biomechanical techniques, researchers are beginning to examine KP as a source of error information.

For now, we will assume that the mechanisms of KP and KR are essentially the same. That is, we assume that what the learner does with these two kinds of information is identical, the major difference being that the two kinds of information refer to different aspects of the response. Thus, the principles that have been discovered for KR would be applicable to practical situations when KP would be given. This could be incorrect, of course, but until evidence appears to the contrary, I think this assumption is reasonable.

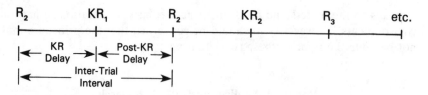

Figure 13-2. Temporal placement of events in the KR paradigm.

Temporal Aspects of KR

Most of the experiments on KR and motor learning are structured so that the temporal relationships among the events in a trial are closely controlled. These events are shown in Figure 13-2. The subject performs Response 1 (R_1), then after a delay called the *KR-delay interval,* the KR for that trial (KR_1) is delivered by the experimenter. The delay from the presentation of KR until the next response is termed the *post-KR delay,* during which presumably the person is processing the KR and deciding on the next movement. The sum of the KR-delay and post-KR delay intervals is termed the *intertrial interval* (or inter-response interval). Usually the intertrial interval is on the order of 10 to 20 sec, but of course these intervals can be practically any length to serve the purposes of a particular experimental situation.

SOME LAWS OF KR

In the next section, some of the fundamental principles of KR for motor learning situations are presented. A number of relatively "solid" conclusions can be drawn from the KR literature, probably because this area has received a great deal of study in motor skills research, and because the effects found are so robust and large relative to other variables considered. First, I treat the basic question of whether or not KR is a variable affecting performance and/or learning.

Learning versus Performance Effects of KR

KR is a Learning Variable

It is perhaps not necessary to document the fact that KR is a variable important in learning; but we have been fooled by our assumptions before, so I have provided some of the evidence here. Using the paradigm just described, Bilodeau, Bilodeau, and Schumsky (1959) used a linear-positioning task with four groups of subjects. One group had KR after each of the 20 trials, and a second group had no KR in these 20 trials. Two other groups received KR for two and six trials, respectively, before having KR withdrawn for the remainder of the 20 practice trials.

The main findings are shown in Figure 13-3, where absolute error is plotted as a function of trials for these four groups. Group 19 (with 19 KRs, after all but the 20th trial) showed an initial rapid decrease in error, fol-

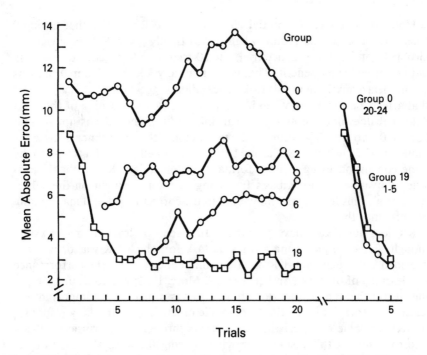

Figure 13-3. Absolute errors in a linear-positioning response as a function of KR. (The group numbers indicate the number of KRs received before KR withdrawal; Group 0 is switched to a KR condition at the right, where its performance is compared to Group 19's first five trials replotted from the left.) (from Bilodeau, Bilodeau, & Schumsky, 1959).

lowed by a more gradual decrease. On the other hand, Group 0, which had no KR at all, showed essentially no change in performance over the 20 practice trials. For the remaining two groups, improvement occurred on trials that followed the administration of KR, but the improvement stopped when KR was withdrawn, with slight decrements in performance afterward.

Did KR affect the learning in this task? As with any other variable that could affect learning and/or performance, these data can be interpreted in at least two ways. First, we could conclude that Group 19 learned more than Group 0 (as evidenced by the fact that they performed more effectively) and that KR is a variable that affects learning. But an equally likely possibility is that KR has affected performance only temporarily, perhaps through some kind of motivational or "energizing" effect. Thus, it could be that when these temporary effects of KR are allowed to dissipate with rest (as with fatigue effects), the temporary effects of KR would vanish and performance would regress to the original level (see Chapter 11).

A partial answer to this question was provided by Bilodeau et al. (1959) when they transferred their Group 0 subjects to the KR conditions for an additional five trials. In the right portion of Figure 13-3, the absolute errors on these five trials are plotted together with the first five trials of Group 19. The size of the errors, as well as the pattern of change with trials, was practically identical for these two sets of trials. That is, Group 0, receiving the KR after 20 trials without KR, performed nearly the same as Group 19, which had never received any previous practice on this task.

How effective were the initial 20 trials of no-KR practice that Group 0 received? Because this group, when it was finally given KR, behaved like Group 19 on its first practice trial, the 20-trial no-KR practice of this task did not provide any benefit. That is, without any KR, the Group 0 subjects did not learn anything in this task. These data suggest that KR is a variable that affects performance when it is present, as well as learning of the task. And, KR does not simply *affect* learning; rather, when KR is not present (Group 0), no learning occurs in the task at all. Other experiments show the same thing (Trowbridge & Cason, 1932), and Newell (1974) has come to the same conclusion using a more formal transfer design. KR probably provided the subjects with a basis for changing the movement on the subsequent trial, thus leading the individual to the correct target and maintaining performance there.

KR does not always have such dramatic effects on learning motor skills, though. For example, using a tracking task for which KR was or was not provided after each trial, KR had only minimal effects on the performance and learning of the task (Archer, Kent, & Mote, 1956; I. Bilodeau, 1966). Is the answer that the information about errors is somehow not important for learning to track? I don't think so. While practicing the tracking response, subjects are able to detect their own errors through the intrinsic feedback (mostly visual in this instance) provided during the normal course of the trial. For example, when a person makes a move to track the target after contact is lost, the result of that move (in terms of whether or not the target was recontacted) can be seen directly; this visual information probably served the same function as the verbal KR did here and in the positioning experiment described earlier. This observation is in accord with the idea that the presentation of information about errors to the learner is more effectively studied in situations in which learners cannot evaluate their own errors.

Some form of error information is important, if not critical, for motor learning, and without such information little or no learning will occur. Such error information can be provided by KR (as in the positioning response) where it is the only information that the subject can use for learning, or the error information can be provided in the form of intrinsic feedback in those tasks for which such feedback gives meaningful information. Thus, designers of learning situations should do everything possible to ensure that such error information is available to learners.

Performance Effects of KR

Are there performance effects of KR in addition to the learning effects? It is reasonable to think so. One of these possible effects can be thought of as motivating. One component of KR presented to subjects has the effect of providing increased interest in the task and a desire to do well. The converse seems correct also; never providing KR often seems to result in the learner's losing interest, becoming bored, and perhaps ceasing to practice. Closely related to this motivating effect is an *energizing* effect, whereby the KR can be seen as providing an activating role for the learner. This effect is similar to "waking up" the subject, so that more effort is brought to the task on the subsequent trials. KR may also have a motivational effect through goal-setting (see Chapter 12), whereby KR establishes new and higher performance goals for ther person (Locke, Cartledge, & Koeppel, 1968).

Is Error Information Absolutely Essential for Learning?

From the point of view of practical application, we could stop right here, as it has been demonstrated that error information undoubtedly helps in the learning process. But a larger issue is at stake that has to do with theories of learning. A number of learning theories are absolutely firm in saying that error information (either intrinsic or extrinsic) is critical for motor learning and that without it no learning can occur (e.g., theories by Adams, 1971; Schmidt, 1975b; and others discussed in Chapter 14). However, a number of experiments (on the surface, at least) *appear* to show that error information may not be critical for learning. Because of the importance of this kind of generalization for theory, I treat two of these lines of evidence next. It should become clear that error information is, in fact, a critical variable for learning, as suspected.

Deafferentation Studies

One example came from Taub and Berman (1968; Taub, 1976) in a program of research described in Chapter 6 related to deafferentation and movement control. A deafferented monkey is placed firmly in an apparatus with a rubber bulb taped to the deafferented hand. An electrode is attached to the (normally afferented) cheek area, to which a shock can be delivered. A tone is presented, and then after a short delay the monkey is shocked on the cheek. However, by squeezing the bulb (which the animal cannot feel, remember), the shock can be turned off; by squeezing the bulb after the tone but before the shock, the animal can avoid the shock altogether. The main finding is that with practice, the animals learn to avoid the shock. Yet there is no obvious KR, there is no feedback from the responding limb, and there are no rewards presented by the experimenter.

Because the Taub and Berman findings seem to suggest that learning can occur without external error information, these data are frequently taken as evidence for some kind of internal feedback loops that are important for learning. It is argued that because some form of error information is critical for learning and because no external error information was provided, some kind of internal feedback must have served as the basis for learning the avoidance response. This internal feedback is frequently called *efference copy* or *corrolary discharge* and will be discussed in more detail in Chapter 14 (Miles & Evarts, 1979).

But the fact is that the monkey *does* have feedback about his response. When the bulb is squeezed, the animal receives immediate information about it, in that the shock is turned off. Surely this is little different from having a monkey press a bar and receive a pellet of food as a reward. The action and the information about success are paired closely in time, and learning probably results from this association. But how does the monkey make the movement the first time? It is reasonable to think that when the shock is delivered the monkey engages in random activity in an attempt to avoid it; part of this activity is squeezing the bulb, eliminating the shock. Thus, a motor command is produced (among all the others as well), the shock goes off, and the animal learns that one accompanies the other. So the Taub and Berman findings do not necessarily mean that internal feedback loops exist as a basis for learning.

Error-Detection Mechanisms

Consider another study (Solley, 1956) in which subjects were positioned in a special motorized chair that could tilt from side to side, controlled by a switch near the subject's hand. The experimenter first positioned the subject in a vertical position and then tilted the chair either 30° to the right or left of vertical. Then the subject used the switch to move back to vertical. When the subject thought that the correct position was achieved, the score (in terms of deviations from the vertical) was recorded. Then the subject was randomly moved back and forth, presumably to interfere with the subject's memory of the just-achieved position, then placed in the vertical, and then tipped to 30° again, whereupon the subject attempted to power back to vertical. This procedure was repeated for 30 trials.

The results are presented in Figure 13-4, where absolute errors in position achieved by the subject are plotted against trials. Even though KR was never given, the subjects were clearly able to improve in this task; and these improvements are probably due to learning (although no transfer design was used). How do the subjects learn in this situation?

I believe these data mean that the subjects were developing an error-detection mechanism (Chapter 6) during practice and that this mechanism was responsible for the improvement in performance without KR (Schmidt, 1975b). This task seems highly feedback-based, with the subject moving to that position recognized as correct. Now, the experimenter presented the

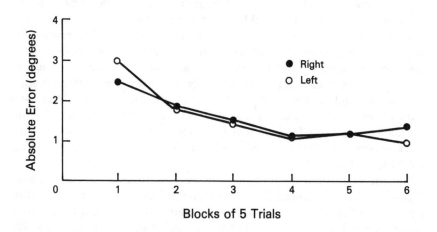

Figure 13-4. Absolute errors in obtaining a vertical position in a tilt-chair apparatus. (The two curves are for subjects tilted to the right and left.) (from Solley, 1956).

correct (vertical) position before every trial. If this experience created a memory of the vertical position, then the subject could try to match that memory with his own feedback on the next trial. With every trial, the experimenter presented additional information about vertical, and thus the memory became stronger with each trial. Thus, with a stronger and more distinct representation of vertical, the subject was able to match it more accurately on each successive trial—even without KR.

Similar results have been produced by Adams and Dijkstra (1966; see Figure 15-4, page 619) and Wrisberg and Schmidt (1975) using linear-positioning responses. Here, the "feel" of the target position was presented before the actual test movements, analogous to presenting the vertical position for Solley's subjects. Puzzling findings come from Henderson (1974, 1975), who showed learning without KR in blindfolded dart throwers. (It is possible that they could hear the impact of the dart, though, thus providing the error information needed for learning.)

The Answer Still Appears To Be "Yes"

If the interpretations I have given about these studies can be accepted, then the original conclusion about the role of error information in learning still remains. It appears that for motor learning to occur, some form of information about errors must be presented to the learner. The evidence suggests, however, that this information can be presented in a wide variety of ways, depending on the task and environmental conditions.

Relative Frequency and Absolute Frequency Effects

Having established that error information is required for learning, we might next ask whether more KR will result in more learning. People who study KR distinguish between two measures of the "amount" of KR that is provided: *absolute frequency* and *relative frequency* of KR.

Absolute frequency of KR is simply the number of KR presentations received over the course of practice. If 80 practice trials are given, and the person receives a KR after every other trial for a total of 40 presentations, then the absolute frequency of KR is 40. On the other hand, relative frequency of KR refers to the percentage of trials on which KR is provided. It is the number of KRs provided divided by the total number of trials and multiplied by 100 to convert to a percentage. In this example, the relative frequency of KR is $(40/80) \times 100 = 50\%$. The relative frequency of 50% means that KR was provided on half the practice trials.

Which of these two KR scheduling measures is the more critical for learning? Bilodeau and Bilodeau (1958) were the first to investigate this question, using a task in which subjects turned a knob to a target position without vision. For four different groups, KR was provided after (a) every trial, (b) every third trial, (c) every fourth trial, and (d) every 10th trial, producing relative frequencies of KR of 100%, 33%, 25%, and 10%, respectively. The number of trials received by these groups, however, was adjusted so that all groups received 10 KRs; for example, the group with 100% relative frequen-

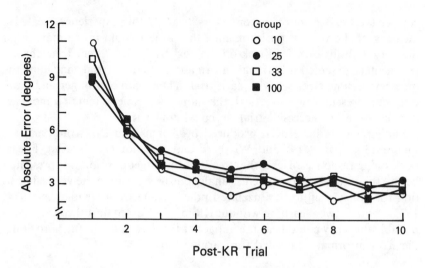

Figure 13-5. Absolute errors in positioning for trials immediately following KR. (Group numbers indicate the total number of trials, KR plus no-KR, received.) (from Bilodeau & Bilodeau, 1958).

cy received 10 trials, and the group with 33% relative frequency received 30 trials. Thus, the experiment involved groups that had different relative frequencies, but constant absolute frequencies (10) of KR.

The important results are shown in Figure 13-5. Here, 10 trials are presented for each of the four groups. Only the trials immediately following the presentation of a KR are plotted. This is, of course, every trial for the group with 100% relative frequency of KR, only one-third of the trials for the group with 33% relative frequency, and so on. The amount of error on each trial, as well as the pattern of change of the errors as trials progressed, was nearly the same for the four groups. Even though the groups differed greatly in terms of the relative frequency of KR, when the absolute frequency was equated, no difference in performance occurred between groups. For performance, the critical feature of KR in this experiment was the number of times that KR was given; the percentage of time that KR was given appeared not to be an important variable. Another way to think of this is that the trials presented between those trials that received KR (i.e., the no-KR trials) were useless, neither contributing to nor distracting from the subject's performance of the task.

Since 1958, and especially since I. Bilodeau's (1966, 1969) review chapters on KR, motor behavior researchers have taken the Bilodeaus' data to mean that lack of performance difference between groups in Figure 13-5 implies that there were no differences in the amount learned under these conditions. If you are alert, you will already have noticed that Bilodeau and Bilodeau (1958) did not use a transfer design; thus the results do not necessarily tell us about learning—only about performance effects. Recently, Johnson, Wicks, and Ben-Sira (Note 22) have performed a similar experiment with a transfer design, and the results are quite surprising.

They used a linear-positioning task and three different schedules of presenting KR. One group had 100% relative frequency for 10 trials (Group

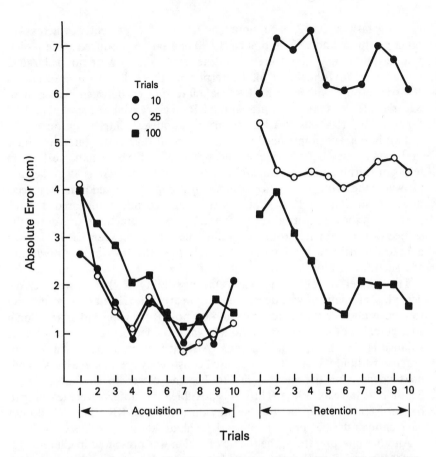

Figure 13-6. Absolute errors in positioning for trials immediately following KR (left) and for every trial in a no-KR retention test. (Group numbers indicate total number of trials, KR plus no-KR, provided in acquisition.) (from Johnson, Wicks, & Ben-Sira, Note 22).

10), another group had 25% relative frequency for 40 trials (Group 40), and a third group had 10% relative frequency for 100 trials (Group 100). The absolute frequency for all groups was equal at 10. Thus these groups differed in terms of the number of no-KR trials that were presented between each of the KR trials (0, 3, and 9, respectively). The relative amount learned was measured on a no-KR transfer test one week after these treatments. If Bilodeau's and Bilodeau's interpretations about learning are correct, no differences should exist between these groups on the transfer test, for they all had the same absolute frequency of KR (i.e., 10 KRs).

The absolute errors in performance are presented in Figure 13-6. In the left half of the figure are the data from trials after a KR presentation, graphed as Bilodeau's and Bilodeau's (1958) data were (see Figure 13-5). Just as in the earlier study, the groups did not differ in performance. But look at the right half of the figure, where the absolute errors on the transfer test are presented. Clear differences existed between the groups, with Group 100 showing the least error and Group 10 showing the most. There was a clear relationship between the number of trials received and the performance level at transfer. And it appeared as though Group 100 continued to learn the task on Day 2, even though no KR was ever presented, whereas the other groups did not. Ho and Shea (1978) had earlier produced some similar findings, although the differences in the retention test were not as large as those found in Johnson et al. I interpret all these data to mean that the 100-trial group, with nine no-KR trials interspersed between each pair of KR trials, learned the most; presenting KR on every trial was least beneficial for learning. This was clearly contrary to Bilodeau's interpretation.

Two important points need to be made about this study. First, as I have said many times before, one should not interpret performance effects in terms of learning unless a transfer design is provided. Here is a good example where the wrong conclusion is made by doing so (massed practice effects discussed in Chapter 12 is another example). Second, it appeared that the practice on the no-KR trials did, after all, provide something useful for the subjects. The 100-trial group, with nine such trials between KR trials, was able to learn the task far more effectively than the 10-trial group without any such trials. How?

The answer is far from clear. One possibility is that a weak error-detection mechanism was developed from early KR trials and that moving to a position near the correct position on no-KR trials provided additional strengthening of it, even though no KR was provided. This is more or less as Adams' (1971) theory would predict. Also, it had been shown earlier that practice without KR results in increased consistency (i.e., decreased VE) but no tendency for the movements to become closer to the target (e.g., Seashore & Bavelas, 1941). Thus, it is possible that subjects were learning to be consistent in Johnson et al.'s study during the no-KR trials. We do not have enough data at present to clearly evaluate these hypotheses.

Another interpretation, the theme of which was presented in Chapter 12, is that the no-KR trials interspersed between the KR trials in the group with 10% relative frequency made the task quite "difficult" for the subjects. The idea is that without KR the subjects had to work hard to discern the relevant task cues, and they probably coded the positional information more completely (i.e., more "deeply") than the 100% relative frequency subjects did. Seen in this way, KR acts as a form of guidance, or as a "crutch," in performing the task. KR has such powerful effects with respect to keeping the subjects on target that the subjects fail to learn the critical elements of the task that are to be responded to when the KR is removed. This hypothesis has been very useful with respect to the guidance literature (Chapter 12). It is possible that this hypothesis applies to the extent that KR acts as a form of guidance.

A few practical implications are possible. First, KR is important for improving performance, and the more the better. But these KR trials should probably be interspersed with no-KR trials, so that the subjects are forced to learn to perform the task without the guidance provided by KR. In this theme, presenting KR every other trial or every third trial might be an effective method. It also seems that a dependency on KR should be avoided, perhaps by making it clear to the learners that they will eventually have to perform the task without any assistance at all from KR, thus forcing the learner to deal with the relevant task cues.

Temporal Locus of KR

This section deals with the questions about when KR should be presented in the learning sequence. The question really concerns three subquestions having to do with the effect of KR delay, post-KR delay, and the so-called trials-delay technique.

KR-Delay Interval

Referring to Figure 13-2, the KR-delay interval is the amount of time that KR is delayed after the movement. We often hear the statement that immediate feedback is more effective than delayed feedback, which makes considerable sense. That is, if KR is delayed too much, it would seem that the learner would have a difficult time remembering what was done so that the information could be used to change the response on the next trial. Otherwise, the response after a delayed KR might produce the same error. Does the evidence support such a viewpoint?

Beginning with an experiment in the 1930s by Lorge and Thorndike (1935) and continuing into the 1960s, many experiments have been conducted to study the delay of KR. In the Lorge-Thorndike study, subjects were asked to toss small loops of chain backward to an unseen target. KR about errors was provided either immediately or after 1, 2, 4, or 6 sec for different groups of subjects. The delay of KR had no negative effect on the performance of this task, as all of the groups' performance curves were nearly the same (there was no transfer design). This was somewhat surprising, because motor behavior researchers had expected to find large KR-delay effects in situations like this.

Perhaps, though, the delay of KR was not long enough. This is certainly a fair criticism, as 6 sec does not seem to be very long to wait for KR. Subsequent experiments have used delays ranging from a few seconds to a few minutes, and one study even delayed KR for one week. This work, most of which has employed slow positioning responses, has generally failed to show that KR delay has any effect on performance (see I. Bilodeau, 1966, 1969, for a review of this work). Thus, for over a decade the prevailing view has been that KR delay had no effect on performance and, therefore, on learning.

Recently, however, this conclusion has been challenged. First, Simmons and Snyder (Note 23) have shown that there was more absolute error for groups with 20-sec KR-delay intervals than for those with zero-sec KR delays, with the task being a rapid ballistic response. It is tempting to suggest that the KR-delay effect might be limited to rapid movements, but recall that Lorge's and Thorndike's (1935) study used ballistic tossing responses (but only very short KR delays). Another, more important problem with all of this work is, again, that transfer designs have not been used to evaluate the relative amount learned for the various KR delay groups. Thus, strictly speaking, the conclusions drawn by I. Bilodeau (1966, 1969) and many others that KR delays have no effect on learning are not based on the proper evidence. Schmidt and Shea (1976) did use a transfer design and a linear positioning task, finding no effect of KR delay on learning.

To summarize, presently there is a great deal of evidence showing that increased KR delay has no effect on performance, some data showing negative effects of KR delay on performance and of KR delay on motor learning. Obviously more research needs to be done, both for practical and theoretical reasons.

Filling the KR-Delay Interval

What is the effect of requiring the learner to perform various activities during an otherwise "empty" KR-delay interval? This question is motivated by an information-processing viewpoint about KR, according to which certain other activities should interfere with various processes that occur during KR delay, and thus the effects should be seen in learning of the task.

Shea and Upton (1976) had subjects perform linear-positioning responses, but the situation was slightly different from the usual case. First, two positions were to be performed on each trial rather than one; these positions were to be learned, and they were the same on every trial. Second, one group was asked to perform other positioning movements during the KR-delay interval, positioning movements that were different from those being learned; another group just rested during KR delay. Thus, on a given trial, the subject would produce Movement 1, then Movement 2, then would engage in the performance of the other movements (or would rest if in the other condition), then after 30 sec receive KR about Movement 1 and Movement 2, then engage in the next trial, and so on. The relative amount learned by these two groups was measured on a transfer test for which KR was never presented.

Figure 13-7 shows the average absolute errors (the two positions are averaged together) for these two groups on the original practice trials and on the no-KR transfer trials. From the left part of the figure, filling the KR-delay

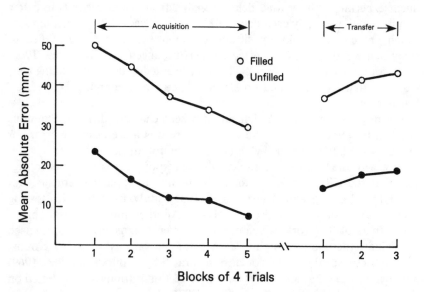

Figure 13-7. Absolute errors in positioning as a function of the processing demands imposed during the KR-delay interval (from Shea & Upton, 1976).

interval increased absolute error on the acquisition trials, indicating that the extraneous movements had a negative effect on performance. Was this due to learning? The relative amount learned can be estimated on the transfer trials in the right-hand portion of the figure. It seemed clear that the decrements in performance caused by the extraneous movements did, in fact, interfere with the learning of the tasks.

What is happening here? Perhaps the most obvious interpretation of these findings is that the subjects were engaging in various information-processing activities during the KR-delay interval and that the requirement of the extraneous movements in some way interfered with this processing, degrading learning of the task. What kinds of processes might they be? One possibility is that the subject must retain in short-term memory the sensory consequences (the "feel") of the movement until the KR is presented, so that these two can be combined in some way. If the other movements are required, then there will be either a blocked capacity to "recycle" the information in short-term memory or a "confusion" about where the target movements were, resulting in less effective use of KR when it is presented. The practice implications are clear. The KR-delay interval should be kept relatively free of other movements that could be confused with the target movements.

Post-KR-Delay Interval

Next, consider the other portion of the inter-response interval—the post-KR-delay interval, or the time between the presentation of KR and the production of the next movement. Unlike the hypothesis that the subject was trying to remember the aspects of the response during the KR-delay interval, during the post-KR-delay interval it appears that different things are going on. In particular, KR has now been delivered, indicating that the movement was incorrect in some way. Now the learner must generate a response that is different from the previous one, hopefully one that is more nearly correct. So, in contrast to the hypothesis that the learner is a holder of information in the KR-delay interval, the learner is thought to be an active and creative movement changer in the post-KR-delay interval.

If the subject is actively processing KR and changing the movement during post-KR delay, then shortening the post-KR-delay interval past a certain point should decrease learning in the task, as the subject would not have the opportunity to develop an effective new response. Some support for this view exists in the verbal learning literature using *concept-formation tasks*. For example, the subject might be presented with a picture containing a number of objects (e.g., squares, triangles, circles, etc.) that vary along dimensions such as color, size, location in the picture, etc. The subject's task is to view this picture on Trial 1 and to state a concept (i.e., a generalization) that accounts for the information in the picture. For example, the concept might be "Things with straight edges are red and things with round edges are blue." This is the subject's response, analogous to R_1, R_2, etc., in Figure 13-2. After this, the experimenter gives KR (e.g., "Wrong"), the subject is shown the picture again and asked to respond again. Here, the problem for the learner is to generate an effective and new concept that will hopefully be the one that the experimenter has in mind.

This is, of course, analogous to developing a new movement pattern that the motor skills experimenter has in mind.

Using these kinds of tasks, various experimenters have found that decreasing the post-KR-delay interval increases the number of trials needed to arrive at the correct concept in both adults (e.g., Bourne & Bunderson, 1963; Bourne, Guy, Dodd, & Justesen, 1965; White & Schmidt, 1972) and in children (Croll, 1970). The principal explanation for these findings is that the limitations in the time for generating a new hypothesis about the concept delayed the discovery of it. But, at the same time, the imposed deadline probably created stress in these laboratory situations, adding to the subjects' problems in coming to the correct concept.

A similar question was studied in the motor behavior realm by Weinberg, Guy, and Tupper (1964), using a linear-positioning task and blindfolded subjects. The post-KR-delay interval was varied at 1, 5, 10, and 20 sec in separate groups. The 1-sec interval produced the least accurate performance in acquisition, with the other intervals producing about equal accuracies. For this task, 1 sec was not long enough to process the KR and to generate a more effective, new response, but 5 sec was. No transfer design was used in this study, though, so these effects might not be learning effects; this possibility needs to be studied in the future. Gallagher and Thomas (1980) found similar effects with children (also with no transfer design). Generally, they found that children were disrupted more than adults by shortening the post-KR-delay interval. When children were given sufficiently long intervals (12 sec), they could perform the task as well as adults. This finding suggests that a major difference between children's and adults' motor learning is in the generation of new and creative solutions to movement problems, not that children are inherently less effective in producing movement responses. Finally, Barclay and Newell (1980) found that children, when allowed to choose their own post-KR-delay intervals, did so with intervals of only 2 or 3 sec. This suggests that the effects of post-KR-delay intervals varied experimentally at 10 sec or more in these simple tasks might be well over the interval length at which learning begins to be affected.

Filling the Post-KR-Delay Interval

If information processing must occur in the post-KR-delay interval in order to select a new response, then processing some additional information from some secondary task should reduce performance and learning. Rogers (1974) found in a positioning task that extra information processing in the post-KR-delay interval interfered with the performance of the position but that increasing the length of the interval tended to nullify this effect. With increased interval length, the subjects could presumably find time to process the information necessary to produce the new action. Boucher (1974) has found similar effects early in practice (but not later in practice) in a positioning task, but Magill (1973) failed to. This issue was discussed clearly by Schendel and Newell (1976); the weight of evidence suggests that performance is depressed with extraneous activities inserted into the post-KR-delay interval. Be careful, though, as none of these studies has used a transfer design, and these effects do not necessarily mean that learning is impaired by these manipulations in post-KR-delay interval.

Again, the practical implications of these findings are relatively clear. After the presentation of KR, the learner needs to have time to generate an effective, new movement, and thus should probably not be interrupted during this processing in the post-KR-delay interval. Presumably, the more complex the task, the more critical the time for processing. Also, with well-learned tasks, for which there are fewer alternative actions to consider, learners appear to suffer considerably less from short or filled post-KR-delay intervals.

Trials-Delay Procedure

The generalizations about the temporal location of KR in a trial sequence need to be qualified somewhat. Most of the evidence shows that increasing KR delay does not degrade performance so long as the KR for a given trial occurs before the next trial (i.e., KR_n occurs before R_{n+1}—Figure 13-2). Lorge and Thorndike (1935) found that their subjects could learn to toss links of chain accurately with 6 sec of empty KR delay but that they could not learn if the KR referred to the second previous throw rather than to the immediately previous one. I. Bilodeau (1956, 1966, 1969) and others have investigated this procedure more completely in what has come to be known as the *trials-delay procedure*.

Discrete tasks. In this method, the KR for a given response does not directly follow (after a delay) the response to which it refers. Rather, one or more other trials is interpolated between a given response and its KR. Thus, in contrast to the usual procedure shown in Figure 13-2, at the top of Figure 13-8, R_1 and KR_1 are separated by R_2, and there is a "one-trial" delay between a given response and its KR. At the bottom of the figure is a two-trial delay, where two trials separate a given response and its KR. A potential problem for the learner is the increased difficulty in "keeping track of" the feedback from the movement and the KR that goes with it. Imagine the difficulty in situations with a 6-trial delay!

Bilodeau (1956) investigated this problem using a lever-positioning task with blindfolded subjects. In two experiments, she varied the number of trials by which KR was delayed; in Experiment 1 she used 0, 1, 2, and 3 trials delay; and in Experiment 2 she used 0, 2, and 5 trials delay. (Remember, a trials delay of 5 means that there were five trials inserted between a

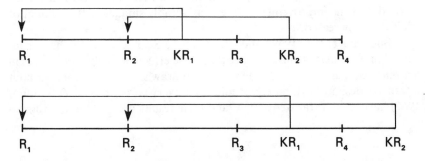

Figure 13-8. The trials-delay technique, showing a trials delay of one (top) and two (bottom). (A given response and its KR are separated by other trials of the same task.)

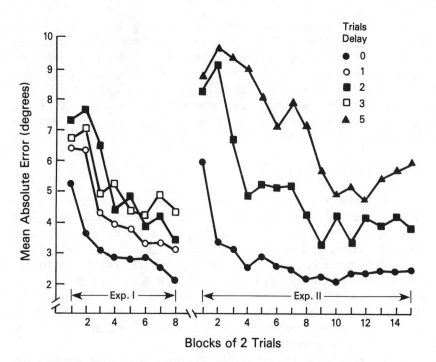

Figure 13-9. Absolute error in positioning as a function of the amount of trials-delay. (The group label indicates the number of trials separating a movement and its KR.) (from Bilodeau, 1956).

given trial and its KR.) Subjects were fully informed about this technique and were questioned to be certain that they understood how KR was being administered.

The data from the two experiments are shown in Figure 13-9, where absolute error in positioning (for trials following KR) is plotted against trials for the various trials-delay conditions. For both experiments, as the trials delay was increased, performance accuracy systematically decreased. This can be seen both in the rate of approach to the final performance level and in the level of final performance. This effect occurred despite the fact that the groups with the largest trials delay had slightly more practice.[2] These findings differed somewhat from the earlier ones by Lorge and Thorndike (1935), in that improvement in performance did occur under the trials-delay method, but the improvements were considerably smaller as the amount of trials delay increased.

I. Bilodeau (1966, 1969) and others (e.g., Schmidt, 1975a) have concluded on the basis of this evidence that these effects were due to changes in learning. But, as I have said, one should not draw such a conclusion without a transfer design. Fortunately, studies by Lavery (1962; Lavery & Suddon, 1962) have used a transfer design, and their results are quite interesting.

---

[2]They had slightly more practice because, with a trials delay of five, an extra five trials had to be used so that the number of KRs given would be the same as in a group with zero trials delay.

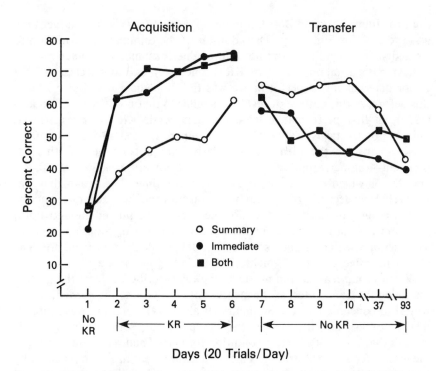

Figure 13-10. Percent correct responses for various trials-delay conditions. (Immediate had KR after every trial, Summary had KR about every trial presented after each block of 20 trials, and Both had both forms of KR.) (from Lavery, 1962).

Lavery (1962) used three tasks: (a) a "pinball" task for which a ball was "shot" up an inclined trackway to a target by the release of a spring-activated plunger, (b) a "hammer ball" task in which a ball was propelled up the same track by a hand-held hammer, and (c) a "puff-ball" task in which a ping-pong ball was moved up a tube by a puff of air via a pipe from the subject's mouth. Three methods were used to give KR. One was the usual condition in which KR is given after every trial, called "Immediate."[3] A second method is "Summary," where the performance on every trial in a 20-trial sequence is shown, but only after the 20th trial had been completed; no KR was given after each trial as in Immediate. This Summary technique was more or less the same as the trials-delay technique, as the KR for Trial 1 was separated from its trial by the other 19 responses in the block, Trial 2 by the other 18, and so on. Finally, the third condition involved both the post-response KR and the Summary score, labeled "Both." Six days of practice were given under these conditions.

Performance on all three tasks averaged together (they were all measured as percentage correct) is shown in Figure 13-10. Consider first the data for the acquisition trials (left side of graph), for which KR was given in the various forms described above. For the two groups with KR after each trial

----

[3]These are my labels, and they do not appear in Lavery's report.

(i.e., for Immediate and Both), number of correct trials was far larger than was the case for Summary. The addition of the Summary information to Immediate to create Both did not improve performance very much relative to having the usual post-response KR (Immediate), and so it is clear that the major determinant of performance was the Immediate KR. But we knew this before, as this pattern of results is similar to that produced by Bilodeau (1956), in that performance in acquisition (while KR was present) was hindered by the trials-delay technique (compare Figures 13-9 and 13-10).

Now consider the measure of relative amount learned in this experiment—the performance on the transfer trials on Days 7, 8, 9, 10, 37, and 93 for which no KR was provided at any time. The group that was formerly least accurate (i.e., Summary) was now the most accurate; and the other two groups that were the most accurate (i.e., Immediate and Both) were now the least accurate. Furthermore, the latter two groups appeared to lose accuracy with each successive no-KR day, while Summary did not. The effects persisted to Day 37 but were essentially gone by Day 93.

Which group learned the most? Using (as described earlier) the performance on the transfer test as the measure of relative amount learned, we are forced to conclude that the Summary (trials delay) condition was more effective for learning than either the Immediate or Both conditions. It is curious that the most effective condition for performance in acquisition was the least effective for learning! This basic experiment has been repeated by Lavery and Suddon (1962), but with the same trials-delay methods as used by Bilodeau (1956), and the results were nearly the same as in Figure 13-10. This is yet another example where it is critical to examine learning effects on a transfer test. The general belief about trials delay (based on Bilodeau, 1956) had been that her performance effects were due to differences in learning. Even though people knew about learning-performance effects and transfer designs, Lavery's important results were not taken seriously by those writing in the area (e.g., Adams, 1971; I. Bilodeau, 1966, 1969; Schmidt, 1975a). This examination of Lavery's experiment now reveals that we were incorrect in this regard.

Why should such effects occur? One possibility is that KR, when provided after each trial, serves a function much like that of guidance (see Chapter 12, "Guidance"). KR seems to provide powerful direction for the subject to keep him or her on target. Because the person is performing so well, he or she comes to rely on KR to the exclusion of learning the proper cues in the task; that is, KR is acting as a "crutch" which, when removed, results in large performance decrements. These effects may occur because subjects with KR fail to use the relevant sources of intrinsic feedback or because of some other mechanism yet to be uncovered.

If individuals are not attending to the proper elements in the task, could the problem be remedied by instructions? Some time ago, Sanderson (1929) gave (or did not give) subjects instructions indicating that they would receive a retention test, and learning in a finger maze increased with instructions to retain. Lavery (1962, Experiment 2) used this idea with the Summary and Immediate KR conditions, measuring the effects on learning on a transfer test. Thus, the procedures were mainly the same as in the previous studies.

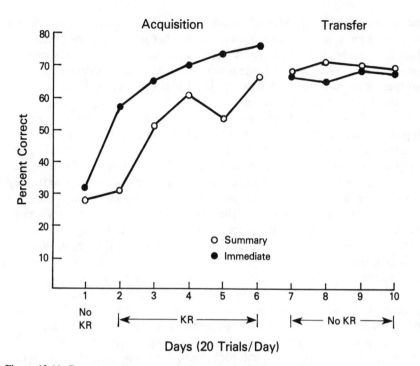

Figure 13-11. Percent correct responses for two trials-delay conditions. (Both groups were warned of an impending transfer test without KR.) (from Lavery, 1962).

The major findings are shown in Figure 13-11. Here again, performance in acquisition was hindered by the Summary condition relative to Immediate. But with instructions to retain, the Immediate condition still learned more (based on the transfer trials) than the Summary condition, but the effect was far smaller than was the case in Figure 13-10. Informing the subjects that a retention test would be given apparently was important in having the subjects learn the task under the Immediate KR technique. Knowing that a retention test would follow may have encouraged the subjects in the Immediate condition to process the cues from the task more effectively, leading to more effective learning.

At the first reading, these Summary KR methods, or the trials-delay techniques, appear to be little "tricks" that serve mostly to keep experimenters interested in their work. But these methods are used far more in practical situations than we might suspect. For example, KR is often given as a summary statement after a large number of trials (e.g., "You were doing much better on those trials"), and trials-delay methods are also used (e.g., "The first trial was good, but the second trial was not"). In earlier textbooks (including Schmidt, 1975a), it was implied that these methods should be avoided, as they seriously impair learning. I now see that this is not correct and that a great deal must be learned about these methods to use them to their fullest advantage in structuring learning sessions.

Continuous tasks. From the previous evidence, trials delay of KR undoubtedly interferes with performance of discrete tasks. It does so probably because the learner has a difficult time associating the actions that he or she produced with the results of those actions (indicated by KR), largely because a given action becomes mixed with other similar actions by the time that KR for the first action is presented. A similar situation exists with continuous tasks for which the feedback from the movement is delayed in time, so that other movements are interpolated between a given movement and the feedback presented to the person.

There are numerous examples. A common one is when a person is speaking into a public address system in an auditorium or gym with poor acoustics and echos occur after a delay of a quarter of a second or so. In these settings and in laboratory simulations of them, speech is very difficult to produce, causing a great deal of halting and stammering on the part of usually effective speakers. One hypothesis is that the feedback from a person's voice, delayed by the duration of the sound's travel during the echo, arrives back to the ear after the next voice command is issued. The speaker is confused because the sound heard does not "agree with" the action that was just produced.

Another example that is not so familiar relates to the space program. In the recent unmanned U.S. moon landings, a small tractor-like device was placed on the moon's surface, controlled remotely from Houston. It was designed to pick up materials and to perform certain tests. The tractor was viewed by a TV camera in the spacecraft on the moon's surface, and the messages were sent back to earth for viewing by a controller (Figure 13-12). The problem was that these visual feedback signals were delayed by approximately 2-sec involved in sending the signals through space to the receiver in Houston. Furthermore, any command (e.g., to stop) was also delayed by the same amount, as this command would have to travel back to the moon. Thus, a 4-sec feedback delay existed between the actions of the people in Houston and the visual consequences of that action seen on their TV screen.

The problem was that the controller did not want the tractor to fall off a cliff or turn itself over, so the use of normal ongoing control movements (such as might be used in controlling a bulldozer) could not be used. The ac-

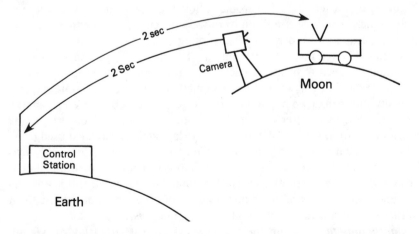

Figure 13-12. Motor control problems with feedback delays. (The feedback delay in controlling a device on the moon is about 4 sec, 2 sec for a command to be received on the moon and 2 sec for the TV picture of it to be transmitted to Earth.)

tions of the controller and the vision of the subsequent actions of the tractor were separated, so that a number of control actions would come between a given movement by the controller and the resulting vision of it from the moon. A strategy was used in which the controller would make a single movement and then stop; in a few seconds, the controller would see the tractor move and then stop. Thus, the future movements of the device could be determined more safely.

This kind of problem is involved to some extent in the control of many vehicles, particularly submarines (for which the delay is on the order of 13 sec) or supertankers (with delays in minutes), and these delays are some of the most powerful determinants of performance in these situations. Unfortunately, no one has used a retention test to determine whether or not the delays in feedback are related to learning as well as to immediate performance (as Lavery, 1962, did for the discrete tasks), so we do not know if the findings from the two kinds of responses would agree. There is no doubt about the clear performance effects in both situations, however.

Forms of KR

Having discussed the temporal placement of KR in the practice sequence, we now turn to the nature of the KR that can be presented. This discussion really takes two separate directions: (a) issues about the precision of KR (or its accuracy in describing the movement outcome), and (b) issues about the mode in which the KR is presented (verbally, pictorially, etc.).

Precision of KR

The *precision* of KR refers to the amount of accuracy contained in it. For example, if the subject is attempting to make a 10-cm movement and the actual movement was 10.13 cm, I could report this error in a variety of ways. First, I could define a band of correctness (say 1 cm wide), and the KR in this instance would be "Right." Or I could say "Long," meaning that the person moved too far. I could say "Wrong by 1," meaning 1 mm off. Or, I could say "Long 1," meaning that it was 1 mm too long. I could say "Long 13," meaning that it was 1.3 mm too long. I could be even more accurate than this if I wanted to, measuring movement accuracy to a very fine degree.

Two sub-issues are involved here. First, the information is presented about the *direction* of the error in some, but not all, of these forms of KR. Second, there is information provided about the *magnitude* of the error in some of them. Some of these forms of KR have information about both factors (e.g., "Long 13"). Generally, the evidence suggests that there is some benefit to providing information about magnitude of error, but this information is far more useful if the direction is also specified. Knowing that I made an error in some direction gives a strong indication of the ways in which the movement must be modified next time; giving the information only about magnitude does not give such a clear indication. Giving information only about direction is clearly better than giving it only about magnitude, although this might depend on the level of learning of the subjects.

Overall, the evidence suggests it is most effective to give information about both the direction and magnitude of errors. Limitations in one or both of these aspects seem to reduce performance. Thus, as a practical principle, clearly both should be used. But be careful in interpreting these principles in terms of learning, as no transfer designs have been employed.

The second issue relates to the precision of the KR report in terms of the accuracy. With adult subjects, Trowbridge and Cason (1932) studied precision of KR, showing essentially that quantitative KR (e.g., "Long 3") was more effective for performance than qualitative KR (e.g., "Right). These techniques do not permit the separation of information about precision of KR from information about the direction of reported error. Studies conducted since the Trowbridge and Cason study have separated these effects and have generally shown that the more precise the KR, the more accurate the performance, up to a point, beyond which no further increases in accuracy are found as KR is made more precise. (See Newell, in press, for a more complete review.) Subjects presumably know that they cannot be responsible for errors smaller than a certain size (e.g., .1mm), as the movement control mechanisms themselves are more variable than this. Apparently, subjects "round off" the very precise KR given to them to some meaningful level of precision, ignoring the more precise information. While we might think that too much KR precision is harmful for adults, the evidence does not support such a claim.

These data are supported by the fact that, in adults, it appears not to matter what units of measurement are used for KR. Interestingly, it does not make much difference whether the KR is presented in units of centimeters, inches, feet, yards, or miles. Adult subjects apparently are capable of adjusting their behavior to the size of the scale that is used by the experimenter, and they do this without any apparent difficulty. Denny, Allard, Hall, and Rokeach (1960) even gave KR in nonsense units called "Glubs," where a Glub was 1/20 in. Even though subjects were not told this relationship, they responded effectively when given KR like "Long 8 Glubs."

Not so with children. Apparently, children are less capable of dealing with imaginary units of measurement or ignoring the nonuseful parts of a very precise KR and are confused by it during learning. For example, Newell and Kennedy (1978) studied children of various ages (1st, 3rd, and 9th graders) on a linear-positioning task, for which the precision of KR was varied. Unlike the behavior of the adults, there was an optimal level of precision for the children, with performance being less accurate if KR was either less or more precise than this optimum. Furthermore, they found that this optimal level of precision increased as the ages of the subjects increased. It appears that, unlike the situation with adults, one must be careful about how KR is provided to children, as too much accuracy can actually lead to less effective performance. This is probably related to the idea that providing too much KR about various aspects of the task (e.g., information presented together about what the arms, head, feet, etc., are doing) can lead to ineffective learning, as children have a more difficult time in dealing rapidly with large "doses" of information than adults do. However, this study is hampered by the failure to use a transfer design, and the interpretations about the precision of KR in children should be limited to performance effects. Such skepticism is warranted by the findings of Salmoni (Note 24), who showed that, with a transfer design, the relative amount learned was largest for the conditions that produced the poorest performance in acquisition, and was smallest for the conditions that produced the best performance in acquisition.

Modes of KR

KR can be presented to learners through a wide variety of modes other than the usual one in which errors are verbalized. Some of the more important modes are videotape replays of performance and the presentation of KR through the kinematics or kinetics of the movement pattern.

Videotape replays. It would certainly seem reasonable that videotape replays would be a powerful mode in which to present KR. The information can be returned by a TV screen after only a few seconds, there will be no trials delay, and there will be a strong interest generated on the part of the learner who will have satisfied a little of his or her desire to be a Hollywood star. From a motor skills viewpoint, there will be a record of many of the errors made, and the individual can detect these directly and attempt to correct them on the next trial.

For all the logic leading to the use of videotape replays, as well as their use in many sports situations (e.g., gymnastics), little research evidence exists that this method of presenting KR is very effective. Rothstein and Arnold (1976) and Newell (in press) have reviewed this work, finding that experiments fail to show very much positive effect of this feedback technique. One suggestion is that the videotape perhaps might supply too much information to the learner and that the observer does not have sufficient viewing skill to separate the relevant aspects of the action from all the others. Also, if the skill is complex, then errors will occur in perhaps more than one dimension of the skill (e.g., arms, legs, foot placement, gaze, etc.), and the learner might wish to change them all at once, leading to confusion. Rothstein and Arnold pointed out that studies using *cuing*, in which subjects were directed to examine certain aspects of the TV display during replay, showed more positive effects of videotape replays than did studies not using cuing, which supports the interpretation about the replay having too much information.

It would seem reasonable to use videotape replays accompanied by an instructor who could pick out the relevant details, while instructing the learner to ignore the irrelevant details of the response. The focus could be on what the hips are doing for a number of responses and then attention could be switched to some other aspect. On the other hand, viewing the total movement may be useful in situations where aspects of the response such as "style" or "emphasis" are required, as is the case in ice skating, gymnastics, dance, and so on. In these cases, it would seem to be effective to provide a videotape replay of the performance, as KR in words would seem to lose information about the details of the movement that should be conveyed.

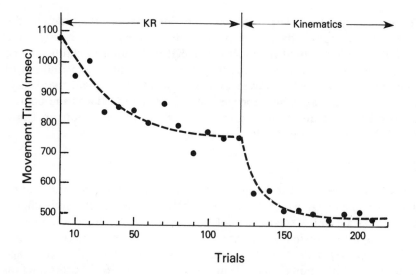

Figure 13-13. Performance of a foot-kick task before and after kinematic KR (from Hatze, 1976).

Kinetics and kinematics. In addition to providing KR about the outcome of the movement in the environment or even about the errors in the motion that the person has made, a few successful attempts have been made to use information about far more subtle aspects of the movement. One aspect of this kind of KR deals with the *kinetics* of the movement (i.e., with the patterns of forces that were applied), while the other deals with the *kinematics* of the movement (i.e., with the motions of the various limb segments). These methods hold considerable promise, even though they have not been studied extensively yet.

Howell (1956) had subjects learn a runner's sprint start and recorded the forces applied against a strain gauge (a force sensor) which was attached to the foot plate in the starting blocks. With this technique, the pattern of forces produced as a function of time could be recorded, resulting in a *force-time curve*. After each trial, these curves were shown to the subjects as a form of KR, and subjects attempted to modify the pattern of forces they applied to achieve a criterion that Howell imposed (a maximum impulse). Given these representations of the forces applied, learners were capable of modifying their own force-time patterns so as to achieve a more effective output; Walter (1981) has provided another example. Here, then, is an example in which aspects of the movement that are not easily perceived consciously can be modified once some knowledge of them is presented to the subjects. In a way, it is like the recent developments in biofeedback, whereby other aspects of the body's functions such as finger temperature can be changed "at will" by proper feedback of the finger's temperature. These methods could have strong practical implications. The force-time patterns of champions, or even some "ideal" force-time curve generated from biomechanical analysis, could be used as the goal for individuals learning these skills.

A second way to report information about movement is through kinematics, descriptions of the movements that are produced by the forces applied to the limbs (i.e., produced by the kinetics). In a way, this is but a variation of videotape replay. Hatze (1976) has provided a demonstration of a specific application of these techniques, although films were used instead of videotape. The subject's task (only one subject was used) was to begin in a standing position, with the heels against a switch, and kick the right foot forward and upward to strike a target. The goal was to move in minimum time. This task, like most tasks, has a variety of movement patterns that could accomplish the goal; there are countless variations in terms of the timing of the hip flexion and knee extension, the amount of the flexion in the two major joints, and so on. Hatze provided KR in the usual way, giving the MT after each trial; and the subject reduced the MT as would be expected. The plot of MT against trials is shown in the left portion of Figure 13-13. The subject probably reduced MT by selecting (among other things) more appropriate combinations of actions of the hip and knee joint. We see that the subject stopped improving at a plateau of about 760 msec.

At this point, Hatze showed the subject some films of the theoretically derived optimal way to do this task.[4] These films showed a stick figure doing the response in the optimal way. The relationship between the knee and hip angles and their timing relationships could be seen clearly. Also, this stick figure was superimposed on film of this subject doing the task, and it was clear that the subject was not doing the task with the same knee-hip pattern as the stick figure was. After viewing the film, the subject then returned to the task for additional practice, and the MTs for this sequence of trials is shown in the right half of Figure 13-13. An immediate improvement in performance is seen, and the application of the specific movement KR in pictorial form was probably responsible for this gain (unless it was motivational in origin).

Such techniques have not been studied extensively, but from the demonstration provided by Hatze, they appear to have potential for application to practical situations. Again, the problem is the determination of what the optimum pattern is. We could use either the patterns from outstanding performers or from biomechanically derived optimal patterns. The latter are certainly more difficult to generate, but they are probably to be preferred as long as the fundamental principles relating to the kinematics of the movement have been worked out, as they appeared to have been in Hatze's case.

THEORETICAL ISSUES ABOUT KR

In the previous sections, various separate facts have been presented relative to the functioning of KR in motor-learning situations. Some of these have had obvious relevance for practical situations. Yet, other facts have distinct implications for how we believe KR operates in humans to produce learning. In this section, I consider some of these implications.

---

[4]This theoretical optimal method was determined by a complex and time-consuming analysis of the muscular and mechanical properties of this subject. These data were then used to develop a theoretically optimal movement pattern. This is why only one subject was used.

Informational versus Rewarding Aspects

In previous sections, I have drawn attention to a number of features that KR in human motor learning situations and reward in animal learning situations have in common. Both KR and reward are presented contingent on the nature of the response, and both are given after the response. What is the evidence that KR and reward are really different?

That KR and reward might be similar is not a new idea at all, and it is the foundation of the empirical Law of Effect stated by Thorndike (1927) over a half century ago (see Adams, 1978). It states that the organism tends to repeat those responses that are followed by a reward and tends to extinguish (or avoid) those responses that are followed by either no reward or by some sort of aversive feedback (e.g., punishment). This idea was thought to be relevant for motor learning situations, where the KR indicating small errors or no error was thought of as a reward and KR indicating large errors was thought of as "punishment." In this way, the responses followed by nonreward were thought to be be eliminated, and those followed by reward (i.e., zero or small error) tended to be repeated, leading to decreasing errors with practice that one commonly sees in experimental situations.

Numerous lines of evidence suggest that humans do not use KR as proposed by this interpretation of the Law of Effect. First, when KR is not presented (on no-KR trials), subjects tend to repeat those movements rather than to eliminate them. Only when KR is presented do subjects change their movements, and then quite clearly in the direction of the target. It would seem that subjects are not using the KR as a reward, but rather as information about what to do next.

This view is supported in other ways as well. For example, numerous studies using animals have been concerned with the effect of delaying the presentation of the food reward after the instrumental response (e.g., a bar press response to a tone). The usual finding is that even a little delay of reward severely retards learning, and delaying reward by 30 sec or so can eliminate learning of the response. Of course, we do not find these effects at all in humans, as the delay of KR seems to have no effect on performance of the task (see the KR delay section, this chapter). Thus, reward in laboratory rats and KR in laboratory humans seems to have fundamentally different principles of operation.

For these major reasons, the current belief about augmented feedback is that it produces learning not by the rewarding of correct responses and the "punishment" of incorrect ones, as it appears to in animals, but rather by the provision of information about what was wrong with the previous trials and a suggestion of how to change the response on the next trial (see also Wallace & Hagler, 1979). This information-processing orientation about KR is quite important for practical applications. Knowing that KR is informational will tend to bias teachers away from post-response statements such as "Nice job" (which is rewarding) to statements such as "Nice job, but you need to keep your head up" (which is rewarding and informational). Such notions about KR are important as well for the development of theories of motor learning, as the mechanisms by which KR "works" to produce learning will be fundamental to how the learning process is conceptualized. I treat some of these issues in the next section.

How Does KR "Work?"

Given that KR is largely informational, what does KR do to produce learning in humans? The research presented in this chapter suggests two possible ways that KR operates in motor learning, and theories of motor learning have generally adopted one of these two positions. KR has been considered to have a function much like *guidance*, and KR has been thought of as forming *associations*. These two viewpoints are presented next.

Guidance Functions of KR

One view of how KR "works" is that it guides the learner to the proper response. Thus, when the learner makes a movement, KR informs the person about how the movement was inadequate, and the learner then changes the movement to one which (hopefully) will be more adequate. KR thus provides inherent "instructions" about which aspects of the movement should be changed, as well as the directions that those changes should take. In this way, KR guides the learner toward the proper response, much in the same way that I can guide you through a maze by giving you verbal instructions about what direction to move next time. According to this view, KR does not provide any direct strengthening of the response, but results in it indirectly by guiding the person to the proper action. Once the proper actions are being produced, other processes take over to help the person learn the task.

Such a point of view is a fundamental part of a theory of motor learning proposed by Adams (1971). Adams' theory says that KR presented after each trial of a slow-positioning response provides a means by which the learner can make the movement different on the next trial, thus progressively guiding the person toward the correct location. Then, as the person achieves positions close to the target, he or she also receives feedback associated with the proper position, and this feedback forms an internal representation of being at the proper position (a reference of correctness). This internal representation, which Adams called the *perceptual trace*, becomes stronger with each successive trial near the target. Then, on successive trials, the learner uses the intrinsic feedback compared with the perceptual trace as a basis for positioning the lever. In other words, the subject moves to that position for which the difference between the feedback received and the perceptual trace is minimized. As you may recall, that is what Solley's (1956) subjects appeared to do in learning to position themselves vertically in the tilt chair. Thus, according to Adams, KR serves only a guidance role in driving the subject closer and closer to the target so that a proper perceptual trace can be formed.

Associational Functions of KR

A different view is that KR is associational, providing associations between stimuli and responses. One view of this was provided in schema theory (Schmidt, 1975b), in which KR is thought to operate associationally as well as in the ways that Adams (1971) has suggested. In schema theory, considering rapid movements that are presumably controlled by motor programs, the person associates the KR received on a trial (a measure of what happened in the environment) with the parameters of the motor program that were issued to produce that outcome in the environment. KR, indicating what happened, is paired with the "instructions" that the person gave to himself in producing the action; with practice, the person comes to develop a *rule* (or *schema*) about the relationship between what the limbs were "told to do" and "what they did when told to do it." On this basis, knowing what kinds of internal commands tend to produce certain kinds of responses, the learner has a basis for selecting the parameters of the response on future trials. Thus, in this view, KR provides more than a guidance function toward the target; it also provides a rule about the relationship between internal commands and the outcomes that were produced in the environment.

Other Mechanisms of KR

It is probably not fair on the basis of the present evidence to suggest that KR operates in one way versus another way. I think that Adams (1971) is correct when he argues that, in positioning responses, KR provides a guidance function. But I think KR has an associational role as well, as suggested by the research surrounding schema theory (to be discussed in Chapter 14). Moreover, as discussed earlier, KR has a motivating or energizing role, keeping the learner alert and interested, leading to more practice and more learning. Finally, KR may also have a rewarding function such as food pellets do for animals, and we can perhaps think of situations in which KR might operate in fundamentally the same ways in man and animal (e.g., as in punishment; see Adams, 1978).

We do not have adequate theories of how KR works, and we are forced at this stage to consider that KR might have a number of different, separate functions. Perhaps these functions change as the nature of the learner changes, as the task changes, or as situations change. Perhaps the explanation for why KR is such a powerful variable for motor (and other) learning is that it appears to operate in so many different ways at the same time. Whatever its exact function, clearly it is important for learning, and it must be carefully considered in the design of an effective learning environment.

SUMMARY

Feedback is that class of sensory information that is movement-related, and it can be classified into two basic categories—*intrinsic* (inherent in the task) and *extrinsic* (supplementary to the task). A major class of extrinsic feedback is knowledge of results (KR), which is verbal post-response information about performance outcome. Much research suggests that information about performance is the single most important variable for motor learning (except for practice itself, of course). In those situations in which no information is available, no learning occurs. Studies that appear to show learning without such information can, under closer inspection, be interpreted as consistent with this fundamental law of motor learning.

The effect of KR delay, the interval from the movement until KR is presented, has been found to be negligible in terms of performance of most motor tasks. Transfer designs have not been used in this research, however, so effects on learning cannot be determined. If the post-KR-delay interval—the interval from the KR until the next response is called for—is too short, subjects appear to have difficulty generating a new and different movement on the next trial. For both intervals, information-processing activities inserted in them decrease performance and learning, presumably because other important information-processing activities are blocked.

Early research indicated that the *relative frequency* of KR (the percentage of trials on which KR was given) was irrelevant for learning, whereas the absolute frequency (the number of KRs given) was the critical determinant. More recent data using transfer designs contradicts this position, indicating that both are clearly important. Trials on which no KR is given appear to contribute to learning in the task, but not as much as the KR trials do. Such effects can probably be explained by the development of error-detection mechanisms. The trials-delay procedure, in which the KR for a given response is separated from it by other trials, was shown to produce detrimental effects on motor performance, but positive effects on learning, suggesting that KR might work as guidance to keep the learner on target.

KR precision refers to the accuracy with which the KR is given. Research with adults shows that performance increases with increases in precision up to a point, with no further increases in performance thereafter. Children, on the other hand, seem to suffer from too much precision, as if they are being overloaded in terms of information processing. KR can be given through videotape replays, recordings of the force-time characteristics of the movement (kinetics), or representations of the movement trajectories (kinematics); and all appear to have positive effects on performance and perhaps on learning.

KR appears to have at least four possible mechanisms for producing learning. It acts as *guidance*. It acts to form *associations* between response parameters and resulting action. It acts as a *reward* or *punishment*. And it acts in a *motivational* role. Much more research is needed to understand which of these roles are most important, depending on the learner, the task, and the movement situation.

GLOSSARY

Absolute frequency of KR. The absolute number of KRs given in a sequence of trials.

Accumulated feedback. Information presented after a series of responses that represents a summary of those performances.

Augmented feedback. Feedback that is added to that typically received in the task; extrinsic feedback.

Concurrent feedback. Feedback that is presented simultaneously with the action.

Extrinsic feedback. Feedback that is added to that typically received in the task; augmented feedback.

Feedback. Sensory information that is contingent on having produced a movement.

Intertrial interval. The interval of time from one response to the next in the KR paradigm; inter-response interval.

Intrinsic feedback. That feedback normally received in the conduct of a particular task.

Kinematic feedback. Feedback about the movement characteristics or movement pattern produced.

Kinetic feedback. Feedback about the force characteristics of a movement.

Knowledge of performance. Augmented feedback related to the nature of the movement pattern produced.

Knowledge of results (KR). Augmented feedback related to the nature of the result produced in the environment.

KR delay. The interval from the production of a movement to the presentation of KR.

Post-KR delay. The interval of time from the presentation of KR to the production of the next response.

Precision of KR. The level of accuracy with which KR represents the movement outcome produced.

Relative frequency of KR. The percentage of trials on which KR is given; the absolute frequency divided by the number of trials.

Separate feedback. KR that refers to separate trials rather than to the summarization of a number of trials; opposite of accumulated KR.

Subjective reinforcement. Term used to describe the subject's self-generated error signal, based on comparing feedback against a reference of correctness.

Terminal feedback. Feedback given after the movement; opposite of concurrent feedback.

Trials-delay technique. A procedure of giving KR in which KR is separated from its response by one or more other response(s).

CHAPTER 14

The Processes of Learning

So far in this section on motor learning, the major concern has been with the most important empirical findings about the acquisition of skills. Some of these empirical relationships can even be considered as *laws* (see Chapter 2), so stable and dependable are they. It is time now to consider the underlying reasons why these laws seem to hold and to ask about the nature of the motor learning processes that cause the motor system to behave in the ways defined in the previous chapters. In this chapter, I consider the many ways that the processes of motor learning have been conceptualized by various individuals at various times in the history of the field. In some cases, the conceptualizations have the character of a vague statement about how motor learning might operate, while in others rather explicit statements are made about the proposed nature of the learning processes which form full-fledged theories of motor learning.

In all of the conceptualizations or theories presented here, the main theme is the understanding of what happens inside us when we learn motor skills. You will, I think, be impressed by the wide variety of ways that motor learning processes have been considered. These viewpoints range from the stages that the learner passes through as learning progresses, to the use of attentional mechanisms, to the shifts in abilities with practice, and so on.

Next, you will find that most of the concepts presented in this chapter are familiar to you already, having been introduced in the first half of the book. In many cases, the ideas about motor learning are based on the changes thought to occur in the fundamental motor performance processes as a result of practice; one example is the notion of "building" a motor program through practice, and another is the increased proficiency of error-detection processes. Indeed, because the ideas about motor learning are founded on the ideas about performance, it makes most sense to present a chapter on motor learning theory quite late in the textbook. Most of the hard work in learning the fundamental concepts is behind you now, and you should find this chapter quite easy to understand.

CHANGES IN OVERALL PERFORMANCE

The most obvious change occurring in individuals when they practice is increased proficiency at the task. In many cases this is obvious and hardly needs to be discussed. In other cases, the changes are more subtle and may require careful study of the skills in order to observe them. In such situations, the proficiency can often be estimated by observing the learners on a secondary task, as discussed in Chapter 11. Because many of these obvious changes in proficiency appear to occur relatively early in practice, some may think that learning is a relatively short-term process. Statements such as "I learned to do the crawl stroke today" give the impression that the learning has been completed and that no more learning will occur.

Actually, substantial evidence suggests that learning is probably never completed. Snoddy (1926), for example, had subjects learn to draw figures while viewing only the mirror image of their drawing hand and showed that learning continued for 100 practice days (see Figure 14-1). Another famous example comes from Crossman (1959), who studied factory workers who made cigars using a small hand-operated jig. Figure 14-2 is a graph of the average cycle time for the production of cigars plotted against the amount of experience that the workers had on the job. As you can see, improvement in performance occurred over the entire range of the graph. This is an impressive finding in that this amount of practice is equivalent to 7 years on

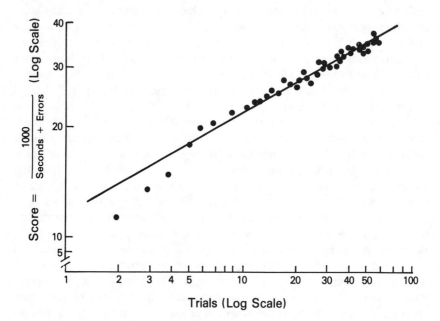

Figure 14-1. Scores in a mirror-tracing task as a function of extended practice (from Snoddy, 1926).

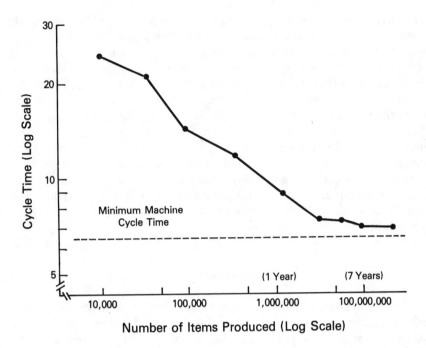

Figure 14-2. Completion time in making cigars as a function of extended practice (from Crossman, 1959).

the job or to the manufacture of 10 million cigars!

Other tasks, though, appear to show relatively stable performance after only a few trials. These tasks are usually very simple, and not much learning is required to perform them (e.g., simple-RT tasks, arm movements). As a principle, it is probably correct to say that the more complicated and unfamiliar a movement is, the longer the period over which improvements can be easily seen. But remember that though improvements in the task are not obvious, changes may still be occurring in learners. To this body of evidence we can add many examples of champion athletes, industrial workers, musicians, etc., who perform at high levels only after many years of hard work and practice.

STAGES OF MOTOR LEARNING

Many have noticed that learners appear to pass through relatively distinct stages or phases as they practice a skill, and Fitts (1964; Fitts & Posner, 1967) has described one set of phases that is quite useful for descriptive purposes. These are called the *cognitive phase*, the *associative phase*, and the *autonomous phase*.

Cognitive Phase

When the learner is new to the task, the primary concern is to understand what is to be done, how the performance is to be scored, and how best to attempt the first few trials. Naturally, considerable cognitive activity is required, so that the learner can determine appropriate strategies. Good strategies are retained, and inappropriate ones are quickly discarded. As a result, the performance gains during this phase are dramatic and generally larger than at any other single period in the learning process. Performance is usually very inconsistent, perhaps because the learner is trying many different ways of solving the problem. As you might imagine, during this phase the use of instructions, film loops, and various other teaching techniques discussed in Chapters 12 and 13 are most effective. Probably most of the improvements in the cognitive stage can be thought of as verbal-cognitive in nature, with the major gains being in terms of what to do rather than in the motor patterns themselves. For this reason, Adams (1971) has termed this stage the *verbal-motor stage*.

Associative Phase

The second phase of motor learning begins when the individual has determined the most effective way of doing the task and begins to make more subtle adjustments in how the skill is performed. Performance improvements are more gradual, and movements become more consistent. This phase can persist for many days or weeks, with the performer gradually producing small changes in the motor patterns that will allow more effective performance. Many writers (e.g., Adams, 1971; Fitts, 1964) think that the verbal-cognitive aspects of the task have largely dropped out by this stage, with the performer concentrating on how to do the particular pattern, rather than on which pattern of action should be produced. This stage is the one that is most often studied in experiments on motor learning, and it is called the *motor stage* by Adams (1971).

Autonomous Phase

After many months, perhaps years, of practice, the learner enters the autonomous phase, so named because the skill has become largely *automatic*. In the chapters on information processing, automatic implied a marked reduction in the attention required for the skill, so that the movements seemed to be performed almost "by themselves," with only minimal involvement from the central attentional mechanisms. Thus, when the task has been so well learned that it does not require attention, "spare" capacity can be devoted to other tasks, it can be devoted to higher-order elements in the skill such as strategy in tennis or style in gymnastics, or it can be "saved" so that the individual does not become fatigued.

We have all seen examples of people in the autonomous phase. One that comes to mind occurred at a field trip to the Detroit post office. In the mail-sorting section, many people sit at typewriter-like machines (e.g., Baddeley & Longman, 1978; Figure 12-6). A piece of mail comes into view in a window and the operator reads the postal code and presses one of 13 buttons, determining for which of the Detroit areas that the letter is destined. The letter is then removed, to be replace 1 sec later by another. And so it goes. In the early stages of practice, it probably required considerable attention just to press the correct key before the next letter appeared. But with experience, these workers could press the proper key, almost never making an error, with plenty of time to spare. In fact, when they knew they were being observed, the operators began to show off. Between button presses the workers would clap their hands in unison, press the buttons with their elbows, and so on, demonstrating the nearly complete mastery that they had over the task. The 125-word/min typist (Shaffer, 1971), the drummer in the rock band, and the quarterback in professional football show similar automaticity in their actions.

A major problem for motor behavior research is that this stage, which is of immense importance for understanding high-level skills, is almost never studied in experiments on motor learning. The reasons are nearly obvious. Using motor learning tasks, as we must, requires that experimental subjects perform for months, and it is extremely difficult to convince our subjects to do this. Other realistic tasks can be studied, such as in industry, in the military, in sports, and the like, but it is difficult to do experiments that can isolate the effect of a particular independent variable. As a result, the principles that govern motor learning in the autonomous phase are nearly completely unknown, and we must assume that the methods and principles that apply to the associative phase are the same ones that apply in the autonomous phase. As you might guess, this assumption could easily be incorrect.

OLD SKILLS COMBINE TO FORM NEW ONES

A reasonable, but largely untested, viewpoint about skill learning is that a new skill learned as an adult is not really new at all, but is a new combination of skills that the individual has learned earlier. An extreme variant of this basic idea is that all motor learning is over by about the age of 4, and that the learning that occurs after this time is mainly the recombination of these basic "building blocks" into other new skills. Scientists who study the learning of skills in children like to speak of these building blocks as subroutines, in an anology to the computer program. Here, a subroutine is a small program for doing a particular operation (e.g., adding a series of numbers), and the subroutine can be called on when needed in the course of executing a larger program. In the area of children's motor learning, such subroutines would seem to be those having to do with reaching, grasping, releasing, placing objects, and the like. Combined into a larger set, these individual subroutines can be made to "look like" a large skill, such as reaching for a cookie and placing it in the mouth. For a review of this kind of thinking, see Connolly (1970).

Such a general hypothesis about skill learning has considerable potential in certain skills. For example, learning to throw effectively provides the performer with a skill that can be transferred to many playground activities; the case is the same for running, jumping, catching, etc. But in other situations, apparently totally new patterns of skills can be learned by adults, patterns that seem to have little if anything to do with previously acquired skills. Learning gymnastics and how to fly a helicopter are just two of many possible examples. This hypothesis is difficult to evaluate scientifically, because presently there is no effective method for determining whether or not an earlier skill is "contained in" the newer one.

INDIVIDUAL DIFFERENCES AND MOTOR LEARNING

Some important hypotheses for motor learning are framed in the language and methods of individual differences research (review Chapter 10). Beginning with the concept that a given motor performance is based upon some small set of underlying motor abilities, one hypothesis simply states that this set of abilities changes in its make-up as practice continues. Now, the abilities themselves do not change, as this would violate the assumption in Chapter 10 that abilities are largely genetically defined and unmodifiable by practice. But what does change, according to this view, are the particular abilities that are in the collection that underlies the skill.

At one level, this hypothesis seems almost certainly to be correct. Early in practice the task should be based on abilities having to do with thinking, reasoning, mechanical knowledge, etc. Later in practice, these abilities should not be involved, as perhaps less cognitive abilities such as movement speed, reaction time, strength, steadiness, etc., become the most important. Also, according to this analysis, the abilities relating to attentional capacity should be less involved in the skill as the learning progresses into the autonomous phase.

As reasonable as this might sound, we should still demand evidence that this viewpoint is correct before we believe too strongly in it. As with much of the work in motor skills related to individual differences and abilities, most of our knowledge comes from the work of Fleishman (e.g., 1965), with contributions from Jones (1966) and Bechtoldt (1970). Basically, this viewpoint is supported by two separate lines of evidence and they are presented next.

Studies Using Individual Difference Variables

Fleishman and Hempel (1955) and Fleishman and Rich (1963) have contributed important investigations in this area. In the Fleishman-Rich study, subjects learned to perform the two-hand coordination task, in which two crank handles had to be manipulated to cause a pointer to follow a moving target on a target board (Figure 3-8, page 72). One handle controlled the left-right movements of the pointer, and the other controlled the forward-backward movements, so that diagonal movements could be made with suitable combinations of the two. Forty males performed the task under identical conditions for 40 1-min trials.

Separately from the practice on the two-hand coordination test, the same subjects were given two additional tests. In one of these, subjects were asked to lift light weights and to judge whether a given weight was heavier, lighter, or the same as a standard weight. This test was called *kinesthetic sensitivity* by Fleishman and Rich, and it seemed to be based on abilities related to how sensitive the motor system was to applied tensions. A second test called *spatial orientation* was a paper-and-pencil test designed to assess the abilities related to the subject's orientation in space.

First, Fleishman and Rich divided their group of people into two, based on their performance on the kinesthetic-sensitivity test, and then they plotted the performances of these two groups of people separately for the two-hand coordination test. Remember, these two groups of people were not treated differently on the two-hand coordination test, but their performances were plotted separately based on the level of proficiency in the kinesthetic-sensitivity test. The top of Figure 14-3 has the performance curves for this contrast. The subjects classed as high and low on the kinesthetic-sensitivity measure were not different on the two-hand coordination test in early trials; but later in practice the subjects high in kinesthetic sensitivity began to outperform those low in kinesthetic sensitivity. Was kinesthetic sensitivity an important ability for the two-hand coordination test? The answer depends on the level of practice that you would like to discuss. For early practice, kinesthetic sensitivity was not important, but it became so as practice increased. Thus, kinesthetic sensitivity is an ability increasing in importance with practice.

Next, consider the spatial-orientation test. The situation is the same as before, with the groups classified as high and low on this test being plotted separately on the two-hand coordination test (Figure 14-3, bottom). Now, though, the subjects classed as high on this test were better performers on the two-hand coordination test than were subjects classed as low, but only for initial performance. This advantage disappeared with practice, so that at the end of practice the advantage for being classed as high in spatial orientation disappeared. Is spatial orientation important for performance of this task? Again, the answer depends on the stage of practice. Here, then, is an ability that is important for early proficiency in this task but appears to have nothing to do with performance in later practice.

Another way to view these results is this. For the two-hand coordination test, there is some collection of abilities that underlies it on Trial 1. This collection of abilities may be quite large, but it includes some abilities related to the spatial orientation measure, and it does not include any abilities related to the kinesthetic sensitivity measure. As practice continues, the *collection* of abilities (not the abilities themselves) changes, so that at the end of practice the task is made up of a somewhat different set of abilities. This group could have some of the same abilities as in early practice; but it now has abilities related to kinesthetic sensitivity, and it does not have abilities related to spatial orientation. When performers are skilled, they apparently use different abilities to produce an action than when they are unskilled.

All of this suggests that the factor structure of this task has changed with practice. This means that the collection of factors (or abilities) underlying the task late in practice and early in practice are not the same. It turns out that more direct evidence of this assertion has been provided by Fleishman and his colleagues using factor-analytic methods, and some of the most im-

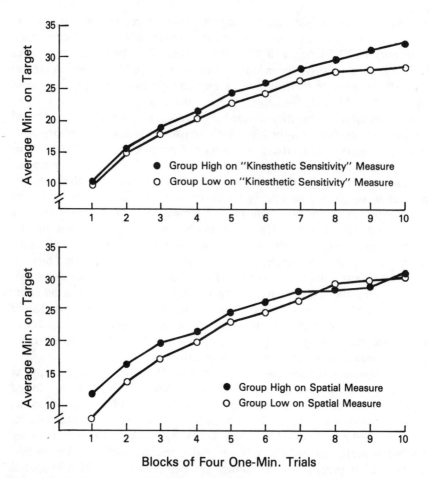

Figure 14-3. Performance on the two-hand coordination test as a function of practice trials. (Top, groups classed as high and low on a kinesthetic sensitivity test are plotted separately; bottom, groups classed as high and low on spatial orientation are plotted separately) (from Fleishman & Rich, 1963).

portant findings are presented next.

Factor-Analytic Methods

Fleishman and Hempel (1955) used the discrimination reaction-time (RT) test, which is similar to an incompatible choice-RT task, as the learning task. They also used a series of *reference tests*, relatively well-studied tests whose underlying abilities are reasonably well understood. Some of these reference tests, such as Reaction Time, Movement Time, Spatial Relations, etc., were based on earlier factor analyses, which showed them to be fairly good measures of the underlying ability. With this method, from 10 to 20 of these reference tests, each representing different abilities, were administered to the group of subjects. In addition, the subjects also performed 15 trials on the discrimination RT test, and the eight odd-numbered trials are included as additional tests in the factor analysis. Because the reference tests

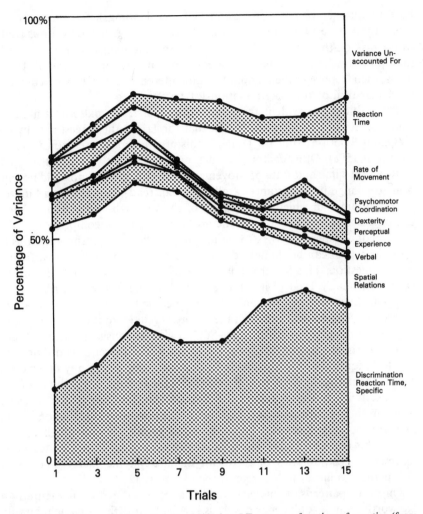

Figure 14-4. Abilities underlying the discrimination RT test as a function of practice (from Fleishman & Hempel, 1955).

are deliberately designed to represent different abilities, these different abilities naturally "come out" in the factor analysis in the form of different factors. Then, by noting which of these factors represent the different trials of the discrimination-RT test, the factor structure of the discrimination RT test can be estimated (see also Chapter 10, Taxonomies).

Figure 14-4 is one of the most famous figures from this work. The trials of the discrimination-RT test are represented on the horizontal axis, and the percentage of variance accounted for by the various reference factors is given on the vertical axis. This percentage of variance score can be understood with the help of an example. Consider the reference test called Spatial Relations. For Trial 1, the shaded area goes from about 20% to slightly more than 50%, indicating that this factor accounted for approximately 30% of the variance for Trial 1; this percentage is the square of the factor loading for Trial 1 on the Spatial Relations factor (multiplied by 100), so that the factor loading in this instance was approximately .55 (refer back to Chapter 10 for a discussion of factor loadings). So what is really plotted in Figure 14-4 is the size of the factor loadings for the various trials of the task on the reference factors, where these loadings are first squared, multiplied by 100, and then represented as an area on the graph. These areas, then, represent the amount that the reference tests are involved in the particular trial of the discrimination-RT test.

Three things are evident from this figure. First, the pattern of abilities changes with successive trials. Notice that for Trial 1 the biggest area by far is Spatial Relations. But by Trial 15, this area has decreased considerably (to about 15%). Other factors become more important with practice, such as Reaction Time and Rate of Movement, and still other factors did not appear to change in importance at all. One can read the graph as a kind of "pie diagram," in which the make-up of the whole discrimination-RT test can be described by the sizes of the areas (factors) that comprise it.

A second aspect of these findings is the factor Discrimination RT, Specific, which can be thought of as having only to do with the particular task in question. This factor is relatively small on Trial 1 (about 20% of the variance), but by Trial 15 it is the largest of all the factors contributing to this skill. In a way, we can think of these specific factors as special abilities that are developed with practice; the ability is related to the task but not to any of the other reference factors. Such a view is consistent with the idea that in learning a motor task a person learns a specific set of coordinations and techniques that are applicable to that task, but not to any other task. This is the particular view that Henry (1958-1968) proposed with respect to the specificity theory (Chapter 10). These specific factors are typically found in these factor analyses, and the most reasonable explanation is that they are specially developed "abilities" that permit the individuals to succeed in this particular task. The area labeled "Variance Unaccounted For" represents those abilities that are not included in the factor analysis at all—perhaps abilities that are yet to be discovered.

Third, the patterns of change in the variance accounted for in Figure 14-4 are worth noting. A tendency develops for the factors that we might be willing to class as non-motor (i.e., verbal or cognitive) to decrease in importance with practice, while the motor abilities seem to increase in their importance with practice. This is certainly in keeping with the findings from Fleishman and Rich (1963), and it agrees nicely with the idea that cognitive abilities drop out as the subjects move from the cognitive stage to the associative or autonomous stages of practice.

Implications for Prediction of Skills

The findings about the changes in component abilities have important implications for the process of prediction (Chapter 10). First, I mentioned in Chapter 10 that a task can be characterized by the abilities that underlie it, so that driving a race car could be described as 30% Ability I, 22% Ability II, and 15% Ability III, analogous to a prescription from the druggist. Using this thinking, how would you describe the discrimination RT task shown in Figure 14-4? Again, it depends on where you look in the practice sequence. On Trial 1, it is about 30% Spatial Relations, but on Trial 15 it is only about 10% Spatial Relations.

The reason this has implications for prediction is that we would like to base the prediction batteries on the make-up of the task to be predicted. That is, knowing that Spatial Relations is the most important ability would lead us to weigh Spatial Relations quite heavily in the design of a battery of tests to predict success in this task. Because the pattern of abilities is continually changing, the design of test batteries becomes even more difficult, as presumably a different battery of tests must be developed to predict success at each level of practice. What should be clear, which has been emphasized in Chapter 10, is that a battery of tests to predict success on Trial 1 will be woefully ineffective in predicting success in later practice.

One final difficulty can now be added to the already-too-long list of difficulties for prediction that I started in Chapter 10. Notice in Figure 14-4 the size and rate of increase in importance of the factor specific to the task. By definition, these factors are not related to any of the other reference factors and are probably related only to the development of skills on the tasks themselves. In the example given, the specific factor, after only 15 trials, accounted for about 40% of the variance in this task, leaving only 60% that is potentially predictable from other reference tests. The task is becoming more and more specific (or unique) with practice, making success on it more and more difficult to predict. But it is just this high-level proficiency that we want to predict in selecting pilots or quarterbacks. The problem is that the higher the level of proficiency, the less well we are able to predict success. It is possible that these specific abilities do have predictable components to them, but they have not been discovered and it appears unlikely that they ever will be, given the other evidence about the specificity of skills.

Intertrial Correlation Analyses

One additional finding about individual differences and learning should be discussed before leaving this topic. Take any motor task you like, and measure each of a large number of subjects on each of a series of trials. Then correlate every trial with every other trial and place these values in a matrix called an *intertrial correlation matrix*. Such a matrix is shown in Table 14-1, reproduced from Jones' (1962, 1966) work on the two-hand coordination test. The bottom half of the matrix is omitted for simplicity, and the table simply gives the correlation of any trial with any other trial. (This is a form of reliability as discussed in Chapter 3.) There are a number of interesting features of these tables, as has been pointed out by Jones (1966).

Remoteness Effects

First, notice that across any row of the table, the correlations become systematically smaller; they drop from .79 to .70 in the first row, from .87 to .82 in the second row, and so on. But this top row represents the correlations between Trial 1 with Trial 2, Trial 1 with Trial 3, Trial 1 with Trial 4, and so on up to Trial 1 with Trial 8. Thus, there is an increasing number of

Table 14-1

An Intertrial Correlation Matrix (adapted from Jones, 1966)

Trial	1	2	3	4	5	6	7	8
1	□	.79	.77	.74	.73	.71	.71	.70
2		□	.87	.87	.84	.82	.82	.82
3			□	.91	.89	.87	.85	.86
4				□	.91	.88	.86	.88
5					□	.89	.90	.90
6						□	.93	.93
7							□	.94
8								□

Note: The boxed-in section forms the diagonal of the matrix, and the shaded portion is the "superdiagonal."

trials between the two trials being correlated as we move to the right along any row; the correlation of .70 between Trials 1 and 8 has six intervening trials (i.e., Trials 2-7), whereas the correlation of .79 between Trial 1 and Trial 2 has no intervening trials. As a general rule, as the number of intervening trials increases, the correlation between any two trials decreases. This effect is often called the *remoteness effect*, because the correlations between trials depend on how remote (how separated) the trials are from each other.

What is the meaning of this well-established remoteness effect? First, remember that the correlation between two tests (in this case, two trials of the "same" test) is related to the number of common abilities shared by them. As two tests become more separated in the practice sequence, and their correlations systematically drop, it is possible to say that the performance mechanisms on these trials are becoming more and more different, being dependent on fewer and fewer of the same abilities. In this sense, the remoteness effect is just another way to say that the motor task is being changed with practice, the changes being in the make-up of the set of underlying abilities. Yet another interpretation, which means basically the same thing, is that the lowered correlations mean that the ordering (from best to worst) of individuals in the group are systematically changing, with subjects' orders becoming systematically more different (relative to Trial 1) as practice continues.

Adjacent-Trial Effects

Examine the data in Table 14-1 again, this time concentrating on the correlations between adjacent trials—i.e., between Trial 1 and 2, between Trial 2 and 3, and so on. These correlations can be found on what is called the *superdiagonal* (the shaded area), or the line of correlations that lies just above the diagonal of the matrix. Notice that as the adjacent trials are placed later and later in the sequence the correlations steadily increase. The correlation between Trials 1 and 2 is .79, whereas the correlation between Trials 7 and 8 is .94, the highest in the entire matrix.

This also is a well-known finding, and it can be interpreted in terms of the specific factor seen in Figure 14-4. Notice that as the correlations between any two tests increases the two tests can be said to contain more and more abilities in common. Thus, as the trials progress and the correlations between adjacent trials increase, the trials can be said to be more and more representative of a stable set of abilities. (Or it could as well be said that people don't reorder themselves from trial to trial to the same extent later in practice as they do earlier in practice.) Furthermore, this stable set of abilities was found to be unrelated to the reference abilities from which performance could be predicted in early practice. Thus, the increased adjacent-trial correlations say that the specific factor in Figure 14-4 is increasing in its importance with practice.

Practice as a Process of Simplification

As pointed out by Jones (1966), almost every task studied so far has these characteristics in the intertrial correlation matrices: decreasing correlations with remoteness and increasing correlations for later and later adjacent trials. However, an even more restrictive descriptor of the correlation matrix is what is called the *superdiagonal form*. For a matrix to have this particular form, any four arbitrarily chosen correlations within the matrix must possess a particular mathematical relationship. (A discussion of the nature of this relationship is beyond the scope of the text, but see Jones, 1966, for a discussion.) For Jones, the important point is that this restrictive relationship among correlations is predictable from (i.e., can be derived from) the hypothesis that the number of abilities systematically decreases with practice, so that the task comes to depend on just a few abilities at the end of practice. This viewpoint is related to the idea that practice strengthens an ability specific to the task itself, as was shown in Figure 14-4. But it seems inconsistent with the idea that some other factors would become increasingly important with practice. Notice that in Figure 14-4 the factor called Rate of Movement began with no relationship to the task and appeared to increase its importance to the point that it accounted for about 15% of the variance on Trial 15. The idea that a factor can emerge as important does not fit well with Jones' notions.

On purely intuitive grounds, it seems unreasonable that none but a specific factor could increase its importance with practice, as many tasks seem to have various abilities required as the nature of the performances and the requirements of the information-processing system are altered with practice (Jones, 1980). The Jones simplification hypothesis has not been as well received as the Fleishman changing-component-abilities view has for this and other reasons. But another view is that these hypotheses are not all that different, because they both say that (a) the make-up of abilities changes with practice and (b) the specific factor grows with practice. They only differ in that the Jones' view calls for systematic simplification, where

Fleishman's view argues that there is mostly simplification, with the possibility that factors can emerge in particular stages of practice. For more on the difference between these two views and the evidence for them, see Jones (1966) and the rebuttal to his paper by Fleishman (1966).

ERROR DETECTION CAPABILITIES

It is well known that a major outcome of practice is the capability to produce more effective movement behaviors, but an additional outcome of practice is that the learners become more capable of evaluating their own movement behaviors. That is, it seems that learners develop a kind of error-detection capability with practice and experience and that this error-detection can then be substituted for KR to inform the individual about erroneous responses.

Supporting Evidence

Rapid Responses

What is the evidence that error-detection capability can be learned with practice? White and I (Schmidt & White, 1972) used a ballistic-timing task, in which the subjects were to move a slide from a starting position through a distance of 23 cm, with a follow-through, so that the MT was as close to 150 msec as possible. We provided 170 trials of this task over two days of practice. The procedure was to have the subject make a movement, then to have the subject guess his or her score in milliseconds, and then to give KR in milliseconds. The subject's guess was termed *subjective error*, and the actual score was termed *objective error*. We reasoned that if people have increased capability to detect their own errors with practice, the agreement between the subject's subjective and objective scores should increase. That is, the subjective score should be an increasingly accurate estimator of the subject's actual performance.

The statistic we used to estimate this agreement was a form of correlation. For a group of 10 trials, each subject would have 10 objective scores and 10 subjective scores. We correlated these two arrays of scores for each subject separately, and for each of the 17 blocks of 10 trials in the experiment separately. Those within-subject correlations should be sensitive to the extent to which the objective scores and subjective scores agreed. If the error detection capability is weak, nearly no agreement should exist between them, and the correlation should be nearly zero. But if error-detection has increased in accuracy with practice, then the objective and subjective scores should agree to a greater extent, and the correlation should approach 1.0.[1]

---

[1]Actually, there is no requirement that the objective and subjective scores agree, only that they differ by a constant, in order that the correlation between them be 1.0. For this reason, Newell (1974) has argued that it is better to use this correlation along with the absolute difference between objective and subjective error as a measure of error-detection accuracy.

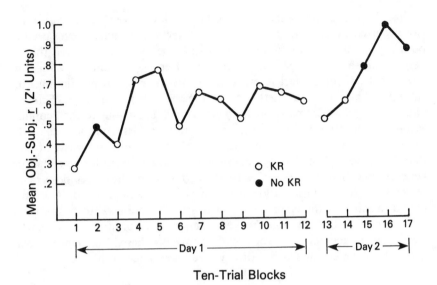

Figure 14-5. Average within-subject correlation between objective and subjective error as a function of practice trials. (Increased correlation is interpreted as gains in capability to detect errors; correlations are transformed to Z' units; from Schmidt & White, 1972).

The major results of the study are shown in Figure 14-5. Here, the average within-subject correlation for each of the 17 trial blocks is presented. On the first block, the average correlation was about .30, indicating a relatively weak association between objective and subjective errors. But as practice continued in this task, the average correlation increased to the point that on Day 2 the values approached 1.0. This evidence suggests that the learners became more and more sensitive to their own errors through the development of error-detection processes.

How does the performer use the error detection? It is reasonable to assume, based on the information about closed-loop processes presented in Chapter 6, that if the movement is rapid, such as was the case in the Schmidt-White study, the subject would use the feedback from the movement compared to the reference of correctness to define an error after the response. Error-detection is not responsible for producing the action, and it only evaluates its correctness after the movement has been completed. For reasons discussed before, time is insufficient for the performer to take in the feedback, evaluate it, and make corrections before the movement is completed. So the motor program is thought to produce the movements, and the comparison of response-produced feedback with the learned reference of correctness is responsible for evaluating the movement afterwards.

Slow Responses

Not so with slow movements. It appears that, for some slow movements at least, the error-detection processes may be responsible for actually producing the action. Because there is plenty of time to use feedback, the subject in a positioning movement is thought to evaluate intrinsic feedback against the learned reference of correctness and to move to the position that is recognized as correct. If so, the error-detection capacity, being used to position the limb at the target, cannot then be used again to tell the experimenter about the error in positioning after the movement. With slow movements, if the subject is asked to report the error in positioning, the subject will have no idea whether or not the response was on target. Schmidt and Russell (Note 25) performed an experiment analogous to the Schmidt-White study, but using a slow linear-positioning task. In contrast to the findings from Schmidt and White (Figure 14-5), Schmidt and Russell found that the subjects demonstrated consistently low within-subject correlations between objective and subjective errors, with most of the correlations being only about .20, even after 100 trials of practice. We interpreted these findings to mean that the error detection processes were used to position the limb in the slow task and that further estimates of error after the movement were based largely on guesswork by the subjects. These ideas figure heavily in the development of schema theory, presented later in this chapter.

Potential Applications

The issues about error-detection are important for theoretical reasons, as will be discussed shortly, but there is a strong practical application to them as well. We can think of the self-generated error as a kind of substitute for KR, as it informs the subject about the size and direction of the error he or she has just made (for programmed responses only). Earlier, I defined such self-generated error information as *subjective reinforcement* (e.g., Adams, 1971; Adams & Bray, 1970; Schmidt, 1975b) and indicated that it can serve as a substitute for KR in certain situations. It is unfortunate that nearly all of the focus in learning environments is on performance and that nearly no concern is present for the development of the learner's error-detection capacity. If procedures could be developed for increasing the strength of error-detection, then the learner could provide KR to him- or herself, even if the teacher or coach were not present, thus enabling the individual to learn without KR.

One such method was provided by Hogan and Yanowitz (1978). The task was ballistic timing again, and during learning some subjects were required to guess their own scores (as Schmidt & White, 1972, had their subjects do), while other subjects learned the task without this requirement. The major results are presented in Figure 14-6. When KR was present in the first phase, no difference was found between the group that reported their scores and the group that did not. But when the KR was taken away in the next phase of the study (the subjects did not have to guess their errors in these trials), a clear performance advantage was observed for the subjects who had previously been asked to guess their errors. Why?

One possibility is that during the acquisition trials the subjects who are asked to guess their errors are learning error-detection, while those subjects not asked to guess their errors are not (or are learning it less well). The subjects who guessed their errors do not show a performance advantage because KR is so strong in its guidance function (see Chapter 13) that sub-

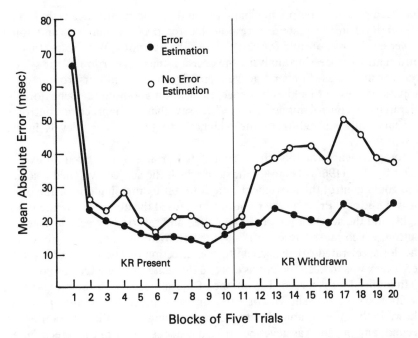

Figure 14-6. Absolute error in a ballistic timing task in KR and no-KR trials. (The group required to estimate their own errors in acquisition performs best when KR is withdrawn.) (from Hogan & Yanowitz, 1978).

jective error information can be ignored. But when the KR is withdrawn the subjects must rely on the subjective error information to hold them on target, and the subjects made to guess their errors in earlier practice are better performers because they learned to detect their own errors more completely in acquisiton.

Requiring learners in practical situations to guess their own errors should have strong positive effects on the development of error detection, probably because it requires that the subjects focus attention on the response-produced feedback stimuli, so they can be learned. These methods could be used easily in teaching programs, and the payoff should be both increased performance levels when the teacher is not providing KR and continued learning of the task without KR. This basic research is only now beginning to be considered in the design of practical learning environments.

HIERARCHICAL CONTROL MODEL

One thing that appears to happen as people learn, at least with some tasks, is a shift in the method of motor control to progressively "lower" levels in the nervous system. The idea that motor behavior is hierarchical[2]

---

[2]It is probably incorrect to assume that there are permanently situated "higher" and "lower" levels in the system. We normally think of decision mechanisms being at a "higher" level acting to control movement, but we can just as easily say that actions are at a "higher" level and act to control decisions (e.g., an incorrect action leads to a decision to correct). Turvey (1977) has argued that we should think of motor behavior as coalitional, whereby the levels of control can be easily reversed in terms of what is "higher."

has been presented before in Chapters 6 and 7. Briefly, the idea is that some higher level in the system is responsible for decision making, and some lower level is responsible for carrying out the decisions. With respect to the information-processing analysis, the decision-making portion of the system was considered as "higher" in the hierarchy than the motor-programming apparatus. Given this kind of conceptualization about motor behavior, the hierarchical control model goes on to say that with practice control is systematically shifted from the "higher" to the "lower" levels in the system.

Some evidence for this kind of view of learning comes from an experiment by Pew (1966). He used a task in which the subject watched a screen and could control the movement of a dot on it by pressing one or the other of two buttons. Pressing the right button caused the dot to accelerate to the right, and the acceleration could be halted and reversed by pressing the left button, which caused acceleration to the left. Without pressing any buttons, the dot accelerated off the screen to one direction or another, and the subject's task was to keep the dot as close to the center of the screen as possible.

In Figure 14-7 is a record from one of the subjects, with the velocity and position of the dot shown for early and late practice. In early practice, shown in the upper graph, the subject was making about three responses per second, and the dot was never positioned near the center of the screen for an appreciable length of time. The mode of control for this record seems to be that the subject pressed the other button, waited for the feedback from the screen, decided that the dot was accelerating off the screen, then planned a response to reverse it, pressed the button, etc. Here, the subject is using the

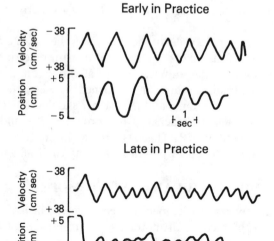

Figure 14-7. Performance records from a button-press tracking task in early (top) and late (bottom) practice. (Top records show instantaneous velocity, and bottom records show position with target represented as zero; responding is more rapid and more accurate in later practice.) (from Pew, 1966).

executive (i.e., the information-processing stages) level predominantly, so that the highest level in the system is consistently involved in the production of every movement.

Compare this record to the one below it, which is from the same subject but later in practice on this task. Here, the motor behavior is quite different. First, the rate of responding is much faster, about eight movements per second. Next, the dot is much closer to the target area, because the button was pressed to reverse the direction of the dot before the dot got very far away from the target. Although we cannot be absolutely certain, the mode of control appears to have changed in this case. From Chapters 5 and 6, we know that stimuli cannot be processed through the information-processing stages as rapidly as eight times each second, as each time through requires at least 200 msec, and probably more because of psychological refractoriness. So how does the subject produce the movement? In this case, it appears that a long string of movements is prestructured as a unit, perhaps governed by the motor program. Thus, each of the button presses is not controlled by a separate decision from the executive level. Pew viewed this finding as evidence for the hypothesis that, with practice, the subject shifted the control to the lower-level control of the motor program, both freeing the decision mechanism for other activities and making the movement more effective.

Pew (1966) gives some examples of various strategies that the learners produced in doing this task. In one of them, the subjects responded at a relatively high rate until the dot began to move unacceptably far from the target. Then, the subject would simply stop responding, picking up the rhythm of rapid responding again when the dot was in the proper location. A more "sophisticated" strategy involved the modulation of the duration of one or both of the button hold-down times. Thus, if the dot were drifting to the left, the subject would correct by holding down the right-hand button slightly longer than the left-hand one, all without stopping the alternate button pressing. Thus, the basic pattern of alterations was retained, but it was modified by changing its phasing slightly to control the position of the dot. Clearly, such a strategy was to be preferred in terms of producing accurate responding on the task, and it represents a very different approach to the problem as compared to the strategy in early practice.

It is easy to see the advantages of shifting the control from the decision-making level to the motor program level. Foremost is the freeing of the attentional mechanisms for use on higher-order aspects of the task (e.g., strategy), for doing other simultaneous tasks, or for simply resting so that the organism does not become fatigued. This freeing of attention is one of the major events that occurs when people learn, and it is discussed further in the next sections.

DECREASING ATTENTIONAL DEMANDS

So much evidence for the decreased attentional requirements of the task with practice has been presented in previous chapters that it hardly needs to be documented again, but I include a brief mention of it here for completeness. We can think of these decreased attention demands in two different ways: (a) through a shift to other mechanisms and (b) by making the response to task stimuli more compatible or predictable.

Shifts to Other Mechanisms

According to the hierarchical control model, with practice, longer and longer motor programs develop which govern increasingly longer sequences of behavior. We know from earlier analyses of motor programming that the selection and initiation of a program of action is highly attention demanding, but the actual execution of the program (once initiated) may not be attention demanding at all; if it is attention demanding, the demands are thought to be quite low (review Chapter 5). So, if the motor system generates longer and longer motor programs, fewer programs need to be initiated, less and less effort will have to be devoted to program initiation, and the attention demands of the total task will have been reduced as a result. We see these kinds of effects with the musician at a piano bar who seems to play long strings of music while carrying on meaningful conversation with the customers; we also saw these effects in Pew's (1966) experiment.

Increased Compatibility and Predictability

Another mechanism for reducing the attention demand of tasks with practice is that the stimuli and the responses that they evoke seem to become more S-R compatible (see Chapter 5). In a way, the stimuli which in early practice required considerable processing in order to generate a response seem after extensive practice to evoke the response almost "automatically." Thus, to the extent that the stimulus-response pairs in the task are becoming less foreign to the learners, less attention and effort will be required.

A similar sort of process happens if the stimuli are predictable, as they usually are in real-world situations and sometimes are in laboratory situations (Bahrick & Shelly, 1958). As the subjects learn the regularities of the stimulus patterns, they come to anticipate that a certain stimulus may occur in a certain place, in a certain form (visually, via touch, etc.) and/or at a certain time. Knowing that a stimulus will not occur can allow the person to relax and avoid attending, thus saving attentional capacities for other activities or allowing the subject to rest to prevent fatigue. These decreased attention demands produce a situation in which the performers are doing the task in an effortless and unhurried manner after practice.

CREATING MOTOR PROGRAMS

Throughout the discussions of motor performance and learning, I have repeatedly alluded to the idea that motor programs of increasing length, precision, and complexity are in some way structured through practice. Motor behavior researchers typically assume that such structuring takes place with practice, but almost no research studies shed light on how this structuring takes place. How is it that I have a program to type the word "university" as if it were a single unit? That these questions have no good answer is a sign of weakness for a motor program viewpoint about skilled behavior. Some hypotheses have been suggested, however, and some research has begun to test them.

The Gearshift Analogy

Keele (Note 26) suggested rather informally that motor programs might be generated by stringing together smaller programmed units of behavior, so that eventually this string of behavior is controllable as a single unit. He thought of this idea in relationship to learning to shift gears in a car. As you probably recall, the act of shifting gears was, when you were first learning, a slow, jerky, step-by-step process; you lifted the foot from the accelerator, then depressed the clutch, then moved the shift lever (probably in three distinct movements as well), until the entire act was completed (or until the car rolled to a stop on the hill). Contrast this behavior to that of the race-car driver, who shifts gears in a single rapid action; the movement not only occurs much more quickly, but elements of the action are performed with precise timing, and the actions of the hands and both feet are coordinated in relatively complex ways. In contrast to the behavior of the early learner, the action seems to be controlled in a very different way, perhaps as a single programmed unit.

Keele suggested that the various elements are combined in a progressive way to form the entire action. Figure 14-8 is a diagram of how this might work. Assume there are seven elements in the entire sequence and that these

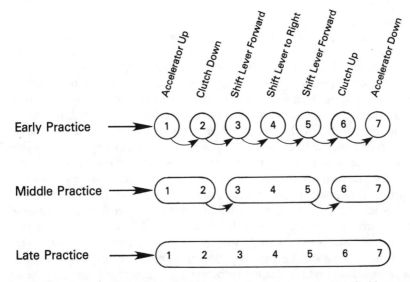

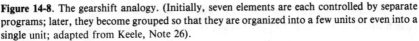

Figure 14-8. The gearshift analogy. (Initially, seven elements are each controlled by separate programs; later, they become grouped so that they are organized into a few units or even into a single unit; adapted from Keele, Note 26).

are, at first, controlled one at a time, each by a separate motor program. With some practice, the first two elements might come to be controlled as a single unit, the next three elements could comprise another, and the last two could comprise a third. Finally, with considerable experience, the entire sequence might be controlled as a single unit. This view is similar to the hierarchical control model presented in the previous section, but it goes further to specify how the programs are structured. An alternative to this view is that the program is structured from the beginning, progressively growing in length by adding parts. Other possibilities exist as well.

According to Keele (Note 26), we should be able to see evidence of the changes in these structures by using a fundamental principle of variability: The variability (inconsistency) of the elements within a unit should be considerably smaller than the variability between units. Return to Figure 14-8 for a moment and focus on the line labeled "Middle Practice." If we were to measure the interval from the end of Element 2 to the beginning of Element 3, the variability of this interval from trial to trial would be greater than the variability from the end of Element 3 to the beginning of Element 4. This is because the first two elements (2 and 3) are in different units (controlled by different programs), while the latter two (3 and 4) are supposedly in the same program. Turning this logic around, if we found intervals in the sequence where variability was very high, this could be taken as evidence that the behavior occurring at the opposite ends of this interval of time are members of different motor programs.

This strategy has been tried by Marteniuk (Note 27) and Shapiro (1978), but not with encouraging results. Considerable problems arose with the analysis in both studies, however, and it is possible that future attempts with different tasks and analytic methods will produce something more definitive. For now, though, as appealing as the gearshift analogy might be, almost no evidence indicates that it might be on the right track.

Subroutine Program

As mentioned before in this chapter, many investigators believe that much motor responding is made up of pre-existing subroutines, such as grasping, reaching, releasing, etc., in the case of arm movements in infants. Good evidence suggests that infant motor behavior is structured in this way (Connolly, 1970), but far less evidence exists that adult motor behavior is made up of these small elements. It is possible that as children develop into adulthood commonly used programs progressively combine into larger units (e.g., throwing, shifting gears in the car) and that even these units can in turn be combined to form larger units. If the idea of subroutine formation has relevance for adult motor behavior, it would seem to apply most to those relatively complex tasks performed for the first time. Here, the performer must combine previously learned elements in some new way to accomplish the goal on the first try. But on subsequent attempts, it seems more reasonable that these subunits become grouped into larger units. This has the advantage that information-processing stages are not required between units, with the entire sequence, or at least very large parts of it, being run off as a single movement. Obviously much more research needs to be done with respect to this idea of subroutines.

Combinations of Reflexes

A third way that motor programs are thought to be formed through practice is through the combination of fundamental reflexes. Easton (1972, 1978) is probably the strongest proponent of this point of view. According to Easton, higher levels in the motor system are capable of tuning or adjusting lower spinal levels so that the existing reflexes (e.g., the stretch reflex) can be controlled in ways that result in skilled actions. Thus, rather than hypothesizing that the motor system builds a set of commands that come to exist as a stored motor program, Easton's view is that the "commands" are really ways of controlling the pre-existing reflexes. Such emphases on reflexes are also a part of the views of Fukuda (1961) and Hellebrandt et al. (1956), as discussed in Chapter 6 (see Figures 6-16, 6-17). In these cases, the reflexes are thought to be of assistance to the overall programmed action when increased force or speed is required, but they are not the fundamental basis of it. Also, Easton's viewpoint has a great deal in common with the ideas of Greene (1972) and Turvey (1977), each of whom argue that rapid movements consist of controlling structures that are constrained to act as a single unit, perhaps by tuning of spinal systems or by utilization of reflexes. In all these cases, though, the drawback is that these hypotheses do not account well for the data on deafferentation, mainly that deafferented animals are not always seriously impaired (Chapter 7). If these hypotheses are correct, how can such behaviors occur if no spinal reflexes exist? Any theory of program learning which places too much emphasis on the reflexes seems to contradict these basic deafferentation findings.

It is intriguing that one of the most fundamental problems in motor learning—how rapid, prestructured movements are acquired through practice—has almost no research that can give us solid answers. Much of this will change as newer biomechanical and neurophysiological methods are used in conjunction with hypotheses such as the gearshift analogy.

PROGRESSION-REGRESSION HYPOTHESIS

Fuchs (1962) presented an hypothesis about the changes in motor behavior with practice that has particular relevance to tracking tasks. In many tracking responses, both in the laboratory and in the outside world, the movements of the track to be followed are made up of a number of components that can be described according to the physical principles of motion. At the most simple level is the position of the track at any moment. The next most complex aspect of the track is its velocity at any moment. A third and yet more complex aspect of the track is its acceleration at any moment. In designing servo systems to regulate some mechanical system, engineers can design a simple system that only responds to the position of the track, a system that responds to the position and velocity, or a highly complex system that responds to the position, velocity, and acceleration. With each increase in the components being tracked, progressive increases are required in the complexity and expense of the mechanical or electronic devices that are to track them.

The progression-regression hypothesis for humans holds that as the learner practices on a tracking task, a progression develops in the learner's behavior in the direction of acting more and more like a complex tracking system. Early in practice, the individual responds only to the most simple elements of the display (position). With increased practice, the learner becomes able to use velocity information, and even later comes to use information about acceleration as well. The regression portion of the hypothesis refers to what happens to the learner under stressful conditions or when forgetting of the response has occurred (perhaps as a result of a long layoff). Here, according to the hypothesis, the individual regresses to a more simple level of control, from acceleration to velocity, or from velocity to position, with systematically reduced accuracy as a consequence.

Fuchs (1962) has presented some tracking data that are generally in keeping with the hypothesis. But there has not been enough study of this interesting view of skill learning to be able to evaluate it well. It does provide some appealing ideas with respect to tracking, and more work is needed on this notion of tracking and other motor tasks.

THEORIES OF MOTOR LEARNING

The ideas presented earlier in this chapter are probably best described as hypotheses—or miniature theories—about the learning of motor skills (Chapter 2). They really do not satisfy the basic criteria for a full-blown theory for a number of reasons. First, many of them are directed at only certain kinds of tasks, such as tracking tasks, positioning tasks, etc., and more generality is usually required for a theory. Next, many of them are concerned with only a few experimental variables, and theories are usually thought to have more complete structures that are capable of explaining the effects of a variety of independent variables. Finally, many of these hypotheses are based mainly on speculation about the nature of motor learning and are not as well grounded as they could be in the empirical laws of learning, such as those laws presented in Chapters 12 and 13. Of course, a good theory of motor learning should, in a single structure, be able to explain as many of these laws as possible. And there should be no contradictions with the laws. A single repeatable contradiction will cast serious doubt on the effectiveness of a theory, as I have mentioned in Chapter 2.

A theory dealing exclusively with motor learning was presented by Adams (1971). Because it does satisfy most of the criteria of a theory as mentioned above and in Chapter 2, and because it generated enormous interest in the 1970s, it is deserving of somewhat more space than earlier ideas. I will present some of the major theoretical propositions of Adams' theory, some of the empirical support for it, and then some of the major lines of evidence that seem to indicate that it is not correct. Following the discussion of

Adams' theory, I will present the same sort of discussion for a theory that I proposed in 1975 that was intended as a replacement for Adams' theory. After all this, I hope you will have a fairly good idea of the kind of theorizing occurring in the motor learning field. You will also realize that, unfortunately, no theory yet proposed is capable of explaining the kinds of learning phenomena and principles that I have presented in Chapters 12 and 13.

Adams' Theory

Adams (1971) developed his closed-loop theory of motor learning using a well-established set of empirical laws of motor learning, most of which were based on slow, linear-positioning responses. He believed that the principles of performance and learning that applied to these responses were the same as for any other kind of response (a belief that I will challenge shortly) and that using a well-established set of empirical laws from positioning responses would produce a solid basis for theorizing. Also, the literature that dealt with other kinds of tasks (tracking, ballistic actions, etc.) was not nearly as well developed as the literature for the positioning responses, which provided an additional justification for using them as a starting point. With this set of laws in hand, he set out to create a theoretical system that could explain the kinds of findings that occurred in learning experiments on positioning.

A Closed-Loop Emphasis

A major aspect of the theory that distinguishes it from others is that it is *closed-loop*, and all of the elements of closed-loop systems discussed in Chapter 6 are present. Adams believed that all movements are made by comparing the ongoing feedback from the limbs during the motion to a reference of correctness that is learned during practice. He termed this reference of correctness the *perceptual trace*. For positioning responses, for which the individual must learn to locate the limb at a proper position in space, the perceptual trace represents the feedback qualities of the correct position. Therefore, minimizing the difference between the feedback received and the reference of correctness (the perceptual trace) means that the limb is brought to the correct position by the kinds of closed-loop processes discussed in Chapter 6. In some of his writings, Adams implies that the perceptual trace represents the path of the action toward the target as well as the target endpoint, with feedback being used to guide the movement along this proper trajectory. But one point is clear in the theory: The perceptual trace is the most important element of all, and the accuracy of responding is dependent on the "strength" (or quality) of this trace.

Perceptual-trace formation. Given the critical role of the perceptual trace in performance, how is the reference of correctness learned with practice or experience? The basic idea is quite simple. When the individual makes a positioning movement, intrinsic feedback stimuli are produced that represent the particular locations of the limb in space. These stimuli are retained in some way, and it is said that they "leave a trace" in the central nervous system (hence the name perceptual trace). With repeated responses with KR, the individual comes closer and closer to the target on repeated trials; and on each of the trials another trace is laid down, so that eventually a kind of "collection" of traces develops. Because with KR the learner is responding close to the target after only a few trials, each trial provides feedback stimuli that tend to represent the correct movement. In turn, the collection of traces (perceptual trace) comes to represent the feedback qualities of the correct movement. Then, on subsequent trials, the learner moves to that position in space for which the difference between the ongoing feedback produced and the perceptual trace is minimal. The difference between the perceptual trace and the feedback represents an error in the movement, and the individual seeks to produce an action that produces minimal error on each trial. Since the perceptual trace is stronger with each KR trial, the errors in performance decrease with KR practice.

When KR is withdrawn, the perceptual trace begins to be degraded because of "decay" or because some slightly errant responses and their feedback are being produced; the result is the slight decrements in performance with further no-KR trials. Given more KR practice, the decrements in no-KR trials should be less severe because the perceptual trace is stronger and less resistant to this degradation from errant responses. See Bilodeau, Bilodeau, and Schumsky (1959) in Chapter 13 (Figure 13-3), or Newell (1974) for evidence on this point.

KR and the perceptual trace. KR, as should be clear from Chapter 13, is a critical variable for motor learning, and any theory of motor learning must be able to explain how KR acts on the theory's constructs (i.e., on the perceptual trace in Adams' case). Adams rejected the long-standing reinforcement position about KR (see Chapter 13), in which KR was thought of as mainly rewarding. He believed that there was far more to it than this. Learners, according to Adams, are not passive recipients of reward, but rather are actively engaged in forming hypotheses about the task to be learned. Learners engage in considerable verbalization (especially in early learning), and they use many strategies to make the next response different (hopefully better) from the previous ones. To Adams, KR provides information about errors, and the individual uses the information to solve the motor problem, rather than using it as a reward that in some way was thought to "strengthen" the response.

In particular, Adams provided a guidance role for KR, although his writings do not use this term. After a given trial, KR is given which provides information about how the next movement should be made differently. In early learning, the learner uses KR in relation to the perceptual trace to make the movement more precise, so that KR guides the movement to the target on successive trials. In such a view, KR does not produce learning directly. Rather, it creates the appropriate situation (i.e., being on target) so that the actual learning mechanisms (i.e., the feedback producing an increment in "strength" for the perceptual trace) can operate.

Subjective reinforcement. Adams' theory sought to explain how individuals develop error-detection capacities, or how it is that we come to know when we have made an error. He was led strongly by verbal-learning work and the common "slips of the tongue" that are quickly corrected, such as the person who says "John left no turn unstoned—I mean stone unturned." Such effects were present in the motor work as well, such as the work by West (1967) on skilled typists and by Rabbitt (1967) on RT performances, both of whom showed evidence that people can detect and correct motor errors rather quickly. More research has been done since 1971 that shows the same thing (see Chapter 13, Rapid Error Corrections). Adams argued that after the movement was completed the individual could compare the feedback received against the perceptual trace, the difference representing the error in responding that the person could report to him- or herself or to the experimenter as subjective reinforcement. White and I (1972) showed that this error-detection capability is strengthened with practice as predicted by Adams' theory, but we used rapid ballistic actions (see also the section on "Limitations and Contradictory Evidence" later in this chapter). Presumably, this subjective reinforcement can be used to keep the movement on target without KR; and, according to the theory, keeping the movement on target can provide gains in learning because the feedback continues to add to the perceptual trace, again without KR in later learning.

A two-state theory. Contrary to earlier closed-loop theorists, Adams realized that in order to have the capacity for the system to detect its own errors, two memory states must be present—one to produce the action and one to evaluate the outcome. What if the same state that produced the movement also evaluated it? If the movement were chosen incorrectly, the feedback from the movement and the reference of correctness would always match, producing a report of no error on every attempt. In Adams' theory, though, the reference of correctness (the perceptual trace) represents the correct response, and the movement is selected and initiated by another memory state that Adams called the *memory trace*. According to Adams, the memory trace is a "modest motor program" that is responsible for choosing the direction of the action, initiating it, and giving it a "shove" toward the target location. Then, the perceptual trace takes over the control of the movement to cause it to come to a stop at the final target location.

The role of errors. One of the interesting implications of Adams' theory is that any errors produced during the course of training are harmful to learning. This is because, when an error is made, the feedback from it is necessarily different from that which is associated with a correct response, and the perceptual trace will be degraded a little bit as a result. One prediction, then, is that guidance should be particularly useful as a training method, as it prevents errors. What does the evidence on guidance say (Chapter 12)? This aspect of the theory is one of the ways that Adams' theory and schema theory (to be presented next) are quite different.

Predictions and Supporting Evidence

Adams has pointed out a number of predictions from the theory, and many of them appear to be supported rather well. These have been presented in many other places (e.g., Adams, 1971, 1976a, 1976b) so I will mention them only briefly here. The two main areas in which these predictions lie are presented next.

Effects of KR. A major class of predictions has to do with the effects of KR and of the various temporal intervals in the KR paradigm. Adams (1971) argued that (a) there should be no effect of lengthening the KR-delay interval, (b) there should be negative effects on learning when the post-KR-delay interval is too short, and (c) there should be negative effects on learning when the inter-trial interval is too long. These predictions, plus additional predictions about the precision and withdrawal of KR, seem reasonably well supported in the literature on KR, without contradictory findings (review Chapter 13).

Effects of feedback. Because the theory holds that the development of the perceptual trace—the most critical element in the theory—is dependent on feedback from the responding limb, the theory naturally predicts that factors increasing such feedback should enhance learning, and factors degrading or eliminating feedback should retard learning. In a series of experiments using positioning tasks, Adams and his colleagues have shown that these predictions are well supported (e.g., Adams & Goetz, 1973; Adams, Goetz, & Marshall, 1972). Further, these experiments have implicated feedback in the development of error-detection and correction, as is predicted by the theory. In these ways, and particularly for slow, linear-positioning responses, Adams has claimed a number of lines of support for his theory.

Limitations and Contradictory Evidence

At the time Adams' theory was published, the theory accounted for a great deal of the existing data on motor learning. Naturally, additional experiments have been done in the decade since the theory was presented, some of which were directly motivated by predictions from the theory and some of which were motivated by various other reasons. The result is that now a number of findings suggest that the theory is incorrect or inadequate in various ways. Here are some of the reasons why the theory seems incorrect.

Logical inconsistencies. One characteristic of "good" theories is that they have internal consistency; that is, there should be no contradictions among the logically derived predictions from the theory. A logical inconsistency does appear to exist in Adams' theory, though, regarding subjective reinforcement for slow positioning responses. Adams has the perceptual trace providing (a) the basis for placing the limb at the correct target location and (b) a basis for knowing how far that movement was away from the target location after the movement is completed. I have argued (Schmidt, 1975b; see also the section on "Error Detection Capabilities" earlier in this chapter) that, if the perceptual trace is used to position the limb, then no additional information can be available about the amount of actual error produced. And, empirically, Schmidt and Russell (Note 25) provided evidence that no error-detection mechanism exists after slow positioning responses, even after 100 trials of practice, contrary to Adams' predictions. However, Schmidt and White (1972) found strong error-detection mechanisms after rapid movements for which the perceptual trace presumably cannot be used during the response to guide the limb. Adams does not make a distinction between these fast and slow movements, yet the evidence shows that they develop and use error detection mechanisms very differently (e.g., Newell, 1976).

Limitations in scope. A major limitation for the theory is that it focuses almost entirely on slow, linear-positioning responses—responses that a number of writers in the area feel are simply not sufficiently representative of the many other kinds of skills that we see in everyday actions (e.g., ballistic responses, tracking, etc.). While the theory has potential applicability to slower responses, most would not agree that it is applicable to all motor learning. Indeed, a number of predictions from rapid movements (e.g., that mentioned about error-detection capability) do not hold in the laboratory. And Adams' insistence that rapid movements be governed by feedback mechanisms seems to be contradictory to the body of literature dealing with deafferentation, some of the details of which are presented next.

Contradictory evidence. Certainly one of the most damaging lines of evidence for Adams' theory is the work on deafferentation in animals (Taub, 1976) and in humans (Lashley, 1917). This work was reviewed in Chapter 7. Briefly, the findings are that organisms deprived of all sensory feedback from the limbs can respond skillfully, and they can even learn new actions (e.g., Taub & Berman, 1968). If the only mechanism for controlling skilled actions was the use of feedback in relationship to a perceptual trace, then these individuals should not have been able to produce the actions they did. Adams (1976b) has countered this argument by saying that the animals may have shifted to some other source of feedback, such as vision, to substitute for the lost sensations from the responding limbs. This may be the case in some of these studies, but it seems not to apply to all of them (e.g., Polit & Bizzi, 1978, 1979; Taub & Berman, 1968). Also, Adams' theory ignores the data from various species showing the existence of central (spinal) pattern generators, structures apparently capable of causing complex actions without feedback from the responding limbs (see Gallistel, 1980, or Grillner, 1975, for reviews).

The failure to recognize the obvious role of open-loop processes in movement control is a serious drawback for the Adams' theory. The best that can be said for Adams' theory in this regard is that not all movements are controlled in the ways he specified; at worst, these data say that the theory is wrong. At the same time, these lines of evidence provide strong support for motor programming theories—viewpoints which are direct rivals to Adams' closed-loop view.

A second line of evidence against Adams' theory was provided by the literature on variability in practice (review the section in Chapter 12). Because the perceptual trace is the feedback representation of the correct action, making movements different than the correct action (in variable practice) will not result in the development of an increment of perceptual trace strength. Thus, Adams' theory predicts that variability-in-practice sequences, in which the learner experiences a number of targets around a central criterion target, should be less effective in learning the criterion target than practice at the target itself. In the literature that Shapiro and I (1982) reviewed on this topic, we found no clear evidence that, for adults, variable practice was less effective than practice at the transfer target; for children, the evidence said that variability in practice was superior to practicing the transfer target itself! Thus, the literature on variability-in-practice effects suggests that it is not necessary to have experience at the target in order for a movement to the target to be learned. Because Adams' theory explicity claims that such experience is critical for the development of the perceptual trace, this evidence is quite damaging to his position.

Summary

At the time Adams' theory was proposed, it represented a major step forward for motor learning, as it presented a plausible, empirically based theory for researchers to evaluate. I believe that such evaluations have shown it to have a number of limitations (such as being tied to positioning responses), a logical inconsistency dealing with subjective reinforcement, and a number of predictions that have not held up in the laboratory. Adams' theory, after 10 years of study, no longer seems to account for the currently available evidence on motor learning. But the theory served its intended purpose—generating substantial research and thinking directed at showing that the theory was incorrect and paving the way for newer theories which account for the older data and the newer data as well. One such newer theory is schema theory, and it followed Adams' theory by approximately five years. It is represented next.

Schema Theory

In 1975, largely because of my dissatisfaction with Adams' position (mentioned in the previous sections), I formulated a theory that can be considered as a rival to Adams'. My primary concern with Adams' position was (and is) the lack of emphasis on open-loop control processes, and the schema theory has a strong open-loop dependency. Yet, at the same time, many aspects of Adams' theory are very appealing, such as the emphasis on subjective reinforcement, the concern for slow responses, and the need to have one memory state that is responsible for producing the response and another that is responsible for evaluating it. Thus, schema theory borrowed heavily from the ideas of Adams and others in hopes of keeping the most effective parts and eliminating defective ones. Also, the theory is based heavily on our knowledge about motor control such as was presented in Chapters 6 and 7, and it uses these concepts in conjunction with ideas about learning processes to attempt to explain the learning of both rapid and slower movements (see also Schmidt, 1980).

Two States of Memory

Schema theory holds that there are two states of memory, a *recall memory* that is responsible for the production of movement, and a *recognition memory* that is responsible for response evaluation. For rapid, ballistic movements, recall memory is involved with the motor programs and parameters, structured in advance to carry out the movement with but minimal involvement from peripheral feedback (review Chapters 7 and 8 for the details of the motor program idea). Recognition memory, on the other hand, is a sensory system capable of evaluating the response-produced feedback after the movement is completed, thereby informing the subject about the amount and direction of any errors in responding. Such structures satisfy the goal of having the agent that produces the action be different from the agent that evaluates its correctness, one of Adams' main ideas.

Now consider slow positioning responses. Here, recall memory is thought not to have an important role, and the major problem for the learner is the comparison of response-produced feedback and the reference of correctness. In these movements, the recall state merely pushes the limb along in small bursts, with the individual stopping the responding when the response-produced feedback and the reference of correctness match.[3] Here, the agent that produces the action is the same as the agent that evaluates it, and hence no post-response subjective reinforcement can exist as is the case for the rapid responses. I have already presented evidence that rapid responses do, and slow responses do not, provide post-response subjective reinforcement.

The Emphasis on Motor Programming

At the heart of schema theory is the idea of the generalized motor program, discussed at some length in Chapters 7 and 8. The generalized motor program, you will recall, is thought to be structured with phasing and (perhaps) relative force, and parameters are required in order to specify the particular way that the program is to be executed. For example, an overall-duration parameter specifies the time required to go through the total sequence of action, an overall-force (or gain) parameter is responsible for defining the level of intensity with which the muscular action is to be carried out, and a muscle-selection parameter defines which muscles or limbs will be involved. When these parameters have been chosen, the movement can be carried out by the program as specified by them.

Like most programming theories, the schema theory does not specify from where the motor programs come. This is an important problem, but the level of knowledge at this time does not allow much to be said about this process. So, the theory has had to assume that programs are developed in some way and that they can be carried out by executing them with the proper parameters. Review Chapter 8 for the details of this argument and the evidence supporting it.

---

[3]After the theory was presented, evidence was produced indicating that not all slow movements are feedback-based. In some instances these slower movements appear to be preprogrammed by one of a number of different mechanisms described in Chapters 7 and 8. See Kelso (1977) for some examples.

The Concept of a Schema

An important part of schema theory, naturally, is the schema. The schema concept is an old one in psychology, being introduced by Head (1926) and later popularized by Bartlett (1932). The term was used for the abstract memory representations for events, stories, skilled actions, etc., where the representation could be thought of as a concept, generalization, or rule about the event lacking in many of the actual details. Popularity of the idea faded in the 1940s through 1960s, but it generated new interest as a result of experiments by Posner and Keele (1968, 1970) and Edmonds, Evans, and Mueller (1966) that were conducted at a time when cognitive psychology was becoming a dominant direction for psychology. I attempted to use the basic idea of the schema (or rule) in combination with the ideas of the generalized motor program to form a theory of how skills are learned.

Schema Learning

I assumed that, after a movement is made with a generalized motor program, the individual briefly stores four things. First, the individual stores the initial conditions (bodily positions, weight of thrown objects, etc.) that existed before the movement. Next, the individual stores the parameters that were assigned to the generalized motor program. Third, the individual stores the outcome of the movement in the environment in terms of KR. And, finally, the learner stores the sensory consequences of the movement, that is, how the movement felt, looked, sounded, etc. These four sources of information are not stored permanently (as this would lead to a serious storage problem as mentioned in Chapter 8) but are stored only long enough so that the performer can abstract some relationships among them. Two such relationships, or schemas, are thought to be formed, and they are listed next.

Recall schema. The first of these relationships is called the recall schema because it is concerned with the production of movements. Figure 14-9 is a graph that represents the kind of process that could be occurring. On the horizontal axis the outcomes in the environment are represented, such as the number of feet that a softball traveled when it was thrown. On the vertical axis are the parameters that an individual could provide for the motor program. When the individual produces a movement, the brief storage of the parameter and the movement outcome produces a "data point" on the graph. With repeated responses using different parameters and producing different outcomes, other data points are established, and the individual begins to define a relationship between the size of the parameter and the nature of the movement outcome; this relationship is represented in the diagram by the regression line drawn through the points (as in situations involving empirical equations, Chapter 3). With each successive movement using the program, a new data point is produced, and the location of the line (the relationship) is adjusted slightly. After each of these adjustments, the stored data are "thrown away," so all that remains of the movement is the relationship. This relationship is the recall schema.

The relationship is also thought to comprise information about the initial

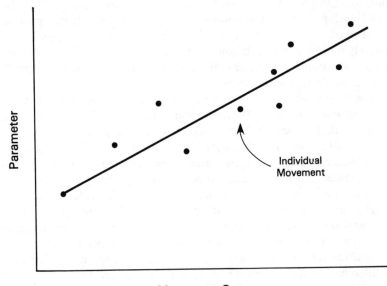

Figure 14-9. The hypothetical relationship between movement outcomes in the environment and the parameters that were used to produce them (adapted from Schmidt, 1982).

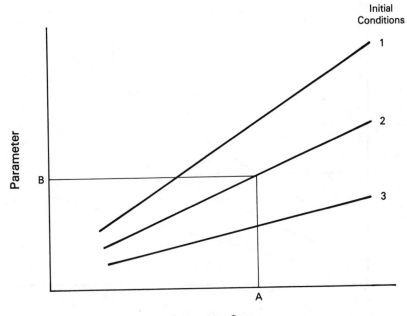

Figure 14-10. The hypothetical relationship between movement outcomes in the environment and the parameters that were used to produce them for various initial conditions: the recall schema (adapted from Schmidt, 1982).

conditions of the movement, and this idea is shown in Figure 14-10. Here, the relationship between the parameters used and the outcome produced will depend on the nature of the initial conditions, and one can then imagine a relatively more complex relationship being formed among the initial conditions, the response parameters, and the outcome in the environment that resulted from these combinations.

How does the individual use this schema? On a future trial using this generalized motor program, the individual notes the particular environmental outcome that is desired, labeled as Point A on Figure 14-10. Also, the particular initial conditions are noted (e.g., the weight of the object to be thrown), which might fit into the category represented by the second line. Then, using the relationship established by past experience with these initial conditions and parameters, the individual uses the rule to select the parameter that will come closest to accomplishing the particular environmental outcome. This parameter is labeled as Point B in the figure. The parameter is then applied to the program to produce the action.

Recognition schema. The recognition schema, for response evaluation, is thought to be formed and used in a similar way. Figure 14-11 is a diagram representing this process. Here, the schema is comprised of the relationship between the initial conditions, the environmental outcomes, and the sensory consequences (rather than the parameters as in Figures 14-9 and 14-10). Because these elements are assumed to be present after each trial, the relationship among them is established, perhaps reflecting the fact that faster movements have had more "intense" sensory consequences. This relationship is represented as the three lines shown in the figure.

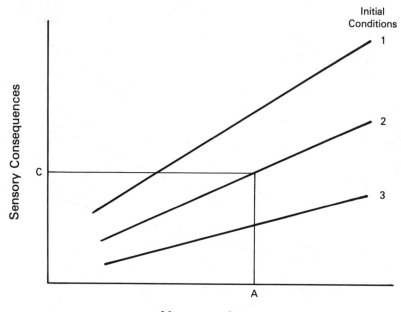

Figure 14-11. The hypothetical relationship between movement outcomes in the environment and the sensory consequences produced for them by various initial conditions: the recognition schema (adapted from Schmidt, 1982).

The recognition schema is thought to be used in a way analogous to the recall schema. Before the response, the individual decides which of the movement outcomes is desired and determines the nature of the initial conditions. Then, with the recognition schema, the individual can estimate the sensory consequences that will be present if that movement outcome is produced. These are called the *expected sensory consequences* (labeled as Point C) and serve as the basis for determining (after the movement) whether or not the movement that will be produced is correct. The expected sensory consequences are analogous to Adams' perceptual trace discussed earlier.

Recall and Recognition Processes in Movement

The entire system can perhaps be visualized more easily by referring to Figure 14-12. This diagram is very similar to one presented during the discussions of motor programs in Chapter 6 (Figure 6-10), but now the ideas of recognition and recall are included. For fast movements, the initial conditions and desired outcomes are inputs to the system and give rise to the parameters (called response specifications in the theory) and the expected sensory consequences (expected proprioceptive feedback and expected exteroceptive feedback in the diagram). After the movement is run off by the program, the feedback from the limbs and environment is fed back and compared to their respective expected states; any difference represents an error which is labeled and is then delivered back to the information-processing mechanisms as subjective reinforcement.

For slow movements, the theory says that the subjective reinforcement is actually used to produce the action. Here, the expected feedback sources represent the criterion of correctness, and the feedback compared to them gives ongoing information about errors during the response. Then, the individual moves in such a way that the error signalled to the information-processing mechanisms is as small as possible, indicating that the individual's limbs are on target. Thus, even though the slow movement is actively produced by the individual, it is thought to be governed by recognition memory and the recognition schema.

Variables Important for Schema Learning

The theory says that we learn skills by learning rules about the functioning of our bodies. With experience, we come to form relationships between how our muscles are activated, what they actually do, and how those actions feel. As such, responses for which any of four stored elements are missing will result in degraded learning of the rules. One of the most critical is movement-outcome information (or KR). If movements are made in which the individual does not receive information about the movement outcome, then even if the other features are present, no strengthening of the schema can occur because the location on the horizontal axis will not be known (Figure 14-10). Similarly, if sensory consequences are missing (e.g., in temporary deafferentation), then no recognition schema development can occur. In passive movements, no parameters are issued to the program (indeed, no program is to be run off), so no recall schema updating can oc-

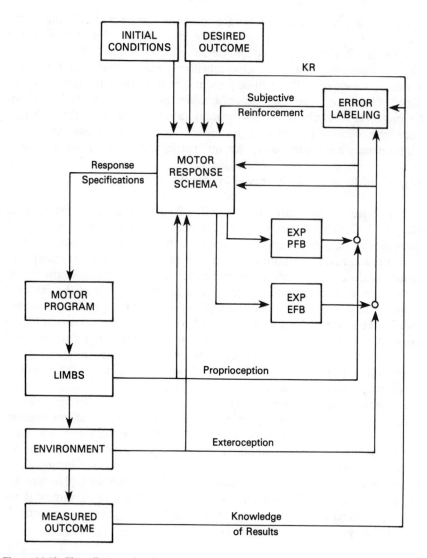

Figure 14-12. Flow diagram showing critical elements in a movement performance from the point of view of schema theory (EXP PFB = expected proprioceptive feedback, EXP EFB = expected exteroceptive feedback) (from Schmidt, 1975b).

cur. These hypothetical mechanisms provide ways of testing the theory, and many of these kinds of experiments have been done already.

The Role of Errors

In contrast to Adams' theory, schema theory has positive benefits from the production of movements whether they are correct or not. This is because the schema is the rule based on the relationship among stored elements, and this relationship is present just as much for incorrect movements as for correct ones. Producing an incorrect response just gives additional information about how the body functions. Adams' theory, as you may remember, views errors as disruptive, as they degrade the perceptual trace.

Predictions and Supporting Evidence

Predictions from the theory are numerous, and many of these have been discussed in other places (Schmidt, 1975b, 1976b; Shapiro & Schmidt, 1982). For brevity, I will list only a few of the major ones.

Variability in practice. The theory predicts that practicing a variety of movement outcomes with the same program (i.e., by using a variety of parameters) will provide a widely based set of experiences upon which a rule or schema can be built. In graphic form, this can be seen in Figure 14-9. When the range of movement outcomes and parameters is small, all of the "data points" are clustered together in the center of the diagram, and less certainty will exist about the placement of the line. So when a new movement is required, greater error will occur in estimating the proper parameters and/or expected sensory consequences. In recently reviewing the literature on variability of practice, Shapiro and I (1982) found considerable evidence that practice variability is a positive factor in motor learning, especially so for children's motor learning (see the "Variability in Practice" section, Chapter 12). These relatively new data are predictable from schema theory, but are not predictable from Adams' theory.

Novel responses. The theory says that a particular movement outcome (specified by a particular value of the parameter) need not be produced previously in order to be produced in the future. This is related to the variability-in-practice prediction, because the basis for producing a new movement is a rule about parameter selection based on the performance of earlier similar movements. Research has shown that after varied practice novel responses can be produced nearly as accurately as they can be if the novel response had been practiced repeatedly, and other studies show that the two are about equivalent. Studies with children suggest that it is more effective to practice responses other than the particular one that is to be learned. All of this evidence suggests that motor learning may be primarily rule learning and not the learning of specific responses.

These kinds of effects seem particularly strong in open skills, for which the movements are never repeated exactly on two consequetive trials. In a batting task, for example, the ball is never in the same place with the same velocity on two occasions, and thus the individual would seem to have to generate a novel response on each trial. Such ideas have been used for a long time in movement education situations with children, where the pupils are encouraged to make as many different movements as they can. By such procedures, the children are presumably developing a strong set of rules or schemas about their motor behaviors, consequently helping them to be more proficient performers in novel situations in the future. See Schmidt (1976b, 1977) for more on the relationship between schema theory and movement education.

Error detection. The theory predicts that there should be no capability for error detection after a slow movement, while such capability should exist after a rapid movement. This is so because the error detection capability is actually used to produce the slow response, leaving none afterwards with which to detect errors. As mentioned during the discussion of Adams' theory, empirical evidence supports this kind of prediction (Schmidt & Russell, Note 25; Schmidt & White, 1972).

Limitations and Contradictory Evidence

Limitations. One major strength (and limitation) of the theory is in relationship to the emphasis of the generalized motor program. While I believe that the evidence strongly supports such a view (see Chapter 8), the entire structure is quite vague in relationship to how the program is formed in the first place, how the rules about parameters and sensory consequences are developed and used, how the individual makes the first response before any schema can exist, and so on. Also, to the extent that the generalized motor program idea might later be shown to be incorrect, so too will be schema theory, as the theory depends strongly on the programming notion. Certainly, more work needs to be done on the nature of motor programs, and such research will surely have a bearing on schema theory.

Logical inconsistencies. Like Adams' theory, the schema theory is not without logical problems. The theory seems well suited to the explanation of how the basis for novel responses is learned, particularly in situations that are classified as open skills, such as fielding a baseball. A stable relationship is built over a lifetime of practice at similar skills using the same programs, and each new response in this class is another variant of these previous ones. But what about the learning that goes on within motor learning experiments, which is one of the most important experimental outcomes that must be explained by a theory of learning? Here, the theory says that the schema changes radically with each practice trial, so that the parameters come to be chosen more effectively with practice. This is inconsistent with the idea that the schema is a stable rule established over the course of many years, however, and this represents a serious contradiction in the theory. Shapiro and Schmidt (1982) provided one kind of theoretical solution to this problem, but it will remain to be seen whether this solution creates more problems than it solves.

Contradictory evidence. One of the predictions from schema theory is that the recall schema and recognition schema are separate states and that they should develop more or less independently. Some evidence exists that variables strengthening motor recall do not have effects on recognition and vice versa, supporting the separation of recognition and recall (e.g., Schmidt, Christenson, & Rogers, 1975). But there is also evidence that factors which, according to the theory, should affect only motor recognition also affect recall (Wallace & McGhee, 1979; Zelaznik, Shapiro, & Newell, 1978); but McGhee (Note 28) has provided data that tend to negate this criticism. It is, however, clear that the separation of recognition and recall is not as complete as the theory suggests.

Summary

Schema theory has provided an alternative to Adams' closed-loop theory of motor learning. Compared to Adams' theory, it has the advantage that it accounts for more kinds of movements, it seems to account for error-detection capabilities more effectively, and it seems to explain the production of novel responses in open-skills situations. Some logical problems need to be solved, but it is not clear that this can be done without discarding the entire theoretical structure. There are some apparent failures of the evidence to agree with the theoretical predictions as well. While I think that the theory was a step forward, it should be clear that it does not provide a complete understanding of the data on motor learning. But ignoring these failures, the theory does seem to provide a useful framework with for thinking about skill learning, because it is so consistent with the literature on the generalized motor program. While schema theory may be wrong, it should be recognized that a future theory, to be more effective, must account for all of the data (variability in practice, error detection, etc.) more effectively than schema theory does as well as encompass the data that do not fit the predictions from schema theory.

SUMMARY

The empirical laws of motor learning presented in previous chapters are the focus of a number of hypotheses or theories that are directed at explaining them, and this chapter presents some of the more important ones. A preliminary analysis of skills learning shows that learning is an ongoing process that is probably not ever completed. Also, learners appear to pass through various phases when acquiring a skill; a *cognitive phase* in which emphasis is on discovering what to do, an *associative phase* in which the concern is with perfecting the movement patterns, and an *autonomous phase* in which the attentional requirements of the response appear to be reduced or even eliminated.

A major direction for understanding skill learning has been provided by the individual differences tradition. A significant finding is that the set of abilities underlying a skill appears to change with practice, so that the factor structure of the skill is systematically different in practiced and unpracticed subjects. The change is in the direction of less involvement of cognitive abilties and greater involvement of motor abilities with practice. In addition, the strength of an ability that is specific to the particular task in question increases. These characteristics of abilities and learning provide insight into why the accurate prediction of high-level motor behavior is so difficult to achieve.

These notions are somewhat similar to those in the hierarchical control model, which holds that the control of the skill is systematically shifted from higher-level control processes involving attention to lower-level processes involving motor programming. Such a view is consistent with the well-known notion that the attentional requirement of movements tends to decrease with practice. Motor programs are assumed to be constructed through practice, but it is not known how such structuring occurs. As well, there is an increase in the capability of the learner to detect his or her own errors, leading to subjective reinforcement that can be a substitute for KR in later learning.

Two theories of motor learning are *Adams' theory* and *schema theory*. Adams' theory holds that the learner acquires a reference of correctness (called the *perceptual trace*) through practice and that the improvements in motor responding result from the increased capability of the performer to use the reference in closed-loop control. Schema theory, on the other hand, is based largely on the idea that slow movements are feedback-based, with rapid movements being program-based; with learning, the subject develops rules (or schemas) that allow for the generation of parameters to produce novel responses. Both theories can claim a number of lines of experimental support, but neither of them is capable of explaining all of the available evidence on motor learning.

GLOSSARY

Adams' theory. A closed-loop theory of motor learning proposed by Adams in 1971, focusing heavily on the learning of slow positioning movements.

Adjacent-trial effect. With intertrial correlation matrices, the tendency for the correlations between adjacent trials to increase with practice.

Associative phase. The second of three phases of learning proposed by Fitts, in which learners establish important motor patterns.

Autonomous phase. The third of three phases of learning proposed by Fitts, in which learners have greatly reduced the attention demands of the task.

Changing component abilities hypothesis. The hypothesis that the set of abilities underlying a skill shifts systematically as practice continues.

Cognitive phase. The first of three phases of learning proposed by Fitts, in which learners' performances are heavily based on cognitive or verbal processes.

Expected sensory consequences. A construct in schema theory, the anticipated sensations that should be received if the movement is correct.

Gearshift analogy. An idea presented by Keele about the learning of motor programs, analogous to learning to change gears in an automobile.

Hierarchical control model. The idea that with practice the control of the response shifts systematically from attention demanding higher levels to less attention demanding motor program levels.

Initial conditions. A construct in schema theory, the nature of the task and environment prior to the production of a response.

Intertrial correlation matrix. A table or matrix of correlations between performances on all pairs of trials in a practice sequence.

Memory trace. A construct in Adams' theory, a modest motor program for determining the initial direction of the movement and initiating it.

Movement outcome. A construct in schema theory, the result of the movement in the environment, usually signaled by intrinsic feedback or KR.

Perceptual trace. A construct in Adams' theory, the reference of correctness based on feedback from experience at the correct target position.

Progression-regression hypothesis. The idea that learning produces a progression to more complex control strategies and that stress or forgetting produces a regression to more simple levels.

Recall schema. A construct in schema theory, the relationship between past parameters, past initial conditions, and the movement outcomes produced by these combinations.

Recognition schema. A construct in schema theory, the relationship between past initial conditions, past movement outcomes, and the sensory consequences produced by these combinations.

Remoteness effect. In intertrial correlation matrices, the tendency for trials that are progressively more separated in the practice sequence to correlate systematically lower with each other.

Schema. A rule, concept, or relationship formed on the basis of experience; the basis of schema theory.

Simplification hypothesis. The idea that the factor structure of a skill becomes progressively simpler with practice.

Subroutines. Simple discrete elements or actions that are thought to be combined to form the basis of larger more complicated movements.

CHAPTER 15

Motor Memory

Up to this point, the major concern has been with the variables, principles, and processes that have to do with the acquisition of motor skills with practice. To be able to perform a skill well enough to call it "learned" is but one part of the problem, however, as usually a strong need exists to perform the skill at some time in the future, hopefully without having to relearn it from the original levels of performance. Such concerns for how well skills are retained over time are of both theoretical and practical importance—theoretical because of the need to understand how the motor system is structured so that skills can be produced "on demand," and practical because usually a great deal of time and effort have gone into the learning of the skills in the first place. We need to know how such investments can be protected from loss. So this chapter is about the empirical relationships and principles that have to do with motor memory.

FUNDAMENTAL DISTINCTIONS AND DEFINITIONS

You may have the impression that motor learning and motor memory are two different aspects of the problem, one having to do with gains in skills, the other with losses. This is because memory is often thought of by psychologists and others as a place where information is stored. Statements like "I have a good memory for names and dates" or "The subject placed the phone number in long-term memory" are representative of this use of the term. The implication is that some set of processes has led to the acquisition of the materials, and now some other set of processes is responsible for keeping them "in" memory.

Memory

The more common meaning of the term *memory* is "the persistence of the acquired capability for responding." In this sense habit (Chapter 11) and memory are conceptually similar. Remember, the usual test for learning of a task was related to whether or not the individual could produce it on a transfer test (or retention test). That is, an item has been learned if and only if it can be retained "relatively permanently" (see Chapter 11). If I can still perform a skill after not having practiced it for a year, then I have a memory of the skill. Thus, the memory is the capability for responding, not a place where that capability is stored. Depending on one's theoretical orientation about motor learning, memory is a motor program, a reference of correctness, or a schema that was acquired during practice. As you can see from this viewpoint, learning and memory are, as Adams (1976a) has put it, just "different sides of the same behavioral coin" (p. 223).

Forgetting

Another term used in this context is *forgetting*. Forgetting is used as the opposite of learning, in that learning refers to the acquisition of the capability for responding, while forgetting refers to the loss of such capability. It is likely that the processes and principles having to do with gains and losses in the capability for responding will be different, but the terms refer to the different directions of the change in this capability. Finally, forgetting is a term that has to do with theoretical constructs, just as learning does. Memory is a construct, forgetting is the loss of memory, so forgetting is a concept at a theoretical, rather than a behavioral, level of thinking.

Retention, on the other hand, refers to the persistence or lack of persistence of the performance, and it is at the behavioral, rather than the theoretical, level. It is the test that tells me whether or not memory has been lost. The test on which decisions about retention are based is called the *retention test*, performed after some *retention interval*, and the data from such a test are all that behaviorists have to find out about memory or forgetting.[1] If performance on the retention test is as proficient as at the end of original learning, then we say no memory loss (no forgetting) has occurred. If performance on the retention is poor, then we may decide that a memory loss has occurred. However, because the test for memory (the retention test) is a performance test, it is subject to all of the variations that cause performances to change in temporary ways. Thus, it could be that performance is poor on the retention test for some temporary reason (fatigue, anxiety), and

---

[1]For all practical purposes, a retention test and a transfer test (defined in Chapter 11 for measuring the relative amount learned) are very similar. In both cases, the concern is for the persistence of the acquired capability for responding (habit). They differ in that the transfer test has subjects switching from different tasks or conditions, whereas the retention test usually involves the retesting of subjects on the same task or conditions.

Table 15-1

**The Analogous States of Motor Learning
and Motor Forgetting**

	Theoretical Level	Behavioral Level
Motor Learning	Acquiring the capability for responding, gains in memory	Relatively permanent gains in performance with practice
Motor Forgetting	Losing the capability for responding, or forgetting, loss of memory	Relatively permanent losses in performance, or retention losses

thus I could falsely conclude that a memory loss occurred.

As shown in Table 15-1, the analogy to the study of learning is a close one. At the theoretical level, learning is a gain in the capability to respond, while forgetting is the loss of same. And, on the behavioral level, learning is evidenced by relatively permanent gains in performance, while forgetting is evidenced by relatively permanent losses in performance, or losses in retention. So, if you understand how measures of behavior tell about learning, then you also understand the same about forgetting.

MEASURING RETENTION

In motor memory research, a number of different measures of retention have been used, and these different methods provide somewhat different interpretations about the underlying forgetting processes. Chief among these methods are *absolute retention* and various forms of *relative retention*.

Absolute Retention

By far the most simple and scientifically justifiable measure of retention is absolute retention, defined simply as the level of performance on the initial trial(s) of the retention test. Figure 15-1 shows the hypothetical scores of a group of subjects who practiced the pursuit rotor followed by a retention interval and a retention test with relearning. The absolute retention is approximately 20 sec of time on target (TOT). Notice that the absolute retention score is not based on the level of performance from which the retention losses began in original learning.

Relative Retention

Various measures of relative retention are possible, such as those using a

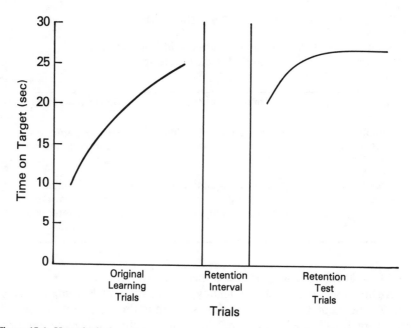

Figure 15-1. Hypothetical performance curves on the pursuit rotor for original-learning and retention-test trials.

difference score and those using *percentage scores*. These are described below.

Difference Scores

Probably the most common relative-retention score is a difference score (or a drop-off score) that represents the amount of loss in skill over the retention interval. It is computed by taking the difference between the performance levels at the end of the original learning session and the beginning of the retention test. In the example given in Figure 15-1, the difference score is 5 sec TOT, as the group had 25 sec TOT before the retention interval and 20 sec afterwards. Such measures are esthetically pleasing to many investigators because they seem (erroneously) to represent the forgetting processes more or less directly.

Percentage Scores

A second kind of relative-retention score is a percentage score, which represents the amount of the loss in retention over the retention interval relative to the amount of learning that occurred on the task in the original learning session. That is, the percentage score is the difference score defined above divided by the amount of change in original performance (another difference score) and multiplied by 100 to convert it into a percentage. In the example in Figure 15-1, the percentage score is the drop-off score (5 sec) divided by the learning score ($25 - 10 = 15$ sec TOT) and multiplied by 100, or $5/15 \times 100 = 33.3\%$. The meaning of this score is that one-third of the amount of original improvement was lost over the retention interval. These scores are sometimes useful where the retention on two different skills with different scoring systems is to be compared. Reducing each to a percentage value allows some of these comparisons to be made, as will become evident later in the chapter.

Contrasting the Various Measures

While it may seem that these various methods merely provide subtle differences in the measurement of a single process (forgetting), this is not the case. According to my analysis of the problem several years ago (Schmidt, 1971a, 1972a), the relative-retention scores are flawed by a variety of factors. The basis of the problem is that all of these measures are performance measures, with changes in performance being used to infer something about the changes in the internal state (memory) that underlies the performance. Therefore, all of the problems with performance curves that I have mentioned with respect to the measurement of learning (ceiling and floor effects, etc., in Chapter 11) also apply to the measurement of forgetting. In particular, difference scores are subject to a variety of influences that cloud the interpretations about forgetting, casting doubt on the usefulness of the difference-score method described above. Moreover, the percentage score uses two difference scores and then divides them by each other to gain the percentage, which clouds the issue even further. The absolute-retention score seems to be the most simple and straightforward score to use.

As I have pointed out (Schmidt, 1971a), the problem is not just a technical or academic one. Some of the most fundamental variables in forgetting have empirical effects that seem to depend completely on the ways in which retention is measured. For example, consider the variable of amount of original learning, or the number of practice trials on the original learning session shown in Figure 15-1. If forgetting is measured by the absolute retention method, then numerous studies show that absolute retention increases as the amount of original learning increases, just as we might suspect; that is, the better the performance in original learning, the better the performance on the retention test. But if retention is measured by the relative-retention methods, then relative retention (computed from the same set of data) decreases as the amount of original learning increases (see Schmidt, 1972a; see also Lewis et al., 1951, in Chapter 12, Figure 12-12). Thus, the statement of the law relating retention of skills to the amount of original practice is completely different depending on how retention is measured. Obviously, this has caused, and will continue to cause, many confusing situations for students who are attempting to understand the principles of motor forgetting.

One final method for measuring forgetting involves the idea that the relearning of a task on the retention test (after a retention interval) should be faster if the retention of the response is greater. One very common finding (evidence will be presented later; see Figure 15-3) in motor retention studies is that the "steepness" of the performance curve is greater in the relearning trials (during the retention test) than it was in original learning.

This increased slope means that even though performance of the task on the retention test is poor, subjects have retained something that has enabled them to improve more quickly than they did originally. Using this logic, an additional measure of retention is the "rate" of relearning, such as the number of trials required to achieve the original performance level at the end of acquisition. These methods have not been used as often as the other retention measures (described earlier) have. But they are of use in various situations, especially when the initial performance on the retention test is rendered insensitive to the internal level of learning (e.g., if the initial performance level is near a "floor"). Such measures, as I have pointed out, are sensitive to all the things that make performance curves "impure" measures of the amount learned (Chapter 11), so they should be interpreted carefully.

THEORIES OF FORGETTING

We all know that information or skills are sometimes lost over periods of no practice, and considerable research has been devoted to understanding why such losses in memory occur. Little of this work has been concerned with the processes of motor forgetting, so most of the theoretical ideas apply most strongly to verbal skills. In this regard, two theories of forgetting, each with related subtheories, can be distinguished: a *trace-decay theory* and an *interference theory*.

Trace-Decay Theory

Clearly the oldest theory of forgetting, and the one with the most intuitive appeal, is the trace-decay theory. It is a passive theory in which the reason that information is forgotten is because it is not practiced, and it therefore "decays" with time. The memory of an item, event, or skill is thought to be represented as a neurological trace, and this trace becomes weaker with time, much in the same way that iron rusts or milk turns sour. Then, when the information or skill is demanded at some future time, the trace is too weak or ill-defined to be able to produce performance effectively, if at all. These theories, based upon little other than speculation about how forgetting seems to occur, account well for the common effects of disuse and, of course, for the fact that time seems to be a strong factor in retention.

Interference Theory

The mere passage of time is not all that happens during the retention interval, though, as there are many other events, tasks to be learned, etc., that can intervene between the original learning of the response and its retention. Thus, it is possible that the cause of forgetting has something to do with these events, rather than mere passage of time as trace-decay theory would have it. Thus, interference theory is an active theory of forgetting, in which memory is actively degraded by other events. Such events can be, according

Table 15-2

**Experimental Designs for Retroactive and
Proactive Interference**

Group	Prior Experiences	Original Learning	Retention Interval	Retention Test
I	—	Task B	Task A	Task B
II	—	Task B	—	Task B
III	Task A	Task B	—	Task B

R I Design: Groups I and II

P I Design: Groups II and III

to the theory, of two basic kinds: retroactive interference and proactive interference.

Retroactive Interference

The most obvious way that one event can be thought of as interfering with some learned information or skill is for the interfering event to come between the original learning and the retention of the to-be-remembered materials. These processes can be studied in special, experimental designs that were presented earlier in Chapter 11. As we shall see, retroactive interference (RI) is really the same as negative retroactive transfer, and so the two notions can be studied in the same experimental designs. In Table 15-2 (also Table 11-2, page 468) is shown the common experimental design for retroactive interference (or negative transfer). Two groups are used (I and II), both of which learn some Task B in an original learning situation. Then, during the retention interval, Group II rests (or performs some "neutral" activity) while Group I performs some potentially interfering Task A. Then, both groups are given a retention test on Task B. If Group I with the interfering activity performs less well on the retention test than Group II without this activity, then retroactive interference is inferred from the interfering Task A to Task B. The reason that the term *retroactive* is used is that the interfering Task A is thought to "work backwards" on the earlier-learned Task B; of course, it does not "work backwards" at all, but it and the earlier-learned task interfere with each other during the retention interval or on the retention test. Because this retroactive-interference paradigm is really just a negative-transfer design, evidence for negative transfer is taken as evidence for retroactive interference (review "Negative Transfer," Chapter 12).

Proactive Interference

A less obvious way that two skills can interfere with each other is through proactive interference. Here, the skills learned before the learning of the criterion skill—perhaps skills learned through a lifetime of motor behavior—interfere with the newly learned skill during the retention interval, so that the result is a loss of skill at the retention test. Analogous to retroactive interference, proactive interference (PI) is really the same as proactive negative transfer discussed in Chapter 11. Table 15-1 has the experimental design used in proactive interference studies. Two groups are again used, with Group II serving also in this proactive interference (PI) design. Group III learns a potentially interfering Task A and then learns (transfers to) Task B. Group II does not have Task A experience and then learns Task B. Then, after a retention interval, if the group with practice at Task A (Group III) performs less well on the retention test (i.e., Task B practice) than Group II, the proactive negative transfer is inferred from Task A to Task B. The term *proactive* is used to imply that Task A worked "forward" on Task B, while we again should see that there was probably mutual interference because the memory for Task A and Task B existed together after Task B was learned.

Evidence for the Interference Theory

As I pointed out earlier, the evidence and thinking about forgetting and interference has mainly come from studies of verbal behavior. An analysis of verbal behavior, however, is beyond the scope of this book; for a review of this work on interference the reader should consult Adams (1967, 1976a). However, this work can be summarized rather easily. Clear and unmistakable retroactive and proactive interference occur, based on experiments using designs such as shown in Table 15-1. Generally speaking, scientists in the verbal-behavior area are convinced that most if not all of the forgetting seen in verbal responses is due to either proactive or retroactive interference, or both, and that little evidence supports a trace-decay viewpoint for forgetting. Such support for the interference theory has led to a number of hypotheses about how interference might function, and substantial debate is currently being heard on these issues (see Adams, 1976a).

There is one logical difficulty with this evidence for interference theory, however. First, evidence of proactive and retroactive interference merely provides "support" for the interference theory and does not prove that the interference theory is correct. Perhaps this can be seen in terms of the faulty logic from the "All crows are black" syllogism discussed in Chapter 2 and mentioned by Adams (1967, p.120):

> A decrement in retention is caused by interference.
> Forgetting leads to a decrement in retention.
> Therefore, all forgetting is caused by interference.

Of course, it could be that the mechanisms causing retention losses in these experiments are totally different from those that cause us to forget everyday skills. Certainly, the evidence supports the interference theory rather well, but it cannot provide proof of it.

LONG-TERM MOTOR MEMORY

A commonly studied memory for motor skills is that for relatively well-learned tasks with retention intervals measuring in the months, or even years. According to the distinction made in Chapter 4, such well-learned skills are thought to have a long-term memory representation.

Continuous Tasks

It is almost cliché in writings about motor skills that many motor responses are nearly never forgotten. Examples such as swimming and riding a bicycle are frequently cited, where performance after many years is nearly as proficient as it was originally. Such examples, though, are seldom based on acceptable measures of performance, but many laboratory examples of these situations have been studied and seem to say the same thing.

Although many examples could be cited, a representative study with long retention intervals by Fleishman and Parker (1962) is presented. They used a three-dimensional compensatory tracking task (Mashburn task, Figure 3-8, page 72), with movements of the hands in forward-backward and left-right dimensions, and the feet in a left-right dimension. They gave subjects 17 daily sessions, and then separate groups were retested after either 9, 14, or 24 months.

The scores for original learning and the retention test are shown in Figure 15-2, where all three retention groups have been averaged together in original learning. After the retention intervals, the various groups were nearly equivalent, and none had shown any appreciable losses in proficiency, even after 2 years of layoff. Some tendency is seen for the 2-year group to have slightly less proficiency than the groups with shorter retention inter-

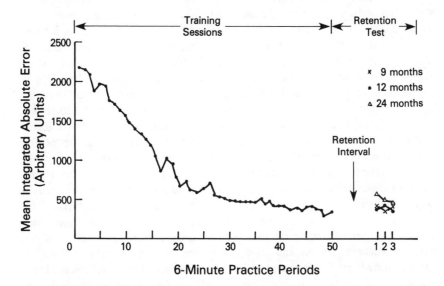

Figure 15-2. Mean performance on a three-dimensional tracking task in original learning and after three retention intervals (from Fleishman & Parker, 1962).

vals, but the differences were small and the losses were regained completely in three sessions. These small differences are not very meaningful when one compares the retention-test performance to the level of performance at the start of practice. Certainly this continuous task was retained nearly perfectly for 2 years.

Other studies, using different tasks, have shown very similar effects. Meyers (1967), using the Bachman ladder-climb task, showed nearly no loss in performance for retention intervals of up to 12 weeks; Ryan (1962), using the pursuit rotor and stabilometer tasks, found nearly no retention losses after retention intervals of 21 days; later, Ryan (1965) found only small losses in performance on the stabilometer task with retention intervals of up to 1 year. There are many other examples, and the generalization continues to hold. Continuous motor tasks are extremely well retained over very long retention intervals, just as the cliché about the bicycle would have us believe.

It is interesting to note our own forgetting of motor skills, although we must be careful about the conclusions because the methods and measurements are usually not up to scientific standards. My father started me skiing when I was 4 years old, and I skied every winter until I was 15, whereupon I stopped completely for 14 years. When I returned after this retention interval, I was particularly interested in how I would do, as I had some knowledge of the research literature on the problem. It seems safe to say that within about 15 min of practice I was skiing as well as I ever did, and that by the end of the day I was skiing better. I was amazed at the retention of skill possible after the retention interval of 14 years.

Discrete Responses

While there is ample evidence of nearly complete retention of continuous skills, the picture appears to be quite different for discrete responses. Consider an example by Neumann and Ammons (1957). The subject sat in front of a large display with eight pairs of switches located in a circular pattern. The subject was to turn the innner switch "on" and then discover which switch in the outer circle was paired with it; a buzzer sounded when the correct match was made. Subjects learned the task to a criterion of two consecutive errorless trials, and then retention intervals of 1 min, 20 min, 2 days, 7 weeks, and 1 year were imposed for different groups of subjects.

The main findings are presented in Figure 15-3. Some losses in performance appeared after only 20 min, and the losses became progressively greater as the length of the retention interval increased. In fact, after 1 year, the performance was actually poorer than the initial performance was in original learning, suggesting that the forgetting was nearly complete. However, notice that in all cases the relearning of the task was more rapid than the original learning (as indicated by the slopes of the relearning and original learning curves), indicating that some memory for the skill was retained, allowing a faster reacquisition with practice. The faster relearning as compared to original learning after a layoff is a typical finding in the verbal retention studies, and it appears to be present for motor retention as well.

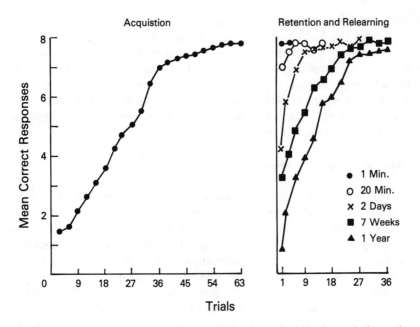

Figure 15-3. Mean performance of a discrete response in original learning and after various retention intervals (from Neumann & Ammons, 1957).

Continuous versus Discrete Tasks

Why is there such a large difference in the retention characteristics of continuous and discrete responses, with continuous tasks having nearly perfect retention and discrete tasks having such poor retention? A number of hypotheses have been proposed to explain these differences, and they are discussed in brief form next. See also Adams (1967, Chapter 8) or Schmidt (1975a, Chapter 8).

Verbal-Cognitive Components

One hypothesis is that verbal-cognitive components are somehow more quickly forgotten than motor components; because discrete tasks in the literature seem to have a heavier emphasis on verbal-cognitive elements (learning which switch goes with which light in the Neumann-Ammons study, for example), there is more loss for the discrete tasks over time. While it is correct that most of the discrete tasks that have been studied in retention situtations seem highly verbal-cognitive in nature, there is no reason that discrete tasks have to be. Certainly, one can think of many discrete tasks that have little reliance on verbal-cognitive abilities (e.g., throwing, striking, pole vaulting). What would be the retention characteristics of a discrete task that was highly "motor" in nature?

Lersten (1969) used an arm-movement task (rho task), in which a circular and a linear movement component had to be performed as quickly as possible; this task has few verbal-cognitive components, or so it would seem. He found approximately 80% loss (of the original amount of improvement) in the circular phase, and a 30% loss for the linear component, with retention intervals of 1 year. Similarly, Martin (1970) used a task in which the subjects moved the hand over two barriers and then returned to a starting switch as quickly as possible, finding approximately 50% retention loss for a 4-month retention interval. The amount of loss in retention for discrete skills that can be considered as "mostly motor" in nature is quite similar to the loss experienced by Neumann's and Ammons' subjects (Figure 15-3), suggesting that there is more to the cognitive-discrete difference in retention than the "motorness" of the tasks.

Amount of Original Learning

One of the major factors determining absolute retention is the amount of original learning, with retention increasing as the amount of original learning increases. In the typical continuous task, there might be trials of 30 sec in duration, with each trial consisting of many separate "discrete" responses. In tracking, for example, many instances occur where the pointer and track become separated, each requiring a separate adjustment. Contrast this situation to the discrete responses, where a trial typically consists of but a single adjustment or action. It is reasonable, therefore, that the continuous task, with the same number of learning trials as the discrete task, has been far more highly practiced than the discrete task. This extra level of original learning, according to this hypothesis, leads to increased retention, since it is well known that absolute retention is directly related to the amount of original practice.

What Is a "Trial"?

Another notion, related to the one just presented, is that the definition of *trial* is quite arbitrary; trial can refer to anything from a 200-msec RT performance to a 2-min bout of performance on a tracking task. This is a problem in defining the amount of original learning for the task, and it too is a problem in discussing the retention test. Remember, the level of absolute retention was measured in terms of the performance on the first few "trials" of retention-test performance. Now if a "trial" is a 2-min performance, then there could be a great deal of relearning that occurs within a trial for the continuous task, with no relearning within a trial for a rapid discrete performance. So the initial movements within the trial for the continuous task could show considerable retention loss, but the experimenter would never detect it because the poor initial performance would be "averaged" with the later portions of the trial on which performance was more proficient. Because this could not occur for the discrete task, it is possible that the amount of forgetting is typically underestimated for the continuous task and not for the discrete task, making the two kinds of tasks appear to be different in their retention characteristics when they might otherwise not be. Fleishman and Parker (1962) have found a great deal of relearning within a continuous task trial, as might be suspected from this kind of analysis.

PROCESSES OF MOTOR FORGETTING

What is the source of forgetting that is seen in varying degrees in different classes of motor behavior? This question did not seem to require an answer because so little forgetting seemed to occur in many motor tasks that there appeared to be nothing to explain. However, a few studies have been directed at motor forgetting processes, and a few generalizations can be made about them.

Retroactive and Proactive Interference

In the context of the interference theory of forgetting, a number of investigations have been directed at retroactive interference as a primary mechanism. From the earlier section on interference theory, recall that the retroactive-interference paradigm was really a negative-transfer paradigm (see Table 15-1), and thus the studies that can be taken in support of negative transfer are generally the same ones supporting the concept of retroactive interference. Primary among these is the study, discussed in Chapter 12, by Lewis, McAllister, and Adams (1951). Here, subjects learned the Mashburn task, for which three movement dimensions had to be controlled separately to control the movements of a display. Negative transfer, or retroactive interference, was produced by reversing the direction of the relationship between the control movement and the display movement. Providing this reversed-task practice after the learning of the task with the standard control-display relationship caused marked retroactive interference, supporting the interference theory of forgetting for motor tasks. (Review Figure 12-2, page 478, and related text.) Generally, the absolute retention was greater if the amount of original learning was increased and smaller as the amount of reversed-task practice was increased. Other studies, using similar designs and motor tasks, generally show the same things (e.g., Lewis, 1947; McAllister & Lewis, 1951).

These studies of retroactive interference have not been paralleled by studies of proactive interference at all, and I know of no evidence that proactive interference is a factor in motor forgetting. But judging from its relatively strong effects in verbal behavior (e.g., Underwood, 1957), it would certainly be a candidate for one of the mechanisms of motor forgetting. As you can see, motor forgetting has not been studied extensively, and is not very well understood as a result.

Motor Specificity and Forgetting

Another implication of the interference theory is that motor skills may interfere with each other to the extent that they have common elements associated either with conflicting stimuli or responses. But the analysis of individual differences in skills (Chapter 10) suggests that skills are very specific, so even similar-appearing skills do not have many elements that can be regarded as common. I mentioned earlier that this feature of skills fits well with the findings about motor transfer (Chapter 12), and it also fits with these findings about forgetting. If, indeed, motor skills are specific, then skills that are learned will not have interfering elements for others that have been learned, leading to the rather high levels of retention typically seen for motor skills. This evidence also fits well with the findings that motor negative transfer is quite small (Chapter 12), again suggesting it is quite difficult to interfere with learned motor acts. Thus, while it may be that the interference theory is the most effective one for explaining motor forgetting, it is also probable that motor interference is quite small because of the specific nature of most motor tasks. Not so for verbal responses, however, as there seem to be far more sources of verbal interference that can lead to forgetting. This is the dominant explanation for the large difference seen between the retention of verbal and motor tasks.

SHORT-TERM MOTOR MEMORY

Recently, as a direct result of the short-term memory research using verbal tasks, an interest in motor short-term memory processes has been created. As you will recall from Chapter 4, the initial research on verbal short-term memory came quite recently (in contrast to the long-standing interest in long-term memory), early studies of it being conducted by Brown (1958) and Peterson and Peterson (1959). Briefly, these investigators studied the retention of once-presented nonsense materials, for which rehearsal of the information was not permitted. The recall was quite poor, with almost complete losses in memory over retention intervals as short as 18 sec. Almost inevitably, such important research directions with verbal skills lead to the conduct of analogous studies with motor behavior, and pioneering work in the motor area was done by Posner and Konick (1966) and Adams and Dijkstra (1966; Adams, 1969).

Early Motor Short-Term Memory Studies

Adams and Dijkstra used a linear-positioning response, in which the subject was to move to a stop that defined a target position, then return to a starting location for a retention interval, then attempt to move to the target positon again (but with the stop removed). Subjects were blindfolded and were never given KR about their movement accuracy. In addition, subjects were given various numbers of "reinforcements," whereby the position was presented 1, 6, or 15 times before the retention interval. So the procedures were analogous to those in the verbal short-term memory paradigm; short retention intervals, no KR, prevention of rehearsal, and once-presented items (except for the conditions with multiple "reinforcements").

The major findings of Adams' and Dijkstra's (1966, Experiment 2) study are presented in Figure 15-4. The absolute errors on the recall trials are presented as a function of the number of "reinforcements" and the length of the retention interval. As the length of the retention interval increased, the error in recall also increased, with the increases nearly maximized by the

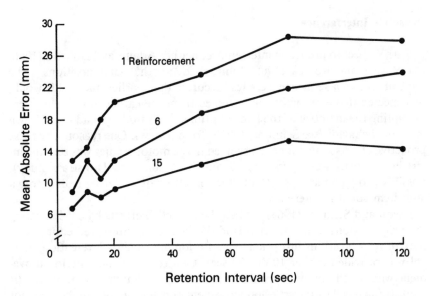

Figure 15-4. Mean absolute error in positioning as a function of the retention interval and the number of "reinforcements" (from Adams & Dijkstra, 1966).

time the retention interval was 80 sec in length and with no further increases thereafter. Similar to verbal responses, the memory for motor responses appears to have a forgetting process that was nearly complete in about 1 min. Also, this forgetting process can apparently be retarded by practice, as the errors were systematically smaller as the number of times that the subject moved to the stop increased. (Notice that this is an example of learning without KR, as pointed out in Chapter 13.) One interpretation is this: The movement to the stop created a short-term memory representation of the feedback qualities of the correct position, and this representation was weakened over the course of the empty retention interval so that the individual had a progressively more "faint" reference of correctness to which to compare the feedback from the limb during the retention test. This experiment, plus a similar one by Posner and Konick (1966), established what has come to be known as the motor short-term memory paradigm. During the course of the late 1960s and early 1970s, extensive research was done using this general method, and some of the major accomplishments of this work are presented in the following sections. (See Laabs & Simmons, 1981, Schmidt, 1972b, or Stelmach, 1974, for a review of this work.)

Proactive and Retroactive Interference Effects

The mechanisms causing forgetting in these motor short-term memory experiments have been examined in relation to the interference theory. Investigators have generally asked about proactive and retroactive interference effects in ways analogous to the work in verbal behavior.

Proactive Interference

With respect to proactive interference, neither Adams and Dijkstra (1966) nor Posner and Konick (1966) found evidence that later positions to be remembered in a sequence were less accurate than earlier ones. This would be expected if the proactive interference from the earlier movements were disrupting the memory of the later positions; such findings had been shown in verbal behavior (see Schmidt, 1972b, for a review). One reason why these proactive effects may not have occurred in the motor studies was that the intertrial intervals were very long (3 min in Adams and Dijkstra's study), possibly providing an opportunity for forgetting of an earlier item before a later item could be presented.

Ascoli and Schmidt (1969) studied the proactive effects by concentrating the prior responses in a short period of time. They presented either zero, two, or four positions just prior to a criterion movement. A retention interval was provided (either 10 or 120 sec), then recall of the criterion movement was tested followed by the recall of the preliminary movements (if any). If the recall of the criterion movement depends on the number of prior positions, support for proactive interference would be provided.

The results are shown in Figure 15-5, where absolute errors in recall are presented for the two retention intervals and for the various numbers of prior movements. As in the Adams-Dijkstra study, errors increased as the length of the retention interval increased. But of more interest was the finding that the four-prior-position condition showed more error than either the zero- or two-prior-position conditions. The major effect was on the constant error (Chapter 3), with increased prior positions making the movements systematically too short. These general aspects of the results were also shown by Stelmach (1969b). The data can be interpreted to mean that proactive interference is a factor in the retention of these positioning movements, supporting the interference theory.

Retroactive Interference

With respect to retroactive interference, various authors had failed to find effects of activities placed between the presentation and recall of the test movements, casting serious doubt on the interference theory (see Pepper & Herman, 1970, for a review). But none of these studies reported constant errors, and the finding that proactive interference had its major effects on constant error raised the possibility that retroactive effects would be seen in the same way. In a reanalysis of earlier data, Pepper and Herman (1970) found that movements produced during the retention interval tended to have negative effects on the movement accuracy, when measured in terms of constant (signed) error. Subsequently, Patrick (1971) and Milone (1971) provided support for retroactive interference.

To summarize, interfering activities can degrade the accuracy of positioning responses, thus providing support for both retroactive and proactive interference in motor short-term memory. This is not to say that other sources of forgetting are not operating, such as trace decay. It appears that the interference theory cannot account for all of the forgetting seen in these situations.

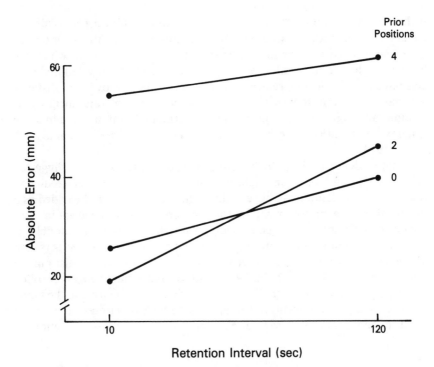

Figure 15-5. Mean absolute error in positioning as a function of the retention interval and the number of previous positions (from Ascoli & Schmidt, 1969).

Cue-Separation Techniques

What does the performer remember and recall in these positioning tasks? One possibility, mentioned earlier, is that the person remembers the sensory qualities of the target position and attempts to match these sensations through a closed-loop process during the recall movement. That is, the person might be attempting to move to that position that is recognized as correct (see Chapter 14, Schema Theory). Another possibility, however, is that the person remembers the distance moved rather than the location of the target; it is also possible that the person remembers some kind of program that will move the limb a certain distance. These two possible cues (location or distance cues) were confounded in the earlier experiments on motor short-term memory. However, Keele and Ells (1972), Marteniuk (1973), and Laabs (1973) used an ingenious but simple method for unraveling these two potential cues.

For example, Laabs (1973) had subjects move to a stop (just as in the Adams-Dijkstra study) for the presentation of the stimulus materials. Then he formed two different conditions for recall. In both of these conditions, subjects were moved to a different starting position for the beginning of the recall movement. In one condition, subjects were asked to recall the same location on the track as before, so the distance of the recall movement was different from that of the presentation movement, rendering information about distance less effective. In the other condition, the subject was asked to move the same distance as in the presentation movement, so the location of the presentation movement was less useful to the subject for recall.

Laabs' major findings were that the condition in which the location cue had to be recalled was far more accurate than the condition in which the distance cue had to be recalled. Subsequent research has suggested that subjects have a difficult time remembering the cues about movement distance and that positioning movements are probably based on some memory of location, although location and distance information may be used in some complex combination in certain instances (Walsh, Russell, Imanaka, & James, 1979).

Recent evidence (Kelso, 1977; Kelso, Holt, & Flatt, 1980) has suggested that remembering a position might be handled other than by the feedback-based processes mentioned above and that the position might be coded as a specification in a motor program for the action. Such a viewpoint was discussed in Chapter 8, in conjunction with the mass-spring model for motor programming; here, the idea was that the subject remembers and programs an *equilibrium point* between the agonist and antagonist muscle groups (e.g., Polit & Bizzi, 1978, 1979), with the movement being controlled open-loop at recall. The method of remembering the response and the mode of the response at the retention test appears to be a function of the way in which the movement is presented, as discussed in the following section.

The Preselection Paradigm

In the usual paradigm for motor short-term memory studies, the subject is asked to move to a stop that is defined by the experimenter, and thus the subject does not have any advance knowledge about where the movement endpoint will be until he or she hits the stop. Marteniuk (1973) and Stelmach, Kelso, and Wallace (1975) broke tradition with this method when they asked subjects to choose their own movement endpoints. In effect, the instruction was to move to a position of the subject's choice (a stop was not provided), then the subject returned to the starting position and was asked to reproduce the position after a retention interval. When this so-called "preselection" method was compared to the experimenter-selected method, the recall of the target position was much more accurate in the preselected technique.

When the subject is faced with these reproduction situations, it is likely that the nature of the paradigm will influence the way in which the person codes the information. For example, if the person does not know where the target will be (standard paradigm), then this could force the individual to process sensory cues about the target location, perhaps leading to a strategy wherein the recall of the movement is through closed-loop processes. In the preselection method, however, the performer can generate a response in advance, perhaps programming it, and thus ignore the sensory consequences of the movement, simply re-running the program at the retention test. These notions are supported in experiments by Kelso (1977). The preselection effect is also present in verbal behavior (e.g., Slamecka & Graf, 1978; see also Lee & Gallagher, 1981), providing one instance (among many contradictions) in which the motor short-term memory research has led the work on similar problems in verbal short-term memory.

Contributions of the Motor Short-Term Memory Work

Considerable excitement accompanied the early motor short-term memory research, and it tended to dominate the field of motor behavior for a number of years (approximately 1968 to 1976). The initial excitement was due to the belief that the nature of the codes that defined what was learned and what was retained in a movement seemed close to being understood; and, with the short-term motor memory paradigm, these questions could be answered in future research. While a number of interesting and important findings did emerge from this work (some of which have been already mentioned; see Stelmach, 1974, for others), this research direction did not live up to the expectations, and it is largely dormant today.

The major problem seemed to be a dissatisfaction with the slow, self-paced, linear-positioning responses. There are, of course, many other kinds of movements available in the outside world, and many investigators felt that these slow responses were simply not sufficiently representative of the vast majority of everyday tasks to justify their continued study. Also, many experimental-design problems emerged (as would be the case in any new area), and these seemed to prevent a clean understanding of the processes underlying the motor short-term memory paradigm. Suspicion grew that much of the motor short-term memory was not motor at all but rather was concerned with the retention of sensory information about the feedback associated with the target position (but see Kelso, 1977). In spite of these criticisms (which I feel are valid), the area of research did dominate thinking in motor behavior for nearly a decade, and the educated student of motor behavior should know something of its rise and fall.

WARM-UP DECREMENT

To this point in the chapter, the concern has been with memory losses. As mentioned earlier, numerous retention losses are not due to memory losses, including such temporary factors as loss of motivation, day-to-day fluctuations in performance, effects of drugs, illness, and so on. Many of these have been discussed with respect to the measurement of performance (Chapter 3) and learning (Chapter 11), and they are all involved in motor retention as well. But a special kind of decrement in motor performance has had a small literature of its own, and it deserves mention. This decrement is called *warm-up decrement*.

The phenomenon can be easily introduced with an example. Adams (1952, 1961) studied a large group of subjects on the pursuit rotor task, provided 36 30-sec trials per day for five days, and the performance data are shown in Figure 15-6. The typical improvement with practice during a run of trials is seen, but a relatively large decrement in performance is produced after each of the longer rest periods. This decrement appears to be quite severe, and it is equivalent in size to the gains experienced in three or four trials; and the decrement is rather short-lived, being eliminated in only a few

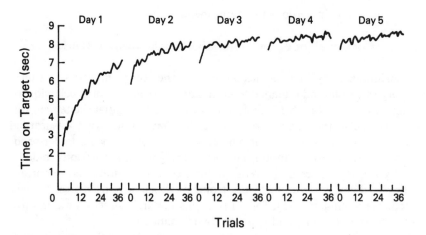

Figure 15-6. Mean performance on the pursuit rotor task for five days. (The decrements in performance from the end of one day until the beginning of the next are termed "warm-up decrement"; from Adams, 1952, 1961.)

practice trials. The phenomenon has been known about for a long time, and has been found in nearly every motor task that has been studied (see Adams, 1961, for a review). At that time, this decrement was thought to be related in some way to the need to "warm up" for the task again after the rest, and the phenomenon came to be called *warm-up decrement*.

This relatively large decrement is of potential importance when individuals are asked to perform after a rest period, such as the worker operating a dangerous machine after a coffee break or the athlete going into the game from the bench. Some of the major hypotheses to explain warm-up decrement are presented next.

Hypotheses for Warm-Up Decrement

Warm-Up Decrement as Forgetting

One major hypothesis is that warm-up decrement is simply forgetting, or the loss of memory for the skill. In this view, the rest period allows certain forgetting processes to occur, with the initial phases of these processes being relatively rapid. These account for the rather large performance decrements seen in only a few minutes of rest. The improvements in performance with resumed practice are, under this view, due to relearning of the task whose memory was lost over the rest period. This hypothesis is probably the most simple of the notions to explain warm-up decrement, as it sees the decrements in skill as just another example of the well-known forgetting processes discussed earlier; no special theoretical status for warm-up decrement is required.

Set Hypothesis

In this view, the loss of skill is related to the loss of some temporary internal state(s), or *set*, that underlies and supports the skill in question. Warm-up decrement is caused by the loss (or disruption) of this set over the rest period. This hypothesis says that memory of the skill is not lost over the rest period (or perhaps very small losses, far too small to account for the large decrements seen). With practice resumed on the task after the rest, the individual regains the lost set and performance is improved.

Early Evidence for the Set Hypothesis

The set hypothesis seemed reasonable for many years, as it is easy to imagine how such a process might disrupt skills with rest, especially in the face of the nearly perfect retention of skills like the pursuit rotor discussed earlier. Yet no evidence existed for these set-loss phenomena until Irion's (1948) data with verbal skills suggested a way to study the problem. Irion's idea was that if the set hypothesis is correct, then the lost set should be able to be reinstated by certain activities that are related to the action in question but which cannot be thought of as contributing to the memory for the task. Irion used verbal-learning as the main task, with two treatment groups; both practiced the verbal task, then had a rest, then resumed practice again. One of the groups remained inactive in the rest period. The second group engaged in color-naming during the end of the rest period, presumably a nonmemory activity presented on the same apparatus and with the same rhythms as the verbal-learning task but using none of the learned items for the verbal task. If the set hypothesis is correct, color-naming should reinstate the lost set produced by the rest, and the initial performance on the verbal-learning task should be more accurate than for the group that simply rested. It was. Since the color-naming cannot be thought of as creating increased memory strength for the paired associates task, the implication is that color-naming reinstated the lost set, in some way preparing the subjects for the upcoming verbal task.

Numerous studies were done to evaluate the set hypothesis with motor skills, and the successes for the hypothesis were few. As an example, Ammons (1951) used the pursuit rotor; during the rest he had subjects watch another active subject or follow the target area with the finger, etc., in an attempt to eliminate the warm-up decrement. No procedures were found that would eliminate the decrement (see Adams, 1955). These data seemed to say that either (a) the set hypothesis was wrong for motor behavior or (b) the appropriate nonmemory set-reinstating activities had not been discovered. In either case, the set hypothesis was not well supported. All this evidence is reviewed more completely in Adams (1961, 1964) and in Nacson and Schmidt (1971).

Recent Evidence on the Set Hypothesis

Recently, a number of experiments tested a slightly different view of the set hypothesis and provided considerable support for it. The notion, originally called the *activity-set hypothesis* by Nacson and Schmidt (1971), is closely related to the ideas about the inverted-U hypothesis discussed in Chapter 5. Motor performance is thought to be supported by a number of adjustments (or "sets"), such as arousal being adjusted to the most effective level for the particular task and subject, attention being directed at the proper source of input, and so on. When the subject practices the task, various supportive mechanisms are constantly adjusted so that performance in the task is maximized; but then the rest period is presented, and these functions are adjusted to different levels, perhaps to those levels most compatible with rest, leading to an ineffective pattern of adjustment when the task is resumed. If so, then practicing a task requiring the same adjustments (set) as the main task just before returning to it should reinstate those adjustments, leading to an elimination or reduction in the warm-up decrement.

Nacson and Schmidt (1971) used essentially this procedure. The main task was a right-hand force-production response, in which the subject had to learn to squeeze a handle with a 45.4-lb (20.6-kg) force, with KR given after each trial and 10 sec rest between trials. After Trial 20, a 10-min rest was given, and then practice resumed for another 10 trials. The independent variable was the nature of the activities presented in the 10-min rest period. One group (REST) was allowed to rest for 10 min. Another (EXP) group had 5 min of rest, followed by 5 min of another force-estimation task; this task, though, involved the left arm rather than the right, elbow flexors rather than the gripping action, and a different level of force (20 lb, or 9.1 kg). So it could not be argued that this task would contribute to the memory of the right-hand grip task. After 18 trials of this task with the same intertrial interval and KR, subjects were shifted immediately to the right-hand grip task for the retention test.

The major findings are shown in Figure 15-7. The absolute errors in the main (right-hand gripping) task are shown for the two groups before and after the rest period. Immediately after the rest, the group that simply rested (REST) for 10 min showed the typical warm-up decrement effect, and the losses were regained in the next few post-rest practice trials. But the group with the left-hand activities (EXP) showed almost no warm-up effect, suggesting that the activities in the rest period reinstated the lost set, enabling accurate performance to occur on the first post-rest trial. Similar findings have been shown for a linear-positioning response (with a positioning task as the warm-up task) by Nacson and Schmidt (1971; Schmidt & Nacson, 1971), and by Schmidt and Wrisberg (1971) using a movement-speed task (with another movement speed task as the warm-up task). These data support the set hypothesis rather well, suggesting that warm-up decrement is the loss of some critical adjustments over the rest period. These data also argue against the hypothesis that warm-up decrement is simply forgetting, because a forgetting hypothesis cannot explain why the performance of a few trials of a different warm-up task (which seems to have no memory elements in common with the main task) should produce improvements in main task performance.

Other data (Schmidt & Nacson, 1971) show that the reinstated set is rather transient in nature. If as few as 25 sec of rest are inserted between the reinstatement of the set and the resumption of practice on the main task, the

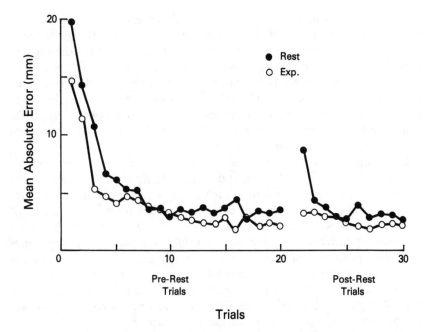

Figure 15-7. Absolute error in a force-estimation task for original learning and after a 10-min rest (Group REST rested during the interval, and Group EXP performed a left-hand force-estimation task; error is measured as polygraph pen displacement.) (from Nacson & Schmidt, 1971).

set is completely lost again. Activities can be designed that will increase warm-up decrement even more than resting does. For example, Schmidt and Nacson (1971) showed that a right-hand grip-strength task (with maximum force) performed just before the resumption of practice on a linear-positioning task caused a very large increase in error on the first post-rest trial, an error even larger than on the original trial of practice before the rest. This finding suggests that the maximum grip force task required a different set, one which was incompatible with careful linear positioning.

All of these experiments are rather consistent in saying that the warm-up effect is caused by some loss of internal adjustments (or set) over the rest period. These adjustments are critical to effective performance in the task, but they are not a part of the memory for it. Just as the race car has to be brought to the proper state of tuning before maximal performance can be achieved, so too must the human be brought into the proper state of adjustment for high-level skilled performance. It is not clear just what is being adjusted in these experiments, but probable candidates are the level of arousal, the rhythm and timing for the trial cycle, the attention to the proper sources of feedback, and so on.

Implications for High-Level Performances

I believe that these findings have considerable relevance for high-level performances, especially after performance is interrupted by rest or when major changes in performance are required. For example, it would seem that a number of different sets should be achieved at different times in many games. In golf, there will probably be different sets for driving and putting, as well as for walking between shots, and each of these sets must be re-established before the shot or large errors may occur. In basketball, the player must shift quickly from an offensive set when her team has the ball to a defensive set when a pass is intercepted. Failure to adopt the proper set could result in ineffective performance for a few seconds, long enough that her opponents could score an easy goal.

Can people adjust their own sets? There is absolutely no evidence on this point, but it would seem they might be able to. In many skills situations, the performer seems to engage in some preliminary activities, perhaps a practice putt at an imaginary ball in golf or actual practice serves in tennis, all of which might have the effect of reducing warm-up decrement on the first actual performance trial. In some cases, it would even appear that some kinds of mental-practice activities have this set-reinstating effect, and this is perhaps one of the reasons that mental practice is so effective in producing gains in skills (see Chapter 12, "Mental Practice"). It is also possible that these self-generated set-reinstating activities must be learned and that biofeedback training could be of assistance in learning (e.g., biofeedback of one's arousal level). There are many unanswered questions in this area, but the payoffs for finding the answers should be great because the sizes of the decrements are particularly large and damaging for performers who demand high-level proficiency on the first performance attempt after a rest.

SUMMARY

Motor learning and motor memory are very closely related concepts. *Motor memory* usually refers to the persistence of the acquired capability for responding, and losses in memory are called *forgetting*. Forgetting is usually measured by performance losses on a *retention test*, administered after a *retention interval*.

Forgetting of verbal materials is probably caused largely by interference. Forgetting of an item is thought to occur from other tasks learned between the original learning and retention (retroactive interference), or from other tasks learned prior to the original learning (proactive interference). These mechanisms of forgetting have not been studied in motor skills extensively and, while some evidence of retroactive interference exists, mechanisms of motor forgetting are not well understood.

Continuous skills are retained nearly perfectly over long retention intervals. Discrete skills, on the other hand, can show marked performance losses during the same retention intervals. The reasons for this continuous-discrete difference in retention are not clear, but they are probably not based on the tendency for continuous tasks to be more "motor" than discrete tasks. It is possible that the difference is based on the possibility that continuous tasks, with more practice time in a typical experiment, have more resistance to forgetting because they are learned more completely.

Parallel to the research in verbal memory, work on motor short-term memory has been quite active in the 1970s. Using once-presented movements, linear-positioning tasks, prevention of rehearsal, and no KR, numerous studies show rather rapid retention losses, increased retention loss as the retention interval is increased to about 60 sec, and decreased losses as the experience at the target is increased. Forgetting appears to be due, in part, to interference from other positions. The code for the position of a movement endpoint location is more effectively remembered than the code for a movement distance, and allowing a subject to select the target results in better retention than having the experimenter select it (*preselection effect*).

Warm-up decrement is a retention loss caused by the imposition of a short rest in a series of practice trials. Recent research supports the *set hypothesis*, which holds that warm-up decrement is a loss over rest of a pattern of nonmemory adjustments that are critical to the performance of the task.

GLOSSARY

Absolute retention. A measure of retention based only on the level of performance on the retention test.

Forgetting. The loss of memory, or the loss of the acquired capability for responding.

Interference theory. A theory holding that forgetting is caused by interference from other learned materials.

Memory. The persistence of habit—the acquired capability for responding.

Motor memory. The memory for movements or motor information.

Preselection effect. In short-term motor memory work, the phenomenon that the memory for subject-selected movements is stronger than for experimenter-selected movements.

Proactive interference. In the interference theory, a source of forgetting caused by learning imposed before the original learning of some to-be-remembered task.

Relative retention. A group of measures of retention in which the performance on the retention test is evaluated in relationship to the level of performance reached in original learning.

Retention interval. The interval between the end of original learning and the retention test.

Retention test. A performance test administered after a retention interval; similar to a transfer test.

Retroactive interference. In the interference theory, a source of forgetting caused by learning imposed between the original learning and the retention test for a to-be-remembered task.

Set. A nonmemory pattern of adjustments that supports performance.

Set hypothesis. A hypothesis holding that warm-up decrement is caused by loss of set.

Short-term motor memory. The short-term memory for motor information or motor tasks, analogous to verbal short-term memory.

Trace-decay theory. A theory holding that forgetting is caused by the spontaneous "decay" or weakening of memory over time.

Warm-up decrement. A decrement in performance occurring after a brief rest period.

APPENDIX

Logarithms to the Base 2

[To find the $Log_2(23.5)$, for example, enter the row labeled 23, then move to the right under the column headed .5; the result is 4.55.]

NUMBER   PLUS DECIMAL

	.0	.1	.2	.3	.4	.5	.6	.7	.8	.9
0.	0.00	− 3.32	− 2.32	− 1.74	− 1.32	− 1.00	− 0.74	− 0.51	− 0.32	− 0.15
1.	0.00	0.14	0.26	0.38	0.49	0.58	0.68	0.77	0.85	0.93
2.	1.00	1.07	1.14	1.20	1.26	1.32	1.38	1.43	1.49	1.54
3.	1.58	1.63	1.68	1.72	1.77	1.81	1.85	1.89	1.93	1.96
4.	2.00	2.04	2.07	2.10	2.14	2.17	2.20	2.23	2.26	2.29
5.	2.32	2.35	2.38	2.41	2.43	2.46	2.49	2.51	2.54	2.56
6.	2.58	2.61	2.63	2.66	2.68	2.70	2.72	2.74	2.77	2.79
7.	2.81	2.83	2.85	2.87	2.89	2.91	2.93	2.94	2.96	2.98
8.	3.00	3.02	3.04	3.05	3.07	3.09	3.10	3.12	3.14	3.15
9.	3.17	3.19	3.20	3.22	3.23	3.25	3.26	3.28	3.29	3.31
10.	3.32	3.34	3.35	3.36	3.38	3.39	3.41	3.42	3.43	3.45
11.	3.46	3.47	3.49	3.50	3.51	3.52	3.54	3.55	3.56	3.57
12.	3.58	3.60	3.61	3.62	3.63	3.64	3.66	3.67	3.68	3.69
13.	3.70	3.71	3.72	3.73	3.74	3.75	3.77	3.78	3.79	3.80
14.	3.81	3.82	3.83	3.84	3.85	3.86	3.87	3.88	3.89	3.90
15.	3.91	3.92	3.93	3.94	3.94	3.95	3.96	3.97	3.98	3.99
16.	4.00	4.01	4.02	4.03	4.04	4.04	4.05	4.06	4.07	4.08
17.	4.09	4.10	4.10	4.11	4.12	4.13	4.14	4.15	4.15	4.16
18.	4.17	4.18	4.19	4.19	4.20	4.21	4.22	4.22	4.23	4.24
19.	4.25	4.26	4.26	4.27	4.28	4.29	4.29	4.30	4.31	4.31
20.	4.32	4.33	4.34	4.34	4.35	4.36	4.36	4.37	4.38	4.39
21.	4.39	4.40	4.41	4.41	4.42	4.43	4.43	4.44	4.45	4.45
22.	4.46	4.47	4.47	4.48	4.49	4.49	4.50	4.50	4.51	4.52
23.	4.52	4.53	4.54	4.54	4.55	4.55	4.56	4.57	4.57	4.58
24.	4.58	4.59	4.60	4.60	4.61	4.61	4.62	4.63	4.63	4.64
25.	4.64	4.65	4.66	4.66	4.67	4.67	4.68	4.68	4.69	4.69
26.	4.70	4.71	4.71	4.72	4.72	4.73	4.73	4.74	4.74	4.75
27.	4.75	4.76	4.77	4.77	4.78	4.78	4.79	4.79	4.80	4.80
28.	4.81	4.81	4.82	4.82	4.83	4.83	4.84	4.84	4.85	4.85
29.	4.86	4.86	4.87	4.87	4.88	4.88	4.89	4.89	4.90	4.90
30.	4.91	4.91	4.92	4.92	4.93	4.93	4.94	4.94	4.94	4.95
31.	4.95	4.96	4.96	4.97	4.97	4.98	4.98	4.99	4.99	5.00
32.	5.00	5.00	5.01	5.01	5.02	5.02	5.03	5.03	5.04	5.04
33.	5.04	5.05	5.05	5.06	5.06	5.07	5.07	5.07	5.08	5.08
34.	5.09	5.09	5.10	5.10	5.10	5.11	5.11	5.12	5.12	5.13
35.	5.13	5.13	5.14	5.14	5.15	5.15	5.15	5.16	5.16	5.17
36.	5.17	5.17	5.18	5.18	5.19	5.19	5.19	5.20	5.20	5.21
37.	5.21	5.21	5.22	5.22	5.22	5.23	5.23	5.24	5.24	5.24
38.	5.25	5.25	5.26	5.26	5.26	5.27	5.27	5.27	5.28	5.28
39.	5.29	5.29	5.29	5.30	5.30	5.30	5.31	5.31	5.31	5.32
40.	5.32	5.33	5.33	5.33	5.34	5.34	5.34	5.35	5.35	5.35
41.	5.36	5.36	5.36	5.37	5.37	5.38	5.38	5.38	5.39	5.39
42.	5.39	5.40	5.40	5.40	5.41	5.41	5.41	5.42	5.42	5.42
43.	5.43	5.43	5.43	5.44	5.44	5.44	5.45	5.45	5.45	5.46
44.	5.46	5.46	5.47	5.47	5.47	5.48	5.48	5.48	5.49	5.49

NUMBER   PLUS DECIMAL

	.0	.1	.2	.3	.4	.5	.6	.7	.8	.9
45.	5.49	5.50	5.50	5.50	5.50	5.51	5.51	5.51	5.52	5.52
46.	5.52	5.53	5.53	5.53	5.54	5.54	5.54	5.55	5.55	5.55
47.	5.55	5.56	5.56	5.56	5.57	5.57	5.57	5.58	5.58	5.58
48.	5.58	5.59	5.59	5.59	5.60	5.60	5.60	5.61	5.61	5.61
49.	5.61	5.62	5.62	5.62	5.63	5.63	5.63	5.64	5.64	5.64
50.	5.64	5.65	5.65	5.65	5.66	5.66	5.66	5.66	5.67	5.67
51.	5.67	5.68	5.68	5.68	5.68	5.69	5.69	5.69	5.69	5.70
52.	5.70	5.70	5.71	5.71	5.71	5.71	5.72	5.72	5.72	5.73
53.	5.73	5.73	5.73	5.74	5.74	5.74	5.74	5.75	5.75	5.75
54.	5.75	5.76	5.76	5.76	5.77	5.77	5.77	5.77	5.78	5.78
55.	5.78	5.78	5.79	5.79	5.79	5.79	5.80	5.80	5.80	5.80
56.	5.81	5.81	5.81	5.82	5.82	5.82	5.82	5.83	5.83	5.83
57.	5.83	5.84	5.84	5.84	5.84	5.85	5.85	5.85	5.85	5.86
58.	5.86	5.86	5.86	5.87	5.87	5.87	5.87	5.88	5.88	5.88
59.	5.88	5.89	5.89	5.89	5.89	5.89	5.90	5.90	5.90	5.90
60.	5.91	5.91	5.91	5.91	5.92	5.92	5.92	5.92	5.93	5.93
61.	5.93	5.93	5.94	5.94	5.94	5.94	5.94	5.95	5.95	5.95
62.	5.95	5.96	5.96	5.96	5.96	5.97	5.97	5.97	5.97	5.97
63.	5.98	5.98	5.98	5.98	5.99	5.99	5.99	5.99	6.00	6.00
64.	6.00	6.00	6.00	6.01	6.01	6.01	6.01	6.02	6.02	6.02
65.	6.02	6.02	6.03	6.03	6.03	6.03	6.04	6.04	6.04	6.04
66.	6.04	6.05	6.05	6.05	6.05	6.06	6.06	6.06	6.06	6.06
67.	6.07	6.07	6.07	6.07	6.07	6.08	6.08	6.08	6.08	6.09
68.	6.09	6.09	6.09	6.09	6.10	6.10	6.10	6.10	6.10	6.11
69.	6.11	6.11	6.11	6.11	6.12	6.12	6.12	6.12	6.13	6.13
70.	6.13	6.13	6.13	6.14	6.14	6.14	6.14	6.14	6.15	6.15
71.	6.15	6.15	6.15	6.16	6.16	6.16	6.16	6.16	6.17	6.17
72.	6.17	6.17	6.17	6.18	6.18	6.18	6.18	6.18	6.19	6.19
73.	6.19	6.19	6.19	6.20	6.20	6.20	6.20	6.20	6.21	6.21
74.	6.21	6.21	6.21	6.22	6.22	6.22	6.22	6.22	6.22	6.23
75.	6.23	6.23	6.23	6.23	6.24	6.24	6.24	6.24	6.24	6.25
76.	6.25	6.25	6.25	6.25	6.26	6.26	6.26	6.26	6.26	6.26
77.	6.27	6.27	6.27	6.27	6.27	6.28	6.28	6.28	6.28	6.28
78.	6.29	6.29	6.29	6.29	6.29	6.29	6.30	6.30	6.30	6.30
79.	6.30	6.31	6.31	6.31	6.31	6.31	6.31	6.32	6.32	6.32
80.	6.32	6.32	6.33	6.33	6.33	6.33	6.33	6.33	6.34	6.34
81.	6.34	6.34	6.34	6.35	6.35	6.35	6.35	6.35	6.35	6.36
82.	6.36	6.36	6.36	6.36	6.36	6.37	6.37	6.37	6.37	6.37
83.	6.38	6.38	6.38	6.38	6.38	6.38	6.39	6.39	6.39	6.39
84.	6.39	6.39	6.40	6.40	6.40	6.40	6.40	6.40	6.41	6.41
85.	6.41	6.41	6.41	6.41	6.42	6.42	6.42	6.42	6.42	6.42
86.	6.43	6.43	6.43	6.43	6.43	6.43	6.44	6.44	6.44	6.44
87.	6.44	6.44	6.45	6.45	6.45	6.45	6.45	6.45	6.46	6.46
88.	6.46	6.46	6.46	6.46	6.47	6.47	6.47	6.47	6.47	6.47
89.	6.48	6.48	6.48	6.48	6.48	6.48	6.49	6.49	6.49	6.49
90.	6.49	6.49	6.50	6.50	6.50	6.50	6.50	6.50	6.50	6.51
91.	6.51	6.51	6.51	6.51	6.51	6.52	6.52	6.52	6.52	6.52
92.	6.52	6.53	6.53	6.53	6.53	6.53	6.53	6.53	6.54	6.54
93.	6.54	6.54	6.54	6.54	6.55	6.55	6.55	6.55	6.55	6.55
94.	6.55	6.56	6.56	6.56	6.56	6.56	6.56	6.57	6.57	6.57
95.	6.57	6.57	6.57	6.57	6.58	6.58	6.58	6.58	6.58	6.58
96.	6.58	6.59	6.59	6.59	6.59	6.59	6.59	6.60	6.60	6.60
97.	6.60	6.60	6.60	6.60	6.61	6.61	6.61	6.61	6.61	6.61

NUMBER

PLUS DECIMAL

	.0	.1	.2	.3	.4	.5	.6	.7	.8	.9
98.	6.61	6.62	6.62	6.62	6.62	6.62	6.62	6.62	6.63	6.63
99.	6.63	6.63	6.63	6.63	6.64	6.64	6.64	6.64	6.64	6.64
100.	6.64	6.65	6.65	6.65	6.65	6.65	6.65	6.65	6.66	6.66
101.	6.66	6.66	6.66	6.66	6.66	6.67	6.67	6.67	6.67	6.67
102.	6.67	6.67	6.68	6.68	6.68	6.68	6.68	6.68	6.68	6.69
103.	6.69	6.69	6.69	6.69	6.69	6.69	6.69	6.70	6.70	6.70
104.	6.70	6.70	6.70	6.70	6.71	6.71	6.71	6.71	6.71	6.71
105.	6.71	6.72	6.72	6.72	6.72	6.72	6.72	6.72	6.73	6.73
106.	6.73	6.73	6.73	6.73	6.73	6.73	6.74	6.74	6.74	6.74
107.	6.74	6.74	6.74	6.75	6.75	6.75	6.75	6.75	6.75	6.75
108.	6.75	6.76	6.76	6.76	6.76	6.76	6.76	6.76	6.77	6.77
109.	6.77	6.77	6.77	6.77	6.77	6.77	6.78	6.78	6.78	6.78
110.	6.78	6.78	6.78	6.79	6.79	6.79	6.79	6.79	6.79	6.79
111.	6.79	6.80	6.80	6.80	6.80	6.80	6.80	6.80	6.80	6.81
112.	6.81	6.81	6.81	6.81	6.81	6.81	6.82	6.82	6.82	6.82
113.	6.82	6.82	6.82	6.82	6.83	6.83	6.83	6.83	6.83	6.83
114.	6.83	6.83	6.84	6.84	6.84	6.84	6.84	6.84	6.84	6.84
115.	6.85	6.85	6.85	6.85	6.85	6.85	6.85	6.85	6.86	6.86
116.	6.86	6.86	6.86	6.86	6.86	6.86	6.87	6.87	6.87	6.87
117.	6.87	6.87	6.87	6.87	6.88	6.88	6.88	6.88	6.88	6.88
118.	6.88	6.88	6.89	6.89	6.89	6.89	6.89	6.89	6.89	6.89
119.	6.89	6.90	6.90	6.90	6.90	6.90	6.90	6.90	6.90	6.91
120.	6.91	6.91	6.91	6.91	6.91	6.91	6.91	6.92	6.92	6.92
121.	6.92	6.92	6.92	6.92	6.92	6.92	6.93	6.93	6.93	6.93
122.	6.93	6.93	6.93	6.93	6.94	6.94	6.94	6.94	6.94	6.94
123.	6.94	6.94	6.94	6.95	6.95	6.95	6.95	6.95	6.95	6.95
124.	6.95	6.96	6.96	6.96	6.96	6.96	6.96	6.96	6.96	6.96
125.	6.97	6.97	6.97	6.97	6.97	6.97	6.97	6.97	6.97	6.98
126.	6.98	6.98	6.98	6.98	6.98	6.98	6.98	6.99	6.99	6.99
127.	6.99	6.99	6.99	6.99	6.99	6.99	7.00	7.00	7.00	7.00
128.	7.00	7.00	7.00	7.00	7.00	7.01	7.01	7.01	7.01	7.01
129.	7.01	7.01	7.01	7.01	7.02	7.02	7.02	7.02	7.02	7.02
130.	7.02	7.02	7.02	7.03	7.03	7.03	7.03	7.03	7.03	7.03
131.	7.03	7.03	7.04	7.04	7.04	7.04	7.04	7.04	7.04	7.04
132.	7.04	7.05	7.05	7.05	7.05	7.05	7.05	7.05	7.05	7.05
133.	7.06	7.06	7.06	7.06	7.06	7.06	7.06	7.06	7.06	7.07
134.	7.07	7.07	7.07	7.07	7.07	7.07	7.07	7.07	7.07	7.08
135.	7.08	7.08	7.08	7.08	7.08	7.08	7.08	7.08	7.09	7.09
136.	7.09	7.09	7.09	7.09	7.09	7.09	7.09	7.09	7.10	7.10
137.	7.10	7.10	7.10	7.10	7.10	7.10	7.10	7.11	7.11	7.11
138.	7.11	7.11	7.11	7.11	7.11	7.11	7.11	7.12	7.12	7.12
139.	7.12	7.12	7.12	7.12	7.12	7.12	7.13	7.13	7.13	7.13
140.	7.13	7.13	7.13	7.13	7.13	7.13	7.14	7.14	7.14	7.14
141.	7.14	7.14	7.14	7.14	7.14	7.14	7.15	7.15	7.15	7.15
142.	7.15	7.15	7.15	7.15	7.15	7.15	7.16	7.16	7.16	7.16
143.	7.16	7.16	7.16	7.16	7.16	7.16	7.17	7.17	7.17	7.17
144.	7.17	7.17	7.17	7.17	7.17	7.17	7.18	7.18	7.18	7.18
145.	7.18	7.18	7.18	7.18	7.18	7.18	7.19	7.19	7.19	7.19
146.	7.19	7.19	7.19	7.19	7.19	7.19	7.20	7.20	7.20	7.20
147.	7.20	7.20	7.20	7.20	7.20	7.20	7.21	7.21	7.21	7.21
148.	7.21	7.21	7.21	7.21	7.21	7.21	7.22	7.22	7.22	7.22
149.	7.22	7.22	7.22	7.22	7.22	7.22	7.22	7.23	7.23	7.23
150.	7.23	7.23	7.23	7.23	7.23	7.23	7.23	7.24	7.24	7.24

REFERENCE NOTES

1. Carter, M.C., & Shapiro, D.C. *Invariant properties of sequential movements*. Paper presented at the annual meeting of the North American Society for the Psychology of Sport and Physical Activity, Asilomar, CA, June 1981.
2. Bender, P.A. Unpublished data, University of Southern California, 1979.
3. Keele, S.W. Personal communication, University of Oregon, 1980.
4. Rosenbaum, D.A. Unpublished observations, Bell Laboratories, 1978.
5. Larish, D.D. *On the relationship between response organization processes and response programming*. Unpublished manuscript, University of Iowa, 1981.
6. Herman, R. Personal communication, Temple University Medical School, 1979.
7. Hawkins, B., Zelaznik, H.N., & Kisselburgh, L. *The effects of concurrent visual feedback on the spatial accuracy of single-aiming movements*. Manuscript in preparation, UCLA, 1981.
8. Crossman, E.R.F.W., & Goodeve, P.J. *Feedback control of hand movements and Fitt's [sic] law*. Communication to the Experimental Psychology Society, 1963.
9. Schmidt, R.A., & McGown, C.M. *Phasing in unidirectional movements*. Paper presented at the annual meeting of the Psychonomic Society, Phoenix, AZ, November 1979.
10. MacKay, W. *Programmable motor control loops passing through posterior parietal lobe*. Paper presented at the Organization of Movements Symposium, Good Samaritan Hospital, Portland, OR, 1980.
11. Armstrong, T.R. *Training for the production of memorized movement patterns*. (Technical Report No. 26). Human Performance Center, Uni-

versity of Michigan, 1970.

12. Kelso, J.A.S., Goodman, D., & Putnam, C.A. *Human interlimb coordination. I. A kinematic analysis.* Manuscript in preparation, Haskins Laboratories, 1981.

13. McGown, C.M., & Schmidt, R.A. *Coordination in two-handed movements.* Paper presented at the annual meeting of the North American Society for the Psychology of Sport and Physical Activity, Asilomar, CA, June 1981.

14. Shapiro, D.C. *Bilateral transfer of a motor program.* Paper presented at the annual meeting of the American Alliance for Health, Physical Education, and Recreation, Seattle, WA, March 1977.

15. Quinn, J.T., & Sherwood, D.E. *Time requirements of changes in program and parameter variables in rapid movements.* Paper presented at the annual meeting of the North American Society for the Psychology of Sport and Physical Activity, Boulder, CO, May 1980.

16. Wallace, S.A. *An EMG and kinematic analysis of rapid movements.* Paper presented at the Conference on the Neural Basis of Motor Control, Columbia University, 1980.

17. Gottsdanker, R. Personal communication, University of California, Santa Barbara, 1977.

18. Eysenck, H.J. Remarks presented in a Faculty Colloquium, University of Southern California, 1979.

19. Schmidt, R.A., & Pew, R.W. *Predicting motor-manipulative performances in the manufacture of dental appliances.* Final Report submitted to Heritage Laboratories, 1974.

20. McGown, C. *Massed and distributed practice revisited.* Unpublished manuscript, Brigham Young University, 1980.

21. Johnson, R.W. Personal communication, University of Minnesota, 1981.

22. Johnson, R.W., Wicks, G.G., & Ben-Sira, D. *Practice in the absence of knowledge of results: Acquisition and transfer.* Unpublished manuscript, University of Minnesota, 1980.

23. Simmons, R.W., & Snyder, R.J. *Acquisition of a ballistic skill as a function of length of KR-delay, post-KR delay, and intertrial interval.* Unpublished manuscript, San Diego State University, 1980.

24. Salmoni, A.W. Unpublished observations, Laurentian University, 1981.

25. Schmidt, R.A., & Russell, D.G. *Error detection in positioning responses.* Unpublished manuscript, University of Michigan, 1972.

26. Keele, S.W. Personal communication of ideas based on conversations between S.W. Keele and D. MacKay, 1976.

27. Marteniuk, R.G. Unpublished observations, University of Waterloo, 1978.

28. McGhee, R.C. *The contribution of sensory feedback to response production ability.* Paper presented at the annual meeting of the North American Society for the Psychology of Sport and Physical Activity, Asilomar, CA, June 1981.

REFERENCES

Adams, J.A. Warm-up decrement in performance on the pursuit rotor. *American Journal of Psychology*, 1952, **65**, 404-414.

Adams, J.A. A source of decrement in psychomotor performance. *Journal of Experimental Psychology*, 1955, **49**, 390-394.

Adams, J.A. *An evaluation of test items measuring motor abilities*. Research Report AFPTRC-TN-56-55. Lackland Air Force Base, 1956.

Adams, J.A. The second facet of forgetting: A review of warm-up decrement. *Psychological Bulletin*, 1961, **58**, 257-273.

Adams J.A. Motor skills. *Annual Review of Psychology*, 1964, **15**, 181-202.

Adams, J.A. Some mechanisms of motor responding: An examination of attention. In E.A. Bilodeau (Ed.), *Acquisition of skill*. New York: Academic Press, 1966.

Adams, J.A. *Human memory*. New York: McGraw-Hill, 1967.

Adams, J.A. Response feedback and learning. *Psychological Bulletin*, 1968, **70**, 486-504.

Adams, J.A. Motor behavior. Section VII in M.H. Marx (Ed.), *Learning processes*. London: MacMillan, 1969.

Adams, J.A. A closed-loop theory of motor learning. *Journal of Motor Behavior*, 1971, **3**, 111-150.

Adams, J.A. *Learning and memory: An introduction*. Homewood, IL: Dorsey, 1976. (a)

Adams, J.A. Issues for a closed-loop theory of motor learning. In G.E. Stelmach (Ed.), *Motor control: Issues and trends*. New York: Academic Press, 1976. (b)

Adams, J.A. Feedback theory of how joint receptors regulate the timing and positioning of a limb. *Psychological Review*, 1977, **84**, 504-523.

Adams, J.A. Theoretical issues for knowledge of results. In G.E. Stelmach

(Ed.), *Information processing in motor control and learning*. New York: Academic Press, 1978.

Adams, J.A., & Bray, N.W. A closed-loop theory of paired associate verbal learning. *Psychological Review*, 1970, **77**, 385-405.

Adams, J.A., & Creamer, L.R. Anticipatory timing of continuous and discrete responses. *Journal of Experimental Psychology*, 1962, **63**, 84-90.

Adams, J.A., & Dijkstra, S. Short-term memory for motor responses. *Journal of Experimental Psychology*, 1966, **71**, 314-318.

Adams, J.A., & Goetz, E.T. Feedback and practice as variables in error detection and correction. *Journal of Motor Behavior*, 1973, **5**, 217-224.

Adams, J.A., Goetz, E.T., & Marshall, P.H. Response feedback and motor learning. *Journal of Experimental Psychology*, 1972, **92**, 391-397.

Adams, J.A., & Hufford, L.E. Contributions of a part-task trainer to the learning and relearning of a time-shared flight maneuver. *Human Factors*, 1962, **4**, 159-170.

Adams, J.A., & Reynolds, B. Effect of shift in distribution of practice conditions following interpolated rest. *Journal of Experimental Psychology*, 1954, **47**, 32-36.

Aiken, L.R. Reaction time and the expectancy hypothesis. *Perceptual and Motor Skills*, 1964, **19**, 655-661.

Allen, L. *Variability in practice and schema development in children*. M.A. Thesis, University of Southern California, 1978.

Allport, D.A., Antonis, B., & Reynolds, P. On the division of attention: A disproof of the single channel hypothesis. *Quarterly Journal of Experimental Psychology*, 1972, **24**, 225-235.

Ammons, R.B. Effects of pre-practice activities on rotary pursuit performance. *Journal of Experimental Psychology*, 1951, **41**, 187-191.

Angel, R.W. Antagonist muscle activity during rapid movements: Central versus proprioceptive influences. *Journal of Neurology, Neurosurgery, and Psychiatry*, 1977, **40**, 683-686.

Angel, R.W., & Higgins, J.R. Correction of false moves in pursuit tracking. *Journal of Experimental Psychology*, 1969, **82**, 185-187.

Archer, E.J., Kent, G.W., & Mote, F.A. Effect of long-term practice and time-on-target information feedback on a complex tracking task. *Journal of Experimental Psychology*, 1956, **51**, 103-112.

Asatryan, D.G., & Fel'dman, A.G. Biophysics of complex systems and mathematical models. Functional tuning of nervous system with control of movement or maintenance of a steady posture. I. Mechanographic analysis of the work of the joint on execution of a postural task. *Biophysics*, 1965, **10**, 925-935.

Ascoli, K.M., & Schmidt, R.A. Proactive interference in short-term motor retention. *Journal of Motor Behavior*, 1969, **1**, 29-35.

Atkinson, R.C., & Shiffrin, R.M. The control of short-term memory. *Scientific American*, 1971, **225**, 82-90.

Bachman, J.C. Specificity vs. generality in learning and performing two large muscle motor tasks. *Research Quarterly*, 1961, **32**, 3-11.

Bachrach, A.J. Diving behavior. In Scripps Institute of Oceanography, *Human performance and scuba diving*. Proceedings of the Symposium on Underwater Physiology, LaJolla, CA, 1970. Chicago: The Athletic Institute, 1970.

Baddeley, A.D. *The psychology of memory*. New York: Basic Books, 1976.

Baddeley, A.D., & Longman, D.J.A. The influence of length and frequency of training session on the rate of learning to type. *Ergonomics*, 1978, **21**, 627-635.

Bahrick, H.P. An analysis of stimulus variables influencing the proprioceptive control of movements. *Psychological Review*, 1957, **64**, 324-328.

Bahrick, H.P., Fitts, P.M., & Briggs, G.E. Learning curves—facts or artifacts. *Psychological Bulletin*, 1957, **54**, 256-268.

Bahrick, H.P., & Shelly, C.H. Time-sharing as an index of automatization. *Journal of Experimental Psychology*, 1958, **56**, 288-293.

Bandura, A. *Principles of behavior modification*. New York: Holt, Rinehart, and Winston, 1969.

Bandura, A., Blanchard, E.B., & Ritter, B. Relative efficacy of desensitization and modeling approaches for inducing behavioral, affective, and attitudinal changes. *Journal of Personality and Social Psychology*, 1969, **13**, 173-199.

Barclay, C.R., & Newell, K.M. Children's processing of information in motor skill acquisition. *Journal of Experimental Child Psychology*, 1980, **30**, 98-108.

Barnett, M.L., Ross, D., Schmidt, R.A., & Todd, B. Motor skills learning and the specificity of training principle. *Research Quarterly*, 1973, **44**, 440-447.

Bartlett, F.C. *Remembering: A study in experimental and social psychology*. Cambridge: Cambridge University Press, 1932.

Battig, W.F. Transfer from verbal pre-training to motor performance as a function of motor task complexity. *Journal of Experimental Psychology*, 1956, **51**, 371-378.

Battig, W.F. Facilitation and interference. In E.A. Bilodeau (Ed.), *Acquisition of skill*. New York: Academic Press, 1966.

Bayley, N. The development of motor abilities during the first three years. *Monographs of the Society for Research in Child Development*, 1935, **1**, 1-26.

Beatty, J., & Wagoner, B.L. Pupillometric signs of brain activation vary with level of cognitive processing. *Science*, 1978, **199**, 1216-1218.

Bechtoldt, H.P. Motor abilities in studies of motor learning. In L.E. Smith (Ed.), *Psychology of motor learning*. Chicago: The Athletic Institute, 1970.

Beevor, C.E., & Horsely, V. A minute analysis (experimental) of the various movements producd by stimulating in the monkey different regions of the cortical centre for the upper limb as defined by Professor Ferrier. *Philosophical Transactions*, 1887, **178**, 153.

Beevor, C.E., & Horsely, V. A record of the results obtained by electrical excitation of the so-called motor cortex and internal capsule in the orangutang. *Philosophical Transactions*, 1890, **181**, 129.

Beggs, W.D.A., & Howarth, C.I. The accuracy of aiming at a target: Some further evidence for a theory of intermittent control. *Acta Psychologica*, 1972, **36**, 171-177.

Beggs, W.D.A., Sakstein, R., & Howarth, C.I. The generality of a theory of intermittent control of accurate movements. *Ergonomics*, 1974, **17**, 757-768.

Belen'kii, V.Y., Gurfinkel, V.S., & Pal'tsev, Y.I. Elements of control of voluntary movements. *Biofizika*, 1967, **12**, 135-141.

Bernstein (Bernshtein), N.A. [*On the structure of movements.*] Moscow: State Medical Publishing House, 1947. (In Russian)

Bernstein, N. *The co-ordination and regulation of movements.* Oxford: Pergamon Press, 1967.

Bilodeau, E.A. (Ed.), *Acquisition of skill.* New York: Academic Press, 1966.

Bilodeau, E.A., & Bilodeau, I.M. Variable frequency knowledge of results and the learning of simple skill. *Journal of Experimental Psychology*, 1958, **55**, 379-383.

Bilodeau, E.A., & Bilodeau, I.M. Motor skills learning. *Annual Review of Psychology*, 1961, **12**, 243-280.

Bilodeau, E.A., Bilodeau, I.M., & Schumsky, D.A. Some effects of introducing and withdrawing knowledge of results early and late in practice. *Journal of Experimental Psychology*, 1959, **58**, 142-144.

Bilodeau, I.M. Accuracy of a simple positioning response with variation in the number of trials by which knowledge of results is delayed. *American Journal of Psychology*, 1956, **69**, 434-437.

Bilodeau, I.M. Information feedback. In E.A. Bilodeau (Ed.), *Acquisition of skill.* New York: Academic Press, 1966.

Bilodeau, I.M. Information feedback. In E.A. Bilodeau (Ed.), *Principles of skill acquisition.* New York: Academic Press, 1969.

Bird, A.M. Effects of social facilitation upon females' performance of two psychomotor tasks. *Research Quarterly*, 1973, **44**, 322-330.

Birren, J.E. *The psychology of aging.* Englewood Cliffs, NJ: Prentice-Hall, 1964.

Bizzi, E., Dev, P., Morasso, P., & Polit, A. Effect of load disturbances during centrally initiated movements. *Journal of Neurophysiology*, 1978, **41**, 542-556.

Bizzi, E., Polit, A., & Morasso, P. Mechanisms underlying achievement of final head position. *Journal of Neurophysiology*, 1976, **39**, 435-444.

Blankenship, W.C. *Transfer effects in neuro-muscular responses involving choice.* M.A. Thesis, University of California, 1952.

Bliss, C.B. Investigations in reaction time and attention. *Studies from the Yale Psychological Laboratory*, 1892-1893, **1**, 1-55.

Bliss, J.C., Crane, H.D., Mansfield, K., & Townsend, J.T. Information available in brief tactile presentations. *Perception & Psychophysics*, 1966, **1**, 273-283.

Boder, D.P. The influence of concomitant activity and fatigue upon certain forms of reciprocal hand movement and its fundamental components. *Comparative Psychology Monographs*, 1935, **11**, No. 4.

Book, W.F. The psychology of skill. *University of Montana Studies in Psychology* (Vol. 1), 1908. (Reprinted, New York: Gregg, 1925.)

Boring, E.G. *A history of experimental psychology.* New York: Appleton-Century-Crofts, 1950.

Boucher, J.-L. Higher processes in motor learning. *Journal of Motor Behavior*, 1974, **6**, 131-137.

Bourne, L.E., Jr., & Bunderson, C.U. Effects of delay of informative feedback and length of postfeedback interval on concept identification. *Journal of Experimental Psychology*, 1963, **65**, 1-5.

Bourne, L.E., Jr., Guy, D.E., Dodd, D.H., & Justesen, D.R. Concept identification: The effects of varying length and informational components of the intertrial interval. *Journal of Experimental Psychology*, 1965, **69**, 624-629.

Bowditch, H.P., & Southard, W.F. A comparison of sight and touch. *Journal of Physiology*, 1882, **3**, 232-254.

Boyd, I.A., & Roberts, T.D.M. Proprioceptive discharges from stretch receptors in the knee joint of the cat. *Journal of Physiology*, 1953, **122**, 38-58.

Brame, J.M. The effects of expectancy and previous task cues on motor performance. *Journal of Motor Behavior*, 1979, **11**, 215-223.

Briggs, G.E., & Brogden, W.J. The effect of component practice on performance of a lever-positioning skill. *Journal of Experimental Psychology*, 1954, **48**, 375-380.

Briggs, G.E., & Waters, L.K. Training and transfer as a function of component interaction. *Journal of Experimental Psychology*, 1958, **56**, 492-500.

Broadbent, D.E. *Perception and communication*. London: Pergamon Press, 1958.

Brooks, V.B. Roles of cerebellum and basal ganglia and control of movements. *Le Journal Canadien Des Sciences Neurologiques*, 1975, **2**, 265-277.

Brooks, V.B. Motor programs revisited. In R.E. Talbot & D.R. Humphrey (Eds.), *Posture and movement*. New York: Raven Press, 1979.

Brown, J. Some tests of the decay theory of immediate memory. *Quarterly Journal of Experimental Psychology*, 1958, **10**, 12-21.

Brown, I.D. Measuring the "spare mental capacity" of car drivers by a subsidiary auditory task. *Ergonomics*, 1962, **5**, 247-250.

Brown, I.D. Measurement of control skills, vigilance, and performance on a subsidiary task during 12 hours of car driving. *Ergonomics*, 1967, **10**, 665-673.

Bryan, W., & Harter, N. Studies in the physiology and psychology of telegraphic language. *Psychological Review*, 1897, **4**, 27-53.

Bryan, W.L., & Harter, N. Studies on the telegraphic language: The acquisition of a hierarchy of habits. *Psychological Review*, 1899, **6**, 345-375.

Burgess, P.R., & Clark, F.J. Characteristics of knee joint receptors in the cat. *Journal of Physiology*, 1969, **203**, 317-335.

Buss, A. *Psychology: Man in perspective*. New York: Wiley, 1973.

Carlton, L.G. Control processes in the production of discrete aiming responses. *Journal of Human Movement Studies*, 1979, **5**, 115-124.

Carron, A.V. *Performance and learning in a discrete motor task under massed versus distributed conditions*. Doctoral dissertation, University of California, 1967.

Carron, A.V. Performance and learning in a discrete motor task under massed vs. distributed practice. *Research Quarterly*, 1969, **40**, 481-489.

Chambers, J.W., Jr., & Schumsky, D.A. The compression block technique: Use and misuse in the study of motor skills. *Journal of Motor Behavior*,

1978, **10**, 301-311.

Chapanis, A. *Man-machine engineering*. Belmont, CA: Wadsworth, 1965.

Chase, W.G., & Simon, H.A. Perception in chess. *Cognitive Psychology*, 1973, **4**, 55-81.

Chernikoff, R., & Taylor, F.V. Reaction time to kinesthetic stimulation resulting from sudden arm displacement. *Journal of Experimental Psychology*, 1952, **43**, 1-8.

Cherry, E.C. Some experiments on the recognition of speech, with one and two ears. *Journal of the Acoustical Society of America*, 1953, **25**, 975-979.

Clarke, D.H., & Stull, G.A. Strength recovery patterns following isometric and isotonic exercise. *Journal of Motor Behavior*, 1969, **1**, 233-243.

Coggeshall, R.E., Coulter, J.D., & Willis, W.D. Unmyelinated axons in the ventral roots of the cat lumbosacral enlargement. *Journal of Comparative Neurology*, 1974, **153**, 39-58.

Connolly, K. (Ed.). *Mechanisms of motor skill development*. New York: Academic Press, 1970.

Cooke, J.D. The organization of simple, skilled movements. In G.E. Stelmach & J. Requin (Eds.), *Tutorials in motor behavior*. Amsterdam: North-Holland, 1980.

Corbin, C.B. Mental practice. In W.P. Morgan (Ed.), *Ergogenic aids and muscular performance*. New York: Academic Press, 1972.

Crago, P.E., Houk, J.C., & Hasan, Z. Regulatory actions of the human stretch reflex. *Journal of Neurophysiology*, 1976, **39**, 925-935.

Craik, F.I.M., & Lockhart, R.S. Levels of processing: A framework for memory research. *Journal of Verbal Learning and Verbal Behavior*, 1972, **11**, 671-684.

Craik, K.J.W. The theory of the human operator in control systems: II. Man as an element in a control system. *British Journal of Psychology*, 1948, **38**, 142-148.

Cratty, B.J. *Movement behavior and motor learning*. Philadelphia: Lea & Febiger, 1964.

Cratty, B.J. A three level theory of perceptual-motor behavior. *Quest*, 1966, **6**, 3-10.

Creamer, L.R. Event uncertainty, psychological refractory period, and human data processing. *Journal of Experimental Psychology*, 1963, **66**, 187-194.

Croll, W.L. Children's discrimination learning as a function of intertrial interval duration. *Psychonomic Science*, 1970, **18**, 321-322.

Cronbach, L.J. The two disciplines of scientific psychology. *American Psychologist*, 1957, **12**, 671-684.

Crossman, E.R.F.W. A theory of the acquisition of speed skill. *Ergonomics*, 1959, **2**, 153-166.

Davis, R. The role of "attention" in the psychological refractory period. *Quarterly Journal of Experimental Psychology*, 1959, **11**, 211-220.

DeGroot, A.D. *Thought and choice in chess*. The Hague: Mouton, 1965.

Denier van der Gon, J.J. & Wadman, W.J. Control of fast ballistic arm movements. *Journal of Physiology*, 1977, **271**, 28-29.

Denier van der Gon, J.J., & Thuring, J. The guiding of human writing movements. *Kybernetik*, 1965, **2**, 145-148.

Denier van der Gon, J.J., Thuring, J.P., & Strackee, J. A handwriting simulator. *Physics in Medicine and Biology*, 1962, **6**, 407-414.

Denny, M.R., Allard, M., Hall, E., & Rokeach, M. Supplementary report: Delay of knowledge of results, knowledge of task, and intertrial interval. *Journal of Experimental Psychology*, 1960, **60**, 327.

Desmedt, J.E., & Godaux, E. Voluntary commands in human ballistic movements. *Annals of Neurology*, 1979, **5**, 415-421.

Deutsch, J.A., & Deutsch, D. Attention: Some theoretical considerations. *Psychological Review*, 1963, **70**, 80-90.

Dewhurst, D.J. Neuromuscular control system. *IEEE Transactions on Biomedical Engineering*, 1967, **14**, 167-171.

Dickinson, J. Incidental motor learning. *Journal of Motor Behavior*, 1977, **9**, 135-138.

Donders, F.C. [On the speed of mental processes.] In W.G. Koster (Ed. & trans.), *Attention and performance II*. Amsterdam: North-Holland, 1969. (Originally published, 1868)

Drazin, D.H. Effects of foreperiod, foreperiod variability, and probability of stimulus occurrence on simple reaction time. *Journal of Experimental Psychology*, 1961, **62**, 43-50.

DuBois, P.H. The design of correlational studies in training. In R. Glaser (Ed.), *Training research and education*. New York: Wiley, 1965.

Duffy, E. *Activation and behavior*. New York: Wiley, 1962.

Dunham, P. Learning and performance. *Research Quarterly*, 1971, **42**, 334-337.

Dunham, P. Distribution of practice as a factor affecting learning and/or performance. *Journal of Motor Behavior*, 1976, **8**, 305-307.

Easterbrook, J.A. The effect of emotion on cue utilization and the organization of behavior. *Psychological Review*, 1959, **66**, 183-201.

Easton, T.A. On the normal use of reflexes. *American Scientist*, 1972, **60**, 591-599.

Easton, T.A. Coordinative structures—The basis for a motor program. In D.M. Landers & R.W. Christina (Eds.), *Psychology of motor behavior and sport*. Champaign, IL: Human Kinetics, 1978.

Eco, U., & Zorzoli, G.B. *The picture history of inventions*. New York: Macmillan, 1963.

Edmonds, E.M., Evans, S.H., & Mueller, M.R. Learning how to learn schemata. *Psychonomic Science*, 1966, **6**, 177-178.

Ellis, H.C. *The transfer of learning*. New York: Macmillan, 1965.

Ells, J.G. Analysis of temporal and attentional aspects of movement control. *Journal of Experimental Psychology*, 1973, **99**, 10-21.

Ericsson, K.A., Chase, W.G., & Faloon, S. Acquisition of a memory skill. *Science*, 1980, **208**, 1181-1182.

Espenschade, A. Motor performance in adolescence including the study of relationships with measures of physical growth and maturity. *Monographs of the Society for Research in Child Development*, 1940, **5**, 1-126.

Estes, W.K. The problem of inference from curves based on group data. *Psychological Bulletin*, 1956, **53**, 134-140.

Evarts, E.V. Contrasts between activity of precentral and postcentral neurons of the cerebral cortex during movement in the monkey. *Brain Research*, 1972, **40**, 25-31.

Evarts, E.V. Motor cortex reflexes associated with learned movement. *Science*, 1973, **179**, 501-503.

Evarts, E.V., & Tanji, J. Gating of motor-cortex reflexes by prior instruction. *Brain Research*, 1974, **71**, 479-494.

Falls, J. *The Boston marathon*. New York: Collier, 1977.

Farina, A.J., Jr., & Wheaton, G.R. Development of a taxonomy of human performance: The task characteristics approach to performance prediction. *American Institutes for Research*, 1970, pp. 726-727 (Technical Report). *See also Catalog of Selected Documents in Psychology,* 1973, **3**, 26-27.)

Farrell, J.E. The classification of physical education skills. *Quest*, 1975, **24**, 63-68 (Monograph XXIV).

Fel'dman, A.G. Functional tuning of the nervous system with control of movement or maintenance of a steady posture. II. Controllable parameters of the muscles. *Biophysics*, 1966, **11**, 565-578. (a)

Fel'dman, A.G. Functional tuning of the nervous system with control of movement or maintenance of a steady posture. III. Mechanographic analysis of the execution by man of the simplest motor tasks. *Biophysics*, 1966, **11**, 667-675. (b)

Fentress, J.C. Development of grooming in mice with amputated forelimbs. *Science*, 1973, **179**, 704-705.

Fenz, W.D., & Jones, G.B. Individual differences in physiologic arousal and performance in sport parachutists. *Psychosomatic Medicine*, 1972, **34**, 1-8.

Ferrier, D. Discussions on cerebral localization. *Transactions of the Congress of American Physicians and Surgeons*, 1888, **1**, 337-340.

Fitch, H.L., Tuller, B., & Turvey, M.T. The Berstein perspective: III. The specification and tuning of coordinative structures. In J.A.S. Kelso (Ed.), *Human motor behavior: An introduction*. Hillsdale, NJ: Erlbaum, 1982.

Fitts, P.M. The information capacity of the human motor system in controlling the amplitude of movement. *Journal of Experimental Psychology*, 1954, **47**, 381-391.

Fitts, P.M. Perceptual-motor skills learning. In A.W. Melton (Ed.), *Categories of human learning*. New York: Academic Press, 1964.

Fitts, P.M., & Peterson, J.R. Information capacity of discrete motor responses. *Journal of Experimental Psychology*, 1964, **67**, 103-112.

Fitts, P.M., & Posner, M.I. *Human performance*. Belmont, CA: Brooks/Cole, 1967.

Fitts, P.M., & Seeger, C.M. S-R compatibility: Spatial characteristics of stimulus and response codes. *Journal of Experimental Psychology*, 1953, **46**, 199-210.

Fleishman, E.A. Psychomotor selection tests: Research and application in the United States Air Force. *Personnel Psychology*, 1956, **9**, 449-467.

Fleishman, E.A. A comparative study of aptitude patterns in unskilled and skilled psychomotor performances. *Journal of Applied Psychology*, 1957, **41**, 263-272.

Fleishman, E.A. A relationship between incentive motivation and ability level in psychomotor performance. *Journal of Experimental Psychology*, 1958, **56**, 78-81.

Fleishman, E.A. *The structure and measurement of physical fitness.* Englewood Cliffs, NJ: Prentice-Hall, 1964.

Fleishman, E.A. The description and prediction of perceptual-motor skill learning. In R. Glaser (Ed.), *Training research and education.* New York: Wiley, 1965.

Fleishman, E.A. Human abilities and the acquisition of skill. Comments on Professor Jones' paper. In E.A. Bilodeau (Ed.), *Acquisition of skill.* New York: Academic Press, 1966.

Fleishman, E.A. Individual differences and motor learning. In R.M. Gagne (Ed.), *Learning and individual differences.* Columbus, OH: Merrill, 1967.

Fleishman, E.A. Toward a taxonomy of human performance. *American Psychologist*, 1975, **30**, 1127-1149.

Fleishman, E.A., & Bartlett, C.J. Human abilities. *Annual Review of Psychology*, 1969, **20**, 349-380.

Fleishman, E.A., & Hempel, W.E. The relation between abilities and improvement with practice in a visual discrimination task. *Journal of Experimental Psychology*, 1955, **49**, 301-312.

Fleishman, E.A., & Hempel, W.E. Factorial analysis of complex psychomotor performance and related skills. *Journal of Applied Psychology*, 1956, **40**, 96-104.

Fleishman, E.A., & Parker, J.F. Factors in the retention and relearning of perceptual motor skill. *Journal of Experimental Psychology*, 1962, **64**, 215-226.

Fleishman, E.A., & Rich, S. Role of kinesthetic and spatial-visual abilities in perceptual motor learning. *Journal of Experimental Psychology*, 1963, **66**, 6-11.

Fleishman, E.A., & Stephenson, R.W. *Development of a taxonomy of human performance: A review of the third year's progress. American Institutes for Research*, 1970, 726-TPR3 (Technical Report). (See also *Catalog of Selected Documents in Psychology*, 1972, **2**, 40-41.)

Forscher, B.K. Chaos in the brickyard. *Science*, 1963, **142**, 339.

Forssberg, H., Grillner, S., & Rossignol, S. Phase dependent reflex reversal during walking in chronic spinal cats. *Brain Research*, 1975, **85**, 103-107.

Frank, J.S. *Spinal motoneuron tuning during anticipation of motor output.* Ph.D. dissertation, University of Southern California, 1980.

Frank, J.S., Williams, I.D., & Hayes, K.C. The ischemic nerve block and skilled movement. *Journal of Motor Behavior*, 1977, **9**, 217-224.

Frey, H.J., & Keeney, C.J. *Elementary gymnastics apparatus skills.* New York: Ronald Press, 1964.

Fritsch, G., & Hitzig, E. Uber die elektrische Errerbarkeit des Grosshirns. *Archiv Anatomie Physiologie*, 1870, **37**, 300-332.

Fuchs, A.H. The progression-regression hypothesis in perceptual-motor skill learning. *Journal of Experimental Psychology*, 1962, **63**, 177-182.

Fukson, O.I., Berkinblit, M.B., & Feldman, A.G. The spinal frog takes into account the scheme of its body during the wiping reflex. *Science*, 1980, **209**, 1261-1263.

Fukuda, T. Studies on human dynamic postures from the viewpoint of postural reflexes. *Acta Oto-Laryngologica*, 1961, **161**, 1-52.

Gallagher, J.D., & Thomas, J.R. Effects of varying post-KR intervals upon children's motor performance. *Journal of Motor Behavior*, 1980, **12**, 41-46.

Gallistel, C.R. *The organization of action*. Hillsdale, NJ: Erlbaum, 1980.

Gelfan, S., & Carter, S. Muscle sense in man. *Experimental Neurology*, 1967, **18**, 469-473.

Gelfand, I.M., Gurfinkel, V.S., Tomin, S.V., & Tsetlin, M.L. *Models of the structural-functional organization of certain biological systems*. Cambridge, MA: MIT Press, 1971.

Gentile, A.M. A working model of skill acquisition with application to teaching. *Quest*, 1972, **17**, 3-23.

Ghez, C., & Vicario, D. The control of limb movement in the cat. II. Scaling of isometric force adjustments. *Experimental Brain Research*, 1978, **33**, 191-202.

Gibson, J.J. *The senses considered as perceptual systems*. Boston: Houghton Mifflin, 1966.

Gill, D.L. The prediction of group motor performance from individual member abilities. *Journal of Motor Behavior*, 1979, **11**, 113-122.

Godwin, M.A., & Schmidt, R.A. Muscular fatigue and learning a discrete motor skill. *Research Quarterly*, 1971, **42**, 374-382.

Goodwin, G.M., McCloskey, D.I., & Matthews, P.B.C. The contribution of muscle afferents to kinesthesia shown by vibration-induced illustrations of movement and by the effects of paralyzing joint afferents. *Brain*, 1972, **95**, 705-748.

Goslow, G.E., Reinking, R.M., & Stuart, D.G. The cat step cycle: Hind limb joint angles and muscle lengths during unrestrained locomotion. *Journal of Morphology*, 1973, **141**, 1-41.

Gottsdanker, R. Uncertainty, timekeeping, and simple reaction time. *Journal of Motor Behavior*, 1970, **2**, 245-260.

Gottsdanker, R. Psychological refractoriness and the organization of step-tracking responses. *Perception & Psychophysics*, 1973, **14**, 60-70.

Granit, R. *The basis of motor control*. New York: Academic Press, 1970.

Graw, H.M.A. *The most efficient usage of a fixed work plus rest practice period in motor learning*. Doctoral dissertation, University of California, 1968.

Greene, P.H. Problems of organization of motor systems. In R. Rosen & F.M. Snell (Eds.), *Progress in theoretical biology* (Vol. 2). New York: Academic Press, 1972.

Greenwald, A.G. Sensory feedback mechanisms in performance control: With special reference to the ideo-motor mechanism. *Psychological Review*, 1970, **77**, 73-99.

Grillner, S. The role of muscle stiffness in meeting the changing postural and locomotor requirements for force development by the ankle extensors. *Acta Physiologica Scandinavica*, 1972, **86**, 92-108.

Grillner, S. Locomotion in vertebrates: Central mechanisms and reflex interaction. *Physiological Reviews*, 1975, **55**, 247-304.

Gullicksen, H. *Theory of mental tests*. New York: Wiley, 1950.

Gurfinkel, V.S., Kots, Y.M., Krinskiy, V.I., Pal'tsev, Y.I., Fel'dman, A.G., Tsetlin, M.L., & Shik, M.L. Concerning the tuning before movement. In I.M. Gelfand, V.S. Gurfinkel, V. Fomin, & M.L. Tsetlin (Eds.), *Models of the structural-functional organization of certain biological systems*. Cambridge, MA: MIT Press, 1971.

Hatze, H. Biomechanical aspects of a successful motion optimization. In P.V. Komi (Ed.), *Biomechanics V-B*. Baltimore: University Park Press, 1976.

Head, H. *Aphasia and kindred disorders of speech*. Cambridge: Cambridge University Press, 1926.

Hellebrandt, F.A., Houtz, S.J., Partridge, M.J., & Walters, C.E. Tonic neck reflexes in exercises of stress in man. *American Journal of Physical Medicine*, 1956, **35**, 144-159.

Hellyer, S. Stimulus-response coding and amount of information as determinants of reaction time. *Journal of Experimental Psychology*, 1963, **65**, 521-522.

Henderson, S.E. *The role of feedback in the development and maintenance of a complex motor skill*. Ph.D. thesis, University of Waterloo, 1974.

Henderson, S.E. Predicting the accuracy of a throw without visual feedback. *Journal of Human Movement Studies*, 1975, **1**, 183-189.

Henry, F.M. Dynamic kinesthetic perception and adjustment. *Research Quarterly*, 1953, **24**, 176-187.

Henry, F.M. Reliability, measurement error, and intra-individual difference. *Research Quarterly*, 1959, **30**, 21-24.

Henry, F.M. Reaction time—movement time correlations. *Perceptual and Motor Skills*, 1961, **12**, 63-66.

Henry, F.M. Specificity vs. generality in learning motor skill. In R.C. Brown & G.S. Kenyon (Eds.), *Classical studies on physical activity*. Englewood Cliffs, NJ: Prentice-Hall, 1968. (Originally published, 1958)

Henry, F.M. Absolute error versus "E" in target accuracy. *Journal of Motor Behavior*, 1975, **7**, 227-228.

Henry, F.M. Use of simple reaction time in motor programming studies: A reply to Klapp, Wyatt, and Lingo. *Journal of Motor Behavior*, 1980, **12**, 163-168.

Henry, F.M., & Harrison, J.S. Refractoriness of a fast movement. *Perceptual and Motor Skills*, 1961, **13**, 351-354.

Henry, F.M., & Rogers, D.E. Increased response latency for complicated movements and a "memory drum" theory of neuromotor reaction. *Research Quarterly*, 1960, **31**, 448-458.

Herrick, C.J. Origins and evolution of the cerebellum. *Archives of Neurology and Psychiatry*, 1924, **11**, 621-652.

Hick, W.E. On the rate of gain of information. *Quarterly Journal of Experimental Psychology*, 1952, **4**, 11-26.

Higgins, J.R., & Angel, R.W. Correction of tracking errors without sensory feedback. *Journal of Experimental Psychology*, 1970, **84**, 412-416.

Ho, L., & Shea, J.B. Effects of relative frequency of knowledge of results on retention of a motor skill. *Perceptual and Motor Skills*, 1978, **46**, 859-866.

Hodgkins, J. Influence of age on the speed of reaction and movement in females. *Journal of Gerontology*, 1962, **17**, 385-389.

Hoffman, P. *Untersuchen uber die Eigenreflexe (sehnreflexe) menschlicher Muskeln*. Berlin: Springer-Verlag, 1922.

Hogan, J.C., & Yanowitz, B.A. The role of verbal estimates of movement error in ballistic skill acquisition. *Journal of Motor Behavior*, 1978, **10**, 133-138.

Holding, D.H. *Principles of training*. Oxford: Pergamon Press, 1965.

Holding, D.H. Learning without errors. In L.E. Smith (Ed.), *Psychology of motor learning*. Chicago: Athletic Institute, 1970.

Holding, D.H. An approximate transfer surface. *Journal of Motor Behavior*, 1976, **8**, 1-9.

Holding, D.H., & Macrae, A.W. Guidance, restriction, and knowledge of results. *Ergonomics*, 1964, **7**, 289-295.

Hollerbach, J.M. *A study of human motor control through analysis and systhesis of handwriting*. Ph.D. dissertation, Massachusetts Institute of Technology, 1978.

Hollerbach, J.M. An oscillation theory of handwriting. *Biological Cybernetics*, 1981, **39**, 139-156.

Hollingworth, H.L. The inaccuracy of movement. *Archives of Psychology*, 1909, **13**, 1-87.

Holmes, G. The cerebellum of man. *Brain*, 1939, **62**, 1-30.

Houk, J.C. Regulation of stiffness by skeletomotor reflexes. *Annual Review of Physiology*, 1979, **41**, 99-114.

Houk, J.C., & Henneman, E. Responses of Golgi tendon organs to active contractions of the soleus muscle of the cat. *Journal of Neurophysiology*, 1967, **30**, 466-481.

Howarth, C.I., Beggs, W.D.A., & Bowden, J.M. The relationship between speed and accuracy of a movement aimed at a target. *Acta Psychologica*, 1971, **35**, 207-218.

Howell, M.L. Use of force-time graphs for performance analysis in facilitating motor learning. *Research Quarterly*, 1956, **27**, 12-22.

Hubbard, A.W. Homokinetics: Muscular function in human movement. In W.R. Johnson (Ed.), *Science and medicine of exercise and sports*. New York: Harper and Brothers, 1960.

Hubbard, A. W., & Seng, C.N. Visual movements of batters. *Research Quarterly*, 1954, **25**, 42-57.

Hull, C.L. *Principles of behavior*. New York: Appleton-Century-Crofts, 1943.

Huxley, H.E. The mechanism of muscular contraction. *Scientific American*, 1965, **213**, 18-27.

Hyman, R. Stimulus information as a determinant of reaction time. *Journal of Experimental Psychology*, 1953, **45**, 188-196.

Ikai, M., & Steinhaus, A.H. Some factors modifying the expression of human strength. *Journal of Applied Physiology*, 1961, **16**, 157-163.

Irion, A.L. The relation of set to retention. *Psychological Review*, 1948, **55**, 336-341.

Ismail, A., Kephart, N., & Cowell, C.C. *Utilization of motor aptitude tests in predicting academic achievement*. Technical Report No. 1, Purdue University Research Foundation, 1963. (P.U. 879-64-838)

Jagacinski, R.J., Hartzell, E.J., Ward, S., & Bishop, K. Fitts' law as a function of system dynamics and target uncertainty. *Journal of Motor Behavior*, 1978, **10**, 123-131.

James, W. *The principles of psychology* (Vol. 1). New York: Holt, 1890.

Jeeves, M.A. Changes in performance at a serial reaction task under conditions of advance and delay of information. *Ergonomics*, 1961, **4**, 329-338.

Jensen, A.R. The heritability of intelligence. *Engineering and Science*, 1970, **33**, 1-4.

Jensen, A.R. The current status of the IQ controversy. *Australian Psychologist*, 1978, **13**, 7-27.

Jones, M.B. Practice as a process of simplification. *Psychological Review*, 1962, **69**, 274-294.

Jones, M.B. Individual differences. In E.A. Bilodeau (Ed.), *Acquisition of skill*. New York: Academic Press, 1966.

Jones, M.B. Sequential precession and diminishing returns in the acquisition of a motor skill. *Journal of Motor Behavior*, 1980, **12**, 69-73.

Judd, C.H. The relation of special training to general intelligence. *Educational Review*, 1908, **36**, 28-42.

Kahneman, D. *Attention and effort*. Englewood Cliffs, NJ: Prentice-Hall, 1973.

Keele, S.W. Movement control in skilled motor performance. *Psychological Bulletin*, 1968, **70**, 387-403.

Keele, S.W. Attention demands of memory retrieval. *Journal of Experimental Psychology*, 1972, **93**, 245-248.

Keele, S.W. *Attention and human performance*. Pacific Palisades, CA: Goodyear, 1973.

Keele, S.W. Behavioral analysis of motor control. In V. Brooks (Ed.), *Handbook of physiology: Motor control*. In press.

Keele, S.W., & Ells, J.G. Memory characteristics of kinesthetic information. *Journal of Motor Behavior*, 1972, **4**, 127-134.

Keele, S.W., & Posner, M.I. Processing of visual feedback in rapid movements. *Journal of Experimental Psychology*, 1968, **77**, 155-158.

Keele, S.W., & Summers, J.J. The structure of motor programs. In G.E. Stelmach (Ed.), *Motor control: Issues and trends*. New York: Academic Press, 1976.

Kelso, J.A.S. Motor control mechanisms underlying human movement production. *Journal of Experimental Psychology: Human Perception and Performance*, 1977, **3**, 529-543.

Kelso, J.A.S., & Holt, K.G. Exploring a vibratory systems analysis of human movement production. *Journal of Neurophysiology*, 1980, **43**, 1183-1196.

Kelso, J.A.S., Holt, K.G., & Flatt, A.E. The role of proprioception in the perception and control of human movement: Toward a theoretical reassessment. *Perception & Psychophysics*, 1980, **28**, 45-52. (a)

Kelso, J.A.S., Holt, K.G., Kugler, P.N., & Turvey, M.T. On the concept of coordinative structures as dissipative structures: II. Empirical lines of convergency. In G.E. Stelmach & J. Requin (Eds.), *Tutorials in motor behavior*. Amsterdam: North-Holland, 1980. (b)

Kelso, J.A.S., Southard, D.L., & Goodman, D. On the nature of human interlimb coordination. *Science*, 1979, **203**, 1029-1031.

Kelso, J.A.S., & Stelmach, G.E. Central and peripheral mechanisms in motor control. In G.E. Stelmach (Ed.), *Motor control: Issues and trends*. New York: Academic Press, 1976.

Kelso, J.A.S., Stelmach, G.E., & Wannamaker, W.M. The continuing saga of the nerve compression block technique. *Journal of Motor Behavior*, 1976, **8**, 155-160.

Kerlinger, F.N. *Foundations of behavioral research* (2nd ed.). New York: Holt, Rinehart, and Winston, 1973.

Kerr, B. Processing demands during mental operations. *Memory & Cognition*, 1973, **1**, 401-412.

Kerr, B. Processing demands during movement. *Journal of Motor Behavior*, 1975, **7**, 15-27.

Kerr, B. Task factors that influence selection and preparation for voluntary movements. In G.E. Stelmach (Ed.), *Information processing in motor control and learning*. New York: Academic Press, 1978.

Kerr, R., & Booth, B. Skill acquisition in elementary school children and schema theory. In D.M. Landers & R.W. Christina (Eds.), *Psychology of motor behavior and sport* (Vol. 2). Champaign, IL: Human Kinetics, 1977.

Kerr, R., & Booth, B. Specific and varied practice of motor skill. *Perceptual and Motor Skills*, 1978, **46**, 395-401.

Klapp, S.T. Short-term memory as a response-preparation state. *Memory & Cognition*, 1976, **4**, 721-729.

Klapp, S.T. Reaction time analysis of programmed control. *Exercise and Sport Sciences Reviews*, 1977, **5**, 231-253. (a)

Klapp, S.T. Response programming, as assessed by reaction time, does not establish commands for particular muscles. *Journal of Motor Behavior*, 1977, **9**, 301-312. (b)

Klapp, S.T. The memory drum theory after twenty years: Comments on Henry's note. *Journal of Motor Behavior*, 1980, **12**, 169-171.

Klapp, S.T., & Erwin, C.I. Relation between programming time and duration of the response being programmed. *Journal of Experimental Psychology: Human Perception and Performance*, 1976, **2**, 591-598.

Klapp, S.T., & Wyatt, E.P. Motor programming within a sequence of responses. *Journal of Motor Behavior*, 1976, **8**, 19-26.

Klein, R. Attention and movement. In G.E. Stelmach (Ed.), *Motor control: Issues and trends*. New York: Academic Press, 1976.

Klemmer, E.T. Time uncertainty in simple reaction time. *Journal of Experimental Psychology*, 1956, **51**, 179-184.

Knight, A.A., & Dagnall, P.R. Precision in movements. *Ergonomics*, 1967, **10**, 321-330.

Kots, Y.M. Supraspinal control of the segmental centres of muscle antagonists in man: I. Reflex excitability of the motor neurones of muscle antagonists in the period of organization of voluntary movement. *Biophysics*, 1969, **14**, 176-183.

Kots, Y.M. *The organization of voluntary movement: Neurophysiological mechanisms*. New York: Plenum, 1977.

Kots, Y.M., & Zhukov, V.I. Supra-spinal control of the segmental centres of muscle antagonists in man: III. "Tuning" of the spinal apparatus of reciprocal inhibition in the period of organization of voluntary movement. *Biophysics*, 1971, **16**, 1129-1136.

Kugler, P.N., Kelso, J.A.S., & Turvey, M.T. On the concept of coordinative structures as dissipative structures: I. Theoretical line. In G.E. Stelmach & J. Requin (Eds.), *Tutorials in motor behavior*. Amsterdam: North-Holland, 1980.

Kupferman, I., & Weiss, K.R. The command neuron concept. *The Behavioral and Brain Sciences*, 1978, **1**, 3-10.

Laabs, G.J. Retention characteristics of different reproduction cues in motor short-term memory. *Journal of Experimental Psychology*, 1973, **100**, 168-177.

Laabs, G.J., & Simmons, R.W. Motor memory. In D.H. Holding (Ed.), *Human skills*. Chichester, England: Wiley, 1981.

Laban, R. *Principles of dance and movement notation*. London: MacDonald and Evans, 1956.

LaBerge, D. Indentification of two components of the time to switch attention: A test of a serial and a parallel model of attention. In S. Kornblum (Ed.), *Attention and performance IV*. New York: Academic Press, 1973.

Lachman, R. The model in theory construction. *Psychological Review*, 1960, **67**, 113-129.

Landers, D.M. Observational learning of a motor skill: Temporal spacing of demonstrations and audience presence. *Journal of Motor Behavior*, 1975, **7**, 281-287.

Landers, D.M. Motivation and performance: The role of arousal and attentional factors. In W.F. Straub (Ed.), *Sport psychology: An analysis of athlete behavior*. Ithaca, NY: Mouvement Publications, 1978.

Landers, D.M. The arousal-performance relationship revisited. *Research Quarterly for Exercise and Sport*, 1980, **51**, 77-90.

Landers, D.M., & Landers, D.M. Teacher versus peer models: Effect of model's presence and performance level on motor behavior. *Journal of Motor Behavior*, 1973, **5**, 129-139.

Langolf, G.D., Chaffin, D.B., & Foulke, J.A. An investigation of Fitts' law using a wide range of movement amplitudes. *Journal of Motor Behavior*, 1976, **8**, 113-128.

Lashley, K.S. The accuracy of movement in the absence of excitation from the moving organ. *The American Journal of Physiology*, 1917, **43**, 169-194.

Lashley, K.S. The problem of serial order in behavior. In L.A. Jeffress (Ed.), *Cerebral mechanisms in behavior: The Hixon Symposium*. New York: Wiley, 1951.

Laszlo, J.I. Training of fast tapping with reduction of kinaesthetic, tactile, visual, and auditory sensations. *Quarterly Journal of Experimental Psychology*, 1967, **19**, 344-349.

Laszlo, J.I., & Bairstow, P.J. The compression-block technique: A reply to Chambers and Schumsky (1978). *Journal of Motor Behavior*, 1979, **11**, 283-284.

Laszlo, J.I., Bairstow, P.J., Ward, G.R., & Bancroft, H. Distracting information, motor performance, and sex differences. *Nature*, 1980, **283**, 377-378.

Lavery, J.J. Retention of simple motor skills as a function of type of knowledge of results. *Canadian Journal of Psychology*, 1962, **16**, 300-311.

Lavery, J.J., & Suddon, F.H. Retention of simple motor skills as a function of the number of trials by which KR is delayed. *Perceptual and Motor Skills*, 1962, **15**, 231-237.

Lawther, J.D. *The learning of physical skills*. Englewood Cliffs, NJ: Prentice-Hall, 1968.

Lee, D.N. Visuo-motor coordination in space-time. In G.E. Stelmach & J. Requin (Eds.), *Tutorials in motor behavior*. Amsterdam: North-Holland, 1980.

Lee, D.N., & Aronson, E. Visual proprioceptive control of standing in human infants. *Perception & Psychophysics*, 1974, **15**, 527-532.

Lee, T.D., & Gallagher, J.D. A parallel between the preselection effect in psychomotor memory and the generation effect in verbal memory. *Journal of Experimental Psychology: Human Learning and Memory*, 1981, **7**, 77-78.

Lee, W.A. Anticipatory control of postural and task muscles during rapid arm flexion. *Journal of Motor Behavior*, 1980, **12**, 185-196.

Leonard, J.A. Advance information in sensorimotor skills. *Quarterly Journal of Experimental Psychology*, 1953, **5**, 141-149.

Leonard, J.A. An experiment with occasional false information. *Quarterly Journal of Experimental Psychology*, 1954, **6**, 79-85.

Leonard, J.A. Tactual choice reactions: I. *Quarterly Journal of Experimental Psychology*, 1959, **11**, 76-83.

Lersten, K.C. Transfer of movement components in a motor learning task. *Research Quarterly*, 1968, **39**, 575-581.

Lersten, K.C. Retention of skill on the Rho apparatus after one year. *Research Quarterly*, 1969, **40**, 418-419.

Leuba, J.H. The influence of the duration and of the rate of arm movements upon the judgment of their length. *American Journal of Psychology*, 1909, **20**, 374-385.

Lewis, D. Positive and negative transfer in motor learning. *American Psychologist*, 1947, **2**, 423.

Lewis, D., McAllister, D.E., & Adams, J.A. Facilitation and interference in performance on the modified Mashburn apparatus: I. The effects of varying the amount of original learning. *Journal of Experimental Psychology*, 1951, **41**, 247-260.

Lindeburg, F.A. A study of the degree of transfer between quickening exercises and other coordinated movements. *Research Quarterly*, 1949, **20**, 180-195.

Locke, E.A. & Bryan, J.F. Cognitive aspects of psychomotor performance: The effects of performance goals on level of performance. *Journal of Applied Psychology*, 1966, **50**, 286-291.

Locke, E.A., Cartledge, N., & Koeppel, J. Motivational effects of knowledge of results: A goal-setting phenomenon. *Psychological Bulletin*, 1968, **70**, 474-485.

Lordahl, D.S., & Archer, E.J. Transfer effects on a rotary pursuit task as a function of first-task difficulty. *Journal of Experimental Psychology*, 1958, **56**, 421-426.

Lorenz, K. *Evolution and modification of behavior*. Chicago: University of Chicago Press, 1965.

Lorge, I., & Thorndike, E.L. The influence of delay in the after-effect of a connection. *Journal of Experimental Psychology*, 1935, **18**, 186-194.

Lotter, W.S. Interrelationships among reaction times and speeds of movement in different limbs. *Research Quarterly*, 1960, **31**, 147-155.

Macrae, A.W., & Holding, D.H. Method and task in motor guidance. *Ergonomics*, 1965, **8**, 315-320.

Macrae, A.W., & Holding, D.H. Transfer of training after guidance or practice. *The Quarterly Journal of Experimental Psychology*, 1966, **18**, 327-333.

Magill, R.A. The post-KR interval: Time and activity effects and the relationship of motor short-term memory theory. *Journal of Motor Behavior*, 1973, **5**, 49-56.

Marsden, C.D., Merton, P.A., & Morton, H.B. Servo action in human voluntary movement. *Nature*, 1972, **238**, 140-143.

Marteniuk, R.G. Retention characteristics of motor short-term memory cues. *Journal of Motor Behavior*, 1973, **5**, 249-259.

Marteniuk, R.G. *Information processing in motor skills*. New York: Holt, Rinehart, and Winston, 1976.

Marteniuk, R.G., & MacKenzie, C.L. A preliminary theory of two-hand coordinated control. In G.E. Stelmach & J. Requin (Eds.), *Tutorials in motor behavior*. Amsterdam: North-Holland, 1980.

Martens, R. Anxiety and motor behavior: A review. *Journal of Motor Behavior*, 1971, **3**, 151-180.

Martens, R. Arousal and motor performance. *Exercise and Sport Sciences Reviews*, 1974, **2**, 155-188.

Martens, R. *Social psychology and physical activity*. New York: Harper and Row, 1975.

Martens, R., & Landers, D.M. Effect of anxiety, competition and failure on performance of a complex motor task. *Journal of Motor Behavior*, 1969, **1**, 1-9.

Martens, R., & Landers, D.M. Motor performance under stress: A test of the inverted-U hypothesis. *Journal of Personality and Social Psychology*, 1970, **16**, 29-37.

Martin, H.A. *Long-term retention of a discrete motor task*. M.A. thesis, University of Maryland, 1970.

Matthews, P.B.C. Muscle spindles and their motor control. *Physiological Reviews*, 1964, **44**, 219-288.

Mays, L.E., & Sparks, D.L. Saccades are spatially, not retinocentrically, coded. *Science*, 1980, **208**, 1163-1165.

McAllister, D.E., & Lewis, D. Facilitation and interference in performance on the modified mashburn apparatus: II. The effects of varying the amount of interpolated learning. *Journal of Experimental Psychology*, 1951, **41**, 356-363.

McCloy, C.H. The measurement of general motor capacity and general motor ability. *Research Quarterly*, 1934, **5**, (Supplement 5), 46-61.

McCloy, C.H. An analytical study of the stunt type test as a measure of motor educability. *Research Quarterly*, 1937, **8**, 46-55.

McCracken, H.D., & Stelmach, G.E. A test of the schema theory of discrete motor learning. *Journal of Motor Behavior*, 1977, **9**, 193-201.

McGraw, M.B. *Growth: A study of Johnny and Jimmy.* New York: Appleton-Century, 1935.

McGraw, M.B. Later development of children specially trained during infancy: Johnny and Jimmy at school age. *Child Development*, 1939, **10**, 1-19.

McLeod, P. A dual task response modality effect: Support for multi-processor models of attention. *Quarterly Journal of Experimental Psychology*, 1977, **29**, 651-668.

McLeod, P. Does probe RT measure central processing demand? *Quarterly Journal of Experimental Psychology*, 1978, **30**, 83-89.

McLeod, P. What can RT tell us about the attentional demands of movement? In G.E. Stelmach & J. Requin (Eds.), *Tutorials in motor behavior.* Amsterdam: North-Holland, 1980.

Megaw, E.D. Directional errors and their correction in a discrete tracking task. *Ergonomics*, 1972, **15**, 633-643.

Melton, A.W. (Ed.). *Apparatus tests.* Washington, DC: United States Government Printing Office, 1947.

Merkel, J. Die zeitlichen verhaltnisse der sillensthatig-keit. *Philosophische Studien*, 1885, **2**, 73-127. (Cited in Woodworth, R.S. *Experimental psychology.* New York: Holt, 1938)

Merton, P.A. Speculations on the servo control of movement. In G.E.W. Wolstenholme (Ed.), *The spinal cord.* London: Churchill, 1953.

Merton, P.A. How we control the contraction of our muscles. *Scientific American*, 1972, **226**, 30-37.

Meyers, J. Retention of balance coordination learning as influenced by extended lay-offs. *Research Quarterly*, 1967, **38**, 72-78.

Michon, J.A. Tapping regularity as a measure of perceptual motor load. *Ergonomics*, 1966, **9**, 401-412.

Michon, J.A. *Timing in temporal tracking.* Soesterberg, The Netherlands: Institute for Perception, RNO-TNO, 1967.

Miles, F.A., & Evarts, E.V. Concepts of motor organization. *Annual Review of Psychology*, 1979, **30**, 327-362.

Miller, G.A. The magical number seven, plus or minus two: Some limits on our capacity for processing information. *Psychological Review*, 1956, **63**, 81-97.

Milone, F. *Interference in motor short-term memory.* M.A. thesis, Penn State University, 1971.

Minas, S.C. Mental practice of a complex perceptual motor skill. *Journal of Human Movement Studies*, 1978, **4**, 102-107.

Minas, S.C. Acquisition of a motor skill following guided mental and physical practice. *Journal of Human Movement Studies*, 1980, **6**, 127-141.

Moray, N. *Attention: Selective processes in vision and hearing.* New York: Academic Press, 1970.

Morgan, C.T., & King, R.A. *Introduction to psychology* (4th ed.). New York: McGraw-Hill, 1971.

Mowbray, G.H., & Rhoades, M.U. On the reduction of choice reaction-times with practice. *Quarterly Journal of Experimental Psychology*, 1959, **11**, 16-23.

Mowrer, O.H. Preparatory set (expectancy): Some methods of measurement. *Psychological Monographs*, 1940, **52**, No. 233.

Näätänen, R. The inverted U relationship between activation and performance: A critical review. In S. Kornblum (Ed.), *Attention and performance* IV. New York: Academic Press, 1973.

Nacson, J., & Schmidt, R.A. The activity-set hypothesis for warm-up decrement. *Journal of Motor Behavior*, 1971, **3**, 1-15.

Namikas, G., & Archer, S.E. Motor skill transfer as a function of intertask interval and pre-transfer task difficulty. *Journal of Experimental Psychology*, 1960, **59**, 109-112.

Nashner, L.M., & Woollacott, M. The organization of rapid postural adjustments of standing humans: An experimental-conceptual model. In R.E. Talbott & D.R. Humphrey (Eds.), *Posture and movement*. New York: Raven, 1979.

Navon, D., & Gopher, D. On the economy of the human processing system. *Psychological Review*, 1979, **86**, 214-255.

Neisser, U. *Cognitive psychology*. New York: Appleton-Century-Crofts, 1967.

Nelson, J.K. *An analysis of the effects of applying various motivation situations to college men subjected to a stressful physical performance*. Ph.D. dissertation, University of Oregon, 1962.

Neumann, E., & Ammons, R.B. Acquisition and long term retention of a simple serial perception motor skill. *Journal of Experimental Psychology*, 1957, **53**, 159-161.

Newell, K.M. Knowledge of results and motor learning. *Journal of Motor Behavior*, 1974, **6**, 235-244.

Newell, K.M. Motor learning without knowledge of results through the development of a response recognition mechanism. *Journal of Motor Behavior*, 1976, **8**, 209-217.

Newell, K.M. The speed-accuracy paradox in movement control: Error of time and space. In G.E. Stelmach (Ed.), *Tutorials in motor behavior*. Amsterdam: North-Holland, 1980.

Newell, K.M. Skill learning. In D.H. Holding (Ed.), *Human skills*. New York: Wiley, in press.

Newell, K.M., Carlton, L.G., Carlton, M.J., & Halbert, J.A. Velocity as a factor in movement timing accuracy. *Journal of Motor Behavior*, 1980, **12**, 47-56.

Newell, K.M., Carlton, L.G., & Carlton, M.J. The relationship of impulse to timing error. *Journal of Motor Behavior*, in press.

Newell, K.M., Hoshizaki, L.E.F., Carlton, M.J., & Halbert, J.A. Movement time and velocity as determinants of movement timing accuracy. *Journal of Motor Behavior*, 1979, **11**, 49-58.

Newell, K.M., & Kennedy, J.A. Knowledge of results and children's motor learning. *Developmental Psychology*, 1978, **14**, 531-536.

Nichols, T.R., & Houk, J.C. The improvement of linearity and the regulation of stiffness that results from the actions of the stretch reflex. *Journal of Neurophysiology*, 1976, **39**, 119-142.

Nideffer, R.M. *The inner athlete: Mind plus muscle for winning.* New York: Crowell, 1976.

Noble, C.E. Age, race, and sex in the learning and performance of psychomotor skills. In R.T. Osborne, C.E. Noble, & N. Weyl (Eds.), *Human variation: The biopsychology of age, race, and sex.* New York: Academic Press, 1978.

Noble, M., & Trumbo, D. The organization of skilled response. *Organizational Behavior and Human Performance*, 1967, **2**, 1-25.

Norman, D.A. Memory while shadowing. *Quarterly Journal of Experimental Psychology*, 1969, **21**, 85-93.

Norman, D.A. *Memory and attention* (2nd ed.). New York: Wiley, 1976.

Norman, D.A., & Bobrow, D.G. On data-limited and resource-limited processes. *Cognitive Psychology*, 1975, **7**, 44-64.

Nottebohm, F. Ontogeny of bird song. *Science*, 1970, **167**, 950-956.

O'Brian, F. *Force and time variability as predictors of the variability in the endpoint of an aiming movement.* M.A. thesis, University of Southern California, 1979.

Osborne, R.T., Noble, C.E., & Weyl, N. *Human variation: The biopsychology of age, race, and sex.* New York: Academic Press, 1978.

Osgood, C.E. The similarity paradox in human learning: A resolution. *Psychological Review*, 1949, **56**, 132-143.

Paillard, J., & Bruchon, M. Active and passive movements in the calibration of position sense. In S.J. Freedman (Ed.), *The neuropsychology of spatially oriented behavior.* New York: Dorsey, 1968.

Parker, J.F., & Fleishman, E.A. Ability factors and component performance measures as predictors of complex tracking behavior. *Psychological Monographs*, 1960, **74** (Whole No. 503).

Partridge, L.D. Muscle properties: A problem for the motor physiologist. In R.E. Talbot & D.R. Humphrey (Eds.), *Posture and movement.* New York: Raven, 1979.

Patrick, J. The effect of interpolated motor activities in short-term motor memory. *Journal of Motor Behavior*, 1971, **3**, 39-48.

Penfield, W. *The excitable cortex in conscious man.* Springfield, IL: Thomas, 1958.

Pepper, R.L., & Herman, L.M. Decay and interference effects in the short-term retention of a discrete motor act. *Journal of Experimental Psychology*, 1970, **83** (Monograph Supplement 2).

Peterson, L.R., & Peterson, M.J. Short-term retention of individual verbal items. *Journal of Experimental Psychology*, 1959, **58**, 193-198.

Pew, R.W. Acquisition of hierarchical control over the temporal organization of a skill. *Journal of Experimental Psychology*, 1966, **71**, 764-771.

Pew, R.W. Toward a process-oriented theory of human skilled performance. *Journal of Motor Behavior*, 1970, **2**, 8-24.

Pew, R.W. Human perceptual-motor performance. In B.H. Kantowitz (Ed.), *Human information processing: Tutorials in performance and cognition.* New York: Erlbaum, 1974.

Philippson, M. L'autonomie et la centralisation dans le system animaux. *Trav. Lab. Physiol. Inst. Solvay (Bruxelles)*, 1905, **7**, 1-208.

Plagenhoef, S. *Patterns of human motion: A cinematographic analysis.* Englewood Cliffs, NJ: Prentice-Hall, 1971.

Platt, J.R. Strong inference. *Science*, 1964, **146**, 347-353.

Polanyi, M. *Personal knowledge: Towards a post-critical philosophy.* London: Routledge and Kegan Paul, 1958.

Polit, A., & Bizzi, E. Processes controlling arm movements in monkeys. *Science*, 1978, **201**, 1235-1237.

Polit, A., & Bizzi, E. Characteristics of motor programs underlying arm movements in monkeys. *Journal of Neurophysiology*, 1979, **42**, 183-194.

Polya, G. *Mathematics and plausible reasoning.* Princeton, NJ: Princeton University Press, 1954.

Posner, M.I. Reduced attention and the performance of "automated" movements. *Journal of Motor Behavior*, 1969, **1**, 245-258.

Posner, M.I. *Cognition: An introduction.* Glenview, IL: Scott, Foresman, 1973.

Posner, M.I. *Chronometric explorations of mind.* Hillsdale, NJ: Erlbaum, 1978.

Posner, M.I., & Keele, S.W. On the genesis of abstract ideas. *Journal of Experimental Psychology*, 1968, **77**, 353-363.

Posner, M.I., & Keele, S.W. Attentional demands of movement. *Proceedings of the 16th Congress of Applied Psychology.* Amsterdam: Swets and Zeittinger, 1969.

Posner, M.I., & Keele, S.W. Retention of abstract ideas. *Journal of Experimental Psychology*, 1970, **83**, 304-308.

Posner, M.I., & Konick, A.E. On the role of interference in short-term retention. *Journal of Experimental Psychology*, 1966, **72**, 221-231.

Posner, M.I., Nissen, M.J., & Ogden, W.C. Attended and unattended processing modes: The role of set for spatial location. In H.L. Pick & I.J. Saltzman (Eds.), *Modes of perceiving and processing information.* Hillsdale, NJ: Erlbaum, 1978.

Posner, M.I., & Snyder, C.R. Attention and cognitive control. In R.L. Solso (Ed.), *Information processing and cognition.* Hillsdale, NJ: Erlbaum, 1975.

Poulton, E.C. Perceptual anticipation and reaction time. *Quarterly Journal of Experimental Psychology*, 1950, **2**, 99-112.

Poulton, E.C. On prediction in skilled movements. *Psychological Bulletin*, 1957, **54**, 467-478.

Poulton, E.C. *Tracking skill and manual control.* New York: Academic Press, 1974.

Provins, K.A. The effect of peripheral nerve block in the appreciation and execution of finger movements. *Journal of Physiology*, 1958, **143**, 55-61.

Quesada, D.C., & Schmidt, R.A. A test of the Adams-Creamer decay hypothesis for the timing of motor responses. *Journal of Motor Behavior*, 1970, **2**, 273-283.

Quinn, J.T., Jr., Schmidt, R.A., Zelaznik, H.N., Hawkins, B., & McFarquhar, R. Target-size influences on reaction time with movement time controlled. *Journal of Motor Behavior*, 1980, **12**, 239-261.

Rabbitt, P. Time to detect errors as a function of factors affecting choice-response time. *Acta Psychologica*, 1967, **27**, 131-142.

Rack, P.M.H., & Westbury, D.R. The effects of length and stimulus rate on tension in the isometric cat soleus muscle. *Journal of Physiology*, 1969, **204**, 443-460.

Raibert, M.H. *Motor control and learning by the state-space model.* Technical Report, Artificial Intelligence Laboratory, MIT, 1977, (A I - T R - 4 3 9).

Rawlings, E.I., Rawlings, I.L., Chen, C.S., & Yilk, M.D. The facilitating effects of mental rehearsal in the acquisition of rotary pursuit tracking. *Psychonomic Science*, 1972, **26**, 71-73.

Reynolds, B., & Adams, J.A. Effect of distribution and shift in distribution of practice within a single training session. *Journal of Experimental Psychology*, 1953, **46**, 137-145.

Richardson, A. Mental practice: A review and discussion I. *Research Quarterly*, 1967, **38**, 95-107. (a)

Richardson, A. Mental practice: A review and discussion II. *Research Quarterly*, 1967, **38**, 263-273. (b)

Roethlisberger, F.J., & Dickson, W.J. *Management and the worker.* Cambridge, MA: Harvard University Press, 1939.

Rogers, C.A., Jr. Feedback precision and postfeedback interval duration. *Journal of Experimental Psychology*, 1974, **102**, 604-608.

Rosenbaum, D.A. Human movement initiation: Specification of arm, direction, and extent. *Journal of Experimental Psychology: General*, 1980, **109**, 444-474.

Rosenbaum, D.A., & Patashnik, O. Time to time in the human motor system. In R.S. Nickerson (Ed.), *Attention and performance VIII.* Hillsdale, NJ: Erlbaum, 1980.

Rosenthal, R. *Experimenter effects in behavioral research.* New York: Appleton-Century-Crofts, 1966.

Ross, I.D. *Interference in discrete motor tasks: A test of the theory.* Ph.D. dissertation, University of Michigan, 1974.

Rothstein, A.L. Effect of temporal expectancy of the position of a selected foreperiod within a range. *Research Quarterly*, 1973, **44**, 132-139.

Rothstein, A.L., & Arnold, R.K. Bridging the gap: Application of research on videotape feedback and bowling. *Motor Skills: Theory into Practice*, 1976, **1**, 35-62.

Rushall, B.S., & Siedentop, D. *The development and control of behavior in sport and physical education.* Philadelphia: Lea & Febiger, 1972.

Ryan, E.D. Retention of stabilometer and pursuit rotor skills. *Research Quarterly*, 1962, **33**, 593-598.

Ryan, E.D. Relative academic achievement and stabilometer performance. *Research Quarterly*, 1963, **34**, 185-190.

Ryan, E.D. Retention of stabilometer performance over extended periods of time. *Research Quarterly*, 1965, **36**, 46-51.

Sage, G.H. *Introduction to motor-behavior: A neurophysiological approach.* Reading, MA: Addison-Wesley, 1977.

Salmoni, A.W., Sullivan, S.J., & Starkes, J.L. The attention demands of movements: A critique of the probe technique. *Journal of Motor Be-*

havior, 1976, **8**, 161-169.

Sanderson, S. Intention in motor learning. *Journal of Experimental Psychology*, 1929, **12**, 463-489.

Scanlan, T.K., & Passer, M.W. Factors related to competitive stress among male youth sports participants. *Medicine and Science in Sports*, 1978, **10**, 103-108.

Schendel, J.D., & Newell, K.M. On processing the information from knowledge of results. *Journal of Motor Behavior*, 1976, **8**, 251-255.

Schleidt, W. Uber die auslosung der flucht vor raubvogeln bei truthahn. *Naturwissenschaften*, 1961, **48**, 141-142. (Cited in Marler, P., & Hamilton, W.J., III, *Mechanisms of animal behavior*. New York: Wiley, 1966)

Schmidt, R.A. *Motor factors in coincident timing*. Ph.D. thesis, University of Illinois, 1967.

Schmidt, R.A. Anticipation and timing in human motor performance. *Psychological Bulletin*, 1968, **70**, 631-646.

Schmidt, R.A. Intra-limb specificity of motor response consistency. *Journal of Motor Behavior*, 1969, **1**, 89-99. (a)

Schmidt, R.A. Consistency of response components as a function of selected motor variables. *Research Quarterly*, 1969, **40**, 561-566. (b)

Schmidt, R.A. Movement time as a determiner of timing accuracy. *Journal of Experimental Psychology*, 1969, **79**, 43-47. (c)

Schmidt, R.A. Retroactive interference and amount of original learning in verbal and motor tasks. *Research Quarterly*, 1971, **42**, 314-326. (a)

Schmidt, R.A. Proprioception and the timing of motor responses. *Psychological Bulletin*, 1971, **76**, 383-393. (b)

Schmidt, R.A. The case against learning and forgetting scores. *Journal of Motor Behavior*, 1972, **4**, 79-88. (a)

Schmidt, R.A. Experimental psychology. In R.N. Singer (Ed.), *The psychomotor domain: Movement behavior*. Philadelphia: Lea and Febiger, 1972. (b)

Schmidt, R.A. The index of preprogramming (IP): A statistical method for evaluating the role of feedback in simple movements. *Psychonomic Science*, 1972, **27**, 83-85. (c)

Schmidt, R.A. *Motor skills*. New York: Harper and Row, 1975. (a)

Schmidt, R.A. A schema theory of discrete motor skill learning. *Psychological Review*, 1975, **82**, 225-260. (b)

Schmidt, R.A. Control processes in motor skills. *Exercise and Sport Sciences Reviews*, 1976, **4**, 229-261. (a)

Schmidt, R.A. Movement education and the schema theory. In E. Crawford (Ed.), *Report of the 1976 Conference June 3-8*. Cedar Falls, IA: National Association for Physical Education of College Women, 1976. (b)

Schmidt, R.A. Schema theory: Implications for movement education. *Motor Skills: Theory into Practice*, 1977, **2**, 36-38.

Schmidt, R.A. Past and future issues in motor programming. *Research Quarterly for Exercise and Sport*, 1980, **51**, 122-140.

Schmidt, R.A. More on motor programs. In J.A.S. Kelso (Ed.), *Human motor behavior: An introduction*. Hillsdale, NJ: Erlbaum, 1982.

Schmidt, R.A. The schema concept. In J.A.S. Kelso (Ed.), *Human motor behavior: An introduction*. Hillsdale, NJ: Erlbaum, 1982.

Schmidt, R.A., Christenson, R., & Rogers, P. Some evidence for the independence of recall and recognition in motor behavior. In D.M. Landers, D.V. Harris, & R.W. Christina, (Eds.), *Psychology of motor behavior and sport II*. State College, PA: Penn State HPER Series, 1975.

Schmidt, R.A., & Gordon, G.B. Errors in motor responding, "rapid" corrections, and false anticipations. *Journal of Motor Behavior*, 1977, **9**, 101-111.

Schmidt, R.A., & McGown, C.M. Terminal accuracy of unexpectedly loaded rapid movements: Evidence for a mass-spring mechanism in programming. *Journal of Motor Behavior*, 1980, **12**, 149-161.

Schmidt, R.A., & Nacson, J. Further tests of the activity-set hypothesis for warm-up decrement. *Journal of Experimental Psychology*, 1971, **90**, 56-64.

Schmidt, R.A., & Russell, D.G. Movement velocity and movement time as determiners of degree of preprogramming in simple movements. *Journal of Experimental Psychology*, 1972, **96**, 315-320.

Schmidt, R.A., & Shea, J.B. A note on delay of knowledge of results in positioning responses. *Journal of Motor Behavior*, 1976, **8**, 129-132.

Schmidt, R.A., & Sherwood, D.E. An inverted-U relation between spatial error and force requirements in rapid limb movements: Further evidence for the impulse-variability model. *Journal of Experimental Psychology: Human Perception and Performance*, in press.

Schmidt, R.A., & White, J.L. Evidence for an error detection mechanism in motor skills: A test of Adams' closed-loop theory. *Journal of Motor Behavior*, 1972, **4**, 143-153.

Schmidt, R.A., & Wrisberg, C.A. The activity-set hypothesis for warm-up decrement in a movement-speed task. *Journal of Motor Behavior*, 1971, **3**, 318-325.

Schmidt, R.A., Zelaznik, H.N., & Frank, J.S. Sources of inaccuracy in rapid movement. In G.E. Stelmach (Ed.), *Information processing in motor control and learning*. New York: Academic Press, 1978.

Schmidt, R.A., Zelaznik, H.N., Hawkins, B., Frank, J.S., & Quinn, J.T., Jr. Motor-output variability: A theory for the accuracy of rapid motor acts. *Psychological Review*, 1979, **86**, 415-451.

Schneider, W., & Shiffrin, R. Controlled and automatic human information processing: I. Detection, search, and attention. *Psychological Review*, 1977, **84**, 1-66.

Schutz, R.W., & Roy, E.A. Absolute error: The devil in disguise. *Journal of Motor Behavior*, 1973, **5**, 141-153.

Sears, T.A., & Newson-Davis, J. The control of respiratory muscles during voluntary breathing. *Annals of the New York Academy of Sciences*, 1968, **155**, 183-190.

Seashore, H., & Bavelas, A. The functioning of knowledge of results in Thorndike's line-drawing experiment. *Psychological Review*, 1941, **48**, 155-164.

Severin, F.V., Orlovskii, G.N., & Shik, M.L. Work of the muscle receptors during controlled locomotion. *Biophysics*, 1967, **12**, 575-586.

Seymour, W.D. Experiments on the acquisition of industrial skills. *Occupa-

tional Psychology, 1954, **28**, 77-89.

Shaffer, L.H. Attention in transcription skill. *Quarterly Journal of Experimental Psychology*, 1971, **23**, 107-112.

Shaffer, L.H. Analyzing piano performance. A study of concert pianists. In G.E. Stelmach & J. Requin (Eds.), *Tutorials in motor behavior*. Amsterdam: North-Holland, 1980.

Shannon, C.E., & Weaver, W. *The mathematical theory of communication*. Urbana, IL: University of Illinois Press, 1949.

Shapiro, D.C. A preliminary attempt to determine the duration of a motor program. In D.M. Landers & R.W. Christina (Eds.), *Psychology of motor behavior and sport* (Vol. 1). Urbana, IL: Human Kinetics, 1977.

Shapiro, D.C. *The learning of generalized motor programs*. Ph.D. dissertation, University of Southern California, 1978.

Shapiro, D.C., & Schmidt, R.A. The schema theory: Recent evidence and developmental implications. In J.A.S. Kelso & J.E. Clark (Eds.), *The development of movement control and coordination*. New York: Wiley, 1981.

Shapiro D.C., Zernicke, R.F., Gregor, R.J., & Diestal, J.D. Evidence for generalized motor programs using gait-pattern analysis. *Journal of Motor Behavior*, 1981, **13**, 33-47.

Shea, J.B., & Morgan, R.L. Contextual interference effects on the acquisition, retention, and transfer of a motor skill. *Journal of Experimental Psychology: Human Learning and Memory*, 1979, **5**, 179-187.

Shea, J.B., & Upton, G. The effects on skill acquisition of an interpolated motor short-term memory task during the KR-delay interval. *Journal of Motor Behavior*, 1976, **8**, 277-281.

Sherrington, C.S. *The integrative action of the nervous system*. New Haven: Yale University Press, 1906. (Reprinted, 1947)

Sherwood, D.E., & Schmidt, R.A. The relationship between force and force variability in minimal and near-maximal static and dynamic contractions. *Journal of Motor Behavior*, 1980, **12**, 75-89.

Shiffrin, R.M., & Schneider, W. Controlled and automatic human information processing: II. Perceptual learning, automatic attending, and a general theory. *Psychological Review*, 1977, **84**, 127-190.

Shik, M.L., & Orlovskii, G.N. Neurophysiology of a locomotor automatism. *Physiological Reviews*, 1976, **56**, 465-501.

Shik, M.L., Orlovskii, G.N., & Severin, F.V. Locomotion of the mesencephalic cat elicited by stimulation of the pyramids. *Biofizika*, 1968, **13**, 127-135. (English translation, 143-152).

Shirley, M.M. *The first two years* (Vol. 1). Minneapolis, MN: University of Minnesota Press, 1931.

Sidman, M. A note on functional relations obtained from group data. *Psychological Bulletin*, 1952, **49**, 263-269.

Simon, J.R. Reactions toward the source of stimulation. *Journal of Experimental Psychology*, 1969, **81**, 174-176. (a)

Simon, J.R. Stereotypic reaction in information processing. In L.E. Smith (Ed.), *Psychology of motor learning*. Chicago: Athletic Institute, 1969. (b)

Singer, R.N. Effect of an audience on performance of a motor task. *Jour-*

nal of Motor Behavior, 1970, **2**, 88-95.

Singer, R.N. *Motor learning and human performance* (2nd ed.). New York: Macmillan, 1975.

Singer, R.N. *Motor learning and human performance* (3rd ed.). New York: Macmillan, 1980.

Skinner, B.F. A case history in scientific method. *American Psychologist*, 1956, **11**, 221-233.

Skoglund, S. Anatomical and physiological studies of the knee joint innervation in the cat. *Acta Physiologica Scandinavica*, 1956, **36**, Supplement 124.

Slamecka, N.J., & Graf, P. The generation effect: Delineation of a phenomenon. *Journal of Experimental Psychology: Human Learning and Memory*, 1978, **4**, 592-604.

Slater-Hammel, A.T. Reliability, accuracy and refractoriness of a transit reaction. *Research Quarterly*, 1960, **31**, 217-228.

Smith, J.L. *Fusimotor neuron block and voluntary arm movement in man.* Ph.D. dissertation, University of Wisconsin, 1969.

Smith, J.L. *Mechanisms of neuromuscular control.* Los Angeles: UCLA Printing and Production, 1977.

Smith, J.L. Sensorimotor integrations during motor programming. In G.E. Stelmach (Ed.), *Information processing in motor control and learning.* New York: Academic Press, 1978.

Smith, J.L., Roberts, E.M., & Atkins, E. Fusimotor neuron block and voluntary arm movement in man. *American Journal of Physical Medicine*, 1972, **5**, 225-239.

Smith, M.C. The effect of varying information on the psychological refractory period. In W.G. Koster (Ed.), *Attention and performance II.* Amsterdam: North-Holland, 1969.

Smith, W.M., & Bowen, K.F. The effects of delayed and displaced visual feedback on motor control. *Journal of Motor Behavior*, 1980, **12**, 91-101.

Snoddy, G.S. Learning and stability. *Journal of Applied Psychology*, 1926, **10**, 1-36.

Snoddy, G.S. *Evidence for two opposed processes in mental growth.* Lancaster, PA: Science Press, 1935.

Solley, C.M. Reduction of error with practice in perception of the postural vertical. *Journal of Experimental Psychology*, 1956, **52**, 329-333.

Sperling, G. The information available in brief visual presentations. *Psychological Monographs*, 1960, **74** (11, Whole No. 498).

Sperry, R.W. Neural basis of the spontaneous optokinetic response produced by visual inversion. *Journal of Comparative and Physiological Psychology*, 1950, **43**, 482-489.

Spielberger, C.D. Anxiety as an emotional state. In C.D. Spielberger (Ed.), *Anxiety: Current trends in theory and research.* New York: Academic Press, 1966.

Start, K.B. Intelligence and improvement in a gross motor skill after mental practice. *British Journal of Educational Psychology*, 1964, **34**, 85-90.

Stelmach, G.E. Efficiency of motor learning as a function of intertrial rest. *Research Quarterly*, 1969, **40**, 198-202. (a)

Stelmach, G.E. Prior positioning responses as a factor in short-term retention of a simple motor task. *Journal of Experimental Psychology*, 1969, **81**, 523-526. (b)

Stelmach, G.E. Retention of motor skills. *Exercise and Sport Sciences Reviews*, 1974, 2, 1-31.

Stelmach, G.E., Kelso, J.A.S., & Wallace, S.A. Preselection in short-term motor memory. *Journal of Experimental Psychology: Human Learning and Memory*, 1975, **1**, 745-755.

Sternberg, S. The discovery of processing stages: Extensions of Donders' method. In W.G. Koster (Ed.), *Attention and performance II*. Amsterdam: North-Holland, 1969.

Sternberg, S., Monsell, S., Knoll, R.L., & Wright, C.E. The latency and duration of rapid movement sequences: Comparisons of speech and typewriting. In G.E. Stelmach (Ed.), *Information processing in motor control and learning*. New York: Academic Press, 1978.

Stroop, J.R. Studies of interference in serial verbal reactions. *Journal of Experimental Psychology*, 1935, **18**, 643-662.

Stuart, D.G., Mosher, C.G., Gerlack, R.L., & Reinking, R.M. Mechanical arrangement and transducing properties of Golgi tendon organs. *Experimental Brain Research*, 1972, **14**, 274-292.

Suinn, R.M. *Psychology in sports: Methods and applications*. Minneapolis, MN: Burgess, 1980.

Summers, J.J. The relationship between the sequencing and timing components of a skill. *Journal of Motor Behavior*, 1977, **9**, 49-59.

Suzuki, S. *Nurtured by love: A new approach to education*. New York: Exposition Press, 1969.

Swets, J.A. *Signal detection and recognition by human observers*. New York: Wiley, 1964.

Taub, E. Movements in nonhuman primates deprived of somatosensory feedback. *Exercise and Sport Sciences Reviews*, 1976, **4**, 335-374.

Taub, E., & Berman, A.J. Movement and learning in the absence of sensory feedback. In S.J. Freedman (Ed.), *The neuropsychology of spatially oriented behavior*. Homewood, IL: Dorsey Press, 1968.

Telford, C.W. The refractory phase of voluntary and associative responses. *Journal of Experimental Psychology*, 1931, **14**, 1-36.

Terzuolo, C.A., & Viviani, P. The central representation of learning motor programs. In R.E. Talbot & D.R. Humphrey (Eds.), *Posture and movement*. New York: Raven Press, 1979.

Thomas, J.R. Acquisition of motor skills: Information processing differences between children and adults. *Research Quarterly for Exercise and Sport*, 1980, **51**, 158-173.

Thomas, J.R., & Chissom, B.S. Relationships as assessed by canonical correlation between perceptual-motor and intellectual abilities for pre-school and early elementary age children. *Journal of Motor Behavior*, 1972, **4**, 23-29.

Thorndike, E.L. *Educational psychology*. New York: Columbia University, 1914.

Thorndike, E.L. The law of effect. *American Journal of Psychology*, 1927, **39**, 212-222.

Thorndike, E.L., & Woodworth, R.S. The influence of improvement in one mental function upon the efficiency of other functions. *Psychological Review*, 1901, **8**, 247-261.

Treisman, A. Strategies and models of selective attention. *Psychological Review*, 1969, **76**, 282-299.

Trowbridge, M.H., & Cason, H. An experimental study of Thorndike's theory of learning. *Journal of General Psychology*, 1932, **7**, 245-260.

Trumbo, D., Ulrich, L., & Noble, M. Verbal coding and display coding in the acquisition and retention of tracking skill. *Journal of Applied Psychology*, 1965, **49**, 368-375.

Tuller, B., Fitch, H., & Turvey, M.T. The Bernstein perspective: II. The concept of muscle linkages or coordinative structures. In J.A.S. Kelso (Ed.), *Human motor behavior: An introduction*. Hillsdale, NJ: Erlbaum, 1982.

Turvey, M.T. On peripheral and central processes in vision: Inferences from an information-processing analysis of masking with patterned stimuli. *Psychological Review*, 1973, **80**, 1-52.

Turvey, M.T. Preliminaries to a theory of action with reference to vision. In R. Shaw & J. Bransford (Eds.), *Perceiving, acting, and knowing*. Hillsdale, NJ: Erlbaum, 1977.

Underwood, B.J. Interference and forgetting. *Psychological Review*, 1957, **64**, 49-60.

Underwood, B.J. Individual differences as a crucible in theory construction. *American Psychologist*, 1975, **30**, 128-134.

Vallbo, A.B. Human muscle spindle discharge during isometric voluntary contractions: Amplitude relations between spindle frequency and torque. *Acta Physiologica Scandinavica*, 1974, **90**, 319-336.

Van Rossen, D.P. *The effects of diversions on repetitive swimming performance*. Ph.D. dissertation, University of Illinois, 1968.

Vince, M.A., & Welford, A.T. Time taken to change the speed of a response. *Nature*, 1967, **213**, 532-533.

von Holst, E. Relations between the central nervous system and the peripheral organs. *British Journal of Animal Behavior*, 1954, **2**, 89-94.

Vredenbregt, J., & Koster, W.G. Analysis and synthesis of handwriting. *Philips Technical Review*, 1971, **32**, 73-78.

Wadman, W.J., Denier van der Gon, J.J., Geuze, R.H., & Mol, C.R. Control of fast goal-directed arm movements. *Journal of Human Movement Studies*, 1979, **5**, 3-17.

Wallace, S.A., & Hagler, R.W. Knowledge of performance and the learning of a closed motor skill. *Research Quarterly*, 1979, **50**, 265-271.

Wallace, S.A., & McGhee, R.C. The independence of recall and recognition in motor learning. *Journal of Motor Behavior*, 1979, **11**, 141-151.

Walsh, W.D., Russell, D.G., Imanaka, K., & James, B. Memory for constrained and preselected movement location and distance: Effects of starting position and length. *Journal of Motor Behavior*, 1979, **11**, 201-214.

Walter, C.B. *Contrasting information feedback parameters for learning a simple rapid response*. M.S. thesis, University of Illinois, 1981.

Weinberg, D.R., Guy, D.E., & Tupper, R.W. Variation of postfeedback interval in simple motor learning. *Journal of Experimental Psychology*, 1964, **67**, 98-99.

Weinberg, R.S., & Hunt, V.V. The interrelationships between anxiety, motor performance, and electromyography. *Journal of Motor Behavior*, 1976, **8**, 219-224.

Weinberg, R.S., & Ragan, J. Motor performance under three levels of trait anxiety and stress. *Journal of Motor Behavior*, 1978, **10**, 169-176.

Weiss, A.D. The locus of reaction time change with set, motivation, and age. *Journal of Gerontology*, 1965, **20**, 60-64.

Welch, J.C. On the measurement of mental activity through muscular activity and the determination of a constant of attention. *American Journal of Physiology*, 1898, **1**, 283-306.

Welford, A.T. The psychological refractory period and the timing of high-speed performance—A review and a theory. *British Journal of Psychology*, 1952, **43**, 2-19.

Welford, A.T. *Fundamentals of skill*. London: Methuen, 1968.

Weltman, G., & Egstrom, G.H. Perceptual narrowing in novice divers. *Human Factors*, 1966, **8**, 499-505.

West, L.J. Vision and kinesthesis in the acquisition of typewriting skill. *Journal of Applied Psychology*, 1967, **51**, 161-166.

Wetzel, M.C., & Stuart, D.G. Ensemble characteristics of cat locomotion and its neural control. *Progress in Neurobiology*, 1976, **7**, 1-98.

White, R.M., Jr., & Schmidt, S.W. Preresponse intervals versus postinformative feedback intervals in concept identification. *Journal of Experimental Psychology*, 1972, **94**, 350-352.

Whitley, J.D. Effects of practice distribution on learning a fine motor task. *Research Quarterly*, 1970, **41**, 576-583.

Whiting, H.T.A. *Acquiring ball skill*. London: Pergamon Press, 1972.

Wickens, C.D. The effects of divided attention on information processing in manual tracking. *Journal of Experimental Psychology: Human Perception and Performance*, 1976, **2**, 1-13.

Wickens, C.D. The structure of processing resources. In R. Nickerson & R. Pew (Eds.), *Attention and Performance VIII*. Hillsdale, NJ: Erlbaum, 1980.

Wiener, N. *Cybernetics*. New York: Wiley, 1948.

Wilson, D.M. The central nervous control of flight in a locust. *Journal of Experimental Biology*, 1961, **38**, 471-490.

Wing, A. M. Response timing in handwriting. In G.E. Stelmach (Ed.), *Information processing in motor control and learning*. New York: Academic Press, 1978.

Witkin, H.A. Perception of body position and of the position of the visual field. *Psychological Monographs*, 1949, **63** (7, Whole No. 302).

Woodworth, R.S. The accuracy of voluntary movement. *Psychological Review*, 1899, **3** (Supplement 2).

Woodworth, R.S. *Le mouvement*. Paris: Doin, 1903.

Woodworth, R.S. *Experimental psychology*. New York: Holt, 1938.

Wrisberg, C.A., & Ragsdale, M.R. Further tests of Schmidt's schema theory: Development of a schema rule for a coincident timing task. *Journal of Motor Behavior*, 1979, **11**, 159-166.

Wrisberg, C.A., & Schmidt, R.A. A note on motor learning without postresponse knowledge of results. *Journal of Motor Behavior*, 1975, **7**, 221-225.

Yerkes, R.M., & Dodson, J.D. The relation of strength of stimulus to rapidity of habit-formation. *Journal of Comparative Neurology of Psychology*, 1908, **18**, 459-482.

Zajonc, R.B. Social facilitation. *Science*, 1965, **149**, 269-274.

Zavala, A., Locke, E.A., Van Cott, H.P., & Fleishman, E.A. *The analysis of helicopter pilot performance*. Technical Report AIR-E-29-6/65-TR, American Institutes for Research, Washington, DC, 1965.

Zelaznik, H.N., Shapiro, D.C., & McColsky, D. Effects of a secondary task on the accuracy of single aiming movements. *Journal of Experimental Psychology: Human Perception and Performance*, 1981, **7**, 1007-1018.

Zelaznik, H.N., Shapiro, D.C., & Newell, K.M. On the structure of motor recognition memory. *Journal of Motor Behavior*, 1978, **10**, 313-323.

Zelaznik, H.N., & Spring, J. Feedback in response recognition and production. *Journal of Motor Behavior*, 1976, **8**, 309-312.

Zernicke, R.F., & Roberts, E.M. Lower extremity forces and torques during systematic variation of non-weight bearing motion. *Medicine and Science in Sports*, 1978, **10**, 21-26.

Zukav, G. *The dancing Wu Li masters. An overview of the new physics.* New York: Morrow, 1979.

AUTHOR INDEX

SUBJECT INDEX